ADDRESSES AND PUBLIC PAPERS

OF

JAMES BAXTER HUNT JR.

ADDRESSES AND PUBLIC PAPERS

OF

JAMES BAXTER HUNT JR.
GOVERNOR OF NORTH CAROLINA

Volume III

1993-1997

JAN-MICHAEL POFF, EDITOR

Raleigh
Division of Archives and History
Department of Cultural Resources
2000

NORTH CAROLINA DEPARTMENT OF CULTURAL RESOURCES

Betty Ray McCain
Secretary

Elizabeth F. Buford
Deputy Secretary

DIVISION OF ARCHIVES AND HISTORY

Jeffrey J. Crow
Director

David J. Olson
Deputy Director

NORTH CAROLINA HISTORICAL COMMISSION

William S. Powell (2001)
Chairman

Alan D. Watson (2003)
Vice-Chairman

ISBN 0-86526-289-6

STATUTORY AUTHORIZATION

Section 121-6(b) of the *General Statutes of North Carolina* requires that a copy of "all official messages delivered to the General Assembly, addresses, speeches, statements, news releases, proclamations, executive orders, weekly calendars, articles, transcripts of news conferences, lists of appointments, and other official releases and papers of the Governor" be provided to the Department of Cultural Resources. From these records a selection is made by "a skilled and competent editor" who "shall edit according to scholarly standards the selected materials which shall be published in a documentary volume as soon as practicable after the conclusion of the term of office of each Governor."

4,000 copies of this volume were printed at a cost of $40,619.20, or $10.15 each.

FOREWORD

In accordance with G.S. 121-6(b) of the *General Statutes of North Carolina*, the Division of Archives and History, Department of Cultural Resources, has published Volume III of the *Addresses and Public Papers of James Baxter Hunt Jr., Governor of North Carolina, 1993-1997*. Together with the *Addresses and Public Papers of James Baxter Hunt Jr., Governor of North Carolina, 1977-1981* (Volume I) edited by Memory F. Mitchell, and the *Addresses and Papers of James Baxter Hunt Jr., Governor of North Carolina, 1981-1985* (Volume II) edited by Jan-Michael Poff and Jeffrey J. Crow, these documentaries provide an extensive and important record of twelve eventful years in the history of twentieth-century North Carolina.

Jan-Michael Poff, editor of the third Hunt volume, has edited the governors' papers since 1983. Besides two collections of Hunt papers, he also edited the *Addresses and Public Papers of James Grubbs Martin, Governor of North Carolina, 1985-1989* and *1989-1993* (2 volumes). A seasoned editor, Mr. Poff brings a wealth of knowledge and experience to these projects. His skill in gathering, selecting, and annotating such a large collection of significant documents is evident throughout. The quality and depth of his research and knowledge of political events are amply reflected in his many thorough notations to the papers of both governors.

North Carolina has published, since 1923, the official papers of its chief executives. The timely publication of those materials has earned the state the praise of historians, political scientists, and the general public. The *Addresses and Public Papers of James Baxter Hunt Jr., Governor of North Carolina, 1993-1997* (Volume III) continues that proud tradition.

Joe A. Mobley
Administrator
Historical Publications Section
Division of Archives and History

October 2000

ACKNOWLEDGMENTS

Everyone who aided in the completion of the *Addresses and Public Papers of James Baxter Hunt Jr., Governor of North Carolina, 1993-1997*, has earned my sincere thanks. Among those many people, the following deserve special mention for their generous cooperation: Mary Ann Dusenbury and Patrice Swinton, Governor's Press Office; Dana Pope and Kathy Zeisel, Governor's Policy Office; Janice Shearin, executive assistant to First Lady Carolyn Hunt; Jan Parker, director, and Libby Haggerty, Boards and Commissions Office, Office of the Governor.

The advice, skill, and good humor of Joe A. Mobley and Robert M. Topkins, administrator and general publications editor, respectively, of the Historical Publications Section, North Carolina Department of Cultural Resources, are appreciated more than they know. I am also grateful to the section's perpetually busy proofreader, Lisa D. Bailey, for casting her sharp eyes over the text of this documentary.

Others in the public and the private sectors who graciously shared their knowledge, abilities, and time include Rebecca Banks, associate director, Support Our Students, Office of Juvenile Justice, Raleigh; Dianne Beasley, assistant director, North Carolina Division of Forest Resources, Raleigh; Kim Brooks, public affairs director, North Carolina Department of Revenue, Raleigh; Stephanie D. Fanjul, director, Division of Child Development, North Carolina Department of Health and Human Services, Raleigh; Billy Ray Hall, president, North Carolina Rural Economic Development Center, Raleigh; Leah Jung, principal, Vista Environmental, Evergreen, Colorado; Russell Koonts, North Carolina State University Archives, Raleigh; Diane Lamb, *Greensboro News and Record*; Holly MacKenzie, *Asheville Citizen-Times*; Paul Magann, *News and Observer*, Raleigh; Roberta Mazer, director of development, Planned Parenthood of the Capital and Coast, Raleigh; Richard M. Rodero Jr., corporate development, National Alliance of Business, Washington, D.C.; Michael Sampair, Bleu Aura Productions, Raleigh; Sammie L. Shine and William H. Brown, Archives and Records Section, North Carolina Department of Cultural Resources, Raleigh; Lynn Wilson, communications director, State Employees Association of North Carolina, Raleigh; and Alicia Wright, executive assistant to Secretary C. Robin Britt Sr., North Carolina Department of Human Resources, Raleigh.

Jan-Michael Poff

October 2000

EDITORIAL METHOD

Texts or notes exist for more than 1,020 of the addresses James Baxter Hunt Jr. delivered during his third term as governor. Add to them the scores of news releases issued by his Press Office, and one has amassed a body of material too large to be reprinted in the single-volume documentary permitted each of the state's chief executives, per four-year term, by North Carolina law. The 254 items ultimately selected to appear in the *Addresses of Hunt* most comprehensively reflect the scope of the governor's official activities during the 1993-1997 period. They discuss the aspirations and accomplishments of his administration, explain policies, focus on developments in the state and the issues he confronted, effectively illuminate some aspect of his occupational or political philosophy, or contain significant autobiographical elements. Whenever possible, transcripts of speeches meeting those criteria were published. If transcripts were unavailable or multiple versions of an address were prepared for a single event, the text bearing Governor Hunt's handwritten emendations was favored over unadorned copy.

The clear text method of transcription generally was followed. Although the diplomatic format would have enabled users of this volume to distinguish the governor's additions to, and deletions from, the material prepared for him, sigla-strewn prose characteristic of the diplomatic rendition impedes speedy comprehension of the documents themselves. Researchers eager to examine speeches fine tuned by Hunt are directed to the originals kept at the Division of Archives and History, North Carolina Department of Cultural Resources.

While most of the governor's textual emendations were incorporated silently into the documents selected for the *Addresses of Hunt*, there have been exceptions to the rule. Marginalia and interlinear notes that Hunt added to his speeches, but which could not be incorporated elegantly into the body of a published document, were reprinted as annotations, their corresponding footnote numbers placed at the point in the text where the governor made his original insertion. Some of his jottings were so fragmentary that they defied accurate interpretation; no attempt was made to reproduce them. Extrapolation was kept to an absolute minimum, and all of the editor's supplemental words have been placed in square brackets.

Overall, the documents were edited to ensure consistent spelling, capitalization, punctuation, and use of numbers. Headings were standardized. Salutations of addresses were deleted unless they contained information or a particular nuance that greatly enhanced the reader's understanding of the audience, occasion, or main text of the speech. Ampersands and esoteric abbreviations have been expanded, and typographical errors in the originals have been corrected.

Every effort was made to identify persons, legislation, reports, and quotations the first time they appear in the documentary. Presidents of the United States and others whose names are immediately recognizable did not receive biographical annotations. The editor mailed letters requesting biographical information to individuals the governor mentioned but for whom such data was not available in standard directories. Occasionally those who failed to reply could not be footnoted. Although extensive measures were employed to locate and cite all bills, laws, and studies to which the governor referred, and to check the accuracy of quotations he used, not every one could be identified.

Naturally, it is inevitable that some of the same conceptual currents flow through more than one address, thus demonstrating the continuing importance Governor Hunt assigned to specific issues. Annotations accompanying the documents reprinted herein mention textually identical and thematically similar items that were omitted. Deleted speeches and statements, press releases consisting primarily of Hunt's direct quotations, and speaking engagements for which there were no prepared texts, are listed by date, title, and place of delivery, on pages 626-659.

Finally, all North Carolina governors are statutorily required to deposit their official papers with the Department of Cultural Resources—and it is upon official papers, like Governor Hunt's, that documentaries such as this are based. The manner of disposal of personal records, however, is left to the discretion of the chief executive. Hunt's private papers are housed at Joyner Library, East Carolina University, Greenville.

TABLE OF CONTENTS

1994

1996

LIST OF ILLUSTRATIONS

JAMES BAXTER HUNT JR.
By Gary Pearce*

It was one of the great second acts in American politics: Jim Hunt's public career seemed finished after he lost a bitter, brutal United States Senate race to Jesse Helms in 1984. But by 1993, he was back—back for a third term as governor of North Carolina, and back with the same energy, drive, and determination as before.

Hunt was not back for "more of the same," however. He returned with new ideas about children and education, new approaches for how government should work, and a new willingness to cross party lines. More focused than ever, he fought for his goals more fiercely than ever. And he was more effective than ever:

—He launched one of the most sweeping education reform initiatives in the nation.

—He established Smart Start, one of the most innovative early childhood initiatives in the nation.

—He passed comprehensive anti-crime legislation, started a landmark welfare-to-work plan, and made the state more competitive for economic growth.

—He once again transformed the office of governor. Twenty years before, he had pushed through a constitutional amendment permitting governors to run for consecutive terms. Now he was able to pass an amendment finally giving governors veto power.

By 1997, as Hunt took the oath of office for a fourth time, he was not only the nation's most experienced governor, he was also recognized as one of its most effective, successful, and popular chief executives.

* * *

---

*James Gary Pearce (1949-   ), former political reporter, Raleigh *News and Observer*; press secretary, speech writer, Jim Hunt for Governor, 1976; press secretary to Governor Hunt, 1977-1984; communications consultant from 1985; political consultant to Hunt (U.S. Senate campaign, 1984, and third and fourth terms as governor), Lieutenant Governor Bob Jordan (campaign for governor, 1988), John Edwards (campaign for U.S. Senate, 1998), and Lieutenant Governor Dennis Wicker (Democratic gubernatorial primary, 2000). Tim Gray, "Consultant: Small—Not Medium—Is The Message," *Business North Carolina* (June 2000): 26-28; Jan-Michael Poff and Jeffrey J. Crow, eds., *Addresses and Public Papers of James Baxter Hunt Jr., Governor of North Carolina*, Vol. II, *1981-1985* (Raleigh: Division of Archives and History, Department of Cultural Resources, 1987), xix.

The opportunity for an administration spokesman to furnish an introduction reviewing the accomplishments of the chief executive traditionally has been extended as a courtesy by the editors of previous volumes of modern governors' papers. The introduction represents the views of the writer and is a supplement to, rather than an official part of, the documentary.

Jim Hunt grew up with North Carolina. He was raised on a farm at a time when the state's economy was based largely upon agriculture and manufacturing. The policies he pursued as lieutenant governor (1973-1977) and governor (1977-1981, 1981-1985) were shaped by his experiences as a youth: waiting for hours to see a doctor, seeing the paving of the dirt road past his home after Governor Kerr Scott pledged to get farmers out of the mud, and discovering how inadequately rural schools had prepared him for his studies at North Carolina State University.

In his first two terms as governor, Hunt aggressively recruited new industry, campaigned for better schools to equip graduates with new skills for a changing economy, pushed for expanded health services, and fought for progress on racial issues and women's rights. But when he ran for the United States Senate in 1984, the riptides of social, economic, and political change pulled him under. A career that could have led to the White House seemed over. Many of his initiatives received little support from his successor.

Hunt began a new life as a corporate attorney and cattle farmer. Characteristically, he put in long hours at his law firm. He traveled extensively, meeting with clients and serving on national commissions. On weekends he worked his Wilson County farm alongside his wife, Carolyn, who managed the operation during the week.

Just as he was achieving new success in private life, North Carolina was heading in the other direction. Hit hard by a national recession, the state faced a massive budget shortfall in 1991. The Republican governor and a Democratic General Assembly were at loggerheads.

Hunt believed that North Carolina was losing its edge. It was faltering in the competition for new jobs. Student test scores lagged far behind the nation and the South.

"I was really worried about what was happening to North Carolina," Governor Hunt recalled in an interview near the end of his fourth term. "I believed that I knew what we needed to do."

He had passed up opportunities to run for the United States Senate in 1986 and 1990. But eventually, the idea of running again for governor of North Carolina took root. It grew out of two passions: first, studying the challenges facing the nation's schools; and second, his grandchildren.

* * *

"Those years in between my terms as governor were in many ways the busiest and most productive years of my life," Hunt said later. "I spent them learning."

He learned how the private sector worked. "I was involved with a lot of CEOs and good managers, and I learned a lot from them about planning and achieving goals."

He also learned how to make public education work better. The teacher's son from Rock Ridge found his cause after joining the Carnegie Forum on Education and the Economy in 1985. A key recommendation was to upgrade the profession of teaching. With typical zeal, Hunt spent a year assembling a national organization on teaching. He recruited board members, raised money, and sold the project to foundations, business leaders, and teachers. He founded the National Board for Professional Teaching Standards and served as its chairman for ten years, including three years while he was governor.

Some teachers were skeptical. Their relations with Governor Hunt had been strained in his previous administration. One recession year, his budget included no pay raise for teachers. Angry and bitter, they organized torchlight protests at the Executive Mansion, and the North Carolina Association of Educators gave only lukewarm support to his race against Senator Helms.

Now he would spend hours at meetings, listening as teachers talked about what members of their profession needed to know and be able to do. He led the development of a national process for board-certifying teachers: a rigorous, professional examination that demonstrated a teacher's proficiency, much like board certification for doctors.

Hunt became an expert on what it took to be a great teacher. And in 1992, the North Carolina Association of Educators enthusiastically endorsed him for governor.

*　*　*

"The key to making schools work is, first, for kids to have a great teacher," Hunt said. "Second is for them to get a good start, to start school ready to succeed and not destined to fail."

He had championed early childhood initiatives during his first two terms, but now his eyes were opened by watching his own grandchildren grow.

"When you're raising your own kids, especially when you're in politics, you're gone a lot, and you're going as hard as you can go to make a living and keep your family together," he recalled. "But it's different when you're a grandparent. You have more time. You don't take care of them [grandchildren] because you have to, you want to do it. You reflect on it more, and you're grateful for them. You consider them a gift."

He acknowledged he was late to learn what Carolyn had long known: the importance of a child's early years. Hunt wrote about seeing a small child, wearing only a diaper in winter, on the front porch of a shack near his farm: "The child was holding a bottle, always empty, trying to suck out one last drop of milk. He looked malnourished and was certainly cold. And I never once saw an adult come out for that child, wrap him up in warm clothes, and take him back inside. In my mind, that child became the poster child for Smart Start."

The Smart Start early childhood education and health program was a vision unique to Jim Hunt. North Carolina had a strong child-advocacy movement, but he felt it focused too much on building a large state government bureaucracy. He had become less enamored of big-government solutions during his years away from political office and was convinced that the most vital source of public action was at the local level.

"It just came to me that the need is there and that state government has a responsibility to put up resources," Hunt said. "But the answer was not a bureaucracy run out of Raleigh—and surely not out of Washington. The answer was something new. The answer was to capture all the knowledge, ideas, commitment, and energy of people at the local level, where they lived and worked. Let them own it. That's why I insisted on Smart Start being owned and operated at the local level."

His choice to lead Smart Start was revealing of his approach: Jim Goodmon, of Raleigh, was a conservative Republican, CEO of Capitol Broadcasting Company, and owner of WRAL-TV, the station that gave Jesse Helms his start. Goodmon helped Hunt sell Smart Start to local leaders and to a sometimes doubtful General Assembly. They established the Partnership for Children, a public-private effort that recruited community support and millions of dollars in contributions from businesses and individuals. They focused on local initiatives to improve child care, early education, and health services. Every local Smart Start program had its own partnership of business and civic leaders, foundations, churches, child-care groups, and literacy programs. Each program grew deep roots in the community.

* * *

Was there a new Jim Hunt? Critics scoffed when he announced he would run for governor in 1992. Conventional wisdom held that he was too bloodied by the 1984 Senate race, but Hunt offered a simple and compelling rationale for his candidacy: "I love this state too much to watch it fall behind." He built a coalition of conservative business leaders and progressive education supporters and won the election against Lieutenant Governor Jim Gardner by a 53 percent-43 percent margin.

He said in his Inaugural Address: "Today, people ask if there's a new Jim Hunt—or if it's the same old Jim Hunt. Well, it's an older Jim Hunt, but not quite the same old Jim Hunt.

"I hope I am wiser and more mature. I am less partisan, but I am more committed to the principles that led me into public life. I am less confident that the answers to our problems can be found in government, but I am more certain that the answers will be found in our people. I am less ambitious for myself, but I am more ambitious for our state."

The *Almanac of American Politics* described him this way: "Forceful, articulate, disciplined and well-organized, Hunt seems by nature an executive; he might not have found the Senate congenial. He became governor here two years before Bill Clinton did in Arkansas and had success much sooner than Clinton; had he beaten Helms, Hunt might have been the moderate Democrat elected president in the 1990s."

In the 1990s, there was much talk of the "third way," a centrist style of governing that could not be neatly labeled liberal or conservative. Jim Hunt had been blazing a third way before anybody knew what it was. Smart Start combined statewide goals with local action and won support from liberals and conservatives. One of its strongest proponents was David Flaherty, a Republican who ran against Hunt for governor in 1976 and had been a bitter political opponent.

Governor Hunt took the same approach to education reform. "When I ran for governor in 1992," he said, "I ran on the promise of raising standards for our students and holding our schools accountable for real progress. I knew the business community and parents, as well as teachers, wanted higher standards and were willing to look at new ways to reach them." So he pushed for a Standards and Accountability Act and set up a commission to implement the goals of higher standards for schools and greater accountability. He held hearings across the state and listened to hundreds of parents, business leaders, and educators talk about what was needed to ensure that all of North Carolina's students graduated with skills that would result in college acceptance, good jobs, and brighter futures.

The governor's emphasis on standards led to the State Board of Education's establishment of the North Carolina ABCs of Public Education, a program that, for the first time, set clear standards for what students should be learning and how to measure their progress and their schools' progress. At the same time he was focusing on higher standards for schools, Governor Hunt was chairing the National Commission on Teaching and America's Future. This work would later lead him to propose the Excellent Schools Act, a plan to raise teacher standards and pay in North Carolina. It became the centerpiece of his fourth term.

Governor Hunt cut the education bureaucracy in Raleigh and put more money into classrooms. He championed a tough school-discipline crackdown, made it a felony to bring guns to school, and started Support Our Students, an after-school plan to recruit tutors and mentors for troubled youths. Just as they had during his first eight years as governor, he and Carolyn worked every week as school volunteers.

The governor's less-partisan approach did not always sit well with fellow Democrats. Some resisted when he called a special legislative session on crime in early 1994; they even delayed taking up Hunt's bills. A prolonged, testy session resulted. That fall, in the first off-year elections of Bill Clinton's presidency, Democrats in North Carolina and across the nation suffered historic losses. Republicans took over the North Carolina House of Representatives for the first time in the twentieth century and nearly seized control of the senate.

Hunt kept his balance despite the political earthquake. He proposed a tax cut even larger than the Republicans'. When the legislature deadlocked on welfare reform, he issued an executive order establishing the Work First program. He even won the Republicans' reluctant agreement to expand Smart Start. That victory came after Republicans forced a showdown in 1996, adjourning the General Assembly without adopting a state budget. The governor barnstormed the state to spell out the consequences for education, children's programs, and health care, and mobilized business and community support. The Republicans gave in and passed his budget. Hunt cruised to re-election over Representative Robin Hayes in a year when Republican candidate Bob Dole carried North Carolina in the presidential race and Jesse Helms was re-elected to the Senate.

Voters also overwhelmingly approved the proposition giving governors the veto for the first time since statehood. For years, Democratic legislative leaders had blocked the veto, and Republicans had pushed for it. Once Republicans controlled the House, the governor challenged them to put the veto up for a statewide vote. They did, and it passed.

Governor Hunt took pride that the legislature passed every major piece of legislation he proposed. For all his focus on Smart Start and schools, he had an ambitious and far-reaching agenda nevertheless:

Economic development. Hunt pushed through new incentives for industrial development and the biggest tax cut in state history. He launched Transportation 2001, a program to accelerate construction of major highways, step up maintenance, and increase the availability of public transportation.

Environmental protection. He led the campaign to pass a clean water bond issue, increased oversight of hog farms and other animal-waste operations, and attacked water-pollution problems.

Crime. The legislature approved longer sentences for serious crimes, and the state dramatically increased the number of inmates on work details. The crime rate, which had been rising in the early 1990s, was dropping by the end of his term.

Child Support. The governor started the "Crackdown for Children" that significantly increased the amount of child support collected from deadbeat parents.

* * *

In January 1997, Jim Hunt was inaugurated for a fourth time to an office he had transformed. Twenty years before, when he first took the oath, North Carolina governors were limited to one term and had no veto power. Now it was a position of strong leadership, so identified with him that one columnist dubbed him "Governor-for-Life."

North Carolina was transformed, too. It had gone from an agricultural and manufacturing state to a leader in research, technology, and finance. Business investment was up, and unemployment was down. Crime was dropping, and welfare rolls were shrinking. The public schools were undergoing dramatic change. With its booming economy, growing population, and diverse culture, North Carolina was on the leading edge of where the nation was going. A new century of challenges and opportunities lay ahead.

The stage was set for a final act. Jim Hunt was ready with new ideas for North Carolina's future.

Above: With his swearing-in on January 9, 1993, James Baxter Hunt Jr. became twentieth-century North Carolina's only three-term governor. First Lady Carolyn Hunt shared in the historic event as Chief Justice James Gooden Exum Jr., of the state supreme court, administered the oath of office. (Photograph courtesy of the Office of the Governor, James Baxter Hunt Jr.) *Left:* Hunt vowed, in his inaugural address, to lead a crusade for children. (Photograph by Scott Sharpe, Raleigh *News and Observer*.)

As he outlined his legislative agenda to state lawmakers in his 1993 State of the State message, Hunt emphasized three topics: jobs, education, and children. (Photograph courtesy of the Office of the Governor, James Baxter Hunt Jr.)

INAUGURAL ADDRESS

JANUARY 9, 1993

Two weeks ago, in Warsaw, Carolyn and I read the Christmas story to three grandchildren named Stephanie, Lindsey, and James Baxter Hunt IV.[1] Today, I take the oath of office before two grandchildren named Hannah and Joseph Hawley.[2] It is to them, and to all of your children and to all of your grandchildren, that this day is dedicated. It is to them that this administration will be dedicated. Their future is our future. Their future is in our hands, and their future must be our cause, our commitment, and our crusade in North Carolina these next four years.

Twice before I have taken the oath of office as your governor. Today, people ask if there's a new Jim Hunt—or if it's the same old Jim Hunt. Well, it's an older Jim Hunt, but not quite the same old Jim Hunt.

I hope I am wiser and more mature. I am less partisan, but I am more committed to the principles that led me into public life. I am less confident that the answers to our problems can be found in government, but I am more certain that the answers will be found in our people. I am less ambitious for myself, but I am more ambitious for our state.

I am more optimistic about what we can do together. I am more confident that we can change North Carolina. I am more certain that we can build a better future for our children. I believe North Carolina can do more for its children than we have done before. I believe we can do more for young children than any other state has done, and I am ready to lead a crusade for the future of our children and our state!

We have not done as well as we have wanted in North Carolina. We have not done better because we have started too late. We lose too many children too early. We lose them in their first five years of life. We lose them before they show up for the first day of school. They may be hungry, or starved for love, or scared, or sick, or hurting.

As they grow up, they don't find love at home, so they find escape in drink and drugs. As they grow up, they don't have good families, so they have their own babies before they're ready. As they grow up, they don't learn to read, and study, and apply themselves. So they learn to steal, and hurt, and take from others.

It is more than a cycle of poverty. It is a cycle of drugs, and violence, and neglect, and abuse, and irresponsibility in too many families. It is a cycle of apathy, and cynicism, and hopelessness in too much of our society. If we don't change this, nothing else we do will make much difference. If we do change it, nothing else we do will make a greater difference. If we don't change it, we will just keep throwing more and more money into an ocean of crime, and ignorance, and disease, and despair. If we do change it, we can spend our money for better schools, and better health care, and better child care.

If we don't change, we will keep on fighting the same old battles. If we do change, we will change our state's future. But change will not be measured overnight, or in the next four years. It will be measured over decades to come.

Change will not be measured by what happens in Raleigh. It will be measured by what happens in your homes and your communities. Change will not be measured by the laws we pass. It will be measured by the lives we touch. It will be measured in the lives and in the lifetimes of our children—not just the children of poverty, not just the children of the middle class, but every single child, in every single family, in every single city, and corner, and community of North Carolina!

Think what North Carolina can be if we do change. Think what our schools can be if every child shows up that first day healthy, strong, ready to learn, and excited about life. Think what our state can be if every child goes to a school that challenges them, and inspires them, and helps them achieve high standards. Think what our economy can be if every student graduates, and is ready to compete, and keep up, and keep learning for the rest of their lives. Think what our state can be if every person can get a good job, and take care of their children, and provide for their families' future. Think what our neighborhoods and communities can be if they are safe from crime, and drugs, and guns, and violence, and fear.

Think what North Carolina can be if every individual learns the value of education, work, family, faith, and responsibility. Look at Kristen Culler and what she has done at the United States Naval Academy.[3] Look at Angela Jernigan, Aaron McNally, and Wes Schollander and what they have done.[4] Look at them, for they are what North Carolina can be, and the time has come to make our state all that it can be!

If you want to see what we can do in North Carolina, look at what North Carolinians are doing today. There are parents working hard and sacrificing all they have—for their children. There are teachers working long hours and giving all they have—for their students.

There are hundreds of thousands of people who know what must be done, who are ready to work together, who are ready to change our state, save our children, and shape our future. There is Robin Britt, dedicating his life to uplifting the lives of young children and their families. There is Carolyn Hunt, serving on a school board and leading our church day-care program. There are Governor Jim Martin and First Lady Dottie Martin, dedicating themselves to fighting for at-risk children; for myself and for all North Carolinians, I thank them for their years of service to our state.[5]

The time has come. The time has come when good intentions are not enough. The time has come when it is no longer sufficient just to talk about what must be done. The time has come to start earlier than we have started before. The time has come to aim higher than we have aimed before. The time has come for action; for leadership; for change.

The time has come to be a voice for those too small to have a voice. The time has come to conceive a new compact, in North Carolina, between our generation and their generation. The time has come for a new compact with James, and Stephanie, and Lindsey, and Hannah, and Joseph—a new compact with your children and your grandchildren, a new compact with every child in this state. The time has come to make their dreams our dreams, their cause our cause, and their future our abiding commitment.

The future of our children, and the future of our state, depend on what we do with the time now in our hands. Let us dedicate this time in our lives to them, for their time has come, and our time has come to lift them up. Thank you, and God bless you.

---

[1] Governor-elect Hunt and the future First Lady flew to the Polish capital to visit their son, a U.S. Foreign Service officer, and his family. James Baxter Hunt III and his wife, Deborah Lynn Derrick, were the parents of Stephanie Davies Hunt (born Nov. 6, 1990), and Lindsey Derrick and James Baxter Hunt IV (both born Nov. 27, 1991).

Carolyn Leonard Hunt (1937-   ), native of Mingo, Iowa; A.B. in elementary education, University of North Carolina at Chapel Hill, 1964; married James Baxter Hunt Jr., 1958. Schoolteacher in Katmandu, Nepal, 1964-1966; First Lady of North Carolina, 1977-1985, and since 1993; member, Wilson County School Board, 1986-1990; established N.C. International Friendship Force program; member, N.C. Teaching Fellows Commission and board of visitors, UNC-Chapel Hill School of Social Work; volunteer tutor/mentor, Communities in Schools and Save Our Students programs; honorary chair, N.C. Partnership for Children.

James Baxter Hunt III (1963-   ), born in Washington, D.C.; resident of Arlington, Va.; bachelor's degree in international studies, University of North Carolina at Chapel Hill, 1985; master's degree, international studies and public policy, Princeton University, 1987. U.S. Foreign Service officer, served in Warsaw (1991-1993) and at U.S. Consulate General in Durban, South Africa (1993-1995), before being posted to Washington, D.C. Wife Deborah Lynn Derrick worked for C-SPAN cable television network. Janice Shearin, executive assistant to First Lady Carolyn Hunt, letters to Jan-Michael Poff, August 16, September 17, 1996; "The Naked Soul:" Polish Paintings from the National Museum, Raleigh, April 28, 1993, Governors Papers, James Baxter Hunt Jr., State Archives, Division of Archives and History, Raleigh; Jan-Michael Poff and Jeffrey J. Crow, eds., *Addresses and Public Papers of James Baxter Hunt, Jr., Governor of North Carolina*, Vol. II, *1981-1985* (Raleigh: Division of Archives and History, Department of Cultural Resources, 1987), 227n-228n.

[2] Hannah Streeter (born Jan. 3, 1986) and Joseph Thornton (born Dec. 23, 1988) were the children of the Hunts' eldest daughter, Rebecca Joyce Hunt Hawley, and Jimmy Lee Hawley.

Rebecca Joyce Hunt Hawley (1959-   ), born in Raleigh; resident of Lucama; bachelor's degree, nursing, Atlantic Christian College (later Barton College), 1981; master's degree, public health policy and administration, University of North Carolina at Chapel Hill, 1988.

Nurse, Wake Medical Center, Raleigh, 1982-1983, and at Wilson Memorial Hospital, 1983-1995; later employed by Developmental Evaluation Center, Rocky Mount. Husband Jimmy Lee Hawley operates and manages the Hunt-Hawley Simmental Cattle Farm in Wilson County. Shearin correspondence.

[3] Kristen Culler, resident of Fayetteville and 1989 graduate of the North Carolina School of Science and Mathematics, was the highest-ranking midshipman at the United States Naval Academy when Hunt named her grand marshal of his inaugural parade. A winner of the Hunt Youth Award for leadership, she was also senior class brigade commander at the academy. *News and Observer* (Raleigh), December 31, 1992.

[4] Angela Jernigan, Aaron McNally, and Wes Schollander won James B. Hunt Jr. Young Citizen Awards in 1992, 1990, and 1991, respectively. Candidates eligible for the annual prize were sophomores or juniors in North Carolina high schools who demonstrated high ethical and moral standards; a "dedication to public service, citizenship, and leadership" outside school; "creativity and imagination within the context of leadership/citizenship"; the talent "to enlist peers in a service or cause"; and "effective communication within the community." A panel of community and business leaders chose a winner from each county in the state, and the top three recipients earned scholarships to be used at any college or university.

Thomas K. Hearn, president of Wake Forest University, and former governor Hunt announced the establishment of the awards in 1989; Hunt donated funds to launch the program, and the university pledged continuing financial support. In view of the burgeoning number of stories in the media critical of the educational, motivational, and moral failings of youth, Hunt declared it was past time to accentuate the positive. "'Instead of knocking our young people, we need to honor those students who are success stories—who study hard in school and work hard to make their communities better places to live. This program will recognize and celebrate students in every county who are role models of citizenship and hold them up for others to follow.'" Mary Ann Dusenbury, Office of the Governor, undated written reply to inquiry of October 9, 1996, from Jan-Michael Poff; *Henderson Daily Dispatch*, October 5, 1996; *News and Observer*, September 20, 1989.

[5] Charles Robin Britt Sr. (1942-   ), born in San Antonio, Tex.; resident of Greensboro; B.A., 1963, J.D., 1973, University of North Carolina at Chapel Hill; LL.M., New York University, 1976; U.S. Naval Reserve, 1963-1987 (capt., ret.). Attorney; member, U.S. House of Representatives, 1983-1985; secretary, N.C. Dept. of Human Resources, 1993-1997; special adviser to the governor for children and families, since 1997. Hunt's mentioning Britt's dedication to "uplifting lives" is a reference to Project Uplift, a model organization the former congressman founded in 1987, in Greensboro, and which he served as president and board member, 1987-1993. Project Uplift readied impoverished four-year-olds for school, helped parents earn high school diplomas, and generally aided families in finding "avenues out of poverty." *Biographical Directory of the United States Congress, 1774-1989* (Washington, D.C.: United States Government Printing Office, 1989), 671-672; *News and Observer*, September 29, 1991, December 15, 1992, January 16, 18, 1997; *North Carolina Manual, 1995-1996* (Raleigh: Rufus L. Edmisten, Secretary of State, n.d.), 394; Alicia Wright, executive assistant to Secretary Robin C. Britt Sr., electronic correspondence with Jan-Michael Poff, September 24, 1996.

James Grubbs Martin (1935-   ), born in Savannah, Ga.; B.S., Davidson College, 1957; Ph.D., Princeton University, 1960. Associate professor of chemistry, Davidson College, 1960-1972; member, 1966-1972, chairman, 1966-1969, 1971, Mecklenburg Board of County Commissioners; member, U.S. House of Representatives, 1973-1984; only Republican to succeed himself as governor of North Carolina during twentieth century, elected 1984, reelected 1988; chairman, since 1993, Research Development Board, James G. Cannon Research Center, Carolinas Medical Center, Charlotte; Republican. Jan-Michael Poff, ed., *Addresses and Public Papers of James Grubbs Martin, Governor of North Carolina*, Vol. I, *1985-1989* (Raleigh: Division of Archives and History, Department of Cultural Resources, 1992), xxiii-xlii; Jan-Michael Poff, ed., *Addresses and Public Papers of James Grubbs Martin, Governor of North Carolina*, Vol. II, *1989-1993* (Raleigh: Division of Archives and History, Department of Cultural Resources, 1996), 438; *North Carolina Manual, 1991-1992*, 15.

Dorothy McAulay Martin (1937-   ), born Dorothy Ann McAulay, in Charlotte; was educated at Queens College and University of South Carolina; was married to James Grubbs Martin, June 1, 1957. Assistant, Industrial Relations Dept., Princeton University, 1957-1960; Davidson kindergarten teacher, 1960-1972; realtor, Mount Vernon Realty, Alexandria, Va., 1972-1984. During her husband's two administrations as chief executive, Mrs. Martin chaired the Governor's Commission on Child Victimization, the Commission on Children and the Family, and the Governor's Commission for the Family. Poff, *Addresses of Martin, 1985-1989*, 8n, and *Addresses of Martin, 1989-1993*, 333, 397, 399n.

MESSAGES TO THE GENERAL ASSEMBLY

STATE OF THE STATE

FEBRUARY 15, 1993

I

Mr. President,[1] Mr. Speaker,[2] Mr. President Pro-Tem,[3] the Council of State, Justices, Judges, Members of the Cabinet, My Fellow North Carolinians, and especially, Members of the General Assembly:

You invited me here to speak to you tonight, but I come here to make sure you know that I am ready to listen to you during this session. The General Assembly's invitation to the governor for this address symbolizes the relationship that should exist between two equal branches of government—a relationship built not on confrontation, but on cooperation. It is in this spirit of cooperation that I intend to work with you, in this session and in future sessions.

It is not my intention to do all the talking. It is my intention to do more listening. It is not my intention to impose my ideas. It is my intention to respect your ideas. It is not my intention to twist arms. It is my intention to join hands.

II

I would be presumptuous if I pretended to have all the answers, for those of you who served before proved what this legislature can do. When you convened two years ago, North Carolina faced one of the most serious fiscal crises of any state in the nation. Today, North Carolina has done more to solve its budget problems and protect its fiscal integrity than any state in the nation, and you deserve great credit for this achievement.[4]

You sustained the difficult process of education reform. You moved the Basic Education Program forward despite hard times.[5] You put our transportation program on a sound, long-term course. You refused to sacrifice environmental protection for short-term economic gain. You started putting children first because you knew it was the right thing to do and because you had the courage and vision to do it!

You did all this in a time when the governor and the General Assembly were too often at odds. Just think what we can do for North Carolina if we work together. As Speaker Blue said, "Now that we have laid the foundation, it is time to build the house."[6]

In the 100 days since the election, reporters have asked me if the people have given me a mandate. My answer is no: The people have given us a chance.

In the campaign, all of us listened to the people of North Carolina. We would not be here if we had not listened. The people want us, the governor and the General Assembly, to work together and bring real progress to our state.

The people want constructive action, not conflict. They want change, not business as usual. They want us to put their future first and our politics second. They are right. They deserve no less, and my commitment, to them and to you, is that action and change are what they will get!

In these 100 days, I have met with many of you. We talked about our hopes for North Carolina and for this session, and we listened to each other. We share many of the same goals. On the opening day of the session, we heard Lieutenant Governor Wicker, Speaker Blue, and Senator Basnight speak eloquently and passionately about the needs of our children and all our people.

But talking to each other is not an end in itself. As Senator Basnight said, "It is time to stop speaking and start acting."[7] The measure of our success this year will not be what happens to you and me—who's up, who's down; who's in, who's out; who's hot, who's not. The measure of our success will not be the legislation we pass. It will be the lives we touch.

This must be our greater goal: concerted action for the people of North Carolina. They gave us this chance. Their future comes first, and this year, together, we can begin to shape that future.

III

With our action or inaction, we will choose the kind of future North Carolina will have. The choice is stark. We could choose a future of low-skill, low-wage jobs; educational underachievement; and a growing gap between the prosperous and the poor North Carolina. Or we could choose a future in which every child comes to school healthy and ready to learn; every youngster graduates from high school; every graduate gets the training and higher education required for a good job; and every family can provide a better future for their children.

Which future will we choose? That depends on how we answer many issues in this legislative session. We will answer it by:

—How we respond to the crime crisis in our state;

—How we provide access to good health, especially for every child;

—How we all respond to the challenge set out by the Government Performance Audit to make government more effective and more efficient;[8]

—How we treat state employees and whether we involve them in making government work better to serve our citizens;

—How we fulfill our responsibilities to our children as stewards of the environment.

But tonight I will focus on three areas of action, for these are the most critical to our future in North Carolina. They are jobs, education, and children.

Jobs

In the last month, we have seen economic changes take jobs from hundreds of North Carolinians. To all of them and to all working people in this state, we must pledge to be more aggressive and more creative in building our economic future. We want North Carolina to be a place where business wants to do business. We want business leaders and economic leaders all over the nation and the world to know about, and be talking about, what we are doing in North Carolina, and I believe we can do that.

Our economic development approach will include:

—A new charge to the Department of Commerce, led by Dave Phillips, and the Economic Development Board, led by Bob Jordan, to develop a long-range, highly competitive strategy;[9]

—A Workforce Preparedness Council, led by Sandy Babb, to give new leadership and new direction to our skill-training efforts;[10]

—An Entrepreneurial Development Board, led by Bob Luddy, to multiply our number of start-up companies and emerging businesses;[11]

—A Small Business Development Council, led by Lieutenant Governor Dennis Wicker, to assist small businesses, which are the backbone of our economy.[12]

This is our economic development team. We expect them to think creatively and act boldly, and we give them this charge: create more jobs, and more good jobs, for North Carolinians.

Education

North Carolinians will get the best jobs if, and only if, we have the education and the skills that the jobs of the twenty-first century will require. So, we must make sure every child starts school ready to learn. Then we must make sure that every student graduates; then make sure that every graduate has mastered what they must know, and be able to do, to work in the modern economy; then make sure that every graduate has a chance to go to a community college or a four-year college or university. Then, and only then, will North Carolina be able to compete in the twenty-first century.

The biennial budget that I propose will have very limited new resources, as you know.[13] So, we must make state government more efficient and more effective. This budget commits us to achieving efficiencies of at least $100 million each year. If we carry through on the performance audit recommendations, if we involve state employees in making changes, and if we work together, we can make state government work better for the taxpayers. Then we must apply our limited dollars to where they will yield the greatest returns:

—$105 million for a greater commitment to our university system, because this system must be excellent if we want North Carolina to excel;

—$113 million for a greater commitment to workforce preparedness and to our community college system. We must make our workforce competitive with any in the world;[14]

—$60 million for a greater commitment to the Basic Education Program, with a special emphasis on low-wealth and small school systems;[15]

—And $200 million for a greater commitment to teachers and educators in our public schools, so they can do the job they know how to do for our children and our future!

We ask a lot of our schools, but we have not made clear what we expect of them. We should change that during these next four years. Educators are willing to be held accountable if they are given a clear mission and the resources they need to achieve their mission. The key to great schools is great teachers, and we have great teachers in North Carolina. It is time to give them the clear mission, the decision-making authority, and the tools they need to do their job!

We must set higher standards and instill greater accountability. So, our budget proposes an Education Standards and Accountability Commission that will involve educators, parents, and business people in setting standards. The standards must define what our graduates should know and be able to do to compete in the twenty-first century economy. The standards must be high, they must be specific, and they must be measurable. Then, and only then, will we be able to hold our schools accountable for results![16]

Children

We know that the work teachers do in the classroom too often is overwhelmed by the problems children bring to the classroom. So, we must start earlier to prepare our children for school and for life. We can give every child a better start, and we can do it by making these investments:

—$5 million to enact the Baby Bill, strengthen the child-staff ratios for child-care centers, and demonstrate that we in North Carolina are committed to doing the most of any state for the least among us;[17]

—$16 million to guarantee that every child receives immunizations against disease. President Clinton has made a commitment to do this for many children. I applaud him for that, but we can do it for every child. If we can afford to pave every road in North Carolina that carries 100 automobiles a day, we can afford to vaccinate every child in this state;[18]

—$3 million to expand financial help for the working poor who too often cannot afford quality child care;

—$8 million to provide greater child-care tax credits for middle-income families;[19]

—And let's begin, this year, the most ambitious partnership for children of any state in America. Our budget proposes $60 million to establish this ambitious new public-private initiative. Leading it will be the North Carolina Partnership for Children.[20]

This Partnership for Children will bring together parents, churches, the nonprofit sector, business, and government to develop statewide goals and a strategic vision for our early childhood initiatives. It will challenge people in local communities to think creatively and come up with innovative ways of providing health care, child care, and other essential services to children. Local people, whether in Gates County or Mecklenburg County, can best decide what works in their communities.

It will chart our course for the next four years and for the next generation. It will make North Carolina a state where children come first. It will lay a foundation that will give our children the best start, the highest hopes, and the best chance for success of children in any state in this nation!

IV

These are ambitious goals, but we can be satisfied with nothing less. We are building for the next generation. We are building the house of which Dan Blue spoke. It is the house that our children and our grandchildren will inhabit.

Regardless of what we do this year, as long as we fail one child in North Carolina, we have not done our job. As long as one child cannot get a decent meal, we have not done our job. As long as one child cannot see a doctor, we have not done our job. As long as one child contracts a disease that could have been prevented, we have not done our job. As long as one child grows up without love and learning, we have not done our job. As long as one child's growth, and health, and enjoyment of life are threatened by pollution, we have not done our job. As long as one child's parents are unable to get a good job and make a decent living, we have not done our job. As long as one child's teacher is held back in any way from doing the job of teaching, we have not done our job. As long as one child cannot get a public education that paves the way for success in life, we have not done our job. As long as one child cannot grow up healthy and happy, smart and skilled, ready to think for a living and solve problems, able to do a good job and even create other jobs, we have not done our job.

I am realistic enough to know that our job will not be finished this session or in the next four years. But I am optimistic enough to believe that all of us in this great chamber tonight, and all of us in this great state, will not rest until we have built this house for every child in North Carolina: a house of healthy starts; a house of education; a house where the air is clean, and the water is fresh, and the land is green; a house where we are safe; a house where our children can grow, and work, and earn, and provide a better future for their families.

This is our great challenge. This is our chance. This is our time. Let us begin now to build this house for our children, for their children, and for the future of North Carolina.

Thank you. I look forward to working with you.

---

[1] Dennis Alvin Wicker (1952-   ), born in Sanford; B.A., University of North Carolina at Chapel Hill, 1974; was graduated from Wake Forest University School of Law, 1978. Attorney; member, state House of Representatives, 1980-1992; lieutenant governor and senate president, elected 1992, reelected 1996; Democrat. *News and Observer*, November 6, 1996; *North Carolina Manual, 1995-1996*, 221.

[2] Daniel Terry Blue Jr. (1949-   ), born in Robeson County; resident of Wake County; B.S., N.C. Central University, 1970; J.D., Duke University, 1973. Attorney; member, since 1981, Speaker, 1991-1994, state House of Representatives; Democrat. *News and Observer*, November 10, 11, December 9, 1994; *North Carolina Manual, 1995-1996*, 549-550.

[3] Marc Basnight (1947-   ), born in Manteo; resident of Dare County; was graduated from Manteo High School, 1966. President, co-owner, Basnight Construction Co., Manteo; state senate member, since 1985, and president pro tempore, since 1992; Democrat. *North Carolina Manual, 1995-1996*, 448, 451.

[4] An economic recession during the late 1980s and early 1990s, diminishing income and sales tax collections, federal budget cuts, and unfunded federal mandates dried up much of the revenue stream to state and local governments across the country. Even with its normally robust economy, North Carolina faced a major financial crisis during three consecutive fiscal years beginning July 1, 1989, and ending June 30, 1992. Actual income fell far short of the revenue projections upon which state budgets already adopted for those

years were based, and the North Carolina Constitution required the governor, as budget administrator, to keep the state from running a deficit. Governor Martin used spending cuts, funding shifts, and a hiring freeze to stabilize the F.Y. 1989-1990 budget then in effect. To help balance the F.Y. 1990-1991 budget, he recommended 3 percent reductions in departmental and institutional operating budgets, totaling $244.5 million, and a negative reserve for lapsed salaries and excess receipts to save another $97.9 million; the General Assembly adopted both measures, along with increases in fees due the state, changes in tax collection strategies, and postponing the June 1991 payday for state employees until the next month—and the start of a new fiscal year. State lawmakers cut spending by $557 million, and raised taxes by $617 million, to prevent a $1.2 billion shortfall in the budget approved for F.Y. 1991-1992.

Having replenished the revenue flow, the General Assembly reviewed the Executive Budget Act, which established the entire state budget process. For a description of budget reform legislation passed in 1991 and 1992, and an overview of the state's fiscal crisis, see Joseph S. Ferrell, ed., *North Carolina Legislation, 1993* (Chapel Hill: Institute of Government, University of North Carolina at Chapel Hill, 1993), 9-12; see also *Our State, Our Future: The Report of the North Carolina Government Performance Audit Committee* (Raleigh: [The Committee], February 1993), 3-7, and Poff, *Addresses of Martin, 1989-1993*, 27-41.

[5] Devised to improve the quality and consistency of public schooling, from the core curriculum to support services, the Basic Education Program was described and implemented under *Session Laws of North Carolina, 1985*, c. 479, s. 55. The plan itself was an outgrowth of the Elementary and Secondary School Reform Act of 1984—which in turn was inspired by a report from the North Carolina Commission on Education for Economic Growth, a board Hunt established in October 1983. See *Education for Economic Growth: An Action Plan for North Carolina* ([Raleigh]: North Carolina Commission on Education for Economic Growth, April 1984); *N.C. Session Laws, 1983*, 1448-1450; and *N.C. Session Laws, 1983, Extra and Regular Sessions, 1984*, c. 1103.

[6] Accepting the speakership of the state House, January 27, 1993, Daniel T. Blue Jr. told convened legislators:

> Because of the courage of many of you sitting here today, our state now remains one of a handful in the nation with a balanced budget, a Triple A bond rating from all of the agencies, and revenues coming in ahead of projections. Our workplace safety laws are the model for all the states in this country.
>
> Now that we have laid the foundation, it is time to build the house. That's what Maya Angelou told us all last week at the presidential inauguration, in her poem, *A Rock, A River, A Tree*. Listen to this verse: "Lift up your hearts, each new house holds new chances for new beginnings. Do not be wedded forever to fear, eternally yoked to brutishness. The horizon leans forward, offering you space to place new steps of change. Here on the pulse of this fine day, you may have the courage to look up and out upon me, the rock, the river, the tree, your country."

Quotation from *Journal of the House of Representatives of the 1993 General Assembly of the State of North Carolina, First Session, 1993*, 22.

[7] "We speak continuously of the 'Year of the Child.' We speak continuously of opportunity for all people, but it is time to stop speaking and start acting in offering solutions to the very problems that are real and facing our citizens as they are children today." Excerpt of address by Senator Marc Basnight, acceptance of post of president pro tempore, January 27, 1993, from *Journal of the Senate of the General Assembly of the State of North Carolina, Session 1993*, 15.

[8] As a consequence of the fiscal difficulties of the early 1990s, the North Carolina General Assembly established the Government Performance Audit Committee to oversee "the nation's first legislatively driven efficiency study" of an executive branch of state government. Legislators requested the twenty-seven-member committee to look anew at governmental operating procedures and recommend methods "to improve the quality of state services"; propose "better management practices"; "restructure, reallocate, or reform

service delivery systems"; and "set priorities for future state spending." The committee conducted its mission between October 1991 and February 1993, when it submitted to state lawmakers 350 recommendations for action. *Our State, Our Future*, iii, 1-11; the government performance audit was authorized under "An Act to Make Base Budget and Expansion Budget Appropriations for Current Operations of State Departments, Institutions, and Agencies; to Make Appropriations for Capital Improvements for State Departments, Institutions, and Agencies; to Make Appropriations for Other Purposes; to Provide for Budget Reform; and to Provide for Revenue Reconciliation," *N.C. Session Laws, 1991*, II, c. 689, s. 347, ratified July 13, 1991.

[9] The General Assembly instructed the Economic Development Board, a component of the Commerce Department, to prepare a statewide comprehensive strategic economic development plan by April 1, 1994. The board was to identify "distressed areas," document business development concerns, and assemble an economic database for the state. It also was to review and update the four-year plan annually. Rick Carlisle, Hunt's economic policy adviser, led the effort. See "An Act to Make Continuation and Expansion Budget Appropriations for Current Operations of State Departments, Institutions, and Agencies, and for Other Purposes," *N.C. Session Laws, 1993*, I, c. 321, s. 313, ratified July 9, 1993; "The Capital Improvements Appropriations Act of 1993" [short title], *N.C. Session Laws, 1993*, II, c. 561, s. 12, ratified July 24, 1993; and *News and Observer*, September 24, 1993.

Incidentally, state legislators renamed the Department of Commerce, in 1989, as the Department of Economic and Community Development. The new appellation lasted until January 1, 1993, when the agency reverted to its former title. "An Act to Change the Name of the Department of Commerce to the Department of Economic and Community Development . . . and to Make Technical and Conforming Amendments to Various Laws," *N.C. Session Laws, 1989*, II, c. 751; and "An Act to Change the Name of the Department of Economic and Community Development, and to Make Technical and Conforming Amendments to Various Laws," *N.C Session Laws, Extra Session, 1991, Regular Session, 1992*, III, c. 959.

S. Davis Phillips (1942-   ) born in High Point; was educated at University of North Carolina at Chapel Hill. President, chief executive officer, Phillips Industries, Inc., textile manufacturing and factoring services holding company; partner, Market Square Partnership, High Point; past chairman, High Point Economic Development Corp., Piedmont Triad Development Corp., Piedmont Triad Partnership, N.C. Zoological Society, and of Babcock School of Management Board of Trustees, Wake Forest University; state commerce secretary, 1993-1997. *News and Observer*, December 15, 1992, January 16, 1997; *North Carolina Manual, 1995-1996*, 334.

Robert Byrd Jordan III (1932-   ), born in Mt. Gilead; B.S., North Carolina State College (later University), 1954; U.S. Army, 1955-1957, and Reserve, 1957-1962. President, Jordan Lumber and Supply; state senator, 1977-1984; elected lieutenant governor, 1984; Democratic candidate for governor, 1988; chairman, N.C. Economic Development Board, 1993-1995. *News and Observer*, November 9, 1988, April 17, 1993, June 17, 1995; *North Carolina Manual, 1987-1988*, 567, 570.

[10] Executive Order Number 4, signed March 10, 1993, established the Commission on Workforce Preparedness. *N.C. Session Laws, 1993*, 2:3187-3194. See also press release, Hunt Creates Commission on Workforce Preparedness, Raleigh, March 17, 1993, Governors Papers, James Baxter Hunt Jr.

Sandra Porter Babb (1940-   ), born in Pitt County; resident of Raleigh; B.S., 1960, M.A., 1962, East Carolina University; M.A., University of North Carolina at Chapel Hill, 1970. Public schoolteacher in N.C., Fla., and Calif., 1960-1967; instructor, Dept. of Social Sciences, St. Augustine's College, 1967-1969, and in Dept. of History, N.C. State University, 1969-1973; director, Raleigh Action City Program, 1974-1977; director, Outdoor Recreation Funding, 1977-1980, and director, Division of Community Assistance, 1980-1983, N.C. Dept. of Natural Resources and Community Development; member, Raleigh City Council, 1981-1985; director, government and member relations, HealthAmerica, Cary, 1983-1986; N.C. plan manager, Equicor Health Plan, Raleigh, 1986-1988; president, executive director,

NC Equity, Raleigh, 1988-1993; executive director, Governor's Commission on Workforce Preparedness, appointed 1993. Sandra Porter Babb, letter to Jan-Michael Poff, April 4, 1996.

[11] Hunt signed Executive Order Number 6, creating the Entrepreneurial Development Board, on April 12, 1993. *N.C. Session Laws, 1993,* 2:3198-3201; see also Entrepreneurial Development Board Charge, Raleigh, April 28, 199[3], Governors Papers, James Baxter Hunt Jr.

Robert L. Luddy (1945-   ), born in Miami, Fla.; B.S., LaSalle University, 1967; U.S. Army, 1967-1968. Founder, chief executive officer, Atlantic Fire Systems, 1976-1983, Raleigh; founder, developer, Triangle Entrepreneurial Development Center, Raleigh, since 1989; developer, Franklin Industrial Park, Youngsville, since 1989; founder, president, chief executive officer, Captive-Aire Systems, Inc., Youngsville, since 1979; chairman, Entrepreneurial Development Board, 1993-1995. *News and Observer,* December 18, 1994, August 16, 1995.

[12] Although Hunt referred to the entity Wicker led as the Small Business Development Council, its official designation was the North Carolina Small Business Council. See Executive Order Number 2, signed February 11, 1993, *N.C. Session Laws, 1993,* 2:3180-3184.

[13] The governor officially unveiled his spending proposals for the coming biennium on February 16, 1993. His remarks on that occasion are reprinted elsewhere in this volume. *North Carolina State Budget, 1993-1995 Biennium: Supplemental Budget Recommendations, James B. Hunt, Jr., Governor* (Raleigh: Office of State Budget and Management, February 1993) summarizes his fiscal proposals. For an outline of appropriations approved by state lawmakers, see *North Carolina State Budget, Post-Legislative Budget Summary, 1993-1995 Biennium, James B. Hunt, Jr., Governor* (Raleigh: Office of State Budget and Management, October 1993), and *Overview: Fiscal and Budgetary Actions, North Carolina General Assembly, 1993 Session and 1994 Sessions* (Raleigh: Fiscal Research Division, N.C. General Assembly, n.d.).

[14] Legislators earmarked $25.4 million for workforce preparedness programs at the state's community colleges during the 1993-1995 period. The governor, however, reserved almost $59 million for those purposes in his proposed $112.6 million spending increase for community colleges. *North Carolina State Budget, 1993-95 Biennium: Supplemental Budget Recommendations,* 24-26, and *North Carolina State Budget, Post-Legislative Budget Summary, 1993-95 Biennium,* 25.

[15] Lawmakers appropriated $18 million in supplemental funding for low-wealth school systems and another $8 million to bolster the state's small school systems for 1993-1995. Ashe and Jackson Counties, combined, received a further $600,565. Hunt had hoped to obtain $30 million for each year in the biennium. *North Carolina State Budget, 1993-95 Biennium: Supplemental Budget Recommendations,* 20; *North Carolina State Budget, Post-Legislative Budget Summary, 1993-95 Biennium,* 37-38, 47; *N.C. Session Laws, 1993,* I, c. 321, secs. 138, 138.1.

[16] "An Act to Create the North Carolina Education Standards and Accountability Commission" was ratified June 3, 1993; see *N.C. Session Laws, 1993,* I, c. 117. The legislation was amended under *N.C. Session Laws, 1993,* I, c. 321, s. 39.3, ratified July 9, 1993.

[17] The General Assembly lowered day care child-staff ratios under *N.C. Session Laws, 1993,* I, c. 321, s. 254.

[18] The governor requested $15.9 million for drugs, staff, and other necessities to provide all of the state's children, from birth to age nineteen, with a full regimen of inoculations; see North Carolina Hospital Association Winter Meeting, February 18, 1993, below. He also urged that the program be initiated during 1993-1994 and be fully operational in 1994-1995. State lawmakers ultimately approved $10.7 million for a statewide childhood inoculation program and instructed the Department of Environment, Health, and Natural Resources to draw up an eight-year plan for implementing the project. "Capital Improvements Appropriations Act of 1993" [short title], *N.C. Session Laws, 1993,* II, c. 561, s. 109; *N.C. Session Laws, 1993,* I, c. 321, s. 287; *North Carolina State Budget, 1993-95 Biennium: Supplemental Budget Recommendations,* 60-61; *North Carolina State Budget, Post-Legislative Budget Summary, 1993-95 Biennium,* 206; see also press release, Hunt's Immunization Plan Passes General

Assembly, Raleigh, July 6, 1993, and Healthy Start, Raleigh, February 25, 1994, Governors Papers, James B. Hunt Jr.

Hours after Hunt proposed a vaccination plan in his "State of the State" message, President Bill Clinton broadcast a television address from the Oval Office of the White House in which he repeated an earlier call for increased protection from childhood diseases: "And as we make deep cuts in existing government programs, we'll make new investments where they'll do the most good . . . a fairer tax system to ensure that parents who work full time will no longer raise their children in poverty, welfare reform to move people from welfare to work, vaccinations and Head Start opportunities for all children who need them, and a system of affordable quality health care for all Americans." Two days later, February 17, 1993, Clinton said in his "State of the Union" address, "Each day we delay really making a commitment to our children carries a dear cost. Half of the two-year-olds in this country today don't receive the immunizations they need against deadly diseases. Our plan will provide them for every eligible child. And we know now that we will save $10 later for every $1 we spend by eliminating preventable childhood diseases. That's a good investment no matter how you measure it." *Congressional Quarterly Almanac, 103rd Congress, 1st Session, 1993* (Washington, D.C.: Congressional Quarterly, Inc., 1994), 8D, 10D-11D.

[19] "An Act to Increase the Income Tax Credit for Child and Dependent Care Expense for Families with Income Below Forty Thousand Dollars a Year," *N.C. Session Laws, 1993,* I, c. 432, ratified July 22, 1993, became effective for taxable years beginning January 1, 1994. See also *North Carolina State Budget, 1993-95 Biennium: Supplemental Budget Recommendations,* 42, and *North Carolina State Budget, Post-Legislative Budget Summary, 1993-95 Biennium,* 143.

[20] *N.C. Session Laws, 1993,* I, c. 321, s. 254, set forth the General Assembly's conditions for funding the North Carolina Partnership for Children, Inc.

OPENING ADDRESS
SPECIAL LEGISLATIVE SESSION ON CRIME

FEBRUARY 8, 1994

[In the weeks leading to, and then during, the special legislative session on crime, Hunt worked hard to build support among a variety of audiences across the state for his thirty-six-point prevention/punishment package. For example, see: Notes for Comments to State Senators, Raleigh, January 4; N.C. DARE Fifth Annual Conference, Raleigh, January 6; Kiwanis Speech, Greensboro, January 13; Substance-Abuse Center Groundbreaking, Greensboro, January (13)14; Governor's Teleconference on Crime (draft script), Raleigh, January 18; African American Ministers, Raleigh, January 21; Charlotte Rotary Club, Charlotte, January 25; Legislative Meeting Talking Points, Charlotte, January 25; Teacher Advisory Committee, Charlotte, January 25; NCAE Summit on School Violence, Raleigh, January 26; Governor's Educators' Forum on Crime (draft script), Raleigh, January 27; N.C. Press Association, Chapel Hill, January 27; Liberty Middle School, Liberty, February 4; Crime Forum, Research Triangle Park, February 8(9); Law Enforcement/Victims Advocates Press Conference, Raleigh, February 14; Briefing for Chamber of Commerce Representatives, Raleigh, February 15; N.C. Democratic Chairs Lobbying Day, Raleigh, February 16; Prevention Briefing, Raleigh, February 16; Victims' Briefing Talking Points, Raleigh, February 17; Special Session Update, Raleigh, March 3; Sentencing

Statement, Raleigh, March 8; N.C. Conference of Superior Court Judges Banquet, Raleigh, March 18.

Press releases and media advisories on the governor's crime prevention and punishment proposals include: Governor Hunt to Call Special Session on Crime, Raleigh, December 23, 1993; Governor Details 36-Point Crime Plan, Raleigh, January 13, 1994; Governor Hunt to Hold Statewide SOS Briefing for Educators, Raleigh, January 21, 1994; Governor Hunt's Crime Plan Available to Public, Raleigh, January 26, 1994; Governor Hunt to Address Joint Session of General Assembly, Raleigh, February 4, 1994; Governor Hunt to Keynote Leadership Council Meeting on Crime, Raleigh, February 4, 1994; Hunt Urges General Assembly to Take "Strong, Tough" Action on Crime, Raleigh, February 8, 1994; Law Enforcement, Victims' Advocates Support Governor Hunt, Raleigh, February 8, 1994; Hunt Challenges Citizens to Fight Crime, Research Triangle Park, February 9, 1994; Hunt's Crime Plan Endorsed by Law Enforcement, Victims, Raleigh, February 14, 1994; Chambers Endorse Governor's Crime-Fighting Plan, Raleigh, February 15, 1994; Prevention Groups Urge Support for Governor's SOS Program, Raleigh, February 16, 1994; Senate Passes Hunt's "Three Strikes You're Out," Raleigh, February 25, 1994; Police Chiefs Endorse Governor's Punishment Bills, Raleigh, March 8, 1994; Text of Letter to House Members, Raleigh, March 15, 1994; Governor Hunt's No-Parole Bill for Murderers Approved, Raleigh, March 23, 1994; Governor Hunt's Crime Package Passed into Law, Raleigh, March 28, 1994; Governor Hunt Plans Citizens' Forums on Crime, Raleigh, April 4, 1994; Governor Hunt's Proposals Step Up Prevention Efforts for Youth, Raleigh, April 27, 1994; Governor Hunt Takes "New Approach" to Substance Abuse Programs, Raleigh, April 27, 1994; New Crime Session Laws to Take Effect, Raleigh, September 29, 1994, Governors Papers, James Baxter Hunt Jr.]

This is a unique session of the General Assembly. In a real sense, it was called by the people of North Carolina.

It was called because of what is happening in the communities where you and I live. In the last three months, three police officers in the Charlotte area have been shot down in cold blood.[1] Three weeks ago, a Winston-Salem policeman was killed by a parolee who had served only ten months on a ten-year sentence.[2] In the last ten days of January, eight people were murdered in the city of Raleigh, some only blocks from where you sit today.[3]

Our people are afraid, and they have told us that very clearly. One legislator told me that he had heard more from constituents about crime than any issue in his long legislative career.

In three months of hearings and meetings, Speaker Blue, Senator Basnight, and I listened to crime victims, police officers and sheriffs, district attorneys, and child advocates. I have walked with cops on the beat, heard the gunfire in dangerous communities, and heard little girls cry as they told me about being violently attacked.[4] If you have not talked to people in your community who have felt the pain and agony of crime, you should do so before you vote in this session.

You should talk to someone like Tyrone. Tyrone is the eleven-year-old boy I talked about in my television address last month. Tyrone lives with his mother in a public housing community in Durham and sees violence all around him. He saw his own father shot and killed. He told me that he is often afraid.[5]

Let me tell you about one of the 8,000 calls and letters I've received in the last few months about crime. Tyler Coleman is a ten-year-old girl who lives in Garner, in a safe neighborhood, with a family dog and an alarm system at her house. Her father is in law enforcement. Yet, she is also afraid. Her mother wrote me that Tyler is afraid to go to sleep at night. She's afraid someone will come into her house and hurt her. She's afraid to go to the shopping mall. She's even afraid to ride her bike down the street.[6]

Tyler and Tyrone are not alone. People fear what is happening in their communities and our state. They fear for their safety and their families' safety. They are looking to us for action. You and I have heard their voices. It is now time to heed their call.

You know what my plan of action is. The thirty-six recommendations that I have made will be introduced as legislation today.[7]

The cynics doubt our ability to take effective action. They don't think we can do it, but I believe we can, and you in this legislature have shown that we can. You showed it last year. You began Smart Start. You began an ambitious effort to raise standards and put more accountability in our schools. You began a new economic development strategy built on high skills and high-wage jobs.

You took important steps to make our state safer. You authorized 5,000 new prison spaces.[8] You passed a structured sentencing law that will give us truth in sentencing.[9] You passed tough laws to keep guns and violence out of schools.

But the people do not believe we have done enough, and they are right. They know that government is failing to meet its most basic responsibility: to keep them safe. They know that we have not done enough to make sure dangerous criminals do their time—even with the new prisons. They know that we have not done enough to make the criminal justice system more efficient and effective, even with structured sentencing. They know that we have not done enough for children and families in our state—even with Smart Start, and higher standards, and higher skills. We have not done enough to give our kids a chance for more than drugs, and guns, and crime, and prison.

As elected representatives of the people, you and I have a responsibility to do everything we can to keep our people safe. We owe it to them to make their safety our top priority. We owe it to Tyrone and Tyler.

I believe we must set three goals for this session. Our first goal: keep violent criminals behind bars longer and show them that crime does not pay. Nothing else will work unless we have real punishment. This means no parole for first-degree murderers. They should get the death penalty or they should get life without parole, period. They should never get out.[10]

It means "three strikes and you're out" for violent felons.[11] It means five more years in prison if you use a gun when committing a felony.[12] It means trying fourteen- and fifteen-year-olds, who commit the most violent crimes, as adults, and no longer keeping their criminal records secret.[13] And it means raising the prison cap so that more than 3,000 criminals, many of them violent, do not walk out of prison and return to your neighborhoods and mine in the next month.[14]

Our second goal: change the criminal justice system so prosecutors have the tools they need and victims are put first. This means trying drug dealers quickly and making drug users get treatment.

Our third goal: reach out in North Carolina and help youngsters who can be saved from a life of crime. This means starting the SOS [Save Our Students] program to give middle-school kids something positive and constructive to do in the afternoons—a safe place to be, with adults who can teach them values and discipline. It means family resource centers in elementary schools.[15] It means getting thousands of North Carolinians involved in these and other programs to help save our students.

It means putting inmates to work and learning skills, so they'll have an opportunity to earn an honest living when they get out. No excuses for returning to crime.

I believe the plan I've put before you will meet these three goals. I believe we can afford to fund this plan. We can't afford not to.

I believe we can pay for it without raising taxes, and we can do it without hurting Smart Start, education standards, job training, and economic development. This plan carries a price tag of $27 million in one-time capital costs next year and $91 million in recurring expenditures. This will take some new money, but I am committed to fiscal responsibility. That's why I will recommend during the short session at least $45 million in specific, permanent cuts to finance the operating costs of this plan.

Let me talk to you now, as leaders of North Carolina, about our duty in this special session. We start with a sense of urgency. The people feel it, and I feel it. I know that you feel it. I urge you to act with that sense of urgency. Never before has our legislature had an opportunity to focus on a single issue of such importance to so many people. Never before have the people of North Carolina been watching so closely.

I told you about the letter I got from Tyler Coleman's mother. It is an eloquent and moving letter. I want you to hear part of it. She wrote, "No child in our state should be afraid to go to sleep in their own bed, or ride their bike in their own neighborhood. Please urge our legislature to pass this crime package, for our children. I do not want my daughter growing up in fear of her safety. Give us back that sense of safety.

"We live in the greatest nation on earth, blessed with the greatest resources," she wrote. "We must put some of those resources into this anti-crime package in order to secure our future. I love our state, and I pray that our leaders will realize how serious crime is affecting its citizens."[16]

We owe it to Alice Coleman and her daughter to take strong, tough, and effective action—and make no mistake about it, the people of this state will tolerate nothing less. They will not tolerate excuses. They will not tolerate wasting time and money. They will not tolerate distraction by other issues. They will not tolerate inaction. They know that we cannot solve the problem from Raleigh, but they also know that the battle begins here, today.

Today we have a responsibility, a responsibility to answer the call of the people, a responsibility to Tyrone and Tyler. Today we have an opportunity, an opportunity to work together, bringing together both parties, both houses of this legislature and all branches of government. Today we face a challenge, a challenge to get tougher with dangerous criminals, but also a challenge to save a generation of young people from a life of crime.

We must meet our responsibility. We must seize this opportunity, and we must rise to the challenge. I am ready to work with you. I am as serious about this, and as determined, as I have ever been. So are the people of North Carolina: They are waiting, and they are watching. It is time for action.

---

[1] Two law enforcement officers from Charlotte and another from nearby Kannapolis were murdered during the last quarter of 1993. Responding to a report of a stolen/suspicious van, Charlotte policemen Anthony Alford Nobles and John Thomas Burnette were shot by Aldon Jerome Harden, an occupant of the vehicle. Harden had been arrested nineteen times since March 1984 and was on probation for a robbery conviction at the time of the killings. *Charlotte Observer*, October 6, 7, 8, 1993.

Tony Edwin Sherrill shot Kannapolis policeman Roger Dale Carter eight times with an assault-style weapon, on New Year's Eve, 1993, before killing himself. Earlier, Sherrill had called police "to turn himself in on outstanding arrest warrants." Carter was the first officer killed in Kannapolis Police Department history. *Charlotte Observer*, January 4, 1994.

[2] Robert Buitrago, an off-duty Winston-Salem policeman, was in the checkout aisle of a Food Lion grocery store when he witnessed the robbery of a cashier by a gun-carrying thief. Unarmed and dressed in civilian clothes, he nevertheless attempted to apprehend the gunman, who shot him in the chest. Buitrago was declared dead on arrival at Baptist Hospital, Winston-Salem.
The arrest record of Buitrago's killer, Thomas Michael Larry, stretched back to 1972. Larry was released from prison in September 1990 after serving thirty-six months of a ten-year sentence for armed robbery. *Winston-Salem Journal*, January 16, 17, 18, 19, 1994.
[3] The worst string of murders in Raleigh history claimed eight lives from January 21-31, 1994. Nearly all of the perpetrators had criminal records, and one was on probation for a drug conviction. *News and Observer*, February 5, 1994.
[4] See press releases, Hunt Holding Series of Meetings with State Crime Experts, Raleigh, October 27, 1993; Hunt Continues Anti-Crime Meetings, Raleigh, November 8, 1993; and Hunt Continues Anti-Crime Meetings, Raleigh, November 29, 1993, Governors Papers, James Baxter Hunt Jr.
[5] The governor first mentioned Tyrone Turrentine in his "Televised Address: Special Legislative Session on Crime," Raleigh, January 12, 1994, reprinted below. Tyrone's father went for a pack of cigarettes one night and never returned home. The next day, five-year-old Tyrone and his brother found him lying in a creek, shot in the back. *Independent Weekly* (Durham), February 16, 1994; *News and Observer*, January 13, 1994.
[6] "Just this week my daughter told me she thought someone was going to come into our house and hurt her. She also revealed she was afraid of going to the shopping mall anymore and did not even want to ride her bike down the street to her friend's house. I tried to explain to her that she was safe. We live in a 'safe neighborhood.' My husband is in law enforcement and is trained to protect people. We have an alarm system in our home and a dog that barks at anything unusual. As I explained all of this to Tyler, I began to think of all the children that don't have all of these assurances and, if my child is frightened, how they must feel each day." Letter, Alice Coleman to Governor Hunt, reprinted in *News and Observer*, February 9, 1994; see also footnote 16, below.
[7] Although Hunt touched on some of his thirty-six anti-crime proposals later in this address, a more complete component listing accompanies his text, Press Conference on Crime-Fighting Program, January 13, 1994, reprinted elsewhere in this volume.
[8] Lawmakers approved spending $87.5 million to house 3,712 inmates under "An Act to Appropriate the Balance of the Funds from the Proceeds of the Two Hundred Million Dollars in General Obligation Bonds Authorized for the Construction of State Prison and Youth Services Facilities, and to Provide for the Use of Inmates in Prison Construction," *N.C. Session Laws, 1993*, II, c. 550, ratified July 24, 1993. The legislation lists the projects and inmate capacity of each. Hunt, on February 25, 1993, recommended building space for 4,200 additional inmates with the remaining bond funds; the press release accompanying that announcement is reprinted elsewhere in this volume. Legislators allocated the initial $112.5 million, from the $200 million prison bond referendum approved by state voters on November 6, 1990, under *N.C. Session Laws, 1991*, II, c. 689, secs. 239-240.
[9] "An Act to Provide for Structured Sentencing in North Carolina Consistent with the Standard Operating Capacity of the Department of Correction and Local Confinement Facilities and to Redefine State and County Responsibilities for the Confinement of Misdemeanants," was ratified July 24, 1993, and became effective on January 1, 1995; see *N.C. Session Laws, 1993*, II, c. 538. The law was revised by "An Act to Make Technical Amendments and Conforming Changes to the General Statutes and Session Laws Relating to Structured Sentencing, Misdemeanors, and Felonies," *N.C. Session Laws, 1993, Extra and Regular Sessions, 1994*, c. 14, ratified March 15, 1994.
[10] "An Act to Provide for Life Imprisonment Without Parole for First Degree Murder and to Provide That, After a Defendant has Served Twenty-Five Years of Imprisonment and Every Two Years Thereafter, the Defendant's Sentence of Life Imprisonment Without Parole Shall be Reviewed by a Resident Superior Court Judge for the County in Which the Defendant was Convicted and the Judge Shall Make a Recommendation to the Governor or an Executive Agency Designated by the Governor as to Whether or not the Defendant's

Sentence Should be Altered or Commuted," *N.C. Session Laws, 1993, Extra and Regular Sessions, 1994*, c. 21, ratified March 23, 1994; press releases, Gov. Hunt's No-Parole Bill for Murderers Approved, Raleigh, March 23, 1994, and Gov. Hunt's Proposal to End Parole for First-Degree Murderers Now Law, Raleigh, April 19, 1994, Governors Papers, James Baxter Hunt Jr.

[11] Legislators adopted, on March 24, 1994, a "Three Strikes You're In" provision for sentencing violent habitual felons. Anyone convicted of two violent felonies in North Carolina or anywhere else in the United States was considered a "violent habitual felon." Conviction on charges of a third violent felony carried a sentence of life imprisonment without parole. "Crime Control Act of 1994" (short title), *N.C. Session Laws, 1993, Extra and Regular Sessions, 1994*, c. 22, s. 31, was effective upon ratification. See also press release, Senate Passes Hunt's "Three Strikes You're Out," Raleigh, February 25, 1994, Governors Papers, James Baxter Hunt Jr.

[12] *N.C. Session Laws, 1993, Extra and Regular Sessions, 1994*, c. 22, secs. 18-24, increased firearm penalties. Mentioned first among them was the provision that a person convicted of a felony and "who used, displayed, or threatened to use or display a firearm during the commission of the felony," received a five-year prison term in addition to the sentence merited for the "underlying" crime. See also press release, Gov. Hunt's Proposals Toughen Gun Laws, Raleigh, May 13, 1994, Governors Papers, James Baxter Hunt Jr.

[13] S.B. 28, which Hunt supported, would have required "judges to try especially violent fourteen- and fifteen-year-olds as adults." It cleared the senate, but its companion proposal in the House did not fare as well. See Attachment, Special Session Statement, Raleigh, March 25, 1994, Governors Papers, James Baxter Hunt Jr.; *N.C. Senate Journal, 1993, Extra and Second Sessions, 1994*, 20, 90, 92, 476. "An Act to Provide that a Court May Order that Juvenile Records of Juveniles Adjudicated or Convicted of Class A-E Felonies May be Used at a Subsequent Criminal Trial Either in the Guilt Phase or to Provide an Aggravating Factor at Sentencing," *N.C. Session Laws, 1993, Extra and Regular Sessions, 1994*, c. 7, was ratified March 8, 1994.

[14] "An Act to Provide that the Governor Shall Set the Prison Population Cap and to Provide that in Paroling Inmates Under the Prison Population Cap the Parole Commission May Release Nonviolent Inmates Who Would Not Otherwise be Eligible for Release," *N.C. Session Laws, 1993, Extra and Regular Sessions, 1994*, c. 15, ratified March 15, 1994. See also Press Release: Hunt Raises Prison Cap to Avert Parole Deadline, March 15, 1994, reprinted below; other related press releases include Governor Hunt, Attorney General Can't Declare Cap Unconstitutional, Raleigh, January 10, 1994, and Governor Hunt Says State Will Oppose Loss of Prison Beds, Raleigh, June 29, 1994, Governors Papers, James Baxter Hunt Jr.

[15] Hunt's "Save Our Students" proposal was adopted by the General Assembly as "Support Our Students." The program was established within the Department of Human Resources by "An Act to Adjust the Appropriations Made for the 1993-94 Fiscal Year and the 1994-95 Fiscal Year to Aid in the Control and Prevention of Crime," *N.C. Session Laws, 1993, Extra and Regular Sessions, 1994*, c. 24, s. 30. The act, ratified March 26, 1994, also founded the Family Resource Center Grant Program; see sections 4, 31.

[16] "No child in our State should be afraid to go to sleep in their own bed, or ride their bike in their neighborhood. Please urge our Legislature to pass this crime package—for our children. I do not want my daughter growing up in fear of her safety on a daily basis. Please, help us provide a safe and nurturing environment for all children in North Carolina. Give us back a sense of safety. We live in the greatest Nation on earth—blessed with the greatest resources. We must put some of these resources into this anti-crime package in order to secure our future. I love our state and I pray that our leaders will realize how serious crime is affecting its citizens." Letter, Alice Coleman to Governor Hunt, reprinted in *News and Observer*, February 9, 1994.

STATE OF THE STATE

FEBRUARY 9, 1995

[Governor Hunt foreshadowed the contents of this address in his Statement on Tax Relief, December 8, 1994, and in speeches to NC FREE, December 15, 1994; Charlotte Business Roundtable, January 9; North Carolina Education Commission, January 12; John Locke Foundation, January 19; Laurinburg/Scotland County Chamber of Commerce, January 19; Raleigh Business Roundtable, January 23; North Carolina Press Association, January 26; and N.C. Citizens for Business and Industry Legislative Forum, February 2, 1995; see also press release, Governor Hunt Outlines Legislative Priorities for '95 Session, Charlotte, January 9, 1995. He also delivered condensed versions of his 1995 State of the State address on a number of occasions, including the Wilmington Business Roundtable, February 27; Greenville Business Roundtable, March 6; the Cleveland County Chamber of Commerce, March 15; Hickory Business Roundtable, March 20; Forsyth County Elected Officials, May 5; and Davidson County Council of Chambers of Commerce, May 31, 1995. Governors Papers, James Baxter Hunt Jr.]

Mr. President,[1] Mr. Speaker,[2] Mr. President Pro Tem,[3] Members of the Council of State, Justices of the Supreme Court, Judges of the Court of Appeals, Members of the Cabinet, Members of the General Assembly:

I want to begin by introducing some people who are sitting in the galleries with the First Lady. You won't recognize their names. They aren't famous. They haven't been in the news. But they are the most important people here today.

They are the citizens of North Carolina. They are the taxpayers. They are the reason we are here.

—First are Pamela Cross and her boys, Jacob and Steve. Pamela works for an insurance company in Charlotte.

—Next are Brent and Sheila Gerald from Greensboro. He's a firefighter, and she's at home with their daughter, Alexandria.

—Then there are George and Evelyn Schnupp, who retired to New Bern after running a marina and boatyard in New York.

—In front of them is the Williams family, Franklin and Jo Ann, with their daughters Laura Jane and Mary Elizabeth. Franklin is a farmer in Duplin County, and Jo Ann works as a home economics extension agent.

—Jessie Copeland is a seventy-one-year-old grandmother here in Raleigh who's working to make Chavis Heights a place where children can be safe.[4]

—And next are the Bartolos. Staff Sergeant [Scott] Bartolo is stationed at Fort Bragg, and his wife Petra is working toward her college degree and caring for their sons, Anthony and Nicholas.[5] Let's welcome these families to their capital.

I introduce these people to make a point: For the last three months, Election Day has been *the* issue for most of us in this chamber.[6] We care a lot about what happened, and why, and what it means, and what this session will be like. But these people care a lot more about their families and their future than they do about our politics. They care about their jobs, the safety of their families, and the education of their children. And that's what we should care about this year.

Our job is to put these people first—and our politics last. Our job is to move beyond campaign rhetoric and partisan turf fighting. Our job is to find common ground where we can discuss important issues on their merits, listen to each other, and learn from each other. You and I may never get another chance like this one to build a better future for North Carolina. Let's make up our minds today that we're going to do what's right for these people.

We're building a better future in North Carolina today because of what the General Assembly did in the last two years, Democrats and Republicans together:

—Tough laws against crime and smart programs to prevent crime;

—An aggressive economic development strategy;

—Smaller classes, better teaching, and higher standards in the public schools, and better early childhood education;

—A bond issue that is building new libraries, and classrooms, and labs, and other facilities at our universities and community colleges.[7]

All of that was done without raising taxes. Democrats and Republicans together built that foundation. This year, let's work together to build a better future.

Let's make this a productive session. Let's concentrate on doing three things: First, cut taxes. Second, fight crime. Third, and most important, help children.

Taxes

We should cut taxes because it is the right thing to do. It is the right thing for our economy. It is the right thing for the record number of men and women who have jobs in this state today, and it is the right thing for their children. So let's give the most tax relief to the hard-working families who deserve it most. I have proposed a $483 million tax cut.[8] Three-fourths of it would go to families like these, because working families raising children need the most help.

We should raise the personal exemption for every member of a household by $500. We should create a tax credit of $50 per child—and we should remember that these families need the money.[9] The Geralds need the money: They want to put their tax savings toward Alexandria's college education. Pamela Cross needs the money for food and clothing for her boys, and maybe a few extras like a baseball glove or karate lessons.

We should also make tax cuts that will build our economy and build our children's economic future. North Carolina's already one of the best places in the country to live and do business. This year, we can make it even more attractive and competitive. We should repeal the intangibles tax on stocks and bonds, so George and Evelyn Schnupp can have a little more in their retirement years.[10] We should reduce the corporate income tax, and we should pass it this year so we can use it right now to recruit business and jobs to North Carolina.[11]

Now this is a big tax cut—nearly half a billion dollars. It'll require tough choices and new priorities, and it must be done with the help, and involvement, and participation of state employees who care just as much as we do about giving taxpayers their money's worth. It won't be easy, but we can do it, because state government can get by with less; and we ought to do it, because these families and their children deserve it.

Crime[12]

We should continue our efforts to fight crime, because it is the right thing to do. It is the right thing for the law-abiding people who are the backbone of our state, and it is the right thing to do for their children.

Children can't learn in schools that aren't safe. Families can't live in neighborhoods that aren't safe. Our state won't ever be safe if more and more young people get involved in drugs and crime.

Even in small towns like Wallace, crime is a problem. Franklin and Jo Ann Williams know that. Franklin is the treasurer at his church. Last summer, thieves broke into their house and stole $300 in church collections. The Williamses weren't home at the time, so they weren't hurt. But a lot of victims aren't that lucky.

We need to do a lot more to help keep communities safe, in Duplin County and all over North Carolina. I believe fighting crime starts with tougher sentences for violent criminals. When a dangerous criminal is locked up behind bars, every North Carolinian is safer. So we should pass longer sentences for violent crimes, like second-degree murder, rape, armed robbery, and other felonies. I will propose increasing these sentences by 30 percent.

We need to build more prisons, and find faster and cheaper ways to do it. My budget will propose more than 2,000 more prison beds over the next two years, part of a plan to build more than 4,000 new beds in four years.[13] We need to put more prisoners to work in North Carolina.[14] We need to repeal the prison cap.[15]

We should pass a victims' rights amendment to our state constitution. If criminals have rights, victims of crime should have rights, too.[16] We should pass a law requiring registration of sex offenders and notifying communities where they live. Families have a right to know when dangerous sex offenders move in next door or down the street. [17]

We need to make all our communities safer, and public housing communities need special efforts. They need more police officers and tougher laws to evict those who put their neighbors in danger.[18] Jessie Copeland knows how important it is to get guns, and drugs, and dangerous people out of public housing. She's helped hundreds of young people stay out of crime, and more of us need to get involved in that.

All of us, not just government, need to do more to prevent crime and keep a better eye on our children. That's what the SOS [Support Our Students] program is all about. That's what a lot of these people are about. They've been volunteering at their schools and churches. They've worked as Big Buddies, and Big Sisters, and mentors to troubled teens. This year, I've started volunteering in a Wake County SOS program, working with a young man here in Raleigh. I'm not proposing more tax dollars for this, but I am saying that we need more people and more volunteer time devoted to our children.

Children[19]

Fighting crime will build a safer North Carolina. Cutting taxes will build a stronger economy and stronger families. But there is more we can do and should do to build our future. We have to build up our children so they will be healthy, and smart, and productive, and law-abiding citizens in the twenty-first century. That means we have to make fundamental changes in our public schools so North Carolina's graduates will compete and succeed in the modern economy.

We need to do five things to make our schools better. Some will take legislation, and some will take action by the State Board of Education and Department of Public Instruction. All will take hard work in every single school in this state.

First, we must restore discipline and make our schools safe places to learn and teach. That means more support for principals and teachers to keep schools safe. More school resource officers on campuses. It means zero tolerance for guns, drugs, and weapons. And zero tolerance for students who put others in danger: We should automatically expel those students for up to a full year. But don't put them on the streets. Put them in alternative schools, or even in education boot camps, where they learn to read, and write, and do math—and do what they're told.[20]

Second, we must give teachers the tools they need to do their jobs. Next to parents, teachers are the most important influence on children. Teachers need better pay. They need better training. They need more time for planning, and they need more voice in how schools are run. If we want good schools in North Carolina, we've got to have good teachers.

Third, we must go back to basics—emphasizing reading, writing, and math. It's most important to do this in the early years, and smaller class size can help us do it. Burke County has shown what can happen to test scores when class size is cut dramatically.[21] We can do that all across North Carolina.

Last year the legislature cut class size in kindergarten down to twenty-three students. This year we should do the same in the first grade, and we should give schools the flexibility to cut class size even more dramatically. If we let them, local schools can have one teacher for every seventeen children in kindergarten through third grade. Then we'll really see progress in North Carolina's schools.[22]

Fourth, we must set higher standards for what our students should know and be able to do, so they graduate with the skills they need to be good workers and good citizens.

Fifth, we must improve job training, especially for the many young people who go straight from school to work. Schools and businesses must join together in new partnerships to help us do that.

To make these changes in our schools, we need more support for principals and teachers. We need more involvement by parents. And my budget will propose shifting millions of dollars from administration to local schools, because we need to spend less money in bureaucracy and more in the classrooms of North Carolina.[23]

We must build a better education system, and we must help build stronger families. That's why we need to scrap the present welfare system and replace it with a system that works—a system that puts people to work, requires personal responsibility, and protects children from poverty. We must teach children and teenagers what it takes to be a good parent and why they ought to wait until they're ready to take on those responsibilities.[24]

We must go after deadbeat dads—and moms. I ask you to pass a tough child support enforcement law. We owe it to single mothers to see that fathers meet their obligations, and we'll do whatever it takes. We'll take away their drivers licenses, their hunting and fishing licenses, their professional and business licenses. We'll track them down in ways they never dreamed of. We'll even put their faces on wanted posters. We are going to see that parents support their children in North Carolina.[25]

Building stronger families is critically important, but there is more we can do. We can do more for children in those vital early years before they start school. When I gave my inaugural speech two years ago, I said that if we want to change North Carolina, we have to start earlier. We're doing that now. We're doing it because of Smart Start, and we need to do more of it.

The Bartolos can tell you what Smart Start is doing. They were worried about Nicky, because at age 2 he wouldn't talk, or play, or respond the way other children do. Three months ago they found a Smart Start program in Fayetteville that helps children like theirs.

The other day I got a letter from Sergeant Bartolo. He said that Nicky has "really blossomed," and he ended his letter with this: "I see Nicholas developing more and more every day. The Smart Start program at Dorothy Spainhour is responsible for these developments. Nicholas is now going to have a chance to develop like other children his age. I am deeply indebted to Nicholas' teachers and the Smart Start program, which has allowed the funding for this to occur. Where we have tried, Smart Start has succeeded. Our heartfelt thanks."

That's just one story. There are thousands more. Because of Smart Start, people across North Carolina are working together to see that children get preventive health care, and immunizations, and vision screening, and hearing checkups. Because of Smart Start, people are working together to see that there's good day care for every family that needs it. Because of Smart Start, business leaders, and ministers, and parents, and teachers, and elected officials, and community leaders are working together. Doctors and dentists are giving their services to children.

People who never talked to each other before are working together. Democrats and Republicans are working together.

Even Jim Hunt and Dave Flaherty are working together—because of Smart Start. Over the last twenty years, we've been on opposite sides in a lot of political battles. This year, we're on the same side, because of Smart Start.[26]

Here is what Dave told the nation's governors about Smart Start last month: "This is the kind of approach that requires a new way of thinking and a new way of working. It requires new partnerships—between public and private sectors, between community interests, between political parties. It requires us to make changes in how we do things, so we can make changes for our children."[27]

That's what we have to do this year: make changes in how we do things so we can make changes for our children. That's what Smart Start is about. It's not Raleigh telling people what to do. It's people deciding what to do in their communities and working together to do it.

Smart Start is helping children grow up healthy and able to learn. It's making schools better, making our state safer, and making the economy stronger. It's building our future. That's why I'm going to ask this legislature to keep Smart Start working in the thirty-two counties where it's working today, and that's why I'm going to ask you to expand it to twenty-four more counties over the next two years.[28]

As Dave Flaherty said, Smart Start is a new way of doing things, and we need new ways of doing things: new ways of building our economy and helping working people; new ways of protecting against crime; new ways of educating children and giving them a good start in life; new ways of government working together with the private sector, with the nonprofit sector, with communities, and with people. We need a new approach for a new century.

This is a time of great change. You can look around this chamber and see that. The people of North Carolina certainly aren't afraid of change. Now they want to know if we can change. They want to know if we can put aside partisanship and politics. They want to know if we can work together to build a better state and a better future for our children.

They're doing it. They're working together, and we can do it, too. Let's resolve to do it this year, Democrats and Republicans together. Let's join hands to build a better state, Democrats and Republicans together. Let's build a better future, Democrats and Republicans together, for these families and for all North Carolinians.

---

[1] Dennis Alvin Wicker.

[2] Harold James Brubaker (1946-   ), born in Mount Joy, Pa.; resident of Asheboro; B.S., Penn State University, 1969; Masters (Economics), N.C. State University, 1971. President, Brubaker and Associates, Inc., real estate appraisals and consulting; member, since 1977, minority leader, 1981-1984, Speaker, from 1995, N.C. House of Representatives; first Republican Speaker of N.C. House in twentieth century. *North Carolina Manual, 1995-1996*, 529; *News and Observer*, November 16, 20, 1994, January 26, 1995.

[3] Marc Basnight.

[4] Jessie Copeland was a youth mentor in the Chavis Heights public housing project. Press release, Governor Hunt's State of the State Puts People over Politics, Raleigh, February 9, 1995, Governors Papers, James B. Hunt Jr.

[5] Staff Sergeant Bartolo's first name was verified in press release, Governor Hunt's State of the State Puts People over Politics, February 9, 1995.

[6] Across the country, voters gave Republicans reason to celebrate, and Democrats cause for concern, on election day 1994. Congress was fully in the control of the GOP: As a result of the November 8 balloting, the U.S. House of Representatives had a Republican majority for the first time in forty years; previously, the Democrat-led House and Republican-held Senate acted as a check on each other. Perhaps more newsworthy was the end of ninety-six years of Democratic domination over the North Carolina House of Representatives. In the state senate, the Democratic majority dwindled to two seats. Paul Luebke, *Tar Heel Politics 2000* (Chapel Hill: University of North Carolina Press, 1998), 26-27, 47-48, 49-50, 61-62.

[7] For more on the 1993 bond referendums, see North Carolina League of Municipalities, October 18, and North Carolinians for Education, Jobs, and Progress, October 21, 1993, reprinted elsewhere in this volume.

[8] Hunt unveiled his $483 million tax-cut plan a month after the November 1994 elections that saw the Democratic Party lose control of the state House for the first time in the twentieth century; see Statement on Tax Relief, December 8, 1994, reprinted below. Although Republicans won the House and had a near majority in the senate, in large part due to the anti-tax component of their campaigns, the General Assembly could muster only a $364 million tax cut. Luebke, *Tar Heel Politics 2000*, 61; *News and Observer*, February 14, April 18, 25, August 2, 1995.

[9] "An Act to Reduce Income Taxes for the Lower and Middle-Income People of North Carolina by Increasing the Personal Exemption Deduction by Five Hundred Dollars and by Allowing a Tax Credit of Sixty Dollars per Dependent Child" was ratified April 18, 1995. *N.C. Session Laws, 1995*, I, c. 42.

[10] "An Act to Repeal the Intangibles Tax and to Reimburse Local Governments for Their Resulting Revenue Loss" was ratified April 18, 1995. *N.C. Session Laws, 1995*, I, c. 41; see also *News and Observer*, April 18, 25, 1995.

[11] State House and senate negotiators focused on cutting personal income taxes and eliminating the intangibles tax for 1995. The revenue stream simply would not float the reduction in the corporate income tax rate, from 7.75 percent to 7 percent, that Hunt requested. House Finance Committee co-chairman Lyons Gray, a Republican, said of the corporate tax cut, "'We may be able to come back in the short session next year and have a look at it. But I think we're also being prudent and saying let's see what we can accomplish this year without putting this state in jeopardy and then come back and have another look at it.'" John Kerr, co-chair of the Senate Finance Committee and a Democrat, added, "'Frankly, I haven't had very many people talking about the corporate rate to me. Most small corporations are able to control the taxable income. I know it looks bad when you compare our rates to the other states in the Southeast. I just haven't had the demand.'" *News and Observer*, April 16, August 2, 1995.

[12] Speeches focusing on Hunt's 1995 anti-crime package, as outlined in this section of the State of the State address, include: Town Meeting Talking Points, Charlotte, June 1, 1995; *Governing* Magazine Conference on Crime, Research Triangle Park, July 21, 1995 (reprinted below); North Carolina Sheriff's Association, Atlantic Beach, August 7, 1995. For related press releases, see Governor Hunt Asks N.C. Congressional Delegation for Help with Prisons, January 13, 1995; N.C. House Passes Governor Hunt's Law Enforcement Officer Assault Bill, May 10, 1995; Governor Hunt's Crime-Fighting Bills Move through Senate, May 12, 1995; House Passes Governor Hunt's Alternative Sentencing Bill, June 16, 1995; Governor Hunt's Bill to Maximize Use of Boot Camps Passes House, July 13, 1995; Radio Advisory on Sex Offender Bill, Raleigh, July 20, 1995; Governor Hunt's Bills Requiring Criminal Background Checks Pass House, July 21, 1995; Governor Hunt's Sex Offender Registration Law Takes Effect January 1, December 29, 1995. Governors Papers, James Baxter Hunt Jr.

[13] "I know all of you have been feeling the effects of prison overcrowding," the governor told the N.C. Sheriffs Association on August 7, 1995. "So I'm sure you were glad to see the legislature pass my proposal to provide $100 million, over the next two years, to build almost 2,500 new prison beds, the first phase of a 3,800-bed, $200 million prison construction program to be phased in over the next four years. The General Assembly also passed my proposals to allow for the privatization of prisons and allow double-bunking in single cells."

[14] See press release, Governor Hunt's Proposal Will Put Over 400 More Prisoners to Work, Raleigh, August 3, 1995, reprinted elsewhere in this volume.

[15] The prison cap was repealed under "An Act to Appropriate Funds for the Continuation Budget Operations of State Departments, Institutions, and Agencies, and for Other Purposes," *N.C. Session Laws, 1995*, I, c. 324, s. 19.9(e), effective January 1, 1996.

[16] Speaking at the commissioning of the Marion Correctional Institution, April 7, 1995, the governor elaborated on his victims' rights proposals. The constitutional amendment

"would guarantee victims the right to be heard in court and the right to be informed of and involved in court proceedings related to their case. We're pushing for mandatory impact statements so judges will know exactly what victims have gone through before they hand down a sentence, and we're pushing to increase our victim restitution efforts to make sure more victims are reimbursed for their losses."

Seventy-eight percent of the ballots cast in a November 5, 1996, referendum approved the adoption of a victims' rights amendment; see *North Carolina Manual, 1997-1998*, 1260-1262. State legislators set out the text of the amendment and authorized the referendum under "An Act to Amend the Constitution of North Carolina to Establish Rights for Victims of Crime," *N.C. Session Laws, 1995*, I, c. 439, ratified July 17, 1995.

[17] See "An Act to Require the Registration of Persons Convicted of Certain Criminal Sexual Offenses," *N.C. Session Laws, 1995*, II, c. 545, ratified July 29, 1995, and press release, Governor Hunt Outlines Crime Proposals to Help Victims, Raleigh, January 19, 1995, Governors Papers, James Baxter Hunt Jr.

[18] See Crime Prevention in Public Housing Conference, January 17, 1996, reprinted below.

[19] This section of the speech was previewed in Hunt's remarks to the N.C. Education Commission, Research Triangle Park, January 12, 1995, and in the press release, Governor Hunt Lays Out Education Goals for '95, Raleigh, January 13, 1995, Governors Papers, James Baxter Hunt Jr.

[20] "An Act to Require a One-Year Suspension for Any Student Who Brings Certain Weapons onto School Property and to Allow the Superintendent to Modify the Suspension for Children with Special Needs, or by Providing an Alternative School Setting," was ratified June 20, 1995. *N.C. Session Laws, 1995*, I, c. 293; see also press releases, Senate Passes Governor Hunt's Automatic Suspension Bill, Raleigh, May 5, and House Passes Governor Hunt's Automatic Suspension Bill, June 15, 1995, Governors Papers, James Baxter Hunt Jr.

[21] Most primary school classrooms in Burke County had a 15:1 pupil-teacher ratio. As a result, the county discovered that third-graders in smaller classes scored markedly higher on statewide reading and math tests than their counterparts in more-crowded classrooms. *News and Observer*, January 22, 1995.

[22] Legislators cut first-grade class sizes from 26 to 23 students per teacher, as Hunt requested. They also enabled schools to reallocate funds to reduce the student-teacher ratio to 17:1 in grades K-3. *N.C. Session Laws, 1995*, II, c. 507, sec. 17.12; see also press release, Governor Jim Hunt's Plan to Reduce Class Size Clears General Assembly, Raleigh, August 2, 1995, Governors Papers, James Baxter Hunt Jr. Kindergarten class sizes had been reduced under c. 769, s. 19.17, *N.C. Session Laws, 1993, Extra and Regular Sessions, 1994*.

[23] For related press release, see House Passes Governor Hunt's Plan to Give Parents, Teachers Bigger Role in Education, Raleigh, June 16, 1995, Governors Papers, James Baxter Hunt Jr.

[24] The governor revealed his welfare reform proposal, Work First, in his March 27, 1995, address to the Greater Raleigh Chamber of Commerce, reprinted below.

[25] Chapter 538, "An Act to Improve the Enforcement of Child Support by Creating Additional Remedies," *N.C. Session Laws, 1995*, II, was ratified July 29, 1995; see also press release, Governor Hunt's Bill to Crack Down on Deadbeat Parents Passes House, Raleigh, June 28, 1995, Governors Papers, James Baxter Hunt Jr.

[26] As Caldwell County manager, David Thomas Flaherty Sr. backed Smart Start enthusiastically. As a Republican, however, he and Hunt often found themselves on opposite sides of the political fence. Flaherty lost the 1976 gubernatorial election to Hunt; eight years later he repaid the favor, working diligently on behalf of Jesse Helms to defeat Hunt in a bruising race for U.S. Senate. David Thomas Flaherty Sr. (1928-   ), born in Boston, Mass.; B.A., Boston University, 1955; U.S. Army, 1949-1952. Various positions with Broyhill Industries, including national advertising manager, and manager, Plastics Division; elected to N.C. Senate from Caldwell County, 1968, reelected 1970; secretary, state Dept. of Human Resources, 1973-1976, 1987-1993; Republican gubernatorial candidate, 1976; chairman, state Republican Party, 1981-1983; chairman, state Employment Security

Commission, 1985-1987; became Caldwell County manager in 1993. *North Carolina Manual, 1969,* 585, *1987-1988,* 1313-1319, *1991-1992,* 180-181, *1997-1998,* 361; Poff and Crow, *Addresses of Hunt, 1981-1985,* 506, 508n, 509; press releases, Governor Hunt and Ex-Political Foe to Pitch Smart Start to NGA, Raleigh, January 26, 1995, Governor Hunt Joins Forces with Former Political Foe on Behalf of Smart Start, Raleigh, January 30, 1995, and Flaherty Joins Governor Hunt in Smart Start Presentation, Raleigh February 1, 1995, Governors Papers, James Baxter Hunt Jr.

[27] The first two sentences of the quotation attributed to Flaherty appeared in the press release, Flaherty Joins Governor Hunt in Smart Start Presentation, Raleigh, February 1, 1995, Governors Papers, James Baxter Hunt Jr. He and Hunt testified January 29, 1995, in support of Smart Start during a meeting of the National Governors Association. *News and Observer,* January 29, 1995; and press release, Governor Hunt Joins Forces with Former Political Foe on Behalf of Smart Start, Raleigh, January 30, 1995, Governors Papers, James Baxter Hunt Jr.

[28] Hunt wanted more than $51 million for his Smart Start expansion proposal, but legislators gave him only $3.5 million "in planning money" for the following twelve counties: Alleghany, Buncombe, New Hanover, Pamlico, Randolph, Robeson, Rutherford, Stokes, Surry, Wake, Washington, and Wilson. Media Advisory on House Smart Start Vote, April 28, 1995, Governors Papers, James Baxter Hunt Jr.; *News and Observer,* August 2, 1995.

EDUCATION CONFERENCE

It is appropriate that this is my first speech outside Raleigh since taking office, because the education of our children will be the first concern of this administration.

During the transition and during the inaugural activities, I sensed a readiness to work together and build a better future for our state. Parents, teachers, business people, elected leaders—all are ready. You, school board members and the superintendents, are ready to lead.

I want to express my thanks and my respect to you, and to those across the state, who have fought for education reform the last eight years. Credit should go to Governor Martin, General Assembly members, Superintendent Bob Etheridge,[1] State Board [of Education] members, and most of all, the elected and appointed leaders of our local school systems.

Real reform will not happen in Raleigh. It can happen only in your [school] systems and in your schools. My responsibility as governor is not to dictate to you, but to support you, work with you, and enable you to bring about real reform. As I have watched school reform efforts across North Carolina and the nation the last eight years, I have developed a real appreciation for the people on the front line.

We know what we must do. We are ready to do it. We have an army of support across the state. Now we have the opportunity and the obligation to make it happen. So I'm here today, and for the next four years, to listen more than I talk, to answer your questions, and respond to your needs and problems.

First, here are my key goals for our public schools:

—Education is economic development. We will focus on education and on [the] first five years, because that will have the greatest long-term impact on our state's economic future. If we do this job well, we will have less crime and unemployment—and better jobs, stronger families, and a brighter future.

—Our first goal must be raising standards. The modern global economy demands smarter people. Jobs will follow brains. Education will be a magnet for economic growth. We must set out standards that clearly define what students should know, and be able to do, to compete in this economy.

—Then we must develop accountability measures. These measures must adequately address the standards we set. This is why I want to work toward an exit exam, why I want us to offer employers a written guarantee that our graduates are ready to go to work.

—We must continue to decentralize education authority. Decisions must be made in your communities, not in Raleigh. We need to make more progress in reducing funding categories.

—As I said in my inaugural speech Saturday, we must start earlier. We cannot wait until children show up at school. Too often, that is too late. So we will launch in these four years a comprehensive and coordinated early-childhood crusade.

This is an ambitious agenda, but I know we can do it if we work to-gether—Raleigh and every school district, education and business leaders, the governor, legislators, the state Department [of Public Instruction], the State Board, local school board members, superintendents, principals, and most important, the parents, teachers, and students themselves.

This is an exciting time. I thank you for how far you have brought our schools. I challenge you to think anew and commit yourselves anew to the course of reforming and revitalizing public education in North Carolina. For this is the time to lift up our children, our schools, and our state.

---

[1] Bob R. Etheridge (1941-   ), born in Sampson County; B.S., Campbell College (later University), 1965; U.S. Army, 1965-1967. Businessman; licensed realtor; director, North Carolina National Bank, Lillington; Harnett County commissioner, 1973-1976, commission chairman, 1974-1976; member, N.C. House of Representatives, 1979-1988; state superintendent of public instruction, 1989-1996; was elected from Second N.C. Congressional District to U.S. House of Representatives, 1996; Democrat. *News and Observer*, November 6, 1996; *North Carolina Manual, 1995-1996*, 263-264.

NONPROFIT SUMMIT

RALEIGH, JANUARY 14, 1993

[Governor Hunt met with approximately 250 representatives of nonprofit agencies and foundations from across the state, on January 14, 1993, to establish a public-private "partnership for action in North Carolina." The first-ever Nonprofit Summit focused on devising new methods of improving public schools, early childhood education, crime control, and state government reform. Press release, Hunt Nonprofit Summit Tomorrow, Raleigh, January 13, 1993, Governors Papers, James Baxter Hunt Jr.]

I want to welcome you, this morning, and thank you for taking the time to be here. I also want to thank Billy Ray Hall,[1] with the Rural Economic Development Center, Blair Levin, and the Center for Nonprofits for their help in putting on this summit, along with the Z. Smith Reynolds and Mary Reynolds Babcock Foundations for helping us in so many ways.

Today is a first. It's the first time such a summit has been held. It's the first time many of you have been in the same room together. It's the first sentence in a continuing dialogue between the Hunt administration and the state's nonprofit sector, and it's the first step to building the public-private partnership that we need to make our state a better place to live.

You know better than I what challenges face North Carolina in the next four years and in the next generation. We must improve the quality of life for our children. We must reform their schools; improve their early childhood education; create high-skill, high-wage jobs for them; make their neighborhoods safer; and make their state government work better.

This is an ambitious agenda, but it's not one that state government can meet alone. As I've said many times in the last eighteen months, all wisdom does not reside in Raleigh. All answers do not lie in state government, nor do all funding sources lie in the state's coffers. Instead, state government must serve as a catalyst, nurturing new ideas and leveraging public dollars with the help of the nonprofit community, the business community, the religious community, and others in our state who are committed to change. This is particularly true for the nonprofit sector. Each of you here today represents the best of North Carolina's community spirit. You and the thousands of others involved in nonprofit work are making a difference in the lives of our people.

You are innovators, devising and encouraging creative ways to serve the public interest, and you are a vehicle for community involvement; through you, North Carolinians can get involved and help make their community a better place to live. That community spirit is one I want to inject into all levels of state government. That spirit is reflected in Robin Britt, founder of Project Uplift and my new secretary of human resources.

It is in that spirit that we gather here today. To meet the challenges ahead, I need your help, your ideas, your energy, and your commitment to help us translate this agenda for action into policy. Today, as you participate in the working sessions, keep in mind that I'm looking to you for creativity and that entrepreneurial spirit. I'm also looking to you for expertise and experience. You are problem solvers, and you can help us determine what policies would work in your communities.

Finally, I'm looking to you for a voice—to tell the people in your communities about these policy issues, the tough choices we're facing, and to help us build support for our public-private programs. I want all of us to work together, as partners, to come up with a new way: new ways of thinking, new ways of serving our people, and new ways to pay for that service delivery. We all know there are limits to what each of us, here today, can do. But if we join together as a public-private partnership, starting right here, right now, we can transcend those limits. We can do more than North Carolina has ever done before. That's the challenge before us today, and I look forward to spending the day with you in that effort.

---

[1] Billy Ray Hall (1948-   ), born in Duplin County; B.A., 1969, M.A., 1970, N.C. State University. Chief economist, Office of State Planning, 1972-1974, assistant director for policy development, 1977-1981, N.C. Dept. of Administration; director, Community Assistance Division, N.C. Dept. of Natural and Economic Resources, 1974-1977; assistant secretary for policy coordination, 1981-1983, deputy secretary, 1983-1985, N.C. Dept. of Natural Resources and Community Development; assistant town manager, Town of Cary, 1985; executive director, N.C. Commission on Jobs and Economic Growth, 1985-1987; president, N.C. Rural Economic Development Center, since 1987; chairman, N.C. Rural Economic Development Council, since 1993; author. Billy Ray Hall, letter to Jan-Michael Poff, April 1, 1996.

CHILDREN'S SUMMIT

RESEARCH TRIANGLE PARK, JANUARY 29, 1993

[Although dated January 29, Hunt delivered this address the following day. Media Advisory for January 29, 1993, Governor Hunt's Schedule for January 30-February 5, Governors Papers, James Baxter Hunt Jr.]

I'm honored to be here, today, and to take part in North Carolina's first Children's Summit. I want to commend the Child Advocacy Institute and WUNC-TV for bringing this distinguished group of state leaders and policy makers together and for its efforts on behalf of North Carolina's children. When the planning for this summit began two years ago, no one could have imagined the hope, the anticipation, and the expectation that 1993 would bring to the children's agenda.

Today is a new day. It's a hopeful day for children. No one could have known that this country would have a president so committed to investing in our people—not to mention a First Lady who is a national leader for children![1]

The General Assembly's commitment to children has been evident, but no one could have known that the next governor would have an equally strong commitment to children. The leaders of our General Assembly, who have long been children's advocates, and I share a common vision for children. Together we'll be working, side by side, to make our children's lives better.

All of us here today share a common vision for North Carolina's children. We believe that children are North Carolina's most precious resource. Our children embody our hopes, our dreams, and our future.

If we are to make the most of our state, we must make the most of our children. This is more than rhetoric, it's a principle that should guide all of us in the next four years and beyond. We want to provide our children with affordable, quality day care, basic health care, proper nutrition and education in the early years. We want to make sure our children are safe in our schools, and we must make sure they graduate from high school ready to compete in today's world. Finally, we must make sure our children become skilled workers, so they can help us bring high-wage, high-skill industries to North Carolina.

Each and every one of you here today—civic leaders, business leaders, elected officials, and [non]profit representatives—have worked hard to make that vision a reality. You have helped move our state forward in the right direction. Our legislative leaders have set aside partisan differences to work for North Carolina's children, and we should pay tribute to their efforts. House Speaker Dan Blue has been a forceful leader in making children a priority. In education, child abuse protection, mental health, family preservation, and health services, North Carolina legislative leaders have looked after our children. At the same time, nonprofit groups like the [Child] Advocacy Institute have helped train our focus on children. Nonprofits can pla[y] an important role, as advocates, partners with state government, and as innovators, in translating our vision for children into reality.

We've made great strides for children, but we haven't done enough. Our state ranks forty-first among all fifty states in the health and well-being of its children. You've heard the grim statistics: more than 200,000 children living in poverty in our state; more than 300,000 children lacking affordable, quality day care; almost 75,000 children suffering from abuse or neglect; more than 150,000 children lacking health insurance.

These numbers paint a tragic picture. North Carolina can do better by our children. We must do better. Our state has a highway system second to none and one of the strongest manufacturing economies in the nation. We have become a leader in science and technology. But we have failed to develop a common vision and blueprint for our children.

We're beginning to develop that blueprint. In recent weeks, the Speaker of the House and the senate president pro-tem have spoken eloquently about the need to do better for our children.[2] I look forward to working with them to translate that vision into policy. Today we can start by setting specific goals for North Carolina children by the year 2000. I commend the Child Advocacy Institute for the goals it has set out in its comprehensive vision document, and I share your urgency in meeting those goals.[3]

Let's start with early childhood education. There's no question that we need quality comprehensive day care for all children. We must reach our children before the age of five, so they can come to school ready to learn. But we cannot wait. Our children cannot wait. We must start today if we are to provide affordable, quality day care for every child who needs it in North Carolina.

I want to work with Secretary Britt and our legislative leaders to map out a creative new plan for early childhood education that builds a strong public-private partnership for North Carolina children. In the meantime, I hope we can pass legislative measures to boost day care. The Baby Bill is a first step, improving our child-staff ratios—which are among the worst in the nation.

We cannot wait until the year 2000 to protect our children in the schools. Our children deserve to be safe from violence, drugs, and abuse in the classroom. We must stem the tide of violence. Every week, news reports tell us another tragic story of a child shot or stabbed in our schools. Students cannot learn in a violent environment. Teachers cannot teach in a violent environment. School violence is an issue that must be dealt with today. It may be one of the greatest challenges facing us here today. I ask you to help us make our schools safe for our children.

We cannot wait until the year 2000 to provide basic health care for our children. It's unacceptable that half of our two-year-olds don't get the shots they need. I've proposed that the state pay for immunizations for those children who need it [sic]. If we can afford to pave every road that carries more than 100 cars a day, then we can afford to give our babies their measles shots.

Other goals laid out in this vision document are equally important: access to basic health care, especially prenatal and well-baby care; child abuse prevention; safe homes and neighborhoods; better parent education; improved mental health plan for children; loving, nurturing families; family-friendly workplaces. This is an ambitious agenda, but I believe it is one that we can accomplish if we work in the spirit of partnership. This is North Carolina. We have long dedicated ourselves to children, education, and a better quality of life, and we can do better.

Last month, I spoke to North Carolinians about leading a crusade for children. Many of you have spent years fighting for children. Today I ask you to join me in this crusade. I ask you to enlist others in our crusade: parents, teachers, religious leaders, businessmen and women, community activists, elected officials. Every North Carolinian who cares about children and about our state should be part of our crusade.

Together, we can build a partnership for children, and our children will
be better off.

----

[1] The governor was referring to William Jefferson Clinton, president of the United
States, and his wife, Hillary Rodham Clinton.
[2] Speaker Daniel T. Blue and Marc Basnight, president pro-tem of the senate, were
identified earlier in this volume.
[3] The document Hunt cited was *The Vision for Children and Families in North Carolina*
(Raleigh: North Carolina Child Advocacy Institute, 1993).

STATEMENT ON SCHOOL VIOLENCE

RALEIGH, FEBRUARY 3, 1993

We're here this morning to witness two fine men take the oath of office.
I welcome Franklin Freeman and Thurman Hampton to my cabinet and
welcome their friends and family here this morning. We're fortunate
to have Franklin Freeman coming aboard as secretary of correction. As
administrative officer of the courts, he has spent years cutting fat and
containing costs while running an effective and efficient operation. I know
he'll bring the same skills to the Correction Department, and he'll help
us get that agency back on track.[1] And we're fortunate to have Thurman
Hampton taking the oath today as secretary of crime control and public
safety. His experience as a district attorney in Eden gives him special
insight into the importance of preventing crime; and his work in the
community is critically important, especially his efforts to keep young
people out of trouble.[2]

Our young people are the focus, today, and should be the focus of
our administration for the next four years. We must build a brighter future
for our youngsters, and we must keep them safe. We must keep our
children safe in our streets and safe in our schools.

Every week, news reports tell another tragic story of school violence
and another tragic story of a child in danger. Just yesterday, a seventeen-
year-old was sentenced to life in prison for murdering a young girl as
she sat in a Randolph County classroom last year.[3] Last Monday, a star
football player was shot in the corridors of a Richmond County high
school.[4] On Thursday, students were assaulted and robbed in the school
yard of Sanderson High School, and a Raleigh police officer was wounded
after a subsequent shoot-out.[5] Just as frightening are the reports of guns,
knives, and other weapons in the schools. In this school year alone, more
than 100 Mecklenburg County students have been caught bringing
weapons into school.

As governor, and as a parent and grandparent, I say enough is enough. Our children cannot learn surrounded by violence. Our teachers cannot teach in classrooms surrounded by violence. Our public schools cannot thrive surrounded by violence, and our state cannot realize its potential in an environment of violence. In short, school violence victimizes all of us, and we must all band together to fight it. All of us—elected officials, law enforcement officers, educators, parents, religious and community leaders—must join hands to stem the tide of school violence. It is our responsibility to make our schools safe.

We must join our attorney general, Mike Easley, who has led the way in fighting school violence. He made this issue a tenet of his campaign, and he is now working on legislative proposals to address this problem. I commend Mike for his efforts and will do all I can to help him.[6]

I also want to commend Superintendent Bob Etheridge, who is now conducting a survey of school violence in twenty school systems. These figures are critical to our efforts, because no state agency is now tracking the number of weapons confiscated in our schools, and no state agency is now devoting its efforts and resources to fighting school violence. Today, that's changing.

We must develop a comprehensive approach to preventing violence in our classrooms, and we must put the resources of state government squarely behind this effort. I've asked my new secretary of crime control, Thurman Hampton, to make school violence his number-one priority. I've asked him to identify federal and state money in his department to target school violence and to make school violence a fundamental part of the crime prevention plan he's drawing up.

Today I'm asking Secretary Hampton to form a special Task Force on School Violence, and I'm asking Attorney General Easley and Superintendent Etheridge to join with him in putting this task force together. The four of us will be meeting this morning to begin work on our joint effort. I'm looking to North Carolina's leading law enforcement officers and our top education official to bring their unique perspectives and expertise to this critical task.

It's my hope that this task force will conduct hearings across North Carolina in the next sixty days—in places like Rockingham, Durham, Charlotte, Greensboro, and Raleigh. We must hear from local law enforcement officials, parents, students, teachers, school administrators, judges, legislators, and others involved in the fight against school violence. We must find out what local school systems are doing to fight violence in their classrooms. We must find out what works and what doesn't. We must develop a statewide approach to prevent school violence and to make our classrooms safe again. I'm hopeful that with

Secretary Hampton, Attorney General Easley, and Superintendent
Etheridge working together, we can take the first step today.

---

[1] Franklin Edward Freeman Jr. (1945-   ), born in Dobson; B.A., 1967, J.D., 1970,
University of North Carolina at Chapel Hill. Assistant district attorney, 1971-1973, district
attorney, 1979-1981, Seventeenth N.C. Judicial District (Caswell, Rockingham, Surry, and
Stokes Counties); assistant director, 1973-1978, director, 1981-1993, Administrative Office
of the Courts; was appointed secretary, N.C. Dept. of Correction, 1993; author. As AOC
chief, Freeman managed the financial and business operations of the state's judicial branch,
the latter having 4,700 employees and a $220 million budget. *North Carolina Manual, 1995-
1996,* 342; press release, Hunt Names Freeman as Correction Secretary, January 15, 1993,
Governors Papers, James Baxter Hunt Jr.
    [2] Thurman B. Hampton (1949-   ), born in Chatham County; B.A., N.C. A&T State
University, 1970; J.D., State University of Iowa, 1973; U.S. Army, 1973-1976; U.S. Army
Reserve, Judge Advocate General Corps. Assistant professor of law, N.C. Central University,
1976-1979; attorney in private practice, 1979-1982, 1985-1986; assistant district attorney,
1982-1985, district attorney, 1986-1993, District 17A (Rockingham and Caswell Counties);
N.C. crime control and public safety secretary, 1993-1995. *News and Observer,* January 18,
June 25, August 12, 1995; *North Carolina Manual, 1993-1994,* 266.
    [3] Willis Odell "Junior" Gravely declared if he could not have Patricia Ann Mounce, no
one would. The sixteen-year-old forced his way into an eighth-grade science class at
Archdale-Trinity Middle School in northwestern Randolph County, February 25, 1992, and
stabbed his former girlfriend in the heart as her incredulous classmates and teacher
watched. Mounce, age fourteen, died just over an hour after the attack. Gravely pleaded
guilty to murder and was sentenced to prison for life. *Greensboro News and Record,*
February 26, 27, 1992; *News and Observer,* March 4, 1993.
    [4] Students taking the basement hallway to first-period classes at Richmond County
Senior High School, Monday, January 25, 1993, screamed and scattered when they saw
James Richard Goodwin pull out a .32-caliber revolver. Amid the panic, Goodwin
encountered senior Orrick McDougald, a tailback on the varsity football squad, and shot
him in the chest. Although it appeared he might die, McDougald survived the shooting,
his dreams of playing college football postponed indefinitely. His sixteen-year-old assailant
faced trial as an adult and a maximum of thirty-four years in jail.
    Goodwin brought the gun to school, he said, to defend himself against some boys who
had beaten a friend of his the previous Friday night at a Rockingham nightclub. He said
McDougald was involved in the fight, a claim McDougald denied. *News and Observer,*
January 26, June 13, 1993.
    [5] A group of teenagers in a stolen Honda Accord stopped some students on the
Sanderson High School campus, January 28, 1993, and asked if they wanted to buy
marijuana. One student was hit in the head with a gun and had his jacket stolen after he
declined their offer. Notified of the assault and theft, Raleigh police later spotted the
Honda, gave chase, and ultimately stopped it a mile from the high school. As the suspects
fled the car, the driver began shooting a .25-caliber pistol at the policemen, hitting Sergeant
Stephen B. Price in the shoulder. Officers returned fire, twice wounding a suspect in the
leg. The injuries suffered by Price and the youth were not fatal. One of the teenagers
charged in the incident, Jason Lamont Landis, nineteen, had been convicted of felony
larceny in January 1991. *News and Observer,* January 29, 1993.
    [6] Michael F. Easley (1950-   ), born in Rocky Mount; B.A., University of North
Carolina at Chapel Hill, 1972; cum laude graduate of N.C. Central University School of
Law, 1976. Sworn in as assistant district attorney, 1976, was elected district attorney, 1982,
Thirteenth N.C. Judicial District; candidate for Democratic nomination, 1990 U.S. Senate
race; was elected N.C. attorney general, 1992, re-elected in 1996. *News and Observer,*
November 6, 1996; *North Carolina Manual, 1995-1996,* 277.

EMERGING ISSUES FORUM

RALEIGH, FEBRUARY 11, 1993

In the best southern tradition, I want to start with a story: About ten years ago, I went to Greensboro for the ribbon-cutting of Analog Devices, the computer lab division of a Boston semiconductor chip manufacturer. During a tour of the plant, I met a young fellow who was introduced to me as the developer of a new microelectronic device, which had brought in the first American contract with NTT [Nippon Telegraph and Telephone Public Corp.], Japan's telephone company. In chatting with this fellow, I asked him where he'd gone to school. I expected him to be an engineer with multiple degrees from a fine university—perhaps a graduate of my own alma mater, N.C. State.[1] But he told me proudly that he had graduated from the Guilford County school system and had a two-year degree from Guilford Technical Community College. Now this young man was directly responsible for creating hundreds of new jobs, and more new ideas, in North Carolina. That's what I'd call a good return on the state's investment!

I tell you that story because it illustrates the link between investing in our people and investing in our state. To make our state competitive in the global marketplace, I believe we must pursue parallel strategies of investment. In the short run, we must invest in our infrastructure so that our communities can recruit industry. We must invest in technology, then link it to the factory floor, and we must encourage our industries to invest in skill training. In the long run, we must invest in our people. We must build a world-class workforce, one that can compete and help our state compete.

We must invest in our children early on, so that they can come to school ready to learn. We must invest in our students, raising standards in our schools, setting up a tough exit exam as a graduation requirement, then offering an unconditional guarantee to employers to back up our commitment. And we must invest in training and retraining of our present and future workers.

Like any wise investments, these require a little foresight and a lot of discipline. But consider the potential returns. Consider the NTT contract at Analog Devices and the jobs it created. Consider that young man who made it happen. Consider what North Carolina could achieve if we duplicated that success across our state.

Just as that young man's training at Guilford Technical Community College was a foundation of his success, I believe skill training is a foundation for North Carolina's success. Today we're laying the cornerstone of this foundation. I ask each of you to serve as stonemasons in this effort, to help us build this foundation in every single community across North Carolina. With your help, we can fashion a comprehensive workforce preparedness effort and a long-range economic development plan that will make our state all it can be.

In the next few days I will be creating, by executive order, the Governor's Commission on Workforce Preparedness. I will ask Sandy Babb, head of N.C. Equity and a leader in workforce and community development issues, to serve as executive director. Sandy will help us develop a coordinated effort on workforce preparedness and will bring new efficiency and accountability to this area.

As part of this foundation, we must also expand our fine Tech Prep program, putting it in place in every single county across our state. The budget I'll take to the General Assembly next week will include money to make that happen. Pioneered in Richmond County by my friend, Joe Grimsley, Tech Prep shines as an example of innovative new ways to prepare students for the jobs in the factories, labs, and offices of tomorrow.[2]

Our foundation must include youth apprenticeship programs, giving high school students the hands-on training they need. I've asked Secretary Reich and the Labor Department to work with North Carolina to develop a model apprenticeship program that will combine classroom experience with work experience. As a model state we can get federal assistance, and we can show the country how it's done.[3]

Community colleges make up a critical piece of this foundation as well. We must upgrade our community college system's ability to provide the kind of education, training, and retraining that the workplace demands. North Carolina has pioneered the linkage of community colleges and economic development, but in recent years we have not invested in our community colleges as we should. Today, community colleges get less than 8 cents of the state's education dollar. Many campuses are turning away students for lack of space or teachers. Salaries are forty-seventh in the nation. Equipment has not kept pace with technology.

The budget I'm presenting next week will include, also, funds for additional community college enrollments, and funds for better salaries, better books, and better equipment. But at the same time, we must maximize the resources we do have for community colleges, making sure each dollar is spent wisely and taking a hard look at cost savings recommended by the Government Performance Audit Committee.

In short, we must invest in our people to invest in our state—and we must invest in our industries and communities as well. We must strengthen North Carolina's manufacturing base and help our industries modernize and stay competitive. North Carolina has a higher percentage of workers employed in manufacturing plants than any other state. More than one-fourth of our people work in some 12,000 manufacturing plants, making North Carolina a leader in textiles, furniture, and other traditional manufacturing industries. At the same time, we have the finest universities in the nation, with some of the most advanced research and development under way. N.C. State is just one example, conducting much of the nation's textile research. But [we] must do a better job of linking the two, so that our traditional industries have the benefit of cutting-edge technology to help them stay competitive. I've proposed a technology extension service, modeled after the successful Agriculture Extension Service, to link university research to the factory floor. My budget will include funds to start up this extension service this year.[4]

I've asked Bob Jordan, chairman of the state's Economic Development Board, to investigate incentives to encourage new and expanding industry to our state. Efforts are already under way to develop a comprehensive package of incentives, which will make us more competitive with other states and other countries.

Finally, we must invest in North Carolina by investing in North Carolina's entrepreneurs. I will be establishing, by executive order, an Entrepreneurial Development Board to help start-up companies get capital, management help, and export assistance. Bob Luddy, who built one of the nation's leading kitchen ventilation manufacturing companies, will head this effort.

Bob Jordan, Bob Luddy, and my commerce secretary, Dave Phillips, will be working closely together to hammer out a comprehensive economic development strategy for the state. The three of them, key players on our state's economic development team, will be talking more about that later this morning. This strategy will also include attention to rural economic development and women and minority business development. We're serious about leveling the playing field for all North Carolinians to create a better economic future. You'll be hearing from Billy Ray Hall, head of the Rural Economic Development Center, on this later.

Finally, our investment strategy must include more planning for growth. The first step is to develop a state economic development strategy. Then we must work with local governments to build the infrastructure needed to draw new and expanding industry. Too many of our communities, especially in rural areas, are forced to "sell out of an empty wagon" because they lack water, sewer, and natural gas services and the necessary industrial sites. As part of this effort to address local needs, we are going to develop an economic development institute to provide world-class instruction for our economic development professionals and allies.

These investment strategies are the strategies I believe North Carolina must pursue in the next four years and beyond. I believe these programs will pay rich dividends in future years: a world class [work]force and a high-skill, high-wage economy with good jobs for our people. But I also believe that we on this stage cannot do it alone. All of you here today are investors in North Carolina. You must help us make this investment in our people and our state, and you will share in the dividends that will result.

Each of you here today—educators, business leaders, economic developers, elected officials, religious and community leaders, and the nonprofit sector—can help us boost education and economic development. I ask you to join with me today to form a partnership for economic growth; a partnership for investment; a partnership for our people; a partnership for the future. Together, we can make it happen.

---

[1] Hunt earned his bachelor of science degree in agricultural education, in 1959, and a master of science in agricultural economics, in 1962, from N.C. State University. *North Carolina Manual, 1995-1996*, 203-204. Neither Analog Devices nor the Governor's Press Office could identify the man to whom Hunt referred in this address.

[2] The General Assembly approved funds to assist "local education agencies and community colleges in planning and implementing 'Tech Prep' across the State"; see *N.C. Session Laws, 1993*, I, c. 321, s. 114. Created for high school students not planning to attend a four-year college, Tech Prep aimed to prepare them better for the workplace. The program combined technology-oriented vocational training with a stringent academic curriculum. It also dovetailed into further coursework at community colleges, which Tech Prep students were encouraged to attend. Joseph W. Grimsley, president of Richmond Community College, and M. Douglas James, Richmond County schools superintendent, devised the program. *News and Observer*, March 3, 1991.

Joseph Wayne Grimsley (1936-   ), born in Wilson; B.A., University of North Carolina at Chapel Hill, 1961; Fulbright scholar, University of the Andes, Bogata, Colombia, 1962; M.A., George Washington University, 1964; U.S. Army, 1954-1957. U.S. Peace Corps staff, 1963-1968; assistant field director, U.S. Coastal Plains Regional Commission, 1968-1971; director of Hunt's campaigns for lieutenant governor, 1972, governor, 1976, 1980, and U.S. Senate, 1984; assistant secretary, 1971, 1973-1974, secretary, 1977-1979, 1981, N.C. Dept. of Administration; secretary, N.C. Dept. of Natural Resources and Community Development, 1981-1983; president, Richmond Community College, since 1985. *News and Observer*, May 17, 1985, March 3, 1991.

[3] Robert Bernard Reich (1946-   ), born in Scranton, Pa.; B.A., Dartmouth College, 1968; Rhodes scholar, 1968, M.A., 1970, Oxford University, England; J.D., Yale University, 1973. Attorney; political economics educator; assistant solicitor general, U.S. Justice Department, 1974-1976; policy planning director, Federal Trade Commission, 1976-1981; faculty member, John F. Kennedy School of Government, Harvard University, since 1981; chairman, biotechnology section, U.S. Office of Technology Assessment, 1990-1991; appointed U.S. labor secretary by President Clinton, 1993; author. *Who's Who in America, 1996*, s.v. "Reich, Robert Bernard."

[4] State lawmakers provided development funds for the Technology Extension Project under *N.C. Session Laws, 1993*, I, c. 321, s. 311. Hunt outlined the proposal in *North Carolina State Budget, 1993-1995 Biennium: Supplemental Budget Recommendations, James B. Hunt, Jr., Governor*, 24-25.

NORTH CAROLINA SMALL BUSINESS DEVELOPMENT COUNCIL

RALEIGH, FEBRUARY 12, 1993

I've spent the last two days talking about economic development and outlining North Carolina's economic development strategies. Today I want to talk about the role that small businesses play and how we can expand that role.

Almost 75 percent of North Carolina's new jobs are created by small businesses. Some 97 percent of our state's employers are small businesses, and more than half our state's workers are employed by small businesses. In the last decade, small businesses have created nearly all of North Carolina's net jobs and still produce about half of our goods and services. It's no exaggeration to say that our state's economy depends on the vitality of small businesses, and it's no exaggeration to say that the growth of our state's economy is linked to the growth of small business.

How can we help small businesses grow? Boosting education and skill training. Strengthening our manufacturing base and helping industries of all size[s] compete. Encouraging growth from within by encouraging entrepreneurs. Planning for growth and making state government more effective and efficient.

We can also serve small business more effectively. We must refocus attention in the Commerce Department on the needs of small business. We must consolidate small-business agencies within state government. We must look for ways to reduce regulatory burdens on small businesses, and we must do a better job coordinating all of these efforts.[1]

Most of all, we must bring small businesses to the table. We must give them a voice in our decision making, and we must listen to that voice. Today we're taking the first step in that direction. I am creating, by executive order, the North Carolina Small Business Development Council. This council will be made up of fifteen small businessmen and -women and will be led by our lieutenant governor, Dennis Wicker.

Under the lieutenant governor's leadership, this council will be a voice for small businesses across North Carolina, and they will have this governor's ear. I will look to the Small Business Council to advise me, the General Assembly, and the state's Economic Development Board on small-business issues. I will look to the council to help us develop and implement policies to nurture small-business growth and development across our state. I will look to the council to recommend changes in laws, and regulations, and tax policies affecting small business, including an examination of one-stop permitting to streamline the regulatory process. I will look to the council to bring direction and coordination to our state's public and private programs for small businesses. I will look to the council to target needs in small businesses for education, training, marketing, funding resources, exports, purchases and contracts.

Most of all, I will look to the state's top small-business advocate, Lieutenant Governor Wicker, to lead the way in helping our state help small businesses. With Dennis Wicker's energy, time, and commitment to small business, I believe this council will make real progress. His role as a policy troubleshooter is a valuable one to me and to North Carolina's small businesses.

---

[1] Excessive paperwork and overlapping regulations were among the targets of a Clinton administration pilot project "to streamline the regulatory process" affecting small businesses. Press release, North Carolina Chosen for Pilot Program to Help Small Businesses, Raleigh, July 28, 1994, Governors Papers, James Baxter Hunt Jr.

PRESS RELEASE: GOVERNOR HUNT TO BE FEATURED ON NEW MONTHLY RADIO CALL-IN SHOW

RALEIGH, FEBRUARY 15, 1993

Keeping a campaign promise to stay in tune with North Carolinians, Governor Jim Hunt will launch a monthly call-in show on statewide radio next week. The show, called "Capitol Ideas with Governor Jim Hunt," will be aired on Monday, February 22, from 8:00 P.M. to 9:00 P.M. Produced by the North Carolina News Network, the show will be carried live on the last Monday of every month by North Carolina News Network radio stations across the state, including: WSKY, Asheville; WBT, Charlotte; WMFR, High Point, Greensboro; WNHW-FM, Nags Head; WTRG-FM, Raleigh, Rocky Mount; WAYN, Rockingham; WTOB, Winston-Salem.

During the hour-long show, Hunt will take questions from callers across the state. Listeners can reach the governor during the show by calling 1-800-. . . .

"Part of my responsibility as governor is to keep in touch with the people of this state," Hunt said. "That means I need to hear people's views, comments, and concerns. This call-in show will be a learning experience for me. It will give me a chance to be educated by North Carolinians, and it will help me do a better job as governor of their state.

"During the next four years, I plan to take every opportunity I can to talk directly to North Carolinians, through call-in shows, public meetings, and other forums," Hunt said. "The people of this state deserve no less."

Hunt is also appearing on two other live call-in shows next week:

—The governor and House Speaker Dan Blue, Senate president pro tem Marc Basnight, Senate minority leader Bob Shaw,[1] and House minority leader David Balmer[2] will be featured on a public radio call-in show on Tuesday, February 23, from 7:00 to 8:30 P.M. The show, called "The North Carolina Agenda," will be produced by WFAE, a Charlotte public radio station. It will be aired on eleven public radio stations in the state. Callers can talk to Hunt and the legislative leaders at 1-800- . . . . The show will be broadcast out of the Governor's Press Conference Room in the Administration Building, 116 West Jones Street.

In addition to WFAE, participating radio stations include WCQS, in Asheville; WUNC, Chapel Hill; WDAV, Davidson; WFSS, Fayetteville; WNAA, Greensboro; WTEB, New Bern; WNCW, Spindale; WHQR, Wilmington; WFDD, Winston-Salem; and WSNC, Winston-Salem.

"This is the first time that North Carolina's legislative leaders have come together to talk to the people on statewide radio," Hunt said. "North Carolinians want us to set aside partisan bickering to address the real issues, and I'm hopeful that this effort will be an important step in that direction."

—Hunt and Jane Kendall, executive director of the North Carolina Center for Nonprofits, will answer questions from cable [television] viewers on Open Net from 9:00 P.M. to 10:00 P.M. on Thursday, February 25.[3] Callers can talk to Hunt and Kendall by calling (919) 733- . . . . The show will be aired on most local cable channels. The call-in portion of the show will be preceded by an excerpt of Hunt's January 14 Nonprofit Summit, which brought together some 300 representatives of nonprofit agencies and foundations. The summit, the first of its kind, was designed to build a public-private partnership to help improve schools, boost early childhood education, control crime, and reform state government.

"Jane Kendall and I will be discussing the role that nonprofits can play in moving our state forward," Hunt said, "and we hope to hear from many North Carolinians on this and other issues." Open Net is produced by the Open Public Events Network and is designed to give North Carolinians access to their elected officials. Open Net is part of the North Carolina Agency for Telecommunications, a division of the state's Department of Administration.

[1] Robert G. Shaw (1924-   ), born in Erwin; resident of Greensboro; was educated at Campbell College (later University) and University of North Carolina at Chapel Hill; U.S. Army Air Force, 1943-1946. Restaurateur; member, 1968-1976, former chairman, Guilford County Board of Commissioners; state Republican Party chairman, 1975-1977; chairman, N.C. Council on Community and Economic Development, 1975-1977; elected to N.C. Senate, 1984, and was returned in subsequent elections; Senate minority leader. *North Carolina Manual, 1995-1996*, 504.

[2] David Gregory Balmer (1962-   ), born in Charlotte; B.A., University of North Carolina at Chapel Hill, 1984; J.D., Wake Forest University, 1988; U.S. Army; N.C. National Guard. Attorney; assistant press secretary to Gov. James G. Martin; member, 1989-1994, minority leader, 1993-1994, state House of Representatives; Republican. *News and Observer*, April 30, May 4, 11, 15, 17, 28, June 1, July 11, 1994, October 18, 19, 1995; *North Carolina Manual, 1993-1994*, 453.

[3] Jane C. Kendall (1951-   ), born in Nashville, Tenn.; resident of Raleigh; B.A., 1972, M.A., 1977, University of North Carolina at Chapel Hill. Counselor, 1973-1974, assistant director, 1974-1978, Career Planning and Placement, University of North Carolina at Chapel Hill; director, Southern Economic Development Intern Program, 1978-1981; associate executive director, 1978-1983, executive director, 1983-1990, National Society for Experiential Education; founder, president, N.C. Center for Nonprofits, since 1990; author; consultant. Jane C. Kendall, letter to Jan-Michael Poff, April 28, 1996.

BUDGET STATEMENT

RALEIGH, FEBRUARY 16, 1993

Well, folks, there aren't many surprises here. If you compare these two documents, you'll see that the priorities I laid out in my "Agenda for Action" are the same priorities I've laid out in my biennial budget. I think the people of North Carolina should know that their governor is doing what he said he'd do.[1]

Putting together a budget that addresses the real needs of our people in these times of fiscal constraint is a tough job for the governor and the General Assembly. Our dollars are few, and our needs are great. To deliver services to our people, and to do a better job delivering those services, we must rethink the way we operate in state government. That means we should do more than create new programs. We must also look outside the framework of state government. That's the intent of the North Carolina Partnership for Children, the new public-private partnership that will lead our early childhood efforts.

That also means we should look to individual state departments and individuals within each department to find the most effective, efficient way to operate. As you know, I've asked every single department to take a hard look at its budget and to recommend efficiencies in the form of 1 percent and 2 percent cost savings. Dick Futrell and the rest of my budget team have been meeting with the cabinet, the Council of State, and the leaders of the community colleges and universities.[2] In the next week, they'll put together a list of recommendations, and we will work together to find those savings throughout the budget review process.[3] Of course, the incentive to find those savings is great, because the programs that will be funded by the savings are greatly needed.

Over the next two years, I'm recommending $60 million to begin providing quality, affordable day care, health care, and early childhood education to every child in North Carolina who needs it. This is seed money for the North Carolina Partnership for Children, the public-private partnership I described last night. I'm not proposing a new government program. I'm proposing a new approach outside government.

At the same time, government must do its share. I'm recommending $5 million, over two years, to reduce the child-staff ratios in day-care centers; almost $12 million for day-care subsidies and tax credits, to ease the cost of day care for the working poor and for middle-income families; and almost $16 million to immunize every child in our state. This budget recommends $2 million to step up child protective services, as recommended by the Child Fatality Task Force.[4] In addition, I've recommended $5.6 million to boost health care in rural and poor areas of our state. Senator Daniel's rural health care and primary care initiatives (S.B. 6),[5] along with $16 million in expansion money to immunize our children, is the first step to providing basic health care for our children.

I promised during my campaign to give teachers the tools they need, to raise standards in schools, and set up new ways to meet those standards. To fulfill our pledge to help teachers do a better job, this budget recommends a 2 percent salary schedule increase, along with the 2 percent differentiated pay increase under S.B. 2, longevity pay, and staff development assistance.[6] And it recommends a new education standards and accountability commission that will develop a set of high school graduation standards.

I promised during the campaign to boost skill training for our present and future workers. This budget recommends implementing Tech Prep statewide, providing almost $60 million for worker training programs at community colleges, and I'm recommending a tough new exit exam for community college graduates as well, so that high school and community college graduates enter the workforce equipped with the skills they need to compete.[7] Worker training is a vital component of our state's new economic development strategy, so I'm looking to Sandy Babb and the workforce preparedness council to help us do a better job targeting state and federal skill-training dollars.

I've already outlined much of my economic development strategies. This budget does recommend new incentives, in the form of an industrial recruitment competitiveness fund. This will be a discretionary fund to be used to help recruit industries, depending on the individual industry and its needs.[8]

I promised during the campaign to establish a technology extension service, to set up a furniture export office, to boost travel and tourism, [along with] trade and film industry efforts. All of that is reflected in this budget—and this budget also reflects my commitment to give economically distressed areas the help they need. We're increasing support for those areas, and we're recommending assistance for western North Carolina and the coast, as well.[9]

I promised during the campaign to step up our fight against crime. I proposed a rape strike force, prison boot camps, and putting prisoners to work.[10] Again, it's in the budget. I'll be meeting with Correction secretary Franklin Freeman this week to discuss our plan to spend the remaining prison bond money, so there will be more to come. We may come out with a special crime package, along with some supplemental budget recommendations, later this year.

Finally, let me say a word about state employees. We cannot achieve any of these goals without a strong, effective team built around the front-line state employee. I promised state employees that I'd engage in a dialogue with them, not a one-way conversation. I promised to seek their input and encourage them to bring their good, creative ideas to the forefront; and I promised them that we'd work together to develop a pay plan that rewards career service and top performance.[11] In addition to a 2 percent salary increase and a 1 percent performance pay bonus, we're setting aside additional money to provide flexibility for higher salaries when the marketplace demands it.[12] We're recommending funds for a Total Quality Management program, to lead all of us in the direction of greater effectiveness and efficiency.[13] We're recommending funds for a state employees' study on compensation, to bring state employees to the decision-making table; and we're recommending funds for a state employees' ombudsman, to serve as a direct link between the governor and state employees.[14]

In short, this budget reflects my campaign commitments. I consider it a promise kept, and I look forward to working with the General Assembly to deliver on this promise.

---

[1] "A North Carolina Agenda for Action, 1992" (Raleigh: Citizens for Jim Hunt, n.d.) was a 40-page campaign document that outlined Hunt's priorities for a third term as governor. It was divided into three chapters: "An Education Compact for North Carolina: A Strategy for Competing in the Modern Global Economy"; "Building North Carolina's Economic Future: A Strategy for High-Skill, High-Wage Jobs and a High-Growth Economy"; and "Protecting North Carolinians against Crime: A Strategy for Making Prisons and Prisoners Work."

[2] J. Richard Futrell Jr., native of Hertford, N.C.; A.B., University of North Carolina at Chapel Hill, 1953; was graduated from Graduate School of Banking of the South, Louisiana State University. Banker; initial chairman and chief executive officer, 1990-1993, of Centura Banks, Inc., and Centura Bank following merger of Peoples Bancorporation and Planters Corporation; retired from post and withdrew as chairman-elect, N.C. Citizens for Business and Industry, to serve as state budget officer, 1993-1994; is currently Executive Committee chairman, Centura Banks, Inc., Rocky Mount. J. Richard Futrell Jr., letter to Jan-Michael Poff, August 13, 1996.

[3] At this point in his text, Hunt jotted, "In add[ition] to work[ing] closely w[ith] leg[islature] on GPAC."

[4] Among its recommendations for preventing the deaths of abused children, the North Carolina Child Fatality Task Force urged the hiring of additional child protective services workers in all counties and setting a state-mandated limit on the number of cases each worker could oversee. Hunt requested $2 million to hire more of those workers during the 1993-1995 period, but state lawmakers approved spending that amount for each year of the biennium. A case load limit was not established. N.C. Session Laws, 1993, c. 321, s. 234; North Carolina State Budget, 1993-1995 Biennium: Supplemental Budget Recommendations, James B. Hunt, Jr., Governor, 30; "Our Children, Our Future, Our Responsibility: Report of the North Carolina Child Fatality Task Force" ([Raleigh: The Task Force], February 1993), 31. The General Assembly established the twenty-nine-member North Carolina Child Fatality Task Force in 1991; see N.C. Session Laws, 1991, c. 689, s. 233.

[5] George Berkley Daniel (1951-   ), born in Raleigh; resident of Caswell County; B.S., N.C. State University, 1973; J.D., Wake Forest University, 1976. Attorney; farmer; member, state senate, 1987-1994, and chairman, Appropriations Committee; Democrat. News and Observer, November 10, 11, 1994; North Carolina Manual, 1993-1994, 383.

S.B. 6, "A Bill to Define Primary Care Hospital and Rural Hospital Network, and Appropriate Funds for Encouraging Health Care Providers to Practice Primary Care and Provide Services to Rural Areas," was incorporated into N.C. Session Laws, 1993, I, as c. 321, s. 101.3; see also North Carolina Senate Journal, 1993, 29, 79, 1576. Senators Betsy L. Cochrane, Chancy R. Edwards, James S. Forrester, David R. Parnell, Beverly M. Perdue, Lura S. Tally, and Ed N. Warren joined Daniel as cosponsors of S.B. 6.

[6] The governor's proposed differentiated pay raises for teachers participating in S.B. 2 pilot programs; pay increases for all teachers; longevity pay; and three days' school leave for staff development, plus funding to hire substitute teachers as replacements, are outlined in North Carolina State Budget, 1993-1995 Biennium: Supplemental Budget Recommendations, 19-20. S.B. 2 was the popular abbreviation for the School Improvement and Accountability Act of 1989; see N.C. Session Laws, 1989, II, c. 778.

The General Assembly approved teacher pay raises averaging 3 percent and revised the salary schedule upward as a reflection of the new $20,020 base pay for a teacher with a bachelor's degree. A Task Force on Teacher Staff Development was also established. N.C. Session Laws, 1993, I, c. 321, secs. 127, 141; Overview: Fiscal and Budgetary Actions, North Carolina General Assembly, 1993 Session and 1994 Session, 353. For longevity and differentiated pay funding, see North Carolina State Budget, Post-Legislative Budget Summary, 1993-1995 Biennium, 35-36, 47.

[7] The $58.7 million Hunt proposed for worker training programs at community colleges included funds for equipment and books, child care grants for students, improvements in literacy education, hiring more instructors and instructional support personnel, and pay raises. He also wanted to set aside $1 million for a "workforce competitiveness exam." Financing for the exam was not included among the $25.4 million the General Assembly approved for workforce preparedness during 1993-1995. North Carolina State Budget, 1993-1995 Biennium: Supplemental Budget Recommendations, 24-25; North Carolina State Budget, Post-Legislative Budget Summary, 1993-1995 Biennium, 25.

[8] Creation of the Industrial Recruitment Competitive Fund enabled the governor to offer financial aid to "businesses and industries [he] deemed . . . to be vital to a healthy and growing State economy and that are making significant efforts to establish or expand in North Carolina." State lawmakers stocked the fund with $5 million for F.Y. 1993-1994,

matching Hunt's request, and established guidelines for its use. *N.C. Session Laws, 1993,* I, c. 321, s. 314.3; *North Carolina State Budget, 1993-1995 Biennium: Supplemental Budget Recommendations,* 54.

[9] For the 1993-1995 period, the governor wanted $2.2 million to establish a technology extension service; $500,000 to set up furniture export offices in Raleigh and High Point; a $3 million increase in travel and tourism funding; trade offices on the West Coast and in Mexico at $300,000 each; $100,000 to start a film industry council; and $4 million to support business development in economically depressed parts of the state, with a further $240,000 earmarked for western North Carolina. According to the *North Carolina State Budget, Post-Legislative Budget Summary, 1993-1995 Biennium,* 188-191, lawmakers funded the film industry council ($100,000); planning for the technology extension project ($250,000); Mexican ($300,000) and West Coast ($316,426) trade offices; expansion of travel and tourism promotions ($1.5 million); development programs to reverse economic stagnation in various regions across the state; and creation of a furniture export office ($400,000). The furniture export office was established in High Point. Its first chief, Bill Fenn, was a member of the Board of Directors of Ladd Furniture, Inc., and former president of Stanley Furniture Co. Attachment, Budget Statement, Raleigh, February 16, 1993; High Point Furniture Market, High Point, October 16, 1993; and High Point Chamber of Commerce, December 13, 1993, Governors Papers, James Baxter Hunt Jr. See also *North Carolina State Budget, 1993-1995 Biennium: Supplemental Budget Recommendations,* 54-58.

[10] The proposed budget allocated $260,000 for a rape strike force. Instead, the General Assembly approved an additional $220,000 for the Rape Victims' Assistance Program, enabling the program to handle an increasing case load better and to obtain rape evidence kits for hospitals. *North Carolina State Budget, 1993-1995 Biennium: Supplemental Budget Recommendations,* 49-50; *North Carolina State Budget, Post-Legislative Budget Summary, 1993-1995 Biennium,* 166. See "Press Release: Governor Hunt Announces Prison Construction Plan," February 25, 1993, reprinted below, for specific prison building and inmate work program proposals.

[11] See "An Act to Establish a Comprehensive Compensation System for State Employees Subject to Chapter 126 of the General Statutes and to Direct the Distribution of Appropriations for Implementation of this Comprehensive Compensation System," *N.C. Session Laws, 1993,* I, c. 388, ratified July 18, 1993.

[12] State employees received a 2 percent wage increase, effective July 1, 1993, the first across-the-board percentage pay hike in three years. The compensation bonus, payable in December 1993, amounted to 1 percent of their annual salary; see Ferrell, *North Carolina Legislation, 1993,* 180; *N.C. Session Laws, 1993,* I, c. 321, secs. 63, 69. *N.C. Session Laws, 1993,* II, c. 561, s. 6, authorized $950,000 in F.Y. 1993-1994 for a state government pay disparity study.

[13] Total Quality Management was an increasingly popular business practice that Hunt wanted to apply to state government. Simply put, the process was "designed and implemented for the sole purpose of continuously improving the performance of an organization by emphasizing quality and customer satisfaction, encouraging cooperation among employees, and basing decisions on precise data and analysis." The governor hoped to draft "top management from the private sector" to assist in establishing the state's program. *North Carolina State Budget, 1993-1995 Biennium: Supplemental Budget Recommendations,* 36.

[14] Blanche Critcher, of Chapel Hill, was hired by Hunt to be the state employees' ombudsman. A retired state employee, she had been an aide to state senator Joe Johnson (D-Wake) and an assistant to the Psychology Department chairman at the University of North Carolina-Chapel Hill. The job of ombudsman resided in the Governor's Office. *News and Observer,* August 14, 1993; *North Carolina State Budget, 1993-1995 Biennium: Supplemental Budget Recommendations,* 36.

NORTH CAROLINA HOSPITAL ASSOCIATION

RALEIGH, FEBRUARY 18, 1993

I want to commend you for your work in delivering vital health care services to North Carolinians. The mission of health care professionals was captured eloquently by Louis Pasteur in his speech at the opening of the Pasteur Institute in Paris in 1888. He said, "Two contrary laws seem to be wrestling with each other nowadays; the one, a law of blood and death, ever imagining new means of destruction and forcing nations to be constantly ready for the battlefield—the other a law of peace, work, and health, ever evolving new means of delivering man from the scourges which beset him. . . . The one seeks violent conquests; the other, the relief of humanity. The former would sacrifice hundreds of thousands of lives to the ambition of one; while the latter places one human life above any victory."

Two contrary laws are wrestling today in North Carolina, also—the first sacrifices health care for millions to the financial ambition of a few, while the other places one human life above any financial ambition. We see this in the 1.2 million North Carolinians who are uninsured and the 750,000 who are underinsured, and we see it in those fighting for change.

There's no question we need to change. Every North Carolinian deserves access to quality, affordable health care, especially our children.

The first step in health care reform is containing costs. As you know, Senator George Daniel, who spoke here yesterday, chaired the commission of access to health insurance, and they concluded that we can't afford to insure everybody unless we first bring down costs. Well, friends, that makes good, sound sense. Imagine you had a leak in your roof during a rainy spell. You might begin by mopping up the puddles every so often. Once the puddles became ponds, you might put a bucket under the leak. But as the leak gets worse and you get tired of emptying buckets, you go on up and fix the roof.

Our taxpayers can't continue to mop up the spillage from this leaky health care system. We must fix it. In Washington, our new president has made health care reform one of his top priorities.[1] I'm glad to see this emphasis, but we can't wait for Washington.

Many talk about change and health care reform. I commend you for your efforts to be part of that reform. I commend you for your work on Senate Bill 10 to limit purchases of expensive medical equipment and keep down costs of treatment.[2] Until every child has access to the basic preventive care they need, I'm not sure that every hospital, clinic, and doctor's office needs a magnetic resonance imaging and positron emission tomography scanner. I believe we should target our dollars and technology very carefully, ensuring first that every citizen enjoys a basic level of care.

Let me also commend you for your support of the Healthy Carolinians 2000 task force and your action on preventive health care.[3] We can take care of our people by increasing preventive care, improving access to primary care, increasing the number of medical professionals in rural areas, and enhancing child and maternal health care.

I am pleased to report that the expansion budget submitted to the General Assembly this week included the task force recommendations that all mandated immunizations be provided from public funds. Immunizations represent preventive care at its most basic. It's an investment we must make. If we can afford to pave every road that carries over a hundred cars a day, we can afford to give every two-year-old his measles shots. We are providing $15.9 million over the next two years for that purpose. This would include a complete series of all vaccines recommended by the National Vaccine Advisory Committee, U.S. Public Health Service, and the American Academy for Pediatrics.

We have also included measures in the budget to remedy the primary care physician shortage in rural areas by recommending funding for Senator Daniel's rural health care and primary care initiatives, S.B. 6. We have recommended $900,000 to be paid out, in $10,000-a-year stipends, to students in the health professions if they do their residency or practical training in underserved areas of the state. Their stipend is forgiven at the rate of $10,000 a year if they serve in the area after completing their training. We have also recommended $1 million over two years to induce primary care professionals to work in underserved areas. There is also over $2 million, over the next two years, recommended for the Office of Rural Health to provide support for fifty-four health centers and to establish ten scholarships for North Carolina medical students who agree to work in rural and medically underserved areas. We also have recommended $320,000 for grants to encourage the development of primary care clinics.[4]

Finally, let me commend you for your willingness to take a stand for insurance reform. This is the most controversial plank of every health care platform. While I have yet to see a reform plan I can endorse 100 percent, I can endorse the central principle of your platform: Everyone must have health insurance. This is not just a moral issue; it is an economic issue. Illnesses that go untreated early are very expensive to treat later.

Now, having said all that, I don't want to appear to be taking an adversarial position. We all must work together to solve this problem.

While there is little money, there is enough ingenuity and human kindness among us to work out a system where all are covered and none are bankrupted. The shrill voices on either side are an impediment to fruitful discussion. For my part, I will be watching Hillary Clinton's efforts with the keenest interest.[5] But despite my great respect for her, I think it would be a mistake to abdicate our responsibilities to North Carolina in the hopes that our problems will be solved by the federal government.

We must continue to discuss and debate this issue, both in the General Assembly and in forums like this. With good sense and goodwill on all sides, a consensus will emerge. Congratulations on taking a leading role in this dialogue and also for taking the lead role in delivering health care to our people. You do a heroic job for those you see, but you know there are some you don't see—who may have no insurance, who may have insurance but no money for co-payments, who may be sick but might have been spared their sickness with preventive care. You are here today because you want to heal them, too. You are a credit to your profession and to your state, and I thank you.

---

[1] For a full discussion of President William Jefferson Clinton's plan to reform America's system of health care, provide universal insurance coverage, and reduce the costs of care, see *Congressional Quarterly Almanac, 1994*, 319-355.

[2] The General Assembly adopted Senate Bill 10 on March 18, 1993. See *N.C. Session Laws, 1993*, I, c. 7, "An Act to Modify the Certificate of Need Law."

[3] The "Healthy Carolinians 2000 task force" was the Governor's Task Force on Health Objectives for the Year 2000, established on August 6, 1991, by Governor Martin. It was reestablished under Hunt's Executive Order Number 56, issued July 13, 1993. *Healthy Carolinians 2000: The Report of the Governor's Task Force on Health Objectives for the Year 2000* ([Carrboro, N.C.: The Task Force], November 1992); *N.C. Session Laws, 1995*, 2:2080-2082; Poff, *Addresses of Martin, 1989-1993*, 493-496, 538.

[4] S.B. 6 was enacted as c. 321, s. 101.3, *N.C. Session Laws, 1993*, I. The legislative conference report on c. 321 designated the following rural health care expenditures for each year of the 1993-1995 biennium: $500,000 in financial incentives to cover expenses such as relocation costs and loan payments of "primary care providers," and $450,000 to fund "stipends to medical residents, nurse midwives, physician assistants, and family nurse practitioners, who agree to work in underserved areas"; $800,000 "for health centers in rural and underserved areas," and an additional $160,000 for a community primary care program to make planning grants available "to communities that want to develop primary care facilities"; and $250,000 to establish "a scholarship fund for medical students who agree to practice in underserved areas." Ferrell, *North Carolina Legislation, 1993*, 76.

[5] The president placed his wife, First Lady Hillary Rodham Clinton, at the head of the Task Force on National Health Care Reform. *Congressional Quarterly Almanac, 1994*, 321-322.

NORTH CAROLINA FARMWRITERS AND BROADCASTERS

Raleigh, February 19, 1993

It's great to be with my friends today. Some of you may know I'm a lifetime member of this organization and always enjoy getting together with you. As most of you know, I'm a cattleman with deep roots in rural Wilson County. My father is a soil and water conservationist, and he taught me, early on, to love this state and its land.[1]

During high school, I served as president of the Future Farmers of America. I went through N.C. State [University] in agricultural education, along with Bill Johnson and Carlyle Teague and some others of you, and my master's from there is in agricultural economics.[2] Then I had the good sense to marry a woman who could teach me even more about farming: My wife Carolyn grew up on an Iowa farm. These days at my farm in Wilson County, our Simmentals have just finished calving season, and we're getting one of our heifers ready for next month's beef exposition in Fayetteville.

Folks, there's no question about it, this is a challenging time to be making your living off the land. Last summer's flooding ruined crops in ten counties, and Jim Wilder can tell you what our rainy fall and winter did to our soybean crops.[3] Farmers with erodible land have been scrambling to get their land management plans finished—to hold onto those program benefits. And we're all watching the progress of the GATT [General Agreement on Tariffs and Trade] negotiations to see if we can increase agricultural exports.

These are our challenges in North Carolina agribusiness, but we also have plenty of good news. Last year we opened one of the largest cold-storage facilities in the country, in Tar Heel, for preserving fruits, vegetables, [and] pork and poultry products. For the first time in five years, state cattle farmers, with a little help from Wilson County, are raising more than a million head of cattle. Thanks in large part to the efforts of my good friend, Jim Graham,[4] we're still the top state in the nation in sales of farm forest products, turkeys raised, tobacco, and sweet potatoes.

But our market here in North Carolina is no longer just the United States. Most of the world's population lives outside of the United States. They have to eat. We here in North Carolina should go after that world market aggressively, and I aim to do everything I can to make that happen. We've already made a good start of it. In 1991, for the first time, our exports to all seven continents topped $1 billion for the first time [sic], and we can do even better than that! We do that by paying constant attention to our existing markets in Japan, Canada, and Mexico, and by working hard to find new markets.

Back here at home, we have to work hard to find a delicate balance. We need to protect our farmlands and our wetlands, our rivers and streams. But we need to make sure our farmers can keep producing their crops. That means you folks need to help us—by writing about the success our people are having with no-till farming and land terracing to save our topsoil. That means you need to keep telling people about the work of the people, at our state's research facilities, to learn more about integrated pest management and pheromone traps. Some of you are doing that research at N.C. State right now, and we're finding that those traps can make a big difference: Last year, our farmers were able to plant ten times as much cotton as they could fifteen years ago, because they didn't have to worry about the boll weevil anymore![5]

As I've traveled the state over the past year, a lot of our farmers tell me of their concerns about disaster protection. They tell me about their falling profits because of foreign trade barriers. They tell me they want imported products to pass the same tests for pesticide residue as the products grown in the United States.

Make no mistake about it: Agriculture is a cornerstone of our economic development in this state. In the next couple of weeks, I'll be announcing an agricultural adviser who will be part of my staff, just as I did in my first administrations.[6] And I'll be counting on that person, and you, to keep us working together—to make sure that goodness keeps growing in North Carolina!

While my vision for this state goes beyond agriculture, it's rooted in an appreciation for reaping what one sows. As a child I learned early on that to raise any good crop, you need to start early. If you want good yields in the summer, you prepare in the winter. That's the secret of our emphasis on early intervention: to get day care to the young children of this state, whose parents can't afford it, early. You reach kids before they go to kindergarten, and you make sure that every child has quality, affordable day care, early childhood education, basic health care, and the nutrition they need. If we do that, our kids will come to school ready to learn, grow, and thrive.

Another thing I learned a long time ago: You can't neglect your crops once they're in the fields. We will not abandon our children. We will challenge our educators to challenge our students as they make their way through school. We will raise our standards and hold educators accountable for meeting those standards.

As a master's student at N.C. State, I learned the importance of marketing crops once we've raised them. When we find out good news about agriculture in this state, we tell you folks, and you tell the world—or anyone else who'll listen. That's what we're going to be doing with our high school and community college graduates: telling the world about them. We're going to guarantee that our workers have the skills to do the jobs they want done when they move their companies here. If they don't, we'll send them back to school to get those skills.

We'll tell the automotive company that wants to locate here that we want them, and that Sam and Cindy in Charlotte have the skills to do the job for them. We'll tell the computer software company that Robert and Renee in Rockingham can compute and compete with the people in any other state. And we'll tell the new farm chemical company that wants to locate here that Ken and Karen in Kinston know how to do the job. We'll tell that company we have the best-educated, most highly skilled agricultural community in the world—right here in North Carolina.

As a cattleman in Wilson County, I know that we have to be aware of the ever-changing markets in our counties, our state, our nation, and the world. As a governor starting his third term, I am keenly aware of that. As agriculturists and as responsible citizens, we must continue to adapt to our new world markets and make sure our agricultural community, and all of our workforce, gets the training and retraining necessary to serve those markets. You folks call it professional development. I call it economic common sense. All of the good things won't happen overnight, any more than any crop grows overnight, but we are starting right now to prepare the fields for future students, to nurture the minds of our current children, to get our current job seekers to the right markets at the right time, and to make sure our current workforce is ready for the new world markets.

These are challenging times, but exciting times. You, as journalists, are lucky. You get to watch, and listen, and report as this state takes off. I'm excited about the next four years, too, as we do our best to make a difference in this state, to build something new, and lasting, and good. I hope you'll join us as we plant the seeds for a bright future.

---

[1] James Baxter Hunt Sr. (1911-   ), native of Greensboro; resident of Wilson County; B.S., North Carolina State College (later University), 1934. Tree and tobacco farmer; U.S. Dept. of Agriculture, Soil Conservation Service, 1934-1966; member, Tobacco Marketing Committee, 1966-1972, and Coastal Plains Regional Commission, 1966-1981; member, since 1964, chairman, 1974-1989, Mt. Olive College Board of Trustees. Jan-Michael Poff and Jeffrey J. Crow, eds., *Addresses and Public Papers of James Baxter Hunt, Jr., Governor of North Carolina*, Vol. II, *1981-1985* (Raleigh: Division of Archives and History, Dept. of Cultural Resources, 1987), 93n; Gardner M. Nason, Mt. Olive College public information director, letter to Jan-Michael Poff, April 24, 1997.

[2] Billy G. Johnson (1936-   ), born in High Point; resident of Randolph County; B.S., N.C. State University, 1960; U.S. Army Reserve. Director of communications, Carolina Milk Producers Assn., Greensboro, 1960-1965; manager, member and employee relations, Central Carolina Farmers, Durham, 1965-1966; regional editor, *Progressive Farmer* magazine, Raleigh; cattle production and investment management, Ramseur, since 1987. Billy G. Johnson, letter to Jan-Michael Poff, September 30, 1997.

F. Carlyle Teague (1936-   ), born in Alamance County; resident of Raleigh; B.S., N.C. State University, 1958. Public affairs dir., 1969-1981, N.C. Dept. of Agriculture; president, since 1981, Cooperative Council of N.C. F. Carlyle Teague, letter to Jan-Michael Poff, September 1, 1997.

[3] Tar Heel farmers helpless to save their drowning crops in 1992 suffered again the following year—not from an excess of rain, but from much too little. Hunt surveyed drought-withered fields in July 1993 and steadily lobbied the Clinton administration for disaster relief. By August 11, United States agriculture secretary Mike Espy had declared eighty-nine North Carolina counties primary disaster areas; he designated the remaining counties as contiguous disaster areas. The declaration enabled farmers to obtain federal low-interest emergency loans.

Further assistance to North Carolina farmers came in emergency disaster-aid legislation that President Clinton signed into law on August 12. Initially conceived to cover crop losses resulting from massive flooding in nine Midwestern states, the bill was broadened to include North Carolina and other parched areas of the Southeast. Funds made available under the law did not have to be reimbursed. The value of crops lost to drought in North Carolina exceeded $161 million by August 1993. *Congressional Quarterly Almanac, 103rd Congress, 1st Session, 1993* (Washington, D.C.: Congressional Quarterly Inc., 1994), 714-717; *News and Observer*, August 11, 1993; press releases, Hunt Inspects Crop Damage at Wake and Wilson County Farms [letter from Hunt to Secretary Mike Espy, U.S. Dept. of Agriculture, July 13, 1993, attached], Raleigh, July 13, 1993, N.C. Farmers Eligible for Federal Drought Assistance, Raleigh, July 15, 1993, Hunt Requests Federal Disaster Relief for Drought-Stricken Farmers, Raleigh, July 27, 1993, and N.C. Farmers Receive Federal Disaster Declaration, Raleigh, August 11, 1993, Governors Papers, James Baxter Hunt Jr.

James Franklin Wilder (1936-   ), born in Franklin County; resident of Raleigh; B.S., N.C. State University, 1961. Former Linotype operator/printer, store manager, farmer; poultry marketing specialist, N.C. Farm Bureau Federation, Raleigh, 1967-1969; agricultural technician, N.C. State University, 1969; assistant director, advertising and public relations, FCX, Inc., Raleigh, 1969-1972; executive vice-president, N.C. Soybean Producers Assn., Inc., Raleigh, from 1972. James Franklin Wilder, letter to Jan-Michael Poff, October 24, 1997.

[4] James Allen Graham (1921-   ), born in Cleveland, Rowan County; B.S., N.C. State College (later University), 1942. Farmer; Iredell County vocational agriculture teacher, 1942-1945; superintendent, Upper Mountain Research Station, 1946-1952; head, Beef Cattle and Sheep Dept., N.C. State Fair, 1946-1952; manager, State Farmers Market, Raleigh, 1957-1964; was appointed state agriculture commissioner by Gov. Sanford, 1964, to fill term of L. Y. Ballentine; was elected agriculture commissioner, 1964, and reelected in subsequent elections, 1968-1992; Democrat. *North Carolina Manual, 1995-1996*, 297-198.

[5] Hunt also discussed agriculture and the environment in his remarks to the N.C. Agribusiness Council, December 9, 1993.

[6] R. W. Wilkins was Hunt's agriculture adviser, 1993-1995. *News and Observer*, March 15, 18, 24, 25, April 5, 25, August 18, October 4, November 18, 1995, March 17, 1996.

PRESS RELEASE: GOVERNOR HUNT ANNOUNCES
PRISON CONSTRUCTION PLAN

Raleigh, February 25, 1993

[In announcing his appointment of Franklin Freeman as correction secretary, January 15, 1993, Hunt briefly discussed the objectives for the state's prison system that he advocated during his campaign for governor. Inmates should receive job training, educational opportunities, and substance-abuse rehabilitation, he said; they also should be responsible for the construction and upkeep of their own prisons, grow and process the food they ate, and perform community-service projects such as removing litter from roads and parks. To obtain the best use of prison construction bonds approved by public referendum in 1990, Hunt recommended building "less-costly prisons, such as work farms, barrack-style prisons, and boot camps for nonviolent and first-time youth offenders." He also espoused "a state-local partnership to build and operate county and regional prison farms." Above all, it was vital to build sufficient space to keep violent and career criminals incarcerated.

The governor gave substance to those general recommendations in the prison construction proposal he described for reporters on February 25, 1993. Poff, *Addresses of Martin, 1989-1993*, 50-51, 62n, 445-449, 449-453; Statement on Correction Secretary, January 15, 1993, Governors Papers, James Baxter Hunt Jr.]

Governor Jim Hunt today proposed building 4,200 new prison beds, including two prison work farms and a boot camp for youthful offenders, with the state's $87.5 million in prison bond money.

"During my campaign I promised voters that we'd put more criminals in jail, build less-costly prisons, and put prisoners to work," Hunt said. "Today I'm delivering to the General Assembly a prison construction plan that significantly increases the number of prison beds in North Carolina, using prison labor to build less-costly prisons. I consider this a promise kept."

Hunt and Correction secretary Franklin Freeman outlined the administration's prison construction plan at a press conference today. That plan recommends building 4,200 prison beds, some 1,600 more than proposed by former governor Jim Martin, with the state's remaining prison bond money.

"Our prison system has a great many needs, but too few resources," Hunt said. "No matter what sentencing philosophy our state adopts, we can count on an increasing number of criminals. We need to get those criminals off the streets and into an appropriate setting, whether that's jail, a prison work farm, or an alternative that requires them to work and change their behavior.

"Getting criminals off the streets is a critical first step in making our neighborhoods safer," he said. "I believe that criminals should serve their sentences, and spend their time productively while serving that sentence. I believe this prison construction plan meets those goals and will help North Carolina combat our crime crisis."

Hunt's prison construction plan recommends spending:

—$15 million for two, 500-bed, minimum-security prison work farms, built with inmate labor. Hunt's 1993-1995 budget recommendation calls for a $10.8 million inmate construction program so that prison labor can be used to build and maintain prisons across the state.[1]

—$1.1 million to build a 90-bed boot camp in Burke County for first-time youthful offenders. Hunt's 1993-1995 budget recommendation also includes $5.6 million to expand Richmond County's IMPACT [Intensive Motivational Program for Alternative Correctional Treatment] program by 180 beds and to finance operating costs for the boot camps.[2]

—$3.5 million to build 192 additional close-custody cells at Marion Correction Institution.

—$20.6 million for a processing center in eastern North Carolina, which will allow another 200 beds, now used to process inmates, to be used for close-custody cells.[3]

—$8.6 million to add 150 beds and otherwise improve women's prison facilities, bringing them up to par with men's facilities.

—$13 million for 1,600 additional minimum- and medium-security prison beds, built in barrack-style buildings, at seventeen existing sites.

—$11.8 million for a medium-security prison, with 416 beds, in Hyde County.

—$3.8 million to build 104 medium-security beds at Harnett Correctional Institution, along with an operations center, a gatehouse, and an electronic perimeter security system.

—$1.2 million to complete the Lumberton Correctional Center, adding 104 new medium-security beds.

—$8.6 million to add more than 200 beds for youthful offenders at Morrison and Polk youth institutions.

Hunt has also called for putting more first-time offenders to work on community service projects and establishing a comprehensive range of community-based correction programs and exploring more alternatives to incarceration. And he has also called for stepping up drug treatment facilities for prisoners. Freeman has already submitted a proposal to the General Assembly for a 500-bed drug treatment center.

---

[1] N.C. Session Laws, 1993, II, c. 550, authorized two minimum-security work facilities, one each for the eastern and western parts of the state and both with a 500-bed capacity. The inmate construction program received funding of $4.4 million, versus Hunt's proposed $10.8 million. North Carolina State Budget, 1993-1995 Biennium: Supplemental Budget

Recommendations, 49; *North Carolina State Budget, Post-Legislative Budget Summary, 1993-1995 Biennium,* 162.

   [2] Hunt's proposed budget would have expanded the capacity of the state's boot camp program from 90 to 360 "slots." The IMPACT program at Morrison Youth Institution, Richmond County, would have increased from 90 to 270 beds, while a new 90-bed boot camp was envisioned for Western Youth Institution, Burke County. Lawmakers supported Western's ninety beds but restricted the expansion at Morrison to half the number Hunt requested.

   IMPACT, the state's first boot camp program for youthful, nonviolent offenders, admitted its first class on October 30, 1989. Young men, from sixteen to twenty-five years old, were assigned to a ninety-day "shock incarceration program" at Morrison Youth Institution in which they performed manual labor and schoolwork in a military, basic-training-type setting. *North Carolina State Budget, 1993-1995 Biennium: Supplemental Budget Recommendations,* 49; *North Carolina State Budget, Post-Legislative Budget Summary, 1993-1995 Biennium,* 162; Poff, *Addresses of Martin,* II, 207n.

   [3] Funds for planning, design, and construction of the Eastern Processing Center in Vanceboro were authorized under *N.C. Session Laws, 1993,* II, c. 550, and *N.C. Session Laws, 1993, Extra and Regular Sessions, 1994,* c. 24, s. 5.

BUDGET STATEMENT

RALEIGH, MARCH 10, 1993

When I presented my budget recommendation three weeks ago, I laid out a plan to finance improvements in education, early childhood education, economic development, and crime control. That budget was a modest, conservative one, based on the concept of doing more with less in state government. I promised then that I'd come back with a line-by-line recommendation, detailing $100 million in annual cost savings. Today, I'm doing that.

I said we could pay for these new programs without raising taxes, and we're doing that. I said we could save money by making every state agency more effective and efficient, and we're doing that. I said we would squeeze every available dollar out of GPAC [Government Performance Audit Committee recommendations] for the biennium, using conservative estimates, and we're doing that. What we're doing is practicing entrepreneurial government. We're shifting resources from less-productive areas to more-productive areas, and we're encouraging those on the front lines to look for additional efficiencies and cost savings.

Every cabinet secretary, every Council of State member, and the General Assembly have come up with an average of 1 percent in cost savings each year. Some offices, including the Governor's Office, are achieving 2 percent in savings each year. Together, we were able to find $100 million in real savings in 1993-1994, and $104.7 million in real savings the next year. That's real money—no lapsed salaries, no smoke and mirrors. That includes $74.8 million in state agency efficiencies the first year and $75.1 million in the second year, with very little reduction in services.

We're recommending more than 270 specific savings, including:

—Cutting 18 percent, over three years, in central administrative staff at the Department of Public Instruction;

—Closing fourteen regional state offices, including four economic development offices in Commerce and ten field offices in Revenue;

—Eliminating 364 positions over the biennium, mostly in the Department of Correction;

—Eliminating a 5 percent automatic pay hike for court personnel, a pay hike that's on top of raises other state employees get; and

—Closing the Department of Agriculture's Morehead City seafood office.

But that's only the first step to a more effective, efficient government. The second step is GPAC. Let me say very plainly that I support GPAC. I support the General Assembly's efforts to push the audit through, and I will work with legislative leaders to adopt as many of the recommendations as we can. And I will work to continue to search for other efficiencies.

Today I'm endorsing GPAC recommendations that GPAC estimates could save $188.3 million the first year and $173.5 million the second year. But this is a conservative budget, and we're using conservative accounting methods to come up with at least $100 million in cost savings a year. We are only counting on those GPAC recommendations that we're confident will mean actual savings in the next two years: $25.1 million the first year and $29.5 million the second year.

I believe we can save a great deal more with GPAC, including cost savings in outlying years, and I've endorsed those recommendations in this document. And I believe we may be able to achieve even more savings with additional study of the remaining recommendations. I'm taking a look at those now. As I see it, this is just the beginning of the GPAC process, and it's just the beginning of our effort to reinvent government during the Hunt administration.

Over the next four years, we must continue to find new ways to operate state government more effectively and efficiently, and state employees must play a key role. As I told DOT workers at our brown-bag lunch last week, front-line workers know better than any of us how to save money.[1] That's why I want to adopt a Total Quality approach, encouraging innovative efficiencies at all levels. In fact, I believe that we can do more with less, and without raising taxes. We can cut waste. We can deliver services more effectively and efficiently. We can adopt a new approach to state government, with state employees actively involved, year in and year out, in re-evaluating and improving our operations.

This new approach can help us make fundamental changes in how state government works, and it can help us free up resources to make changes in education, children's programs, economic development, and crime prevention. Doing more with less in state government can help us do more in North Carolina.

---

[1] The noon meeting with Department of Transportation employees, March 1, 1993, was the first in Hunt's series of hour-long mealtime visits to each state agency. The governor wanted to hear workers' "'ideas on how we can all do a better job,'" and they were encouraged to "bring their lunch, along with any questions, comments, and concerns" about government operations and employment. Press release, Governor Hunt to Hold "Brown Bag" Lunches with State Employees, Raleigh, February 18, 1993, Governors Papers, James Baxter Hunt Jr.

NORTH CAROLINA CITIZENS FOR BUSINESS AND INDUSTRY

RALEIGH, MARCH 17, 1993

[The governor discussed the relationship between the state's schools and businesses in his remarks to NCCBI, below, and in addresses to the N.C. Business Committee for Education, February 11 and October 14, and the Total Quality Education Kickoff Luncheon, October 25, 1993.]

I'm honored to be here today, especially given the letter of invitation that I got from Phil Kirk in June.[1] I got Phil's letter some five months before the election, congratulating me on my primary victory and inviting me to speak to you today—on the condition that I won in November. I can tell you, no one is happier to be here today than I am!

But I won't be here for the rest of your annual meeting, so let me take a moment to commend Roger Soles,[2] who will be honored later today with the distinguished citizen award; and let me commend my friend, Smedes York,[3] who will be nominated as president to replace Dick Futrell. Although Dick has been in his new job for only two months, he's doing a terrific job as state budget administrator. And let me commend all of you and the work you've done in your communities. In my third term, I see more clearly that the efforts of North Carolina's business leaders to improve the lives of our people is key to our state's success.

Perhaps there's no greater example of leadership by the business community than in the area of education. Across this state, business leaders have sounded the call for improved workforce training and have devoted their efforts to improving our schools. As I traveled across the state during the campaign, I saw business leaders literally rolling up their sleeves to tackle local problems on the school board. I saw companies "adopting" schools to provide sorely needed computers in the classroom. I saw corporate executives encourage their employees to volunteer in schools, then spend their own time tutoring at-risk children as well.

Why this outpouring of effort? Everywhere I went, business leaders told me the same thing: that economic development in our state depends on education. As they put it, if we want to create jobs, we've got to start in the schools.

Folks, you're preaching to the choir. In the eight years I was out of the Governor's Office, I spent a lot of time thinking about that very issue. In between having five grandchildren, starting a beef cattle farm, and practicing business law, I served on the Commission on the Skills of the American Workforce. We issued a report three years ago that summed up the choice before our country in its title: *America's Choice: High Skills or Low Wages*.[4]

After eight years of governing and eight years of studying, I'm convinced that we cannot provide a prosperous future for our state if we don't dramatically upgrade the education and skill training of our workers. We must make sure our children graduate from high school with the skills they need to think for a living and to compete in the offices, factories, and labs of tomorrow.

If our workers can't compete, our state can't compete. Let's not forget the lesson of BMW. BMW chose South Carolina as the site for its first American manufacturing plant, not for tax incentives, but because South Carolina can provide a better-trained, better-educated workforce.[5]

We can do better, and we must. We are a state that has always excelled in education, the first to found a state-supported university and a pioneer in linking community colleges to economic development. We can build a world-class workforce as a foundation for a world-class economy, and we must. That's why I ran for governor, and that's why I'm here today. That's what my administration will be about for the next four years. That's what you'll hear me talk about, argue about, and advocate for in the next four years.

Why aren't we doing better? First, I believe we've got to start earlier to educate the workforce of the future. We must reach our children before the age of five, before their personalities and brains have been fully formed. We must give them the right start in life so they come to school healthy, and eager, and ready to learn.

Now, families are primarily responsible for early childhood education. But many families need help, and I believe that all of us in this room must join together to provide that help and to make sure our children get the right early childhood education, health care, nutrition, and parenting they need in the first five years. In a few weeks, I'll be unveiling the North Carolina Partnership for Children, a public-private initiative designed to help give children that healthy start. This partnership will include top leaders from across our state—including many of you, I hope—who will map out a comprehensive blueprint for early childhood education. Our goal is to provide affordable, quality, early childhood education to every child who needs it in the next four years and to do that outside the framework of government. In my budget, I've recommended about $60 million in state seed money to encourage counties to set up similar public-private partnerships in the next two years, developing their own innovative approach to early childhood education, nutrition, health care, and parenting.

Just think what the children of Gates County could do if business leaders, religious leaders, educators, nonprofit organizations, parents, and government joined together to ensure that every child in Gates County got the early childhood education they needed. Just think what it would mean to the schools of Gates County if every child came to school ready to learn. Just think what this could do down the road for our children, our schools, our workforce, and our state.

This Partnership for Children is a partnership for North Carolina, and a partnership that I ask all of you to join in your counties over the next four years. But it's only the first step. Once our children have come to school ready to learn, we must make sure that our schools are preparing our students to compete for the best jobs in the world and to be the productive workers that you need. That requires fundamental change in our schools.

We must raise the standards in our schools to define what a student needs to know to work in our modern economy. Then we must hold ourselves accountable, to make sure that every graduate, and every school, meets those standards. I'm now putting the final touches on legislation to set up a Standards and Accountability Commission, made up of educators, parents, and business leaders, to develop a set of standards and a tough new exit exam measuring these standards.

After we've set these higher standards, I want us to do something no other state in the nation has done. I want [to] offer employers an unconditional guarantee: If our graduates can't do what we say they can, then we'll take them back and retrain them at the state's cost.

Your businesses and industries can grow and expand, new ventures will start up, and other industries will come to North Carolina.

Fundamental change in our schools also requires more local control and clear standards of accountability, so that parents, teachers, and educators have more flexibility to address local problems—with incentives for success and consequences for failure. Fundamental change in our schools also means cutting centralized bureaucracy in Raleigh. I've already recommended that we follow the recommendations of GPAC [Government Performance Audit Committee] by cutting central administrative staff at DPI [Department of Public Instruction] by 18 percent over three years, and I commend Superintendent Bob Etheridge for his efforts in this area and to shift DPI's role to one of research and support for local schools.

Finally, I believe we cannot achieve fundamental change in our schools without resolving the issue of education governance. The governor of North Carolina is the CEO of the state and must be held accountable for education results along with the General Assembly. I believe the superintendent should be appointed, and that the governor should have veto power. I know you in this organization share my view on the governance issue, and I appreciate your support. I may be coming back to you to ask for your help in pushing this issue forward.

I want to commend the General Assembly for its work in charting a clear course of school reform. With strong leadership from the governor, we can help bring reform into every classroom across North Carolina.

Once we have achieved fundamental change in our schools, and we are producing skilled graduates, we must boost our skill training and retraining efforts. I've proposed boosting community college workforce training programs in my budget and implementing a workforce competitiveness exam, as well. In addition, I want to expand Tech Prep statewide and set up apprenticeship programs to link employers and schools; and I want to make sure our universities remain the finest in the nation, with the best libraries, technology, professors, and other support they need.

But we cannot achieve any of these changes in workforce training if we stray from the path of fiscal responsibility. I believe we can invest in our schools and our children without raising taxes, but we have to do more with less, as business[es] have been doing for years. Last week, I proposed $100 million in budget cuts to provide funds to balance my budget, and my proposed investments in children, jobs, and education, by shifting resources from less-productive areas to more-productive areas. We cut the average state agency by 1 percent, and many, including the Governor's Office, by 2 percent in 1993-1995. I recommended closing fourteen regional state offices, eliminating almost 500 jobs, doing away with a 5 percent automatic pay hike for court personnel, and closing a seafood office in Morehead City.

I want to continue to find ways to do more with less, in state government, by adopting as many GPAC recommendations as we can. I've already endorsed some $188 million in GPAC recommendations next year and some $173 million the next. By using the Total Quality Management approach to encourage state employees to find innovative efficiencies at all levels [sic], and we will put TQM into effect in state government. If we can make our government more effective and more efficient, we can invest in our children, our schools, and our workers, and we can build the high-skill, high-wage economy that will ensure North Carolina's success.

But economic growth is going to require us, in North Carolina, to be more competitive than in the recent past. We need more tools in the form of incentives to compete with Kentucky, South Carolina, with states around the country, and countries around the world. There are many decisions being made by companies that can favor North Carolina—more than I expected. Pepsi Cola, which announced a new customer service center in Winston-Salem this week, is just one example.

I know, perhaps as well as anyone, that to build North Carolina up, government must form a partnership—with business leaders, educators, nonprofit organizations, religious and community leaders—for North Carolina's future. Today, I ask each of you here to join that partnership for our state's future. Help us come up with innovative ways to reach children and to provide early childhood education in your community. Help us set these new standards in our schools and define the competencies our graduates must have. Help us set goals and develop strategies for educational excellence at the local level. Help us find new and innovative ways to improve our schools, help our children, and create new jobs. Help us restore North Carolina's margin of excellence, and fix our sights on what we can do, not what we cannot.

Help us make North Carolina a better state for our children and for our grandchildren. If we can do that, together, then we leave a fitting legacy. Our state, and our children, deserve no less.

---

[1] Phillip James Kirk Jr. (1944-   ), born in Salisbury; resident of Raleigh; B.A., Catawba College, 1967. English and journalism teacher, 1967-1972; former radio announcer, newspaper reporter; state chairman, N.C. Young Republicans, 1969-1971; member, N.C. Senate, 1970-1973; chief of staff to Governor James E. Holshouser, 1973-1977, to Congressman James T. Broyhill, 1977-1984, and to Governor James G. Martin, 1987-1989; secretary, N.C. Dept. of Human Resources, 1976, 1985-1987; president and secretary, N.C. Citizens for Business and Industry, and publisher, North Carolina magazine, from 1989; appointed by Governor Hunt to chair State Board of Education, 1997. Phillip J. Kirk Jr., letter to Jan-Michael Poff, February 28, 1998.

[2] William Roger Soles (1920-   ), born in Whiteville; resident of Greensboro; B.S., University of North Carolina at Chapel Hill, 1947; honorary degrees; U.S. Army Air Force, 1941-1945. Insurance co. executive, retired 1993; career with Jefferson Standard Life Insurance Co., Greensboro, since 1947, included positions in Securities Dept. (vice-president and manager, 1964-1966, executive vice-president and manager, 1966), assistant to the president, 1964-1966, and president and director, 1967-1986; chairman, president, CEO, Jefferson-Pilot Life Insurance Co.; chairman and president, Jefferson-Pilot Corp.; board chairman, Jefferson-Pilot Fire and Casualty Co., Jefferson-Pilot Title Insurance Co., and Jefferson-Pilot Communications Co. of N.C. and Va. William Roger Soles, letter to Jan-Michael Poff, March 6, 1998.

[3] Smedes York (1941-   ), resident of Raleigh; B.S., N.C. State University, 1963; M.B.A., University of North Carolina at Chapel Hill, 1968; U.S. Army, 1964-1966, and Army Reserve. Real estate developer; president, York Properties; Raleigh city councilman, 1977-1979, and mayor, 1979-1983; chairman, N.C. Amateur Sports; past chairman, N.C. Citizens for Business and Industry, Wake County Planning Board, Greater Raleigh Chamber of Commerce, and of Raleigh-Durham Airport Authority; winner, numerous professional and public-service awards. Peggy Jones (for Smedes York), letter to Jan-Michael Poff, September 3, 1998.

[4] *America's Choice: High Skills or Low Wages! Report of the Commission on the Skills of the American Workforce* ([Rochester, N.Y.]: National Center on Education and the Economy, June 1990).

[5] German carmaker Bayerische Motoren Werke announced, on June 23, 1992, the construction of an assembly plant for its popular 3-Series sedans near Greer, South Carolina. North Carolina had been a candidate for the facility. But when he learned that Nebraska and South Carolina were the finalists, then-Governor Jim Martin threw his support behind the Palmetto State location, realizing that the new plant could pay economic dividends for the 238 automotive components manufacturers operating in North Carolina. *News and Observer*, June 24, 1992; Poff, *Addresses of Martin, 1989-1993*, 454-456; *The Week in Germany*, June 26, 1992.

BMW was not the only German automaker to decline an invitation to set up shop in North Carolina. See "Statement on Decision by Mercedes-Benz," September 29, 1993, reprinted elsewhere in this volume.

GOVERNOR'S CONFERENCE ON TRAVEL AND TOURISM

RESEARCH TRIANGLE PARK, MARCH 17, 1993

Before I begin tonight, I must say how good it is to be in Durham—home of the North Carolina Museum of Life and Science, the world-famous Durham Bulls, and the internationally renowned Duke University. With all you have to offer in Durham, the title "City of Medicine" is just one of your many distinctions.

I've had the privilege before of addressing the Governor's Conference on Travel and Tourism, but I've never been more impressed with the strides North Carolina is making and the promise we have for the future in this crucial area of our economy. In 1992, travel and tourism was the second-largest industry in North Carolina, a $7.3 billion industry with an annual payroll of more than $2 billion and more than a quarter million jobs. As Ralph Peters has pointed out, almost $400 million in state and local tax revenues can be traced directly to travel expenditures. Folks, $400 million pays for an awful lot of education, and health care, and highways, and the things we need to build this state up.

We should be proud of our performance in the travel industry, but we have slipped a bit over the past few years. We must now fight to recapture and expand our market share, and we're doing that in several ways. We must employ state-of-the-art marketing techniques to draw visitors to North Carolina. We must increase the state's advertising budget to remain competitive with other states. We must develop an even tighter public-private partnership between government and the travel industry, and we must protect and enhance North Carolina's unique environment.

I'm here tonight to tell you we are taking strong action on every one of these important points. In marketing: The millions of people who vacation in North Carolina weren't born knowing about our wonderful climate, our fine hospitality, our great natural beauty, and our world-class attractions. They had to be told about it, and I want to commend you for the job you've been doing in the telling.

But we can do even better, and we must. A few hours ago, Secretary Phillips introduced a draft of the new five-year travel industry marketing plan. This document is a comprehensive, long-term, strategic marketing plan based on state-of-the-art research on what travelers want. It calls for a public-private marketing team. It proposes a specific marketing image of North Carolina, based on research. It outlines explicit programs. It itemizes concrete goals, and it articulates clear measures of success.

This is an exciting and innovative approach, and I commend the authors for drafting the plan and for soliciting comments on it. I encourage all of you to read the plan carefully and send your comments to Dick Trammell, because that's the way a world-class, public-private partnership ought to work.[1]

I want you to know I think your plan and approach are right on target, and I stand behind you 100 percent. That's why I recommended an additional $3 million in my budget, over the next biennium, to help you implement these programs in advertising and promotion. We are facing tough times in North Carolina, and I've had to recommend some budget cuts, but this new money for travel and tourism is going to pay for itself.

In your hands at this conference, you all have a copy of the Division of Travel and Tourism's first annual report. If you look through that document, you'll see that we have studied vacation patterns, redesigned our strategy, and restructured our Division of Travel and Tourism to meet changing needs. We are buying targeted cable advertising, creating a positive perception of North Carolina, and encouraging travel writers to write about our state. The front-page spread on North Carolina in the *New York Times* travel section two Sundays ago shows we are doing our job.[2]

Clearly, the marketing plan and annual report are models of what government and industry can produce when we work together. Working together, we can make North Carolina the number-one travel destination in the Southeast. I want that to be our goal. Now, I know people say Florida is mighty tough competition, but we haven't been fighting with all our weapons. We're no longer just marketing ourselves as a summer destination. We are a year-round travel destination. We've got all four seasons in North Carolina!

In autumn, people flock to our state to see our fall colors. We have the most brilliant autumn of any state in the country, and it lasts longer, too! Last year, 22 million tourists visited the Blue Ridge Parkway, and many came for the changing leaves. For brilliant autumn hikes on the Appalachian Trail, no place is more colorful than North Carolina.

In winter, we offer terrific skiing in some of the world's most beautiful settings. The beauty of Biltmore Estate at Christmastime is unforgettable. For cross-country skiing, wintertime hiking, or just cozying up to the fireplace in a charming country inn, no place is more inviting than North Carolina.

In springtime, flowers bloom earlier and prettier in North Carolina. Rhododendrons, mountain laurel, wildflowers, and azaleas charm painters and poets with their beauty. For beautiful springtime blossoms, no place is prettier than North Carolina.

In our long North Carolina summer, we offer our glorious seashore. Our coast draws people from distant points for sunning, surfing, boating, fishing, or just sitting by the sea. For the magic of a sunny, sandy beach and the salty ocean breeze, no place is more soothing than North Carolina.

Our changing seasons make North Carolina a marvelous year-round destination, but many of our attractions don't change with the season. Here in North Carolina, we are the golf capital of the world. With nearly 500 golf courses, some known round the world, we can attract international golfers to tee up in the Old North State and visit the World Golf Hall of Fame in Pinehurst.

Golf is a marvelous way to market our state internationally. We are going to trade shows in Canada; talking to group tour operators in Japan; inviting travel writers from Europe to come to North Carolina. We are pushing our state internationally more than ever before, and I don't have to tell you that I'm doing all I can to keep those flight schedules into RDU and Charlotte just as convenient as they can be.

But golf is not our only international draw. Here in North Carolina, we are the motorsports capital of the world. We lead the nation in the number of NASCAR speedways. Our tracks at Charlotte, North Wilkesboro, and Rockingham make North Carolina home to the Winston Cup series.

And here in North Carolina, we are the college basketball capital of the world. The top sports question in the month of March is, "Which North Carolina team is going to win the NCAA championship?"

Hunting, fishing, horseback riding, and hiking span the seasons in our wonderful climate, and people can still mine for gems and pan for gold here in the state where gold was first discovered in the New World. We have riches in North Carolina. Let's invite the world to come mine them!

But like any riches or resources, they must be protected. The national seashore, the Great Smoky Mountains, the Appalachian Trail—these are preserves of remarkable beauty, God-given, but they are also very fragile. That's why I've fought to protect our Outer Banks. That's why I support our state parks and state forests. That's why I support the protection of the federal parks and wildlife refuges across North Carolina. We must remember that natural beauty cannot be created by human beings, but it can be destroyed by them. All of us interested in travel and tourism need to help protect the natural resources of our state, as well as encourage people to come and enjoy them.

When the Englishman, John Lawson, visited North Carolina in 1700, he wrote that North Carolina was ". . . a delicious country . . . (with) sweet air, moderate climate, and fertile soil . . . that spin out the thread of life to its utmost extent, and crown our days with the sweets of health and plenty . . . which render the possessors the happiest race of (people) upon earth."[3] Three centuries have passed since John Lawson wrote that passage, but I still recognize my home state in his words. North Carolina is a land of great beauty, and we have every reason to be optimistic about the future of our travel industry. I intend for these years ahead to be the best for travel and tourism in our history. You work hard. We'll be beside you.

---

[1] Richard Douglas Trammell (1946-   ), born in Winston-Salem; resident of Raleigh; was educated at Chowan College and at Davidson County Community College. Director, Asheville Convention and Visitors Bureau, 1975-1983; director, Charleston (S.C.) Convention and Visitors Bureau, 1983-1989; executive director, N.C. Division of Travel and Tourism, N.C. Dept. of Commerce, 1989-1995; founder, president, Travel and Tourism Development Group, Ltd., Raleigh, 1995; author. Richard Douglas Trammell, letter to Jan-Michael Poff, March 28, 1999.
[2] "Rambling the Carolinas," the feature topping the March 7, 1993, *New York Times* travel section, included articles on North Carolina's Albemarle and Cape Fear regions, as well as Aiken, South Carolina.

[3] "When we consider the Latitude and convenient Situation of Carolina, had we no farther Confirmation thereof, our Reason would inform us, that such a Place lay fairly to be a delicious Country, being placed in that Girdle of the World which affords Wine, Oil, Fruit, Grain, and Silk, with other rich Commodities, besides a sweet Air, moderate Climate, and fertile Soil; these are the Blessings (under Heaven's Protection) that spin out the Thread of Life to its utmost Extent, and crown our Days with the Sweets of Health and Plenty, which, when join'd with Content, renders the Possessors the happiest Race of Men upon Earth." John Lawson, *A New Voyage to Carolina*, ed. Hugh Talmage Lefler (Chapel Hill: University of North Carolina Press, 1967), 86.

John Lawson (1674-1711), explorer, naturalist, surveyor; born in England; was captured and killed by Tuscarora Indians while exploring Neuse River Valley, in what is now eastern North Carolina, with Baron Christoph von Graffenreid; journal of exploration of Piedmont region of Carolina colony, 1700-1701, formed basis of his book, *A New Voyage to Carolina* (London, 1709); laid out towns of Bath, New Bern, and encouraged settlement of both; became Bath County clerk of court and public register, established gristmill, 1707; official surveyor for Lords Proprietors of Carolina, 1708, and published map of colony in 1709. *Dictionary of North Carolina Biography*, s.v. "Lawson, John."

GOVERNOR'S CRIME COMMISSION

RALEIGH, MARCH 18, 1993

You have one of the most important jobs in the state ahead of you: helping us tackle North Carolina's crime crisis. Our crime rate is increasing at three times the national average. Every day we hear about another incident of violence in our state. Last night on the news, a Fayetteville teenager said she was worried about going to school every day. She said, "A bullet doesn't ask what your name is."

We can't go on like this. We've got to make sure our citizens are safe—in their homes, in their schools, on the street. I'm looking to you to help give them that protection.

First, we must develop a comprehensive plan to prevent crime in our state. I'm looking to Sis Kaplan to lead this effort, as she led the Mecklenburg County Criminal Justice Commission in their efforts to fight drugs.[1] She'll be joined by Judge Bill Jones, from Charlotte, who works closely with juvenile court cases, and Linda Hayes, a past chair of the North Carolina Juvenile Justice Committee and a past member of this commission.[2] All of you will be working closely with Secretary of Crime Control and Public Safety Thurman Hampton to develop a plan that helps our crime-fighting agencies work together, that recognizes the best way to fight crime is to prevent crime—by targeting at-risk children early on, before they have a chance to become criminals.

Second, we're going to launch a comprehensive attack against drugs in this state. I got a firsthand look at Charlotte's drug court when I was in Charlotte with Sis Kaplan last month.[3] This is an exciting, innovative concept, one that could work in other parts of our state, too. One important factor: coordination and cooperation between agencies. The war on drugs shouldn't [be] fought in Raleigh among agencies; it should be fought on the street against dealers.

Third, we're going to get more people involved. You've already heard about my Task Force on School Violence, and a little bit later today you'll be hearing how serious a problem we're having in our schools. The task force, chaired by Secretary Thurman Hampton, Superintendent of Public Instruction Bobby Etheridge, and Attorney General Mike Easley, is touring the state asking for ideas from the people—about the problems and the solutions—and they're going to find some answers.

Fourth, in the meantime, our Department of Correction is working to find new ways to get criminals off the streets, and into jail, and keep them there. That means building more prisons and putting more prisoners to work. I've called for building two prison work farms, expanding the Richmond County boot camp, and building another one. I've called for establishing an inmate construction program so that prison labor can be used to build and maintain prisons, as in South Carolina.

The job of this commission is to come up with ideas—about how to make our state safer. I ask you to listen to your friends and neighbors, educators, those in law enforcement and correction. Not every idea will work, but as Linus Pauling said, "The best way to have a great idea is to have a lot of ideas."[4] I'm looking to you to share those ideas. I want the hallmark of this commission to be cooperation, for if we work together, we can take back our most basic right: the right to be safe and secure in North Carolina.

---

[1] Sis Atlass Kaplan, resident of Charlotte; award-winning program producer, WBBM Radio and TV, Chicago, 1957-1960; radio/television director, Aaron D. Cushman and Associates, Chicago, 1960-1964. As president of SIS Radio, Inc., 1965-1989, she co-owned and was general manager of WAYS Radio, Charlotte, 1965-1986; owned and operated WAPE, Jacksonville, Florida, 1970-1980; owned and was general manager of WROQ FM, Charlotte, 1973-1986; and started a group of weekly newspapers, 1975, that had been transformed into the *Charlotte Leader* by 1985. Sold *Charlotte Leader* to Shaw Publications, 1988; president, Leader Newspaper, Inc., Charlotte, from 1994. President, National Radio Broadcasters Assn., 1980-1984; former chairwoman, Charlotte/Mecklenburg County Community Relations Committee; former co-chair, National Conference of Christians and Jews; chair, Governor's Crime Commission, appointed March 18, 1993, resigned November 22, 1994. Sis Atlass Kaplan, letter to Jan-Michael Poff, May 23, 1996.

[2] William G. Jones (1945-   ), born in Weston, W.Va.; B.A., Davidson College, 1967; J.D., University of North Carolina, 1970. Attorney, Mecklenburg County Public Defender's Office, 1975-1976; judge, Twenty-sixth District, N.C. District Court, was elected in 1976 and re-elected in 1980, 1984, 1988, 1992, and 1996. *The American Bench, 1997/98: Judges of the Nation,* s.v. "Jones, William G."

Linda Wheeler Hayes (1947-   ), resident of Dunn; was educated at Greensboro College. Office administrator, Stewart, Hayes, and Williams, P.A., attorneys-at-law;

member, 1983-1986, and from 1993, was appointed chair, 1994 and 1998, Governor's Crime Commission; former chair, Crime Commission Juvenile Justice Delinquency Prevention Committee; chair-elect, National Coalition of Juvenile Justice Advisory Groups; active in civic, community, and church programs; Democrat. Linda W. Hayes, letter to Jan-Michael Poff, February 5, 1998; Poff and Crow, *Addresses of Hunt, 1981-1985,* 622.

[3] The Hunt administration also sought to emulate Miami's intensive drug court program for first-time drug offenders. Participants could avoid prison by completing a court-supervised, one-year, job-training and substance-abuse program. Those who failed to finish it, or pass a drug test, were incarcerated. Press release, Governor Hunt Takes "New Approach" To Substance Abuse Programs, Raleigh, April 27, 1994, Governors Papers, James Baxter Hunt Jr.

[4] Linus Carl Pauling (1901-1994), born in Portland, Ore.; B.A., Oregon State College, 1922; Ph.D., California Institute of Technology, 1925; honorary degrees. Chemist; internationally famous opponent of nuclear weapons testing; assistant professor, 1927-1929, associate professor, 1929-1931, and professor of chemistry, from 1931, Cal Tech; member, numerous boards and commissions; author; winner, Nobel Prize for Chemistry, 1954, and of Nobel Peace Prize, 1962. Charles Moritz, ed., *Current Biography, 1964* (New York: The H. W. Wilson Company, 1965), 339-342; *Who Was Who in America, 1993-1996,* s.v. "Pauling, Linus Carl." Neither the source nor accuracy of the quotation attributed to Pauling could be verified.

NOTES, NORTH CAROLINA ASSOCIATION OF EDUCATORS ANNUAL CONVENTION

RALEIGH, MARCH 19, 1993

There's a saying about teaching some of you may have heard: "The mediocre teacher tells. The good teacher explains. The superior teacher demonstrates. The great teacher inspires."

North Carolina is blessed with great teachers, and I see many of them in the audience today. You inspire, encourage, nurture, and educate our children, and we owe you a tremendous debt in return.

Not only are you great teachers, but you're working every day to reach new heights of excellence. I hope you'll take the chance today to share your inspiration, share your knowledge, learn from others, and set a course of continued excellence for the year ahead.

1. To help you, to help our students, I'm going to need the help of good administrators and good teachers. That's why I've asked Tom Houlihan to help me shape my education policy, and that's why I'm going to be hiring a full-time teacher adviser. I'm beginning interviews now to find a classroom teacher to serve on my staff and advise me on the issues that concern you.[1]

2. Next, I'm committed to developing world-class teachers in this state. That takes money. In my budget, I've proposed that we start our teachers at more than $20,000 a year. For those of you already on the job, I've recommended a 2 percent pay increase, then an additional 2 percent

differentiated pay increase under S.B. 2. I've also asked for additional teacher longevity pay. Then I've recommended that we spend $20 million, over two years, to allow you three days leave each school year, while students are in school, to receive quality staff development.

It also takes a commitment to get better and better teachers into the classroom with you. As most of you know, I helped establish the National Board [for] Professional Teaching Standards, after leaving the Governor's Office, and am currently the chair. I want North Carolina to be the first state in the country to have board-certified teachers—to show the nation what we already know here: that we have the best teachers anywhere![2]

3. To help teachers teach, it's important to raise standards in our schools, to set measures of accountability for students and schools, and to provide local flexibility to meet those standards. I've already proposed funding in my budget and am now drafting legislation to create a Standards and Accountability Commission. This commission of educators, business leaders, and other community leaders will be charged with developing a set of standards to clearly define what a student needs to know to work in a modern economy. The commission will also develop a set of assessments that will test our students for these standards.

4. None of this makes any difference if our schools aren't safe. If you don't feel safe teaching, if you[r] students don't feel safe learning, education can't happen. I've appointed a task force to study school violence, and they've been conducting hearings across the state to listen to you, and your colleagues, and your students and their parents, then report back to me about how to make things better. Then I'll ask all of you to work with us to implement solutions in every school—to get results!

5. If we do all these things, I'm convinced we can turn the mediocre student into good, the good into superior, the superior into great. With great teachers like you, how can we do anything less?

---

[1] George Thomas Houlihan (1950-   ), born in Cincinnati, Ohio; resident of Smithfield; B.S., Indiana University, 1972; M.Ed., N.C. State University, 1975; Ed.D., University of North Carolina at Chapel Hill, 1982. Teacher; guidance counselor; principal, Clayton High School, 1981-1983; special assistant for secondary education, State of N.C., 1983-1984; associate superintendent, Alexander County Schools, 1984-1985; superintendent, Granville County Schools, 1985-1990; president/CEO, Community Leaders Allied for Superior Schools, Indianapolis, Ind., 1990-1991; superintendent, Johnston County Schools, 1991-1993; senior education adviser/education consultant to Governor Hunt, from 1993; president/CEO, N.C. Partnership for Excellence, from 1997; author. G. Thomas Houlihan, letter to Jan-Michael Poff, March 12, 1998.

Karen Garr (1947-   ), born in Hawkinsville, raised in Jackson, Ga.; resident of Raleigh; B.A., Wesleyan College, Macon, Ga., 1969; M.Ed., University of North Carolina at Chapel Hill, 1981. Teacher in Raleigh City and Wake County public schools, since 1969;

president, Wake County Association of Classroom Teachers, 1983-1985; vice-president, 1985-1986, president, 1986-1987, 1988-1989, N.C. Association of Educators; Hunt appointed her as his full-time teacher adviser in 1993. Karen Garr, letter to Jan-Michael Poff, March 3, 1998; press release, Hunt Names Former NCAE President as Teacher Adviser, Raleigh, May 3, 1993, Governors Papers, James B. Hunt Jr.

Hunt also appointed a committee of fifteen classroom teachers to advise him and the Standards and Accountability Commission on changes required to improve the state's schools. See Teacher Advisory Committee, Raleigh, October 29, 1993, and press release, Governor Hunt Creates Teacher Advisory Committee, Raleigh, October 1, 1993, Governors Papers, James Baxter Hunt Jr.

[2] According to the Governor's Press Office, North Carolina was on its way to becoming the first state to employ board-certified teachers, thanks to the adoption by state lawmakers of c. 231 of the *1993 Session Laws*. Passage of the bill coincided with the development, by the National Board for Professional Teaching Standards, of "a system of voluntary advanced certification, similar to the voluntary certification of doctors, architects, and accountants." The board also was creating "state-of-the-art, performance-based assessments" of candidates for certification that included "on-site observations of teachers in classrooms, videotapes of actual teaching, and interviews." Participants earned certification by passing a national teaching exam to be launched in the 1995-1996 academic year. Hunt chaired the National Board for Professional Teaching Standards from its founding in 1987. See press release, National Teaching Exam Bill Becomes Law, Raleigh, June 28, 1993, Governors Papers, James B. Hunt Jr.; and "An Act to Require the State Board of Education to Report on the National Board for Professional Teaching Standards' Program for Identifying Highly Professional Teachers and Recommend a Plan for Providing Monetary Incentives for Teachers to Participate in that Program," *N.C. Session Laws, 1993*, I, c. 231, ratified June 28, 1993.

STANDARDS AND ACCOUNTABILITY ACT

RALEIGH, MARCH 25, 1993

[The proposed Standards and Accountability Act was one of five components comprising the governor's education reform agenda. The other four were safe schools; local decision making; board-certified, or "highly professional" teachers; and his children's initiative: the N.C. Partnership for Children/Smart Start. Hunt discussed that agenda in the following announcement and in his speech to the N.C. Alliance for Public Education, Raleigh, May 12, 1993.]

The single most important task that we must accomplish in this legislative session, and in this administration, is dramatic, fundamental change in our schools. Too many North Carolina high school graduates are not prepared to compete in the modern economy. Employers tell me they're interviewing five or six high school graduates to find a single qualified applicant for any given job! Too many graduates come into the workforce without the basic and technical skills required for a good job in today's world. An auto mechanic can't work on a $20,000 car that's run by a computer if he or she can't read, write, understand computers, operate high-tech equipment, and follow illustrated instructions. Our schools just aren't teaching that. Parents know it. Educators know it. Employers know it.

We can change that, but only if we fundamentally change the way our schools work. Today I'm proposing the Standards and Accountability Act to bring about that change. This bill requires new standards based on what a student needs to know and be able to do in the modern workplace. By 1996, we'll have a new test in place that tells us whether a graduate can meet those standards, and whether that graduate can compete in the modern economy.

By 2000, I want to see one simple rule: If you can't pass that test, you can't graduate from high school. Our goal is not to fail students. Our goal is to help students by forcing change in our schools and to help students meet these new standards. By 2000, I want to guarantee to employers across the state, the country, and the world that every public school graduate has the skills to work in the BMW plants of the world.

I'm proposing real change where it matters the most: in our schools. Senator Perdue and Representative Barnes, the two strongest voices for education in the General Assembly, will sponsor this bill and will be strong voices for change in our schools. Their leadership and their vision of excellence in education will help us bring about that change.[1]

But higher standards and accountability are only part of the solution. I am proposing a comprehensive education reform agenda to bring about the fundamental change we need in our schools. This is an agenda that I'll be fighting for every single day of this legislative session. As part of that agenda, we must combat school violence so that teachers can teach and our students can learn in safety. I'll be proposing legislation based on the recommendations of the Governor's Task Force on School Violence.

We must also help our teachers do the best job they can. We must pay them better, give them more say in their schools, more prestige and respect, and we must provide better pay for better teaching.[2] We have good teachers in North Carolina, and they work hard. But we haven't given our schools clear standards to meet. Once we do that, it's fair to hold them accountable. Teachers want that, parents want that, and employers want that.

We must provide greater flexibility and stronger leadership at the local level. We must waive rules and regulations that hinder a local school's innovation. We must change funding categories to allow local schools to target dollars to local needs.[3]

We must use education dollars more efficiently. We can do that by using Total Quality Management, by conducting a statewide audit of central administration offices, and by strengthening administrator preparation programs as Representative Barnes has proposed.[4]

Finally, we must make sure our children come to school ready to learn, with the early childhood education, nutrition, health care, and other services they need to develop their minds and their potential. You'll be hearing more about that next week.[5]

Why is this education reform agenda so important? I believe education is economic development. I believe that the reforms I've outlined today— along with a renewed commitment to Tech Prep, workforce preparedness programs, and community colleges—will open the door to North Carolina's economic future.

Fundamental change in our schools will help us build world-class schools, a world-class workforce, and a world-class economy. We can bring the best industries to our state, to provide good jobs for our people. We can secure a more prosperous future for our children. We can begin that change by enacting our Standards and Accountability Act and our entire education reform agenda in this session. This is a challenge I set out for this administration, and for the General Assembly. This is a challenge I'll be fighting to meet every single day for the next four years.

---

[1] Beverly Moore Perdue, born in Grundy, Va.; resident of Craven County; B.S., University of Kentucky, 1969; M.Ed., 1974, Ph.D., 1976, University of Florida. Former director of geriatric services, Craven County Hospital; member, N.C. House, 1987-1990, and senate, from 1991; co-chair, N.C. Senate Appropriations Committee; Democrat. *North Carolina Manual, 1995-1996*, 496.

Anne C. Barnes (1932-   ), born in Gaston County; resident of Chapel Hill; was graduated from Mount Holly High School, 1950. Homemaker; former ballet instructor; chair, Orange County Board of Commissioners, 1980-1981; member, N.C. House of Representatives, 1981-1996; Democrat. During the Martin administration she was co-chair of a special committee on prisons and crime that started the momentum for a system of structured sentencing. *News and Observer*, September 4, 5, 1996; *North Carolina Manual 1995-1996*, 545.

[2] An attachment to this text indicates that Hunt was referring to board certification for the state's schoolteachers and his support for differentiated pay as provided under Senate Bill 2.

[3] S.B. 882, "A Bill to Provide Greater Flexibility in Local School Board Expenditures and Provide Incentives for Greater Fiscal Responsibility," would have reduced the number of funding categories and allowed schools more spending leeway. Described as one of the "legislative keystones" of Hunt's education reform package, the bill remained in committee through the end of the 1993 legislative session. *N.C. Senate Journal, 1993*, 289, 369; press release, Key Bills for Hunt's Education Plan Introduced, Raleigh, April 14, 1993, Governors Papers, James Baxter Hunt Jr.

S.B. 380, "A Bill to Implement a Recommendation of the Government Performance Audit Committee to Improve Efficiency in School Operations by Simplifying Funding Formulas and Empowering Local School Administrative Units to Manage for Results," was mentioned specifically in the attachment to this text. It failed to clear the upper house of the legislature; see *N.C. Senate Journal, 1993*, 119, 201.

[4] Hunt established the Public School Administrator Task Force, on May 7, 1993, to perform a review of central administration offices and to determine the percentage of school funding that was reaching teachers and classrooms. Executive Order Number 12,

N.C. Session Laws, 1993, 2:3225-3227; press release, Hunt Creates Task Force to Study School Administrators, Raleigh, May 13, 1993, Governors Papers, James Baxter Hunt Jr.

Rep. Barnes co-sponsored two bills during the 1993 legislative session to improve school administrator preparation programs. H.B. 257 was adopted as "An Act to Implement the Recommendations of the Educational Leadership Task Force and the Joint Legislative Education Oversight Committee Concerning School Administrator Programs at the Constituent University of North Carolina Institutions," *N.C. Session Laws, 1993*, c. 199, ratified June 23, 1993. H.B. 258, "A Bill to be Entitled an Act to Implement a Recommendation of the Education Leadership Task Force and the Joint Legislative Education Oversight Committee to Plan for the Establishment of a School Leadership Academy to Enhance the Quality of Ongoing Professional Development for School Administrators," was incorporated into *N.C. Session Laws, 1993*, c. 321, as s. 86.

[5] Hunt was, of course, referring to the N.C. Partnership for Children. See Children's Initiative, March 31, 1993, below.

NAACP SOUTHERN REGION LEADERSHIP CONFERENCE

FAYETTEVILLE, MARCH 26, 1993

You are here, as branch leaders of the NAACP [National Association for the Advancement of Colored People], to carry on a great and powerful mission begun in 1909 with the founding of the NAACP. The NAACP has fought long and hard to win equal rights for blacks in America. I've worked with many of you over the years, and I've seen that hard work, that courage, and that leadership firsthand. I salute you for all you've done in North Carolina and across the country. As governor of North Carolina, I want you to know I stand behind you 100 percent as you fight for equal rights and equal opportunity in housing, education, health care, and jobs.

Here in North Carolina, we are committed to diversity in the workforce, starting at the top! Those of you who know me are aware of my record in appointing blacks to top positions. Henry Frye, one of our state's great jurists, was one of my appointments to the North Carolina Supreme Court.[1] In the present administration, I have appointed two African Americans as cabinet secretaries: Thurman Hampton, former D.A. in Rockingham County, is my secretary of crime control and public safety; Katie Dorsett, my secretary of administration, is the first African American woman in North Carolina history to serve as cabinet secretary.[2]

Carolyn Coleman, who was the NAACP's southern voter education director, is one of my top aides. Her office in the Capitol is ten steps from mine, and I can tell you those are ten steps she doesn't hesitate to take if she thinks there's something the governor needs to hear! Those of you who know Carolyn know that she gets the job done, and I can tell you she's getting the job done in state government.[3]

Ron Penny, who was assistant legal counsel for the North Carolina NAACP, is my state personnel director.[4] I have also appointed African Americans to top positions in the cabinet departments and prominent boards and commissions.

I believe we have the most diverse administration in the history of our state. But I have not appointed African Americans just for the sake of diversity. I have appointed African Americans because I recognize talent and drive when I see it, and I need both in the Hunt administration—and let me tell you why: In the Hunt administration, we are doing something even more important than getting diversity at the top, we are insisting on equality at the bottom. I'm talking about giving an equal start in school to all children in North Carolina.

Education is the great equalizer. Education can make a poor woman's child the equal of a senator's son, but only if it's equal education. Our schools must offer every child, from every race, from every class, from every creed, an equal opportunity to progress from "Simon says" to "Einstein says." This is what we are committed to in North Carolina.

Next week I will unveil an initiative proposing a public-private partnership to make quality early childhood education, good health care, proper nutrition, parenting classes, and other childhood services available to every child in North Carolina that needs it. When I was lieutenant governor, I fought to make public kindergarten available across the state. Now we're aiming higher. It's not enough that every child attend kindergarten, they must be ready to learn when they get there—not just the rich children, not just the lucky children, not just the gifted children— all children. In our plan, there's only one requirement: You have to live in North Carolina!

Once we get our children to school ready to learn, we must challenge them with rigorous standards and test them to make sure they're learning what we're teaching. I announced legislation, yesterday, to follow that tough talk with tough action. We are putting together a commission to determine exactly what our high school graduates need to know, and be able to do, to compete for high-paying jobs in today's job market; and once we determine those standards, we are going to teach them and test for them. This is more than a competency test; this is a competitiveness test! It will be put together by a diverse group of education and business leaders and will focus on what top businesses are looking for in their employees. We'll train educators to give this test. We'll pilot-test it, and we'll benchmark it to make sure that in earlier grades all students are progressing to that new standard. But by 2000, if you can't pass that test, you can't graduate.

Now, our goal is not to fail students. Our goal is to help students by forcing change in our schools and to help students meet these new standards. It's not just the students who are accountable. We are all in this together, folks!

We are going to hold everyone accountable: students, teachers, parents, administrators, superintendents, even the governor. Everyone is responsible for making sure our students can pass these tests and qualify for high-skill, high-wage jobs. Our students will be qualified to work in any plants and factories in the world, and that quality workforce will draw high-skill, high-wage jobs to North Carolina and make a difference in the lives of all our people. I'm here today to ask North Carolinians to join with me in this partnership for education and for equality, and I ask our friends and neighbors from across the South to go back home and tell folks what we're doing in North Carolina. Join with us in building a bright and prosperous tomorrow.

In closing, I'd like to recall with you the words of poet Langston Hughes, who is a constant and eloquent reminder of the high stakes of our mission:

> What happens to a dream deferred?
>   Does it dry up
>   like a raisin in the sun?
>   Or fester like a sore—
>   and then run?
>   Does it stink like rotten meat?
>   Or crust and sugar over—
>   like a syrupy sweet?
>   Maybe it just sags
>   like a heavy load.
>   Or does it explode?[5]

I'm here as governor to tell you, there will be no more dreams deferred in North Carolina. Let us join together to build a new world of equality. Let us start with our schools, and let us start today.

---

[1] Henry E. Frye (1932-   ), born in Ellerbe; B.S., North Carolina A&T State University, 1953; J.D., University of North Carolina, 1959; U.S. Air Force, 1953-1955. Attorney in private practice, 1959-1963, 1967-1983; assistant U.S. attorney, Middle District of N.C., 1963-1965; law professor, N.C. Central University, 1965-1967; member, N.C. House, 1969-1980, and senate, 1981-1982; appointed to N.C. Supreme Court, February 1983, to replace J. Phil Carlton; elected, 1984, re-elected, 1990, to N.C. Supreme Court. *North Carolina Manual, 1995-1996,* 704.

[2] Katie G. Dorsett (1932-   ), born in Shaw, Miss.; B.S., Alcorn State University, 1953; M.S., Indiana University, 1955; Ed.D., University of North Carolina at Greensboro, 1975. Business teacher, Coahoma Junior College, 1953-1954; associate professor, School of Business and Economics, North Carolina A&T State University, 1955-1987; member, Greensboro City Council, 1983-1986, and of Guilford County Board of Commissioners, 1986-1992; secretary, N.C. Dept. of Administration, from 1993; Democrat. *North Carolina Manual, 1995-1996*, 326.

[3] Carolyn Q. Coleman (1942-   ), born in Savannah, Ga.; resident of Greensboro; B.S., Savannah State College, 1964; M.S., North Carolina A&T State University, 1991. N.C. state director, 1979-1988, southern voter education director, 1988-1992, NAACP; Jim Hunt for Governor campaign, 1992; special assistant to Governor Hunt, since November 1992. Carolyn Q. Coleman, letter to Jan-Michael Poff, March 3, 1998.

[4] Ronald G. Penny, resident of Clayton; B.S., North Carolina A&T State University; was graduated from University of North Carolina School of Law. Attorney, E. I. Du Pont de Nemours and Co., 1978-1980; lecturer in Business and Criminal Justice Depts., 1980-1983, legal counsel to chancellor, 1980-1984, Elizabeth City State University; private law practice, 1984-1993; director, N.C. Office of State Personnel, from 1993; visiting assistant professor, N.C. Central University, from 1993. Ronald G. Penny, letter to Jan-Michael Poff, March 2, 1998.

[5] "Dream Deferred," in Langston Hughes, *The Panther and the Lash: Poems of Our Times* (New York: Alfred A. Knopf, 1967), 14.

ANNOUNCEMENT OF CHILDREN'S INITIATIVE

RALEIGH, MARCH 31, 1993

[With the possible exception of education, few topics dominated Hunt's speeches more than the N.C. Partnership for Children/Smart Start program during 1993. Hunt formally launched the campaign for Smart Start on March 31. Other appearances where he advocated support for his proposal included: Frank Porter Graham Child Development Center, Chapel Hill, April 1; Glaxo-Wake County Infant and Maternal Clinic Dedication, Zebulon, April 8; Testimony before Joint Appropriations Committee, N.C. General Assembly, Raleigh, April 20; Delta Sigma Theta Sorority, Raleigh, April 29; Children's Home Society, Raleigh, May 11; Centennial, Western N.C. Conference, AME Church, Raleigh, May 21; Ministers at the Mansion, Raleigh, June 30; Smart Start Briefing for County Government Leaders, Raleigh, July 28; N.C. Day Care Association Leadership Conference, Chapel Hill, September 13; Smart Start Luncheon, Winston-Salem, September 13(14); Remarks to N.C. Partnership for Children Board, Raleigh, September 23; and American Institute of Banking, Raleigh, November 22(24), 1993. See also press releases, Governor Hunt Unveils Children's Initiative, Raleigh, March 31, and attachment, Smart Start: A Crusade for North Carolina's Children; Hunt, Top Leaders Call for Funding of Children's Initiative, Raleigh, April 20; untitled media advisory, May 4; Governor Hunt's Child Care Tax Credit Bill Advances, Raleigh, July 15; Governor Hunt's Child Care Tax Credit Bill Wins Approval, Raleigh, July 21; Hunt Briefs Government Leaders on Smart Start, Raleigh, July 28; Hunt Names 16 to N.C. Partnership for Children, Raleigh, September 20; and Governor Names First Lady as Smart Start Honorary Chair, Raleigh, September 22, 1993. Governors Papers, James Baxter Hunt Jr.]

Last week I unveiled an education reform plan to help North Carolina build world-class schools, a world-class workforce, and a world-class economy in North Carolina.[1] We're aiming high: higher standards, safer schools, better teachers, and stronger local leadership. But we cannot build that world-class workforce if our children don't come to school ready to learn. What happens in those first five years sets a pattern— for the child, for the school, and for the state.

My granddaughter, Hannah, started kindergarten with a love of learning and an excitement about the world around her. My daughter and her husband have given Hannah the love, nurturing, nutrition, health care, and early childhood education she needs to fully develop in those early years. But Hannah is lucky. Too many children in North Carolina come to school ready to fail, struggling to overcome a family life of poverty, drugs, or neglect. Those failures are North Carolina's failures. We can do better by our children, and we must do better if we want to build the high-skill, high-wage economy we need to improve the quality of life for our children and for all people.

Raising a child is the family's responsibility. But some families need help, and all families should have access to affordable, quality childhood education to give their children the best start in life. Now, the traditional governmental response is to create a government bureaucracy. We could set up a state preschool program for three- and four-year-olds, like we did for kindergarten when I was lieutenant governor.

Today I'm proposing a new approach. This is an approach outside the framework of state government, using government as a catalyst instead of the solution. Today we're setting up a public-private partnership, the North Carolina Partnership for Children, that brings together parents, educators, business leaders, church and community leaders, nonprofits, and government.

This partnership will develop a vision for children that our state now lacks, and it will develop a practical blueprint for action. We'll find out who we're reaching, who we're missing, and what we must do better. Then we'll set about doing better. At the same time, the partnership will encourage similar public-private partnerships in twelve counties next year and eight counties the year after that. Our goal is to have such a partnership in all 100 counties.

Each local partnership will bring together local public and private leaders, and local resources, to develop a local blueprint to provide quality early childhood services, that involve families, to every child who needs it. Our goal is to reach every child in all 100 counties. I'm asking the General Assembly to provide $58 million as incentives for those local partnerships. Most of this money would be in the form of subsidies to make quality child care more affordable.

But we're not just talking about improving early childhood education in twenty counties. We're also taking immediate measures to upgrade the quality of early childhood education across North Carolina and to immunize every single child. I've asked the General Assembly for some $40 million in the biennium to fund measures to ensure higher quality day care, to ease the burden of child care on families, to reach more low-income families, to improve education for child-care teachers, and to step up regulatory monitoring.

Today a bill will be filed that sets out these higher standards for quality and sets out the role of the partnership, as well. This legislation is being sponsored by Senator Russell Walker and Senator Jim Richardson, along with Representatives Howard Hunter, Ruth Easterling, and Edd Nye. Separate legislation will also be introduced to provide that every child in North Carolina, between birth and nineteen, is immunized, and legislation raising child-care tax credits for families making less than $40,000 [sic]. These legislators have been the children's voice and the children's advocate in the General Assembly, and their leadership will help us help children.[2]

The North Carolina Partnership for Children is being created, today, as a nonprofit corporation, and articles of incorporation are being filed. Today I'm issuing a challenge—to the General Assembly, to the business community, to the child-care community, and to everyone else in North Carolina who cares about our children and our future. Here's the challenge: Help us meet the needs of North Carolina's children, but help us do it in a new way, a better way. It's not big government. We know that parents buy most of the child care, and that businesses help a lot, and the state is a relatively small player. We are asking for additional state dollars for this initiative, but we're also asking the business community, the nonprofit community, and everyone in between to help us, as well.

Most importantly, we're not proposing to spend that money in the same old way to do the same old thing. We want to preserve the diversity of our child-care system, and we want to enhance that system. We want to help local communities serve local children and their families, using local resources and local ideas. In short, we want to steer, and we're going to let local communities row.

All of us here, today, know that our children are North Carolina's future. If we are to make the most of our state, we must make the most of our children. Investing in our future requires the same kind of patience, discipline, and occasional sacrifice that children require, and it will require all of us to come together to meet this challenge. Our children will be the better for it, and so will North Carolina.

---

[1] See "Standards and Accountability Act," Raleigh, March 25, 1993, reprinted earlier in this volume.

[2] The General Assembly adopted the early childhood initiatives bill, H.B. 718/S.B. 676, as c. 321, s. 254; the child immunization bill, H.B. 719/S.B. 674, as c. 321, s. 287; and the child-care tax credit bill, H.B. 720/S.B. 675, as c. 432, N.C. Session Laws, 1993; see also N.C. House Journal, 1993, 242, N.C. Senate Journal, 1993, 218, and untitled media advisory, May 4, 1993, Governors Papers, James Baxter Hunt Jr.

The chief sponsors of H.B. 718/S.B. 676, as listed by Hunt, were:

Russell Grady Walker (1918-   ), born in Conetoe; resident of Asheboro; was graduated from High Point High School; pilot, U.S. Army Air Force, 1941-1946; U.S. Air Force Reserve, 1947-1955. Retired supermarket operator; former pres., Food Line Super Markets, Inc.; member, Asheboro City Council, 1961-1965; member, N.C. Senate, 1975-1994, and chairman, Children and Human Resources Committee; chairman, N.C. Democratic Party, 1979-1983. News and Observer, July 11, 1994; North Carolina Manual, 1993-1994, 426.

James Franklin Richardson (1926-   ), born in Charlotte; B.S., Johnson C. Smith University, 1949; U.S. Navy, 1944-1946. Retired postmaster; member, N.C. House, 1985-1986; member, N.C. Senate, 1987-1994, and chairman, Appropriations Subcommittee on Human Resources; Democrat. News and Observer, July 11, 1994; North Carolina Manual, 1993-1994, 416.

Howard J. Hunter Jr. (1946-   ), born in Washington, D.C.; resident of Northampton County; M.S., N.C. Central University, 1971. Vice-president, director, partner/owner, Hunter's Funeral Home, Inc.; former Scoutmaster; Hertford County commissioner, 1978-1988; member, N.C. House of Representatives from 1989, and chairman, House Committee on Children, Youth and Families. North Carolina Manual, 1993-1994, 523-524, 1995-1996, 605.

Ruth M. Easterling (1910-   ), born in Gaffney, S.C.; resident of Charlotte; was graduated from Limestone College, 1932; attended Queens College. Executive assistant to the president, Radiator Specialty Co., 1947-1978; national president, Business and Professional Women, 1970-1971; member, Charlotte City Council, 1972-1973; member, N.C. House of Representatives, from 1977, and co-chair, Appropriations Subcommittee on Human Resources; chair, Legislative Women's Caucus, 1987-1991. North Carolina Manual, 1993-1994, 495-496, 1995-1996, 580-581.

Edd Nye, born in Gulf; resident of Bladen County; A.A., Southeastern Community College, 1969; attended N.C. State University, 1970-1973; served in U.S. Air Force. Insurance executive; member, N.C. Senate, 1975-1976; member, N.C. House, from 1977, and co-chair, Appropriations Subcommittee on Human Resources; Democrat. North Carolina Manual, 1993-1994, 564, 1994-1995, 638.

GLOBAL TRANSPARK CONFERENCE

MOUNT OLIVE, APRIL 5, 1993

[The Global TransPark was envisioned as a 20,000-acre industrial complex integrated with an international air cargo airport. Such an arrangement would permit just-in-time delivery of products, manufactured at the GTP, to any airport worldwide. Rail, highway, and high-speed telecommunications links would connect the facility to off-site customers, as well. Promoters also predicted that it would spur heavier demand for North Carolina agricultural products by allowing food processors and distributors to reach new markets and increase exports.

When fully operational, the Global TransPark was projected to create approximately 50,000 jobs and pump an additional $2.8 billion annually into the state's economy. Eager to land the air-industrial complex, proponents of thirteen different sites from across the state submitted proposals to the Air Cargo Airport Authority for approval. Kinston Regional Jetport, in Lenoir County, offered a combination of assets that resulted in its selection, in May 1992, as the future home of the GTP.

Conceived in 1989 by Dr. Jack Kasarda, director of the Kenan Institute of Private Enterprise at the University of North Carolina at Chapel Hill, the Global TransPark received strong support from Governor Jim Martin early in his second term. Hunt acknowledged the contributions the two men, and others, made to the project in remarks he delivered April 5, 1993, at Mount Olive College. He also expressed on that occasion his determination to ensure the viability of the GTP. The following week Hunt revealed that the Federal Aviation Administration had awarded a $1 million grant to the Kenan Institute to further research the TransPark concept. *News and Observer*, April 13, 1993, March 24, 1996; Poff, *Addresses of Martin, 1989-1993*, xxiv, 385-387, 434-435, 441-443, 458, 473-476; Remarks at Announcement of FAA Grant to Kenan Institute, Chapel Hill, April 12, 1993, Governors Papers, James Baxter Hunt Jr.]

It is certainly a pleasure to be here today in eastern North Carolina, and here at Mount Olive College in this wonderful facility named for Senator Wendell Murphy's family.[1] My father and stepmother are here with us today, and as many of you know, Father has worked tirelessly for this college, as chairman of the board of trustees and, now, as a board member.[2] I'm also personally involved with Mount Olive, too, as chairman of the steering committee of the Road to Excellence Campaign, and I'm proud to tell you that campaign is well on its way to meeting its five-year goal—one year ahead of schedule![3] A lot of that success is due to the leaders you have here: President Burkette Raper, one of the finest college presidents anywhere, has a large vision for this college and region. [He] and Executive Vice-President Bill Byrd are making a real difference at this college, and there's clear evidence of that today, as we come together for Project East 1993.[4]

Our subject, today, is one of the most important economic development opportunities in our state, the Global TransPark, and we can't talk about the TransPark without mentioning several key players:

—Dr. Jack Kasarda, the man with the vision for this park;[5]

—Rusty Goode, for the work he's done to bring this vision into focus, as president and executive director of our Air Cargo Authority;[6]

—Governor Jim Martin has made this project one of his personal priorities and has given his time, energy, and leadership to bring the TransPark to where it is today. He and other members of the Air Cargo Authority Board deserve our heartfelt applause.

—I want to thank Felix Harvey for agreeing to help raise $30 million in private money for Global TransPark, Incorporated, and Henson Barnes for serving as today's moderator and working to raise $20 million in public money. He and the members of the eastern legislative delegation—John Kerr and Phil Baddour, as well as Beverly Perdue and so many others—are working hard to create the eastern economic development zone, covering eleven counties.[7] For the first time ever, these counties are linking arms, saying they will work together because they believe in this project. I commend them for this partnership, one of the best examples of partnership we have seen.

Every single one of you here today is vital to this project. By attending, you're saying you realize the importance of the opportunity we have here, and you want to be a player. You realize the importance of the opportunity we have here, and you want to be a part of it. You've done special things. I know why: Many of us grew up in eastern North Carolina, and we want to do what is right for this region; also, for this state. Just as RTP [Research Triangle Park] [and] University Research Park in Charlotte are statewide resources, this is a North Carolina project.

Let me tell you, there has never been a more important project for this part of the state, and all North Carolina, than this one. There has never been a project that should unite us like this one. There has never been a project with a greater potential to improve our quality of life and our economic future than this one.

Of course, the first thing that comes to mind when people start thinking about the benefits of the Global TransPark is jobs. The counties that are joining the economic development zone know what a project like this can do. It won't just create jobs in Lenoir County. It'll create a ripple effect for all the surrounding counties, spawning new businesses, new opportunities, and tens of thousands of jobs all over North Carolina.

But this is not just a great economic development opportunity. What we are building here is the next century's version of the industrial complex, to put our state on [the] cutting edge of global manufacturing and trade. It is being designed to serve the needs of businesses of the future, to give them the speed and efficiency they need. The TransPark will be a place where global goods will move seamlessly from truck to train; from plane to plant; from Warsaw, North Carolina, to Warsaw, Poland, and back. It will challenge our state's entrepreneurs to solve some of the toughest challenges they will face. They'll have to figure out how to make sure the raw materials they truck in from Tarboro and use for construction in Kinston are ready "just in time" to get on a plane taking off for Tokyo by 2:00 P.M.

We're starting to see some evidence of the TransPark's success already. Recently, two new industrial prospects that have decided to locate in our state have cited the TransPark as one of the reasons. They say they like the idea of being part of a state that has demonstrated such a commitment to progress. Over the next four years I can promise you this: Commerce secretary Dave Phillips, Lieutenant Governor Bob Jordan, and I will be telling every industrial prospect we see what we are doing in this vital part of our state. Let me announce today that I will be saying that as the new chairman of the Air Cargo Authority Board! I will follow the lead of Governor Martin in making this a top priority, and I will work as hard as I can to ensure the success of the TransPark.

The Global TransPark is not just the chance of a lifetime for us, here. It's the chance of many lifetimes, of many generations. This isn't a discussion about building runways; it's about building futures. And if you want to know who we should be thinking about as we get down to business, you don't have to look much further than this table of young folks right down here. Stand up, you students from Wayne County! These Wayne County high school students are here with us today, and I want every one of us to get a picture of them in our minds. These are the people we're working for—and their children, and their grandchildren. Think of your children and grandchildren. The Global TransPark is for them.

But to realize the full potential of the Global TransPark, we must build a world-class workforce. We must work together to bring about dramatic, fundamental change in our schools and make sure every child in eastern North Carolina, and across North Carolina, comes to school ready to learn. If we do that, and if we work together to build up the Global TransPark, we can bring high-skill, high-wage jobs to eastern North Carolina, and all of North Carolina, and we can build a better future for our children. It's up to us, all of us in eastern North Carolina, to make it work, and it's time to get started.

Today is the beginning of the next phase of this great initiative, and it's time to spread the word. We need to make the case for this TransPark in every way we can: at public meetings and in the media, at the feed stores and the coffee shops, in the board rooms and the break rooms. Let's tell people what we're doing here and why it's so important. If we want this project to really take off, like the planes we're planning to have here, each and every one of you has to get on board and then convince your neighbors, and associates, and friends to join you. It won't be easy, but I can't imagine a better team to get this job done than the leaders of eastern North Carolina. Working together, we can make the Global TransPark a success—for our children, our grandchildren, and the generations to come.

---

[1] The Lois K. Murphy Regional Center, dedicated March 31, 1993, on the campus of Mount Olive College, was named in honor of the mother of Sen. Wendell H. Murphy, Joyce

Murphy Norman, and Harry D. "Pete" Murphy. The structure housed the school's main dining hall, student center, private meeting/dining rooms, and the offices of the dean of student development. The Global TransPark Conference of April 5, 1993, was the first public event scheduled for the Murphy Center. Nason correspondence.

Wendell Holmes Murphy (1938-   ), born in Rose Hill; B.S., N.C. State University, 1960. Founder, president, chief executive officer, Murphy Family Farms, Inc., the nation's largest hog producer; member, N.C. House, 1983-1988, and senate, 1989-1992; former teacher; Democrat. *News and Observer*, August 2, 1992, March 5, 1996; *North Carolina Manual, 1991-1992*, 266.

[2] Governor Hunt's stepmother, Pearl Johnson Hunt, was born October 24, 1914, in Smithfield. She married James Baxter Hunt Sr. in February 1991. Janice Shearin, executive assistant to First Lady Carolyn Hunt, letter to Jan-Michael Poff, April 16, 1997.

[3] The goal of the Road to Excellence Campaign was to generate $10 million, between 1989 and 1995, for capital development and educational services at Mount Olive College. Nason correspondence.

[4] William Burkette Raper (1925-   ), born near Wilson; A.B., 1947, M.Div., 1951, Duke University; was ordained as Free Will Baptist minister, 1946. Pastor, Hull Road Free Will Baptist Church, Snow Hill, 1951-1955; promotional director, Free Will Baptist State Convention of N.C., 1953-1954; president, 1954-1995, president emeritus, since 1995, Mount Olive College; president, N.C. Assn. of Colleges and Universities, 1969-1970; secretary, Independent College Fund of N.C., 1976-1978; Democrat. *Who's Who in America, 1997*, s.v. "Raper, William Burkette."

J. William Byrd (1936-   ), B.S., 1959, M.S., 1960, N.C. State University; Ph.D., Pennsylvania State University, 1963. Physics professor, department chair, East Carolina University, 1964-1984; professor, Dept. of Physics and Astronomy, and dean, College of Arts and Sciences, Appalachian State University, 1984-1992. Positions with Mount Olive College, since 1992, included interim president, Oct. 1992-Feb. 1993, executive vice-president, 1993-1995, Executive Council chair, and president-elect; was installed as president, January 31, 1995. Nason correspondence.

[5] John Dale (Jack) Kasarda (1945-   ), born in Wilkes-Barre, Pa.; resident of Chapel Hill; B.S., 1967, M.B.A., 1968, Cornell University; Ph.D., University of North Carolina at Chapel Hill, 1971. Professor of sociology, since 1976, Kenan Distinguished Professor, Sociology Department chairman, 1980-1990, and director, since 1990, Kenan Institute of Private Enterprise, University of North Carolina at Chapel Hill; author. *News and Observer*, April 25, 1993; *Who's Who in America, 1996*, s.v. "Kasarda, John Dale."

[6] Seddon (Rusty) Goode Jr. (1932-   ), born in Clinton; resident of Charlotte; B.S., Davidson College, 1954; M.B.A., University of North Carolina at Chapel Hill, 1957. Vice-president, Southeastern Financial Corp., 1957-1962; president, Mt. Mitchell Broadcasting Corp./WMIT, 1963; vice-president, North Carolina National Bank, 1964-1968; senior vice-president, treasurer, director, Interstate Securities Corp., 1968-1977; chairman, First Charlotte Corp., 1977-1984; president, director, University Research Park, Charlotte, since 1981; president and executive director, 1991-1995, treasurer, since 1995, N.C. Global TransPark Authority. Martha Borden, N.C. Global TransPark Authority, letter to Jan-Michael Poff, September 23, 1994; Poff, *Addresses of Martin, 1985-1989*, 167n; *News and Observer*, February 23, 1995, March 24, 26, 29, 1996.

[7] C. Felix Harvey (1920-   ), born in Kinston; B.S., University of North Carolina at Chapel Hill, 1943; U.S. Navy, 1943-1946. Board chairman, Harvey Enterprises and Affiliates, engaged in farming and agricultural supply, ginning, terminaling, transportation, public utility contracting, real estate, and wholesale and retail petroleum distribution; founder, Life Insurance Co. of North Carolina, 1955; president and chief executive officer, 1969-1971, board chairman, 1971-1972, Georgia International Life Insurance Co.; founder, 1978, chairman, First Financial Savings Bank; local and state civic leader; early believer in GTP concept, became president, N.C. Global TransPark Foundation, in 1993. C. Felix Harvey, letter to Jan-Michael Poff, October 3, 1994; see also autobiographical article on Harvey by Charlie Peek, "Looking Up Down East," *Business North Carolina*, February 1993, 36-45.

Henson Perrymoore Barnes (1934-   ), born in Bladen County; resident of Goldsboro; A.B., 1959, J.D., 1961, University of North Carolina at Chapel Hill; U.S. Army, 1953-1956.

Attorney; farmer; member, state House of Representatives, 1975-1976; member, 1977-1992, president pro tempore, 1989-1992, state senate; attorney, Global TransPark Development Commission; Democrat. *News and Observer*, January 22, 1989, February 28, August 2, 1992, March 29, 1996; *North Carolina Manual, 1991-1992*, 227, 229.

John Hosea Kerr III (1936-   ), born in Richmond, Va.; resident of Wayne County; A.B., 1958, J.D., 1961, University of North Carolina at Chapel Hill; N.C. National Guard, 1954-1962. Attorney; member, state House of Representatives, 1987-1992; was elected to state senate, 1992, and returned in subsequent elections; co-chair, Senate Finance Committee; Democrat. *North Carolina Manual, 1995-1996*, 482.

Philip Augustine Baddour Jr. (1942-   ), born in Goldsboro; resident of Wayne County; A.B., 1964, J.D., 1967, University of North Carolina at Chapel Hill; N.C. National Guard. Attorney; U.S. magistrate, 1970-1971; chair, Wayne County Democratic Party, 1972-1976; member, state House of Representatives, 1993-1994; member, N.C. Courts Commission, 1993-1995; was appointed to N.C. Commission on Business Law and the Economy, 1994, and Southern Growth Policies Board, 1995. Letters of Appointment to Boards and Commissions, Governors Papers, James Baxter Hunt Jr.; *North Carolina Manual, 1993-1994*, 460-461.

Beverly Moore Perdue was identified earlier in this volume.

Legislators created the Global TransPark Development Commission to oversee the GTP Development Zone—which covered Carteret, Craven, Duplin, Edgecombe, Greene, Jones, Lenoir, Nash, New Hanover, Onslow, Pamlico, Pitt, Wayne, and Wilson Counties. "An Act to Authorize Certain Counties that will Derive Economic Benefits from the North Carolina Global TransPark to Form a Global TransPark Development Zone to Promote Economic Development of, and to Encourage Infrastructure Construction in, the Counties of the Zone," *N.C. Session Laws, 1993*, c. 544, ratified July 24, 1993.

STATEMENT ON SCHOOL VIOLENCE TASK FORCE REPORT

RALEIGH, APRIL 8, 1993

When my four children were attending school in Wilson County and here in Raleigh, they carried books, notebooks, and pencils in their book bags. These days, children carry guns, knives, and switchblades in their backpacks. Those are not the tools of learning. They are tools of fear, tools of violence, and tools of destruction.

We cannot tolerate this any longer, and we must not. We must make our classrooms safe, make our teachers safe, and most of all, make our children safe. And we're starting today.

About two months ago, I asked two of the state's toughest district attorneys—Attorney General Mike Easley and Thurman Hampton, secretary of crime control—and state superintendent Bob Etheridge, to serve on the Governor's Task Force on School Violence. I asked them to make school violence their top priority, to assess the problem and find out what communities are doing to solve it. And I asked them to do it quickly, so that we can get to work.

Since then, this task force has held six hearings across the state, from Asheville to Greenville. All told, almost 1,400 people have spent almost twenty hours telling us how school violence has hurt them and hurt the ones they love. We've heard stories from parents, principals, students, law enforcement officers, and community leaders—stories about children shot on campus, teachers assaulted, and administrators without the tools they needed to fight back. But we've also heard success stories about community volunteers monitoring the halls, students offering peer mediation, and police officers spending their lunch hours in cafeterias. Across the state, communities are coming together and coming up with innovative ways to combat school violence.

This task force listened, and listened hard. They came away with a lot of ideas, good ideas, that they're recommending in this report.[1] Now, this is a tough report with some tough recommendations. I support them because I believe it's time for some tough action.

We need more accountability and responsibility on the part of parents and students, as this report recommends. I believe parents who let their children bring weapons to school ought to be held accountable. In my campaign, I called for prosecution of those parents, and I'm glad to see the report address that issue. We ought to establish weapon-free school zones and consider ways to limit minors' access to handguns.[2]

Students who are violent in the classroom ought to be held accountable, as well. That could mean losing a driver's license, losing extracurricular privileges, or expulsion.[3] But once a violent child is removed from the classroom, he or she ought to continue learning— the three Rs as well as personal discipline—in a quality alternative program.[4] And we must recognize that students who behave as criminals should be held accountable for their behavior, as well.

At the same time, we need to give educators the encouragement and resources they need to combat school violence and to strengthen the link between schools and law enforcement; and we need to strengthen the system dealing with juvenile crime. I especially like the recommendation for a clearinghouse, under the Department of Crime Control, to help communities and schools tackle school violence.[5] It is critical that we involve communities in the fight against school violence. Teachers can't do it alone. Law enforcement officers can't do it alone. Parents can't do it alone. But together, we can do it.

I believe that we can combat school violence, and this report gives us the tools for this battle. I commend Secretary Hampton, Attorney General Easley, and Superintendent Etheridge for their hard work and their leadership, but we're not done yet! Next I want to sit down with legislative leaders and education leaders. Together, we'll work out a legislative package based on this excellent report,[6] and I want Attorney General Easley, Secretary Hampton, and Superintendent Etheridge to continue to work closely together and to have their staffs and departments do the same. If we do all this, I believe we can make our classrooms safer, and we can make our teachers and our children safer. We must do this if we truly want to reform our schools.

---

[1] For the group's recommendations, see *Executive Summary Report of the Task Force on School Violence* ([Raleigh, N.C.]: Task Force on School Violence, April 1993), and press release, Hunt Task Force Calls for Tough Measures to Reduce School Violence, Raleigh, April 8, 1993, Governors Papers, James Baxter Hunt Jr.

[2] The General Assembly ratified, on July 24, 1993, "An Act to Make it a Class I Felony to Possess or Carry a Firearm or Explosive on Educational Property or to Cause, Encourage, or Aid a Minor to Possess or Carry a Firearm or Explosive on Educational Property, to Make it a Misdemeanor to Cause, Encourage, or Aid a Minor to Take or Possess Other Types of Weapons on Educational Property, to Make it a Misdemeanor to Fail to Store Firearms in a Reasonable Manner for the Protection of Minors, and to Fail to Warn a Person of This Law Upon the Sale or Transfer of a Firearm." The effective date of the legislation was December 1, 1993. *N.C. Session Laws, 1993*, II, c. 558; see also media advisory, May 12, 1993, Governors Papers, James Baxter Hunt Jr. Legislators amended the 1993 law during the special session on crime; see *N.C. Session Laws, 1993, Extra and Regular Sessions, 1994*, c. 14, s. 4.

[3] S.B. 880, "A Bill to Enable Local Boards of Education to Expel from School Those Students Whose Continued Presence in School Constitutes a Clear Threat to the Safety and Health of Other Students or Employees," passed the state senate on April 29, 1993. It did not fare as well in the House. *N.C. House Journal, 1993*, 475, 493, 981, 1083; *N.C. Senate Journal, 1993*, 280, 369, 379.

[4] "A Bill to Be Entitled an Act to Appropriate Funds for Alternative Programs for Suspended Students," H.B. 1300, was introduced May 7, 1993. Sponsored by Representatives Robert J. Hensley Jr. (D-Wake), Howard J. Hunter Jr. (D-Northampton), Paul Luebke (D-Durham), and Peggy Stamey (D-Wake), the bill was routed to the House Appropriations Committee where it remained through the end of the session. *N.C. House Journal, 1993*, 522.

[5] The governor established such a clearinghouse, the Center for the Prevention of School Violence, under Executive Order Number 19, signed June 30, 1993. *N.C. Session Laws, 1993*, 2:3251-3252.

[6] The following press releases tracked the progress of legislation recommended by the report of the Task Force on School Violence: Hunt School Violence Task Force Proposals Introduced in Legislature, Raleigh, April 21, 1993; Hunt School Violence Bills Introduced, Raleigh, May 7, 1993; Governor Hunt Creates School Violence Prevention Center, Raleigh, July 1, 1993; and Governor Hunt's School Violence Bills Advance, Raleigh, July 6, 1993. Governors Papers, James Baxter Hunt Jr.

"OP-ED" BY GOVERNOR JIM HUNT: BUDGET PROPOSALS ARE FIRST STEP IN CHANGING STATE GOVERNMENT

RALEIGH, APRIL 8, 1993

As a candidate for governor last year, I vowed to push for dramatic changes that would make state government more efficient and effective. In fact, I released a position paper, "Making Government Work for North Carolina's Future," spelling out my plans in detail.

In the three months since Inauguration Day, our administration has begun putting forward a series of initiatives to drastically alter the way our tax dollars are spent and our state agencies operate. Critics—many of them well intentioned, but some of them politically motivated—leapt at the chance to dismiss these ideas as, alternately, not enough or too much. Many of our proposals, especially our plan to save $100 million in next year's budget, have been misunderstood and misrepresented. I welcome the chance to debate our proposals, and I invite the media and the public, as well as the General Assembly, to scrutinize them closely and carefully.

Among the new ideas on our administration's agenda:

—Legislation that will lead to the adoption of rigorous new standards for our public schools and fair and effective measures of whether schools are meeting those standards.

—A government-as-catalyst approach to meeting the education and health-care needs of children aged five and under. Rather than a massive and expensive government program, we have proposed a North Carolina Partnership for Children that brings together the private and nonprofit sectors, with government, to determine how each community can best respond to this challenge.

—Consideration of new incentives for companies to locate operations in our state. Automatically dismissing consideration of any new incentives is to risk losing North Carolina's competitive edge in economic development.

—A new prison-construction program that emphasizes the use of inmate labor in building new cells and expanding the use of military-style boot camps for young offenders and work farms for other inmates.

These new ideas have been criticized by various defenders of the status quo across this state. But perhaps no proposal received more heat, and less light, than our plan to achieve $100 million in budget savings and efficiencies next year to pay for our initiatives.

Some history is useful here. In February, just over 100 days after the election, we presented a proposed budget to the legislature. The budget included new initiatives to promote higher education standards and more accountability, more highly professional teachers, the Partnership for Children and other steps forward in early childhood education and health care, economic development incentives, and expanded use of prison labor.

Because of the short time our team had been in office, we acknowledged that we would need to come back to the legislature with more information about how to pay for these initiatives without raising taxes. Less than a month later, we did just that. Our package of efficiencies included these items among almost 200 specific proposals:

—Eliminating 142 positions over three years from the central education office in Raleigh, so more money could go into classrooms.

—Eliminating a special salary bonus for assistant clerks of court and magistrates, one that gives them an automatic 5 percent salary increase on top of what other state employees receive.

—Transferring, from the Highway Fund to the General Fund, interest on money that is collected through the Highway Fund and, at the end of the year, transferred to the General Fund.

—Eliminating over 500 state government positions, many of which were vacant and can be cut without damaging agencies or causing undue hardships to individual employees.

Some critics seemed to be disappointed that the proposed cuts did not cause more pain and anguish. But the package bore out my conviction that $100 million could be saved without taking a meat ax to vital services. In fact, even more can be cut, and will be cut, in the second year of the biennium without doing serious damage.

For those politically motivated critics who claim that the cuts were too easy, I would ask: If that was so, why weren't the cuts made in the prior administration?

Other critics either misunderstood or misrepresented our approach to the proposals put forward by the Government Performance Audit Committee. The committee recommended steps that it estimated could save $275 million a year. Our budget cuts endorsed more than two-thirds of those proposals, an estimated savings of $180 million per year. But, because we budgeted on a conservative basis, we assumed that only $25 million of that would be available next year, because not all the proposals will be adopted or put in place by the time the fiscal year begins July 1. Further, both the State Budget Office and the legislature's Fiscal Research Division were concerned that some GPAC savings estimates might be overstated.

So, our administration has embarked on an aggressive and fiscally sound course. We are determined to achieve large and small efficiencies throughout state government. More importantly, we are committed to proposing and carrying through sweeping changes in how state government is organized and how it operates. Many of the savings and cuts that are so badly needed, in fact, could be achieved more easily if we joined the federal government and the other forty-nine states in allowing the governor of North Carolina to veto legislation.

It is in the nature of politics that some critics will stretch or even ignore the facts to score rhetorical points. But an informed examination of our administration's goals will show a commitment to dramatic changes in our schools, our economy, our prisons, and all of state government.

NORTH CAROLINA BIOTECHNOLOGY CENTER

RESEARCH TRIANGLE PARK, APRIL 13, 1993

[Hunt announced, on November 5, 1981, the establishment of the North Carolina Biotechnology Center. Nearly twelve years later, the governor reviewed the founding, purpose, and progress of the center, and the state's support of the biotechnology industry, as he opened an international biotechnology conference and exhibition at Research Triangle Park. See Governor Hunt's Weekly Schedule for April 11-17, 1993, Governors Papers, James Baxter Hunt Jr.; Poff and Crow, *Addresses of Hunt, 1981-1985*, 170-172.]

Back in 1981, we in North Carolina didn't know exactly what breakthroughs we'd see in biotechnology over the next decade. But we'd seen enough to know we wanted to be on the cutting edge of biotechnology. So we became one of the first states in [the] United States to create a state-sponsored biotechnology center to help develop the industry in the state.

Today the North Carolina Biotechnology Center is a public-private partnership that, I'm told, is one of the best in the country. Supported by federal, state, and private funds, our center has helped lead the way in educating the nation and in encouraging and supporting biotechnology. With its funding, the North Carolina Biotechnology Center encourages our universities to develop their programs, keeps the best database in the United States for information about biotechnology, and helps get our students ready to work in the field.

Most importantly, the center encourages biotechnology companies. Over the years, it has invested $3.5 million in thirty-one biotechnology companies, paving the way for the investment of $158 million from other sources. Add it up, and over the past eleven years, this state has spawned or attracted seventy biotechnology companies. These companies have made a significant contribution to improving the quality of life in North Carolina, and across the nation, with cutting-edge research in medicine [and] environmental and agricultural science.

We know this industry is still young, still growing. You need to know that North Carolina is going to be in the biotechnology development business for a long time to come. North Carolina has built the infrastructure needed to support the long-term growth of your businesses. We have nine major research programs in biotechnology. Some 1,700 scientists are conducting biotechnology research, across our state, in our universities and colleges. On our high school campuses, we've set up what we call Bio-Tech Prep programs to develop future technicians for your workforce, and our community colleges are following up by continuing that training.

We in North Carolina know that many biotech products must be tested—under safe conditions.

In short, North Carolina is committed to biotechnology and to the private enterprise system in which investors put their ingenuity and time. Here in North Carolina, you'll find a skilled workforce. You'll find low construction and energy costs—and in the next few days, I'll be announcing a comprehensive incentives plan we have to convince you to locate here. You'll find we have rational, science-based regulations for biotechnology field tests and the resources of the Research Triangle Park. The North Carolina Biotechnology Center has the nation's only conference and education facility to bring together groups to talk specifically about the scientific, business, and social opportunities in biotechnology. So whether your biotech company is large or small, foreign or domestic, we're convinced we have something special to offer you here in North Carolina. We want your business here. You are on [the] cutting edge for our nation, the field with the most promise to building [our] economy.

JOBS/INCENTIVES STATEMENT

RALEIGH, APRIL 15, 1993

[Unveiled April 15, 1993, Hunt's proposed economic development incentives were the central topic in the following speeches: Economic Development Board Remarks, Raleigh, May 6; Economic Development Briefings, Raleigh, June 15; North Carolina Economic Development Council, Raleigh, July 13(14); North Carolina Economic Developers Association, Winston-Salem, September 1; Elizabeth City Chamber of Commerce, Elizabeth City, September 2; Lenoir County Committee of 100, Kinston, September 15; and North Carolina League of Municipalities, Fayetteville, October 18, 1993. For related press releases, see Governor Hunt Unveils Economic Blueprint, Raleigh, April 15; Hunt Incentives Bill Passes House, Raleigh, May 6; Two Hunt Incentives Bills Introduced in General Assembly, Raleigh, May 11; Hunt Economic Development Bill Becomes Law, Raleigh, May 13; Hunt's Economic Development Financing Bonds Approved by House Finance, Raleigh, June 29; Hunt Investment Tax Credit Passes House Finance, Raleigh, July 1; Governor Hunt To Form Task Force to Assess Incentives, Raleigh, July 1; Hunt's Industrial Development Fund Passes House, Raleigh, July 14; Hunt's Entire Incentives Package Approved by General Assembly, Raleigh, July 21, 1993. Governors Papers, James Baxter Hunt Jr.]

You've heard me say it many times: Education is economic development. Last week, when I flew out to Detroit to meet with the incoming chairman of Mercedes, I got a reminder. Helmut Werner didn't want to talk about the cost of labor, free land, infrastructure, or tax abatement.

He wanted to talk about the quality of North Carolina's workforce. He wanted to know what North Carolina is doing to make sure companies like Mercedes have the well-trained, well-educated workers they need now and in fifteen years.[1]

A world-class workforce is, and always will be, the key to North Carolina's prosperous future. That's why our efforts to reform our schools, improve early childhood education, and improve workforce training are so critical. In the last few weeks, I've put forth initiatives to make sure our children come to school ready to learn, to raise standards in our schools so that students learn what they need to know to compete in the modern workplace, and to make sure our workers have the skill training and retraining they need after high school. I've already proposed $100,000 in my expansion budget for Tech Prep each year of the biennium, and my capital budget will recommend another $2.9 million to put Tech Prep in every single school in our state. I've proposed $112 million to upgrade our community college system, the keystone to our state's workforce training efforts; and I've set up the Commission on Workforce Preparedness, with Sandy Babb coordinating our state's workforce training programs and targeting our dollars more effectively.

We are taking steps to make sure North Carolina produces a world-class workforce so that we can attract world-class companies. But fighting for world-class jobs is a competitive game. North Carolina must do all it can to stay in the game—and to win that game.

We have a strong economic team in place, which is assisting Secretary Dave Phillips in developing a comprehensive economic development strategy. This week I named seventy top business and community leaders to our three economic boards: the Small Business Council, under Lieutenant Governor Dennis Wicker; the Economic Development Board, under Bob Jordan; and the Entrepreneurial Development Board, under Bob Luddy.

To assist our economic development team in their efforts, I've already proposed measures to modernize our existing industry and to encourage small and start-up businesses. Today I'm proposing that we boost financial incentives, now offered by the state, and create new incentives. These are incentives for recruitment that are modest in cost but significant in impact.

First, I'm asking the General Assembly to pass a constitutional amendment to allow economic development financing. This would let local governments use the additional property tax brought in by a new company to finance capital costs and public facilities that benefit that company. This will give a boost to our recruitment efforts and bring in more new jobs.[2]

I'm also proposing that we boost the job creation tax credit, which Bob Jordan initiated in his jobs commission, from thirty-three to fifty counties. This will help us target areas of economic need in our state.[3]

I'm proposing that we increase access to the investment tax credit to boost investment in emerging and start-up businesses. I'll ask the legislature to increase the amount of money available to businesses, under the industrial development fund, and to provide $15 million over two years for an industrial recruitment competitive fund to serve as "flexible funds" to help close the deal with a given company. And I've already endorsed legislation to cut unemployment taxes for businesses by 30 percent.[4]

These incentives will help North Carolina compete. We must become more competitive if we want to bring more high-skill, high-wage jobs to our state. But we're not going to give away the store. I've considered, and rejected, more sweeping measures that other states routinely offer, such as tax abatements or free land. I just don't believe such measures are necessary at this point.

North Carolina has tremendous advantages: good workers, a good business climate, a low business tax burden, and a good quality of life. But we can do better. I believe it is necessary to upgrade our workforce so our people can compete for the jobs of tomorrow, and it's necessary to upgrade our state's economic development strategy to attract, create, and retain the jobs of tomorrow. This economic blueprint, along with our education reform proposals, will send a strong signal to companies across the country and around the world that North Carolina will go the extra mile to create jobs.

---

[1] Helmut Werner, Mercedes-Benz chief executive officer, 1993-1997. Part of Germany's giant Daimler-Benz conglomerate, Mercedes-Benz lost DM800 million in 1992. D-B hoped Werner, a finance specialist who transformed its subsidiary, Freightliner, into the number-one truckmaker in the United States, could halt the flow of red ink at Mercedes. He did not disappoint. Through reorganization, payroll cuts, foreign assembly programs, and a switch to market-driven pricing, he turned Mercedes into Europe's most profitable auto manufacturer by 1995. By the end of 1996, Mercedes enjoyed net profits of DM2.3 billion and was generating 80 percent of D-B's sales and a majority of its profits. But Werner himself could not escape the tide of corporate reorganization. Disagreeing with the restructuring Daimler chief executive Juergen Schrempp planned for the conglomerate, Werner resigned as Mercedes CEO in January 1997. "Daimler Has a New Curve to Negotiate," *BusinessWeek*, November 4, 1996; "Dustup at Daimler," *BusinessWeek*, February 23, 1997; "Mercedes Can't Shift into Cruise Control Yet," *BusinessWeek*, April 17, 1995; "Mercedes is Downsizing—and That Includes the Sticker," *BusinessWeek*, February 8, 1993; "Werner Says He's Sad to Leave Mercedes-Benz," The Auto Channel, January 21, 1997 (http://www.theautochannel.com/news/date/19970121/news02964.html).

[2] Local governments would have been permitted to issue bonds to fund economic development projects under a constitutional amendment approved by the General

Assembly. Despite legislative, business, and gubernatorial support for the amendment, voters rejected ratification by a 4:1 margin because the measure would have allowed local governments to issue the bonds without first obtaining voter consent. "An Act to Amend the Constitution to Permit Cities and Counties to Issue Bonds to Finance the Public Portion of Economic Development Projects and to Authorize Counties and Cities to Accept as Consideration for a Conveyance or Lease of Property to a Private Party the Amount of Increased Tax Revenue Expected to be Generated by the Improvements to be Constructed on the Property," *N.C. Session Laws, 1993*, II, c. 497, July 23, 1993; *News and Observer*, November 3, 1993; and press release, Hunt's Economic Development Financing Bonds Approved by House Finance, Raleigh, June 29, 1993, Governors Papers, James Baxter Hunt Jr.

[3] See "An Act to Expand the Number of Counties in which the Tax Credit for Creating Jobs is Available," *N.C. Session Laws, 1993*, I, c. 45, ratified May 13, 1993.

[4] "An Act to Expand the Tax Credits for Qualified Business Investments and to Provide that the Tax Credits Shall Sunset for Investments Made On or After January 1, 1999," was ratified July 22, 1993; see *N.C. Session Laws, 1993*, I, c. 443. The Industrial Recruitment Competitiveness Fund, to be used at the governor's discretion, was created under *N.C. Session Laws, 1993*, I, c. 321, s. 314.3. "An Act to Reduce the State Unemployment Insurance Tax Rate under Certain Circumstances," *N.C. Session Laws, 1993*, I, c. 85, was ratified May 26, 1993; see also Press Conference: Tax Cut on Unemployment Insurance, Raleigh, April 13, 1993, Governors Papers, James Baxter Hunt Jr.

PRESS RELEASE: HUNT ABOLISHES DRUG CABINET

RALEIGH, APRIL 16, 1993

[The North Carolina Drug Cabinet was established January 10, 1989, by executive order of Governor James Grubbs Martin. Its purpose was to "develop and recommend the most effective strategy" against the trafficking and use of illegal drugs. Martin credited its members as having been key players in the passage of both the Omnibus Drug Act of 1990 and the excise tax on controlled substances.

Critics contended that the Drug Cabinet made scant progress combating the scourge of narcotics and was little more than a "high profile" vehicle to enhance the likely gubernatorial bid of its chairman, Lieutenant Governor James Carson Gardner, in 1992. Martin agreed to Gardner's proposal that he lead the state's war on drugs after the senate, in January 1989, voted to strip the office of lieutenant governor of all but constitutionally required duties. Hunt signed Executive Order Number 7, terminating the North Carolina Drug Cabinet, on April 13, 1993. *Durham Herald-Sun*, January 19, 1992; *News and Observer*, July 2, 1990, May 23, 1991, October 25, 1992, April 17, 1993; *N.C. Session Laws, 1989*, 2:3094-3097, *1993*, 2:3202-3203; Poff, *Addresses of Martin, 1989-1993*, 5, 103, 247-250, 255, 256n-257n, 476-478.]

Governor Jim Hunt abolished the North Carolina Drug Cabinet this week in an effort to streamline the state's war on drugs. Hunt signed an executive order Tuesday that dissolved the Drug Cabinet, set up by Governor Martin in 1989 and chaired by Lieutenant Governor Jim Gardner. [1] Instead, the Drug Cabinet's work will be taken up by the

Governor's Crime Commission, which is devoted to developing a state crime-fighting policy.

During the gubernatorial campaign, Hunt pledged to transfer the Drug Cabinet to the Attorney General's Office as part of a more aggressive, effective, and coordinated offensive against drugs. But Attorney General Mike Easley has told Hunt that the Drug Cabinet is unnecessary and recommended that it be eliminated.

"After talking it over with Attorney General Easley, I don't believe that we need the Drug Cabinet to fight the state's war on drugs," Hunt said. "He believes his agents can continue their good work fighting drug crimes without the Drug Cabinet, and I agree.

"Instead we will redirect federal funds, now going to the Drug Cabinet, to the Governor's Crime Commission, which is developing a comprehensive preventative plan to battle drug crimes and other crime," Hunt said. "I'm confident that the commission can use those funds more effectively than the Drug Cabinet ever did."

Since its inception, the Drug Cabinet had been criticized for seeking publicity instead of fighting drug traffickers. Some 75 percent of its budget went for salaries, mostly for former Gardner campaign workers, until that fact was exposed by the media; and former attorney general [Lacy] Thornburg and key legislators criticized the Drug Cabinet for not taking an active role in pushing anti-drug legislation in the General Assembly. Said Easley, "I want to see our resources used aggressively on the front lines of a real war on drugs. We have to take politics out of fighting crime, and the Drug Cabinet is a good place to start."

In 1992-1993, the Drug Cabinet had a $114,000 budget, along with staff positions on loan from other agencies. Some $33,000 is left in the budget for this fiscal year. No funds were requested by Governor Martin to fund the Drug Cabinet as part of his continuation budget.

The Governor's Crime Commission, which operates under the auspices of the Department of Crime Control and Public Safety, is chaired by Sis Kaplan, of Charlotte. As former director of the Mecklenburg County Criminal Justice Commission, Kaplan was instrumental in establishing the state's first special drug court, devoted to processing drug-related cases quickly, in Mecklenburg County.

---

[1] James Carson Gardner (1933-   ), born in Rocky Mount; attended N.C. State University; U.S. Army, 1953-1955. Co-founder, executive vice-president, 1962-1967, Hardee's Food Systems; president, Gardner Foods, Inc.; chairman, state Republican Party, 1965-1966; elected to U.S. Congress, 1966; GOP gubernatorial candidate, 1968, 1992; lieutenant governor, 1989-1993. *Biographical Directory of Congress*, 1042-1043; *News and Observer*, November 4, 1992.

OCEAN OUTFALL FORUM

ATLANTIC BEACH, APRIL 19, 1993

[Hunt addressed the relationship between environmental protection and economic development in speeches to the Ocean Outfall Forum, below; the presentation of the Governor's Awards for Excellence in Waste Management, April 22; the Environmental Management Commission, July 8; the Coastal Futures Committee, October 14; and the Cape Fear River Assembly, November 15, 1993.]

I would like to thank all of you for your warm welcome and for inviting me here to this important forum. I want to commend all of you for coming together to explore these difficult issues of ocean outfall, wastewater disposal, and growth. Our state has suffered in the past from polarization on this and similar issues. We must find a way to replace conflict and confrontation with consensus and cooperation. We must build a partnership among businesses, environmentalists, and government.

This forum goes a long way toward meeting that goal, and I commend you for that. You've made certain that all voices will be heard by creating this very distinguished panel that will take a prominent role in the forum. In Dr. Peterson, we have a biologist and ecologist who understands how our actions will affect marine life.[1] In Representative Gottovi, we have a state legislator who understands government and state environmental policy.[2] In Dr. Rader,[3] we have a scientist who understands water quality and water quality planning; and in Billy Ray Hall, we have a rural economic development expert who understands how our decisions will affect jobs and growth.

The different perspectives and backgrounds represented here assure that all sides will be heard, [and] that we can move toward a solution that respects all interests. And I firmly believe that we not only can have both economic development and environmental protection, we must have both. But we can only have both if we plan. Unless we plan for growth, instead of react to it, we cannot protect our natural resources. If we don't protect our natural resources, we will destroy the very things that support economic growth in North Carolina—our quality of life and the travel and tourism industry that is so important to coastal North Carolina.

I want you to know that this is not just rhetoric from Raleigh. This is the principle that has guided my cabinet appointments and board selections. Secretary of Environment, Health, and Natural Resources Jonathan Howes has expertise in regional land-use planning, growth management, and environmental planning that can help us balance environmental and economic concerns.[4] Environment, Health, and

Natural Resources deputy secretary Steven Levitas, who is our moderator this morning, is well known as one of North Carolina's leading environmentalists.[5] I have assembled the most diverse Board of Transportation in the state's history and have given environmental advocates and public transportation advocates a stronger voice than ever.

In a short time I will be making appointments to the Coastal Resources Commission, and I guarantee you that board will not be tilted against coastal issues. As with other boards, I will make these appointments only after seeking the recommendations of environmental groups. I am reaching out to environmental groups because it's time we all work together to protect our natural resources, especially coastal resources.

The economic resource here is the environment. We must make sure that growth doesn't threaten that resource. Our policy must allow for growth, but it can't allow haphazard growth that will endanger coastal water quality. It must protect traditional industries like clamming, oystering, and fishing, and it must do so with strong laws that are strictly enforced.

Next year we will celebrate the twentieth anniversary of the North Carolina Coastal Area Management Act. I've appointed a special commission to help us celebrate the twentieth anniversary, and Richardson Preyer has agreed to lead that group.[6] I pushed for passage of CAMA as lieutenant governor, and I've fought against attempts to weaken it. But I want to underscore that my commitment to environmental issues is not at the expense of economic development, but on behalf of economic development! A healthy environment and strong economic development go hand in hand.

Before North Carolina was a state, before we were a nation, men and women fished for a living along our shoreline. There are fishermen down the road in Salter Path who wonder if their grandchildren will be able to fish these waters for a living. We need to be able to tell them that their great-grandchildren can fish those waters.

As governor, I'm working to set a climate that fosters partnership between businesses and environmental groups. I'm working to put the right people in the right places to make the right decisions for North Carolina, people like Jonathan Howes and Steven Levitas. But we must all work together. We must build a partnership based on good faith and goodwill that will protect the legitimate interests of all parties.

This forum is a giant step toward building this partnership, putting polarization behind us, and making sure we all work together to protect the environmental and economic future of coastal North Carolina. Judging from the quality of the group assembled here this morning, I'm convinced that future is in very good hands.

[1] Charles H. Peterson (1946-   ), born in Lawrenceville, N.J.; A.B., Princeton University, 1968; M.A., 1970, Ph.D., 1972, University of California-Santa Barbara. Assistant professor of biological sciences, University of Maryland-Baltimore County, 1972-1976; associate professor of marine sciences and zoology, 1976-1983, professor of marine sciences, biology, and ecology, since 1983, University of North Carolina at Chapel Hill; appointed to Marine Fisheries Commission by Governor Hunt, 1993. Charles H. Peterson, letter to Jan-Michael Poff, May 7, 1996.

[2] Karen Elizabeth Gottovi (1941-   ), born in Rochester, N.Y.; resident of New Hanover County; B.A., Wells College, 1962; M.S.L.S., University of North Carolina, 1972. High school English teacher, 1962-1966; reference librarian, 1973-1975; New Hanover County commissioner, 1976-1984; political consultant, secretary-treasurer, 1985-1990, Independent Opinion Research-Communications; elected to N.C. House of Representatives, 1990, reelected 1992; chair, House Committee on the Environment. *North Carolina Manual, 1993-1994*, 507.

[3] Dr. Doug Rader was associated with the North Carolina Environmental Defense Fund. Steven J. Levitas, letter to Jan-Michael Poff, April 24, 1996.

[4] Jonathan B. Howes (1937-   ), born in Knoxville, Tenn.; resident of Chapel Hill; B.A., Wittenberg University, 1959; Masters of Regional Planning, University of North Carolina at Chapel Hill, 1961; M.P.A., Harvard University, 1966. Director, research professor, Center for Urban and Regional Studies, Dept. of City and Regional Planning, 1970-1993, director of outreach (town-university liaison), from 1997, University of North Carolina at Chapel Hill; town council member, 1975-1987, mayor, 1987-1991, of Chapel Hill; president, N.C. League of Municipalities, 1986-1987; N.C. secretary of environment, health, and natural resources, 1993-1997. *News and Observer*, December 16, 1992, July 4, 5, 9, 1997; *North Carolina Manual, 1993-1994*, 297.

[5] Steven J. Levitas (1954-   ), born in Atlanta; resident of Raleigh; B.A., University of North Carolina at Chapel Hill, 1976; J.D., Harvard Law School, 1982. Attorney in private practice, 1983-1987; Environmental Defense Fund, NCEDF director, senior attorney, 1987-1993; deputy secretary, N.C. Dept. of Environment, Health, and Natural Resources, 1993-1996. Levitas correspondence; *News and Observer*, December 4, 1996.

[6] Hunt officially established the Coastal Futures Committee in July 1993. Charged with arranging the twentieth anniversary commemoration of the Coastal Area Management Act (CAMA), the group also was ordered to compare North Carolina's coastal management program with other states' and "identify major coastal management issues to be analyzed in depth"; see Executive Order Number 20, "To Designate 1994 as the Year of the Coast and to Create a Coastal Futures Committee on Coastal Area Management," July 15, 1993, *N.C. Session Laws, 1993*, 2:3253-3255. The Coastal Area Management Act itself was ratified April 11, 1974; *N.C. Session Laws, 1973, Second Session, 1974*, c. 1284.

Lunsford Richardson Preyer (1919-   ), born in Greensboro; A.B., Princeton University, 1941; LL.B., Harvard Law School, 1949; served in U.S. Navy during World War II. N.C. Superior Court judge, 1956-1961; U.S. District Court judge, 1961-1963; candidate for N.C. governor, 1964; senior vice-president, trust officer, city executive, N.C. National Bank, Greensboro, 1964-1966; member, U.S. House of Representatives, 1969-1981; Democrat. *Biographical Directory of Congress*, 1673; Remarks to Coastal Futures Committee, Raleigh, October 14, 1993, Governors Papers, James Baxter Hunt Jr.

PRESS RELEASE: GOVERNOR HUNT TO DECLARE FEWER EXEMPT POSITIONS THAN MARTIN

Raleigh, April 19, 1993

Governor Jim Hunt plans to exempt 685 state jobs from the State Personnel Act by May 1, compared to 734 exemptions declared by former governor Jim Martin in the spring of 1985. Under state law, Hunt is required to declare all exemptions by May 1, including positions already considered exempt by the previous administration. An exempt job is exempt from the protections of the State Personnel Act, and the person in that job serves at the pleasure of the governor.[1]

Some 90 percent of the positions being declared exempt were also exempt under the Martin administration. "This is simply a reclassification process, required by every new administration by the State Personnel Act," Hunt said. "There is a misconception in some circles that declaring a position exempt is tantamount to firing an individual. That is not the case."

For example, the previous administration had declared only three people in the Governor's Office as exempt. As part of this reclassification, Hunt has declared all eighty positions in the Governor's Office as exempt. All told, some 784 positions will be considered exempt in the Hunt administration, compared to 829 in the Martin administration. Of those, 685 positions are considered to be policy-making positions, forty-nine fewer positions than declared exempt by former governor Martin in May 1985. Another ninety-nine positions are exempt by statute or are automatically exempt because they are confidential assistant or chief deputy positions as defined by state law.[2]

"I promised that there will be no mass firings, and I've kept my word," Hunt said. "We're moving deliberately to put the best people in state government and will continue putting together a strong and effective team to carry out our agenda."

State law allows each department to exempt thirty positions, or 1.2 percent of their total positions, except for those departments affected by statutory exemptions. Of the nine departments, seven will have fewer exempt employees than allowed, and two—DEHNR [Department of Environment, Health, and Natural Resources] and CC&PS [Department of Crime Control and Public Safety]—will have the exact number allowed. The State Personnel Office has sent a letter from Hunt, as required by state law, to all employees in those affected positions.

---

[1] G.S. 126 is commonly known as the State Personnel Act; for exemption guidelines, see G.S. 126-5.

[2] Martin "inherited 1,500 exempt positions" when he was inaugurated in 1985 and subsequently reduced "the number of state employees subject to political firings" to 875 during his first term. By the end of his second term, in January 1993, he had cut to 512 the number of positions without State Personnel Act protection. Poff, *Addresses of Martin*, I, xxv, 83-84, 100; Poff, *Addresses of Martin*, II, xxx.

VISIT TO NORTHERN TELECOM

Research Triangle Park, April 22, 1993

[The governor discussed his administration's pollution prevention and waste-reduction strategies, below, and in remarks recognizing Take Pride in America Award winners, Raleigh, May 5, 1993; Foster-Forbes Recycling Day, Wilson, April 29, 1994; North Carolina Reduce, Reuse, Recycle Campaign, Raleigh, April 22, 1995; and Square D Recycling Center Dedication, Knightdale, October 18, 1995, Governors Papers, James Baxter Hunt Jr.]

I would like to thank all of you for inviting me here on Earth Day. It's an appropriate setting to mark Earth Day, because you at Northern Telecom are genuinely committed to the earth and to the environment. As I was walking through your plant, I was impressed by your commitment to environmental stewardship. This is truly a Total Quality Management approach to a cleaner environment. I want to commend all of you at Northern Telecom for your excellent work. It is a model of the kind of environmental initiative I want to promote during this administration.

I believe we can have a healthy environment and a strong economy. We must put aside the polarized thinking of the past and find ways to achieve both these goals simultaneously. Northern Telecom has played a big role in achieving that balance. I don't have to tell you that. Your company was honored this morning at the Governor's Awards for Excellence in Waste Management for a manufacturing innovation that contributed to a healthy environment and a strong economy: You eliminated CFC-113 from the manufacturing process, and you have simultaneously saved $4 million and reduced hazardous waste by 65 percent. When people tell me that you can't save money and save the planet, I'm going to tell them about Northern Telecom![1]

I'd like to tell you a little about this administration's vision for North Carolina's environment. Pollution prevention has always been a key element of our environmental policy. The state's Pollution Prevention Pays program was started during my last administration. That program is now the model for other states. It has won awards nationally and internationally, and I am proud to have played a role in getting that program off the ground. We need to strengthen that program and do all we can to help industries reduce waste at the source.

Pollution prevention and waste reduction are creative approaches to environmental regulation and are vital to a balanced environmental program. We have re-committed this administration to waste reduction. I've recommended that we put nearly twice the resources behind our state's waste-reduction efforts.

We are also committed to creating markets for recycled goods. But in order to create markets, we must create a demand for products made from recycled materials. To do this, we must look to purchase recycled products for our personal use, and corporations must develop policies that encourage the purchase of recycled products. We in state government will set the example: I signed an executive order this morning that will encourage state government to buy recycled products.[2]

In my last administration, I founded the Alternative Energy Corporation and the Energy Institute to promote the research and development of new energy sources.[3] We are still deeply committed to energy conservation. I have endorsed a package of energy conservation bills that will significantly increase state government's commitment to energy conservation. Through these programs, we can save up to $30 million a year.

But state government cannot do it alone. We must be joined by progressive companies, like Northern Telecom, and energetic private citizens like the group of volunteers I will meet later today who are working to clean the New Hope Creek.[4] All of us must share the commitment to environmental protection. Only then will we make the economic choices that protect the environment. Only then will we make the environmental choices that protect the economy. Only then will we see we not only can have a strong economy and a healthy environment, we must have both! Thank you for inviting me here today, and thank you for your inspiring example.

---

[1] Telephone equipment manufacturer Northern Telecom used chlorofluorocarbon-113, a substance harmful to Earth's ozone layer, to clean circuit boards. Rather than employ a substitute for CFC-113, NT redesigned its production process so that the boards would not require any cleaning. The company effected the change at its Research Triangle Park operations and in its facilities worldwide, then offered the technology to other manufacturers free of charge. Northern Telecom (later Nortel) was headquartered in Mississauga, Ontario. Leah Jung, principal, Vista Environmental, and former Northern Telecom environmental manager, telephone conversation with Jan-Michael Poff, September 22, 1998.

[2] Executive Order Number 8, "State Government Recycling, Reduction of Solid Waste, and Purchase of Products with Recycled Content," signed April 22, 1993, *N.C. Session Laws, 1993*, 2:3204-3211.

[3] During his first term as governor, Hunt lobbied the state Utilities Commission in favor of creating the Alternative Energy Corporation. The agency was founded in 1980. He signed Executive Order Number 17, establishing the North Carolina Energy Institute, on January 3, 1978. Memory F. Mitchell, ed., *Addresses and Public Papers of James Baxter Hunt, Jr., Governor of North Carolina, Volume I, 1977-1981* (Raleigh: Division of Archives and History, Department of Cultural Resources, 1982), xxx, 645-648; *N.C. Session Laws, 1977, Second Session, 1978*, 252-255; Poff and Crow, *Addresses of Hunt, 1981-1985*, 11, 15n, 318-319.

[4] Hunt ate a brown-bag lunch with Streamwatch volunteers in the Wake County portion of Research Triangle Park. Governor's Schedule for April 18-24, 1993, Governors Papers, James Baxter Hunt Jr.

BUDGET STATEMENT

[The Senate Appropriations Committee cautiously juggled uncertain revenue forecasts, existing funding requirements, and requests to finance new and expanded programs as it began laying out the state budget for F.Y. 1993-1994. Claiming insufficient means, the committee revealed on May 5, 1993, that it was recommending only $7.5 million to launch the twelve Smart Start pilot projects Hunt wanted. Indeed, the governor requested nearly three times that amount: $20 million.

The Appropriations Committee's announcement surprised Hunt. Democrats were in the majority in the upper house, and the entire senate cosponsored the Smart Start bill. He quickly called a press conference (text follows) to say that anything less than full funding would shortchange North Carolina's children. After two days of concerted lobbying by the governor, members of his administration, and children's advocates, the committee relented and earmarked $20 million for Smart Start pilots. That amount was included in the budget the General Assembly approved the following July. *News and Observer*, April 22, May 6, 7, 8, 11, 13, July 10, 1993.]

Once again, we're here today to talk about children. The most important issue before the General Assembly is the educational and economic future of our children. I have made it my highest priority, and I believe that most members of the General Assembly agree that children should be our highest priority. So I am disappointed with the recommendation by the Senate Appropriations Subcommittee yesterday on our early childhood initiative.

I respect the senators' concern about fiscal responsibility, but I strongly believe that we can, and we must, make whatever cuts and changes are necessary to meet our obligation to our children. We can afford to provide early childhood education to every child in twenty counties this year and to boost the quality of day care for every child in this state. We can't afford to do anything less.

The fact is, North Carolina is failing its children. Children in thirty-nine other states are better off than children in North Carolina. Just last week, the annual Children's Index showed that too many of our children are suffering from neglect, abuse, poverty, and poor health care.[1] Meanwhile, juvenile crime continues to climb.

How can anything else take a higher priority? And we do have the money: The budget I proposed shows how we can do it. I stand ready to work with members of the Appropriations Committee, the full senate, and the House to change our priorities—to do more for our state's future by doing more for our children. I'll be talking to every member of the Appropriations Committee and urging them to restore these initiatives.

I believe there is very strong support in the senate: All fifty members cosponsored the Smart Start bill, and Senator Basnight has been a strong advocate for children, as well.

The Appropriation Subcommittees did take an important step toward improving education and creating jobs yesterday, but our education reform and economic development efforts will fail if our children don't come to school ready to learn. This is the single most important challenge we face. My administration will work as hard as we can, for as long as it takes, to give the children of North Carolina a better start.

---

[1] The Children's Index, produced by the North Carolina Child Advocacy Institute, was an annual statistical profile of the state's children. It was the first such assessment in the nation. *News and Observer*, April 11, 1993.

NORTH CAROLINA STATE UNIVERSITY COMMENCEMENT ADDRESS

RALEIGH, MAY 8, 1993

Chancellor Monteith,[1] thank you for your generous introduction; President Spangler;[2] Members of the Board of Governors; Members of the Board of Trustees; Members of the Faculty; Parents; Distinguished Guests; and Graduates:

You graduate at a time when America has lost some [of] its momentum and purpose. One-fifth of our children live in poverty. Our infant mortality rate is higher than some third-world countries'. Our schools, K-12, lost one-fourth of their students as dropouts; other[s] come to universities like this and have to take remedial education courses.

I probably don't have to tell you graduates that jobs are scarce. Every day we read of cutbacks and plant closings. Within the last six weeks there was the news that, at a fine neighboring university, only a handful of students graduating this spring had jobs lined up. And pervading on society there is a discontent, a frustration, that we can't seem to solve our problems. The optimistic tone that marked the days following last November's election has turned more negative.

Well, I have come here today to say to you that things don't have to be that way. We can change our course as a nation. The life you begin today, as a new graduate, can be fulfilling in a nation that is on the rebound—if we have the spirit, the determination, and do the right things.

My confidence in that is borne of two experiences I have had at this, your—our—alma mater. In the fall of 1960, a young presidential candidate came to NCSU and spoke in William Neal Reynolds Coliseum. I was there as a student in the crowd, as many of you were when Bill Clinton spoke there last fall.[3]

But that young senator from Massachusetts was not too young to inspire. He did not promise us our lives would be great; he challenged us to make them great. He did not promise us America would lead the world; he challenged us to lead America. He did not promise us that he would be elected president; he challenged us to elect him president, and we did. Here in North Carolina, we gave John F. Kennedy the votes that made a difference across the country; and when he was inaugurated, he gave us a powerful challenge: "Ask not what your country can do for you; ask what you can do for your country!"[4] And America responded. Over the next decade, we set up the Peace Corps, the Job Corps, waged a war on poverty, made education a national priority, provided decent health care for older Americans, and passed the first civil rights laws in our nation's history. We proved that we can change things.

As an alumnus of N.C. State, I was inspired by another young, dynamic leader who came to our campus and challenged us to dream big dreams. He, too, came from the North, but he had a heart as big as all the South. His dreams and his deeds were powered by one simple charge: "Don't ever give up! Don't ever stop fighting!"[5]

Jim Valvano is not here today. All of us wish he were. But the inspiration he gave us through his life and his words will always be with us.

As he said, don't ever give up. Don't ever stop fighting. Don't ever accept anything less than the best—for yourselves, for your future. And the Wolfpack team in 1983 proved it could change things. With double-digit losses, it had to win the ACC [Atlantic Coast Conference] tournament to get into the NCAAs, and then the "Cardiac Pack" proceeded to upset every opponent it played in the NCAA tournament and crowned it with an impossible win against the best basketball team in America to win the national championship. They proved, under Jim Valvano's inspiration, that they could change things! They could create a new order. The old ways could be pushed aside; a new excellence, a winning spirit, could prevail.[6]

It took a vision. It took big dreams! But North Carolina is a state of big dreams. This state harbored the first English settlers to North America; founded the first public university in the nation; launched the flight of the first airplane; built the biggest and best research park in America.

We are still a state of big dreams, despite many problems. We look around North Carolina, and we see more youngsters committing crimes; more babies born to single teenagers; more children abused and neglected; more children in poverty; more children without health care. It is hard to dream big dreams in the face of such realities, but we must. Now is the time to dream. Now is the time to change our lives, and our future, by changing the lives of our children.

I urge that we here in North Carolina dream big in three ways: first, that we become the first state in America to provide quality early childhood education to every child who needs it, from birth to kindergarten. If North Carolina can be the first state in America to offer higher education, then we can be the first state in America to promise early childhood education. We know that children born in poverty who have high-quality early childhood education continue to show higher achievement twenty years later. We know that they have fewer criminal arrests, higher earnings, greater property wealth, and a greater commitment to marriage. We know that early childhood education yields economic benefits of over $7.00 for every dollar invested; that is one dollar that we must invest for our children and for our state.[7]

Second, I urge that we make a new commitment to our public schools and all of our children. We cannot become a great state, a great nation, unless all of our children receive a first-rate education—not a few children from the wealthy families in selected public or private schools, but all of our children, in all of our counties, from the mountains to the coast. Push us to set higher standards in our schools. Help us reform our schools so they are more productive, and finance our schools more strongly so that the hardest-working people in our society—our teachers—are paid well and given the respect, appreciation, and status they deserve.

Third, I urge that we resolve to move our colleges and universities in North Carolina, especially our great research universities, into the very top tier of universities in America. NCSU is doing well. Under an outstanding academic leader, Larry Monteith, it is highly regarded by our state's leadership; it is in the top ten of all American universities as a recipient of private research dollars; and its faculty and researchers are in the top twenty American universities in patents. But we must do better.

I ask you to help us do better because our people need it. We are well below the national average in per-capita income, and too many of our workers are at the minimum wage, or just above it. You, the graduates of this university today—in engineering, in agriculture and life sciences, in forestry and education, and in the sciences and humanities—all of you can help us. I want this university to help North Carolina become known throughout America and beyond as a state on the cutting edge of high technology, with a workforce from our research laboratories to our manufacturing assembly lines that is clearly world class.

We have the opportunity, and duty, to do this. But it is more than our economic duty; it is our moral duty. Both John Kennedy and Jim Valvano taught us how little time we have to make a difference in this world. We must dream big, because we just don't have time to dream small. The example of these good men, who lived short lives, makes me more determined than ever to touch the lives of our children and see that all students have an education that will open the world to them. As you graduate today, I hope you will carry in your hearts and in your minds a personal image of what we need to change—not about yourself, but of someone whom you can help.

You have your own goals, your own dreams, but make them big. Make them noble. Make them about others, and don't ever give up on them. As Jim Valvano said, "Nothing can happen if not first in a dream. If you have someone with a dream, if you have a motivated person with a goal and a vision, if you have someone who never gives up, who has great hope, anything can happen."[8] Nineteen-ninety-three graduates, I wish that "anything" might happen for you. I wish you good luck and Godspeed.

---

[1] Larry K. Monteith (1933-   ), born in Bryson City; resident of Raleigh; B.S., N.C. State University, 1960; M.S., 1962, Ph.D., 1965, Duke University. Career at N.C. State University includes associate professor, 1968-1972, professor, 1972-1989, and head, 1974-1978, Dept. of Electrical Engineering; dean, College of Engineering, 1978-1989; interim chancellor, October 1989-May 1990; chancellor, from May 1990. Before joining the N.C. State faculty, Monteith was a group leader at Research Triangle Institute, 1966-1968. *North Carolina Manual, 1995-1996,* 783.

[2] C. D. Spangler Jr. (1932-   ), born in Charlotte; B.S., University of North Carolina at Chapel Hill, 1954; M.B.A., Harvard University, 1956; honorary degrees; U.S. Army, 1956-1958. President, C. D. Spangler Construction Co., 1958-1986, and of Golden Eagle Industries, 1968-1986; president, University of North Carolina, 1986-1997; board director, BellSouth Corp., since 1987, and of National Gypsum Co., since 1994; former board chair, Bank of North Carolina, 1973-1982; former board director, Hammermill Paper Co., 1982-1986, NCNB Corp., 1983-1986, Jefferson-Pilot Corp., 1987-1989, 1992, and of The Equitable Life Assurance Society, 1989-1991. *News and Observer,* April 10, July 12, 1997; *North Carolina Manual, 1995-1996,* 746-747.

[3] Sometimes it seems as though the road to the White House runs through Reynolds Coliseum. A crowd of 10,000 people packed the building in September 1960 to hear a campaign speech by Senator John F. Kennedy, the Democratic candidate for U.S. president. Thirty-two years later Bill Clinton, another Democrat seeking the nation's highest elected office, addressed a receptive Reynolds audience. Hunt, running for a third term as governor, introduced Clinton and pointed to the seat where he listened to Kennedy decades earlier. Murray Scott Downs and Burton F. Beers, *North Carolina State University: A Pictorial History* (Raleigh: North Carolina State University Alumni Association, 1986), 124; *News and Observer,* October 5, 1992.

[4] John F. Kennedy, Inaugural Address [January 20, 1961], quoted in John Bartlett, *Familiar Quotations,* 14th ed. (Boston: Little, Brown and Company, 1968), 1073.

[5] James Thomas Valvano (1946-1993), native of Queens, N.Y.; died of cancer and was buried in Raleigh; B.A., Rutgers University, 1967. Head basketball coach, 1980-1990, athletic

director, 1986-1989, N.C. State University; coaching record at N.C. State included 209 wins, 114 losses, two ACC titles, and the 1983 NCAA national championship; career coaching record: 346 wins, 212 losses; author. Previously identified in Poff and Crow, *Addresses of Hunt, 1981-1985*, 48n; see also *News and Observer*, April 8, 1990, April 29, 30, May 1, 1993. The quotation Hunt attributed to Valvano is identified in footnote 7, below.

⁶ The N.C. State University men's basketball team stunned the sports world by winning the 1983 National Collegiate Athletic Association national championship in an upset over the University of Houston, 54-52. It was the climax to an amazing post-season performance for the Wolfpack, which won a series of close-scoring games over higher-ranked opponents. Hunt and members of the General Assembly honored Coach Valvano and his victorious team in ceremonies held April 18, 1983. Poff and Crow, *Addresses of Hunt, 1981-1985*, 46-51; Jim Valvano, *Too Soon to Quit: The Story of N.C. State's 1983 National Championship Season* (Raleigh: Coman Publishing Co., 1983), 52-81.

⁷ Hunt made the same argument for the long-term benefits of early childhood education in other speeches during 1993. Remarks at the Winston-Salem Smart Start Luncheon, September 13[14], 1993, indicate the bases for his position: "A study by the High/Scope [Educational Research] Foundation finds that every dollar we spend on early childhood education saves us more than $7.00 down the road. That's $7.00 we don't have to pay on remedial education, welfare, prisons, and crime. A fifteen-year study by the Frank Porter Graham Child Development Center shows that, even at age 15, a child who got high-quality child care at an early age achieves more than other teens." See offprint articles furnished by Stephanie D. Fanjul, director, Division of Child Development, N.C. Dept. of Health and Human Services: Lawrence J. Schweinhart and David P. Weikart, "A Summary of Significant Benefits: The High/Scope Perry Preschool Study Through Age 27," based on Chapter 10 of Schweinhart and Weikart, *Significant Benefits: The High/Scope Perry Preschool Study Through Age 27* (Ypsilanti, Mich.: High/Scope Press, 1993); and Frances A. Campbell and Craig T. Ramey, "Cognitive and School Outcomes for High-Risk African-American Students at Middle Adolescence: Positive Effects of Early Intervention," *American Educational Research Journal* 32 (winter 1995), 743-772. Frances Campbell was a senior investigator at UNC-Chapel Hill's Frank Porter Graham Child Development Center.

⁸ At two different points in his N.C. State commencement address, Hunt borrowed from the following quotation of Valvano: "The '83 team taught me about dreaming, and the importance of dreams, because nothing can happen if not first you dream. If you have someone with a dream, if you have a motivated person with a goal and a vision, if you have someone who never gives up, who has great hope, anything can happen. That team taught me that persistence, the idea of never, ever quitting. Don't ever give up! Don't ever stop fighting!" James Thomas Valvano, speech at championship reunion for 1982-1983 Wolfpack basketball team, February 21, 1993, as quoted in *News and Observer*, April 29, 1993; see also *News and Observer*, February 22, 1993.

INFORMATION HIGHWAY ANNOUNCEMENT

RALEIGH, MAY 10, 1993

Today North Carolina takes a giant step forward into our future. This fall, North Carolina will link up the most advanced telecommunications network of its kind in the world, a network that will ensure that the state will be a leader in the twenty-first century. The network will reach into every corner of our great state. It will connect our cities with our towns, our schoolhouses and our courthouses, our hospitals and clinics—our people all across the state.

Early in this century, North Carolina came to be known as the "Good Roads State." We discovered a new technology and started paving roads. Those roads began moving people and products in ways never before possible. Today we reach out for a new technology, a new kind of highway: the North Carolina Information Highway. This is not a highway of concrete and cars, but one of fiber optics—and information traveling at the speed of light.

Here's the highway surface: Inside this cable are thirty-five tiny, hair-thin, fiber-optic strands, each capable of transmitting the equivalent of 30,000 simultaneous conversations. This fiber can transmit video in two directions simultaneously, without use of satellites! These strands can transmit digital data used by computers so fast that an entire encyclopedia could be transmitted in about the amount of time it takes to say the word *encyclopedia*.

More importantly, it will help us improve education, create jobs, fight crime, and make state government more efficient and effective. Let me give you a few examples:

—A boy in Hyde County will be able to dial up a phone number and join in a class taught by live video, over fiber-optic lines, by the best calculus teacher in the state.

—A woman in Cherokee County can consult with the top doctor in the field without having to travel to North Carolina Memorial Hospital.

—One of the first questions companies ask us when they're considering locating in North Carolina is about our communications systems. Before Pepsi decided to locate a plant in Winston-Salem, they wanted to know about our fiber-optic connections. This Information Highway will allow companies to network between various plant locations across the state and link up with our community colleges and universities for training and retraining.

—It will help streamline our criminal-justice system. Using fiber-optic technology on the network, a man charged with a crime in Pender County can be arraigned from the jailhouse in Hampstead without having a deputy travel across the county to see the judge.

—State government workers in Dare County can be more efficient by avoiding trips to Raleigh for training. Using the Information Highway, they can conduct their seminars over phone lines.

We've already seen how this project can work in Wilmington, where we've linked the university, hospitals, community colleges, and public schools. We've seen how more than 500 million bits of computer data can be transferred, in a second, between North Carolina Memorial Hospital and the state's super computer, so that complicated medical images can be transferred and interpreted instantly. The technology works!

But we do have to invest in it. That's why I'm asking for $4.4 million in my capital budget to pay for extending services to the first 104 locations. This money will pay for technology at schools, medical centers, and universities across the state. Down the road, we imagine a network of 3,300 locations all across the state. Our "Good Roads State" will become a great highways state!

We won't be working alone. The Information Highway will be part of a network designed, built, and operated by the local phone companies of North Carolina, a public-private partnership for North Carolina's future. In the future, other types of companies will be playing a key role: cable companies, broadcasters, computer imaging businesses, the people who sell customer premises equipment. But our purposes will remain the same: to improve education, create jobs, streamline our criminal justice system, improve productivity.

Labor secretary Robert Reich puts it this way: "Brain power, along with roads, airports, computers, and fiber-optic cables connecting it all up, determines a nation's standard of living." We have the brain power, the ground and air transportation, and the computer systems in place. Tonight we put it all together—with our highway to the future.

NORTH CAROLINA WORLD TRADE ASSOCIATION

CHARLOTTE, MAY 11, 1993

[Although dated May 11, the following remarks were actually delivered May 12, 1993.]

I'm reminded of a story about a speech Winston Churchill gave once to a commencement class in England. I think it applies pretty well to the attitude we must take toward world trade in North Carolina. Sir Winston stood up and said simply this: "Never, never, never give up!" Then he sat down.[1]

All of us, here in this room, have been taking that attitude for years, and it is paying off:

—Last year we set another record in this state for exports, more than $10 billion!

—Two years ago, we were the fourteenth-biggest exporting state. Last year we were the twelfth-biggest. Our goal for this year is to rank tenth, and with the help of Commerce secretary Dave Phillips, and Dick Quinlan,[2] the head of our International Trade Division, and so many of you across this room, I think we can do that.

—We continue to hear gloomy reports of our nation's trade deficit, but not in North Carolina. Here, once again, we have a positive trade balance with the rest of the world, and I want that to continue! Boosting North Carolina's world trade helps our economy, helps us provide better jobs, better schools, [and a] better quality of life.

Improving our trade surplus is a challenge, one that North Carolina is meeting successfully. We're improving our trade surplus by our diversity. Last year, we exported more than a billion dollars' worth of products from each of these areas: industrial and commercial machines, $1.6 billion; transportation equipment, $1.2 billion; agricultural products, $1.2 billion; chemicals, $1 billion; tobacco products, $1 billion; electronic products, $1 billion. And we're sending them to a variety of countries. Our top four importing countries are Canada—we sent them $2.2 billion in goods last year; Japan, $1.2 billion in goods; Saudi Arabia, $1.1 billion; Germany, $635 million.

Jacky Musnier has been a tremendous help in developing our trade with France. He's with us tonight, but is getting ready to move on from his role as consul general for the southern states to an ambassadorship. But he has been a tremendous help to us here in the South, and I'd like to recognize him with a round of applause right now.[3]

(Pause.)

I'm glad to say he now includes Southern among the six languages he speaks.

But we need to do more to help boost world trade. Right now, Mexico is our seventh-largest trading partner, and we think there's room for improvement! So this year I'm asking for $150,000 to set up a trade office in Mexico to help us increase our trade with our southern neighbors.[4] I've also asked for state money to help with the education programs at the Research Triangle Park World Trade Center to help businesses in planning their worldwide business activities.[5] And I've requested $750,000 over the next two years to help get your center for language and cultural resources up and running; this public-private partnership would help North Carolina business people learn what they need to know about the languages and customs of the countries they're doing business with—and would give emergency workers and other people in our state a chance to better respond to the people here who don't speak English.[6]

But the critical group to making our world trade work, for both importers and exporters, is the people in this room. You will determine whether we move forward or stand still. I'm confident we will keep moving forward.

[1] At the midpoint of a brief speech at Harrow, his alma mater, Churchill told his audience: "But for everyone, surely, what we have gone through in this period—I am addressing myself to the School—surely from this period of ten months this is the lesson: never give in, never give in, *never, never, never, never*—in nothing, great or small, large or petty—never give in except to convictions of honour and good sense." Speech, "These are Great Days," October 29, 1941, quoted in Robert Rhodes James, ed., *Winston S. Churchill, His Complete Speeches, 1897-1963*, 8 vols. (New York: Chelsea House Publishers/R. R. Bowker Company, 1974), 6:6499.

[2] Richard L. Quinlan (1928-   ), born in Rantoul, Ill.; resident of Raleigh; B.S., University of Illinois; U.S. Army, 1950-1953. Career with International Harvester, from 1950, included posts as president, IH McLeod, Manila, 1975-1978; vice-president, marketing, Europe/Africa/Middle East, Paris, 1978-1981; regional manager, Eastern Region U.S.A., Raleigh, 1981-1988. Director, International Trade Division, N.C. Dept. of Commerce, 1988-1994, retired. Richard L. Quinlan, letter to Jan-Michael Poff, February 4, 1998.

[3] Jacky R. Musnier (1938-   ), born in Champignol, France; resident of Paris; studied German and English literature, University of Dijon, 1958-1960; master of German literature, 1962, master of English literature, 1962, doctorate of American literature, 1964, University of Paris (Sorbonne); was graduated from Institut des Sciences Politiques de Paris, 1964, and from École Nationale d'Administration, 1968; served on staff of French defense minister, 1965-1966. French diplomat: Soviet affairs desk, Ministry of Finance, 1968-1969; commercial attaché, Pakistan, 1970-1972; commercial counselor, Federal Republic of Germany, 1972-1975, Iraq, 1975-1977, Indonesia, 1977-1981, and Brazil, 1981-1984; financial attaché for Southeast Asia, 1984-1987; consul-general of France, posted to Atlanta, 1989-1993; minister counselor to Mexico, 1994-1995; chef du service des accords de reciprocite (multilateral and bilateral treaties and agreements in judicial and immigration matters), Ministry of Foreign Affairs, from January 1996. Chairman, CEO, Thomson SA-South America, 1987-1989. Jacky R. Musnier, letter to Jan-Michael Poff, December 4, 1997.

[4] Hunt later confirmed that the state was establishing new economic development offices in Mexico and California. High Point Chamber [of Commerce] Dinner, High Point, December 13, 1993, Governors Papers, James Baxter Hunt Jr.

[5] *N.C. Session Laws, 1993*, c. 561, s. 6, earmarked $100,000 in the F.Y. 1993-1994 budget for the World Trade Center.

[6] The N.C. Center for World Languages and Cultures was to be established at Pfeiffer College, Misenheimer. The General Assembly authorized $750,000 for the project, "contingent upon the receipt of matching funds." *N.C. Session Laws, 1993*, c. 321, s. 39.1. For more on the center see Poff, *Addresses of Martin, 1989-1993*, 422, 423-425, 426, 490-492.

PLANNED PARENTHOOD OF THE CAPITAL AND COAST

RALEIGH, MAY 13, 1993

[Planned Parenthood of the Capital and Coast presented its annual Margaret Sanger Award to Governor Hunt in 1993. His acceptance speech follows. The award was established to recognize "an individual or organization who has shown courage in the face of adversity and whose work in the community exemplifies a commitment to the mission of Planned Parenthood of the Capital and Coast." Telephone conversation with Roberta Mazer, director of development, Planned Parenthood of the Capital and Coast, April 8, 1998.]

When Margaret Sanger began her brave crusade, the American public did not understand the need for family planning. Times have changed.

Margaret Sanger spoke out for family planning, and they put her in jail.[1] I speak out for family planning, and they put me in the Governor's Mansion!

The public attitude has changed about the importance and value of family planning, and that's because of her work and your work. Over the past seventy-five years, and the past thirteen years in North Carolina, Planned Parenthood has changed the public attitude and made a difference in the lives of millions of children and families. You have laid the groundwork for public understanding of reproductive issues. Now with a pro-choice government in Raleigh, we have been able to:

—Lift the gag order in our county health clinics so we can remove politics from family planning;[2]

—Replenish the state abortion fund for poor women so that the women least able to provide for children are not forced to do so;

—Maintain the state abortion laws so that government does not interfere with a woman's right to choose.

In my Inaugural Address, I committed this administration to children. As I said, "The time has come to start earlier than we have started before." You understand the need to start early for children. You understand that we must make sure our children get the health care, early childhood education, and the other critical services they need.

You understand we can make a lasting difference in the lives of our children if we reach them in the early years. If we can provide quality early childhood education, health care, and other childhood services to all our children, we can change the course of their lives and change the course of our society. With your help, we can make it happen.

I thank you again for this honor. I congratulate you on thirteen years of providing high-quality health care and education here in North Carolina. I thank you for the opportunity of working with you in the past, and I ask you for the privilege of working with you in the future. I'm convinced our past accomplishments are only a hint of what lies ahead.

---

[1] Margaret Sanger (1879-1966), born in Corning, N.Y.; was educated at Nurses Training School of White Plains Hospital (N.Y.) and Manhattan Eye and Ear Hospital. Birth control movement leader; nurse; was indicted, 1915, "for sending birth control pleas through the mails"; court case resulting from her 1916 arrest for operating birth control clinic in Brooklyn made it possible for doctors to dispense birth control advice "for the cure and prevention of disease"; organizer, first American Birth Control Conference, N.Y.C., 1921, and World Population Conference, Geneva, 1927; founder, 1921, first president, American Birth Control League, which became Planned Parenthood Federation of America, 1942; founder, 1928, president, 1928-1937, National Committee on Federal Legislation for Birth Control; launched birth control movement in India, established fifty teaching centers for

birth control in India, China, and Hawaii, 1935-1936; founder, International Planned
Parenthood Federation; author; editor; publisher. Barbara Sicherman et al., eds., *Notable
American Women, The Modern Period: A Biographical Dictionary* (Cambridge, Mass.: Belknap
Press of Harvard University Press, 1980), 623-627; *Who Was Who in America, 1961-1968*, s.v.
"Sanger, Margaret (Mrs. J. Noah H. Slee)."

[2] President George Bush ordered an end to abortion counseling in all federally funded
family-planning clinics in 1992, and North Carolina followed suit. Hunt lifted the state's
"gag order" in late January 1993. *News and Observer*, January 23, 1993.

NORTH CAROLINA BUSINESS ROUNDTABLE

GREENSBORO, MAY 17, 1993

The first thing I want to do today is thank the members of this Business
Roundtable. You are one of the main reasons I am governor today. The
meeting we had here last June gave our campaign tremendous momentum. It forged a powerful coalition for positive, constructive change.
It put our campaign on the right course, and it brought about a new
course and a new energy for our state.[1]

The second thing I want to do is ask you to keep helping me, keep
helping the members of my administration, and keep helping the
members of the General Assembly. North Carolina's future is at stake
this year, and we need your help.

I can report to you today that your administration is doing what we
promised to do last year. You remember this "Agenda for Action" from
our campaign. Well, we've turned it into this "Hunt Legislative Agenda"
that you see on these charts—and that I carry around in my pocket. Let
me report to you on the status of our agenda:

—We started with education, because it comes first.

—We proposed an Education Standards and Accountability Act that
will do something we have never done before in North Carolina: define
exactly what it is we want our students to learn, what standards they
must meet to graduate, and what they must know to succeed in today's
economy; and it will hold our schools accountable for results.

—We proposed safe schools bills to make it a felony to take a gun
to a school, or for parents to knowingly let their child take a gun to school,
and to give the schools the authority they need to expel troublemakers
and put them into alternative programs.

—We proposed higher salaries, higher standards, better training, and
more professional leadership for teachers.

—We proposed changes in the budget that will cut down the
bureaucracy in Raleigh and give local school systems, local schools,
and individual teachers more decision-making authority.

—We proposed a sweeping and innovative initiative, called Smart Start, that will make North Carolina a leader in early childhood education. It's not a state government program; it's a statewide partnership between parents, child care providers, business, government, and the schools. We'll start with twenty counties, working with them to develop their plan to meet the needs of their children. I've named Jim Goodmon, president of Capital Broadcasting Company in Raleigh, to chair this partnership, and you can be sure it will be done in a businesslike way.[2] It is the most ambitious and most innovative early childhood approach any state has taken, and we are going to make sure every child in North Carolina starts school ready and able to learn.

—In economic development, we proposed a skilled-workforce plan that will upgrade the community college system and give stronger leadership to job training programs.

—We proposed incentives to attract more investment and create more jobs in our state: tax credits for job creation, tax credits for investments in startup companies, creative economic development financing, and discretionary funds for industrial recruitment. We proposed a 30 percent cut in unemployment taxes.

—We pledged to fight crime by making prisoners work, and we have a prison construction plan that puts prisoners to work building prisons, work farms, and military-style boot camps.

—And we proposed budget cuts and efficiencies that will enable us to do all these things without raising taxes.

These are the promises we made last year. They are promises we are keeping this year.

We need your help to pass this agenda. That's why we invited you here today. That's why members of the General Assembly need to hear from you, to know the support these changes have. We need your help passing this agenda for action this year.

Let me add one thing before I introduce our speakers today.[3] All of this agenda is important, but nothing is more important than education. Our biggest job is education. Our biggest task is to change the way we educate and train people in North Carolina. Our biggest challenge is to build a workforce and an entrepreneurial force that will build the strongest, most vibrant, and most prosperous economy anywhere in this nation and this world.

This legislature is making great progress, and I want to say a special word of thanks to Lieutenant Governor Dennis Wicker, to Speaker Dan Blue, and to Senate President Pro-Tem Marc Basnight for their leadership.

We have before us, this year, the opportunity to make a major step forward in North Carolina. It's an opportunity that comes along rarely in a lifetime. It's an opportunity that the people of North Carolina ought to have. Right now the legislature is considering letting the people of North Carolina vote on some important issues, including a bond issue for education and a state lottery. I have personal reservations about the lottery. But I believe it's time to let the people decide, and I believe it is essential that any money from a lottery go to education.[4]

I also believe that, if we're going to ask the people to vote for more money, we owe it to them to make their schools and their state government work better. That means four things:

1. The Smart Start early childhood initiative;
2. Higher standards and greater accountability for our public schools;
3. The veto for the governor, so he—or she—can be held accountable;
4. A resolution of the school governance issue, so there will be clear lines of responsibility and authority in education.

If we are going to ask the people to vote for more money, we should make sure it's not just more money for more of the same. We should let the people vote on measures that will mean more accountability, through education governance and the veto.

Money alone is not the answer. The big problem in education and state government today is that the buck doesn't stop anywhere. It's time the buck stopped here.

I didn't run for this office to be governor. I've been governor. I ran because of what we can do as a state. I ran because I believe this state is ready to take a big step forward; ready to stop ranking at the bottom in educational achievement; ready to build the kind of future we should have. This year, in this session of the North Carolina General Assembly, we have that rare opportunity.

I look around this room, and I see the people here. I know you, and I know what you can do. I think about the talent, and ability, and energy that is here [sic]. I think about what we did last year. I think about what we can do together.

We in North Carolina can do anything we dream. That's what this Business Roundtable is about. That's what our administration is about. That is what this legislature is about. This is our great chance and our great opportunity. Our time has come, this year, this legislative session. Let's leave our children and our grandchildren the kind of future they deserve. I ask you to help us do that. It's something we'll be proud of as long as we live.

---

[1] Eleven hundred businessmen and -women joined the North Carolina Business Roundtable to support Hunt's third gubernatorial campaign. Its first meeting, in June 1992, attracted an audience of approximately 450 people. Hunt called the roundtable "an unprecedented effort to involve business leaders in the future of North Carolina. Last year, we established the roundtable as a forum for dialogue between business and government leaders. It's critical that we continue that dialogue if we want to build a consensus for change in our state. Without a strong public-private partnership, we cannot bring about the dramatic, fundamental changes we need in North Carolina." Press release, Governor Hunt to Meet with Top Business Leaders, Raleigh, May 14, 1993, Governors Papers, James Baxter Hunt Jr.

[2] James Fletcher Goodmon (1943-   ), born in St. Petersburg, Fla.; resident of Raleigh; attended Duke University, 1961-1965; honorary doctor of laws degree, Pfeiffer College; U.S. Navy, 1965-1968. Positions with Capitol Broadcasting Co., Inc., included executive vice-president, 1973-1975, president, 1975-1979, and president/CEO, since 1979, as well as WRAL-TV (Raleigh) operations manager, 1968-1973; president, A. J. Fletcher Foundation, Fletcher School of Performing Arts, The Achievement School; former chairman, N.C. Amateur Sports Board of Directors, Open Net Committee—N.C. Agency for Public Telecommunications, and N.C. Salute to the Troops Committee; former president, N.C. Partnership for Children, N.C. Public Television Foundation, N.C. Association of Broadcasters, United Cerebral Palsy of N.C., and N.C. Symphony Foundation. James Fletcher Goodmon, letter to Jan-Michael Poff, January 8, 1998.

[3] The speakers included Erskine Bowles, of Charlotte, U.S. Small Business Administration chief; Sally Price, general manager, Pepsi-Cola customer-service center, Winston-Salem; and Bert Collins, president, N.C. Mutual Life Insurance Co., Durham. Press release, Governor Hunt to Meet with Top Business Leaders, Raleigh, May 14, 1993, Governors Papers, James Baxter Hunt Jr.

[4] Despite numerous polls that showed growing popularity among North Carolinians for a state lottery, legislators never allowed the electorate to decide the issue in a referendum during Hunt's two terms in office. Lottery bills typically passed the senate. But an "unholy alliance"—between liberal Democrats, who believed a lottery amounted to a regressive tax, and conservative Republicans, who opposed a lottery as a form of gambling—repeatedly stymied pro-lottery legislation in the House. Luebke, *North Carolina Politics 2000*, 228.

RECYCLING COORDINATORS

RALEIGH, MAY 18, 1993

[Although this document was dated May 18, Hunt actually delivered the remarks on May 21, 1993.]

You have an important job ahead of you. You are the front line in an effort that can change the way we think about recycling, not just in state government, but across the state. I want you to concentrate on two things as you work on this committee. First, help us find new ways to reduce waste. Second, help us find ways to use more recycled products.

We have to cut back on the amount of waste we send to our landfills every year, and we can. In the past year, the North Carolina Zoo has reduced the amount it sends to the Randolph County landfill by 40 percent—by source reduction, recycling, and composting. We can achieve that kind of reduction all across the state if you make it convenient for people and help people understand how important it is—in our colleges and universities, in our agencies and departments.

Last year we used 2.3 billion sheets of paper in this state: that's *billion* with a *b*. Less than 5 percent of that was recycled paper. We should do better. We can do better, and we will do better.

The executive order I signed on Earth Day gives us clear goals. We want to use 25 percent recycled paper, five times what we do now, beginning next year. Four years from now, we want to use 65 percent recycled paper. I'm convinced these goals will help us become more efficient and effective.[1]

Some of our copy machines won't run with recycled paper. My executive order says we won't buy new machines unless they can run paper with at least 50 percent recycled content. And it says all other things being equal, we'll always buy recycled paper in this state.

If we can meet these goals, we can create a market for recycling in this state. This executive order will create a significant market by showing manufacturers we are serious about buying the recycled-content products they produce.

If we can meet these goals, we'll lead others in the state by example. In my office, we are already dramatically increasing the amount of paper we recycle. At the mansion, we've set up a composting bin for kitchen scraps and yard trimmings.[2]

Many of you are doing those kinds of things in your workplaces, as well. I applaud you for those efforts and look forward to working with you in the coming years. I'm convinced that you'll be working to find even more creative ways for all of us in state government to recycle and reduce waste. Rest assured you have a governor who will support you every step of the way.

---

[1] To further reduce the dependency of state government upon new paper, the governor suggested "using electronic communications, printing or copying on both sides of the page," and "using the backs of discarded one-sided printed material for note pads. The greatest thing about reducing waste at the source is that we not only avoid having to handle the wastepaper and recycle or dispose of it, we also save money by not having to purchase as much paper and ink!" North Carolina Reduce, Reuse, Recycle Campaign, Raleigh, April 22, 1995, Governors Papers, James Baxter Hunt Jr.

[2] Composting "was not a new idea" to Hunt. "Being the country boy that I am, we've always composted everything we could at the farm—or fed the scraps to the hogs! North Carolina is one of only a handful of states that have a backyard composting system at their executive mansions." North Carolina Reduce, Reuse, Recycle Campaign, Raleigh, April 22, 1995, Governors Papers, James Baxter Hunt Jr.

VETO STATEMENT

RALEIGH, MAY 24, 1993

[North Carolina was the only state in the nation whose governor lacked the power of the veto. The state legislature wielded absolute control over the bills that became law.

Governor Jim Martin, a Republican, persistently advocated the need for gubernatorial veto during his two terms in office, 1985-1993. Although Democrats controlled the legislature, the senate approved bills authorizing constitutional referendums on the issue. The House, however, ensured the General Assembly's continued supremacy over the executive branch by stranding the bills in committee and thereby keeping the choice from the voting public, which clearly favored such power for the governor.

In the aftermath of the 1992 elections, veto proponents hoped a Democratic legislature would award the new Democratic governor—Jim Hunt—the power it denied his Republican predecessor. But Speaker Dan Blue, a staunch opponent of gubernatorial veto, appointed like-minded Democrats to the House Constitutional Amendments Committee, thus dimming the prospects that such a bill might actually receive consideration by the full House. Despite Hunt's best lobbying efforts in the days prior to the committee's vote, that body on May 25, 1993, rejected a measure to allow the electorate the opportunity to determine the issue in a referendum.

Support for gubernatorial veto was one of the issues that propelled GOP candidates to victory in the 1994 legislative elections. With the state House in Republican hands, the General Assembly quickly approved a bill allowing a November 5, 1996, referendum on gubernatorial veto. Seventy-five percent of the voters approved, and Jim Hunt began his fourth term as the first governor in state history to be armed with veto power. "An Act to Provide for a Referendum to Amend the Constitution to Provide for a Gubernatorial Veto," c. 5, ratified March 8, 1995, *N.C. Session Laws, 1995*, I; Jack D. Fleer, *North Carolina Government and Politics* (Lincoln: University of Nebraska Press, 1994), 115-116; *N.C. House Journal, 1993*, 545, 678, 682-683; *North Carolina Manual, 1997-1998*, 1262; Raleigh *News and Observer*, March 14, 1992, February 21, April 29, May 5, 6, 7, 11, 18, 19, 20, 25, 26, 1993, February 1, 2, 3, 7, 8, 10, 28, March 8, August 20, 1995, March 27, 28, 30, April 5, 7, 10, 14, 19, June 7, November 3, 1996, February 20, 28, April 19, 1997.]

The House Constitutional Amendments Committee may vote tomorrow on the veto referendum bill, which passed the senate 45-4.[1] Last week, I met with members of the committee about this issue and have met several times with Speaker Blue. Speaker Blue and I stand together on most issues. Dan Blue has been an eloquent advocate for children, he has fought hard for better schools, and he has worked to bring good jobs to our state. On this issue, however, we disagree.

I respect the Speaker, and our disagreement will not affect our relationship. Our disagreement is over means, not ends. We will continue to work together for the progress of North Carolina.

The people of North Carolina elected a governor to make progress for children, schools, and jobs. They made the decision for themselves. The people ought to be able to make the decision on gubernatorial veto for themselves, as well.

The issue is accountability, not power. The veto is a tool of leadership and of accountability. It is needed to enforce discipline and set budget priorities. Two years ago, the legislature took tough and unpopular action to solve a budget crisis. The governor was free to criticize without taking responsibility for leadership. The veto will require the governor to lead and to be more accountable.

Right now, the buck does not stop anywhere in state government. It ought to stop with the governor. Shouldn't the people have the chance to decide for themselves whether they want their governor to be more accountable? I urge the Speaker to allow the full House to debate and vote on the veto referendum this year.

Whatever happens in the committee tomorrow, I will continue to urge the Speaker and the members of the House to give the people of North Carolina a voice—and the right to vote this year. I will urge the people to voice their opinions to their representatives. If the referendum does not pass this year, I will work for it next year. If it does not pass next year, I will work for it in the 1995 session.

Eventually it will pass, because the people want it. They know that money alone is not the answer to our problems. They want reform, they want more efficiency in government, and they want greater accountability. They want the right to vote on veto. I will work as long as it takes, and as hard as it takes, to give them that right.

---

[1] State senators approved the second reading of the veto referendum bill, S.B. 25, by a 45-4 vote on May 4, 1993. The next day they voted 40-2 to pass the bill, following its third and final reading, and sent it to the House for consideration. *N.C. Senate Journal, 1993*, 398, 405.

STATEMENT ON SMART START

RALEIGH, MAY 26, 1993

A deliberate campaign of deception and disinformation has been launched by a small group of political extremists who want to cripple our efforts to make quality child care available to every family that wants it in North Carolina. Over the weekend, we've heard about leaflets, flyers, phone banks, so-called public-service ads—all spreading lies and false rumors about Smart Start, our children's initiative. Here's what they're saying:

Smart Start would abolish home schooling. Do away with Christian schools. Indoctrinate all two-year-olds. Send state regulators to people's homes to tell them how to raise their children. There is absolutely no truth to any of that. The most ridiculous charge is that church centers wouldn't even be able to let children sing "Jesus Loves Me." This is absolutely absurd. The state will in no way prohibit or limit religious instruction at any child-care center.[1]

The intent of this smear campaign is clear: to raise fears in the minds of parents who are concerned about their children and their churches.

I understand the important role that church-run day-care centers play in North Carolina, because my wife, Carolyn, headed up our church's day-care program in Wilson. Well, I'm here to tell you that I'm not letting any band of right-wing extremists stand in the way of a better life and a better education for North Carolina's children. I will not let them stand in the way of giving every family who needs it access to quality early-childhood education. I will not let any [of] them dictate their political agenda to the rest of us.

We've seen these tactics before in North Carolina. You in the press have exposed them before. I've fought them before. It's not going to happen again.

Now, we have heard some concerns from legislators regarding accountability and openness of the North Carolina Partnership for Children. Those are valid concerns, and in fact, we're addressing those concerns in the legislature. At our request, the House Appropriations Committee today amended the bill to require open meetings, public records, and annual audits of the partnership. The senate bill already includes accountability measures. Secretary Robin Britt and his staff have met with numerous legislators to answer specific questions about Smart Start. Secretary Britt and Jim Goodmon will have a press briefing Friday morning to answer questions.

In coming days, we will be meeting with child-care advocates, parents, church leaders, and child-care providers to clear up any misunderstanding. We want them to understand that Smart Start is not a traditional bureaucratic approach or one that would impose a state-run system on local communities. In fact, our approach relies on local decision making—the involvement of parents, religious and community leaders, child-care providers, business leaders, and local government—to meet the pressing needs of our children. Our approach preserves diversity in child care, including public centers, private centers, home day-care centers, church-run centers, and school-housed centers. It does not intrude on that diversity by dictating what songs should be sung or telling parents how to raise their children.

The problem in North Carolina is clear: Too few children have access to quality, affordable, day care. Too many children start school programmed to fail, because they haven't gotten the early childhood education they need in the first five years. There's far too much neglect and abuse.

Our goal is to help every family get access to affordable, quality, child care. That's why we've proposed the Baby Bill, to improve our child-staff ratios, which are now among the worst in the nation. That's why we've proposed expanding the child-care subsidy and tax credit, so more families can afford good care.

This is one of the most important issues before this legislature and our state. It deserves to be debated fully and considered fairly. It does not deserve to die at the hands of a small group of politically motivated extremists.

---

[1] Twelve Christian radio stations from across the state carried a public-service message by Representative Connie Wilson (R-Charlotte) who said of the bill to establish Smart Start: "There has been no exemption allowed for religious facilities, which could threaten a church day care's right to teach the song, 'Jesus Loves Me, This I Know.' " *News and Observer*, May 26, 1993; for more on the dispute between conservative Christians and Smart Start proponents over Hunt's proposal, see *News and Observer*, May 27, 28, 29, June 2, 3, 6, 7, 9, 15, 16, 23, 25, July 11, 1993.

NOTES, GEOGRAPHIC INFORMATION SYSTEMS

RALEIGH, JUNE 1, 1993

This is a tremendous system that could truly help bring our state closer together. The first automated land records system started in my first administration. I watched in the basement of this building as the first land records were being downloaded from Orange County onto our computer here.[1] Since then, this program has stayed alive and flourished, as advances in computer technology have given us even more possibilities.

Today we are poised to implement two systems that could draw our state closer together—the rural and urban areas, the rich and poor, the east, the west, and the Piedmont:

1. Our information highways project would enable all people all across this state to have access to the best teachers, medical equipment, computer databases, and technology over fiber-optic phone lines.

2. This statewide land record system, when completely implemented, would help in

—*Economic development.* Companies from out of state [will be able] to search everywhere in this state with equal effort. They could call our Department of Commerce and tell us their needs, and we could locate potential sites all across the state.

—*Strategic planning.* It would give policymakers in Raleigh much more information about a particular county, with the touch of a few buttons, [and] help in highway and land-use planning.

—*County recordkeeping.* It's much easier to keep up with digitized maps, and this could also simplify disputes about the size of property tracts.

—*Public access.* It would allow people to have access to land records that have been very complicated to find in the past.

I'm interested in knowing more about the project and will look forward to hearing the report of the coordinating council.

---

[1] Data from Orange County land records was transferred to the computer located in the basement of the state Administration Building, 116 West Jones Street, Raleigh. See Governor Hunt's Weekly Schedule for May 28-June 5, 1993, Governors Papers, James Baxter Hunt Jr.

TESTIMONY BEFORE DEFENSE BASE CLOSURE AND REALIGNMENT COMMISSION

Norfolk, Virginia, June 11, 1993

[The United States victory over the Soviet Union in the Cold War, and efforts to balance the federal budget, resulted in a strategy to eliminate superfluous domestic military installations. Three rounds of base closings were approved under U.S. Public Law 101-510, adopted in 1990. According to the statute, the Department of Defense was to compile a list of military facilities to be scaled down or eliminated. An independent base closure commission, appointed by the president with the consent of Congress, would then review the list and make additions and deletions as it deemed necessary. Once it completed its work, the commission was to submit its recommendations to the president. He, in turn, would examine the revised list and then either pass it back to the commission for further study, or send it on to Capitol Hill for final approval. Prohibited from making their own revisions, federal lawmakers could only vote the entire list up or down: PL 101-510 curtailed the power of Congress to "interfere and block the closure of facilities that created local jobs but contributed little to defense operations." The first round of base closures was approved in 1991.

Secretary of Defense Les Aspin launched the second round of closings on March 12, 1993. He proposed to eliminate 31 major military installations, reduce operations at 134 more, and thus save the federal government $3.1 billion a year after the plan was fully implemented. Approximately 91,000 civilian and military jobs would be lost.

The Defense Base Closure and Realignment Commission reviewed Secretary Aspin's controversial list amid a coast-to-coast chorus of people in cities, states, and congressional districts bewailing the threatened loss of jobs. But in North Carolina, government and military officials expressed delight that Craven County would benefit from closings elsewhere. Aspin recommended that the Marine Corps Air Station at Cherry Point receive F/A-18 jets and more than 3,300 personnel from the doomed Cecil Field Naval Air Station in Jacksonville, Florida. Cherry Point Naval Aviation Depot stood to gain approximately 1,900 aircraft maintenance jobs from the three NADEPs proposed for closing: Alameda, California; Norfolk, Virginia; and Pensacola, Florida. But Tar Heel voices joined the chorus of consternation in mid-May, when the closure commission announced it would consider all six naval aviation depots as candidates for elimination, including Cherry Point.

Critics questioned the wisdom of closing NADEP Cherry Point. The facility ranked highest among its peers in a military value rating conducted by the Defense Department. It competed successfully with private enterprise to win contracts for the overhaul of military aircraft, and it was the only profitable aviation depot in the navy. Senator Jesse Helms wondered why it was even being considered for closure, when the proposed transfer of jets from Florida to MCAS Cherry Point meant that half the aircraft in the Marine Corps inventory would be stationed in Craven County.

Supporters of the Cherry Point aircraft maintenance depot were given the opportunity to speak on its behalf at hearings in Norfolk, Virginia, on June 11, 1993. Governor Hunt; Congressman Martin Lancaster; Lieutenant-General D. A. Wells, deputy chief of staff at Marine Corps Headquarters; state senator Beverly Perdue; local government officials from the Craven County area; and scores of depot employees hoped to persuade the commission to keep the facility open. Hunt's remarks are reprinted below.

President Clinton accepted the independent commission's recommendations on July 2, 1993, and Congress later approved them. NADEP Cherry Point was not included among the 35 major and 95 minor domestic military installations chosen to be eliminated. Instead, it was to grow—primarily at the expense of the three naval aviation depots that Aspin had designated originally for closing. But the additional aircraft Cherry Point Marine Corps Air Station seemed to have won in the 1993 closings were withdrawn during the third round of military cutbacks in 1995. *Congressional Quarterly Almanac, 1993*, 465-473; *News and Observer*, March 13, 18, May 26, June 11, 12, 1993, January 3, 1994, March 1, June 24, 1995.]

I am proud to be here, today, with my good friend and outstanding congressman, Martin Lancaster,[1] and in the company of citizens, state legislators, community leaders, elected officials, and most importantly, many of the hardworking eastern North Carolinians who have made the Cherry Point Naval Aviation Depot the undisputed leader in naval aircraft overhaul and maintenance. We welcome this opportunity to demonstrate the quality, diversity, and real military value of NADEP

Cherry Point by sharing with you facts—not subjective opinion, but facts—which support our claim of eminence.

Ladies and gentlemen, I appear before you as the governor of the tenth most populous state in the nation and assure you that I know that making government more efficient is no easy task. I am pushing hard to establish, in the state of North Carolina, the same outstanding level of productivity and efficiency which is so exceptional at NADEP Cherry Point. I recognize that it is our NADEP's total commitment to quality which has earned them the leadership position among naval aviation depots, and I believe that my state and many others can learn a great deal from Cherry Point with respect to embedding quality into every facet of operations.

Of course, NADEP Cherry Point's vital importance to North Carolina extends well beyond its role as a model for quality improvement. Eastern North Carolina is the poorest region in the state, and the depot is the largest civilian employer in the region. A closure of the facility would be devastating to this region, where unemployment rates are already high, incomes are low, and alternative employment is virtually nonexistent. The work ethic and dedication of the employees at Cherry Point is as strong as any workers' in the world, and it would be a travesty if a facility with such an unparalleled trac[k] record for productivity and quality were to be closed.

Our presentation today, however, will not further address economic impacts. Instead, the speakers will address how NADEP Cherry Point is the leader in efficiency, production, and quality among all of the depots in the navy. We welcome the opportunity to compete with any other depot in the navy or Air Force, for that matter.

Clearly, keeping NADEP Cherry Point in business is in North Carolina's best interest. We firmly believe that keeping NADEP Cherry Point is in the best interest of our nation as well. In support of that conviction, we will show you that our naval aviation depot:

—is a world leader in achieving quality;

—is one of the only naval aviation depots in a sound financial position;

—is the only naval aviation depot that reached its defense management review cost savings goals in the fiscal year 1992;

—returns its products to the fleet faster, on average, than any other naval aviation depot;

—is the most diversified naval aviation depot;

—has two times its current acreage available for future expansion;

—is uniquely positioned to support future navy and Marine Corps aviation requirements.

The naval aviation depot at Cherry Point is a superb example of excellence in the federal government. North Carolina is proud of the people of NADEP Cherry Point and what they stand for. We not only look forward to your examination of our NADEP, we approach it with enthusiasm. I am now pleased to introduce Senator Beverly Purdue, who will present to you the excellent quality and cost record of the NADEP at Cherry Point.

---

[1] H. Martin Lancaster (1943-   ), born in Patetown; A.B., 1965, J.D., 1967, University of North Carolina; U.S. Navy, 1967-1970; U.S. Air Force Reserve, 1971-1982; U.S. Navy Reserve, from 1982. Attorney; member, N.C. House of Representatives, 1979-1986; member, U.S. House of Representatives, 1987-1994, and member, House Armed Services Committee; military consultant to Hunt, appointed 1995. *News and Observer*, January 5, 1995; *North Carolina Manual, 1993-1994*, 945.

1992 INFANT MORTALITY STATISTICS

RALEIGH, JULY 8, 1993

[This statement is similar to Hunt's November 17, 1993, remarks recognizing recipients of awards for the reduction of infant mortality.]

The true reflection of any state can be found by looking at how it cares for its children. A few years ago, I'm not sure any of us were comfortable looking at the reflection. We're a state that prides itself on our superlatives, but in 1988, North Carolina had the dubious honor of ranking first in our nation in infant mortality. More babies were dying here than in any state!

But the leadership of former governor Jim Martin, Senator Russell Walker, Representative Dave Diamont,[1] and other legislative leaders helped turn this around. The legislature established a four-year plan to increase funding and improve services. We had leadership from so many people in this room—and leaders from all across the state, in business, academic, health care, the nonprofit sector, and the community leaders—working hard to reverse those numbers, and your joint efforts are paying off. Today we have the lowest infant mortality rate in history! In 1992 we reached a record low of 9.9 deaths per 1,000 live births.[2] That's something some people didn't think North Carolina could do.

Our infant mortality programs have played a key role in this reversal:
—The Baby Love program has helped improve access to health care and social services for pregnant women and infants across our state. By reducing the financial barriers, it encouraged low-income pregnant women to seek prenatal care.
—The First Step campaign has created a toll-free line any pregnant woman can call for information and assistance.

—The WIC [Women, Infants, Children] program has focused on helping provide improved nutrition.

—The Rural Obstetrical Care Incentive Program helps improve service in the less-populated parts of our state;[3]

—And the Commission on the Reduction of Infant Mortality has brought together people from a full range of backgrounds to encourage people to work together to reduce infant mortality.[4]

The statistics prove that these programs are working, but we can do better than that, and we must. We must boost our state's investment to child and maternal health. Today the General Assembly is expected to approve a budget that includes $2.7 million more for programs to reduce infant mortality, including $1.4 million for Healthy Mothers-Healthy Babies programs, like the one run here in the Wake County Health Department.

I commend the General Assembly for its leadership in making a real commitment to these children, and the General Assembly has endorsed my Smart Start proposal to immunize all children from birth to age five. Today they're expected to approve more than $10 million in funding over the next two years to start this ambitious effort. Every year, 40,000 children under the age of two do not get all the shots they need to protect them against childhood diseases. As I've said before, if we can pave every road that carries more than [100] cars, we ought to vaccinate every baby against the measles!

This year the General Assembly is taking another bold step in investing in our children's future. Last night, budget conferees agreed to provide $20 million for Smart Start, our children's initiative.[5] This is the first step in making sure that every child in North Carolina has access to affordable, quality, early childhood education. It's the first step in making sure that all children in North Carolina have a healthy start in life and come to school healthy and ready to learn.

Without the leadership of so many of you people in this room, we could not have made the progress we have. Without your help in the future, we cannot continue to make improvements. So as we celebrate today, we must also commit ourselves to the future, a future committed to all of our children across the state.

---

[1] David Hunter Diamont (1946-   ), born in Greensboro; resident of Pilot Mountain; B.A., Wake Forest University, 1968; M.A., Appalachian State University, 1972. History teacher, 1968-1977, and since 1991, assistant football coach, 1968-1977, football coach, since 1991, Mt. Airy Sr. High School; history teacher, head varsity football coach, East Surry High School, 1977-1990; member, 1975-1994, N.C. House, and Appropriations Committee co-chairman, 1989-1994; Democrat. *News and Observer*, August 22, 1993, July 11, 1994; *North Carolina Manual, 1993-1994*, 492.

[2] The N.C. Center for Health and Environmental Statistics reported that the combined infant mortality rate fell from 10.9 deaths per 1,000 live births, in 1991, to 9.9 per 1,000 in 1992. During 1992, the mortality rate among nonwhite babies also dropped to its lowest level in state history: 15.7 per 1,000 live births. The rate for white infants was 7.2 per 1,000 live births. Press release, Infant Mortality Rate Lowest in History, Raleigh, July 8, 1993, Governors Papers, James Baxter Hunt Jr.

[3] The Rural Obstetrical Care Incentive Program was established under "An Act To Create and Continue Various Committees and Commissions and To Make Changes in the Budget Operations of the State," *N.C. Session Laws, 1987, Regular Session, 1988,* c. 1100, s. 39.3, ratified July 12, 1988.

[4] Governor Martin issued Executive Order Number 99, establishing the Commission on Reduction of Infant Mortality, on December 13, 1989. Hunt prolonged the life of the commission under his own Executive Order Number 41, which he signed April 12, 1994. *N.C. Session Laws, 1989, Extra Session, 1989, Extra and Regular Sessions, 1990,* 1009-1015; *N.C. Session Laws, 1993, Extra and Regular Sessions, 1994,* 3:1011; Poff, *Addresses of Martin, 1989-1993,* 52, 535.

[5] *N.C. Session Laws, 1993,* c. 561, s. 13, authorized $20 million for F.Y. 1993-1994, and $27.64 million for F.Y. 1994-1995, to support the North Carolina Partnership for Children and implement the early childhood education and development initiatives described under *N.C. Session Laws, 1993,* c. 321, s. 254.

GOVERNOR'S LUNCHEON FOR CHILDREN

Charlotte, July 9, 1993

Hugh McColl[1] and I want to thank each and every one of you for coming here, today, for the sake of our children. You may have heard me talk about our crusade for children. You are an important part of our state's crusade.

You are in a position to help us help children, and many of you have been doing just that. NationsBank, Duke Power, Capitol Broadcasting, and some of the other leading corporations represented here today boast some of the most progressive child care and parental leave programs. That means your employees have access to quality, affordable child care. Those children are getting the early childhood education they need, and you're getting the benefit of loyal and committed employees.

Now the state must do the same for all North Carolinians. North Carolina must be a leader in day care, not just because we have one of the highest percentages of working mothers in the nation, but because quality early childhood education is the cornerstone of our vision for improving the quality of life in North Carolina. We see a North Carolina where every child gets the early childhood education he or she needs to start school ready to learn. We see a North Carolina where tough new standards force change in our schools, and classes are geared to what graduates need to know and be able to do to compete in the modern workplace. We see a North Carolina where a high-skill, high-wage economy will offer our graduates jobs that are worthy of their skills and talents.

That vision is built on early childhood education. If our kids don't come to school healthy and ready to learn, nothing else we do will make much difference. Right now, there are children in North Carolina who enter first grade not knowing the alphabet, who don't know their colors—some don't even know their names! As one Charlotte mother said, "These kids start school behind, and they fall further and further behind."

Folks, we can't have that in North Carolina! We can't afford to have students spending twelve years falling further behind. We can't afford to have students spending twelve years catching up. We must have students who start school ready to learn, students who spend twelve years moving ahead!

To do this, we have proposed Smart Start, an ambitious effort to provide early childhood education to every child in North Carolina who needs it. This is a new response to an old problem. Smart Start promises to succeed where big government would fail, if it can enlist the support of schools, businesses, nonprofits, parents, and teachers. To gain this support we've formed the North Carolina Partnership for Children, chaired by Jim Goodmon, CEO of Capitol Broadcasting—a man of talent and achievement who has demonstrated a lifelong commitment to children. And we'll rely on the efforts and expertise of committed children's advocates, like Jack Tate,[2] and the guidance of Department of Human Resources secretary Robin Britt, who has shown with Project Uplift that public-private partnerships can work.

The North Carolina Partnership for Children will map out a blueprint and will encourage counties to develop local public-private partnerships designed to provide quality early childhood education to every child in the county who needs it. It will encourage businesses, churches, and private day-care centers to expand their capacities and open new facilities, depending on local needs.

This is the best investment we can make for North Carolina. We know that children born into poverty who receive quality early childhood education enjoy the benefits for the rest of their lives. They have fewer arrests, higher earnings, greater property wealth, and a greater commitment to marriage. In fact, if you take into account the costs of welfare, unemployment, law enforcement, incarceration, the courts, and lost tax revenue, quality early childhood education yields economic benefits of $7.00 for every dollar invested. As business leaders, you understand the value of investment, and you understand that in North Carolina, we must start spending the one dollar to save the seven.

Now, legitimate questions have been raised about how this program will work. I understand that. It's a new way of doing things in government. I respect the people who raised responsible questions, and we worked with them to improve Smart Start. But some people oppose Smart Start for ideological reasons. They are not trying to improve the program; they are trying to kill it. They have not offered their own program to help our children; they just want to stop ours.

So let me make something clear today: We will not let them stop us. We will not let them stop North Carolina from doing the right thing for children and families. We will not stop working to give every child in North Carolina a better chance in life, because nothing is more important to our state's future and our state's families—and nothing is more important to me, as governor. I urge every one of you in this room to participate in Smart Start. There is no better way to ensure that North Carolina becomes all that it can be, all that it should be, and all that it must be in the years ahead.

---

[1] Hugh Leon McColl Jr. (1935-   ), born in Bennettsville, S.C.; B.S., University of North Carolina at Chapel Hill, 1957; U.S. Marine Corps Reserve, 1957-1959. Started as trainee, 1959-1961, later served as president, 1974-1983, and board chairman, NCNB National Bank; chief executive officer, NationsBank Corp., from 1983. G. D. Gearino, "Rebel Yell," *Business North Carolina*, January 1999, 36-41; *Who's Who in America, 1998*, s.v. "McColl, Hugh Leon, Jr."

[2] John A. Tate Jr. (1917-   ), born in, resident of Charlotte; A.B., University of North Carolina at Chapel Hill, 1937; M.B.A., Harvard University, 1939; United States Navy, 1943-1945. Wachovia Bank and Trust Co., Winston-Salem, 1939-1943; R. S. Dickson and Co., 1946-1949; Freeman-Tate-McClintock Realtors, 1949-1958; North Carolina National Bank, sr. vice-president, 1958-1967; chairman, president, CEO, Piedmont Corp., 1968-1983; sr. consultant, First Union National Bank, 1984-1987. Member of numerous boards and commissions, including: Union Theological Seminary Board of Trustees, 1967-1977, 1980-1984; UNC Consolidated University Board of Trustees, 1967-1969; member, 1970-1983, chairman, 1983, UNC-Chapel Hill Board of Trustees; charter board member, first president, Child Care Resources, Inc., 1983-1992; charter board member, vice-chairman, N.C. Center for the Advancement of Teaching; winner, numerous civic and humanitarian awards, including naming of the UNC School of Social Work building in his honor (Tate-Turner-Kuralt), 1995. Letter, John A. Tate Jr. to Jan-Michael Poff, November 18, 1998.

GOVERNOR'S CRIME COMMISSION

RALEIGH, JULY 15, 1993

Thank you, Sis,[1] for your kind words and for agreeing to head this commission. I know, because I know you, that this group will chart new directions under your leadership and really make a difference in our battle against crime here in North Carolina.

The Governor's Crime Commission has been a weapon against crime since it was placed in the Department of Crime Control and Public Safety in 1977. Since then, it has advised the governor and the secretary of crime control on crime and justice issues. It has also helped put in place many successful statewide programs and distributed grant money to help support federal programs.

You've done an excellent job over the past years, but it is no insult to you to say it just isn't enough. Just a few days ago, a woman and her children were resting in a car on the side of the road as they heard shots ring out. The mother heard her little girl crying in the back seat and said, "It's okay, baby." She thought she had just been scared by the noise. But when she checked, the mother found her daughter shot in the head. It just makes me sick to think about it.

We cannot tolerate this. We cannot tolerate that behavior. We cannot tolerate the conditions that lead to that behavior. We must have radical change in North Carolina.

We must start by getting violent criminals off the streets. That means we must move aggressively to arrest them, prosecute them, and sentence them, and we must insist that they serve that sentence. That's why I support structured sentencing. It guarantees North Carolina's law-abiding citizens that if a criminal is convicted for a given offense, he or she must get a sentence that falls in a fixed range. In other words, if someone is convicted for robbing you on the street, you're guaranteed that for a fixed period of time, you're not going to see that person anywhere but jail.

This is a good proposal, and I support it. But this alone is not enough. It would not even be enough if it kept every known criminal off the street, because there are new criminals every day—young people who turn to crime for the first time. If we are really going to cut [down] on crime, we have to find out how criminals are made and stop making so many!

I believe that criminals are made starting at a very young age. When children are born into poverty, and don't get good health care, and don't get quality early childhood education, and don't get the attention of educated adults, and don't develop self-esteem and the belief that they can succeed, they start school behind and fall further behind every year. Some of them can't ever hold a legal job.

That's the life story of most of the people in our prisons! But here in North Carolina, we have the vision, and the resources, and the commitment to turn that around. We know that children born into poverty, [but] who receive quality early childhood education, enjoy the benefits for the rest of their lives. They have fewer arrests, higher earnings, greater property wealth, and a greater commitment to marriage. In fact, if you take into account the costs of welfare, unemployment, law enforcement, incarceration, the courts, and lost tax revenue, quality early childhood education yields economic benefits of $7.00 for every dollar invested.

In North Carolina, we must start spending the one dollar to save the seven. We must make quality early childhood education available to every child in North Carolina. If we can do that, we can teach at-risk children to earn money instead of steal it, and buy homes instead of rob them.

But we can do more to prevent crime. We can create boot camps for youthful offenders, young people who are tempted by crime but who have not yet gone over the edge. If we can give them some discipline and the self-esteem that comes from it, we can turn them around. We can help them spend their lives building up society instead of tearing it down.

And we must make our schools safe. Violence in schools is worse than violence on the streets, because schools are the only chance many students have to escape the streets. If violence invades schools, there will be no way out at all.

The problems that face us are daunting, and we need the help of all of you on the Governor's Crime Commission. You must do more than you have in the past. You must contribute in research and policy. You must help design new programs, and you must work to implement them. You must help North Carolina keep its criminals in jail, prevent crime through early childhood education, and preserve the peaceful sanctuaries of our schools. By agreeing to serve on this commission, you have accepted an assignment that will be endless, exhausting, but, I hope, rewarding. I thank you. You can perform no higher service for yourselves, your families, and your neighbors across North Carolina.

---

[1] Sis Atlass Kaplan.

PRESS RELEASE: STATEMENT FROM GOVERNOR JIM HUNT IN RESPONSE TO 1993 LEGISLATIVE SESSION

RALEIGH, JULY 24, 1993

["Legislative Overview," the text for Hunt's news conference of July 28, 1993, is similar to the statement reprinted below. See also the related press release, Governor Hunt Outlines Legislative Agenda, Says Job Not Done, Raleigh, July 28, 1993, Governors Papers, James Baxter Hunt Jr.]

In this session, we've taken bold action on the issues most important to the people of North Carolina—education, children, crime, and jobs—and we showed that the governor and the General Assembly can work together to build a better future for North Carolina. I commend the General Assembly for its leadership and vision. Legislators deserve great credit for their willingness to give our people the tools they need to make their lives better.

In my State of the State address five months ago, I said we needed to replace conflict with cooperation. Too often, legislative sessions have ended with the governor and the General Assembly in confrontation. This year we've ended the session with constructive action.

We've passed the Standards and Accountability Act to raise standards in our public schools and to guarantee that our graduates are ready to compete in [the] twenty-first century economy.

We've passed the Smart Start children's initiative to make sure our children come to school healthy and ready to learn. Smart Start encourages local communities to provide every child with quality, affordable day care and basic health care in the earliest years. As I said in my Inaugural Address, investing in our children is investing in North Carolina's future. I believe this is the single most important action we can take to improve education, build a more competitive workforce, prevent crime, and make North Carolina's future a prosperous one.

At the same time, we've got to make our classrooms safer. The safe schools legislative package recommended by the Governor's Task Force on School Violence is an important first step in our fight for safer schools.

To help reduce crime, we will build nearly 4,900 new prison beds, with two 500-man prison work farms and two new boot camps to help youthful offenders turn their lives around; and we've begun a prison labor program to make sure prisoners work.

I'm pleased to see the General Assembly taking a leadership role in health care reform, particularly our need for more preventive care, primary care physicians, rural health care, and affordable health insurance for small businesses. I look forward to working with the General Assembly in developing a comprehensive plan that meets these needs.

We've also laid the groundwork for a higher level of economic development by investing in our workforce and our industries. We've boosted workforce training efforts in our community colleges and begun developing a high-tech training center that will use computer and video technology, along with our new Information Highway, to provide the most sophisticated training for North Carolina's auto workers. And we've stepped up North Carolina's job recruitment efforts with a jobs-incentives package that will help us bring good jobs to our state. In short, the General

Assembly has given us the incentives we need to attract the best jobs and has made sure our workers get the training they need to do the best jobs.

The legislature has given the executive branch and the people of North Carolina the tools we need to build a better future. But the job is not done. Now the challenge for all of us is to use what the General Assembly has given us to make a difference for every school, every child, and every community in North Carolina.

PRESS CONFERENCE ON SCHOOL VIOLENCE

WILMINGTON, AUGUST 9, 1993

[Hunt's address to the North Carolina Sheriff's Association, Wilmington, August 9, 1993, was similar to his statement to the press on that date, reprinted below. For related press release, see Governor Hunt Calls for Local Efforts to Combat School Violence, Wilmington, August 9, 1993, Governors Papers, James Baxter Hunt Jr.]

Here at New Hanover High School, and in every school across the state, teachers are making plans for the new school year. Students are preparing for a year of classes. But the new school year has become a time of trepidation, not anticipation. Too many of our students and teachers are afraid that the start of the school year will be the start of a new wave of guns, knives, and other weapons in our schools.

There's a good reason for their fears. You can't pick up a paper anymore without seeing another story of a teen shooting another teen on a ball field, or knifing someone in a hallway, or bringing a gun to school just to show off. A rising senior in one of our schools says, "If you really look, you can come up with a gun pretty quickly." And he says, "I don't think adults realize how easy it is." It's time we did—and time we did something to make our schools safe again.

Today I want to tell you we are putting the resources of state government behind our law enforcement [agencies] and schools in the fight to reduce school violence. We've begun to do just that. This spring, I convened a Task Force on School Violence to focus the state's attention on the issue of school violence. I appointed Secretary of Crime Control and Public Safety Thurman Hampton, Attorney General Mike Easley, and Superintendent of Public Instruction Bob Etheridge to the task force and charged them with developing an action plan for the prevention of school violence. After public hearings across the state, the task force recommended a set of safe schools bills to the General Assembly. The safe schools bills are now law.

The centerpiece of the new laws is the weapons-free school zone. It's now a felony to bring a weapon onto school grounds or to knowingly allow a minor to bring a weapon to school. It's now a misdemeanor to bring any kind of weapon to school, on the bus, or to a ball game. And it's now illegal for a parent to leave a firearm out where a school-age child can get to it.[1]

Other bills require judicial officers and law enforcement officials to tell schools more about students who've been convicted of violent crimes and require schools to report violent behavior to law enforcement officials.[2] They also authorize a long-overdue review of the state's judicial code for juveniles.[3] And we've created a statewide resource that every school in North Carolina can call on. The Center for the Prevention of School Violence offers a toll-free hot line to provide hands-on technical assistance to schools and communities who need help combating school violence. The center is a statewide clearinghouse staffed by people who know what's working in other schools and know how to make it work in your schools. And the General Assembly has approved $100,000 grants, that every school system can apply for, to finance local school violence prevention programs.[4]

These efforts will provide educators and law enforcement officers with more weapons in the fight against school violence, but new laws are only a first step. All of us—government, law enforcement, educators, parents, students, and community leaders—must come together to rally around our schools. Starting today, we must make a statewide commitment to work together to make our schools safer.

U.S. attorney general Janet Reno said about youth violence: "The best solutions are out in the communities and the neighborhoods of America."[5] Now we challenge you to organize local school violence task forces, to get parents involved as volunteers in the schools. We challenge you to bring more law enforcement officers onto school grounds, as they have here in New Hanover County. Officers here don't just clean up after violence has happened, they prevent it. They get to know the at-risk kids through the DARE [Drug Abuse Resistance Education] program, through tutoring programs, and by volunteering for after-hours programs in the neighborhoods. It's estimated that 80 percent of our children have no one waiting for them at home if they get there at 3:00 P.M. We need more programs like the one Mike Brown is offering, here in New Hanover County, to get at-risk kids into afternoon athletic programs.

We need more students to get involved in our peer mediation and conflict resolution programs to make sure they really work. We have to make it clear to every student, in every school, that schools are places not to shoot, and cut, and threaten, but to learn, and think, and grow. Every one of us must do our part to stop the violence and let our teachers and students return to schools that are free of weapons and full of learning. That means starting right now. In the next thirty days, I'll be going all across our state to challenge school systems to get to work and to see what they're already doing that is working.[6] At the same time, my crime commission will make school violence their top priority this year, and the Task Force on School Violence will continue to meet to review the progress we've made and determine our next step in the state's efforts against school violence. Now the task force members will tell you how their agencies will be stepping up their efforts to combat school violence.

---

[1] See N.C. *Session Laws, 1993*, c. 558, identified earlier in this volume.

[2] See "An Act to Require Juvenile Court Counselors to Notify School Officials in Certain Cases When a Juvenile Is Adjudicated Delinquent and Is Ordered to Attend School as a Condition of Probation," N.C. *Session Laws, 1993*, c. 369, ratified July 17, 1993, effective October 1, 1993, expired October 1, 1995; and "An Act to Require School Principals to Report Certain Acts Occurring on School Property to Law Enforcement," N.C. *Session Laws, 1993*, c. 327, ratified July 9, 1993, effective December 1, 1993.

[3] H.B. 1007, "A Bill to Be Entitled An Act to Establish a Second Juvenile Code Revision Committee to Study the Provisions of the Existing Juvenile Code That Relate to Delinquency and Recommend Necessary Revisions" passed the state House of Representatives on May 13, 1993. Its companion legislation in the senate, S.B. 881, remained in committee through the end of the 1993 session. N.C. *House Journal, 1993*, 616; N.C. *Senate Journal, 1993*, 288.

[4] N.C. *Session Laws, 1993*, c. 321, s. 139, authorized school violence prevention grants. The Center for the Prevention of School Violence was created by Executive Order Number 19, identified earlier in this volume.

[5] Janet Reno (1938-   ), born in Miami, Fla.; A.B., Cornell University, 1960; LL.B., Harvard University, 1963. Attorney; Judiciary Committee staff director, Fla. House of Representatives, 1971; counsel, Criminal Justice Committee for Revision of Fla. Criminal Code, Fla. Senate, 1973; staff member, 1973-1976, state attorney for Dade County, 1978-1993, Eleventh Judicial Circuit of Fla., and first woman to head a county prosecutor's office in Fla.; was appointed U.S. attorney general, 1993. Judith Graham, ed., *Current Biography Yearbook, 1993* (New York: The H. W. Wilson Company, 1993), 485-489; *Who's Who in America, 1997*, s.v. "Reno, Janet."

[6] Between August 13 and September 7, Hunt met with student leaders and held public forums on school violence in Greensboro, Greenville, Charlotte, Asheville, Raleigh, and Fayetteville. Press release, Governor Hunt Announces School Violence Prevention Forums, Raleigh, August 5, 1993. For related speeches, see School Violence Forum, Greenville, August 25, Charlotte School Violence Prevention Forum, August 24 (delivered August 26), and Wake County School Violence Forum (notes), August 31, 1993; the governor's address at the Duke SCOPE Conference, November 12, 1993, covered the same ground. Governors Papers, James Baxter Hunt Jr.

NORTH CAROLINA ASSOCIATION OF
COUNTY COMMISSIONERS

RESEARCH TRIANGLE PARK, AUGUST 13, 1993

[An emphasis on state-local partnerships characterized Hunt's remarks to the N.C. Association of County Commissioners, below, and his earlier N.C. League of Municipalities speech, April 1, 1993.]

Thank you, Tim, for those generous words. I congratulate you on your fine record as president. I've enjoyed working with you, as I'm sure I'll enjoy working with your new president, Moses Carey.[1]

I also want to congratulate all the people who won awards today for efficient and effective government. We are about to launch a Total Quality Management program in state government. If we are able to do for state government what you have been able to do for county government, we will have earned the salaries and the trust of our taxpayers.

I am especially honored to talk to you, this morning, as you begin to discuss so many of the issues that affect our quality of life here in North Carolina. You in local government are in many ways closer to the people, and you understand local needs best. I want you to know that we in state government respect your experience and expertise, and this administration pledges to issue in a new era of cooperation between state and local government. This is not just rhetoric from Raleigh, folks! I have here in my hand a copy of an executive order I just signed establishing the North Carolina Local Government Partnership Council.[2] This council will make sure the governor and the General Assembly understand and respect the concerns of local governments, and I can assure you that the voice of this council will be heard—because Lieutenant Governor Dennis Wicker is going to chair it!

I hope you are as excited as I am about this commitment to renewed cooperation between state and local governments. In that same spirit of cooperation, I want to reassure you about our position on mandates. I am philosophically opposed to the state imposing unfunded mandates on local governments, and I'm going to do everything I can to make sure the practice is reduced.[3]

Also, this year we took the first step toward restoring and stabilizing local government revenues, and we won! State-collected local revenues are coming out of the appropriations process, and you're going to see that revenue growth restored.

Now, I hope that with my news about the local government partnership, my opposition to [unfunded] mandates, and our steps to restore local revenue growth, you're now in the right kind of mood for me to

ask you a favor! I need all of you to help us pass economic development financing bonds this November. This is the one component of the
governor's legislative agenda that we still must work to pass. We already
passed our Smart Start program that will start us on the way to seeing
every child in North Carolina get the early childhood education he or
she needs to start school, ready to learn. We passed the Standards and
Accountability Act that will make sure our graduates learn what they
need to know and be able to do to work in the global marketplace, and
we passed a prison bond package that will help us keep criminals off
the street and put prisoners to work.

But all our efforts in fighting crime and supporting education won't
pay off unless we have the kind of high-paying jobs in North Carolina
that are worthy of our graduates. That's why we worked hard to pass
a judicious package of economic growth incentives that will help bring
good jobs to North Carolina. We are not going to give away the store,
but neither are we going to give away the advantage to our neighboring
states—and so we passed the governor's Industrial Recruitment Fund
that will give the governor some flexible means for meeting the needs
of new companies.[4] We passed the Jobs Tax Credit and the Industrial
Development Fund that will give companies incentives to create jobs
and improve infrastructure in distressed counties. In fact, the Jobs Tax
Credit has already been responsible for bringing one big company,
Schlegel, to North Carolina.[5] We also passed the Business Investment
Tax Credit, which gives a state tax credit to people who are willing to
invest in promising young companies so they can get the start-up capital
they need.

It's a fine record of accomplishment, but as I said, we're not done yet.
You should have in your hands a brochure about economic development
financing bonds. EDF is an economic development tool that will help
us bring new companies and new jobs to the state. It will especially be
helpful for both rural and urban counties who want to recruit or expand
industry but can't afford to build the public infrastructure to attract that
industry. For example, if a company is interested in building a factory
on a particular site, but won't make the move unless water and sewer
lines are put in, EDF allows the local government to sell bonds and use
the bond proceeds to build the water and sewer lines. The bondholders
are then paid back with the additional property tax revenue that comes
from the factory built on that site.

The General Assembly is sold on economic development financing.
It passed the House by an overwhelming bipartisan majority, and it
passed the senate 47-1. That's the kind of margin you would expect on
a resolution approving of motherhood! But it's not enough for the General

Assembly to pass it. The people must pass it, and that's where we need your help. Every one of you knows the need for new jobs, every one of you has influence in your county, and every one of you knows how to get voters to the polls. We need you to talk to your supporters, to the people who helped put you in office, and tell them we need this for North Carolina.

Nearly forty states in the country have this economic development tool. We can't let them leave us behind. We must compete with them, step for step, to make sure the children we are working so hard to educate today will have their choice of the best jobs tomorrow.

Let us work together. In the same cooperative spirit of the Local Government Partnership Council, in the same spirit of cooperative opposition to mandates, let us work to provide North Carolina this competitive advantage. Let us work together, over the next eleven weeks, to add one more success to our efforts to provide good jobs for all our people.

---

[1] Timothy A. Glass (1945-   ), born in North Wilkesboro; resident of Alexander County; was graduated from Wingate College, 1965; attended University of North Carolina-Charlotte, 1965-1967. Poultry, cattle farmer, owner-operator of Glass Farm; elected, 1972, reelected 1976, and chairman, 1978-1980, Alexander County Board of Education; elected, 1986, reelected 1990, 1994, and chairman, 1986-1987, 1991, 1994-1995, Alexander County Board of Commissioners; member, Alexander County Board of Health, 1986-1997; numerous positions, from 1986, with N.C. Association of County Commissioners, including president, 1992-1993. Letter, Timothy A. Glass to Jan-Michael Poff, May 15, 1997.

Moses Carey Jr. (1945-   ), born in Tampa, Fla.; resident of Chapel Hill; B.S., Fort Valley State College, 1967; M.S.P.H., University of North Carolina at Chapel Hill, 1972; J.D., N.C. Central University, 1980. Chairman, 1989-1996, member, Orange County Board of Commissioners; president, N.C. Association of County Commissioners, 1993-1994. Moses Carey Jr., letter to Jan-Michael Poff, May 20, 1997.

[2] Hunt signed Executive Order Number 21, establishing the Local Government Partnership Council, on August 12, 1993. Governors Papers, James Baxter Hunt Jr.

[3] Both the state and federal governments required local governments to carry out or enforce certain programs. Too often, those mandates were unaccompanied by the funds required for their execution. Unfunded mandates cost local governments in North Carolina $7.5 billion annually. *News and Observer*, August 14, 1993; Hunt also discussed the issue of unfunded mandates in remarks before the Local Government Partnership Council, Raleigh, May 17, 1994, Governors Papers, James Baxter Hunt Jr.

[4] Bristol Compressors accepted a $750,000 inducement from the Industrial Recruitment Competitive Fund to locate a new factory, employing 750 workers, in Sparta. Hunt reported that the money, combined with the expanded Jobs Tax Credit, "gave North Carolina the edge in a seven-state search." Groundbreaking for Bristol Compressors Plant, October 20, 1993, Governors Papers, James Baxter Hunt Jr. The Industrial Recruitment Fund was identified earlier in this documentary.

[5] Schlegel, a manufacturer of automotive weatherstripping, expected to hire 800 workers for its new factory in Reidsville. Hunt hoped the company's presence would attract other makers of automotive components to North Carolina. Remarks at Groundbreaking of Schlegel Plant, August 19, 1993, Governors Papers, James Baxter Hunt Jr. The Jobs Tax Credit was identified earlier in this documentary.

GOVERNOR'S AWARD FOR
OUTSTANDING VOLUNTEER SERVICE

ASHEVILLE, AUGUST 27, 1993

[Texts for the Governor's Awards for Outstanding Volunteer Service presentation ceremonies in Greenville, September 16, and Raleigh, October 18, 1993, were identical in many ways to the speech Hunt delivered in Asheville.]

I'd like to thank everyone who had a hand in arranging this event. It's only fitting that we give our volunteers the honor they deserve. The spirit of community and cooperation you bring to your special tasks inspires all of us and reminds us of the power we have when we put aside our own concerns and focus on [those of others].

I firmly believe in volunteerism. I believe that it helps not only the community, but also the volunteer. It teaches patience and compassion, and it teaches us how to be grateful for what we have by teaching us how to give. My wife Carolyn and I have always volunteered, and we have encouraged it in our children. We hope that the careers our children have chosen, including nursing and social work, reflect those values and that emphasis on serving one's fellow man.[1]

Because charity does begin at home, I've also encouraged volunteerism in the Governor's Office. We have launched a volunteer program for Governor's Office employees at the Raleigh Nursery School. Every week, Governor's Office employees will volunteer at the school, working with children under five. We've also adopted a highway that we will police on a regular basis to help keep it clean and free of litter. Both projects were coordinated by Christie Barbee, who [sic] you just met, and who heads the Governor's Office of Citizen Affairs.[2]

In my previous administration, I started the Governor's Office of Citizen Affairs as a way to encourage volunteerism.[3] These awards we're presenting tonight are part of that same spirit. I know that your good works will inspire your neighbors, and friends, and family to follow your example.

I know people will be inspired by Jim Bullins, whose handicapped brother died as a child. Jim began his volunteering by purchasing a wheelchair lift for a handicapped child, then began collecting donations from others. Finally he founded his own nonprofit organization to help handicapped children find the comfort, companionship, and maybe even a cure.

We see inspiration in people like Jackie Blackburn, who traveled to Jamaica to help in hurricane relief. After befriending a Jamaican man who'd lost his legs below the knees twenty years before, Jackie went back to Charlotte and had two high-quality artificial legs made. When Jackie returned to Jamaica with the new legs, his friend was so overcome that he hobbled to him, hugged him around the waist, and lifted him into the air in gratitude.

And we find inspiration in retired teacher Lorelle Martin, who runs the Read to Succeed program at Carver Elementary School in Mount Olive. In three years, Lorelle has recruited more than 100 volunteers and built a reading program that makes a huge difference in the lives of many, many young children.

As a parent and grandparent, I was inspired by Frances Curtis. Frances was licensed as a foster parent seventeen years ago and, since then, has taken in more than 100 children. Many times Frances has gotten out of bed in the middle of the night to open the door for the Department of Social Services and welcome a frightened child with a warm, motherly hug.

We need more like you in this world. When you're governor of a state, you learn all of the problems of your state, and you feel responsible for them; and sometimes it breaks your heart that there isn't enough money or manpower in state government to solve all these problems. But your spirit gives me a sense of confidence and a reason for hope. I'm touched by your ability to reach out and do what the government, business, and schools cannot do alone: heal a sick child, hold a lonely widow, teach a poor man to read. This is what makes us human—to feel the suffering of another human being and to help meet our own needs by reaching out to meet theirs. It is the greatest gift we can give. Thank you for reaching out to our young, our old, and our needy. Thank you for serving as examples of what it means to be good, kind, charitable people.

---

[1] Rebecca Joyce Hunt Hawley had been a nurse in Wake and Wilson Counties, and Elizabeth Brame Hunt Amigh was a social worker for the Wake County Public School System. Shearin correspondence.

[2] Hired in 1993 to lead the Governor's Office of Citizen Affairs, Christie Barbee departed the Hunt administration early in 1994 for the Carolina Asphalt Paving Association, a lobbying organization. Before becoming chief of Citizen Affairs, she served as operations manager for Hunt's 1992 campaign for governor, finance director for Mike Easley's 1990 campaign for U.S. Senate, and finance director for congressional candidate David E. Price in 1988. *News and Observer*, February 12, 1994.

[3] Hunt signed Executive Order Number 3, establishing the Governor's Office of Citizen Affairs, on March 29, 1977. Besides its function as a clearinghouse for volunteers, the office also routed and replied to mail and telephone inquiries directed to Hunt. Mitchell, *Addresses of Hunt, 1977-1981*, 5-6, 10n, 834; *N.C. Session Laws, 1977*, 1525-1526; *News and Observer*, July 7, 1994.

STATE EMPLOYEES ASSOCIATION OF NORTH CAROLINA ANNUAL CONVENTION

CHARLOTTE, SEPTEMBER 10, 1993

I come to you today in a spirit of partnership. As partners, we can build a new era of prosperity for the people of North Carolina. We have begun the process of change. We have passed legislation and established programs to help our children get quality day care, raise standards in our schools, keep violent criminals off the street, and bring high-skill, high-wage jobs to North Carolina.

But these are only the first steps. We need your help to make it happen. Without state employees, we can't make these changes and make our state a better place. We need correctional officers to help us keep dangerous criminals off our streets. We need the economic developers to bring new businesses and new jobs to all parts of our state. We need DOT [Department of Transportation] to improve our roads and rail service and make us more competitive. We need school employees, university and community college employees, to help us educate and train the workers of the next generation. We need emergency management workers to protect our families against hurricanes, storms, and other disasters. We need every single worker in every single agency to help us make our government more efficient and more effective.

You are the heart and soul of our state, and you work hard every day serving the interests of others. I want you to know that I am working hard for your interests. I am working with you to help you get the pay, the health care, the retirement benefits, and the job security you need to help your families live and grow.

I promised you a year ago that, if you did your job as state employees, that your position would not be jeopardized by politics. I have kept that promise. You are professionals, and in my administration you will be treated like professionals.

I promised you a year ago that I would forge a link between the state employees and the Governor's Office by appointing a state employee ombudsman. I have kept that promise. Blanche Critcher, a longtime state employee and former officer of SEANC, is your ombudsman and your link to the governor. I will be asking Blanche to take the lead on drafting the state employee bill of rights, so that the job protections I have promised you will be written into an executive order and serve as a standard for future administrations.

I promise to work hard to preserve the benefits of the State Health Plan and to preserve the core benefits package for state employees. As you may know, state government has launched a Health Planning Commission, which I will convene. I will use that commission as a vehicle to fight for a better, more sensible benefits package. In your current benefits package, if you take a sick child to the doctor, most of the costs are covered. But if you take a healthy child to the doctor for a checkup, you pay almost 75 percent of the cost. That does not encourage preventive care. It does not encourage healthy children, and it does not encourage you to take your children in for checkups. You and your children deserve better, and I intend to see that you get it!

I also support giving you a bigger say in running government. We have recently launched the Partnership for Re-Engineering Government to give frontline state employees a stronger say in how things are run. We need to make government more efficient and effective, and we believe you can show us how to do it.

I also support performance pay. We must have the flexibility we need to encourage excellence, and our state employees must know that exceptional performance will be recognized and rewarded. The taxpayers of North Carolina benefit from exceptional service and so should the employees who render it.

We must also encourage state employees to be good citizens and good workers. I've proposed a new policy for state employees that will give full-time state employees eight hours a year paid leave to visit with your children's teachers, attend a school event, or perform volunteer work in school. This policy, which should be finalized shortly, should help parents stay involved in their children's education. That is the single most important ingredient in a child's success. Our program is similar to policies in other states, and it's something we need here in North Carolina. You, and your children, deserve it.

I want to thank you for giving me this opportunity to address the convention and talk about what we can do, together, for the future of our state. I look forward to working with your new president, Chuck Hunt, who is on our top management team at Revenue.[1] I look forward to working with all of you to help give the people of North Carolina the finest service, and the best government, of any state in the country.

---

[1] E. B. "Chuck" Hunt was president of the State Employees Association of North Carolina from October 1, 1993, through September 30, 1994. Lynn Wilson, communications director, State Employees Association of North Carolina, telephone conversation with Jan-Michael Poff, September 30, 1998.

The governor rotates kitchen scraps and lawn trimmings among the Executive Mansion's three compost bins. A 1993 ban on yard-waste dumping was intended to extend the operating lives of landfills across North Carolina, and Hunt promoted recycling as an environmentally responsible alternative. Naturally, composting was nothing new to Hunt, a cattle farmer who grew up on a farm himself. "Being the country boy that I am, we've always composted everything we could at the farm—or fed the scraps to the hogs. North Carolina is one of only a handful of states that have a backyard composting system at their executive mansions," he said. (Photograph by Lance Powell, Raleigh *News and Observer*.)

Fourth-graders from Apex and Raleigh elementary schools, visiting the Capitol grounds to trim a children's Christmas tree in December 1993, allow Hunt the privilege of hanging the first decoration. (Photograph by Harry Lynch, Raleigh *News and Observer*.)

CHANCELLOR'S FORUM, EAST CAROLINA UNIVERSITY

GREENVILLE, SEPTEMBER 16, 1993

[The following address is much like Hunt's remarks to the N.C. Education Standards and Accountability Commission, September 3, 1993.]

I want to thank Chancellor Eakin for that introduction and for inviting me here to East Carolina University.[1] There is no better setting for talking about education and the opportunities it presents us. The contribution that you all make to Greenville, and Pitt County, and all of eastern North Carolina is the best evidence that our best investment in the future is the investment we make in educating our students.

I want to say how proud I am to be able to follow Dr. Boyer at this podium.[2] He is an education visionary, and I have long admired his work as U.S. commissioner of education and now as president of the Carnegie Foundation for the Advancement of Teaching. The Carnegie Foundation has had a profound influence on my own involvement in education and has spurred reform efforts here in North Carolina. As a member of the Carnegie Forum on Education and the Economy, I served on the Carnegie Task Force on Teaching as a Profession. We issued a 1986 report called *A Nation Prepared: Teachers for the 21st Century*, which recommended the creation of the National Board for Professional Teaching Standards.[3] I helped found, and still chair, that board, and we're busy designing a set of teaching standards to encourage excellent teachers through board certification.

Here in North Carolina, we're working to become the first state with voluntary, board-certified teachers. Our General Assembly has enacted a law to help us reward certified teachers. If doctors, engineers, and architects can distinguish themselves in their fields by becoming board-certified, why not teachers?

The educational contributions of the Carnegie Foundation are more than just theory. They are helping us set new standards for educational excellence here in North Carolina.

The single most important task we must accomplish for our students and for our state is dramatic, fundamental change in our schools—and that means dramatic, fundamental change in what our students know and are able to do when they graduate! That means higher standards for students as well as teachers. Too many North Carolina high school graduates are not prepared to compete in the modern economy. An auto mechanic can't work on a $20,000 car that's run by a computer if he or she can't read, write, understand computers, operate high-tech equipment, or follow illustrated instructions.

Right now, a North Carolina high school diploma is no guarantee that the graduate can do those things. Right now, we don't expect enough from our students. In fact, we demand more from our high school athletes than our high school graduates. We require a high school football player to be able to catch a ball, run a certain distance, and understand certain formations. If the player doesn't meet those standards, a good coach will make him do it over, and over, and over until he gets it right. A good coach will never send his players out on game day without the skills to compete, and a good school should not sent its students out on graduation day without the skills to compete.

A North Carolina diploma should guarantee certain skills: the skill necessary to compete for a good job in the global marketplace. That's the challenge of our new North Carolina Standards and Accountability Commission. Under the leadership of retired UNC-Charlotte chancellor E. K. Fretwell and Sam Houston, former school superintendent of the Mooresville schools, the commission will work to enhance the value and meaning of a North Carolina diploma.[4]

During the next year, the commission will reach out to business leaders, employers, parents, educators, and other real people to define exactly what graduates need to know and be able to do to compete in the real world. We're now scheduling six public hearings across the state to make sure we tap the insight and expertise of people all across North Carolina. I especially want the input of Chancellor Eakin and everyone here today. We hope to hold a hearing in Greenville in January, and we're relying on you all to help us get tough new standards for our schools.

The commission is also talking to employers and educators across the country and the world to make sure that the standards we set in North Carolina are as rigorous and relevant as standards anywhere in the world. By next spring, the commission will recommend a set of specific, concrete standards to the State Board of Education. Once those standards are set, the commission will begin developing a set of assessments that will measure student performance on these standards. By 1996, every high school senior will take this new set of assessments. By the year 2000, every high school senior must pass it to graduate.

By the year 2000, a North Carolina diploma should be a guarantee to employers that the graduate has the knowledge and skills needed for the modern workplace—and we should make that guarantee to all North Carolina employers: Any student who holds a North Carolina diploma will be able to do certain tasks. If they can't, we'll retrain them at the state's expense. No state has ever taken such a far-sighted view of education. No state has ever tied its curriculum to the real demands of the workplace. No state has ever guaranteed its diplomas. North Carolina will be the first, with your help. North Carolina has always led the way in education, and we must continue to set those challenges for our state. I believe our future, and that of our children, depends on it.

---

[1] Richard Ronald Eakin (1938-   ), born in New Castle, Pa.; A.B., Geneva College, 1960; M.A., Ph.D., 1962-1964, Washington State University. University administrator; mathematician; career with Bowling Green State University began in 1964, with appointment to mathematics dept., and ended as vice-president, planning and budgeting, 1983-1987; chancellor, East Carolina University, from 1987. *News and Observer*, January 10, 1987; *North Carolina Manual, 1995-1996*, 755.

[2] Ernest Leroy Boyer (1928-1995), educator; university administrator; U.S. commissioner of education, 1977-1979; president, Carnegie Foundation for the Advancement of Teaching, from 1979; senior fellow, Woodrow Wilson School, Princeton University. Previously identified in Poff and Crow, *Addresses of Hunt, 1981-1985*, 291n; see also *Current Biography Yearbook, 1996*, 656.

[3] Carnegie Forum on Education and the Economy, Task Force on Teaching as a Profession, *A Nation Prepared: Teachers for the 21st Century* (Washington, D.C.: [The Forum], 1986).

[4] E. K. Fretwell Jr. (1923-   ), born in New York City; resident of Charlotte; B.A., Wesleyan University, 1944; M.A., Harvard University, 1948; Ph.D., Columbia University, 1953. U.S. vice-consul, Prague, 1945-1947; career in higher education, from 1953, included dean for academic development, City University of New York, 1964-1967; president, SUNY College at Buffalo, 1967-1978; chancellor, University of North Carolina at Charlotte, 1979-1989; chair, N.C. Education Standards and Accountability Commission, appointed 1993; member, president, chairman of numerous national boards and commissions on higher education; author. *News and Observer*, February 22, 1981, September 26, 1993; *North Carolina Manual, 1987-1988*, 1013.

Samuel H. Houston Jr. (1944-   ), born in Mecklenburg County; resident of Raleigh; B.S., 1965, M.A., 1966, Appalachian State University; Ed.D., University of North Carolina at Greensboro, 1982. Educator; adjunct professor, Appalachian State University, 1974-1975, and at University of North Carolina at Chapel Hill, 1985-1988; principal, Ledford Jr. High School, Thomasville, 1975-1976, and at North Davidson Sr. High School, Lexington, 1976-1981; auxiliary services director, 1981, assistant superintendent, 1981-1983, Davidson County Schools; superintendent, Mooresville City Schools, 1983-1993; executive director, N.C. Education Standards and Accountability Commission, 1993-1998; executive director, UNC Center for School Leadership Development, from 1998; author. Letter, Samuel H. Houston Jr. to Jan-Michael Poff, October 14, 1998.

PRESS CONFERENCE ANNOUNCING
SAFETY BELT INITIATIVE

RALEIGH, SEPTEMBER 22, 1993

["Click It or Ticket," the seat belt law awareness and enforcement campaign the governor announced at his September 22, 1993, press conference, was also the topic of the speech with which he proclaimed Child Passenger Safety Week. See Child Safety Week Proclamation address, Raleigh, February 14, 1996, Governors Papers, James Baxter Hunt Jr.]

I am pleased to be with you today as we announce the launch of a dynamic, new, statewide highway safety initiative. Beginning October 4, all over the state, it's going to be "Click It or Ticket" in North Carolina, as our law enforcement officials begin stepped-up enforcement of our law requiring the use of automobile seat belts and child safety seats.[1] We will be using checkpoints, like the one you will see later this morning, in every part of the state; and if you're caught not wearing your seat belt, you will get a ticket which carries a $25 fine.

I'm strongly supporting this initiative for a simple reason: It will save lives and prevent serious injuries. Research has proven this to be true in North Carolina, beyond a shadow of a doubt, and seat belts save money. Right now, the 35 percent of our citizens who aren't wearing seat belts are costing the rest of us millions of dollars in emergency services and health care costs. We simply can't afford to pay that cost any longer.[2]

Now we have to meet the challenge of increasing seat belt usage. We can do that with high visibility enforcement of the law in all 100 counties of North Carolina. The law enforcement officials of High Point, Elizabeth City, and Haywood County, with the support of local elected officials and the business community, have already shown us earlier this year that we can achieve the highest seat belt usage in the nation. I want to commend those officers and elected officials from the three pilot sites who are with us today.

But I'm here today to tell you what safety belts have meant to me. When I was growing up, my daddy was one of the first supporters of using seat belts. Even before seat belts were a standard feature on cars, he took our car to a garage to have them installed, and he insisted that our family buckle up. So when our car was hit by a drunk driver during my twenties, my life was saved because I was wearing my seat belt. There is not a stronger supporter of wearing seat belts and using child safety seats than Jim Hunt, and I'm living proof that they work.

I also want to express my pride that North Carolina has been selected to be the pilot state for the nation in carrying out this initiative. I understand there are four good reasons why we were chosen. First, we're blessed to have a tradition of excellent law enforcement in North Carolina. At every level—the Highway Patrol, sheriffs, city and county police departments, as well as military police and the Division of Motor Vehicles—we have quality and effective law enforcement. They are working closely together, and that's what it will take to make this initiative a rousing success. So I want to thank our law enforcement officers, who are so well represented here today, for answering the call again, and to say that I, as governor, stand behind you in your efforts 100 percent.

Second, we were selected because our legislature had the foresight and courage to pass a primary seat belt and child safety seat law several years ago. Legislators took a strong stand for safety on our highways, and the nation has recognized that stand by choosing us to kick off this program.

Third, North Carolina is the pilot state because of the aggressive efforts of Commissioner Jim Long and the Insurance Department to hold down insurance premiums by encouraging innovative programs that prevent losses.[3] The insurance industry in our state has embraced the commissioner's philosophy and is a full partner in this initiative.

Fourth, the commitment of our state government to the highest quality in highway safety, through the Governor's Highway Safety Program, has been recognized. Joe Parker and his staff are to be commended for their efforts to make our highways safer every day.[4]

I'm excited about this initiative, because I know that it will ultimately result in thousands of lives being saved, tens of thousands of injuries being prevented, and millions of dollars saved, and I look forward to sharing the results with my fellow governors across the country. Once again, North Carolina is providing leadership for the nation, and I'm proud to announce the statewide launch of the initiative today.

---

[1] See "An Act to Make the Use of Seat Belts in Motor Vehicles Mandatory," *N.C. Session Laws, 1985*, c. 222; "An Act to Require Passenger Restraint Systems for Children under Four Years of Age," *N.C. Session Laws, 1981*, c. 804; and "An Act to Reenact the North Carolina Child Passenger Restraint Law," *N.C. Session Laws, 1985*, c. 218.

[2] By the time the 1993 Click It or Ticket campaign ended in December, the number of Tar Heel travelers who buckled up before driving off had risen from 65 percent to 80 percent, the highest level of compliance in the country. The 15 percent increase in seat belt usage resulted in 100 lives being saved, prevented 1,700 serious traffic-related injuries, and averted $150 million in health care costs. But apart from increasing the awareness of state seat belt and child passenger safety statutes, the campaign proved beneficial in other ways. Click It or Ticket checkpoints caught scores of motorists who were driving while impaired or operating a motor vehicle without a valid license; they also snared twenty-two fugitives: one of them was wanted for murder, another for armed robbery, and a third had thirty-two outstanding arrest warrants. Click It or Ticket News Conference, Raleigh, December 20, 1993, Governors Papers, James Baxter Hunt Jr.

[3] James Eugene Long (1940-   ), born in Burlington; A.B., 1963, J.D., 1966, University of North Carolina at Chapel Hill. Attorney; member, N.C. House of Representatives, 1971-1975; served as state chief deputy insurance commissioner, 1975-1976; was elected state insurance commissioner, 1984, reelected in 1988, 1992; author; cofounder, N.C. Special Olympics movement; Democrat. *North Carolina Manual, 1993-1994*, 237-238.

[4] Joseph Mayon Parker (1931-   ), born in Washington, N.C.; resident of Raleigh; B.A., 1953, M.P.A., 1992, University of North Carolina at Chapel Hill; was also graduated from U.S. Army Command and General Staff College, 1972, and U.S. Army War College, 1980; U.S. Army, 1953-1954, and Reserve, 1954-1988 (col., ret.); N.C. Army National Guard, 1955-1985. Printing and publishing executive; career with Parker Brothers, Inc., Ahoskie, publishers of community newspapers in northeastern N.C. and southeastern Va., included:

manager, print division, 1956-1971, chief editorialist, 1961-1977, general manager, 1971-1977, president, chief executive officer, from 1977. State chairman, National Newspaper Assn., 1976-1983; vice-chairman, N.C. Goals and Policy Board, 1977-1984; chairman, Northeastern N.C. Tomorrow, 1981-1984; television talk show panelist, "North Carolina This Week," 1986-1989; Democrat. Hunt appointed him chairman, Governor's Highway Safety Program, April 5, 1993. Joe Parker, letter to Jan-Michael Poff, June 28, 1996.

SMART START ANNOUNCEMENT

RALEIGH, SEPTEMBER 27, 1993

[North Carolina has one hundred counties. Eighty-nine of them were included among eighty-one competing applications to establish one of the first twelve Smart Start partnerships across the state. As required by state law, the governing board of the North Carolina Partnership for Children chose one proposal from each congressional district. Hunt announced the winners on September 27: Hertford County, First District; Halifax County, Second District; Jones County, Third District; Orange County, Fourth District; Burke County, Fifth District; Davidson County, Sixth District; Cumberland County, Seventh District; Stanly County, Eighth District; Cleveland County, Ninth District; Caldwell County, Tenth District; partnership among Cherokee, Clay, Graham, Haywood, Jackson, Macon, and Swain Counties, Eleventh District; Mecklenburg County, Twelfth District.

Each of the twelve winners was to develop its Smart Start strategies by the spring of 1994. Each partnership "must be coordinated by a local, private, nonprofit organization responsible for developing a comprehensive, collaborative, long-range plan of services to children and families in the area served by the project." To proceed, the projects required the approval of the state secretary of human resources. Ferrell, *North Carolina Legislation, 1993*, 210-211; *N.C. Session Laws, 1993*, I, c. 321, s. 254; press release, Hunt Names First Twelve Smart Start Partnerships, Raleigh, September 27, 1993, Governors Papers, James Baxter Hunt Jr.]

Eight months ago, I stood on the steps of the Archives Building to talk to the people of North Carolina about my vision for this state.[1] I said then that we must invest in our children to invest in our future, and I asked North Carolinians to help us make this a better state for our children. Today I'm proud to say that North Carolina is rising to the challenge.

Today we are launching our Smart Start program. We are launching an historic effort to provide our children with the quality day care, health care, and other critical services they need. Today we are honoring eighteen counties that will be Smart Start pioneers. Today we are celebrating the creativity, enthusiasm, and commitment of these counties, because we all know that the hardest work begins tomorrow.

The eyes of the state and the nation will be on these pioneers as they develop a comprehensive plan to provide quality, affordable day care to every single child who needs it in their communities. These counties truly represent North Carolina—rural and urban, rich and poor, large and small—and the needs of our children. In Hertford County, almost 40 percent of the children are living in poverty, twice the state average. Mecklenburg County is struggling with typical urban problems like crime, and a juvenile crime rate that tops the state's average, but is still working to galvanize the community around at-risk children. In the mountains, seven counties have banded together to develop a campaign to improve children's services, continuing a twenty-one-year tradition of community cooperation that fits within the framework of Smart Start.

But we wouldn't be here today if it were not for the many people who have helped us rise to this challenge. Smart Start would not have gotten off the ground without the visionary leadership of House Speaker Dan Blue and Senate president pro tem Marc Basnight; or the strong support of so many legislators; or the grass-roots work of child advocates like John Niblock;[2] or the support of community, business, religious, and nonprofit leaders from across our state; or the hard work of Jim Goodmon, chairman of the North Carolina Partnership for Children, and the committed board that has worked day and night for the last four days. Most of all, Smart Start owes its existence to one man: Robin Britt. Robin has always been a champion of children and families. He gave up a lucrative law practice to found Project Uplift, a public-private partnership in Greensboro that helps at-risk children and their families. Robin has devoted his life to helping North Carolina's children, and he has brought that dedication, drive, and vision to the Department of Human Resources—and to Smart Start.

Robin's enthusiasm, creativity, and commitment is contagious. It's spread all across North Carolina! Everywhere I go, I see that enthusiasm. Everywhere I go, I see people putting aside political and personal differences for their children. Everywhere I go, I see community leaders committed to coming up with new ways to address the needs of their children. This spirit was evident in every single Smart Start application, all eighty-one of them. As my wife, Carolyn, honorary chair of the partnership, told me, selecting twelve pilot programs was a tough choice.

But this is just the first chapter. We will be putting Smart Start into every county in this state, because our children deserve nothing less. In the meantime, the other counties will be dividing more than $1.5 million to take a closer look at which children they're serving and which they're missing in their communities. And mountain counties that are part of the Appalachian Regional Commission will divide $656,000 to get ready for Smart Start and begin developing small-scale demonstration projects. Another $1 million will be committed to improving teaching of day-care workers, in addition to the money the General Assembly has already provided for the TEACH [Teacher Education and Compensation Helps] program to see that child-care teachers get better training.

Next year, I will ask the General Assembly for additional funds for at least eight more Smart Start counties—and more the year after that. This is a long-term effort, one that will transcend all of us in importance. As Dan Blue put it last week, Smart Start is the most important thing that we can do as leaders of this state.

And now the responsibility for the success of this program is in the hands of those of you from the selected counties. You must design local solutions and gather local resources to help you meet your local needs. Show all of us what can be done when counties pull together for a common goal; and when you go home today, I ask each of you to encourage your friends in neighboring counties to continue their Smart Start committees and to continue their efforts for their children. We must do all we can to continue the community spirit that has been started by this program.

Together, I know North Carolina can do more for our children than ever before. We can do more for our children than any other state. We can make our state a better place and our future a brighter one. Let's get started!

---

[1] The site of Hunt's 1993 inaugural ceremony was the Archives-State Library Building, 109 East Jones Street, Raleigh.

[2] John Sterner Niblock (1936-   ), born in Chicago; B.A., Monmouth College, 1958. Reporter; information director, Learning Institute of N.C., 1972-1977; executive director, Governor's Advocacy Council on Children and Youth, 1977-1983; founder, president, N.C. Child Advocacy Institute, 1983. *News and Observer*, April 11, 1993.

STATEMENT ON DECISION BY MERCEDES-BENZ

RALEIGH, SEPTEMBER 29, 1993

[Americans were developing a seemingly insatiable appetite for sport utility vehicles by the early 1990s, and Mercedes-Benz wanted to help feed the demand. But M-B's utilitarian, 4-wheel-drive trucks, built to conquer mountains and deserts, were unsuited to the realities of the American market, which demanded little more of its SUVs than an image of invincibility combined with a smooth highway ride, luxurious interior appointments, and the ability to survive the occasional curb crossing. Lack of product, and Germany's strong currency and high labor costs, put the company at a competitive disadvantage to Japanese and domestic U.S. manufacturers. A new vehicle, built in a new U.S. factory capable of producing at least 60,000 units a year, was required.

Mercedes-Benz officially announced the search for a plant site in April 1993. Thirty states, eager to be linked to the company's world-renowned reputation for quality and engineering precision, submitted 150 site proposals. The Hunt administration offered a $109 million incentive plan to lure the $300 million SUV plant, and its 1,500 jobs, to the Tar Heel State.

The North Carolina offer contained: land and accompanying improvements, valued at $39 million; an automotive training center, $35 million; road and rail access to the new factory, $24 million; temporary office space and temporary housing, $2 million; fire station near the new factory, air transport for company executives, and a German-language school, $1.5 million; water tank, $1.2 million; and $1 million for advertising featuring M-B. The state also pledged to buy 1,000 of the new SUVs, "build and maintain a 2,500-vehicle state port storage center," and furnish job "applicant screening and training for twenty-four months" for 1,500 new Mercedes hires.

In August 1993, Mercedes announced three finalists for the new factory: North Carolina, South Carolina, and Alabama. Weeks later, the *Washington Post* reported that a 1,000-acre site near Mebane, N.C., was the sure choice. But on September 29 the German car maker revealed the decision its board made a fortnight earlier: It would locate the plant near the village of Vance, Alabama.

What made Vance so attractive? The finalists "were in a dead heat when it came to business climate, education levels, and transportation," according to *BusinessWeek* magazine, and "long-term operating costs were roughly equal" among all three states. Officially, the choice of plant site turned on "zeal" and topographical similarity. The "wooded, rolling hills" that surrounded Vance "reminded Germans of the Swabian countryside" near Mercedes' Stuttgart headquarters, and Mercedes-Benz managing director Dieter Zetsche said, "'We sensed a much higher dedication to our project'" in Alabama. SUV project president Andreas Renschler discounted the power of financial incentives to dictate the choice of site: "'Whether you get $10 million more or less in one state doesn't matter.'"

North Carolina economic development officials, who spent weeks negotiating with Mercedes representatives over the terms of an incentive package, were unmoved by the company's denials that money was the primary factor behind the site decision. Mercedes suggested an array of financial inducements during the summer of 1993, among them a request that the state spend $45 million to pay the first year's wages of the new plant's employees. In the end, Alabama proved its "dedication" to Mercedes by awarding the giant auto maker an incentive deal worth an estimated three to five times the $109 million offered by North Carolina. *News and Observer*, March 12, April 2, 8, 9, May 7, 16, 18, 28, 29, June 6, 14, 17, July 7, 16, 19, 21, 23, 25, 28, August 3, 8, 11, 22, 25, 26, 27, September 2, 9, 10, 16, 17, 18, 21, 22, 23, 24, 25, 26, 28, 29, 30, October 1, 4, 10, November 17, 1993; "Why Mercedes is Alabama Bound," *BusinessWeek*, October 11, 1993, 138-139.]

Well, you win some and you lose some. In this case, Mercedes-Benz is losing out on a dedicated work force, a good business climate, and a state that's truly committed to investing in its people in order to invest in jobs.

Certainly, I'm disappointed, but I want to congratulate Governor Jim Folsom [Jr.] and the state of Alabama for landing this fine company. North Carolina gave it our very best shot. We went after Mercedes aggressively, and we did it responsibly. We put forth an innovative package that banked on our workers and honored our tradition of offering skill training as an incentive. That's always been the North Carolina way, and that's the way it ought to be.

Alabama offered Mercedes a twenty-five-year corporate tax holiday and agreed to withhold 5 percent of workers' salaries to help Mercedes pay off its plant construction debt. Those two incentives alone are worth more than $280 million, but we did not feel that North Carolina should offer those kinds of tax abatements, and I cannot envision that we would ever need to.

We offered a package that we believed was a good investment, one that would have paid off for our state. We will compete by making sure that our workers have the skills they need to compete for good jobs. That's why we built our package around skill training. Our high-tech auto training center would have used cutting-edge technology to train Mercedes workers, community college students, and many of the 50,000 North Carolinians in the automotive industry.[1] It would have boosted the skills of our workers and the quality of our state's workforce. It must have been a good idea, since South Carolina came up with a similar proposal a few months later!

There's no question that North Carolina had an excellent proposal, an excellent site, and a tremendous show of legislative, business, and community support. I want to thank the many people who helped us put together this package. It was truly a team effort, and I take pride in that. The legislature took a bold step by supporting the high-tech training center, which was developed by our community college system. Alamance County and the city of Mebane showed their commitment by agreeing to provide as much as they could for land site preparation. The Department of Transportation carved out $7 million from its budget for new road improvements, and business leaders across the state worked around the clock to make this package an attractive one—especially Duke Power, Norfolk Southern, and USAir and American Airlines. I'm proud of their efforts, and I'm proud of the approach North Carolina has taken.

North Carolina has always been a winner and will continue to be a winner. We've led the nation in industrial recruitment for many years. Now the competition is getting stiffer, and we've got to work harder to stay ahead. But we do not need to risk the future of the franchise to recruit star players. We already have star players. Look at PepsiCo, and Merisel, and Schlegel, and the other companies that are coming to our state, and the many companies that have been prospering here for years. We will continue to go after new jobs aggressively, and we will continue to look for innovative ways to market our state. And we will continue the North Carolina tradition of doing what's right for our people.

---

[1] For more on the proposed $35 million Center for Advanced Automotive Technology, see press release, Governor Jim Hunt Gets OK for High-Tech Worker Training, Raleigh, July 26, 1993, Governors Papers, James Baxter Hunt Jr.; *N.C. Session Laws, 1993*, II, c. 561, s. 27; and *News and Observer*, July 16, 18, 19, 21, 23, 25, August 3, October 10, 1993.

NOTES ON PRESENT STATE OF INVESTMENT: SOUTHEAST UNITED STATES-JAPAN ASSOCIATION

OSAKA, JAPAN, OCTOBER 4, 1993

[Departing North Carolina on October 1, 1993, the governor and a seventy-two-member state economic development delegation spent almost a week exploring trade possibilities in Japan. Hunt's itinerary included the annual meeting of the Southeast U.S.-Japan Association. *News and Observer*, September 28, 1993; Tentative Program of Meetings and Events, XVIII Annual Joint Meeting, Southeast U.S./Japan Association . . . October 3-5, 1993, Osaka, Japan, Governors Papers, James Baxter Hunt Jr.]

Since the late 1970s, the southeast U.S. has benefited from significant Japanese corporate investments, including manufacturing, service sector, and real estate. Each of the seven southeastern states represented at this conference have [sic] seen their respective economies become more diversified because of this increased international investment.[1] Each state acknowledges the tremendous economic benefits these relationships have brought: job creation and an additional tax base.

Competition between our southeastern states to attract new international industries and other investments, especially those planned by Japanese firms, has been intense throughout the years.

You all know about the Southeast's enthusiasm for Japan. That's why this annual conference has endured for eighteen years.

Our federal government is focusing on reducing the international trade deficit. But individual states, particularly in the Southeast, recruit high-tech, value-added manufacturing investments. Each of the southeastern states represented at this conference have [sic] strengthened their economic ties with Japan, either through exports from local companies or the direct investments from the past twelve years.

We recruited North Carolina's first significant Japanese manufacturing investment, Ajinomoto, located in Raleigh, in 1980.[2] Ajinomoto's amino acid fermentation facility led the way for many other Japanese firms to have confidence in North Carolina's strong business environment. As a result, North Carolina today is home to nearly 140 Japanese-affiliated companies. More than 50 percent are manufacturing or research and development. These companies have invested $1.9 billion and created more than 12,000 new jobs since Ajinomoto first arrived.

Japanese investment in the U.S. was intense during the 1980s, especially in the automotive and electronics industries. The last two years' investment activity has been noticeably less. Reasons: Japan's economic downturn, along with the U.S.; a substantial decline in the value of Japanese real estate and stock market values; a rapid appreciation of the yen against the dollar.

United States Department of Commerce statistics show, in 1988, Japan invested about $16 billion in the U.S. That number dropped to $990 million in 1992.

The past eighteen to twenty-four months have been a time for Japanese industries to absorb their expansions, assess their market direction in the U.S., and focus on improving profits among their subsidiaries abroad.

United States corporations have been slower to invest in Japan. Several major American firms have retreated recently from the Japanese market and canceled their listing on the Nikkei stock exchange. Most U.S. companies point to perceived market barriers that limit penetration in Japan. One exception is Motorola: It is investing in a major new semiconductor chip factory near Sendai. Motorola is well respected in this country as a quality competitor in the semiconductor industry.

Future mutual investment trends between our countries may well depend on economic forces like the appreciating yen/dollar exchange rate, known as *endaka*, and political issues like local-content requirements on value-added products such as cars.

North Carolina's present state of investment: workforce. North Carolina's focus for industrial recruitment is education and worker training; education reform; Smart Start early childhood initiative; workforce training/Commission on Workforce Preparedness; high-skill, high-wage jobs.

---

[1] North Carolina, Alabama, Florida, Georgia, South Carolina, Tennessee, and Virginia were the seven states represented. Tentative Program of Meetings and Events, XVIII Annual Joint Meeting, Southeast U.S./Japan Association . . . October 3-5, 1993, Osaka, Japan, Governors Papers, James Baxter Hunt Jr.

[2] Hunt announced, on January 7, 1980, that Ajinomoto Co., Inc., of Tokyo would build its first U.S. plant in Wake County, North Carolina. The groundbreaking ceremony was held the following March, and the completed facility was dedicated in April 1982. Mitchell, *Addresses of Hunt, 1977-1981*, 648-651, 737-738, 827, 843; Poff and Crow, *Addresses of Hunt, 1981-1985*, 535.

INTRODUCTION OF JAMES CARVILLE: VANCE-AYCOCK DINNER

ASHEVILLE, OCTOBER 9, 1993

One of the best things about being a North Carolina Democrat is coming to the mountains in October for Vance-Aycock weekend. I left Japan yesterday and flew halfway around the world to be here with you.

We have a lot to celebrate, this year. Just eleven months ago, we elected a Democratic president and a Democratic governor, and we restored positive, progressive leadership to America and to North Carolina![1]

The people hired us to do a job, and we're doing the job. Bill Clinton's had some rough spots in the road, but he's on the right track. He's coming back strong now, because he's never forgotten what he was elected to do. He's working to get the economy moving. He fought hard to get the deficit down, and he and Hillary Clinton are fighting hard to see that every American gets the health care they deserve, and it's important that they win that fight!

Here in North Carolina, we Democrats are doing the job we were elected to do. I especially want to recognize all the members of the General Assembly who are here tonight. Our legislature passed an agenda this year that can make our state what it ought to be. We launched Smart Start, and we're going to see that every child in North Carolina gets a good start in life. We started an initiative that can transform our public schools by setting higher standards for what our students learn. We started an aggressive new economic development strategy. We're building 5,000 new prison beds, and we're going to see that criminals serve their sentences in North Carolina!

The Democratic Party here in North Carolina has new leadership, new energy, and new direction. They're combining the best of the old ways—grass-roots politics—with the best of the new: fund-raising, technology, research, and training. They're committed to giving our candidates a new level of professional service, and I want us to show Tom Hendrickson and his entire headquarters staff our appreciation.[2]

Campaigns have changed a lot since I first ran twenty years ago, and nobody in America understands that better than our speaker tonight.

James Carville has become something of a legend, so I'm proud to say I knew him "when."[3]

I first met James when I was running against Jesse Helms in 1984. James was working in Texas for a Senate candidate named Lloyd Doggett, and nobody thought he had a chance. So we planned to get James up here after his guy lost the primary. Well, lo and behold, James worked his magic, and Lloyd Doggett won the primary. So, we lost out on James.[4]

Now, I don't think that's the reason I lost in 1984, because I got 48 percent of the vote in November and James's guy in Texas got about 41 percent.[5] Still, I regret that we never got the chance to unleash James against Jesse Helms. So, James, how about keeping North Carolina in your plans for the North Carolina political campaigns in 1996?

Now James is famous. He's won campaigns for Democrats in Georgia, New Jersey, and Pennsylvania. He was the chief strategist for Bill Clinton last year. He's half of the best-known Romeo and Juliet couple in the history of American politics. He's known for the funny way he talks, and acts, and looks. Normally I wouldn't suggest that somebody looks funny, but James's own fiancée says he looks like he spent too much time standing beside a "nuclear reactor."[6]

I'll tell you something else you probably don't know about James. He served as a corporal in the United States Marine Corps, and that makes him the highest-ranking military officer in the Clinton administration. It's a good thing Sam Nunn didn't know about James's record in the marines. If he did, he'd be against heterosexuals serving in the military.[7]

James is funny, and he is entertaining, and you will enjoy hearing him speak. But there's more than that to James. He brought something special to our party last year. We started to sense it when we heard about the sign in the Clinton headquarters: "It's the economy, stupid." Then we heard about the campaign "war room." Then we saw the Clinton campaign hit back hard every time they were attacked, and we realized that we finally had a presidential campaign that wasn't going to lie down and take that stuff. Yes, they were smart, and tough, and aggressive, but there was something even more important. Bill Clinton, and James Carville, and that campaign knew that politics should be about people, and their families, and their lives. They knew that the way to win is to talk honestly to people, to care about them, to work on solving their problems, and to always put them first. That's what politics at its best is all about, and our speaker tonight is one of the best at it. Ladies and gentlemen, Mr. James Carville.

[1] As Hunt noted, 1992 was a banner year for Democrats: Americans sent a Democrat to the White House for the first time in twelve years, while Tar Heel voters returned Hunt to the Governor's Office after eight years of Republican occupancy. Although incumbent George Bush carried North Carolina by a narrow margin, Bill Clinton won the presidential election with 44 percent of the vote, versus 39 percent for Bush and 18 percent for Ross Perot. Hunt earned a third term as governor, handily defeating Republican opponent Jim Gardner by more than 246,000 votes. *News and Observer*, November 4, 1992; *North Carolina Manual, 1993-1994*, 1004-1005, 1041-1042.

[2] C. Thomas Hendrickson (1957-   ), grew up in Pinetops; B.S., N.C. State University, 1979; J.D., Wake Forest University, 1984. Cofounder, Triangle Environmental Inc., Raleigh, an engineering consulting co.; owner, Hendrickson Properties commercial real estate development co.; fund-raiser for Hunt's 1984 Senate campaign; state director, Al Gore for President campaign, 1988; headed Clinton-Gore campaign in N.C., 1992; state Democratic Party chairman, 1993-1995. *News and Observer*, January 31, 1993, February 12, 1995.

[3] Chester James Carville Jr. (1944-   ), born at Ft. Benning, Ga.; resident of Maurertown, Va.; B.S., 1970, law degree, 1973, Louisiana State University; U.S. Marine Corps, 1966-1968. Practicing attorney, 1973-1979; political consultant, since 1980; managed successful political campaigns for Robert P. Casey, Pennsylvania governor (1986, 1990 elections), Wallace Wilkinson, Kentucky governor (1987 election), U.S. senator Frank R. Lautenberg, of New Jersey (1988 election), Zell Miller, Georgia governor (1990 election), U.S. senator Harris Wofford, of Pennsylvania (1991 election), and Bill Clinton, U.S. president (1992 election); co-author, with Mary Joe Matalin, *All's Fair: Love, War, and Running for President* (1994); Democrat. Judith Graham (ed.), *Current Biography Yearbook, 1993* (New York: H. W. Wilson Company, 1993), 105-108, and *Current Biography Yearbook, 1996*, 344-348.

[4] Lloyd Doggett, a Democrat, was a Texas state senator running for the U.S. Senate. *Current Biography Yearbook, 1993*, 106.

[5] The extraordinary popularity of President Ronald Reagan, who sought re-election in 1984, made the year difficult for Democrats nationally. Republican candidates rode the president's coattails to victory as a landslide swept him to a second term. Looking back on his loss to incumbent Jesse Helms in the U.S. Senate race, Hunt acknowledged having been caught in the "avalanche." Helms garnered 52 percent of the vote to the governor's 48 percent, a difference amounting to just 86,280 votes. In Texas, Lloyd Doggett lost his Senate bid to former Democrat Phil Gramm by an 18 percent margin. *Current Biography Yearbook, 1993*, 106; William D. Snider, *Helms and Hunt: The North Carolina Senate Race, 1984* (Chapel Hill: University of North Carolina Press, 1985), 205-206.

[6] For a listing of Carville's campaign successes, see footnote 3, above. While he guided Bill Clinton's quest for the White House in 1992, his fiancée, Mary Matalin, directed the re-election campaign of President George Bush.

Mary Joe Matalin (1953-   ), born in Chicago, Ill.; resident of Maurertown, Va.; B.A., Western Illinois University, 1978; attended Hofstra University School of Law. Former steel-mill worker; political consultant; held various posts with Republican National Committee, from 1981; served on presidential election campaign of George Bush, 1988, and became political director of his presidential re-election campaign, 1991; co-host, CNBC talk show *Equal Time*, 1993-1996; host, *The Mary Matalin Show*, CBS Radio, from early 1996. *Current Biography Yearbook, 1996*, 344-348.

[7] Sam Nunn, a conservative Democrat who chaired the Senate Armed Services Committee, was at the forefront of other like-minded members of Congress who opposed President Clinton's controversial proposal to lift the long-standing ban against homosexuals in the military. Clinton's position struck a nerve, already raw, among many in the armed forces displeased at his having avoided military service during the war in Vietnam. Nunn and his committee championed a more stringent alternative to the president's plan that constituted little more than a "modest revision" of existing military policy: The prohibition against homosexual conduct would remain, but recruits could no longer be questioned about their sexual preference. Also, a commanding officer would need "credible information" of improper conduct by a serviceman or woman before launching an investigation.

Congress overwhelmingly approved the Armed Services Committee's proposal. President Clinton acquiesced and signed it into law on November 30, 1993, as part of the defense authorization bill, P.L. 103-160. But court rulings late in the year kept both the gay ban and the new policy on homosexuals in the military from being enforced. *Congressional Quarterly Almanac, 1993*, 454-462.

Samuel Augustus Nunn (1938-   ), born in, resident of Perry, Ga.; A.B., 1960, LL.B., 1962, Emory University; U.S. Coast Guard, 1959-1960, and Reserve, 1960-1968. Farmer; attorney; legal counsel, U.S. House Armed Services Committee, 1962-1963; member, Ga. House of Representatives, 1968-1972; U.S. senator from Ga., 1972-1996, and chairman, Senate Armed Services Committee, from 1987; Democrat. Michael Barone and Grant Ujifusa, with Richard E. Cohen, *The Almanac of American Politics, 1996* (Washington, D.C.: National Journal, 1995), 357-358; *Biographical Directory of Congress*, 1578-1579.

UNIVERSITY OF NORTH CAROLINA BICENTENNIAL CONVOCATION

UNIVERSITY DAY

CHAPEL HILL, OCTOBER 12, 1993

Chancellor Hardin,[1] President Spangler, President Friday,[2] Members of the Board of Governors and the Board of Trustees, Friends of the University of North Carolina:

Welcome to the oldest public university in America! President Clinton, I am especially pleased to welcome you here today. It has been thirty-two years to the day since the president of the United States last stood on this ground: President John F. Kennedy, through his acts of political and personal courage, inspired you, and me, and many others to answer the call to public service.[3]

Mr. President, you have answered the call with courage and exuberance. You knew it would be politically dangerous for you to tackle issues like the deficit and health care, but you knew it would be even more dangerous for the country if you ignored them; and so you took up these issues and took on the risks. I salute your courage, and I am honored to welcome you as the first United States president to follow JFK to Chapel Hill.

Here on this platform, in this stadium, and in this university, we have a diverse gathering of people and opinions. Many of us hold different opinions about the political, social, and economic issues of the day. But as Thomas Jefferson once said, "Every difference of opinion is not a difference of principle."[4] We are all here today to affirm the principles that gave birth and growth to America's first public university.

We believe now, as the university founders did 200 years ago, that a society grows freer and stronger when opportunity is spread widely among its citizens; and we believe now, as we did 200 years ago, that a public university can do more than any other public institution to encourage opportunity, and freedom, and democracy. In fact, the founding [of] our university and the founding of our democracy are parallel strands of history. In 1776, when the authors of the North Carolina Constitution called for a public university, members of the Continental Congress signed the Declaration of Independence. In 1789, when the North Carolina General Assembly passed the university charter, North Carolina's state convention voted to ratify the United States Constitution. In 1791, when the North Carolina General Assembly extended a building loan to the new university, the United States formally ratified the Bill of Rights; and in 1793, here in North Carolina there was born a university of the people to challenge, to protect, and to guide the government of the people.[5]

For the last 200 years, Carolina has rewarded the vision of its founders by broadening opportunity and encouraging debate on the public issues of the day—debate that has overflowed the libraries and lecture halls and brought genuine improvements in the lives of our citizens. So while we gather here today to honor those visionary founders of Carolina, we must not hold them too much in awe. We must not imagine their responsibilities any greater, or their capabilities any broader, than our own. We, too, must be agents of change. We, too, must strive to author the next great ideas that will light a new torch of liberty. We, too, must go forth, advancing the bold new ideas of our generation, each idea giving birth to newer ideas, yet each new idea owing its birth to their first idea: a public university in North Carolina. Today, then, let us celebrate this public university. May it continue to bring broad opportunity to our citizens and our state; and may that opportunity bring us closer to the society of freedom and justice to which we are called by our conscience, by our creeds, and by the founders of this University of North Carolina.

---

[1] Paul Hardin (1931-   ), born in Charlotte; A.B., 1952, J.D., 1954, Duke University; honorary degrees; U.S. Army, 1954-1956. Attorney in private practice, 1956-1958; law faculty, Duke University, 1958-1968; president, Wofford College, 1968-1972, Southern Methodist University, 1972-1974, and of Drew University, 1975-1988; chancellor, University of North Carolina at Chapel Hill, 1988-1995; author. *News and Observer*, June 28, 30, 1995; *North Carolina Manual, 1993-1994*, 711.

[2] William Clyde Friday (1920-   ), born in Raphine, Va.; resident of Chapel Hill; B.S., North Carolina State College (later University), 1941; LL.B., University of North Carolina, 1948; honorary degrees; served in U.S. Navy during World War II. President, 1956-1986, president emeritus, since 1986, University of North Carolina; chairman, federal Task Force on Education, under Presidents Johnson and Carter; served on numerous state and national education boards and commissions. *News and Observer*, June 19, 1985; *North Carolina Manual, 1985*, 915.

[3] President Kennedy addressed a University Day audience, October 12, 1961, in Kenan Memorial Stadium, on the campus of the University of North Carolina at Chapel Hill.

William S. Powell, *The First State University: A Pictorial History of the University of North Carolina*, 3rd ed. (Chapel Hill: University of North Carolina Press, 1992), 273.

[4] "Every difference of opinion is not a difference of principle. We have called by different names brethren of the same principle. We are all republicans. We are all federalists." Thomas Jefferson, First Inaugural Address (1801), quoted in John P. Foley, ed., *The Jeffersonian Cyclopedia* (New York: Funk and Wagnalls Company, 1900), 660.

[5] Hunt's list of significant dates leading to the opening of the University of North Carolina is accurate. The Fifth Provincial Congress, meeting in Halifax, adopted North Carolina's first state constitution on December 18, 1776; Article LXI, copied almost verbatim from the Pennsylvania Constitution, instructed the state legislature to establish "one or more Universities." The General Assembly chartered the University of North Carolina on December 11, 1789. Late in 1791, university trustees struggled with lawmakers to obtain a $10,000 building loan. The loan was narrowly approved and later converted into a gift, but it was the last appropriation the General Assembly made for the university until 1881.

Funds in hand, the trustees hired a contractor. The cornerstone of the first building, subsequently known as Old East, was laid October 12, 1793. The University of North Carolina opened officially on January 15, 1795, and welcomed its first student, Hinton James of New Hanover (later Pender) County, on February 12. Kemp P. Battle, *History of the University of North Carolina*, 2 vols. (1907; reprint, Spartanburg, S.C.: The Reprint Co., 1974), 1:17; Hugh T. Lefler and Albert R. Newsome, *North Carolina: The History of a Southern State*, 3rd ed. (Chapel Hill: University of North Carolina Press, 1973), 221, 262-264, 284-285; Powell, *First State University*, 4-5, 13, 17.

CRIME STATEMENT

RALEIGH, OCTOBER 13, 1993

[The following address is similar to one Governor Hunt delivered in Charlotte, October 19, 1993.]

I saw my friend Chrissy Gallaher this weekend. Many of you may remember Chrissy, a vivacious young woman from Winston-Salem who was the victim of a brutal attack a year ago that left her near dead. Today Chrissy is confined to a wheelchair, scarred and battered. But she's fighting hard to regain the life her attacker damaged so badly, and we are fighting with her.[1]

Too many of our friends, and family members, and neighbors have been victimized by vicious criminals. Too many have been damaged, like Chrissy. Too many have died.

Enough is enough. The state of North Carolina must do more to protect our people. As governor, I'm determined to do whatever it takes to keep violent criminals off the streets and behind bars. This week, I'm directing state agencies to take immediate steps to keep more criminals in prison and to protect the rights of victims. But the most important step we can take is to obtain relief from the federal courts. At my request, the state has filed a petition in federal court, today, asking for such relief. We must have more flexibility to put more prisoners in existing space. As crime rates spiral, the federal court order is forcing our Paroles Commission to let criminals out on the street. Our people deserve better, and we must do better by them.[2]

I've already spoken with U.S. attorney general Janet Reno about enlisting the Justice Department's help in this effort. Today I've written a letter asking her to join us in requesting help from the courts. While the court considers our request, we can take emergency measures to respond to this crisis. We must explore every alternative and look for new solutions to old problems. That's my goal, and that's my directive to this administration.

The Department of Correction is now negotiating with Georgia, Tennessee, and New Mexico to rent 1,000 prison beds for North Carolina prisoners. Prison officials were in Georgia on Monday and hope to have an agreement in place in the next few weeks. Once we have such an agreement, we hope to put 1,000 more criminals in prison within forty-five to sixty days. The department is also conducting an inventory of federal and state sites that could be used as prisons. We've identified a number of sites, including old schools, empty dormitories, and nursing homes no longer in use, that could be converted quickly and cheaply to house prisoners.

We should also use temporary buildings. If we can put schoolchildren in trailers, we can certainly put prisoners in temporary housing! The Department of Correction is now seeking to identify funds to build ten Quonset huts, housing up to 1,000 inmates, in the yards of existing medium-security prisons. Correction officials are traveling to Texas next week to assess that state's use of Quonset huts and to determine how we can get the most for our money.

Both of these steps would require new appropriations from the General Assembly. The Department of Correction is working to determine the cost, and we'll be talking with legislative leaders about this.

We must move quicker to build new prisons. The General Assembly agreed this summer to build 5,000 prison beds, including less-costly work farms and boot camps. Yesterday I met with the state's property and construction officers and directed them to speed up the prison construction process. That means site selections, the bidding and review process, are on a fast track—from six weeks to three days, in some cases.

What's the bottom line? We can put more dangerous criminals in prison if we undertake these emergency measures and pursue every single alternative. Correction officials say we'll need 30,000 prison beds by the year 2000. Combining new beds under construction, adding 2,000 beds with the emergency measures I described, and the modification we're seeking from the federal courts, we can reach that goal.

That's the least we can do for Chrissy Gallaher and others like her, and we should make sure we put their rights, victims' rights, first. As of today, the Paroles Commission will begin notifying all victims of violent crimes before their assailants are considered for parole, even if they don't request such notification in writing. This is a small price to pay to make sure people know when a violent criminal is up for parole.[3]

All of the steps we are taking are first steps, steps that we can and must take to tackle short-term problems. But we must also take steps to tackle long-term problems. We must make sure that dangerous criminals serve their full sentences, and we must make sure that we do everything we can to turn young children away from drugs and crime. We must do everything we can, for my friend Chrissy and for every single North Carolinian.

---

[1] Christine L. "Chrissy" Gallaher, of Pfafftown, was abducted on September 16, 1992, as she walked from her car to her job as a receptionist for an accounting firm in Winston-Salem. Her attacker, Ernest Ray Cherry, was scheduled to appear that morning before a Forsyth County District Court judge to answer to eleven counts of writing worthless checks. Needing "money for court costs," he chose a robbery victim at random—Gallaher—forced her back into her Chrysler at gunpoint, drove to a side street, raped her, and stuffed her into the car's trunk. Cherry then headed for Columbus County, leaving a trail of fraudulent credit card transactions and forged checks for investigators to follow. South of Fayetteville, he drove his victim's car onto a secluded dirt road, sexually assaulted and attempted to strangle her, and left her on the ground for dead.

The brain damage Gallaher suffered as a result of the attack banished her to a wheelchair and severely limited her ability to speak. The daughter of John K. Gallaher, a former state Board of Transportation member, had only $2.00 in her purse at the time of the robbery.

Cherry received a sentence of life in prison, plus 100 years, for kidnapping, rape, and attempted murder. A decade earlier, he was convicted of assault by pointing a gun, and in 1985 was sentenced to fourteen years in prison for armed robbery. News and Observer, July 27, 28, 1994; Winston-Salem Journal, September 19, 20, 21, 1992.

[2] Among its requirements the December 20, 1988, settlement of the Small v. Martin prison overcrowding lawsuit called upon the state to provide fifty square feet of living area for each minimum- or medium-security inmate. Hunt, confronted with a prison population rising faster than the availability of confinement space, ordered Attorney General Easley to petition the U.S. District Court to change the settlement agreement. Without more prisons or federal permission to house more inmates in existing space, the state would have to release increasingly dangerous criminals to keep the worst felons incarcerated. News and Observer, November 11, December 12, 22, 23, 1988; press release, Hunt Orders Emergency Measures on Crime, Raleigh, October 14, 1993, Governors Papers, James Baxter Hunt Jr.

[3] Appalled that victims of violent crimes were not routinely notified of their attackers' impending parole hearings, Hunt ordered the state Parole Commission to begin such practice immediately. Victims were to be given every chance to oppose parole, either in a public hearing or in writing. Press release, Hunt Orders Emergency Measures on Crime, Raleigh, October 14, 1993.

MARINE FISHERIES SUMMIT

MOREHEAD CITY, OCTOBER 14, 1993

This is an historic occasion. For the first time in the history of our state, the governor, the Marine Fisheries Commission, and members of the General Assembly are coming together to address a common goal: restoring, protecting, and conserving one of our most important natural resources, our marine fisheries. Our fisheries, and all of coastal North Carolina, face some very real problems, and it's time to focus on those problems. This meeting signifies the importance I want us to place on that issue.

I'm here today because the coast, and the fisheries, are important to me, just as they're important to all North Carolinians. More and more tourists are realizing every year what a wonderful resource we have on the North Carolina coast. They want to surf fish or hire our charter boats, and thousands of people on the coast depend on their business. Commercial fishermen depend even more directly on the protection of our natural resources. From Calabash to Wanchese, generations of North Carolina's family fishermen have gone to the sea and to the sound to support their families.

All of these elements have come together to place a tremendous burden on our marine fisheries. We must act now, before it's too late, because there is no doubt that our fisheries are in trouble. Of the twenty-two species of fish monitored by the Division of Marine Fisheries, many are in trouble. Bob Lucas tells me that fourteen are considered "stressed" or worse.[1] More and more people are fishing and shellfishing, even though fisheries populations have declined or are leveling out. And conflicts between the groups who want to use the resources have erupted, from Manteo to Wilmington. Such conflicts require a tremendous amount of effort, time, and patience to solve. Undoubtedly, conflicts will continue to surface as the pressure on the resource grows.

Now is the time to act decisively. Frankly, our past history with marine fisheries isn't a proud one. We haven't been ready to make the hard decisions. We are in a rapidly changing world; and as in the world of education and business, we have to make the hard decisions and changes to adapt to this world, even if they aren't easy. In the past, there has been valid criticism that we weren't willing to make those hard decisions and stand by them. Now is the time to do that. We can't continue to let opportunities sail by, and we haven't planned for the future. We should be planning right now for the next century, and we haven't even developed a resource plan to take us into the year 2000.

We have a perennial funding crisis in Marine Fisheries. We have to find some creative strategy for funding. We need to explore new ideas, like a saltwater fishing license. We need to look at new partnerships to help us leverage our own resources.

We need to look at making all of government, the Division of Marine Resources included, more efficient and effective. Jon Howes, Steve Levitas, and Joan Weld[2] are already addressing many of these issues in their department, and I have faith that they'll make the right decisions.

I've talked with Bob Lucas, Marc Basnight, Secretary Howes, and Bill Hogarth[3] about my interest in this subject. I know that there are some specific issues that you must address in the near future. I'd like to mention one in particular.

Anyone who reads a coastal paper knows that our shellfish are in trouble. Now is the time to step back and take a comprehensive look at our shellfish resource. We need to work with our university researchers and other agencies on aquaculture development to find new ways to protect this vital resource.

We need to reach out to all North Carolinians to tell them about our marine fisheries resource and to educate them on how important it is, to all of us, to protect our environment, because we're all in this together. The commercial fisherman in Wanchese, the recreational fisherman from Southern Pines, and the family in Asheville that relishes fried flounder— all of them are part of this picture, and we need to reach out to all of them.

That's what this meeting is all about. It's about beginning the process that ultimately will help to restore, protect, and conserve our marine fisheries. That can't be done unless all of us work together. It will take a coordinated effort from this administration, the Marine Fisheries Commission, and the members of the North Carolina General Assembly. The issues are too difficult for any one person or group to solve by themselves.

It's time to build consensus. Commercial fishermen, recreational fishermen, coastal residents, and other concerned North Carolinians all need to be involved. We all need to focus on a single goal: restoring, protecting, and conserving our marine fisheries for the good of everyone. As members of the Marine Fisheries Commission and the staff of the Division of Marine Fisheries, you're on the front line. I'm depending on you to make the tough decisions, and I'm depending on you to carry them out.

Rest assured this governor will be behind you in your efforts. I'm proud to be a part of this historic meeting. I thank Bob Lucas and Marc

Basnight for bringing us together today. Together the work we do can, and will, make a difference for all North Carolinians.

---

[1] Hunt appointed Selma resident Robert V. Lucas to the Atlantic States Marine Fisheries Commission (October 29, 1993-November 27, 1995); the N.C. Marine Fisheries Commission (December 20, 1993-September 30, 1999), which he also chaired; and the N.C. Fisheries Association, Inc., Board of Directors (October 29, 1993-October 24, 1995). Letters of Appointment to Boards and Commissions, Governors Papers, James Baxter Hunt Jr.; *News and Observer*, October 15, 1993.

[2] Joan Weld was assistant secretary for natural resources, N.C. Dept. of Environment, Health, and Natural Resources, until February 1, 1996, when she became Governor Hunt's executive assistant. She worked in Hunt's 1992 gubernatorial campaign and, prior to that, served thirteen years as state director for U.S. senator John Glenn (D-Ohio). *News and Observer*, January 13, 1996.

[3] William Thomas Hogarth (1939-   ), born in Jarratt, Va.; B.S., 1963, M.S., 1965, University of Richmond; Ph.D., N.C. State University, 1976. Marine biologist; career with Carolina Power and Light Co., 1973-1984, included managing the Environmental Technology Section, Harris Energy and Environmental Center, New Hill, N.C.; supermarket owner/operator, Jarratt, Va., 1984-1986; director, Division of Marine Fisheries, N.C. Dept. of Natural Resources and Community Development (later Environment, Health, and Natural Resources), 1986-1994; Republican. *News and Observer*, February 15, 1986, August 15, 1993, August 30, 1994, February 14, 1997.

NORTH CAROLINA LEAGUE OF MUNICIPALITIES

FAYETTEVILLE, OCTOBER 18, 1993

[North Carolinians went to the polls November 2, 1993, to vote in a referendum on five statewide bond issues: $310 million to build new classrooms, laboratories, and other facilities to accommodate growing enrollment on UNC system campuses; $250 million for new community college classrooms; $145 million for water-sewer projects; $35 million to improve state parks; and a constitutional amendment permitting cities and counties to issue economic development financing bonds. Thanks to strong backing from urban voters, all the measures passed except the proposed economic development financing bonds amendment; for more on EDF, see "Jobs/Incentives Statement," April 15, 1993, above.

Although EDF, which Hunt vigorously supported, failed at the polls, the governor nevertheless was pleased with the outcome of the balloting. "'I'm proud of the action that the people of North Carolina took yesterday to invest in our state's future. It will move our state forward when others are falling behind,'" he said November 3. *News and Observer*, November 3, 4, 1993; press release, Hunt Urges Municipal Leaders to Campaign for Bonds, Raleigh, October 18, 1993.

In the weeks prior to the November referendum, Governor Hunt gave his reasons for backing the five bond issues in speeches to the N.C. League of Municipalities (text below); N.C. Economic Developers Association, September 1; Elizabeth City Chamber of Commerce, September 2; Lenoir County Committee of 100, September 15; Business and Industry Symposium, September 22; and

Pitt County Memorial Hospital Dedication, October 29, 1993, Governors Papers, James Baxter Hunt Jr.]

Thank you all for inviting me to address the league and the issues that affect our quality of life in every city across North Carolina. Perhaps the toughest issue facing us in every community is crime. We're seeing crime skyrocket in our communities, and we as leaders of this state must make crime—preventing crime and keeping dangerous criminals off the streets—our number-one priority. It is our responsibility to keep our people safe, and we must explore every single alternative in fulfilling that responsibility. That's why my administration took a number of emergency measures last week:

—The state has filed a petition, in federal court, seeking permission to house more prisoners in existing prisons, and I've asked Attorney General Janet Reno for her help, as well;

—The state is also negotiating to rent 1,000 out-of-state prison beds; we're pursuing plans to house another 1,000 criminals in Quonset huts; and we're searching for buildings we can convert, quickly and cheaply, to prisons.

Of course, keeping dangerous criminals behind bars is not the final answer. These are short-term steps designed to address our overcrowding problem. We need to take a more comprehensive approach to crime, both in terms of prevention and punishment. This may well require a special session of the General Assembly to let us focus on issues like youth crime, alternative sentencing, and funding for emergency prison beds.

But crime is not a problem that state government can fight alone. The same is true of most of the problems facing North Carolina cities. We must work as partners to serve our people efficiently and effectively. That's why I have signed an executive order establishing the North Carolina Local Government Partnership Council, to help make sure the governor and the General Assembly understand and respect the concerns of local governments. I know that unfunded mandates and state-collected revenues are among your top concerns. I am philosophically opposed to the state imposing unfunded mandates on local governments, and I am going to do everything I can to make sure that practice is reduced. Also, this year we took the first step toward restoring and stabilizing local government revenues. State-collected local revenues are coming out of the appropriations process, and you're going to see your revenue growth restored.

The Local Government Partnership Council will help us work together on our common interests over the next several years, but there is a more pressing need that you and I must band together to promote in the next two weeks: Fifteen days from today, the voters of our state will make a momentous decision. On November 2, the people will have a chance to have their say. They'll be able to vote for education, jobs, and progress. As you know, the stakes are high. Fiscal constraints and tight budgets over the last several years [have] meant that we've neglected some of our key assets. We haven't invested in our schools, water systems, and parks the way we should. If we don't invest in our assets now, we won't be able to offer our children the quality public education at our universities, or top-notch skill training at community colleges, they deserve. We'll leave them with deteriorating parks and a declining economy grown stagnant because of anemic infrastructure and job recruitment.[1]

The league has already invested time and money in the bond campaign, and I commend you for your resolutions of support. I also commend you for your assistance in the coordinated campaign and your leadership for clean water bonds and EDF [economic development financing]. But now we must make sure that every registered voter understands the stakes and understands their responsibility to promote education, jobs, and progress in North Carolina. No one can carry the message better than you can. Each of you must reach out to people in your community and urge them to support the bonds. If you use your numbers and your resources across the state, you can be our greatest force and our strongest advantage in this referendum.

Each and every one of you must take responsibility for getting these bonds passed in your community. You must, because you are leaders, and you must lead your community forward. You must lead your people forward. You must lead North Carolina forward for education, jobs, and progress. If you don't, no one will, because no one understands the importance better than you.

---

[1] Reviewing the importance of the upcoming bond referendum, Hunt told an audience on September 22, 1993: "University and community college bonds are crucial to our efforts to produce workers who can excel in the workplace of the 90s. The community colleges are the center for much of our workplace training efforts; and the universities not only offer the best value for your tuition dollar anywhere in America, they also serve as a source of research and development, technology, and highly skilled, highly educated employees.

"To ensure good jobs in North Carolina, we must support clean water and sewer bonds and EDF on the ballot, as well. Water and sewer bonds will improve and expand our infrastructure for new and existing business. Economic development financing bonds [are] also an economic development incentive that will help us bring new companies and new jobs to the state, without additional cost to local governments or taxpayers. It will help both rural and urban counties who want to recruit new industry, but can't afford to build the public infrastructure to attract that industry. It's used in some forty other states, and we need that competitive tool here in North Carolina. And our parks bonds are a simple investment in maintaining the natural resources and natural beauty of our state." Business and Industry Symposium, Raleigh, September 22, 1993, Governors Papers, James Baxter Hunt Jr.

GLOBAL TRANSPARK AUTHORITY

CHAPEL HILL, OCTOBER 19, 1993

The quarterly meeting of the directors of the North Carolina Global TransPark Authority is called to order. As we begin today's business agenda, we welcome all of you who are here today.

This is the first Authority meeting I've chaired at the Kenan Center, and it's certainly a pleasure to be in th[is] fine facility. One cannot be here without being mindful of the many contributions made to North Carolina, and our great university system, by the Kenan family; and of course, the Global TransPark owes a special debt of gratitude to the work done here by Dr. Jack Kasarda, who is with us today. [1]

The GTP has made great strides toward reality since it was born as a concept here at the Kenan Institute,[2] and there have been some significant developments and activities to report since our last quarterly meeting in July. In August, the master-plan team made a presentation at the Friday Center[3] on the alternatives for the initial and ultimate development of the airfield-complex portion of the GTP. That presentation was a major milestone for us. It marked the point in time when our master planning moved from its information gathering phase into the stage where it produces the vitally important data and recommendations that will allow us to make the right decisions about the project.

We'll see an abbreviated version of the August presentation today. You'll have a chance to become fully aware of the options that were available and gain an understanding of the direction now being taken by the master-plan team. Also, we'll receive an update on the private fund-raising campaign conducted by the Global TransPark Foundation in Lenoir County. Felix Harvey and the folks working with him did a fantastic job in the Kinston area, and I want them to share their success story with us. And we'll get an update on the GTP Development Commission established by the General Assembly during this year's session.

But before we get started with those matters and other business, I want to report to you concerning some activities that I've had the privilege to participate in on behalf of the Global TransPark. In mid-September, Rusty and I traveled to Washington to meet with Secretary Les Aspin; his deputy, Dr. William Perry; and other key leaders at the Department of Defense. We were very pleased with the reception we received, and I can tell you that the civilian and military leaders at the Pentagon see a growing number of advantages stemming from North Carolina's Global TransPark. They understand how it can help them accomplish their missions, and that understanding will be of great benefit to us as we move forward.[4]

While we were in Washington, I met with the North Carolina congressional delegation, too, and had a chance to provide our members with an update on the GTP. We will certainly work to keep them briefed on our progress and our needs. They are supportive of what we're doing and will play an important role in our future.

Also, since we last met, I have had the privilege of leading the North Carolina trade mission to Japan. I'm very excited about the potential for developing even stronger relationships with that nation's business leaders. I'm convinced that we have the opportunity to expand our partnership with them in a meaningful way, and I am committed to doing just that. The Global TransPark was among the things I shared with them, and I can report that many of them understand the tremendous advantages that we will be able to offer.

---

[1] The Kenan Center opened in 1987 on the campus of the University of North Carolina at Chapel Hill. The five-story brick building housed the William R. Kenan Jr. Charitable Trust, the William R. Kenan Jr. Fund, and the Frank Hawkins Kenan Institute of Private Enterprise, the last of which Hunt mentioned in the following paragraph; see also footnote 2, below. The director of the Kenan Institute of Private Enterprise, John Dale (Jack) Kasarda, devised the Global TransPark concept and was identified earlier in this volume.

Perhaps no family has been allied more closely, or has been more generous, to the University of North Carolina than the Kenans. James Kenan was appointed, in 1790, to the university's first board of trustees and was an original subscriber to the construction fund to erect Old East, the first building on the UNC campus. Four subsequent generations of Kenans served as trustees, and many family members were graduates of the university. Over the years the Kenans and the philanthropies they established donated millions of dollars to Chapel Hill and other schools in the UNC system, for numerous academic and athletic purposes. William Rand Kenan Jr. (1872-1965), Mary Lily Kenan Flagler Bingham (1867-1917), Sarah Kenan (1876-1968), and Jessie Kenan Wise (1870-1968) were major benefactors, and Frank Hawkins Kenan (1912-1996) was responsible for committing more than $85 million to the UNC system. Walter E. Campbell, *Across Fortune's Tracks: A Biography of William Rand Kenan Jr.* (Chapel Hill: University of North Carolina Press, 1996), 4, 194, 221, 223, 228-229, 240, 241-242, 305-307, 331-332; Marion A. Ellis, *The Meaning of Honor: The Life of Frank Hawkins Kenan* (Chapel Hill: Mrs. Frank H. Kenan, 1994), 15-16, 25-32, 49, 51, 53, 65; Powell, *First State University*, 360.

[2] The Frank Hawkins Kenan Institute of Private Enterprise was established at UNC to foster mutual cooperation between the university and business. Ellis, *The Meaning of Honor*, 48-53; Powell, *First State University*, 360.

[3] The Friday Center for Continuing Education, built just east of Chapel Hill, was dedicated April 12, 1991. Named for President Emeritus William C. Friday and his wife, Ida H. Friday, the structure housed UNC's Division of Continuing Education; offices for Independent Study, Elderhostel, Correctional Education, and other programs; and class- and conference rooms. Powell, *First State University*, 365.

⁴ The GTP site was no more than 90 minutes by road from Seymour Johnson Air Force Base, Fort Bragg, and Camp Lejeune. To the governor, the military benefits of the project were obvious. He also knew that Pentagon support for the TransPark would be crucial in convincing the U.S. Department of Transportation to fund as much of the $450 million project as possible. Hunt's private, half-hour meeting with Pentagon officials in September 1993 left him "optimistic" that he could count on the military's backing. *News and Observer,* October 20, 1993.

Seddon (Rusty) Goode Jr. was identified earlier in this volume.

Leslie Aspin Jr. (1938-1995), born in Milwaukee, resident of East Troy, Wis.; B.A., Yale University, 1960; M.A., Oxford University, England, 1962; Ph.D., Massachusetts Institute of Technology, 1965; U.S. Army, 1966-1968. Staff member, 1960, and director, reelection campaign, 1964, of U.S. senator William Proxmire; staff assistant to Chairman Walter Heller, of President Kennedy's Council of Economic Advisers, 1963; economic adviser to U.S. defense secretary, 1966-1968; assistant professor, economics, Marquette University, 1969-1970; member, U.S. House of Representatives from Wisconsin, 1971-1993; U.S. defense secretary, 1993; Democrat. *Biographical Directory of Congress,* 552; *Current Biography Yearbook, 1995,* 612-613.

William James Perry (1927-   ), born in Vandergrift, Pa.; resident of Alexandria, Va.; B.S., 1949, M.S., 1950, Stanford University; Ph.D., Pennsylvania State University, 1957; U.S. Army, 1946-1947. Mathematician; electronic defense labs director, GTE Sylvania Co., 1954-1964; president, ESL Inc., 1964-1977; managing director, Hambrecht and Quist investment bankers, 1981-1985; chair, Technical Strategies and Alliances [co.], 1985-1993; co-director, Center for International Security and Arms Control, Stanford University, 1989-1993; technical consultant, 1967-1977, undersecretary for research and engineering, 1977-1981, deputy secretary, 1993-1994, was appointed secretary, 1994, U.S. Dept. of Defense. *Who's Who in America, 1997,* s.v. "Perry, William James."

NOTES, NORTH CAROLINA RURAL INITIATIVE

RALEIGH, OCTOBER 20, 1993

[The North Carolina Rural Economic Development Center unveiled the North Carolina Rural Initiative, an $85 million rural economic development package "encompassing business finance, water and sewer facilities, housing, and the delivery of government services," on October 20, 1993. The initiative consisted of nine programs: N.C. Capital Access and N.C. Microenterprise Loan Programs (business loans); Supplemental Grants Fund (source of matching funds needed to obtain some types of economic development grants); Capacity Building Grants Program (assistance in preparing federal grant applications); Rural Home Ownership and Catalyst Rental Programs (assistance to first-time home buyers and development of rental housing, respectively); the Indoor Plumbing Installation Program; an effort to streamline government regulations to speed funds and services to rural areas; and the Rural Information Network "to build awareness among local leaders of the resources available to them for rural development." Estimates by the Rural Center indicated the plan would create 10,000 jobs and supply 4,000 small business loans by 1998, as well as build 150 rental housing units and an additional 200 new homes by 1994.

A partnership among federal, state, and local governments; the private sector; and nonprofit organizations made the initiative possible. The Rural Center provided the impetus behind the plan and was its chief sponsor. Cosponsors included eight banks; Governor Hunt, whose notes for the unveiling are reprinted below; the General Assembly; the state's congressional delegation; U.S. Small Business Administration; U.S. Agriculture Department; Appalachian Regional Commission; N.C. Commerce Department; N.C. Housing Finance Agency; and the N.C. Rural Development Council. Press release, N.C. Rural Initiative Pulls Together $85 Million for Economic Development, Raleigh, October 20, 1993, from Billy Ray Hall, president, North Carolina Rural Economic Development Center, Inc.]

Today the state of North Carolina has had an immense challenge placed before it. We've been challenged to unite forces and on behalf of rural people and places, to bring together the resources of state government, federal government, businesses, and nonprofits. I applaud each of you on this podium for your role in this partnership.

[Hunt names them.]

We've also been challenged to think in new and different ways. Our banks and the SBA [Small Business Administration] are working together on our new Capital Access Program, which will free up as much as $60 million to loan to small businesses in rural North Carolina. In doing this, we put North Carolina [at] the cutting edge of a new way of thinking about rural economic development.

And finally, we've been challenged to target our resources to the people and places that need them most. Early in my administration, I pledged to focus my attention on a few critical challenges. Ensuring that our rural communities can survive, and compete, and prosper is another. The Rural Initiative will help us do that.

Rural North Carolina needs our attention, and it needs it now. It's a matter of human decency. It's a matter of economic necessity.

We can't ask an assembly line worker to perform on the job if she's just spent the night in a cold, run-down house. We can't expect a smart young mechanic to start his own business if he has nowhere to go for financing and business advice. We can't expect local officials to lead their communities into the future if they don't have the tax base to support the public facilities required for growth.

I am a product of rural North Carolina, so I know the challenges and the charms of living away from the big cities. You don't always have the natural gas or the water and sewer infrastructure. You don't always feel like Raleigh is listening to you. But you have the potential for greatness, and this program begins to tap that—not with government giveaways, but together with public and private investment.

We must begin, today, to prepare the whole state to compete in the demanding global economy. I've just returned from Japan and, not so long ago, from Europe. With each trip outside the U.S., I become more convinced that for North Carolina to compete in a global economy, we must work together as a team. We must have all 6,644,000 of our team players suited up, well conditioned, and ready to win. More than half of those players will be from rural North Carolina.

What will it take to win in this game? We must start with a globally competitive labor force. That means deciding we won't give up on a single citizen—young or old, black or white, from the city or from the country. Here in this state we are beginning a program, called Smart Start, that will ensure that every child everywhere in this state gets quality, affordable, preschool education, so that every child everywhere in this state comes to school ready to learn.

I have appointed a Commission [on] Standards and Accountability that will redefine what our students need to know to compete for the jobs of the twenty-first century.

And I am supporting, as I urge all of you to, the bond issues we will be voting on November 2. These bond issues will mean millions of dollars for us to help us develop rural water and sewer systems, rural community colleges. The bonds will help us develop our park systems, our universities, and will help rural counties compete more effectively for new jobs.

We must create a globally competitive business environment. We're starting to do that with a series of prudent, appropriate incentives designed to encourage new and expanding businesses to give special consideration to rural North Carolinians as they develop their plans for the future. These include expanding the job creation tax credit from thirty-three counties to fifty counties and doubling the amount of loans they qualify for. The Capital Access Program and Microenterprise Loan Program give businessmen new reasons to consider rural North Carolina.

We must encourage the development of globally competitive communities. We do that by investing in innovative new projects like the Global TransPark, which I serve as chairman of the board. We do that by investing in new technologies, like the Information Superhighway, which will allow rural communities to access the latest medical or educational information via fiber-optic lines. We also do that by making sure you have the water and sewer lines and solid waste facilities you need to be successful, and by encouraging your local businesses and community leaders to join the fight to make rural North Carolina the best it can be.

The North Carolina Rural Initiative is a daring step forward. It's time for our state to stop being first in outhouses and start being first in rural economic development.[1] We have the leaders in Washington. We have the leaders in Raleigh. Most importantly, we have the leaders in each of your communities. You will be on the front lines of making this program work, and now we have the right plan, too.

Today we begin boosting business growth; creating jobs; improving housing; developing infrastructure; streamlining government services; arming local leaders with much-needed resources. Today we lay the foundation for the future, a future in which all people—whether they live in Swain County, or Hoke, or Halifax; whether they work in a factory, or on the farm, or run a business; whether they are born into poverty or blessed with wealth—can enjoy the fruits of their labor and have the chance to live the good life that only North Carolina can offer.

I believe North Carolina's rural counties represent our state's greatest potential for the future. Today we begin to realize that potential, bringing together your public, and private—and people—resources into one group, united for the future of North Carolina.

---

[1] The United States Census Bureau reported, in 1980, that no state had more homes without indoor plumbing than North Carolina. Ten years later, the study *Living Without the Basics* revealed that approximately 250,000 North Carolinians lived in homes without an indoor bathroom or running water. Among the southeastern states, North Carolina had the largest number of inhabited houses without complete plumbing, and the fourth largest nationally. The number of such homes in some North Carolina counties exceeded totals for entire states.

North Carolina's outhouses posed a threat to public health and the environment. They also symbolized a barrier to rural economic development. Inadequate or nonexistent water/sewer systems often prevented new businesses or industries from locating in economically depressed areas, thus denying unemployed or underemployed residents access to jobs that would boost their standard of living. Lacking those jobs—or a state program to improve homes without indoor plumbing, as proposed by the authors of *Living Without the Basics*— the cost of installing a bathroom in a house, digging a new well or septic tank, or hooking onto a water/sewer system lay beyond the means of impoverished families. Kim D. Connelly and Eric J. Stockton, *Living Without the Basics: The Hidden Water and Wastewater Crisis in Rural North Carolina. A Report by the North Carolina Rural Communities Assistance Project and the North Carolina Rural Economic Development Center* (Raleigh, N.C.: [The Center, 1990]), 3-32; see also *News and Observer*, November 25, 1989, June 2, September 4, 1990, May 25, 1998.

One facet of the Rural Initiative, the Indoor Plumbing Installation Program, had as its goal the elimination of all outhouses in the state by the year 2000. The Community Assistance Division of the state Commerce Department was to make $1 million in grants available to begin the process in 1993-1994. Press release, N.C. Rural Initiative Pulls Together $85 Million for Economic Development, Raleigh, October 20, 1993, N.C. Rural Economic Development Center, Inc.

GLOBAL COMPETITIVENESS CONFERENCE

GREENSBORO, OCTOBER 20, 1993

[The following address is an expanded version of Hunt's remarks to the Commission on Workforce Preparedness, July 12, 1993. Other documents that focus on that topic include: press release, Governor Urges Workforce Commission

to Make Apprenticeship "Top Priority," Raleigh, July 12, 1993; Remarks to State
AFL-CIO Convention, Fayetteville, September (22), 1993; press release, Governor
Hunt to Keynote Skills Training Conference, Raleigh, October 7, 1993; Acceptance
Speech, National Alliance of Business "State of the Year" Award, Washington,
D.C., October 25, 1993; press release, North Carolina Named "State of the Year"
for its Workforce, Raleigh, October 26, 1993; and Student Body Presidents Address,
Raleigh, November 18, 1993, Governors Papers, James Baxter Hunt Jr.

Although this speech was dated October 19, 1993, the governor's weekly
schedule indicated that it was delivered the following day.]

Thank you, Chairman Burkhardt.[1] I am truly pleased to be here this
afternoon at the opening of your conference. I am particularly impressed
to see so many professionals and business volunteers concerned about
workforce preparation in North Carolina: nearly 700 people all gathered
here, together, to discuss how to make the future brighter for our citizens.
As governor, I share your concern and interest in preparing our citizens
for good jobs and enabling our state to participate in a worldwide
economy. If we don't have a world-class workforce, there is no way we
can succeed in a worldwide economy. If we do have a world-class
workforce, there is no way we can fail. We will attract high-skill, high-
wage jobs because they know our workers are the best.

How do we get there? I recently appointed the Commission on
Workforce Preparedness, with Sandy Babb as executive director. The
commission will play a key role in addressing workforce development
policy for the state, and for the first time they will be taking a look at
every one of the workforce training programs in our state. I want them
[to] make sure every dollar is well spent, making sure our workforce
is equipped to compete for the offices, factories, and laboratories of
tomorrow. To do that, I've asked them to concentrate on four major policy
areas. The first is the school-to-work transition.

It's time to face facts: Seventy-five percent of our high school students
do not get a four-year college degree, and half our students who graduate
do not get any further training. Right now, that means that those young
people end up in temporary or low-wage jobs for years before they gain
enough skills to earn the salaries that other workers start out with. But
in the past, we've almost ignored them. We've told them, in one way
or another, that the people we really care about are our college students.

We owe these young workers more. Our challenge is to come up with
a system of school-to-work transition to ensure that every youngster
in high school has available a clearly identifiable, accessible, attractive
path into a good job with a good wage.[2] To do that, we will need the
cooperative efforts of the Department of Public Instruction and local
school systems. Over the next four years, our Standards and Account-

ability Commission will be taking a close look at what our workers need to know to become world-class employees—then demanding that each of our high school students meet those new, higher standards.

We need the involvement of Governor Bob Scott and our Department of Community Colleges.[3] Our fifty-eight community colleges will play a critical role in helping our workers learn the specialized skills they will need to make the transition from school to full-time work. And perhaps most importantly, we can no longer afford to operate without the help, and good ideas, of our state's employers. That's why I've named leaders like Bill Burkhardt to chair our Workforce Preparedness Commission.

But we need to go beyond that. We need business leaders contributing their ideas and expertise all across our state. The commission will be holding public hearings all across the state for the next year, to hear some of those ideas, looking at the ideas of people like Buster Humphreys at National Spinning in "little" Washington, who's started his own apprenticeship program.

Our top business leaders know that it requires time and energy to develop a good training program for young workers. But they also know how hard it is to find good long-term employees. Bill Burkhardt says he had to talk to 850 people the last time he wanted to hire 300, and that was even after he eliminated those who didn't have high-school diplomas! Folks, we can turn that around, but it will take the efforts of every one of us to do it!

The second area I've asked my Workforce Preparedness Commission to concentrate on is on developing high-performance workplaces. Tomorrow's workplace will have fewer middle managers and more workers who will be asked to solve problems on the front lines. It will have more workers who can perform a variety of tasks and fewer who just know how to do one thing. It will have more machines to do the repetitive work and will need people to do the things machines can't do: think and solve problems.

At the Freightliner plant here, work station team members might work for two weeks on a custom truck order, and each of those team members know[s] how to do every task necessary to build that truck. The high-performance workplace is already here in some parts of this state—and will be here soon in the rest of our state. We need to be preparing our workers to join it.

The third area I've asked our commission to study is adult literacy. We can't be so concerned about those who are preparing to enter the workforce that we forget the workers who are already on the job. Eighty-five percent of the people who will be in the workforce in the twenty-first century are already in the workforce today. But the latest results from the National Adult Literacy Survey released last month shows [*sic*] that nearly half of those surveyed were below the necessary level to be considered literate in today's workforce.

The definition of workplace literacy is changing. It's not enough to be able to read and write. A mechanic who's working on a $20,000 car run by a computer must be able to read an instructional manual, operate a computer, and apply that technical knowledge. All of us need to recommit, today, to work to determine how to help our workers get those skills.

The fourth area we must study is how to help the people in our state who are least well prepared for the workplace. Some people call it human asset development. I call it a moral wake-up call. We just can't write off our long-term unemployed or underemployed. We must study how the state and every community can help these people move into more productive work lives.

You may have noticed there is one key element in addressing all of these problems: Government can't do all the work. What works in Charlotte will not work in Avery County. What works for a garage with twenty employees won't work for a factory with 2,000 employees. Our Workforce Preparedness Commission will be going throughout the state to listen, and learn, and put together a blueprint of how we can make changes in the way we deliver workforce training. But beyond that, we will be asking local communities to come up with local solutions to local problems.

I'm pleased to see that so many of the panels for this conference include the people that our workforce programs serve. Whether we call these people clients, or students, or participants, or consumers, it is important that we—as educators, professionals, business volunteers, and policy makers—listen to what real people are saying about the services and training they received. We need to hear their successes and failures and to remember how important these programs are to the people they serve.

We can make a difference. We can change things. Tonight, we recognize those who are already succeeding. I won't be here to personally hand out the Governor's Awards for Excellence in Workforce Preparedness, but I want to thank those award winners right now. They are people on the front lines who are operating programs that are working, and we can learn from their insight, hard work, and dedication—and we must.

You must continue your daily struggles on the front lines to find quality day care or transportation for a young mother, so that she can enroll in training or get to a class to finish her high school equivalency.

You must continue to motivate all those who have lost hope of ever finding a good job with decent health coverage. And all of us must work to justify that hope.

I believe we can create a world-class workforce in this state. Our Workforce Preparedness Commission is a good first step. But the next step is even more important. It involves all of us across the state. We have eager, talented teachers, a new focus on higher standards and accountability in public schools, and a new commitment to [align] education with economic development. We have dedicated counselors, job developers, adult educators, and other professionals devoted to this task. And we have committed business leaders who understand the importance of getting involved in education reform, early childhood education, and workforce training. They know that helping to build a world-class workforce is the most important thing that business leaders, and all of us, can do to build a world-class economy and world-class future.

With your help, we can do that. With your help, we can raise expectations. With your help, we can improve our training programs. With your help, we can help meet the workforce challenge and make the lives of our citizens better for everyone. With your help, we can do great things, and I expect nothing less!

I commend you again for your hard work, and I hope that you have an exciting, productive conference.

---

[1] William C. Burkhardt (1937-   ), born in Cleveland, Ohio; B.S., Florida State University. President, director, National Continental Foods, Jamaica, 1972-1976; president, Bakery Division, Beatrice Foods Co., 1976-1980; president, chief executive officer, Austin Quality Foods, Inc., Cary, since 1980; chairman, N.C. Commission on Workforce Preparedness, 1993-1994; *Snack Food* magazine Executive of the Year, 1995. William C. Burkhardt, letter to Jan-Michael Poff, March 29, 1996.

[2] Apprenticeship programs might hold the key to solving the school-to-work challenge, according to the governor. Hunt told the Commission on Workforce Preparedness that he had "gained a new understanding of the need for world-class apprenticeship programs in my conversations with Mercedes officials. Germany pays attention to the students who aren't college-bound, providing them with sophisticated apprenticeship programs beginning in their early high school years. In these programs, businesses and schools work together to give students the skills they need for the modern workplace. Students get practical, hands-on training that prepares them for good jobs, and employers get skilled, experienced workers right out of high school. Yet our country and our state have virtually ignored these students. In North Carolina, we've invested in our public schools, community colleges, and universities, yet we have virtually no efforts underway to invest in apprenticeship programs." Commission on Workforce Preparedness, July 12, 1993, Governors Papers, James Baxter Hunt Jr.

[3] Robert Walter Scott (1929-   ), born near Haw River, Alamance County; attended Duke University, 1947-1949; B.S., N.C. State University, 1952; honorary degrees; U.S. Army, 1953-1955. President, Scott Enterprises, Inc., and owner, manager, Melville Farms, from

1958; master, N.C. Grange, 1961-1963; lt. governor, 1965-1969, governor, 1969-1973, of N.C.; federal chair, Appalachian Regional Commission, 1977-1979; public affairs consultant, 1982-1983; president, N.C. community college system, 1983-1994; Democrat. *News and Observer*, February 19, 1994; *North Carolina Manual, 1993-1994*, 735.

NORTH CAROLINIANS FOR EDUCATION, JOBS, AND PROGRESS

RALEIGH, OCTOBER 21, 1993

Why is North Carolina's Democratic governor standing alongside one of the state's most distinguished Republicans at a campaign kickoff?[1] This is no ordinary campaign. This campaign is not about political power or partisan politics; this is a campaign for the future of North Carolina. This is a campaign for education, jobs, and progress.

That's why Jim Broyhill has agreed to serve as chairman of our coordinated campaign, North Carolinians for Education, Jobs, and Progress. Senator Broyhill—former U.S. congressman, U.S. senator, and secretary of the North Carolina Department of Commerce—understands the importance of investing in North Carolina's future. He understands that our state must invest in its universities, community colleges, natural resources, clean water, and economic development if we are to build a prosperous future for our children.

But Senator Broyhill isn't the only one who understands that we must vote "Yes" to move our state forward. The people here today are from the public sector, private sector, and nonprofit sector. They are from the east and the west, from urban and rural North Carolina; and while they are all experts on one of our bond issues, each one supports all five issues on the ballot. They are energizing their own constituencies and getting the word out around the state, to the grass roots, that a vote for all five bond issues is a vote for North Carolina's future.[2]

The groups represented here today, and others supporting all five bond issues—the North Carolina League of Municipalities, the Association of County Commissioners, NCCBI [North Carolina Citizens for Business and Industry]—are working in every community across the state to educate North Carolinians about the ballot issues and to push for their passage. Media events, mailings, meetings, rallies, you name it and these folks are doing it, together. They know what's at stake. With that, let me turn the podium over to Senator Broyhill.

---

[1] That "most distinguished Republican" was James Thomas Broyhill (1927-   ), native of Lenoir; B.S., University of North Carolina at Chapel Hill, 1950. Furniture manufacturer;

member, U.S. House, 1963-1986, and Senate, 1986; secretary, N.C. Dept. of Economic and Community Development (now Dept. of Commerce), 1989-1991; Republican. Poff, *Addresses of Martin, 1985-1989*, 105n; Poff, *Addresses of Martin, 1989-1993*, 64n.

[2] At this point, Hunt introduced the following bond backers: State Treasurer Harlan Boyles; Bryan Brooks, president, Davidson Community College; Mayor Floyd Brothers Sr., Washington, N.C.; Vic Hackley, chancellor, Fayetteville State University; Mayor Nancy Jenkins, Greenville; Larry Jones, president, Economic Developers Assn.; Margaret Nygard, executive vice-president, Eno River Assn. and board member, Friends of State Parks; Earline W. Parmon, Forsyth County commissioner; Julia Sain, Cleveland County Schools social worker and member, South Mountains State Park Advisory Council; and Betty Lou Ward, Wake County commissioner and first vice-president, N.C. Assn. of County Commissioners. North Carolinians for Education, Jobs, and Progress, October 21, 1993, Governors Papers, James Baxter Hunt Jr.

GOVERNOR'S CONFERENCE ON AGING

RALEIGH, OCTOBER 27, 1993

Before I begin my remarks, I want to give credit to the many people and organizations who have brought all of us here for the fourth Governor's Conference on Aging. I want to thank Secretary Britt; Assistant Secretary Lynne Perrin;[1] Bonnie Cramer and her staff in the Division of Aging.[2] I also want to recognize Bruce Vladeck, director of the Health Care Financing Administration;[3] Senator Beverly Perdue, whose efforts have brought about our Senior Tar Heel Legislature; John Denning, the chairman of the Governor's Council on Aging;[4] and Horace Deets, the national executive director of AARP.[5] I also want to thank Reverend Mattie Walden and John Gebbie for presenting that moving slide show.[6] These were faces of the people who raised us—our parents, grandparents, great-grandparents. Their wisdom, experience, and guidance keeps [*sic*] us from falling prey to short-sightedness and selfishness. I must confess that with every passing year, I grow more and more respectful of the abilities of older Americans.

Our older people are rich in knowledge, skills, and experience. They have seen the problems and mistakes of the past, and if we listen, they can teach us how to avoid them in the future. Many older Americans are working full-time jobs, and many who are retired spend their time volunteering in the community or serving as caregivers for a parent, a spouse, a brother or a sister. Some spend their free time with their grandchildren, and I'm fortunate to be able to watch my five grandkids grow.

The contributions of older Americans are significant, but so are the needs. You all need to feel more secure in your homes and on your streets. You need a robust economy that will continue to offer jobs for those who work and will continue to support public and private pensions for those who don't. You also need to feel secure about your health care. Today, too many Americans spend their entire lives building financial security only to see it shattered by one serious illness.

Bad health can destroy your finances, and bad finances can destroy your health. Some older Americans don't have the means to pay the difference between what health care costs and what Medicare pays, so they go undiagnosed, untreated, and uncared for. We cannot tolerate this in North Carolina.

Just yesterday I chaired the very first meeting of the North Carolina Health Care Planning Commission. The commission was created by the North Carolina General Assembly, which had the courage to act and the responsibility to know that we cannot wait for the federal government to solve North Carolina's problems. This commission will develop a plan to provide all eligible residents a guaranteed package of comprehensive, medically necessary health care services, including primary and preventive care. These health services will be provided through community health plans that will accept all eligible residents regardless of health or finances. We will no longer accept a system where corporations take the profits from insuring the healthy and wealthy, and taxpayers take the losses from insuring the poor, the sick, and the aged![7]

The Health Care Planning Commission will give special attention to long-term care. The fastest-growing age group in our state is eighty-five and up. This means our need for long-term care in North Carolina is going up.

We must do a better job of managing long-term care. Right now, 80 percent of our public money available for long-term care goes to institutional care, even though a small percentage of those who need long-term care are living in institutions. Long-term care is cheaper and better at home. I say this from the heart. My mother lived at home until the day she died.[8] I thank God we were able to provide that comfort for her, and I think we need a plan that gives that comfort to every North Carolinian that wants it.

You know what we need as well as I do—perhaps better than I do. That's why we're going to include you in our Health Care Planning Commission. I said earlier that the experience of older Americans can save us from shortsightedness and selfishness. Here is one instance where I insist on it. We want your input. We want to listen to your fears and frustrations with the present system and hear your advice and counsel about how to fix it. We look forward to the recommendations that will come from this conference.

With your help, we can build a coordinated, efficient system of services that provides care in the least restrictive environment possible, that brings health care consumers into partnership with service and program providers, and treats our older Americans with the dignity and respect that the world's wisest cultures rightly show their elders. You have all had a hand in building up this great nation and this great state of North Carolina. You have raised a generation; some of you have raised several! If we cannot repay that debt by treating you with respect and dignity in your later years, we will have lost the right to expect that treatment from our children, and we will have lost the sense of community that built a great nation. I promise you that I, and others here today, will not let that happen.

---

[1] Lynne Morrow Perrin (1949-   ), born in Baltimore, Md.; resident of Greensboro; B.A., University of North Carolina at Chapel Hill, 1971. Held increasingly responsible positions with Guilford County Dept. of Social Services, 1972-1981; director, Area Agency on Aging, Piedmont Triad Council of Governments, 1981-1988; Case Management Division director, United Services for Older Adults, Greensboro, 1988-1990; executive director, HealthCare Directions, Inc., 1990-1991; finance team member, Citizens for Jim Hunt, 1991-1992; assistant secretary for aging and special needs, N.C. Dept. of Human Resources, since 1993. Lynne Morrow Perrin, letter to Jan-Michael Poff, April 10, 1996.

[2] Bonnie M. Cramer (1946-   ), born in, resident of Raleigh; B.A., State University of New York-New Paltz, 1972; M.S.W., University of North Carolina at Chapel Hill, 1977. Social worker, Durham County Dept. of Social Services, 1973-1977, 1977-1978; staff development coordinator, 1978-1979, chief assistant to the director, 1979-1982, assistant director for program administration, 1982-1988, N.C. Division of Social Services; deputy director, 1988-1990, director, since 1990, N.C. Division of Aging. Bonnie M. Cramer, letter to Jan-Michael Poff, April 9, 1996.

[3] Bruce C. Vladeck (1949-   ), born in New York, N.Y.; resident of Silver Spring, Md.; B.A., Harvard University, 1970; M.A., 1972, Ph.D., 1973, University of Michigan. Associate social scientist, New York City-Rand Institute, 1973-1974; assistant to associate professor of public health, Faculty of Medicine, and associate professor of political science, Columbia University, 1974-1979; assistant commissioner, Health Planning and Resources Development Division, N.J. State Health Dept., 1979-1982; assistant vice-president, Robert Wood Johnson Foundation, 1982-1983; president, United Hospital Fund of N.Y., 1983-1993; administrator, Health Care Financing Administration, U.S. Dept. of Health and Human Services, since May 1993. Bruce C. Vladeck, letter to Jan-Michael Poff, May 6, 1996.

[4] John Thurman Denning (1911-   ), born in Wayne County; resident of Clinton; B.A., Atlantic Christian College (later Barton College), 1935; M.A., University of North Carolina at Chapel Hill, 1964. Teacher; coach; principal; superintendent, Brunswick County Schools, 1947-1953, and of Sampson County Schools, 1953-1971; development officer, Southwood College, 1971-1972; coordinator, Sampson County Dept. of Human Resources, 1973-1977; AARP national president, 1986-1988; chairman, Duke Hospital Human Development Board, 1990-1993; chairman, N.C. Governor's Advisory Council on Aging, since 1993. John Thurman Denning, letter to Jan-Michael Poff, March 28, 1996.

[5] Horace Deets (1938-   ), born in Charleston, S.C.; M.A., Catholic University. Various management posts with American Association of Retired Persons, including executive director and chief operating officer since 1988. *Who's Who in America, 1996*, s.v. "Deets, Horace."

[6] Mattie Matthews Walden (1924-   ), resident of Siler City; was graduated as valedictorian from Chatham County Training School, 1941; bachelor's degrees in divinity and theology, Teamer School of Religion, Charlotte. Former CPA, Fitts Tax School, and Blue Cross-Blue Shield agent; entered ministry, 1963, at Gees Grove AME Zion Church, Siler City; was consecrated as deaconess, 1965; joined AME Zion Central N.C. Annual Conference, 1968; was ordained as deacon, 1971; pastor, Johnsonville AME Zion Church, since 1971; was ordained as elder, 1972; newspaper columnist; radio, television program hostess; active in civic, religious, and health-related organizations. The Reverend Mattie Matthews Walden, letter to Jan-Michael Poff, April 19, 1996.

John Shaw Gebbie (1931-   ), born in Glasgow, Scotland; resident of Raleigh; B.S., Indiana University, 1954; U.S. Army, 1955-1957. Executive marketing representative, Armstrong World Industries, Lancaster, Pa., 1957-1989, retired; consultant. John Shaw Gebbie, letter to Jan-Michael Poff, April 23, 1996.

Focusing on the long-term care needs of the elderly, the slide show Hunt mentioned featured thought-provoking pictures of the faces of aging North Carolinians. Walden and Gebbie provided commentary. Gebbie, Walden correspondence.

[7] The General Assembly established the North Carolina Health Care Planning Commission with the passage of "An Act to Provide for Health Care Reform Planning, Small Employer Purchasing Groups, Reorganization of State Health Functions into a State Department of Health, the Creation of Community Health Districts, Uniform Health Claim Forms, Hospital Cooperation Agreements, and Health Delivery Improvements." *N.C. Session Laws, 1993*, II, c. 529, s. 1.2, ratified July 24, 1993. Hunt also briefly discussed the purpose of the Health Care Planning Commission in his address to the North Carolina Medical Care Commission, November 10, 1993. Governors Papers, James Baxter Hunt Jr.

[8] Elsie Brame Hunt (1903-1990), native of Rock Ridge, Wilson County; A.B., North Carolina College for Women (now University of North Carolina at Greensboro), 1926; library science certificate, East Carolina University. Taught English in Johnston and Guilford County high schools until 1944, when she returned to Wilson County; retired from Rock Ridge High School as English teacher and librarian, 1962; first woman member of N.C. Board of Health, appointed 1948; Sunday school teacher; Grange leader; homemaker. *News and Observer*, June 1, 1990; Poff and Crow, *Addresses of Hunt, 1981-1985*, 93n.

NORTH CAROLINA QUALITY LEADERSHIP AWARD

CHARLOTTE, NOVEMBER 16, 1993

Thank you all for inviting me here tonight. I am happy to be here for the same reasons so many of you are happy to be here. The success stories of some of the most successful and forward-looking companies in our state are very inspiring and redouble my interest in helping to make state government, public schools, and our private industries as efficient and effective as possible.

I would like to recognize Dr. Bill Smith and the Quality Leadership Foundation for all it does to advance Total Quality principles.[1] The foundation is the champion of Total Quality in North Carolina. It serves as a resource to any group—public, private, or nonprofit—that is looking to use its available talent and resources in a more effective way: to leave no stone unturned and no opportunity unexplored to provide better quality to the customer, more involvement to the employee, and a better return to the investor.

You have heard from Jane Patterson, my top policy adviser, on how we are implementing TQM [Total Quality Management] in state government. You have heard from Tom Houlihan, my top education adviser, about how we are implementing Total Quality Education in our school systems. And we are here tonight to recognize those who have done an exceptional job in implementing Total Quality in the private sector.[2]

I would like to take a moment now to recognize the North Carolina Quality Awards Council and the Committee of Examiners who reviewed the many applications for these awards, and selected the companies we are honoring tonight. The council and the committee include quality experts from both public and private sectors. Not only did they review every application, they also provided each applicant with a written summary of their strengths and areas for improvement in their pursuit of Total Quality. I would like to commend them for their efforts in the service of Total Quality principles, and their contributions to the efficiency, effectiveness, and ultimately the prosperity of the companies who have applied for this award.

The importance of Total Quality Management in today's world cannot be overstated. It used to be that a business in North Carolina could count on selling its goods in North Carolina. But goods are mobile, and companies in other states and other countries can ship their goods in here and compete with our industries for the business of our own citizens.

It used to be that money made and held in North Carolina would be invested in North Carolina. But in today's packet-switched, international telecommunications networks, capital is mobile, and North Carolinians can choose to invest in companies in other states or other countries if that promises a better return.

It used to be that factories and businesses were fixtures in our towns and cities. But even factories are mobile. Local workers can no longer expect a lifetime job at the local plant. That plant can move to any state or country that might offer a greater profit.

In the new marketplace, goods, capital, even construction can be moved anywhere on the globe, so every town, state, and nation is competing with every other town, state, and nation for investment. The state whose companies can use Total Quality principles to take advantage of all the talent, intelligence, and ingenuity of its employees, suppliers, and customers will broaden its tax base, offer more jobs to its people, and enjoy greater prosperity.

The state whose government can use Total Quality principles to take advantage of the insights and innovations of its state employees, and its taxpayers, will improve its efficiency and effectiveness, cut costs, improve service, and maintain a lighter tax burden on its citizens and corporations.

The state whose schools can use Total Quality principles to take advantage of the energy and enthusiasm of its administrators, teachers, cafeteria workers, custodians, parents, and students will be able to cut costs, improve instruction, and graduate better-educated, better-informed workers ready to advance the cause of the government, the business, or the nonprofit that employs them. That's why the Quality Leadership Foundation is sponsoring TQM in state government, TQE in our schools, and the Quality Leadership Award here tonight. If we don't do everything we can to keep pace with the changing economy, we will lose the race for the best jobs, the best companies, and the best quality of life.

Tonight we are recognizing companies whose achievements will inspire all of us, companies that have created a culture of excellence that runs through every employee, from the head of the corporation to the most recent hire. They are committed to continuously improving their processes by listening to customers and suppliers, empowering their workforce, and managing based on facts. These companies know the power of listening—to employees, suppliers, and customers—because they know the power you can unleash and the lessons you can learn when you listen.

I remember visiting a day-care center at East Carolina University this summer to learn about the innovative new programs going on there. I had spent a half-hour or so there and was about to leave when a teacher brought a four-year-old girl to me, telling me she had a question for the governor. She was very shy and kept staring down at her shoes. So I crouched down and asked her what she wanted. After a lot of hesitation, she asked, in a very soft voice, "Do you have a hamster?"

I answered, "Why no, I don't have a hamster, but when I was a little boy, I had a white rabbit." She seemed unimpressed and started to turn away. So I tried to keep her attention and said, "I have horses and cows on my farm, and a little baby calf."

By this time, she had turned away completely and buried her face in her teacher's skirt. Then it hit me, and I said, "Do you have a hamster?" And the little girl spun right around, nodded with a big smile, and started telling me about her hamster!

That little girl had something to tell me, but I had to be smart enough to listen. Folks, you and I aren't a whole lot different from that little girl. We have big ideas inside that will stay inside unless someone listens.

The companies we're honoring tonight are perfecting the art of listening. They are committed to quality. They are committed to learning everything they can from every employee, every supplier, and every customer. They are committed to listening, and learning, and improving—continuously. I am proud to be here, tonight, to honor these companies and all of us who persist and persevere—day after day, week after week, year in and year out—to make the very best product, offer the very best service, and inspire the very best performance we can.

_____

[1] William A. Smith Jr. (1929-   ), born in Parkersburg, W.Va.; resident of Cary; B.S., U.S. Naval Academy, 1951; M.S., Lehigh University, 1957; D. Eng. Sc./Industrial Engineering, New York University, 1966; U.S. Navy, 1951-1955, and Reserve, 1955-1981. Award-winning professional engineer; computing laboratory director, 1957-1967, industrial engineering professor, 1968-1973, Lehigh University; industrial engineering professor, 1973-1997, head, Industrial Engineering Dept., 1973-1982, Productivity Research and Extension Program director, 1975-1984, advanced program development coordinator, Industrial Extension Service, 1985-1995, N.C. State University; president and founder, 1989-1992, chairman, 1992-1995, and president and executive director, from 1995, N.C. Quality Leadership Foundation. William A. Smith Jr., letter to Jan-Michael Poff, May 28, 1998.

[2] Jane Smith Patterson (1940-   ), born in Wilmington; resident of Tabor City; A.B., University of North Carolina at Chapel Hill, 1961. Editor, Science Research Associates, 1967; exec. dir., N.C. Civil Liberties Union, 1967-1969; founder, N.C. Women's Political Caucus, 1971; president, N.C. Democratic Women, 1971-1973; real estate broker, 1972-1977; chair, Guilford County Democratic Party, 1974-1977; Democratic National Committee member, 1976-1980; assistant secretary, 1977-1979, secretary, 1980-1984, N.C. Dept. of Administration; vice-president, ITT Corp., 1985-1989; vice-chancellor, UNC-Wilmington, 1990-1992; chief budget and policy adviser/senior adviser on policy, budget, and technology to Gov. Hunt. *News and Observer*, August 8, 1993, December 28, 1994.

AT&T Custom Manufacturing Services earned a commendation "for its extraordinary success in implementing Total Quality principles," and First Union Home Equity Corporation was commended "for significant quality achievements." The Integrated Circuit Connector Products Division of AMP Incorporated won the North Carolina Quality Leadership Award for 1993. Attachment, North Carolina Quality Leadership Award, Charlotte, November 16, 1993, Governors Papers, James B. Hunt Jr.

NORTH CAROLINA SCHOOL BOARDS ASSOCIATION

GREENSBORO, NOVEMBER 17, 1993

We all know that the future of our state depends on the quality of our schools. Our challenge before us is to produce the very best students we can from every school in every part of the state. I believe the key is setting high standards and helping our children meet those standards. That means making sure they come to school ready to learn, through Smart Start, our early childhood initiative; and making sure they all have access to quality education, with a fully funded Basic Education Program, and fair funding for small and low-wealth schools. The philosophy behind Smart Start, high standards, and fair funding is the same: Every child deserves a chance to succeed!

Next month, we'll be launching our effort to set rigorous new standards. Starting December 14th, the Standards Commission will be holding six hearings across the state: in Winston-Salem, Greenville, Charlotte, Wilmington, Raleigh, and Asheville. The commission will find out what high school graduates need to know and be able to do to compete for high-skill, high-wage jobs. The commission will seek out educators, employers, business leaders, and former students. They need to hear from you as well. I urge you to attend when the commission holds a hearing near your town or city.

But all our efforts to raise standards will be wasted if our children are unsafe in the classroom. Children can't learn in an atmosphere of violence!

We've begun to combat school violence. Based on the recommendations of the Governor's Task Force on School Violence, the General Assembly passed a series of safe schools laws. The centerpiece of our new safe schools laws is the weapons-free school zone. We'll be putting these signs up in schools throughout the state, reminding people of the law. It is now a felony to bring any firearm onto school grounds or to knowingly allow a minor to bring a weapon to school, and it's now illegal for a parent to leave a gun where a child can easily get at it and take it to school. Other safe schools laws improve communication between the authorities and school officials so we can keep our eye on students who might be dangerous.

Last month, our new Center for the Prevention of School Violence opened its doors. This statewide clearinghouse will provide hands-on, technical assistance to schools and communities to help them develop local school violence prevention programs. The center will help schools figure out what works in other schools and other states, and how to put that knowledge to use; and we've set up a grants program so that school systems can apply for up to $100,000 to help finance school violence prevention programs. The center's director is Dr. Pamela Riley. She is the former principal of Dalton McMichael High School, so she knows what educators are grappling with every day.[1]

But the center is just a resource. We must first decide that we are going to do something about school violence! When even one or two people join together for a great cause, their enthusiasm can bring hundreds into the fight. Let me tell you about Jason Hill and Michael Williams, two high school students I met from West Charlotte High. Both suffered the grief of having a close friend murdered. Both of them knew the murderers; and both of them have gotten involved, at West Charlotte High, in Students Against Violence Everywhere—SAVE—because they want to do everything they can to make sure they don't bury another friend.

Jason and Michael's first meeting of SAVE brought out 300 students, and those students set up peer mediation and conflict resolution programs at West Charlotte High. In the first year, SAVE cut in half the number of kids who were caught bringing guns into school, and now other schools across the state and nation have begun to copy this program. This is the kind of innovative, broad-based response we need if we are to win the battle against school violence. Tomorrow, a group of people from schools, government, and the private sector will gather in Raleigh to roll up their sleeves and hammer out a blueprint for bringing SAVE chapters to every school in North Carolina. I urge you to go home and spread the word to your student leaders: Help us keep your schools safe!

Thomas Jefferson once said that our land was the only country where every person would meet invasions of the public order as his, or her, own personal concern.[2] Either all of us will face the issue of school violence as our own personal concern; or it will spread in our schools like a deadly infection, robbing our children of a good education, safe surroundings, and a happy and carefree childhood. Let's join together, forming groups, and clubs, and programs that teach our students how to respond to violence, how to avoid violence, and how to resolve problems without violence. With everything else they're being taught in school, that may be the most important lesson they ever learn.

---

[1] Pamela Lewis Riley (1949-   ), born in Wilson; B.A., Meredith College, 1971; M.A.T., Duke University, 1976; Ed.D., University of North Carolina at Greensboro, 1991. Teacher, High Point Public Schools, 1971-1980; education consultant, N.C. Dept. of Public Instruction, 1980-1991; principal, 1991-1993, Dalton L. McMichael High School, Rockingham County Consolidated Schools; director, from 1993, Center for the Prevention of School Violence, College of Education and Psychology, N.C. State University; author. Pamela Lewis Riley, letter to Jan-Michael Poff, October 2, 1998.

[2] Neither Jefferson's authorship nor the accuracy of the text attributed to him could be verified.

MARTIN LUTHER KING JR. COMMISSION AND NORTH CAROLINA HUMAN RELATIONS COMMISSION

RALEIGH, NOVEMBER 19, 1993

The Martin Luther King Jr. Commission will be holding its first meeting ever this afternoon.[1] The Human Relations Commission just held its first meeting under new leadership this morning, and I welcome the chance to speak for a few minutes on the importance of your missions. The two commissions here today are working to advance one of the most important interests of our nation: racial justice and racial harmony.

Race relations have been our nation's tragic flaw. Even in moments of strength, race relations divided us. They divided us black against white. They divided us North against South. They divided us in our hearts and minds, because we held principles of equality we knew to be right, and yet permitted practices of inequality we knew to be wrong.

But we are making progress. Even before the founding of our republic, some people in this land made their living by wringing their bread from the sweat of African faces. Then came the idea of equality—in the Declaration of Independence. Then came the movement toward equality—in the Emancipation Proclamation. Then came the demonstrations for equality—in the Montgomery bus boycott, and in the Woolworth lunch-counter sit-in, and everywhere people had courage and a passion for justice.[2]

Then came 250,000 people to Washington to demand jobs and freedom. Not black people fighting for black rights, but black and white people fighting for human rights. On that day in 1963, when Martin Luther King wrote the words "I have a dream" into every American heart, he also said: "Many of our white brothers, as evidenced by their presence here today, have come to realize that their destiny is tied up with our destiny, and their freedom is inextricably bound to our freedom. We cannot walk alone."[3]

So we must walk together, and work together, for justice and harmony. It is no longer enough to say all men are created equal. It's time that all men and women are regarded [as] equal. When we win that battle, our power will be more than one force times two; our power will multiply many times, because all the energy we've wasted fighting among ourselves can be focused on the goals that really matter: quality early childhood education, higher standards in our schools, safer homes and streets, good health care, high-wage jobs, and a society of racial harmony "where little black boys and black girls will be able to join hands with little white boys and white girls and walk together as sisters and brothers."[4]

---

[1] State lawmakers ratified "An Act to Establish the Martin Luther King Jr. Commission" on July 23, 1993. The legislation was effective immediately. *N.C. Session Laws, 1993,* II, c. 503.

[2] Two landmark events in the struggle for civil rights—the Montgomery, Alabama, bus boycott and the lunch-counter sit-in at a Greensboro, North Carolina, Woolworth's—had a common link: They were inspired by Martin Luther King Jr. The grass-roots movement

for racial equality began in the front of a Montgomery bus, December 1, 1955, when Rosa Parks refused to surrender her seat to a white passenger. Parks was arrested for flouting the state's Jim Crow laws; the next evening, leaders of Montgomery's African American community met at Dexter Avenue Baptist Church to organize a boycott of the city bus system. Overwhelming support among blacks for the boycott rapidly transformed King, its twenty-six-year-old leader and the pastor at Dexter Avenue, into a national figure.

The boycott and the message of "militant nonviolence" preached by King prompted thousands of blacks and whites to "challenge Jim Crow practices with direct action." Four black freshmen at North Carolina A&T State University took that message seriously: On February 1, 1960, they sat down at the "white only" lunch counter at Woolworth's, in Greensboro, and ordered coffee. The students were determined not to budge until they were served; by week's end their sit-in inspired similar protests in a half-dozen North Carolina towns. As February closed, cities in six other states experienced sit-ins. Historian George Brown Tindall wrote that the four young A&T students "had introduced two of the salient styles of the 1960s: civil disobedience and the youth rebellion, two protean phenomena that would assume many different shapes before the decade ended." George Brown Tindall, *America: A Narrative History*, 2 vols. (New York: W. W. Norton and Company, 1984), 2:1243-1244, 1261, 1282-1284.

[3] "The marvelous new militancy which has engulfed the Negro community must not lead us to a distrust of all white people, for many of our white brothers, as evidenced by their presence here today, have come to realize that their destiny is tied up with our destiny and they have come to realize that their freedom is inextricably bound to our freedom. This offense we share mounted to storm the battlements of injustice must be carried forth by a biracial army. We cannot walk alone." "I Have a Dream," Keynote Address to March on Washington for Jobs and Freedom, delivered August 28, 1963; quoted in James Melvin Washington, ed., *A Testament of Hope: The Essential Writings of Martin Luther King, Jr.* (San Francisco: Harper and Row, Publishers, 1986), 218.

[4] "I have a dream that one day, down in Alabama, with its vicious racists, with its governor having his lips dripping with words of interposition and nullification, that one day, right there in Alabama, little black boys and black girls will be able to join hands with little white boys and white girls as sisters and brothers. I have a dream today!" Martin Luther King Jr., "I Have a Dream" Address, quoted in Washington, *A Testament of Hope*, 219.

NOTES, EDUCATION CABINET MEETING

Raleigh, November 30, 1993

[The notes for the Education Cabinet meeting also appear to be the basis for Hunt's address to the State Education Commission, Chapel Hill, January 27, 1994.]

I promise to be brief in these introductory remarks, but I can't promise to match the legendary brevity achieved by President Spangler in his introduction of President Clinton.[1]

The GPAC study said the single largest problem in North Carolina education is the lack of coordination across our three education systems.[2]

We are spending $6.47 billion this fiscal year in North Carolina in public education, community colleges, and universities. That does not include local money. At $6.47 billion a year, we cannot afford to duplicate services!

We must forge a continuum across all ages and stages—and learn to complement one another, instead of compete with one another.

We are here to do that and to erase the lines that divide our educational missions.

The global economy has forced us to recognize the importance of an educational continuum and of lifelong learning.

This Education Cabinet can be our first step in developing a comprehensive plan for lifelong learning and make it easier for people to come back to school to train and retrain for new skills and new careers.[3]

We also must improve early childhood education, raise standards in our schools, ease the school-to-work transition, and the transition from high school to community college and the universities.

We must acknowledge by the actions we take in this cabinet, that the three educational branches represented here are not distinct—that whatever happens in one has a profound effect on the other two. And whatever happens to all three determines what happens to North Carolina.

I'm looking forward to working with you, and doing whatever I can to bring our educational system into a seamless continuum that serves our people from the cradle to the grave, and makes North Carolina a model for the nation.

---

[1] UNC system president C. D. Spangler introduced Clinton, who spoke at the University of North Carolina's bicentennial celebration, October 12, 1993, in Chapel Hill. The *News and Observer* said of Spangler, "There are not many speakers who can resist orating to 50,000. But the UNC president could. His one-line introduction of President Clinton was exactly right. . . ." *News and Observer,* October 17, 1993; see also *Chapel Hill Herald,* October 14, 1993, and *Durham Herald-Sun,* October 13, 1993.

[2] North Carolina Government Performance Audit Committee, *Our State, Our Future,* included the creation of an education cabinet (pages 51-52) among its proposals to improve public schooling (pages 48-60). The General Assembly followed GPAC's lead and established the Education Cabinet, chaired by the governor and also consisting of the president of the UNC system, the president of the community college system, and the state superintendent of public instruction. See "An Act to Implement the Recommendations of the Government Performance Audit Continuum of Education in North Carolina," *N.C. Session Laws, 1993,* I, c. 393, ratified July 19, 1993.

[3] The Education Cabinet, Hunt said, "will be asked to approve a specific plan of action for articulation issues. These include a standardized transcript, a common data system, an articulation manual for all systems, a community college transfer program, and remediation. We will also take up the issue of early childhood preparation programs, so we have the quality early childhood teaching we need to make sure every child enters our system ready to learn." The governor added, "The General Assembly and the Joint Legislative Education Oversight Committee will be watching our progress closely. As stewards of the taxpayers' money, they have the right to insist on our best efforts; as trustees of our children's education, we have the duty to give them that." Remarks to State Education Commission, January 27, 1994, Governors Papers, James Baxter Hunt Jr.

TELEVISED ADDRESS:
SPECIAL LEGISLATIVE SESSION ON CRIME

RALEIGH, JANUARY 12, 1994

Good evening. A few months ago, a woman pumping gas just three blocks from this Executive Mansion was abducted, brutally beaten, raped, and left for dead.[1] Last month, a twenty-eight-year-old Reidsville woman was murdered by a parolee who'd served a fraction of his nineteen-year sentence.[2] A few weeks ago, a police officer in Kannapolis was gunned down, the third policeman killed in the Charlotte area in as many months.[3]

These aren't isolated incidents. They're happening too often, and North Carolinians are afraid. They're afraid when they go to the mall, when they drive to work, when their kids go to school, and even in their own homes.

They have reason to be afraid. In the last decade, North Carolina's crime rate has gone up from thirty-second to sixteenth out of the fifty states, and violent crimes have increased 75 percent. Last year, Charlotte, Raleigh, and Winston-Salem set new murder records.

The time has come to fight back. The time has come to let the criminals know we're not going to stand for it. We're going to do whatever it takes to make our families, our neighborhoods, and our state safer. That's why I'm calling the General Assembly to Raleigh on February 8 for an emergency special session on crime. It's critical that the legislature focus on this single issue and take strong action to protect law-abiding citizens. Last year the legislature took important steps to fight crime. Lieutenant Governor Wicker, House Speaker Dan Blue, and Senate president pro tem Marc Basnight gave our state strong leadership in that session, and they recognize the need for strong action now.

I will propose three goals for the session:

1. Keep violent criminals behind bars longer and make prison a real deterrent;

2. Make the criminal justice system work better and put victims' rights first; and

3. Provide both tough punishment for young offenders and more help for kids who can be turned around.

I've spent three months trying to learn what we can do. I've talked to people in the system: police chiefs, sheriffs, prosecutors, and judges. I've talked with mothers in public housing communities, ministers, community volunteers, teachers, advocates for crime victims, and youngsters in danger of becoming criminals themselves. I've heard some great ideas, and I've gotten a real education.

* * *

I've concluded that the most important goal is to make sure violent criminals stay in prison longer. The prison system today is no deterrent. We know it, and criminals know it. Too often, criminals walk out of the courtroom laughing. Even with a tough sentence, they can be back on the streets in a matter of months, weeks, or even days. Chances are, they'll commit even more crimes. That is wrong, and we must change it.

Right now, a life sentence for first-degree murder means a criminal is eligible for parole after twenty years. The General Assembly should pass a law eliminating parole for first-degree murderers. That means the penalty for first-degree murder will be either death or life without parole.

I believe we can make the death penalty a more effective deterrent to crime by cutting down the length of appeals. Today it takes the state courts as long as two-and-a-half years to resolve an appeal. We need to reduce that time.[4]

Now first-degree rapists are eligible for parole after twenty years. That's wrong. The General Assembly ought to add a harsher sentence that would eliminate parole so that someone who has committed an especially brutal rape never walks the streets again.[5]

I will ask the legislature to pass a "three strikes and you're out" law. That would mean any criminal convicted of a third violent felony would be sentenced to life without parole.

And we've got to do something about the easy availability of guns, especially for young people. Last year we made it a felony to bring a gun to school and made parents more accountable for leaving guns in children's reach. That law is working today. Young people need to know that it's the law, and they need to tell someone when a classmate brings a gun to school.

We should automatically lengthen sentences by five years whenever guns are used to commit a felony, and we should make it harder for criminals to buy guns. Today a convicted felon can have a gun the day he's released from prison. I will ask the legislature to change the law so a convicted felon can't ever get a gun without going to court for permission.

Longer sentences mean we need more prison space. The General Assembly took strong action last year to authorize 5,000 new prison beds, including two work farms and two boot camps. But if the legislature does not act before March 15, our prisons will be forced to release more than 3,000 criminals. I've heard the details of some of these cases. As your governor, I don't think these prisoners ought to be turned loose.

Here's what we can do to prevent that. We've already begun shipping 1,000 prisoners out of state. In this special session, I will ask the legislature to fund new prison barracks to hold 1,000 more prisoners and to provide money to lease another 500 spaces right away in county jails. We've speeded up the construction of 1,000 additional beds in two new prisons, working overtime to open these prisons three months ahead of schedule.

We will need to change the law to raise the current prison cap, which limits how many people can be kept in prison. So I will ask the General Assembly to raise the cap. That means we can keep thousands of dangerous criminals behind bars who would otherwise be out on the streets.

* * *

Our second goal is to make the criminal justice system work better. We've especially got to do more to help the victims of crime. I will ask the legislature to appropriate almost $4 million for the Victims Compensation Fund—which is now out of money—and more money for the Victim Assistance Network.[6] And I want to make it clear in the law that criminals injured while committing a crime have no right to money from that victims' fund.[7]

To help prosecutors do their job better, I will ask the General Assembly to authorize a computerized criminal justice information system, as recommended by Mecklenburg County.[8]

To help our courts deal with the flood of drug cases, I will ask the General Assembly to permanently fund a pilot drug court in Charlotte that's shown how to process these cases faster. I will also ask the legislature to fund Attorney General Mike Easley's proposal for an intensive program that keeps first-time drug offenders out of jail if they stick to a rigorous treatment and job-training program and stay drug-free. The attorney general has proposed other changes that will enable courts to focus more on serious crimes. I hope the legislature will enact his ideas in this special session.

* * *

Our third goal is to deal with the most disturbing aspect of our crime crisis: juvenile crime. We are seeing more and more violent crimes committed by teenagers. In the last decade, the number of North Carolina juveniles arrested for murder has quadrupled. Over the holidays, a thirteen-year-old in Asheville was charged with raping an eighty-four-year-old woman, and a fifteen-year-old in Durham was arrested for using a sawed-off rifle to commit murder.[9]

We must get tougher with juveniles who commit violent crimes. Today a fifteen-year-old charged with second-degree murder could be tried in the juvenile system, released automatically from training school at eighteen, and have his court record sealed so no one will ever know what he did. We must change all that. Although some dangerous criminals are young, it doesn't make them less dangerous. They ought to be tried as adults, and they ought to be kept locked up as long as they're still dangerous. I will propose legislation to do that. And I will ask the General Assembly for more detention center beds, more training school space, two new wilderness camps to teach hard work and discipline, and a new boot camp for first-time young offenders.[10]

* * *

But we can't wait until kids get into trouble. We've got to start earlier. We've got to do more today so there won't be so many criminals tomorrow.

We've got to attack the real problem. Too many kids are growing up without learning values and discipline. They have no respect for other people's lives or property, no sense of responsibility, no respect for authority, no fear of punishment.

Too many kids are growing up in troubled families, without fathers or role models. They're growing up around drugs, gangs, and violence. They have no education, no job skills, no opportunity, no hope.

I believe lots of these kids can be saved. That's why I've worked hard, as governor, for Smart Start, giving preschoolers a better chance to succeed in school and in life. That's why I've pushed for more discipline and higher standards in schools, better job training for kids who don't go to college, and more job opportunities across our state. And that's why I will ask the legislature, in this special session, to authorize a major new initiative aimed at juvenile crime. I call it SOS: Save Our Students.

Specifically, I want us to begin setting up special after-school programs in North Carolina's middle schools. These years, grades six through eight, are a crucial time for many kids. Parents, educators, and other experts tell me this is the last chance to reach some of these boys and girls before they get into real trouble.[11]

The goal of the SOS program will be to get adults and older teenagers working directly with kids who need help, encouraging them, helping them discover their own potential and possibilities, and most of all, building up their values, their self-esteem, and their chances for success. Churches, community organizations, educators, parents, business people, and volunteers can come together to give kids something to do, something to learn, and someone to learn from. These volunteers can provide challenging, enriching activities between the hours of three and six—everything from helping on homework, computer classes, mentoring, and peer mediation to clubs and sports. They can also provide the kind of guidance all young people need.

Like Smart Start, government will put in some money, but SOS shouldn't be a government program. It should be a community program, and I appeal to every one of you personally to volunteer, to help make it work, and save these kids. In the end, all of us have to take more personal responsibility for keeping children from becoming victims— or criminals themselves.

* * *

Tonight I've outlined an approach to crime that I believe will work. It includes tougher punishment and more effective prevention. It can make a difference, and I hope you'll ask your legislators to put aside partisanship and support it.

But government alone can't make us safe. Each of us must work to make our families, our communities, and our state safer. As parents and as citizens, we've got to do a better job of teaching our kids to value hard work, respect for others, and personal responsibility.

I know we can do it, because I've seen you doing it. Just this week, I saw servicemen and -women in Goldsboro spending an afternoon helping kids from troubled families with homework. I've seen police officers in Winston-Salem and Wilmington working around the clock to help single mothers make public housing communities safer. I've seen Charlotte business leaders rallying the African American community to serve as role models for young boys.

And I've seen the kids who need your help. A few months ago, I visited a program called Durham Companions. I met a little boy named Tyrone. He lives in a neighborhood that's plagued with drugs and crime. He's had uncles and cousins killed. He saw his father shot and killed. He's only ten years old. In a few years, Tyrone could end up a crime statistic himself, if we don't reach him today.

We can reach Tyrone, and we can reach thousands of children like him. We can make a difference in these kids' lives and their communities, and that can make a difference in our lives and our communities. We can change their future, and we can change our future. We can save these kids, and we can save our families, our communities, and our state. It's up to you and to me.

[1] A 23-year-old art student was abducted from a Raleigh gas station, near the Executive Mansion, on October 23, 1993. She was raped repeatedly, bludgeoned with a pistol, and robbed of all her cash—a mere $7.00. The teenaged perpetrators, brothers Bobby and Jarmal Myers, were convicted of kidnapping, rape, and assault, and each was sentenced to two life terms in prison. The older of the two Myerses had just been paroled after serving four months of a five-year, common-law robbery sentence. *News and Observer*, January 12, 1994.

[2] Sherry Lynn Wyatt was slain December 1, 1993, in her Reidsville apartment. Her killer was among thirty-four parolees who had been charged with murder in the last half of 1993. *Greensboro News and Record*, January 14, 1994.

[3] Hunt was referring to Kannapolis police officer Roger Dale Carter. See "Special Session on Crime," February 8, 1994, above.

[4] The governor sought to consolidate "appeals in death penalty cases to limit the length of the [appeals] process, but the General Assembly took no action" during the special session. Press release, Hunt Asks N.C. Delegation to Shorten Appeals in Murder Cases, Raleigh, January 30, 1995, Governors Papers, James Baxter Hunt Jr.

[5] Hunt backed S.B. 3, "An Act to Provide that a Person Convicted of a Rape or Sex Offense that the Court Finds to be Especially Heinous, Atrocious, or Cruel shall be Sentenced to Life Imprisonment Without Parole," which passed the senate on February 28, 1994. The measure languished in a House committee through the end of the special legislative session. *N.C. Senate Journal, 1993, Extra and Regular Sessions, 1994*, 16, 71, 81, 82, 85, 475; press release, Letter to House Members, Raleigh, March 15, 1994, Governors Papers, James Baxter Hunt Jr. H.B. 39, another bill the governor supported, lengthened prison sentences for first-time rapists and sex offenders from eight and one-half years to sixteen years. The penalty for aggravated rape and sexual assaults committed as second offenses was increased to life without parole. *N.C. Session Laws, 1993, Extra and Regular Sessions, 1994*, c. 22, secs. 2-4; press release, New Crime Session Laws to Take Effect, Raleigh, September 29, 1994, Governors Papers, James Baxter Hunt Jr.

[6] The Crime Control and Prevention Act of 1994 replenished the Victims Compensation Fund in the amount of $3.8 million. The Victim Assistance Network received $150,000 for F.Y. 1994-1995. *N.C. Session Laws, 1993, Extra and Regular Sessions, 1994*, c. 24, secs. 4, 28.

[7] "An Act to Require the Crime Victims Compensation Commission and its Director to Deny the Claim of a Person who was Participating in a Felony or a Nontraffic Misdemeanor at or About the Time the Person's Injury Occurred," *N.C. Session Laws, 1993, Extra and Regular Sessions, 1994*, c. 3, was ratified February 28, 1994.

[8] Legislators appropriated funds to study the feasibility of a Criminal Justice Information Network under c. 24, s. 13, *N.C. Session Laws, 1993, Extra and Regular Sessions, 1994*.

[9] A thirteen-year-old boy broke into the home of an elderly Asheville woman late on Christmas night, 1993. He demanded money, beat her savagely with a cane, and raped her. Sheriff's deputies charged him with first-degree burglary, assault with intent to kill, first-degree rape, and attempted first-degree sexual offense. Because he was under age 14, the perpetrator could not be tried as an adult. As a juvenile offender, neither his name nor any judgments made in his case could be made public under state law. *Asheville Citizen-Times*, December 30, 31, 1993, January 1, 2, 5, February 20, October 1, 1994. The Durham murder could not be verified.

[10] *N.C. Session Laws, 1993, Extra and Regular Sessions, 1994*, c. 24: Section 5 authorized $750,000 for two wilderness camps and reserved $1.6 million for a 24-bed juvenile detention center. Section 19 provided over $1.5 million for a new boot camp for youthful offenders—the IMPACT (Intensive Motivational Program of Alternative Correctional Treatment) facility was scheduled to open during the 1994-1995 fiscal year.

[11] "Studies show that neighborhoods with after-school programs show reduced drug use, reduced juvenile crime, and less teenage pregnancy, and they have a positive impact on parental involvement and school performance," Hunt said. "Similar programs are being launched, right now, all over the state, but a few model programs are not enough. Without aggressive leadership on the state level, we will continue to have isolated programs in

North Carolina that are not available to the children in the next county or the next neighborhood. We must make these programs available to every child in North Carolina!" SOS Talking Points, Raleigh, February 22, 1994, Governors Papers, James Baxter Hunt Jr.

PRESS CONFERENCE ON CRIME-FIGHTING PROGRAM

RALEIGH, JANUARY 13, 1994

Last night I laid out a program designed to keep dangerous criminals behind bars longer, make the criminal justice system work better, and develop a new approach to juvenile crime that includes tough punishment for young criminals and more help for kids who can be turned around. Today I'm releasing a plan with thirty-six specific recommendations that I will ask the legislature to pass when it comes to Raleigh for the special session. This legislative package builds on a solid foundation that the General Assembly laid last year. Under the leadership of House Speaker Dan Blue and Senate president pro-tem Marc Basnight, the legislature took strong and effective action to provide truth in sentencing, increase prison capacity by almost 5,000, and to keep guns out of schools. The General Assembly also deserves credit for what it did during the previous eight years. Most of the leadership, initiative, and ideas to deal with our prison crisis and our crime problem during that time came from the legislature.

Speaker Blue, Senator Basnight, Lieutenant Governor Dennis Wicker, and Attorney General Mike Easley have all been strong leaders in the effort to make our state safer and to deter our youngsters from crime. They know that we can't solve crime in one session, in a long session, or a special session. They know a new set of laws can't solve crime. They recognize the challenge facing all of the state's leaders, and they're willing to roll up their sleeves and get to work.

The legislative package that I'm presenting to the legislature will provide for tougher punishment and stronger deterrence. It will give our prosecutors new weapons to keep violent criminals behind bars longer. It recognizes that some violent juveniles are criminals, and it treats them appropriately. But it also boosts alternatives to incarceration for juveniles with two new wilderness camps and a new boot camp for sixteen- to twenty-one-year-olds. I'm directing Secretary Robin Britt to conduct an in-depth evaluation of our training schools to make sure we're providing our youngsters with the vocational and skill training they need to have a better chance for success.

On the prevention side, the legislature addressed the root causes of crime last year by passing my Smart Start initiative, pushing forward with education reform, and strengthening economic development in all regions of the state. Now I'm asking the General Assembly to help me launch a major crime prevention initiative, called Save Our Students, or SOS. We need to give troubled kids in the middle school years the same kind of boost we're giving preschoolers with Smart Start. I'm asking that the General Assembly provide $10 million to set up SOS programs in half of our 250 middle and junior high schools in the coming school year, and the other half in the 1995-1996 school year. And we need to challenge North Carolinians across this state to rally around their middle school students to make the SOS program a success. I'll ask the state's leaders to help me do this.

I'm recommending that we expand a program, championed by Representative Dave Diamont, to increase the number of coaches as mentors and bring them into conflict resolution, peer mediation, and violence-prevention efforts in middle schools.[1] Representative Diamont is also pushing for a statewide public education campaign to increase community involvement in crime prevention, and I support an approach like that. I also support establishing family resource centers at elementary schools in every single county across this state, which Senators William Martin and Beverly Purdue, and Representatives Anne Barnes and Aaron Fussell, have been pioneering.[2]

To make the court system work better, I'm recommending that the General Assembly adopt Attorney General Mike Easley's court reforms.[3] And to deal more effectively with drug and alcohol offenders, I'm recommending that the state lease a 500-bed facility for serious drug and alcohol offenders and triple the capacity of the DART [Drug and Alcohol Recovery and Treatment] program for habitual DWI [driving-while-impaired] offenders, as advocated by Lieutenant Governor Dennis Wicker.[4]

This is an ambitious agenda, but I believe we can enact this package into law without unnecessary delays and without partisan rancor. I've been talking with legislative leaders of both parties, and I'm gratified by the response. I'm working with legislators on some of the details, and we will continue to work together during the special session. At the same time, I will be traveling across the state to mobilize support for the plan and to urge North Carolinians to help make a difference in their own communities. My office is already getting dozens of phone calls from people who want to be part of this effort. I take both crusades very seriously.

There are some people who believe that punishment alone is the answer to our crime problems. There are others who believe prevention alone is the answer. We need both. If we fail to do both, we will certainly fail. If we can address both punishment and prevention, and get thousands of people involved in changing the lives of our children, we can make a difference.

Making a difference carries a price tag, in this case about $90 million. As some have said, this is a "whopping big package." But it's nothing compared to the cost of crime. As the *N&O* has documented, the cost of a single shooting can climb to $1 million.[5] In the last six months of last year, thirty parolees were charged with murder. What's the price tag for that—not just in money, but in human suffering? I believe we can take steps in this special session that will save our people that cost and suffering.

Governor Hunt's Crime Fighting Plan

I. Keep Dangerous Criminals Behind Bars Longer and Make Punishment a Real Deterrent

A. Longer Sentences for Violent Criminals

1. *Abolish parole for first-degree murderers:* Right now, a life sentence for first-degree murder means a criminal is eligible for parole after only twenty years. That's not enough. Those who commit first-degree murder should never set foot outside a prison. I will ask the General Assembly to pass a law eliminating parole for first-degree murderers.

2. *Toughen sentences for first-degree rapists:* The toughest sentence for first-degree rape is life, which can mean less than twenty years actual time served. This is wrong. I'm recommending that the legislature change the law so that juries have the option to sentence the most brutal rapists to spend the rest of their lives in prison.

3. *Eliminate good time and community service parole:* Prisoners now receive time off their sentences for good behavior and can be released on parole to perform community service after serving as little as one-eighth of their sentences. As a result, some criminals' sentences are cut in half. While structured sentencing guidelines will change that in 1995, there is no need to wait. I'm recommending that good time and community service parole be eliminated now for violent felons.

4. *Three strikes and you're out:* Too many repeat offenders are being released into North Carolina communities. Consider these statistics: The North Carolina Department of Justice says that, over a three-year period, almost two-thirds of the criminals who walk out of North Carolina's prisons are re-arrested. The average felon serves one-fifth of his sentence. In the last six months of 1993, thirty parolees were charged with murder.

I'm recommending that criminals who are convicted of three separate violent felonies go to prison for life, with no chance for parole.

5. *Strengthen habitual offender statute:* The new structured sentencing law will weaken provisions designed to increase sentences for people who commit three or more lesser felonies. Beginning next year, all class H, I, and J felony convictions—crimes such as assault with a deadly weapon with intent to kill, and child abuse—[would count] as one felony, even if multiple crimes were committed. This would hamper prosecutors' ability to put repeat offenders behind bars. We should restore power to the habitual offender statute.

6. *Make cocaine possession a felony:* Another provision of the structured sentencing law will reduce the sentence for possession of less than a gram of cocaine to a misdemeanor offense. Now possession of any amount of cocaine is a felony. Weakening drug laws is not the path North Carolina should take. I'm recommending that the General Assembly change the law to keep the felony offense in place.[6]

B. Toughen Gun Laws

We must make guns less accessible, especially to young people. The General Assembly passed a set of safe school laws last year, making it a felony to bring a firearm to school and making parents more responsible for keeping guns out of the reach of school-aged children. That law is being enforced today, and police officers tell me it's working.

We must also look at other ways to keep guns out of the hands of criminals. I support the Brady Bill passed by Congress, and during my gubernatorial campaign I supported placing limits on semi-automatic assault weapons like the ones used by drug dealers. I will consider any other measures that could be effective in lessening crime and saving lives.

1. *No guns for felons:* North Carolina has one of the weakest gun laws in the nation. It allows convicted felons to keep guns in their homes or businesses the day they leave prison. After five years, that felon can have a gun anytime, anywhere. Attorney General Easley has called for a change, and I agree. The General Assembly should change the law so that a convicted felon can never have a gun without petitioning the courts.

2. *Longer sentences when guns are used:* Attorney General Easley has proposed that we send a clear signal to criminals. If you use a gun to commit a crime, you will do extra time. I agree. I will recommend to the General Assembly that we automatically add five years to a criminal's sentence when he uses a gun while committing a felony.

3. *Destroy confiscated weapons:* After a crime is committed, law enforcement officers confiscate weapons used in that crime. Many times, the guns are auctioned off. Too often, these guns end up back on the streets. I'm recommending that the legislature change the law to require that these guns be destroyed or returned to their rightful owner, if stolen.[7]

C. Increase Prison Capacity

North Carolina's prison overcrowding crisis is rapidly worsening. Right now, the Department of Correction has 1,400 more prisoners than capacity allows. Some 600 new prisoners are being admitted into the system each week; about 400 are being paroled each week.

Last year, the General Assembly authorized 5,000 new prison beds, including two work farms and two boot camps as I recommended. But we need more space now. On December 15, North Carolina triggered the prison cap, giving the state just three months to reduce its prison population to 20,758. Correction secretary Franklin Freeman says as many as 3,400 dangerous prisoners must be released by March 15 unless prison capacity is raised by then. We must increase prison capacity by at least 3,000 to avoid that. That's why I'm recommending that we—

1. *Build 1,000 new beds:* We must build 1,000 new beds as quickly as possible. The most cost-effective option is to build four, 208-man barracks and two, 104-man barracks, cutting red tape to speed up the construction process. Through an accelerated construction schedule, we could put prisoners in these new facilities within eight months. (Cost: capital, $21.5 million; operating, $15.5 million per year)

2. *Lease county jail space:* County jails now hold prisoners awaiting trial and prisoners serving sentences of 180 days or less. Right now, some 500 county jail beds are available that the state could lease. The state would pay counties up to an average of $40 per day, per inmate. This would save the state substantial funds while allowing the counties to recover their costs. (Cost: $8.3 million per year)[8]

3. *Ship 1,000 prisoners out of state:* Department of Correction officials have already shipped 105 prisoners to Rhode Island and Oklahoma to serve the remainder of their time and are negotiating additional contracts with additional facilities. Our goal is to ship a total of 1,000 prisoners out of state so we can use those beds to make sure dangerous prisoners remain behind bars. All told, North Carolina will pay an average of $60 a day to house these prisoners out of state, compared to $64 per day to house medium-custody prisoners in state. While the state does incur some transportation costs, that is more than offset by the millions we save in construction costs. (Cost: $25 million per year)

4. Add 500 beds for drug and alcohol users: I'm recommending that the state lease 500 treatment beds for inmates who need drug and alcohol treatment. This would effectively free up 500 beds in state prisons for other criminals. (Cost: $5.2 million per year)

5. Expand DART program: Lieutenant Governor Wicker has proposed expanding the Drug and Alcohol Recovery and Treatment (DART) program, adding 270 beds for drug and alcohol habitual offenders. I will ask the legislature for funds to provide 270 more treatment beds for substance abuse offenders. This will free up additional beds in our prisons for more dangerous and career criminals. (Cost: $2.2 million per year; $1.4 million capital)

6. Use existing space more efficiently: About one-third of our state's prisons are not governed by legal agreements, giving the state more flexibility with use of space. The Department of Correction has looked for and found ways to house more inmates in existing space, enabling us to add 500 beds to our current prison capacity. (Cost: $1.6 million per year)

7. Speed up construction of 1,000 new beds: At my directive, we have already speeded up the construction of South Mountain Correctional Center, a 712-bed, single-cell facility in Burke County, and Lumberton Correctional Center, a 312-bed prison in Robeson County. As a result, these are scheduled to open in the spring, three months early, to help accommodate our increasing prison population. (Cost: no additional appropriation needed)

D. Raise the Prison Cap by 2,000

In 1987, the General Assembly established a prison cap to limit the number of prisoners that North Carolina's state prisons could hold at any one time. When the cap is broken, the North Carolina Parole Commission is forced to release criminals before they serve their full sentences. To accommodate the additional prison beds that I'm recommending, and to avoid triggering the prison cap, I will ask the legislature to take immediate action to raise the cap by 2,000.

II. Develop a New Approach to Juvenile Crime

A. Deter Children from Becoming Criminals

1. New after-school program for middle-school students, Save Our Students: I am recommending a major new initiative aimed at preventing juvenile crime, called Save Our Students—or SOS. I will recommend that the General Assembly provide funds to begin setting up after-school programs in every North Carolina middle school and junior high school. Educators, parents, and other experts say that the middle school years, grades six through eight, are the last chance to reach many of our troubled children to turn their lives around.

The goal of SOS will be to get adults and older teenagers working directly with kids who need help, encouraging them, building up their self-esteem, strengthening their values and broadening their horizons, as well as their chances for success. I will urge churches, community organizations, educators, parents, business people, and volunteers of all ages to come together to help provide middle-schoolers in every community with challenging, enriching activities between the hours of 3:00 P.M. and 6:00 P.M. I envision SOS programs in every community, offering everything from homework assistance, computer classes, mentoring, and peer mediation to clubs and sports. Most importantly, I believe SOS volunteers can provide the kind of guidance these young people need.

Like Smart Start, SOS will be a public-private partnership, with the state serving as catalyst but the community making each program work. Like Smart Start, we'll look to communities to come together to develop the best plan for their middle-school children, using local ideas, energy, and resources. I'll recommend that each SOS program be set up and run by a neighborhood council. Neighborhood councils should include local community leaders, students, parents, and educators from that community and will be appointed by local county commissioners and school boards. The neighborhood council would develop, monitor, and implement an after-school program targeting that community's middle school; recruit volunteers; and be accountable with biannual reports to its school board and county commissioners. In addition, the SOS program will be overseen by an interagency steering committee that includes representatives from the Departments of Public Instruction, Human Resources, and Crime Control and Public Safety; the House and Senate Education committees; the Attorney General's Office; the North Carolina Child Advocacy Institute; the North Carolina School-Age Care Coalition; and representatives appointed by the governor, House Speaker, senate president pro tem, state superintendent, and attorney general.

I will recommend that the General Assembly provide grant money so that SOS programs can be started in half of our state's 250 middle schools and junior high schools by the start of the 1994-1995 school year, and the other half the following school year. The middle school communities suffering the greatest crime problem ought to be given first priority for the coming school year. (Cost: $10 million in 1994-1995, $20 million when fully funded)

2. *Finance family resource centers:* Smart Start is designed to give preschoolers the boost they need. SOS is designed to reach out to middle-school students who may be at risk. We must complete that circle by making sure we reach out to address the needs of elementary schoolers and their families.

Last year, Senator William Martin, Representative Anne Barnes, and other legislators have pioneered [*sic*] the idea of family resource centers at, or near, elementary schools across the state, and I commend them for their leadership. Family resource centers would serve as one-stop clearinghouses to provide critical services for families, including child care for young children, after-school child care for elementary students, and would provide parents with health care, referrals to community agencies, and parenting training.

Only by empowering families can we truly make a difference in children's lives. Family resource centers should be a model in this area. I will ask the General Assembly to provide funds to set up a model family resource center in each county. (Cost: $4.3 million in 1994-1995; $8.5 million per year after that)

3. *Build wilderness camps to help youngsters turn their lives around*: North Carolina currently sends some nonviolent juveniles to its four wilderness camps as an alternative to training school. At these remote camps, juveniles learn the value of teamwork, discipline, and hard work, and they build self-esteem and confidence. During the yearlong program, students learn to build their own living shelters, cook their own meals, and plan their own activities—including their own educational activities. The program is designed to provide youngsters with the tools to lead a more responsible and disciplined life. I will recommend that the General Assembly provide funds to build two additional wilderness camps, each serving 60 children who may otherwise be sent to training schools. (Cost: capital, $150,000; operating, $3.2 million each)

4. *Build new boot camp for youthful offenders:* North Carolina is now building one additional boot camp, and expanding another, for first-time, nonviolent, youthful offenders. Boot camps can teach young people the discipline and hard work of life in a military boot camp. These beds will triple our present capacity. Experts say the military atmosphere and training of boot camps, like the IMPACT [Intensive Motivational Program of Alternative Correctional Treatment] program in Richmond County, can help get first-time offenders between sixteen and twenty-one back on the right track. We should build one additional boot camp to provide ninety more beds. (Cost: $1.5 million per year; $1.1 million capital)

5. *Expand mentor training programs for coaches:* The Department of Human Resources, in partnership with the North Carolina High School Athletics Association, now operates an innovative training program for high school coaches to better equip them to help today's children. Championed by Representative David Diamont, a high school football coach, the program teaches coaches how to become an even greater positive influence for young people. Representative Diamont has recommended that we expand this program to include peer mediation, conflict resolution, violence prevention, and other efforts targeting middle schoolers. I will ask the General Assembly to provide that funding. (Cost: $250,000 per year)

6. *Expand the Governor's One-on-One program:* The Governor's One-on-One program matches at-risk children with adult mentors and now provides $20,000 each to forty counties to help defray the cost of these programs. I propose that we expand the program to sixty-five counties and increase funding so that each county receives $30,000 to operate these critical programs. (Cost: $1.2 million per year)

7. *Evaluate state training schools and community-based alternatives program:* We need to take a hard look at North Carolina's training schools and make sure they are teaching our youngsters the education and job skills they need to succeed in life. Training school can be a positive learning experience, and we should make the most of our chance to help these children. They should be learning a trade or job skill that will help them become productive citizens in addition to learning about conflict resolution and other daily life skills.

At the same time, we need to evaluate our community-based alternatives program, which now provides $10 million in grants to counties to boost their programs serving youngsters referred by the court system. We need to make sure that each dollar is being well spent and that our children are being well served. In both cases, I will direct the Department of Human Resources to conduct a detailed study of each program and come up with recommendations for change.

B. Tougher Punishment for Young Criminals

1. *Expand detention center beds:* When juveniles are awaiting trial in the juvenile system or waiting to be placed in training schools, they are held in detention centers. Right now, these detention centers are badly overcrowded and understaffed. In fact, overcrowding in our detention centers reached an all-time high last month. Department of Human Resources officials recommend we add sixty detention beds to the system, for a total of 236 beds. Adding staff to the Mecklenburg County detention

center would let us add twelve beds with minor renovation costs. Another forty-eight beds could be build in other parts of the state, depending on facilities and need. I will ask the General Assembly for the appropriate funding. (Cost: $487,360, operating; capital, $3.2 million)

2. *Expand training school beds:* North Carolina's training schools, which serve as jails for juveniles convicted in juvenile court, are also overcrowded and lack sufficient staff to fill the available beds that some schools do have. Right now, space for 147 training school beds is not being used because there is no money to hire the required staff. With additional staff, DHR could reduce crowding in detention centers and serve students in training schools more effectively. (Cost: $6.7 million per year)

3. *Try violent fourteen- and fifteen-year-olds as adults:* Over the holidays, a thirteen-year-old in Asheville was charged with raping an eighty-four-year-old woman, and a fifteen-year-old in Durham was charged with using a sawed-off rifle to commit murder. More juveniles are committing serious crimes like murder, rape, assault, and burglary. Most times, the courts don't treat them as adults. Currently a fifteen-year-old charged with second-degree murder can be tried in the juvenile court system, sentenced to training school, and be automatically released by age eighteen. He can then have his record sealed so that future court officials will never know what he did. I believe judges and prosecutors ought to have all the information at hand about an adult criminal's prior record, especially regarding violent crime. I will recommend that we open court records for juveniles who commit violent felonies.

I will also recommend to the General Assembly that fourteen- and fifteen-year-olds who commit violent felonies be automatically tried as adults. That way, they can be sentenced to prison and serve a complete sentence. And judges, at their discretion, should be able to try thirteen-year-olds in adult court if they commit violent felonies.[9]

4. *No release before eighteen for violent juveniles:* Now a juvenile convicted of a violent felony can be released from training school anytime before age eighteen. That's not right. We should change the law to require that juveniles who commit violent felonies stay in training school until their eighteenth birthday.[10]

III. Make the Criminal Justice System Work Better

A. Put Victims First

1. *Add $3.8 million to the Victims Compensation Fund:* Crime victims can never be truly compensated for their suffering. Many of them not only suffer physical or emotional trauma that hampers their daily lives, but

also must endure high medical bills, lost wages, and other financial hardships. The Victims Compensation Fund was established to help crime victims overcome the financial burden following a crime, but the fund ran out of money last month, with six months left in the fiscal year, causing longer delays for victims who need help. Due to lack of funds, some crime victims have been waiting for two years or more for assistance. Although the General Assembly provided $500,000 in additional funds in the 1993 session, that's not enough. I'm recommending that the General Assembly provide $3 million to handle unpaid claims and appropriate enough money every year to pay victims what they deserve. (Cost: one-time, $3 million; recurring, $800,000)

2. *Add $150,000 to Victim Assistance Network:* The Victim Assistance Network promotes the rights and needs of victims of violent crime, providing an information and data referral bank, initiating public policy debates and initiatives, and holding statewide education conferences. I'm recommending that the General Assembly appropriate additional money to the network, through the Governor's Crime Commission, so the organization can better conduct its critical work. (Cost: $150,000 per year)

3. *Prevent criminals from using the Victims Compensation Fund:* An administrative law judge ruled recently that a man shot by a convenience store owner after robbing the store should be eligible for restitution from the Victims Compensation Fund. Common sense tells us that criminals who are injured due to their own criminal behavior should not have access to money set aside for victims. I'm recommending to the General Assembly, with Attorney General Easley's support, that the law be changed so that criminals cannot profit from their crimes.

B. Speed Up the Process and Eliminate Loopholes

1. *Speed up death sentence appeals:* Right now, state courts hearing death penalty appeals are taking as long as two and a half years. When the federal appeals process is factored in, an appeal can take as long as fifteen years and tie up our court system. Attorney General Easley has recommended that appeals be consolidated to limit the length of the process. I will recommend that the General Assembly make this change in the law.

2. *Set up statewide criminal justice information system:* If a hard-core criminal is arrested in Mecklenburg County tomorrow, the local judge or prosecutor may not know that he has been convicted of other crimes in other counties. We must tie together existing databases and networks so that everybody can identify dangerous offenders. That requires an

integrated criminal justice information system. I'm recommending that the General Assembly provide funds to develop a broad-based system as recommended by Mecklenburg County. Such a system would link law enforcement agencies with the data they need. (Cost: $500,000 in 1994-1995; $500,000 in 1995-1996)

3. *Make criminal evidence from seat belt checks admissible:* While the Click It or Ticket campaign to increase seat belt usage is saving lives, it could also be used to apprehend criminals more effectively. Although state law enforcement officers arrested twenty-two fugitives and numerous other criminals during seat belt checks last year, some judges have interpreted the law to mean that evidence gathered during seat belt checks is not admissible in court. The General Assembly should change the law to make it clear that any evidence of a crime found in the car during a seat belt check can be used in court.

C. Deal More Effectively with Drug and Alcohol Offenders

1. *Permanently fund Mecklenburg County's drug court:* Mecklenburg County has set up a pilot drug court designed to streamline the heavy flow of drug cases. With a special judge, public defenders, prosecutor, and court staff, this drug court hears only drug and alcohol cases and has taken a significant burden off Mecklenburg County's other courts. It has speeded up resolution of drug cases and lessened the load of other courts. I'm recommending that the General Assembly provide permanent funding to this effort. (Cost: $4.4 million per year, $111,396 in 1994-1995)

2. *Establish drug treatment programs for first-time offenders:* To stop the revolving door of drug offenders, our state needs a treatment component. Attorney General Easley has proposed an innovative effort in our district courts, modeled after a successful program in Miami. This is an intensive program that keeps first-time drug offenders out of jail if they stick to a rigorous, year-long substance-abuse treatment and job-training program under court supervision. Failure to pass a drug test or to complete any portion of the program would land the offender in jail. This new approach could rehabilitate first-time drug offenders as well as free up valuable prison space for more dangerous and violent criminals. I'm recommending that the General Assembly provide funding for five pilot programs in North Carolina. (Cost: $800,000 per year)

3. *Lease 500 substance abuse treatment beds:* We also need to boost the treatment and rehabilitation component for more serious drug offenders. By leasing beds at an existing facility, we can provide that treatment for hard-core offenders without incurring capital costs. So I will recommend that the General Assembly lease 500 beds to treat drug and alcohol abusers. (Cost: $5.2 million in 1994-1995)

4. *Expand DART program:* Lieutenant Governor Wicker has advocated that we boost treatment for habitual DWI and drug offenders, and I commend him for his leadership. The DART program offers an intensive twenty-eight-day treatment program for offenders who would otherwise be sent to prison and released almost immediately. By participating in DART, offenders can work to overcome substance abuse problems and reduce recidivism. Lieutenant Governor Wicker has recommended that the state nearly triple the capacity of the DART program by adding 270 new treatment beds. I will recommend that the General Assembly provide that funding. (Cost: operating, $2.2 million per year; capital, $1.4 million)

---

[1] The General Assembly approved $534,000 to expand the Coach Mentor Training Program of the N.C. High School Athletic Association during 1994-1995. *N.C. Session Laws, 1993, Extra and Regular Sessions, 1994,* c. 24, secs. 4, 32.

[2] William Nelson Martin (1945-   ), born in Eden; resident of Guilford County; B.S., N.C. A&T State University, 1966; J.D., George Washington University, 1973. Attorney; co-founder, 1982, board member, and first president, One Step Further, Inc.; member, state senate, from 1983; board member, from 1986, N.C. Public School Policy Forum; chair, 1988-1989, N.C. At-Risk Children and Youth Task Force; member, numerous other boards and commissions; Democrat. *North Carolina Manual, 1993-1994,* 408.

Aaron Eleazar Fussell (1923-   ), born in Rose Hill; resident of Raleigh; A.B., Atlantic Christian (later Barton) College, 1946; M.Ed., University of North Carolina at Chapel Hill, 1952; U.S. Army, 1943-1945. Retired educator, Wake County schools superintendent; member, N.C. House, 1979-1994; Democrat. *News and Observer,* July 11, 1994; *North Carolina Manual, 1993-1994,* 502.

Senator Beverly Perdue and Representative Anne Barnes were identified earlier in this volume.

[3] Attorney General Easley proposed shifting the case loads in criminal courts to ensure the swifter execution of justice. The most serious offenders faced superior court trials; the cases of lesser felons would move from superior court to district court, and "hundreds of thousands of minor infractions" would be heard in magistrate's court, rather than district court. He also advocated special drug courts, stricter gun-control measures, and "streamlining death penalty appeals." *News and Observer,* November 1, 5, 1993, February 11, 1994.

[4] *N.C. Session Laws, 1993, Extra and Regular Sessions, 1994,* c. 24, s. 20, expanded prison substance abuse programs by up to 100 inmates in each of five correctional facilities.

[5] *News and Observer,* January 2, 1994.

[6] "An Act to Repeal the Provision in the Structured Sentencing Act That Would Have Provided That Possession of Less Than One Gram of Cocaine was not a Felony and to Provide for Deferred Proceedings and Expunction of Records for First-time Simple Possession of Less Than One Gram of Cocaine," *N.C. Session Laws, 1993, Extra and Regular Sessions, 1994,* c. 11, ratified March 14, 1994.

[7] See "An Act to Amend the Laws Regarding the Confiscation, Forfeiture, and Disposition of Firearms," *N.C. Session Laws, 1993, Extra and Regular Sessions, 1994,* c. 16, ratified March 15, 1994.

[8] On February 4, 1994, Hunt announced in Morganton that the state would lease beds at the Burke County Detention Center to hold eighty inmates. "Agreements like this one are a tremendous help to us as we search for the prison beds we need to help keep the people of North Carolina safe. We need to do more to take advantage of this kind of creative cooperation between county and state," the governor said. "I hope this agreement is just the first in a series of leasing arrangements with county jails throughout the state. The problem is too severe to let any of our resources go unused."

⁹ *N.C. Session Laws, 1993, Extra and Regular Sessions, 1994,* c. 22, secs. 25-30, allowed juveniles aged thirteen or older at the time they allegedly committed an offense, which would have been considered a Class A felony were it perpetrated by an adult, to be tried in superior court as adults.

¹⁰ Neither H.B. 29, "A Bill to Provide for Commitment of Juveniles Adjudicated Delinquent for Certain Felony Offenses to Age Eighteen," nor its similarly titled senate counterpart, S.B. 29, escaped committee to become law during the special session. Legislators did, however, assign the issue of confining violent juveniles in training school, until age eighteen, to a study commission. Governor Jim Hunt's Crime-Fighting Plan: Special Session Summary, attachment to Special Session Statement, Raleigh, March 25, 1994, Governors Papers, James Baxter Hunt Jr.; *N.C. Senate Journal, 1993, Extra and Second Sessions, 1994,* 20, 64, 90, 91, 94, 100.

"REBUILDING AMERICA" CONFERENCE

New York City, January 20, 1994

I am honored to take part in this outstanding conference and to debate one of the critical issues facing our nation today. There's more to rebuilding America than bricks and mortar. But without bricks and mortar, we can't lay the foundation for better schools, better jobs, and safer communities.

I'm here as governor of the finest state in the nation. My job is to promote North Carolina and to bring good jobs to our state. I'm happy to talk to you all about our state's industrial recruitment opportunities after this panel. But I'm also here as chairman of the North Carolina Global TransPark Authority. The authority is a state agency working in concert with the private sector and other elements of government to develop a unique project: North Carolina's Global TransPark.

The Global TransPark is a model for twenty-first century industrial and transportation infrastructure. We know that to "rebuild America," we must be innovative. We must be bold. We must address the needs of tomorrow today. This is the foundation upon which we've built the Global TransPark.

Like many of North Carolina's innovations, such as the world-renowned Research Triangle Park, the Global TransPark was conceived in our state university system. In the late 1980s, Dr. Jack Kasarda, the director of the University of North Carolina's Kenan Institute of Private Enterprise, determined that innovative business practices, technological advances, and changes in global trade were combining to reshape commerce. The competitive advantage belongs to companies that respond rapidly to shifting market opportunities. Innovation and flexibility are key in the twenty-first century, and speedy, reliable delivery—of information as well as people and products—are requirements, not goals.

These changes carry opportunities for companies and opportunities for states like North Carolina. Dr. Kasarda realized that opportunity in his vision for a new manufacturing and distribution environment. North Carolina is realizing that opportunity in our Global TransPark.

Conceived in the '80s, the TransPark was born in the '90s, when a bipartisan group of legislative and executive leaders came together to establish a state authority with the power to develop the project. The authority handled the nuts and bolts: commissioning a technical feasibility study of the Kasarda concept, selecting a site, and preparing a master plan that will be released tomorrow. The master plan is really the action plan, proposing infrastructure development and land use for a 15,000-acre site in eastern North Carolina.

North Carolinians don't just sit around and think up great ideas— we turn ideas into action! Now let me pause for about six minutes to show you a videotape that illustrates our exciting project.

(Videotape plays.)

I want you to remember that the Global TransPark won't be an air cargo airport. It will be much more, and it will be the first. It will be a cutting-edge response to the needs of the new global marketplace. It will be a world-class industrial and transportation complex, combining access to the best technology with immediate links to the global market, and it will set a new benchmark of public-private partnership.

I want to emphasize the significance of the public-private partnership. Using "government speak," three entities exist right now to support the TransPark:

—*The Global TransPark Authority.* This is a state agency with statutory responsibility. I serve as chairman of the authority's board of directors, and Tom Bradshaw, of First Boston Corporation, who is certainly no stranger to many of you, is the board's vice-chairman.

—*The Global TransPark Foundation.* This is a private, nonprofit corporation that has been established to provide support to the authority.

—*The Global TransPark Development Commission.* This is an official coalition of twelve counties surrounding the GTP site, which will provide funds for economic development-related improvements.

The TransPark gets marketing support from the state Department of Commerce and significant highway improvements from our Board of Transportation; and the FAA [Federal Aviation Administration] has provided $1 million for several groundbreaking research studies into various aspects of the project, and is the lead agency on our master plan. So far, some $285 million has been committed to the GTP by federal, state, local, and private sources. Without question, private participation in the development of the TransPark is vital to our success.

The Global TransPark Foundation is the heart and soul of our private efforts, with 501(c)(3) status and a $30 million fund-raising goal. The foundation will soon begin to put its resources to use on behalf of the authority. Among the activities it contemplates are land options and land banking; land-oriented location incentives; site improvements; special activities on behalf of the GTP—things better left to a private arm.

But the private-sector role goes beyond the scope of the foundation. When it's fully developed, the Global TransPark will have 10,000 acres under private development; manufacturing and distribution sites; shops, stores, and lodging. Government will do what it does best: provide the infrastructure and support that businesses need to operate most efficiently. That's the North Carolina way.

In North Carolina, we're excited about the prospects for the Global TransPark. You can see why we feel that way. I invite you to North Carolina to learn even more about the TransPark and about our state's other industrial opportunities. Come see for yourself!

FREIGHTLINER CORPORATION PRESS CONFERENCE

CLEVELAND, JANUARY 24, 1994

The news is simple: Freightliner, which already provides some of the very best manufacturing jobs in North Carolina, is providing 800 more. Freightliner currently employs 3,227 workers in North Carolina. Its financial success here has led it to boost its North Carolina workforce to 4,004 by 1996. This will make Freightliner one of the top twenty largest manufacturing employers in our state.

This job announcement is not just good news for Freightliner workers. It's good news for workers at Rockwell Axles, in Asheville, who will be making more axles for Freightliner. It's good news for Cummins Engines, in Rocky Mount, who will be making more engines for Freightliner. And it's good news for the surrounding economies where the new workers will spend the high wages they earn at these plants.

But Freightliner and the state of North Carolina have another announcement. You all know that Freightliner will complete $35 million in improvements in its three North Carolina plants this year. That is a major investment in North Carolina's economy.

Today I am announcing another major investment: in North Carolina's workforce. The state of North Carolina will build a training center, at a cost of $3 million, to train Freightliner workers and thousands of workers all over the state. And we are committing an additional $3.6 million over the next three years to operate the center.

This is the first step in a higher level of economic development for North Carolina: using technology to train our workers to compete for world-class jobs. You've heard me say that North Carolina is not going to compete in the global marketplace on the basis of tax breaks, gimmicks, and giveaways. We're going to compete by investing in our people and our skills. We're going to make sure we can get the best jobs in North Carolina by making sure our workers can do the best jobs.

In North Carolina, we have 50,000 workers producing car parts, equipment, and supplies. We have another 50,000 in industries that supply the auto industry—like textiles, electronics, and machinery. This center can be the first in a series of "Centers of Excellence" that can help train and retrain these workers. This is not a new idea. GPAC [Government Performance Audit Committee] and the Commission on the Future of Community Colleges have recommended regional training centers like this one.

Freightliner will control the scheduling at this center, but it will be available for the training of many other workers in the state. Rowan-Cabarrus and Gaston Community Colleges will provide instructors and support for the center and will make use of it for their own students. The computer technology at the center will allow Freightliner to screen potential employees, train and retrain employees, perform task analyses to help design courses that will train workers for specific jobs, and provide training in safety and general manufacturing practices.

The impact of this center will be multiplied by its hookup with the North Carolina Information Highway.[1] The highway will be the first in the world that can transmit computer words, graphics, video, and voice communications. This will provide workers in distant areas what we call "access to excellence."

Now I want to conclude my remarks and bring forward the man whose commitment to the quality of his products, and the quality of his workforce, have [sic] made his company the number-one truck manufacturer in North America: Jim Hebe.[2]

---

[1] The Freightliner Training Center was "the first industrial application of the N.C. Information Highway," the governor said. "In conjunction with our community colleges and other educational institutions, this center will help train Freightliner's employees and other workers throughout North Carolina via the Information Highway." Freightliner Training Center Dedication, Cleveland, N.C., May 18, 1995, Governors Papers, James Baxter Hunt Jr.

[2] James L. Hebe (1949-), born in Liberty, Pa.; B.S., Lycoming College, 1971. Chairman, president, CEO, Freightliner Corp., Portland, Ore., and chairman, Freightliner of Canada, Ltd.; began career in trucking industry as fire truck salesman for American LaFrance, Elmira, N.Y., 1971; owner, general manager, Kenworth of Tampa, 1978-1984;

national sales manager, 1984-1987, assistant general manager for sales and marketing, 1987-1989, Kenworth Corp., Seattle; sr. vice-president of sales and marketing, from January 1989, executive vice-president, from April 1991, president and CEO, from April 1, 1992, Freightliner Corp. Denise Lane, administrative assistant to James L. Hebe, letter to Jan-Michael Poff, August 12, 1999.

TOTAL QUALITY MANAGEMENT CONFERENCE

RALEIGH, JANUARY 25, 1994

It is heartening to know there is so much interest in Total Quality principles. It is especially encouraging to see that interest among managers in state government. Making state government efficient and effective is one of the top priorities of my administration, and I believe if we adopt the same Total Quality principles that have helped bring Ford Motor Company and other corporations back to prosperity, we can provide world-class service to our customers: the citizens of North Carolina.

I believe it, because I have seen these principles in the private sector. Just yesterday I was down in Rowan and Gaston Counties to announce 800 new manufacturing jobs at the Freightliner plants. In this economy, any corporation that's adding manufacturing jobs has got to have an edge, and Freightliner does. It is the number-one truck manufacturer in North America, and it's achieved that by knowing its customers and empowering its employees. Freightliner's customers have had trouble recruiting and retaining top truck drivers, so Freightliner has custom designed a line of trucks that have greater comfort, productivity, and livability; and they are also helping their customers with driver training!

They also empower their workers. I learned yesterday that the Gastonia plant's door manufacturers recently proposed a reorganization that increased productivity by 100 percent. That's what good workers can do for a company, and that's why we also announced yesterday that North Carolina is building a state-of-the-art training center with Freightliner that will train their workers, and thousands of others across North Carolina, in the latest automotive technologies. This training center will help bring out more employee-led suggestions for improved quality and productivity.

Many of you have followed TQM [Total Quality Management] principles in your own workplaces and achieved similar results. I want us to do it all across state government in North Carolina, but we can't do it alone. We need the people who've made TQM work in the private sector help us make it work in the public sector, and we are getting that help. In fact, Gene Godwin, who is manager of employee involvement at Sprint, and who will be speaking at 10 o'clock today, is the facilitator of the Governor's Task Force on Re-engineering Government.[1] This task force, which includes my top policy advisor, Jane Patterson; my state employee ombudsman, Blanche Critcher; and SEANC executive director Bob Berlam,[2] is mapping a blueprint for introducing TQM across state government.

This spring, every one of my cabinet secretaries will join me in several days of training in TQM principles. In total, over 120 managers in my administration will go through this training and begin applying these principles in their departments and divisions. As soon as we begin seeing the results of TQM, I will visit different departments to meet with workers who've had success with these principles and encourage all workers to keep working at it.

But to achieve broad success in this program, we have to have the support of all our managers. I can assure you I will deliver the cabinet secretaries. I want you to work hard to help us enroll everyone else. TQM in state government is every bit as important as TQM in our corporations. If we can provide better service for fewer dollars, we can help restore our taxpayers' faith in government. This is not just about saving some money. In the long run, it's about saving the strength and vitality of our democracy.

I commend you for your interest in Total Quality, and I commend you for taking your time today to come to this conference. Do your best to get everything you can from it, because we've got a lot of work to do together! Thank you, and have a good conference.

---

[1] Gene Godwin (1936-   ), born in Kenly; resident of Rocky Mount; A.B., Barton College, 1958; N.C. National Guard. Career with Sprint/Carolina Telephone included district commercial manager in Roanoke Rapids, 1961-1969, and New Bern, 1969-1979; corporate communications manager, 1979-1983; manager, employee involvement, 1983-1998; and internal consultant, from 1999. Gene Godwin, letter to Jan-Michael Poff, February 17, 1999.

[2] Robert A. Berlam (1936-   ), born in Providence, R.I.; bachelor's degree, Rhode Island College, 1958; M.A., University of Rhode Island, 1965; Ph.D., Nova University, 1974. Government relations director, National Assn. of State Boards of Education, 1976-1978; managing director, Close-Up Foundation, 1978-1984; staff and faculty development director, N.C. Dept. of Community Colleges, 1985-1989; executive director, State Employees Assn. of North Carolina, from 1989. *News and Observer*, November 5, 1992.

CENTER FOR WORLD LANGUAGES
AND CULTURES BOARD MEETING

RALEIGH, FEBRUARY 2, 1994

This is a great day for North Carolina. In fact, if I used an "okay" sign to show you what I thought about the Center for World Languages and Cultures, you'd all understand I thought this project was a great idea. But if I were speaking in Japan, an audience would think I meant it was too expensive. If I was in France, they'd think I meant it was worthless—and in Brazil, they might take a swing at me!

Knowledge of the cultures and languages of countries we do business with is more than a matter of being polite, these days. It's a necessity. We need to know our friends' languages and business styles, and what they care about, to know what their needs are—and it is vitally important to our economy. Last year, North Carolina exported more than $10 billion worth of goods. Seven hundred seventy foreign companies, from thirty-seven foreign countries, do hundreds of millions of dollars worth of business in North Carolina every year and employ thousands of people. More than a quarter-million North Carolinians do not speak English at home and may need some help learning it.

The World Languages and Cultures Center shows our state recognizes these facts and is addressing them to help all of our people. The furniture manufacturer in High Point who needs to understand the German market will get help. The technician from the Triangle, repairing a switch in the Czech Republic, can acquire a few words and simple skills to make the job go better and faster. Young people who want to improve their job prospects will have a place to go to learn a language as quickly and efficiently as possible. A judge in Cumberland County mediating a family dispute between a Spanish-speaking couple will have someone to assist her. Foreign-language teachers will have a place to go to hone their skills.

This center will succeed because of the need for it and because of the dedication of this distinguished group of leaders. This is a true public-private partnership, bringing together leaders from the government, business, and nonprofit sectors, from public and private colleges and universities. State and federal government will provide seed money, and private donations will truly make this center succeed, and we expect important support from the business community, as well.

Just to give one example of the corporate support we can expect, I'm pleased to announce today that Wachovia Bank of North Carolina has agreed to place receptacles for foreign coins at airports around the state. People would drop off foreign coins and currency in bins labeled "Global

Change" on the way back from foreign countries, and the money will go to support the center.

But our vision is larger than North Carolina. I am very pleased to see representatives from companies and education centers based outside our state, and we can be sure that other states will be looking to this center as a model for this entire region and the country. That's why I urge you to look everywhere, not just in North Carolina or the United States, for advice and assistance. We have government representatives from Germany and Japan here, and former Soviet ambassador Toon.[1] I know they all could tell us how important it is to understand the cultural differences between countries. We need to put the best minds in the country to work for us.

We have a long history of being first, in this state, for innovation. We were first to establish a public university system; first in flight; first to establish a park devoted to research industries. Our schools of science and math and the arts became models for the rest of the country. I want this center to continue our tradition of being on the cutting edge of educational innovation, and I will work with you to make sure this dream becomes reality.

With that in mind, it's my privilege to announce the men who will be leading that effort. Senator Kenneth Royall Jr., my budget advisor, will be your chairman; Tom Lambeth, executive director of the Z. Smith Reynolds Foundation, who could not be here today, will serve as vice-chairman. I cannot imagine two more competent leaders to help this center become all that it can be.[2]

---

[1] Malcolm Toon (1916-   ), born in Troy, N.Y.; resident of Southern Pines; A.B., Tufts University, 1937; M.A., Fletcher School of Law and Diplomacy, 1938; numerous honorary degrees and other awards; U.S. Naval Reserve, 1942-1946. U.S. Foreign Service officer, 1946-1979; U.S. ambassador to Czechoslovakia, 1969-1971, Yugoslavia, 1971-1975, Israel, 1975-1976, and U.S.S.R., 1976-1979; member, U.S. delegation to Nuclear Test Conference, Geneva, 1958-1959, and SALT II, Vienna, 1977-1979; Brennan Professor, University of North Carolina at Asheville, 1981. *Who's Who in America, 1998*, s.v. "Toon, Malcolm."

[2] Kenneth Claiborne Royall Jr. (1918-1999), born in Warsaw; A.B., University of North Carolina at Chapel Hill, 1940; U.S. Marine Corps, 1942-1945. Retired owner, Style Craft Interiors; member, Durham County Board of Education, 1957-1966; member, N.C. House, 1967-1973; member, 1973-1992, majority leader, 1973-1974, 1977-1978, deputy president pro tem, 1987-1992, N.C. Senate; chair, state Advisory Budget Commission, 1981-1992; senior budget adviser to Governor Hunt, 1993-1994; advocate for the mentally ill; Democrat. *News and Observer*, February 12, March 22, 1992, November 19, December 26, 1994, June 6, 1999.

Thomas Willis Lambeth (1935-   ), born in Clayton; A.B., University of North Carolina at Chapel Hill, 1957; U.S. Army and Reserve. *Winston-Salem Journal* reporter, copy editor, 1959; Terry Sanford for Governor campaign, 1959-1960; administrative assistant to Governor Sanford, 1961-1965; administrative staff, H. Smith Richardson Foundation, Greensboro, 1965-1969; administrative assistant to Congressman L. Richardson Preyer, 1969-1978; executive director, Z. Smith Reynolds Foundation, Winston-Salem, from 1978. *News and Observer*, January 12, 1986; *North Carolina Manual, 1963*, 457.

CHALLENGE TO AMERICA: NORTH CAROLINA RESPONDS

Greensboro, February 17, 1994

[The following address is similar to Governor Hunt's texts for the Standards and Accountability Commission Citizens' Forums, Morrisville, February 8, and Wilmington, February 15, 1994, and the BellSouth Leadership Conference on Workforce Preparedness, April 15, 1994. See also related press release, Hunt Opens Conference on Workforce Preparedness, Raleigh, February 17, 1994, Governors Papers, James Baxter Hunt Jr.]

A few months ago, the National Alliance of Business recognized North Carolina as "State of the Year," highlighting our efforts in workforce preparedness.[1] When I look around tonight, and see so many of you who are so committed to improving our workforce, I'm inclined to write the National Alliance of Business and tell them, "You ain't seen nothing yet."

All of us here, tonight, understand the importance of a high-skill workforce and the importance of public-private cooperation in building that workforce. Workforce preparedness is the key to economic competition in the twenty-first century. In the global marketplace, every town, state, and nation is competing with every other town, state, and nation for investment; and we understand that the best way to draw investment to North Carolina is by the quality of our workforce. Every CEO I talk to about our state asks first about our workforce and what we're doing to produce quality workers.

The importance of a high-skilled workforce is a wake-up call for us, because we in the United States don't train our workforce as well as we should. I saw the impact of this when I served on the Commission on the Skills of the American Workforce. Less than half of Americans go to college, and only 25 percent of Americans earn a four-year college degree. Nonetheless, we put almost all our energy and investment in the education of the college-bound. That means our non-college-bound students are ill prepared for the world of work, even though they comprise the majority of our front-line workers.

We must develop a better way to move young people from school to work. Otherwise, the private-sector demand for skilled employees will outstrip the supply, and we're seeing that happen every day. Last week, a businessman told our Standards and Accountability Commission a story that illustrates our problem. He decided to set up a button-making shop in Warren County. Six years before, he had started companies in Hong Kong and China and had hired high-school graduates to analyze and repair the companies' circuit boards. Here, he said, he has to hire an electrical engineer at $40,000 a year to do the same work, and the engineer wants a secretary!

Our high-school graduates are just not competitive. That's why I proposed legislation to establish the Standards and Accountability Commission. The commission, chaired by E. K. Fretwell, former chancellor of UNC-Charlotte, is holding hearings across the state, gathering expert testimony on what students need to know and be able to do to compete for the best jobs.

This is North Carolina's first attempt to tie educational standards to the demands of the workplace. Once these standards are set, assessments will be developed to measure the standards, and by the year 2000, every high-school senior will be required to pass that test in order to graduate. Then we'll put an unconditional guarantee in place, guaranteeing to businesses that our graduates have the specific skills required by the workplace. If not, the state will retrain those workers at our expense.

We are also addressing workforce training from another angle. The Governor's Commission on Workforce Preparedness is designing a comprehensive state workforce development system. The commission, chaired by Bill Burkhardt, CEO of Austin Foods, is streamlining the 45 programs, 8 state agencies, and the $600 million a year that is spent on workforce preparedness programs in North Carolina. They will make sure we know who's doing what and that we're all working together to prepare our students for the best jobs.[2]

Next month the commission will kick off its school-to-work transition program, which we call JobReady. JobReady will involve youth apprenticeships, improved technical education, and a career development program that will begin in the primary grades. This program will help our students start thinking about careers earlier, choose their courses more wisely, and understand the link between school performance and job success. We will need each and every one of you here tonight to be involved in JobReady, because all our efforts to raise standards in schools and connect students to work won't be successful without the support of business and schools. To really get students ready for the jobs of the future, government, business, and schools must work together.

Working together has not always been our greatest strength. Americans are individuals. Our strength as individuals helped us build this country and settle it from east to west. It [has] helped us engineer the greatest inventions and innovations the world has ever seen.

But while individualism is a strength of the American character and culture, we can learn from the strengths of other cultures. In the "Challenge to America" series, Japanese and German parents both said they wanted their children to learn to work well in groups. That's not something most American parents would say, but maybe they should. In fact, many employers who have testified before the Standards and Accountability Commission have said that our students must learn to work well in groups. If the Japanese and Germans learn to work in groups, and our North Carolina employers say our students need to learn to work in groups, then government, business, and schools need to learn to work in groups, too.

If we don't work together to build a better workforce, businesses will be forced to compete for a dwindling pool of high-skill workers, and all of us will fall further behind in the battle of global competition. W. Edwards Deming, the management expert whose techniques helped spur the rise of the Japanese economy, said people used to ask: "How long will it take us to catch up with Japan?" His response: "Do you think they're standing still?"[3]

We are trying to catch up with our top competitors in our workforce training efforts, and they are not standing still. We will always lag behind unless we run faster, work harder, and work together better than they do. It is a tough challenge, but North Carolina has always responded to challenges. As I look around tonight, I am confident we can meet this challenge. Together, we can train a new generation of North Carolina workers. Together, we can help keep our companies competitive throughout the world. Together, we can make North Carolina a model for the nation.

---

[1] Press release, N.C. Named State of the Year for its Workforce, Raleigh, October 25, 1993, Governors Papers, James Baxter Hunt Jr.

[2] Hunt told the commission: "Typical of state government, we have forty-five different programs operating in eight different agencies! We're spending $600 million in federal and state money on workforce preparedness, yet no one group has been overseeing this effort in a comprehensive, coordinated fashion. You will fulfill this critical task, and look for ways to do even more." Commission on Workforce Preparedness, Raleigh, July 12, 1993, Governors Papers, James Baxter Hunt Jr.

William C. Burkhardt (1937-   ), born in Cleveland, Ohio; B.S., Florida State University. President, director, National Continental Foods, Jamaica, 1972-1976; president, Bakery Division, Beatrice Foods Co., 1976-1980; president, CEO, Austin Quality Foods, Inc., Cary, from 1980; named Executive of the Year, 1995, by *Snack Food* magazine; chairman, N.C. Commission on Workforce Preparedness, 1993-1994; member, director, numerous boards and commissions. William C. Burkhardt, letter to Jan-Michael Poff, March 29, 1996.

[3] William Edwards Deming; B.S., University of Wyoming, 1922; M.S., University of Colorado, 1924; Ph.D., Yale University, 1928; honorary degrees. Award-winning consultant; engineering, physics, and statistics educator; mathematical physicist, U.S. Dept. of Agriculture, 1927-1939; adviser in sampling, U.S. Bureau of Census, 1939-1945; professor of statistics, Graduate School of Business Administration, New York University, from 1946; Union of Japanese Scientists and Engineers honored him by establishing Deming Prize; author. *Who's Who in America, 1986-1987*, s.v. "Deming, William Edwards." Source, accuracy of quotation could not be verified.

STATEMENT ON JUVENILE JUSTICE, STATE BUDGET

Raleigh, February 21, 1994

As we enter the third week of this special session, the legislature is making good progress toward a tough but smart crime-fighting plan. Now we must focus on balance: tough punishment and smart prevention. We must move quickly to pass this plan, without distractions. Today I want to address two topics surrounding this crime plan: its fiscal framework and the need for tougher punishment for violent juvenile criminals.

No one is a stronger children's advocate than I am. My administration has put children first from the first day. I've always believed we can change the future if we start with children. That's why I've worked hard to launch new statewide children's initiatives like Smart Start and SOS [Save Our Students].

But I'm also a realist. I know that every good prevention program in the world is not going to replace effective punishment. In our society we encourage our children to do right. If they do wrong, we punish them. If we do not punish, we will not teach right from wrong. It's that simple.

We have not done a good enough job teaching our children right from wrong. As a result, we have a generation of young criminals in North Carolina. It's a fact. Juvenile arrests for violent crimes jumped 80 percent from 1987 through 1992, more than twice that of the overall crime rate. The number of juveniles charged with murder has quadrupled over the last decade.

This special session will make sure that dangerous criminals of all ages are treated with the seriousness their crime deserves. I hope it will also better equip us to handle those youngsters sent by judges to training schools. Rising juvenile crime means our training schools are now overcrowded and understaffed, and our alternative programs do not have the resources they need. My crime plan would add $6.7 million for 215 new staff positions in the state's five training schools. I don't believe communities are the place for our violent juvenile criminals. I don't believe that ignoring overcrowding and understaffing problems will help youngsters who are sent to training school.

Our overcrowding and understaffing problems are real: Look at the Saturday night riot at C. A. Dillon in Butner, the state's only maximum security training school.[1] More than thirty youths got out of control. One of the three staffers in the cottage had to lock herself in a room to call the police. The other two had to be taken to the hospital. This training school doesn't have the staff or resources to control these kids, let alone to give them the counseling, treatment, and vocational education they need. Last month, we had a similar riot at a detention center in Gaston County that was jammed with twice as many kids as it could accommodate. Most of the youngsters were there because they were waiting for spaces at our overcrowded training schools.[2]

This situation will only get worse. There's no question that we need better prevention and rehabilitation efforts for teenagers. As part of my crime package, I've ordered Secretary Robin Britt to evaluate our training schools and community-based alternatives to make sure these programs are doing what they should. We need more space to keep dangerous young criminals off the streets and the staff to handle them appropriately. We need both prevention and punishment. Framing the issue as an either/or choice is a false choice.

By the same token, framing the budget debate as an either/or choice between fighting crime and improving schools and children's programs is a false choice. Let me remind you, North Carolina is suffering a crime crisis, not a budget crisis. The $90 million in recurring money I have proposed to spend on this crime plan is less than 1 percent of our General Fund budget. I will propose specific cuts to finance at least half of that.

On top of that, revenues are increasing. The State Budget Office estimates that we'll have almost $465 million in additional available funds, more than twice the amount anticipated. Unlike 1991, we are in an economic recovery, not a recession. Our economy is growing. More new jobs were created in North Carolina last year than any other year in the last decade.

By the short session in May, it will be clear that we will have significantly more revenue than anticipated last July. Until then, it would be premature and unwise to begin slashing good programs now to pay for our crime plan. We can afford to do what we need to do in the priority areas—crime, education, jobs, health care, and children—and we can afford a fair pay raise for teachers and state employees. But we don't need to spend $50,000 a day during a special session on crime to do what the short session is designed to do: map out the next fiscal year. That would distract the General Assembly from its sole purpose in Raleigh: dealing with crime in a special session on crime.

---

[1] Rampaging juvenile offenders at C. A. Dillon School broke furniture and assaulted two staff members in a twenty-minute riot that began around 3:00 P.M. on February 19, 1994. Butner police were called in to help restore order. James Bowden, chief of the state's five training schools and former director at Dillon, said of the event, "'We have disturbances from time to time, and that will continue as long as we're understaffed.'" *News and Observer,* February 21, 1994.

[2] Gaston Regional Juvenile Detention Center, in Dallas, N.C., was designed to hold twelve offenders. There were twenty-one of them at the facility the night of January 19, 1994, when seventeen boys broke out of their rooms and caused enough damage to close the center temporarily. Gaston County sheriff's deputies quelled the melee. There were no escapes and no injuries. *News and Observer*, January 20, 1994.

FAITH AND VALUES CONFERENCE

RALEIGH, FEBRUARY 25, 1994

[This address is almost identical to one Hunt delivered April 7, 1981, before the Christian Life Council. Poff and Crow, *Addresses of Hunt, 1981-1985*, 91-93.]

When you hear people talking about government today, you hear a lot of cynicism. People talk about government as if there is something inherently bad about it. People joke that only dishonest people run for office, and honest people who win don't remain honest very long. Does that sound familiar to any of you?

People said all those things when I was growing up, too, but I didn't grow up believing that. There were two reasons: The first was my family. Both of my parents were public servants. Mother taught school, and Daddy was a soil conservation agent. They worked for government, but I don't know of anyone who had more honesty and integrity. I knew, by their example, that you could be both a public servant and a Christian.

The second influence was my church. My family attended church regularly, we studied the Bible, we prayed in public, and we sought the leadership of the Holy Spirit in trying to learn and do what was right. After church on Sunday, my parents would quiz me about what had happened and made sure that I listened to the Sunday school teacher and pastor. What I heard, and continue to hear about God, in church and at home, is very important to my personal life-style and to my performance as governor.

I'd like to share with you four ways that my faith influences me. First, my faith teaches me about the importance of stewardship. I learned early on the seriousness of burying one's talent; of missing opportunities; of wasting a life; of destroying a relationship. I was blessed with a strong, secure home life, and as Christ said in Luke 12, "Unto whom much is given, much shall be required."[1] My father made clear to me that a Christian was to be faithful with his time, his talents, and his treasure. He was to be faithful, because what he had was entrusted to him by God.

The second major thing I have learned through my faith is to "love my neighbor as myself."[2] The so-called Golden Rule is a practical way of showing your love and devotion to God, and it is as good a reason as any to serve in public life. We can show our love for others by looking for a cause and pouring our hearts into it. That's what Robin Britt did a few years ago when he started Project Uplift: He found a need in our public housing communities and worked to find the best way of making a difference. That is what he is doing in government right now, as my secretary of human resources, running my Smart Start program. Service to our neighbors is not just an option, it is an obligation we face as Christians. We are, each and every one of us, called upon to be the modern-day Good Samaritans.

A third major element of my faith is that Christians need to live Christian lives. As a boy, my parents often said, "Jimmy, we do or don't do something because we are Christians." I learned, early on, that you couldn't talk the talk if you didn't walk the walk. The verbs in the Bible are significant: do; be; follow; obey; trust; go; work.

A fourth element of my faith is a belief that Christians can change the world. I grew up in a small Baptist church, and we were told that we were like Christ's small band of disciples. We were told that that small band had turned the world upside down, and that we could too. And you know what? I believed our preachers. I believed that changed people ought to change the world. I believe it now more than ever. One person can make a difference. As disciples, we are called not to conform to the world, but to transform it. We can do that.

You have a wonderful weekend ahead of you. You will be hearing from a list of inspiring speakers, and you will be having great discussions among yourselves. Now there are two ways to react to a conference like this: You can listen and get excited and inspired, and you can sit on your hands—or you can do something about it. I want you to do something about it. Talk with these business leaders about how you can find your place, by directing you to where you can serve in your own communities. We need good, mature, enthusiastic volunteers who will be good role models for the statewide after-school programs we are starting in our middle schools. We need concerned, caring teachers, who will work to inspire young students. We need you to volunteer or take full-time jobs that give senior citizens hope, get the hungry food, find the unemployed jobs, and give the families strength.

That sort of commitment may start on the mountaintop, but it becomes reality when you come back down. I hope that as you reach the heights this weekend, you will use the view only to get a better view of the world—then you will make your choices and get involved. That can all start for you this weekend. Unto you much has been given. Now, much is required.

[1] "For unto whosoever much is given, of him shall be much required: and to whom men have committed much, of him they will ask the more." Luke 12:48.
[2] "Thou shalt love thy neighbor as thyself." Leviticus 19:18.

REACTION TO NORTH CAROLINA SENATE FLOOR ACTION

RALEIGH, FEBRUARY 25, 1994

The senate's passage of "three strikes and you're out" takes North Carolina one step closer to keeping violent career criminals behind bars. The North Carolina Conference of District Attorneys has endorsed our crime package, and prosecutors are pushing for this bill because they need more effective tools to put violent career criminals behind bars and keep them there. And prosecutors say this will have a deterrent effect. The [Raleigh] *News and Observer*'s own analysis shows that, right now, 1,242 criminals in this state have committed two violent felonies—such as murder, rape, and armed robbery.[1] We must send these criminals a message: If they commit another violent felony, they will pay the price with life in prison.

Just as importantly, violent criminals of all ages ought to be held responsible for the serious nature of their crimes. Law enforcement officers and DA's tell me that teenagers know how the juvenile justice system works. A 14- or 15-year-old who commits a violent felony—like second-degree murder, rape, and armed robbery—knows he or she may get nothing but a slap on the wrist in a juvenile court and walk out of training school at 18. I believe that 14- and 15-year-olds who commit the most violent felonies ought to be held as accountable for their crimes as adults are.

Critics of this bill have now presented a fiscal note that says it would cost $70 million.[2] That's nothing but a smoke screen. This bill will cost the state virtually nothing. Our package already accounts for any necessary prison and detention center space and staff. What we need is tough action to deal with violent criminals, not more excuses to do nothing.

[1] *News and Observer*, February 24, 1994.
[2] The bill to which Hunt referred would have made 14- and 15-year-olds automatically eligible for trial as adults if accused of committing any of twenty-five types of felonies. But some critics claimed that the proposal would cost too much—$70 million over six years, according to legislative analysts—while some judges argued that it would too severely limit their discretion in handling juvenile offenders. *News and Observer*, February 25, 1994.

PRESS RELEASE: HUNT RAISES PRISON CAP
TO AVERT PAROLE DEADLINE

RALEIGH, MARCH 15, 1994

Governor Jim Hunt today raised the prison cap by 2,100, which means the state will be able to keep some 3,000 criminals behind bars instead of paroling them into North Carolina communities. Hunt raised the cap in time to meet a March 15 deadline that would have forced the state to begin the process of paroling the criminals, many of them considered violent and dangerous by the North Carolina Parole Commission. As a result of Hunt's action, those inmates will now remain in prison. The increased cap is being phased in as new prison beds become available. Today's action increases the cap by 1,100, to 22,500, and provides for an increase to 23,000 on May 15 and a further increase to 23,500 on June 30.

"Raising the prison cap was the single most urgent reason for calling the General Assembly to Raleigh for the special session five weeks ago," Hunt said. "We were facing a real deadline with the forced parole of dangerous criminals. Last night's legislative action allowed this state to narrowly avert a crisis."

Although some critics have questioned the deadline, Parole Commission chairman Juanita Baker reaffirmed the urgency of the March 15 deadline. Had the General Assembly not given Hunt the power to raise the cap, the Parole Commission would have been forced to accelerate its paroles process to begin the paperwork to release the 3,000 inmates— in addition to the 400 to 600 inmates already being released in an average week. The pool of 3,000 would have included inmates with prior convictions for violent crimes, including rape and possibly murder, Baker said.

The prison cap was enacted by the General Assembly to limit prison crowding. The previous cap was set at 21,400. The law requires that when the prison population exceeds 98 percent of that number for 15 straight days, the cap is triggered and the Parole Commission has 90 days to bring the prison population down to 97 percent of the cap. The cap was triggered on December 16, marking March 15 as the 90-day deadline.

COMMISSION FOR A COMPETITIVE NORTH CAROLINA

RALEIGH, MARCH 22, 1994

[Executive Order Number 9, signed on May 5, 1993, by Governor Hunt, established the Commission for a Competitive North Carolina. The full text of the document was published in *N.C. Session Laws, 1993*, 2:3212-3216. For related press release, see Governor Hunt Receives Blueprint for North Carolina's Future, Raleigh, March 23, 1995, Governors Papers, James Baxter Hunt Jr.]

The world is changing, and every change affects North Carolina. Years ago we needed to pay attention only to changes in our own state or country. Today we have to pay attention to changes in remote areas of the globe—China, Japan, Uruguay—because what happens there determines what happens here. The North American Free Trade Agreement has been passed. The General Agreement on Tariffs and Trade has been adopted. New markets are opening around the world, and our competitors are sharpening their teeth to take advantage of them.

We in North Carolina must be ready to take advantage of the changing world. But it's not enough for us to change with the world; we must change ahead of it. The people who anticipated the future of air travel, assembly-line manufacturing, and the rise of computers have made a positive difference in the lives of millions of people. We must anticipate the changes in the world and make a positive difference in the lives of all North Carolinians.

We have asked you to join this commission because you all bring together important perspectives on the future of North Carolina and the world. You must use this perspective to help us set out a clear vision of where we want North Carolina to be in twenty years. This vision must take account of the interests and aspirations of all North Carolinians and cannot depend on the political party or the personality of government leaders. It must be a unifying theme for government, business, and nonprofits in North Carolina.

Once we set these goals, we will not only have a clear direction for the state, we will have a way to hold government accountable. Let's say we set a goal to reduce crime. We can then identify indicators that affect the crime rate—like teen pregnancy, dropout rate, and substance abuse—and set goals for reducing these factors. These goals, if adopted by the General Assembly, can be used in budget allocations for state agencies. An agency that can demonstrate its progress toward a goal will have a stronger argument for more funding.

Setting specific goals will help drive our program to reinvent government. It will provide an immediate check on our progress and help us evaluate our programs. If what we're doing doesn't work, we'll find something that does.

We have the people and the resources we need to make North Carolina a leader in the twenty-first century, but we must agree on where we're going. I charge this commission to bring together its background, experience, and expertise to write a report, due in one year, that sets out a twenty-year vision for North Carolina—with specific, measurable goals that will let the people hold their government accountable.

This is one of the most important projects of this administration. Its impact will be felt in the people's quality of life and in their faith in government. Bear that in mind as you chart the future of our state.

NORTH CAROLINA MIDDLE SCHOOL ASSOCIATION

GREENSBORO, MARCH 23, 1994

["There is no age group whose needs are more poorly addressed than our middle-school students," Governor Hunt said, as he explained the benefits of his proposed Save Our Students program. "Younger students can still make some use of day care. Older students can get jobs and be active in high school sports and activities. Middle-schoolers are caught in the middle. We need to do something for these middle-schoolers, before it's too late."

SOS would provide a structured after-school atmosphere for otherwise unsupervised, and possibly vulnerable, middle-schoolers. "As you know, the middle-school years can be a very awkward time for children. Change is very rapid, and children often get confused and reach out for a feeling of security. All too often, that security is found in a peer group just as confused. The after-school hours can (be) especially dangerous because that's when that peer group takes the place of parents and teachers. We need to give these (children) some kind and loving adult supervision during these hours. We need to give them good, wholesome, enriching activities that can help them at school and help them relate, in a positive way, to adults *and* their peers." SOS Talking Points, Raleigh, February 22, 1994, Governors Papers, James Baxter Hunt Jr. Other documents from 1994 that focused on SOS include Prevention Briefing, Raleigh, February 16; Healthy Mothers-Healthy Babies Networking Conference, Raleigh, September 7; State of the Child Conference, Raleigh, November 1; SOS Talking Points, Ferndale Middle School, High Point, November 2; and press releases, Prevention Groups Urge Support for Governor's SOS Program, Raleigh, February 16, and Governor Hunt's Proposals Step Up Prevention Efforts for Youth, Raleigh, April 27.]

Karen Garr, my teacher adviser, uses one word to describe middle-schoolers: shining. Now, she's referring to the sea of braces in your average sixth-grade classroom. But middle-schoolers also shine with new ideas, unlimited energy, boundless enthusiasm, and with great potential. No other period of life jams as much social, emotional, moral, intellectual, and physical development into such a short period of time—and no other period of life offers such a challenge to teachers and administrators. You all are the ones who channel that energy and who urge them on to greater, shinier things.

But the middle-school years are also becoming an age of danger. Too many middle-schoolers come face to face with crime, guns, and drugs. You see them in your classrooms; in your hallways; on your ball fields.

We can do more to protect our children. The General Assembly passed a series of new laws, last year, designed to make our schools safer. It's now a felony to bring firearms onto school property, and it's illegal to bring any other kind of weapon onto campus. Parents are now held accountable for leaving weapons in reach.

We're helping schools fight violence in other ways. The Center for the Prevention of School Violence, which I created last year, is a resource for schools and communities, providing advice, technical help, and grant money for innovative school violence prevention programs. But all of this ends with the school day. We can do a great deal to boost our middle-schoolers and deter youngsters from crime if we continue enriching activities after school.

You know, and many of you have told me, that the middle schools are the last chance to really turn young lives around. We need good-quality, after-school programs to help our middle-school children. Many of you are doing just that already, and I commend you for it. But I have heard from many middle-school teachers and administrators that we must do more, more to help you help our students.

That's why I've proposed a major new crime prevention initiative that targets middle-schoolers. My SOS program is now before the General Assembly, and I'm hopeful that we'll be able to get it in place for middle schools in high-crime areas by the coming school year. The goal of SOS is to bring adults and older teenagers together with kids who need help—encouraging them, helping them to discover their own potential and possibilities, and most of all, building up their values, their self-esteem, and their chances for success. We can use the hours between 3:00 [P.M.] and 6:00 [P.M.] to provide challenging, enriching activities for our children—everything from helping on homework, computer classes, mentoring, and peer mediation, to clubs and sports. They can also provide the kind of guidance all young people need.

Like Smart Start, the program will be run out of DHR [Department of Human Resources], and the government will put in some money. But SOS isn't a government program. It is a community program, designed by you and other members of your community. You are the experts, and we have designed the program to allow experts on the local level to determine how best to meet the needs of their children. We will look to you, along with churches, community organizations, parents, business people, and volunteers to find ways to give kids something to do, something to learn, and someone to learn from. With you behind it, it will work—and it must work. Our children deserve nothing less.

SPECIAL SESSION STATEMENT

RALEIGH, MARCH 25, 1994

[The text for the Havelock Crime Forum, April 14, and the governor's "Post Crime Session Talking Points" for town meetings in Asheville, April 21, Sylva, April 21, and Charlotte, April 27, and the Wilson County Law Enforcement Association, April 29, 1994, appear to be based on the following statement. For related press release, see Governor Hunt's Crime Package Passed into Law, Raleigh, March 28, 1994, Governors Papers, James Baxter Hunt Jr.]

I called this special session because the people wanted it. The people wanted us to do more to protect them from dangerous criminals and to keep young people from going into crime. I've spent the last seven months talking with the people of this state about crime—and the last seven weeks urging legislators to listen to the people. I believe the people have been heard.

While this has been a lengthy and difficult session, I believe we are making some real changes that will make a real difference. I set out a plan that included both tougher punishment and more prevention and worked hard to bring the two sides of that debate together. We need both. One will not work without the other. In the end, the legislature is addressing both the need for tougher sentences for violent criminals and the need for more effective prevention efforts.

I commend the General Assembly for its actions. I commend Senate president pro tem Marc Basnight and House Speaker Dan Blue for putting policy over politics to pass this package with bipartisan support. By working together, the leaders of this state have responded to the concerns of their people. That is their job, and they are doing their job tonight.

But in the end, our job is not over. This special session and this crime package will not eliminate crime. Lawmakers cannot eliminate crime, but they can create new tools with which to fight crime. This is just the start of what we must do to reclaim our communities.

In the weeks and months to come, I'll be working with law-enforcement officers and the people in communities across the state to build on our new laws and our new prevention efforts. I'm pleased that the legislature is providing $5 million for SOS [Support Our Students], our new crime-prevention program for students. But SOS will not work without the involvement of North Carolinians across this state, and I intend to do all I can to make that happen. With $2 million for family resource centers, new wilderness camps, and more money for the Governor's One-on-One program, we can reach more at-risk youths, and we can prevent a new generation of criminals.

On the punishment side, the General Assembly is taking significant steps to keep dangerous criminals behind bars longer. Most importantly, we are abolishing parole for first-degree murder. No longer can a first-degree murderer be paroled in twenty-five years. *Life* will mean *life*.

We are toughening sentences for rape. We are putting three-time violent felons behind bars for life. We are adding five years to a sentence whenever a gun is used. Together, these new laws will mean that the most dangerous criminals, those violent career criminals who commit most of the crimes, will be kept off the streets where they can't hurt people.

I was disappointed that several proposals were not as tough as I would have liked, including the rape bill. I'm disappointed that my bill to keep guns out of the hands of felons did not pass, and I'm especially disappointed that the Mecklenburg drug court did not get funded: I will push for that in the May session. So, more remains to be done— but we've made a good start. I know the legislature will keep working in future sessions, and I will keep working with legislators, law-enforcement officers, and people across this state to make North Carolina a safer place to live.

NORTH CAROLINA A&T STATE UNIVERSITY INSTITUTE ON URBAN AFFAIRS

GREENSBORO, APRIL 7, 1994

Twenty-five years ago, the Department of Sociology and Social Work at this great university sounded a battle cry for freedom and progress that is still heard across North Carolina. For twenty-five years, people have been drawn to this institute to fight poverty and injustice. We've learned a few lessons in those twenty-five years, including the lesson of partnership—a lesson that is put into practice by my administration and by this institute.

Many of you here fought the battle for civil rights. In the beginning, a few brave souls walked alone. Government was against them; businesses were against them. Sometimes even their neighbors were against them. Sustained by their moral courage, these pioneers persuaded government to pass important laws and launch important programs to combat poverty and injustice.

This was a great step forward. The programs had good aims and good intentions. But these programs weren't a partnership of the people and the public sector. It was government working alone and the people walking alone.

There must be a partnership: That's the lesson. We cannot tackle our urban problems effectively without bringing together the energy, enthusiasm, and commitment of everyone affected by urban problems. My administration is committed to offering the hand of partnership to local government, business, education, church, and community leaders. Together, we're working to solve the problems that plague our cities, problems of troubled schools, too much crime, and too few jobs.

Smart Start, which we hope to expand to twenty counties this year, will give quality day care and health care to every child who needs it, so our children can come to school healthy and ready to learn. That program was proposed by the governor and passed by the General Assembly. But it is being put into practice by people in local communities who understand local needs best. Smart Start brings together all our resources and brings people and government together as partners.

Our Education Standards and Accountability Commission follows the same principle. The standards commission is working to set high standards in our schools so every high-school graduate leaves our schools with the real skills needed for a real job. This commission was proposed by the governor and passed by the General Assembly. But it is driven by business and education leaders, employers, parents, and personnel managers, and the higher standards will be put in place by teachers and principals in schools all across North Carolina.

Smart Start and higher standards will help us bring our people good jobs, the first step in addressing urban problems—and we must build a stronger partnership to fight crime. You all know that crime is ravaging our communities and hurting our people. Last year, Charlotte set a murder record with 122 killings; of those 122 victims, 94 were black. The year before last, you had a record number of murders here in Greensboro.

We can't let our children grow up in violence and fear. Government must work in partnership with the people to protect our children and make their future brighter. That's why I spent seven months talking with the people of this state about crime and asking them, here in Greensboro and in other cities, what they wanted the state to do. In a real sense, the crime package that I proposed in the special session, which was passed by the General Assembly last month, was the people's plan. Now we have new laws to keep dangerous criminals behind bars longer, deter youngsters from crime, and make the criminal justice system work better.

But our work is far from done. Now we must work as partners to make our streets safer, and that's what you are doing this afternoon.

At today's workshop on Public Safety as an Outreach of Church Ministry, three distinguished pastors will talk about what their churches can do to fight crime. These pastors know, as you do, that fighting crime is not just the job of police officers. It's the job of each one of us who has a brother, a sister, a child, or a neighbor. We all must be involved!

This is the kind of community leadership we need to tackle our cities' problems and our state's problems. Every business leader, educator, minister, and government official must work, in partnership, for the welfare of every child born and schooled in our state. Until then, our work continues, and the spirit of partnership promoted here must continue. Good luck and Godspeed.

TESTIMONY BEFORE U.S. HOUSE OF REPRESENTATIVES SUBCOMMITTEE ON COMMERCE, JUSTICE, STATE AND JUDICIARY

RALEIGH, APRIL 11, 1994

Good morning. I appreciate the chance to speak before this subcommittee. I want to thank Congressman Price for his leadership on this area and for focusing congressional attention on the crime problem in North Carolina.[1] As Congressman Price knows, crime is tearing the very fabric of life in North Carolina. We have the sixteenth-highest crime rate in the country, up from thirty-second a decade ago. In that time, violent crimes have increased 75 percent, and the number of juveniles arrested for murder has quadrupled. Last year three of our largest cities, including this one, set new murder rates.

As crime has gotten more violent, more senseless, and more random, North Carolinians have become more afraid. They are afraid to go to the mall, drive down the street, and send their children to school. But people are also angry. They believe the system is stacked against them— and in favor of criminals. They read about criminals who get tough sentences but serve less than 20 percent of their time. They think their government is failing in its most basic responsibility: to protect them. It is the responsibility of all governments—federal, state, and local— to work together to respond to these very real fears.

Last month, the North Carolina General Assembly concluded a seven-week special session on crime. When I called the session, I laid out three goals: Do more to keep dangerous criminals behind bars longer and make prison a real deterrent. Do more to deter youngsters from crime. Do more to make the criminal justice system work better for victims.

The crime package that I presented, and is now law, addresses both the need for tougher sentences for violent criminals and the need for more effective prevention efforts. One will not work without the other. Without the threat of real punishment, all of our innovative prevention programs will fail.

I believe we've begun to restore the threat of punishment. We've abolished parole for first-degree murderers. We've toughened sentences for rape. We increased prison capacity. We are putting three-time violent felons behind bars for life. We are adding five years to a sentence whenever a gun is used. These new laws will mean that the most dangerous criminals, those violent career criminals who commit most of the crimes, will be kept off the streets where they can't hurt people.

On the prevention side, we're launching a major new initiative aimed at young students, called SOS [Support Our Students]. The state will provide seed money for neighborhood and community groups to set up after-school programs for youngsters, from kindergarten through the ninth grade. SOS will bring adults and older teenagers together with kids who need help, encouraging them, helping them discover their own potential and possibilities, and most of all, building up their values, their self-esteem, and their chances for success. And SOS will bring churches, community organizations, educators, parents, business people, and volunteers together to give troubled children something to do, something to learn, and someone to learn from. Volunteers will provide challenging, enriching activities, between the hours of 3:00 P.M. and 6:00 P.M., and will provide the kind of guidance that all young people need.

I've read that Senator Bill Bradley has been looking at similar ideas with a national program in mind, and I would urge Congress to take a very close look at this.[2] We must reach out to our children earlier, and we must engage communities in this effort. We cannot wait, or we will lose children to a life of crime.

North Carolina's special session also provided funds to launch family resource centers at elementary schools. We're adding funds to community programs that help at-risk children, and we're building new wilderness camps and boot camps to give troubled youngsters the discipline they need to turn their lives around. I believe that many of these kids can be saved. In the long run, the best way to prevent a new generation of criminals is to reach children before the age of five, as we are doing with our early childhood initiative, Smart Start.

Smart Start will give North Carolina preschoolers the quality day care and health care they need, as well as a better chance to succeed in life. Our efforts for more discipline and higher standards in schools, and better job training for kids who don't go on to college, will give youngsters an even better chance at success.

But that's not all we need to do. We need to focus attention on public housing communities. I've heard the gunshots in North Carolina's public housing communities, and I've talked with the mothers who fear for their children's safety. These families need help. They need more law enforcement, and security, and community-policing officers. I commend HUD secretary Henry Cisneros for his efforts to do just that and would urge you to do all you can to fund such efforts.[3]

Much of what President Clinton has recommended in his crime bill mirrors our efforts here in North Carolina. I think his approach is a good one, and I have urged our [congressional] delegation to support the president's plan.[4]

More police officers on the street, more community policing, more boot camps, and more prisons are sorely needed. What we don't need are more unfunded mandates.

We do need more cops on the street. I'm glad to see that the federal government proposes to pay 75 percent of the new officers' salary. But no money would be appropriated for training and equipment, as I understand it. In North Carolina, that means that many communities will not be able to afford these new officers.

We do need more prisons. North Carolina suffers from serious prison overcrowding, forcing us to ship prisoners out of state and taking other drastic measures to avoid turning dangerous criminals out early. But we don't need underfunded prisons, and we must have flexibility to allow states to use these prisons.

We do need adequate funding for good programs. North Carolina communities can benefit from the WEED/SEED program that helps clean up bad neighborhoods. Other good programs that deserve more money are the Juvenile Justice Delinquency Program, which boosts juvenile crime prevention programs, and the Victims of Crime Assistance program, which helps compensate our crime victims. In particular, North Carolina relies on the Byrne fund to fund local crime prevention programs. The proposed changes in distribution of Byrne funds is likely to redirect resources to major cities, leaving North Carolina communities out in the cold.

North Carolina received $9 million this year from the Byrne fund, down 14 percent from last year. This money finances the Governor's Crime Commission, which in turn is a catalyst for local community-based efforts to fight crime. The Byrne fund is putting school resource officers on campus to combat school violence. It is launching community-policing programs in crime-stricken towns. It is helping rural counties address juvenile crime. States need the flexibility to direct Byrne funding to communities that need it most. I have joined thirty-six other governors in asking House and Senate appropriations committees to preserve the Byrne formula grant program. Today I urge you to help us keep that flexibility.

In summary, North Carolina is looking to Congress and the federal government as a partner in our fight against crime. Government ought to serve as a catalyst, providing funds for new and innovative programs that can make a real difference at the local level. I urge your support for continued funding for these programs.

----

[1] David Eugene Price (1940-   ), born in Johnson City, Tenn.; A.B., University of North Carolina at Chapel Hill, 1961; B.D., 1964, Ph.D., 1969, Yale University. Assistant professor, political science and American studies, Yale, 1969-1973; professor, political science and public policy, Duke University, 1973-1986, 1994-1996; executive director, 1979-1980, chairman, 1983-1984, N.C. Democratic Party; member, U.S. House of Representatives, from North Carolina's Fourth Congressional District, 1986-1994, and from 1996. *North Carolina Manual, 1993-1994,* 946, *1997-1998,* 1063-1064.

[2] Bill Bradley (1943-   ), born in Crystal City, Mo.; B.A., Princeton University, 1965; M.A., Oxford (England) University, 1968; U.S. Air Force Reserve, 1967-1968. Professional basketball player, New York Knicks, 1967-1977; U.S. senator from New Jersey, 1979-1996; author; candidate for 2000 Democratic presidential nomination. *New York Times,* September 9, 1999; *Who's Who in America, 1998,* s.v. "Bradley, Bill."

[3] Henry G. Cisneros (1947-   ), born in San Antonio, Tex.; B.A., 1969, master's in urban and regional planning, 1970, Texas A&M University; doctor of public administration, George Washington University, 1975. City councilman, 1975-1981, mayor, 1981-1989, of San Antonio; secretary, U.S. Dept. of Housing and Urban Development, 1993-1997; president, CEO, Univision Communications, from 1997. *Who's Who in America, 1998,* s.v. "Cisneros, Henry G."

[4] *Congressional Quarterly Almanac, 1994,* 272-294, recounts the evolution and passage, and describes the provisions, of the omnibus anti-crime bill (P.L. 103-322) President Clinton signed the into law September 13, 1994. For more on Hunt's backing of the president's proposal, see press releases, Governor Jim Hunt Urges Support of Crime Bill, Raleigh, November 3, 1993, and Hunt Named to National Leadership Team on Crime, Raleigh, February 2, 1994, Governors Papers, James Baxter Hunt Jr.

CARNEGIE TASK FORCE ON MEETING THE NEEDS OF YOUNG CHILDREN

Washington, D.C., April 13, 1994

[The governor's appearance before the Carnegie Task Force on Meeting the Needs of Young Children was one of many occasions, during 1994, in which he explained the composition of, and rationale behind, the Smart Start program. Others include the Business and Children Luncheon, Chapel Hill, April 11(12); Foundation Summit, Raleigh, May 17; Healthy Mothers Healthy Babies Networking Conference, Raleigh, September 7; Family Resource Center Grant Announcement, Goldsboro, September 20; Smart Start Announcement, Raleigh, September 21; "State of the Child" Conference, Raleigh, November 1; Acceptance Speech, American Academy of Pediatrics Child Health Advocate Award, Greensboro, November 4; and North Carolina Child Care Corps, Greensboro,

November 9. See also press releases, Hunt's Smart Start Proposals Will Help More North Carolina Children, Raleigh, June 17; and Hunt Receives National Child Health Advocate Award, Raleigh, November 4, 1994. Governors Papers, James Baxter Hunt Jr.]

Thank you for the opportunity to be here, today, as you focus on strategies to nurture this nation's greatest resource: our children. The Carnegie Corporation is to be commended for establishing this task force and for training the spotlight on our greatest challenge: to meet the needs of our young children.

This challenge is perhaps our greatest challenge. The toughest choices that today's parents, communities, and political leaders face revolve around our children. As parents and as leaders, all of us in this room believe that our future depends on our children. We believe that children should come first. But in today's world of very fiscal constraints, that is sometimes easier said than done.

In North Carolina, we're putting our money where our mouth is. From day one, my administration has been dedicated to children. We have made it our number-one priority to improve the quality of life for children and families, and that philosophy has been the foundation of every initiative we have built in our first year.

That philosophy shaped my cabinet, as well. Perhaps the most important decision I made as a new governor was choosing Robin Britt as my secretary of human resources, a man who has always put children and families first. A former congressman, Robin gave up a lucrative career as an attorney to found Project Uplift, a groundbreaking effort that brought public and private support together to bring early childhood education, health, and family services to needy children and families in a Greensboro public housing community. Robin takes very seriously the challenge to build a better future for our children, and he has brought a special spirit, energy, and devotion to North Carolina state government as he spearheads our initiatives for children.

North Carolina is rising to the challenge by launching this nation's most comprehensive initiative for young children. Called Smart Start, this bold crusade seeks to ensure that every child in North Carolina enters school healthy and ready to succeed. Smart Start recognizes that those first years in a child's life are the most crucial and can mean the difference between a child's success and failure. A child who doesn't get the love, nurturing, education, or health care he needs in the first few years too often comes to school programmed to fail. We have lost too many children. In North Carolina, we know that giving these children a good start—a "smart start"—can give them a real chance for success in school and in life; and we're determined to do just that for every child in our state.

Our early childhood initiative takes a dual approach: boosting services statewide while building innovative, public-private partnerships to empower local communities to improve services for children and families. Statewide, Smart Start includes:

—A campaign to see that every young child in North Carolina is immunized at the appropriate age. We are providing state dollars to pay for the vaccine so every child, regardless of family income level, can be immunized. More than 40 percent of our state's two-year-olds have not received all of their immunizations, reflecting a critical need for North Carolina, and as we know from the national Committee for Economic Development, every dollar spent now on childhood immunization programs saves $10 in later medical costs.

—Lower child-care staff ratios for infants and toddlers. North Carolina had some of the worst staff/child ratios in the nation. This first step doesn't solve our problem, but it is a step in the right direction.

—Additional state staff to monitor and provide technical assistance to child-care centers and registered family child-care homes.

—An increased child-care tax credit for families earning less than $40,000 to help make child care more affordable for working families.

—Funds to encourage child-care teachers to get their credentials in early childhood development by paying their tuition and ensuring them a raise once they earn those credentials. This effort, called the TEACH [Teacher Education and Compensation Helps] program, was recognized by *Parenting* magazine last fall as one of the top ten innovative efforts in the nation.

—Leadership development. The state is supporting a comprehensive leadership-training program to provide a core of early childhood professionals, in communities across the state, to help lead the way as we seek to upgrade services to all children.

Those are our statewide initiatives to make sure that every child sees an immediate boost from Smart Start. But that's just one aspect of Smart Start. I want to focus, today, on the innovative thinking that has broken the mold in our state. This innovation is at the very heart of Smart Start and is embodied in our local public-private partnerships for children.

We're using state government as a catalyst to bring about real changes at the local level in how we serve children and their families. Through Smart Start and these local partnership efforts, every child who needs it will have access to quality, affordable child care, health care, and other critical services. Let me tell you how we're making this happen in North Carolina.

Last summer, at my urging, the North Carolina General Assembly provided $20 million to establish a statewide Partnership for Children and twelve local partnerships serving eighteen counties in geographically and economically diverse areas across our state. The state-level partnership is setting broad goals for children and family services across the state. Local partnerships decide how to best accomplish those goals, and substantial state funding helps communities carry out their plans.

These eighteen pioneer counties were announced in September, then spent the fall and winter assessing the needs of their children and determining what resources and services already exist. Now they are crafting comprehensive plans to help provide and link children and families with the services they need. To do this, these counties are setting up nonprofit corporations that unite families, educators, nonprofits, churches, businesses, and local government. These local partnerships bring all parts of the community together and take advantage of all existing resources: Head Start agencies, church programs, child-care centers, resource and referral agencies, schools, and business-supported programs. Smart Start reflects a true entrepreneurial spirit. Instead of designating a "lead agency," we've brought the community together on an equal footing. In fact, low-income families—the key target of Smart Start services—are helping to tailor specific plans to meet specific needs of children in their own community.

Once the local partnership is formed and officially set up as a nonprofit corporation, the state provides $100,000 annually to fund its operations, including a staff to assist the partnership. The rest of the money is divided among the partnerships, based on the number of children and the needs of the county. On average, local demonstration sites receive approximately $1 million for services in the first year and $2 million a year after that. The state provides technical assistance and training in collaboration techniques to help local partnerships unite the community and help them build a consensus on how to best meet local needs.

The first twelve pioneer partnerships are pilot projects, so we can work the bugs out of this new, comprehensive initiative. We hope to get additional funding from the legislature this year to add at least eight more counties, and more every year until all 100 counties are participating in Smart Start. By 1998, Smart Start should be in place in every county, with an annual cost of $325 million, including adjustments for inflation.

I've been excited about Smart Start from the beginning, but the people of North Carolina are even more excited about it. Everywhere I go, people talk to me about Smart Start. More importantly, they talk about what they can do in their communities for their children, even if their county is not participating in Smart Start; and the stories from the twelve pioneer partnerships are even more heartening. Smart Start is making a difference in the lives of our children. Let me give you some examples:

—Child care is becoming more affordable for families through greater access to state subsidies for child care. In Mecklenburg County, our state's largest county, Smart Start is providing child-care subsidies for 550 families who had been on waiting lists.

—Families who need help are getting help, and they're not being forced to go on welfare to get it. Orange County has raised the income level that families can earn and still be eligible for child-care subsidies. As a result, a young, single mother has been able to keep her job, provide quality care for her infant, and stay off welfare. Working at the local hospital, she earns $9,600 a year but was paying almost half of it—some $4,300—for child care. She and her infant were barely making it. Now, with Smart Start, she is paying just $80 a month, instead of $360, for child care.

—The quality of child care is improving. Pioneer counties are providing grants to child-care centers and family child-care homes for technical assistance, renovations to facilities, and new equipment to help them move toward higher quality licensing standards or national accreditation. Some child-care teachers are getting better pay as a result of completing their credentials in early childhood education. One county is providing a pool of substitute teachers to help with high turnover. In North Carolina, the turnover rate for child-care teachers stands at 40 percent.

—Some counties with too few child-care spaces are raising the market rate of state subsidies to encourage more churches, nonprofits, and individuals to open quality child-care centers and family child-care homes. These counties are adding state dollars to federal child-care funding, so low-income children can get higher quality care.

—Children and families will get new services, like transportation for day care, with a new partnership between state, federal, and county governments. Counties can leverage Smart Start dollars to get additional federal and state resources. For example, a county can use Smart Start dollars to pay 15 percent on the cost of a van. The state Department of Transportation then finances the rest with federal and state dollars.

—Children and families will be getting the basic health care they need, at their doorstep, with mobile health vans that will provide health checkups, immunizations, and other health services in some counties.

—And many counties will provide basic family services, like parenting education, support for teen parents, counseling services, and strategies to prevent family violence as part of their Smart Start plan.

We know that Smart Start won't work if the family isn't involved. Smart Start dollars cannot make a difference if the child's daily environment is unsafe, uncaring, and abusive. That's why Smart Start initiatives are centered on the child, yet focused on the family. We want to strengthen and empower families, recognizing and reinforcing them as primary teachers and caregivers of their children. Only by empowering families can we make a real difference for children. That's why one-quarter of our Smart Start dollars target [sic] families who don't need child care. Instead, they need other family support services, like parenting education, child development, health care, literacy, information about jobs and job training, and counseling services.

Some counties are using Smart Start money to set up or expand family resource centers to provide "one-stop shopping" for services children and families need. During a special legislative session on crime last month, our General Assembly provided another $2 million for model family resource centers at elementary schools across the state.[1] These family resource centers help close the gap between family needs and community resources. They're a proven and effective way to ensure that families get the help they need to provide nurturing and supportive homes for children.

Smart Start provides local flexibility, but it also provides for comprehensive evaluation and accountability. Our real measure of success is the bottom line, the effect these services have on children and families. To evaluate, we will track the services delivered and their impact on children's development and family situations. This data will be reported at the state level, but also to local officials and local partnerships to help them do an even better job.

Smart Start is already making headlines. Just last month, *Working Mother* magazine cited North Carolina as the most improved state in the nation in child care and recognized Smart Start for the tremendous progress being made.[2] And Smart Start is making North Carolinians proud. They're proud to be working together, as part of the solution.

I believe Smart Start will be this country's most innovative, successful model for serving young children and their families. I invite you to visit North Carolina to see what we've done, and learn as we learn. The promise of Smart Start is a bright one. It's the promise of healthy, nurtured children who are prepared to burgeon forth in school and in life. The promise of a brighter, better America: That's a promise I invite you to make.

---

[1] The Family Resource Center program was "designed to match needy families with the services that can help them. Grants are going to community centers that match local agency resources with families who need financial assistance, health services, or help with child care." Acceptance Speech, American Academy of Pediatrics Child Health Advocate Award, Greensboro, November 4, 1994, Governors Papers, James Baxter Hunt Jr.

[2] See *Working Mother*, March 1994, and *News and Observer*, February 12, 1994.

PRESS RELEASE: GOVERNOR HUNT
LAUNCHES JOBREADY PROGRAM

WENDELL, APRIL 19, 1994

[For related press release, see Hunt's Budget Recommendations Boost Workforce Development Efforts, Raleigh, June 6, 1994, Governors Papers, James Baxter Hunt Jr.]

Governor Jim Hunt today launched his JobReady program, a long-range blueprint to help students make the transition from school to work. JobReady brings together state, federal, and private resources to strengthen career counseling and promote job training programs across the state. It targets the North Carolina high school graduates who go directly from school into the workplace with little training or assistance. Some 75 percent of North Carolina high school graduates do not graduate from four-year colleges, and 50 percent get no further training beyond high school.

"In the past, we have concentrated most of our attention and resources on those students who are going to college," Hunt said. "That's important, but we must do a better job preparing our youngsters to enter the workforce, to make sure they are ready to compete for high-skill, high-wage jobs. The goal of JobReady is to help every student, particularly those who are not going on to college, get good work at good wages."

Hunt announced the JobReady program Tuesday at East Wake High School, in Wendell, where Siemens Energy and Automation is pioneering an innovative youth apprenticeship program similar to those proposed under JobReady. This fall, Siemens will kick off its program with sixteen seniors who will attend training during regular class hours and work at the plant the next summer. At the end of the program, they will have the skills needed to work at Siemens or other similar companies.

"School-business partnerships like this one are the cornerstone of JobReady," Hunt said. "We need businesses across the state to invest in our youth as never before. The investment will ensure that they have well-trained workers and that our young workers have good jobs to go to."

Specifically, JobReady, designed by the Governor's Commission on Workforce Preparedness, calls for:

—*Promoting school-business partnerships.* JobReady will encourage businesses to form partnerships at schools to help provide youth apprenticeships, mentoring programs, and other training.

—*Putting a "job broker" in every school.* Job brokers will serve as a link between school and work, learning about job prospects, openings, wages, and hiring requirements, and working with employers to help place students in workplaces relevant to their coursework.

—*Funding grants for innovative school-to-work transition programs.* Hunt will ask the General Assembly to approve $1 million to finance grants for well-designed programs.

—*Establishing a statewide clearinghouse on school-to-work transition programs.* The Governor's Commission on Workforce Preparedness will keep a statewide database of programs in North Carolina to help communities improve their school-to-work efforts.

—*Strengthening career counseling for all students, elementary through community colleges.* JobReady will promote career counseling to introduce career options in elementary schools, present specific options in middle school, help students choose career paths and coursework in high school, and encourage more career counseling in community colleges.

—*Training teachers and counselors in school-to-work programs.* JobReady will promote training of teachers and others to help non-college-bound students get the coursework they need to succeed in the workplace.

—*Making Tech Prep available to every student.* The Department of Public Instruction will request $3 million from the General Assembly to award grants to promising Tech Prep programs across the state and match federal grants for the same purpose.

NORTH CAROLINA MUSEUM OF HISTORY RIBBON-CUTTING

RALEIGH, APRIL 23, 1994

Today we celebrate this grand, new, North Carolina Museum of History. The theme of this celebration is "North Carolina Stories," and in that spirit I'd like to start with one of the best North Carolina stories I know. It is the story of a North Carolina mountaineer. The Corps of Engineers came into his area to build a lake and a dam. They got every landowner, except one, to sign away their property. But one man would not move. Finally, an official of the corps went to his house, high on a hill. The man sat there, in a rocking chair on the porch, with an old shotgun across his lap.

"You have to move," the official told him.

"Not gonna do it," was the reply.

The federal official was angry. He said, "I just don't understand."

The mountain man said, "Come in and let me show you."

They went inside, and there was a simple cabin room with a fire burning away on the hearth. The owner said, "My grandfather started that fire and kept it going until he died, my father kept it going until he died, and now I'm responsible for it until I die. It has burned for more than 100 years."

Then the government man understood. He arranged for the entire cabin, with the fire intact, to be moved. It would not, he promised, be allowed to go out. At that the man was satisfied and said simply, "I just figured that the thing I was responsible for in my life was to keep the fire of my father and his father burning."

That's what we're here for today, to celebrate our tradition of keeping those fires burning. Today they burn in a glorious new home. In case you haven't noticed, we North Carolinians take our history seriously. From the original Hall of History in the late 1800s to this majestic new building, the North Carolina Museum of History has been committed to preserving our distinctive heritage in a living museum that represents all our people. This commitment is evident through museum education programs from Manteo to Murphy. It's evident in the painstaking care museum staff members have demonstrated in all the wonderful exhibitions you're about to experience—and the tradition continues, to future generations, through the Tar Heel Junior Historians, a statewide organization that nurtures the love of history in our schoolchildren.

We must not forget the ongoing commitment of the North Carolina Museum of History Associates, the largest state museum support organization in the country, with more than 14,000 members. Not only have they been instrumental in spreading the museum's word, but in raising much-needed private funds: more than $5.9 million for the museum and exhibits and more than $100,000 for this weekend's [grand opening] festival.

There's no question: We all need to learn from our past so we can look wisely into the future. The children you see on stage here today represent each of the twelve North Carolina congressional districts and wrote winning essays about what the new museum of history means to them. I'd like you to listen to a few of them, and hear their keen insight and simple truths.

—From Kelly Fish, Willow Springs, Second Congressional District: "The more we know, the better we are."

—From Reginald Lindsay, Charlotte, Ninth Congressional District: "I have never gotten to touch anything in a museum before. A room just to touch things would bring joy to many hearts."

—From Ryan Holsopple, Pollocksville, First Congressional District: "The exhibits need to show the struggle of trying to make it off of the land, but at the same time, show the love a farmer has for his way of life. North Carolina is so rich in heritage, the museum will never run out of things to put in it."

—From George Ivie Ragsdale, Salisbury, Sixth Congressional District: "For too many people, history is dull and boring. Just facts, no mention of what life meant in the past. This museum will not be that way. It will give visitors the chance to understand the trials and tribulations of our state's history."

—From Carmen Clark, Red Springs, Seventh Congressional District: "The museum should give us a sense of belonging, and it should also be fun!"

It is for the hopes and dreams of these children that this beautiful museum has been built, and it is through their continued efforts to understand history that our future successes will be achieved.

Of course, the study of history has changed considerably since I was a boy back in Rock Ridge. Today's history is painted on a wider canvas, and there's a lot more to it than just great battles and fearless heroes. Today's history embraces the whole of human experience—who we are, and where we came from, and where we hope to go from here—and that's what you'll find in the North Carolina Museum of History: a living record of North Carolina's people, our proudest moments and greatest achievements, our heroic struggles and highest hopes; and yes, a record of our failures, and follies, and injustices, because as a great philosopher once said, "Those who cannot remember the past are condemned to repeat it."[1]

Above all, this museum captures the rich diversity of the North Carolina experience. All of our people are represented here: men and women; black and white; Native American and Hispanic; the famous and the forgotten; the rich and the poor. They all made North Carolina history, and they all have the chance to tell their stories here. May they live forever.

Now I invite you to join me in a festive procession to North Carolina's newest front door. It's a home where that old North Carolina mountaineer's family fires will burn warmly—and so will yours.

---

[1] George Santayana, *Life of Reason* (1905), vol. 2, ch. 12, quoted in Angela Partington, ed., *The Oxford Dictionary of Quotations* (Oxford: Oxford University Press, 1996), 555.

CHARLOTTE COUNCIL ON ALCOHOLISM

Charlotte, April 27, 1994

[For related press release, see Governor Hunt Takes "New Approach" to Substance Abuse Programs, April 27, 1994, Governors Papers, James Baxter

Hunt Jr. Much of the following speech is similar to Hunt's remarks to the Commission on Substance Abuse Treatment and Prevention, November 22, 1994.]

You should be very proud of Martha. In her first term as a legislator, Speaker Dan Blue appointed her as co-chair of the Legislative Research Commission Mental Health Committee. That committee, headed by Representative Alexander and Senator Conder, deals directly with alcohol and drug problems, as well as developmental disabilities and mental illnesses. These problems dramatically affect the lives of almost 1 million of our citizens, and even more than that if you count the families affected. I know you are proud of her, as I am, for her outstanding leadership— and happy to have someone with her experience in this field helping to lead the effort.[1]

I am happy to be here today with the members of this council, which has provided an invaluable service to the community for the past thirty-six years by helping match up clients to services. Already this year, you have met with more than 1,300 clients, taken more than 1,400 calls for counseling, and made more than 800 referrals. You have helped thousands, and you have reason to be proud.

That's why it is especially fitting that I should be here to announce today the creation of two new bodies: the Commission on Substance Abuse Treatment and Prevention and the Office of Substance Abuse Policy.[2] By setting up this commission and office, which will include recovering alcoholics and other drug addicts, family members, professionals, and interested citizens, I can get advice about how to:

—Reduce the demand for alcohol and other drugs;

—Reduce administrative overhead by eliminating redundant activities, interagency conflict, and confusion;

—Increase awareness among citizens, elected officials, and service providers of alcohol and other drug problems;

—Reduce the law enforcement, court, and correction resources required by increasing the effectiveness of alcohol/other drug policy and service;

—Make it easier to get cost-effective treatment for addiction to alcohol and other drugs to all citizens;

—Find new sources of funding by going after new grants.

We need that advice. Alcoholism is a major public health problem in North Carolina. A recent Duke University study finds that 9 percent of our citizens become addicted to alcohol during their lives and 1 percent to drugs.

The good news is that we have thousands of recovering people, many of whom have discovered the twelve steps of Alcoholics Anonymous and Narcotics Anonymous. I am asking the recovering community to plug in, to give me their ideas, to help me lead North Carolina in attacking this terrible problem of addiction. The recovering community understands the issues of addiction from a deeply personal level, and many in that community have made great contributions to our society. Today I want to make it official: We care about your ideas, and we want to hear your solutions.

The Commission on Substance Abuse Treatment and Prevention and the Office of Substance Abuse Policy are not just good ideas for the addicts, and alcoholics, and their families. First, the commission and the council will help cut down on the high cost of addictive disease in the state. According to the Mental Health Study Commission, addictive disease directly and indirectly costs citizens of North Carolina over $5 billion annually.

Second, the commission and the council will help make our state safer. Three quarters of all homicides, rapes, child molestations, and assaults involve alcohol and drugs. The majority of people in prison, on parole, and on probation have serious alcohol and drug problems. We owe it to our people to see to it that these addicts get treatment before they get out, so they won't fall into the same dangerous patterns.

During the recent special session on crime, I proposed, and the General Assembly passed, bills to set up drug treatment programs for first-time offenders, to lease 500 substance abuse facility beds, and to triple the funding for the DART [Drug and Alcohol Rehabilitation Treatment] program. The DART prison treatment program has shown very positive results in reducing recidivism, and we should encourage it.

When these recovering substance abusers get out, we have more work to do. We still need services in the community for the thousands of addicted people on probation, the people getting out of prison, and the population that has not gotten involved in crime. We are continuing to develop drug courts and demonstration projects for high-risk offenders. I hope that the Office of Substance Abuse Policy will make it a priority to increase the availability of accessible and acceptable community services.

The more we do to treat addiction early, the more we can do to prevent crime, homelessness, and child abuse, as well as heart disease, liver damage, and pancreatitis. One of the great principles of recovery from addiction is sponsorship where one person further along in recovery helps an alcoholic or addict less far along. This volunteerism is in the greatest tradition of American giving—giving oneself, carrying the message of recovery to the alcoholic or addict that still suffers.

To those of you who are recovering, we need you! We need you to carry the message that treatment works and that sponsorship has never been more important. We need you to help in prisons and in after-care programs. We need you to help in our early childhood initiatives such as Smart Start. We need you to band together to help address the underlying social issues of inadequate work, poor housing, abusive families, and poor health care that shape most addicts' lives. Supporting the council and the commission, and working together, you can make a tremendous difference and really change our state. And now I would like to officially sign this executive order.

---

[1] Dan Blue was identified earlier in this volume.

Martha Bedell Alexander (1939-   ), born in Jacksonville, Fla.; resident of Mecklenburg Co.; B.S., Florida State University, 1961; Master of Human Development, University of North Carolina at Charlotte, 1979. Chair, N.C. Alcoholism Research Authority, 1988-1990, and member of other substance-abuse prevention, religious, and humanitarian organizations; member, N.C. House of Representatives, from 1993; Democrat. *North Carolina Manual, 1995-1996*, 540.

James Richard Conder (1930-   ), born in Hamlet; B.S., East Carolina University, 1958; attended Graduate School of Banking, Louisiana State University, and N.C. Bankers Assn. School, University of North Carolina at Chapel Hill; U.S. Air Force, 1951-1955, and Reserve, 1955-1959. Vice-president, First Union National Bank; member, 1962-1984, chair, 1964-1984, Richmond County Board of Commissioners; pres., N.C. Assn. of County Commissioners, 1972-1973; pres., National Assn. of Counties, 1981-1982; member, N.C. Senate, since 1985; Democrat. *North Carolina Manual, 1995-1996*, 453.

[2] Executive Order Number 46, Commission on Substance Abuse Treatment and Prevention, also established the Office of Substance Abuse Policy. Hunt's order became effective April 27, 1994. *N.C. Session Laws, 1993, Extra and Regular Sessions, 1994*, 3:1027-1030.

OYSTER SUMMIT

WILMINGTON, APRIL 29, 1994

I, too, want to applaud the farsightedness that has brought us to this point, and I want to tell all of you that you can count on me to support the all-important effort to restore North Carolina's oyster resources. I am committed to righting the wrongs that years of overharvesting, habitat degradation, diminished water quality, and disease have done to our state's oyster resources. The figures are overwhelming: The number of oysters harvested has dropped from 225,000 bushels in 1987 to just 48,000 bushels last year.

We can no longer afford to just talk about the problem. We know there's a problem. Now we need to devote all of our resources to solving that problem.

The decline in resources has been a serious blow for many North Carolina communities. The winter oyster harvest sustained coastal fishing communities in our state for almost 100 years. Now many commercial fishermen in some of the state's poorest counties are struggling. We've got to do something to help those family fishermen, and we've got to do something to help them now. Too many folks are moving away from coastal North Carolina, because they can't earn a living like their parents, and grandparents, and great-grandparents did.

We've got to restore our oyster resources to support those folks, the men and women who labor in our cold winter waters fishing for oysters. They deserve to be able to earn a living like their forefathers did. It's not a question of protecting oysters *or* economic development. We need to find the best way of doing both. New industry and development is [*sic*] vital to the coast, but so are our existing industries.

We can turn our oyster harvest around. Our state still possesses thousands of acres of potentially productive shellfish areas, an abundant natural source of shellfish food, and resilient oyster populations. We need to build on them. We do that in four ways:

—First, we protect existing habitat. The Marine Fisheries Commission has recently adopted rules identifying oyster growing areas as critical habitats in the estuary. Those areas now need to be identified for protection from competing fishing practices and other environmental disturbances.

—Second, we must protect our estuarine waters from further degradation. Without protection, we will lose thousands more acres to oyster harvesting.

—Third, we must explore ways to restore the oysters themselves. We must look at aquaculture and how it can be used to bring back the oyster in North Carolina. We need to have as much knowledge about raising oysters as beef farmers do about raising cattle. We must look to institutions like [North Carolina] Sea Grant and our fine state research universities to help us come up with effective ways to raise more and better oysters.[1]

—Fourth, if our oyster resources are to become viable again, we must develop strategies to deal with parasites like Dermo and MSX. Once again, we'll be looking to our research institutions for help in solving this problem.

Today is only the first step in what must be a long-term commitment and a long process as we revive our oyster industry in coastal North Carolina. I urge all of you to listen to what the experts have to say today. Use that knowledge to help devise an approach that will help the people in the oyster industry. It's going to take the best efforts of everyone in this room to get that job done. . . .

I'm certain that we will get the job done, and this administration is committed to restoring the oyster to North Carolina's coastal economy and environment. We will do all we can to get this job done, so that our commercial fishermen can find oysters in quantity and all of us can enjoy their quality—and appreciate what they mean to our coast.

---

[1] Based at N.C. State University, North Carolina Sea Grant was "a subsidiary of a national network of college programs supported by the National Oceanic and Atmospheric Administration" established to aid fisheries and fishermen. *News and Observer*, March 27, 1996.

COMMUNITY-ORIENTED POLICING CONFERENCE

RALEIGH, MAY 2, 1994

A few months ago, I went to visit a public housing community to learn about what we could do about crime in North Carolina. I visited with a woman who was taking care of eleven children. I got out of the car and saw drug dealers. The whole time I was inside, I heard gunshots. This woman I was visiting wouldn't let her kids leave the apartment after dark. I asked her where the police were. She said she hadn't seen a police officer in six months.

A few days later, I toured the Piedmont Park housing community in Winston-Salem with a man named Steve Hairston.[1] We saw no drug dealers. We didn't hear any gunshots, and we saw a lot of kids playing outside. Steve Hairston was proud of that, and he should be. He's a sergeant in the Winston-Salem Police Department, and he's assigned to foot patrol in Piedmont Park.

Sergeant Hairston told me that since they had started foot patrols, the number of juvenile assault cases had dropped by 50 percent. I asked him what he did as a police officer in the community. He didn't talk about busting drug dealers and breaking down doors, although he has to do that sometimes. He said he helped with clothing and food drives and took kids on field trips.

That's part of what community-oriented policing is about, about members of the law enforcement [agencies] becoming part of the community they serve, about showing you care and letting the people you serve see it. But to be truly effective in community policing, we can't just start a foot patrol in one neighborhood or set up a substation in a high-crime area. The criminals will just find out where the foot patrol ends and move there. To be effective, we must find ways of making our community-oriented policing department-wide.

To be truly effective, we can't just enforce the law; we have to take a holistic approach. Greensboro has established police-neighborhood resource centers in some of its public housing communities. Police officers work alongside with human resources workers, social service providers, and other resident services, and they're seen as part of the solution, not part of the problem.

To be truly effective, we must consider across-the-board changes. We may need to allow deputies to drive their own patrol cars while off duty. We may need to give community police officers the authority to get abandoned cars towed, or trash picked up, without having to unravel red tape.

To be truly effective, we need to re-establish the connection between the law-enforcement community and the law-abiding community. We don't expect doctors to be able to make us feel better if we don't tell them where we hurt. If you want to make your communities better, you need to talk to the people in them, ask them where they hurt, and how you can work together to change things.

In Piedmont Park, police have monthly meetings with the resident council to talk about safety, and they've gotten money from the housing authority to hire community safety coordinators—neighborhood residents who bolster the work of the police in the community. Sergeant Hairston says the great thing about involving the whole neighborhood is that they have great ideas. People in the community know where they need more street lights. They know who the drug dealers are. And when they know you care about their ideas, they'll be more willing to work with you on Community Watch programs and clean-up programs, and your officers will start feeling a greater sense of accomplishment and appreciation from the community.

True community-oriented policing won't happen overnight. It involves a fundamental shift in the way we think about law enforcement, from being reactive to being proactive, from simply answering calls to finding ways of preventing those calls.

In the special session on crime, we launched a new crime prevention program aimed at young students, called SOS [Support Our Students], which calls for setting up neighborhood and community after-school programs designed to give youngsters a place to go, and do and learn things, in the afternoons. We're adding other funds to existing community programs that help at-risk children. We're launching family resource centers at elementary schools. I hope you will investigate how you can help with these programs, as well as examining other ways to prevent crime.

Not everyone will be comfortable with that approach. Harry Dolan, the Lumberton police chief whom you've already heard from this morning, says the biggest problem with changing to a true community-oriented approach is that people will say, "We've always done it the other way." Well, if the other way isn't working, you have to look for new ways.[2]

I won't pretend you will leave this conference with a community-oriented policing plan for your town, or city, or county. You need local people to help you come up with local solutions to local problems. But I'm confident you will leave here with some insight into what makes successful programs work, and some commitment to forming partnerships, partnerships in which you can work together to make your communities safer, stronger, and better.

---

[1] Stephen Anthony Hairston Sr. (1954-   ), native of Winston-Salem; B.S. in education, 1977, B.S. in accounting, 1994, Winston-Salem State University; M.B.A., Appalachian State University, 1999. High school teacher, coach, 1977-1980; police officer, 1980-1985, senior police officer, 1985-1990, sergeant, from 1990, detective sergeant, from 1997, Winston-Salem Police Dept.; established 920 Youth Career Club in a Winston-Salem public housing community; earned local, state, and national recognition for outstanding community work and youth program development. Stephen A. Hairston Sr., letter to Jan-Michael Poff, September 20, 1999.

[2] Harry P. Dolan (1957-   ), born in Teaneck, N.J.; resident of Grand Rapids, Mich.; B.S., Western Carolina University, 1980; master's in organizational leadership and management, University of North Carolina at Pembroke, 1996. Career in law enforcement included deputy sheriff, Buncombe County Sheriff's Dept., Asheville, 1980-1982; Raleigh police officer, 1982-1987; police chief, N.C. Dept. of Human Resources Police Dept., Black Mountain; police chief, Lumberton, 1982-1998; police chief, Grand Rapids, Mich., from April 1998. Jacqueline Bush, administrative secretary to Chief Harry P. Dolan, to Jan-Michael Poff, August 30, 1999.

TALKING POINTS
EASTERN NORTH CAROLINA INDUSTRIAL COUNCIL

GREENVILLE, MAY 3, 1994

This chamber has long played a critical role in the success of the state. You have shepherded eastern North Carolina through a period of change that is probably unprecedented in state history.

The change continues today. Our state is changing daily, not just in urban areas, but in rural parts, as well. The tobacco industry, which has long played such an important role in our state's history, is being challenged nationally as never before. As you know, I have spoken personally to the president about this, and I have made clear to him the serious impact that the proposed taxes would have on our state, particularly eastern North Carolina. I will continue to fight for you and for eastern North Carolina.

At the same time, we need to continue to develop our industrial infrastructure through the hard work of this chamber on projects like the Global TransPark and other initiatives. We have to be prepared to adapt to our changing world. That's why, during my campaign, I called for a new economic strategy that would help us build a strong economic future based on high-skill, high-wage jobs.

As I campaigned across the state, I called for a new economic strategy to help us build a strong economic future based on high-skill, high-wage jobs. The future belongs to those with the best education and the best skills, and we need a new emphasis on technological innovation, entrepreneurial development, and planned quality growth.

We haven't done a good enough job of that in the past. Instead, our economic development strategies have changed from governor to governor. That's why the Government Performance Audit Committee said the state's economic efforts were fragmented, without clear direction and accountability; and that's why the North Carolina General Assembly, under the leadership of Senator Beverly Perdue, acted on GPAC's recommendation by passing legislation that called for the North Carolina Economic Development Board to design a new, statewide, comprehensive, strategic plan.[1]

On April 11, [1994], Bob Jordan, chairman of the North Carolina Economic Development Board, presented me with that plan, developed with the input of people from across the state. This plan brings together the views of educators, business leaders, local government officials, and frontline workers. It is a plan that takes into account the concerns of every North Carolinian and gives us a road map into how we can prepare to compete in the new global economy.[2]

I applaud the tireless effort of the North Carolina Economic Development Board to put this plan together. They formed task forces and committees to focus on special issues like incentives, regions, and the state ports, all of which are important to the growth of our state. You've already heard from Rick Carlisle[3] about the specifics of the plan, so you know some of the 103 specific recommendations it makes and the themes it emphasizes:

—the importance of improving worker training;

—the key role that nurturing small and new business will play in our future;

—the importance of equalizing the chance that every county in this state has to recruit new business, so that economic development doesn't just come to our major cities.

But the plan also, in many ways, hinges on an idea that you understood years ago, when you formed this chamber: regionalism. The idea is to enable the regions of this state to work together to promote themselves, with help from the state, and share the economic wealth. Local industrial recruiters will be able to do what they do with the most passion: recruit local jobs.

Under this plan, we will customize programs and services within the Department of Commerce, including customized marketing and promotion programs, so that we can help you do your jobs:

—We will implement an economic development information system that links regional partnerships with a state-of-the-art information system.

—We will develop a combination grant and loan program to provide funding for water and sewer projects in the less-wealthy areas of the state.

—We will work with the electric utilities, electric co-ops, and the utilit[ies] commission to examine electric rate policies and how to improve economic development, statewide.

—We will work to help increase access to natural gas lines in eastern North Carolina and other places.

—And we will increase the availability to the Targeted Jobs Tax Credit program to make it even more available to economically distressed parts of the state.

There is a lot more to study about this plan, but I am confident that it gives us a strong starting point as we try to build our economic future. It emphasizes the need for higher standards in our schools, better job training, and long-range planning. I think it provides us a beginning point from which we can develop jobs not just for tomorrow, but for our children—and our children's children.

---

[1] For the GPAC recommendation, see *Our State, Our Future: Report of the North Carolina Government Performance Audit Committee*, 39-41. Both Senator Beverly Perdue and the legislation requiring a strategic economic development plan were identified earlier in this volume.

[2] *Making North Carolina a High-Performance State: Comprehensive Economic Development Plan of the North Carolina Economic Development Board* ([Raleigh, N.C.: The Board,] April 1994).

[3] Rick Eugene Carlisle (1949-   ), born in Charlotte; resident of Chapel Hill; B.A., Duke University, 1976; master's in regional planning, University of North Carolina at Chapel Hill, 1978; U.S. Air Force, 1969-1973. Economic development consultant, 1977-1979; chief of program planning and development, 1979-1981, director of community assistance division and of Community Development Block Grant program, 1982-1985, N.C. Dept. of

Natural Resources and Community Development; economist, Western Carolina University, 1981-1982; director, housing and community development policy, National Assn. of Housing and Redevelopment Officials, 1985-1987; vice-president, N.C. Rural Economic Development Center, 1987-1991; sr. fellow, Corp. for Enterprise Development, 1991-1993; economic policy adviser to Governor Hunt, 1993-1997; deputy secretary, 1997-1998, acting secretary, 1998, was appointed secretary, 1998, N.C. Dept. of Commerce. *News and Observer*, April 26, May 1, 2, 1998.

TRANSPORTATION 2001

RALEIGH, MAY 5, 1994

[Texts grounded upon the May 1994 Transportation 2001 speech include those for the Wilson Chamber of Commerce Breakfast, Wilson, August 29, 1995; N.C. Board of Transportation Reception, Charlotte, March 6, 1996; Transportation 2001, Raleigh, May 3, 1996; and U.S. 220/I-73/I-74 Ribbon-Cutting Ceremony, Asheboro, August 27, 1996, Governors Papers, James Baxter Hunt Jr.]

Secretary Hunt, I commend you and this board for your hard work on this plan.[1] This plan is unlike any other transportation program our state has put together in its history. For the first time you have come together to take a comprehensive look at the transportation needs of our entire state. It goes beyond highways to include public transportation. It goes beyond piecemeal road projects to look at North Carolina's future economic development needs and looks at how we can address those needs with transportation. You have represented your regions well, but you have also represented the state well, working with the DOT staff to find efficiencies in the department and taking a look at the big picture of what our state needs to be doing in terms of transportation.

When I appointed Sam Hunt secretary of transportation a little over a year ago, I charged him with:

a) developing a comprehensive transportation program designed to boost North Carolina's economic development;

b) ensuring that our existing highways are well maintained; and

c) paying more attention to public transportation to reduce congestion and pollution.

I challenged you and the NCDOT employees to bring innovative and creative ideas to the table so we could use our tax dollars more effectively. With this Transportation 2001 plan, you have done just that.

First, we [are] adding money to speed up completion of roads to key economic corridors. These roads will bring jobs, industries, and improved quality of life to the people in the areas they serve. There are dozens of projects in the plan, but a few deserve special mention this morning. We're adding:

—$100 million to complete the widening of U.S. 17;

—$200 million to complete the U.S. 74 corridor from Brunswick County to Interstate 26;

—$53 million to complete the U.S. 421 corridor in the northwestern part of the state;

—$113 million to complete the U.S. 64 corridor from Nags Head to Ramseur;

—$60 million added to complete Interstate 26 from Asheville to Tennessee.

This is good news by itself, but there is more to this plan. For the first time in history, the maintenance backlog will be eliminated. You know what that means: fewer potholes, better bridges, better signs, and most of all, safer highways.

The third element of this plan is public transportation. Never before has there been a master plan in North Carolina to address public transportation. This plan outlines the necessary steps to improve travel time on our passenger rail routes between Raleigh and Charlotte. It calls for developing transportation centers for both rail and transit systems, encouraging development of regional transit services, and rewarding productivity and success when providing state funding for transit. These are areas I will remain committed to.

Our transportation system is one of the most vital aspects of our economic development. We are successful because of the hard work of our dedicated employees: those who select our rights-of-way and survey our land; those who pave, and plan, and care about how the people of this state get from one place to another. Now we need your continued hard work so that this ambitious plan can become reality. Then, when we get to 2001, we can look back on today and remember that this is when it all got started, and we began setting a new pace for the new century.

---

[1] *Transportation 2001: Setting a New Pace for a New Century, 1995-2001 Transportation Improvement Program* ([Raleigh: N.C. Department of Transportation, n.d.]).

Rector Samuel Hunt III (1941-   ), born in Burlington; B.A., East Carolina University, 1965; U.S. Army, 1966-1969, and Reserve, 1970. President, Hunt Electric Supply Co., and of Atlas Electric Corp.; past director, Alamance Chamber of Commerce; member, N.C. House of Representatives, 1985-1992; was appointed secretary, state Dept. of Transportation, by Gov. Hunt, 1993; Democrat. *North Carolina Manual, 1993-1994*, 335.

WELFARE REFORM AND
POVERTY REDUCTION CONFERENCE

WINSTON-SALEM, MAY 5, 1994

I'm honored to be part of this conference as you examine one of North Carolina's greatest challenges: reforming the welfare system in our state and moving people from poverty into self-sufficiency. If we meet this challenge, we can bring about positive change for North Carolina's children, and families, and our state's economic future. The collective wisdom in this room will be critical as we shape a comprehensive reform initiative that makes the system work for, not against, children and families.

You just heard an eye-opening account from Kathy Harris. She entered our welfare system as a single mother, after a divorce. She encountered a confusing, bureaucratic, and demoralizing system that failed to serve [her] needs and the needs of her family. It failed to get her back into the workforce. It failed—period.

Our system is failing too many mothers like Kathy. Too many mothers are being forced to choose between work and their children, between work and housing, AFDC and child care. That's no choice. We must find a better way. We must help Kathy cross that bridge from poverty to economic independence. We must not let them drown in a sea of bureaucratic red tape.

I believe the Reynolds Foundation report, *Beyond Poverty*, can help us build such a bridge; and I'm here to tell you, North Carolina is going to seize the moment! We are not going to wait for Washington to decide what's best for Kathy Harris and her family. With your help, I believe that North Carolina can create a system that encourages and rewards work; a system that helps move a family toward self-sufficiency with a sliding scale of benefits; a system that provides the basic support services families need; a system that serves as a bridge to economic independence, not an obstacle.

I'm no engineer, but I know that a good bridge needs a solid foundation. So let me take a few minutes to share with you what I see as the principles, the foundation, of North Carolina's welfare reform efforts:

—I envision a system that encourages and rewards work and encourages families to stay together. We must remove penalties and encourage work, earnings, and assets. We need a flexible system that recognizes the importance of work and family stability.

—We must promote real economic choices and options by providing education and training programs that give people marketable skills and credentials. We must provide child care and health care to families as they make the welfare-to-work transition.

—We must pay special attention to teen parents in the welfare system. We must develop strategies to prevent long-term dependency and to end welfare for the next generation. But forcing the children of young parents into orphanages is not the answer! Instead, we must pioneer new and better approaches for working [parents] and serving families and children.

—We will need to be creative to move families toward self-sufficiency. We'll take advantage of public-private partnerships and involve businesspeople in the planning and implementation of welfare reform strategies.

—We will recognize that true welfare reform takes time. The existing system has evolved over the past fifty years. We can fix it, but we need to be patient and do it right!

—We must make better use of technology to simplify the welfare system and make it more efficient and accountable. That may mean redesigning programs to get a clearer idea of whether a program is succeeding. Technology should promote better, more effective delivery of services.

This is an ambitious set of goals, but I believe we can devise such a system. We have the creativity, energy, and the people in North Carolina to do it. What we need is leadership. That's why I've directed the Governor's Commission on Workforce Preparedness to create a special welfare reform task force to map out a blueprint for action. The task force will work closely with legislative leaders and will bring together those who have a stake in welfare reform—consumers, advocates, business leaders, nonprofits and foundations, and state and local government officials—to be part of this effort.

This task force will craft a comprehensive plan to bring low-income people and communities into the mainstream economy and help us provide a clear and reasonable system of responsibilities and consequences for welfare recipients and those who work with and support welfare recipients. Sandy Babb, executive director of the commission, and I are working hard to find the right leader for this task force, a leader with drive, and energy, and vision.[1] I hope this Welfare Reform Task Force will lay the foundation and pave the way for achieving our vision for North Carolina.

We may not have the benefit of a lot of new federal dollars to reform our system, but we can build on the efforts we already have under way

PUBLIC ADDRESSES AND STATEMENTS

and use existing dollars and resources in new ways. By working collaboratively, we can make the most of what we have, streamlining and improving how we deliver services to children and families. North Carolina is already leading the nation in new ways of tailoring services to meet the needs of families and communities. Smart Start, North Carolina's new early childhood initiative, is a national model in public-private partnership and collaboration to better serve children and families. Smart Start uses the state as [a] catalyst to provide quality, affordable child care and family services, the keys to successful welfare reform.

Earlier this week, I met with local leaders from the eighteen Smart Start pioneer counties. I heard some amazing success stories. Across the state, public-private Smart Start partnerships are making child care more affordable for working families—boosting the quality of child care, increasing the number of child-care spaces available for working families, providing emergency help for families in crisis, encouraging teen parents to stay in school by providing needed services, providing basic health care and screening, providing vans to help poor families overcome transportation barriers to get the services they need. Some counties are using Smart Start dollars to set up family resource centers as one-stop clearinghouses for services. During the recent special legislative session, the General Assembly provided another $2 million in grant money, at my urging, for family resource centers. These centers are a critical ingredient of welfare reform because they streamline services and make them more accessible for families in need.

Health care reform is also part of the welfare reform equation. We have a health planning commission now grappling with the best ways to reform our health system and prepare North Carolina for the national health reform movement. All families must have access to health care for welfare reform to be successful.

So, we're already doing a lot in North Carolina to help children and families to prepare for true welfare reform, and we already have some success stories to show that we are making a difference. Let me tell you about Judith Byers, from Mecklenburg County. Judith overcame so many obstacles: juvenile delinquency, teen pregnancy, battering by her husband, drug addiction. She enrolled in the JOBS [Job Opportunities and Basic Skills] program, which I started as the "Workfare" program in my previous administration to help move folks from welfare to work.[2] She earned an associate degree in her local community college. Now Judith is a substance abuse counselor with the Charlotte Housing Authority and is working nights toward her bachelor's degree.

That's what we can do, folks, but we can't wait. The time for action is now. My administration is committed to making a difference for children and families. We have begun to translate that commitment into policy with Smart Start, family resource centers, and our efforts in education reform. Now we must focus our energies on welfare reform. But we can't do it without you. We need your help, your energy, and your ideas. Together, I believe that we can create a system that really works for the children and families of North Carolina.

---

[1] Bertha Maxwell-Roddey was chosen to lead the thirty-two-member Welfare Reform Task Force. Maxwell-Roddey (1930-   ), born in Seneca, S.C.; B.A., Johnson C. Smith University, 1954; M.Ed., University of North Carolina at Greensboro, 1967; Ph.D., Union Graduate School, Cincinnati, 1974. Career with Charlotte-Mecklenburg School System, 1954-1970, included principal at Morgan Elementary, 1967-1968, and Albemarle Road Elementary, 1968-1970; "teachers corps" she co-founded, 1964, to help disadvantaged children with learning and social skills has been cited as inspiration for federal Head Start program. Career at University of North Carolina at Charlotte, 1970-1987, included Frank Porter Graham Professor, from 1971, and director, Afro-American and African Studies Program; vice-president, administrative affairs and planning, Johnson C. Smith University, Charlotte, 1977-1978; adjunct professor, University of South Carolina at Lancaster, from 1987, and Clinton Jr. College, Rock Hill, S.C., from 1995; instructor, Queens College, Charlotte, 1994; co-founder, National Council for Black Studies, 1977, and of Charlotte's Afro-American Cultural Center. Bertha Maxwell-Roddey, letter to Jan-Michael Poff, September 17, 1999; *Charlotte Observer*, May 26, 1964; *News and Observer*, August 28, 1999; press release, Governor Jim Hunt Creates Welfare Reform Task Force, Raleigh, September 22, 1994, Governors Papers, James Baxter Hunt Jr.

[2] For related press release, see Governor Hunt Pushes to Expand JOBS Program to 100 Counties, Raleigh, July 1, 1994, Governors Papers, James Baxter Hunt Jr.

ADVISORY BUDGET COMMISSION

RALEIGH, MAY 6, 1994

[For related press releases, see Governor Jim Hunt Proposes "Education" Budget, Raleigh, May 6, 1994, and Statement in Reaction to 1994-1995 Budget Passed by the General Assembly, Raleigh, July 16, 1994, Governors Papers, James Baxter Hunt Jr. The governor's notes for his May 25, 1994, news conference echo his presentation, below, to the Advisory Budget Commission.]

We're here today to discuss the 1994-1995 budget, which I intend to present to the Appropriations Committees next week in preparation for the short session [of the General Assembly].[1] I'm looking to the Advisory Budget Commission for advice, guidance, and assistance in this process, and I see this meeting as part of our collaborative effort. I've already met with or talked with many of you, and I look forward to working with you to prepare a budget that meets the needs of North Carolinians.

First, I want to take a few minutes to share with you my thinking as I put this draft document together. This chart is my mission statement. I keep it in my office to remind me what's important. "Education is our future—it's everything." That's what's important.[2]

This budget proposal does what we need to do. It puts education first. I am recommending $446 million, some 47 percent of this budget proposal, for North Carolina's education needs next year. First, we must make sure we pay our educators fairly. We expect a lot from teachers, community college instructors, and university faculty, and we must compensate them in return. I'm proposing a 4 percent pay raise for all state employees and teachers, along with a 1 percent performance pay bonus.[3] The details are in your handout.

We must encourage excellent teachers. I am proposing almost $4 million for a teacher academy to help train 3,000 teachers this summer in critical areas like site-based decision making.[4] I want to encourage teachers to meet higher standards with voluntary board certification, so I'm proposing $500,000 to help 100 teachers get board certified. We'd help them take time off to get certified by the National Board for Professional Teaching Standards, pay their fee and a $5,000 bonus for certification.[5]

We must make sure that our children are trained in high-tech skills, and that all our children in all regions have access to quality education. I am proposing $20 million for new computers in our schools and $800,000 for a distance learning program that will let students across the state take courses at the North Carolina School of Science and Math.[6] At the same time, we must continue our commitment to the Basic Education Program. I am proposing $10 million for the BEP in the short session, building on the $18 million the General Assembly provided during the crime session for new counselors, school social workers, and psychologists. And we must take care of other basics as well, so I've proposed $26 million for school buses, textbooks, and other instructional supplies and equipment.[7]

We must make sure that our high school graduates have the real job skills they need for the real world of work. I'm proposing more than $1 million for Tech Prep, to develop courses, revamp curriculum, and boost equipment needs at high schools across the state. And I'm proposing $1 million for our new JobReady initiative, to encourage school-business partnerships to develop apprenticeships and other school-to-work transition efforts.[8]

We must make sure that our community colleges have the resources they need to provide quality workforce training. Our community colleges are last in the Southeast in salaries, and that's not right. I'm recommending more than $30 million for community college salaries, $6 million for instructional support personnel, $13 million for books and equipment, more than $1 million for literacy education, and $500,000 for specialized technology centers.[9]

And we must make sure our universities stay competitive, so they continue to produce the top-notch graduates and cutting-edge research that's made our universities among the finest in the nation. My budget proposal includes $61 million for university salaries, $70 million for construction projects, and almost $17 million for projects identified as priorities by the Board of Governors, including books, computers, and instructional support.[10]

These budget recommendations build on what we've done together in education in the last sixteen months. We want to build on other innovations, like expanding Smart Start to twelve new counties, and we want to move forward with a more aggressive and more strategic approach to recruiting good jobs to all regions of our state. We have the money to do it—without raising taxes. Revenues look good. Our budget analysts expect some $260 million in additional available revenue. That means some $300 million in available recurring funds and more than $400 million in nonrecurring. But we must make sure to get our priorities right and to shift available resources to our highest-priority areas. This budget recommends a number of adjustments and reductions, largely reflecting lower than expected costs next year in areas like Medicaid and education enrollment.

In addition, we expect managers in state government to achieve greater efficiencies. So I am proposing that each department in state government eliminate roughly 1 percent of their SPA, non-classroom positions or the equivalent in other savings.[11] This means some $16 million that we can shift to education and other priorities.

These are my proposals. I look forward to your suggestions and to working with you to finalize our budget and to work together to do what's right for the future of our people.

---

[1] See *North Carolina State Budget, Recommended Changes to the 1994-95 State Budget, 1993-95 Biennium, James B. Hunt Jr., Governor* ([Raleigh]: Office of State Budget and Management, May 1994).

[2] The governor's mission statement consisted of four points:

"Education is our future—it's everything.
  Protect people from crime: Make punishments real and mobilize
    communities to teach kids values.
  Smart Start + High Standards + High Skills = Good Jobs
  Make state government work better. The status quo is
    unacceptable."

[3] The governor proposed the same salary increase for public schoolteachers and state employees, but by the time the 1994 legislative session closed, the educators' superior lobbying effort made them first among equals in terms of pay. Teachers with three to thirty years' service won pay increases of 7 percent; those with less than three or more than thirty years were given raises of 5 percent. State employees received a 4 percent raise and a one-time, 1 percent bonus. John L. Sanders, ed., *North Carolina Legislation, 1994* (Chapel Hill: Institute of Government, University of North Carolina, 1995), 139-140.

[4] Hunt wanted $3.8 million for the Teacher Academy, a sum the General Assembly approved. Press releases, Governor Jim Hunt Proposes "Education" Budget, Raleigh, May 6, 1994, and Statement in Reaction to 1994-1995 Budget Passed by the General Assembly, Raleigh, July 16, 1994, Governors Papers, James Baxter Hunt Jr.

[5] The General Assembly authorized $500,000 for NBPTS candidates in F.Y. 1994-1995. The appropriation covered the $975 program participation fee, a 4 percent annual bonus, and up to three days' paid leave for each eligible teacher. *N.C. Session Laws, 1993, Extra and Regular Sessions, 1994*, c. 769, s. 19.28; press release, Governor Hunt Applauds Legislature for Supporting High Teaching Standards, Boston, July 18, 1994, Governors Papers, James Baxter Hunt Jr.

[6] Legislators set aside $42 million for school technology needs, more than double the amount Hunt requested. *N.C. Session Laws, 1993, Extra and Regular Sessions, 1994*, c. 769, s. 19.26; press release, Statement in Reaction to 1994-1995 Budget Passed by the General Assembly, Raleigh, July 16, 1994, Governors Papers, James Baxter Hunt Jr.

[7] Basic Education Program funding was increased by at least $36 million during the 1994 regular session: $10 million for school psychologists, social workers, and counselors, and $26 million to cut kindergarten class sizes. State lawmakers found $35.7 million for instructional supplies and school buses. *N.C. Session Laws, 1993, Extra and Regular Sessions, 1994*, c. 769, s. 19.17; press release, Statement in Reaction to 1994-1995 Budget Passed by the General Assembly, Raleigh, July 16, 1994, Governors Papers, James Baxter Hunt Jr.

[8] *North Carolina State Budget, Recommended Changes to the 1994-95 State Budget*, 15, 56.

[9] Hunt won $542,885 for specialized technology centers, $1,552,712 for literacy education, and $13 million for books and equipment that he requested for the community college system. Legislators also granted community college faculty salary increases averaging 8 percent, plus a 1 percent bonus. *North Carolina State Budget, Recommended Changes to the 1994-95 State Budget*, 19-21; *Overview: Fiscal and Budgetary Actions, North Carolina General Assembly, 1993 Session and 1994 Sessions*, 70; Sanders, *North Carolina Legislation, 1994*, 139-140.

[10] Faculty members within the University of North Carolina system saw 6 percent pay increases, on average, plus a 1 percent bonus. State lawmakers supplied $16,631,778 to fund projects listed in the UNC Board of Governors' "Schedule of Priorities" instead of the full $16.8 million Hunt requested. *North Carolina State Budget, Recommended Changes to the 1994-95 State Budget*, 24, 77; *Overview: Fiscal and Budgetary Actions, North Carolina General Assembly, 1993 Session and 1994 Sessions*, 102, 397-399; Sanders, *North Carolina Legislation, 1994*, 139-140.

[11] State government positions subject to the provisions of the State Personnel Act were referred to as SPA.

STATE EMPLOYEES ASSOCIATION OF NORTH CAROLINA NEWSPAPER COLUMN

RALEIGH, MAY 11, 1994

From the first day of this administration, we have worked hard to invest in our people in order to invest in the future of North Carolina.

There's no question in my mind that a smart investment today can reap great dividends tomorrow. Investing in preschoolers through Smart Start today will produce healthier children who are eager to learn tomorrow. Investing in our students by setting rigorous new standards today will produce graduates with real-life job skills tomorrow. Investing in workforce preparedness will train and retrain adult workers so they can compete tomorrow and the day after tomorrow.

By the same token, I believe we must invest in our state employees. We expect a great deal from state employees, and we'll be looking to you for a great deal more in the next few years as we work together to fundamentally change the way state government operates. We expect you to give us your best professional efforts. By the same token, we must treat you like professionals and pay you like professionals.

That has not been the case, recently. As you well know, state employee raises have lagged behind the rate of inflation and behind the private sector in recent years. State employees got no raise in 1991, a flat $522 increase in 1992, and a 2 percent raise, with a 1 percent bonus, in 1993. In comparison, private-sector employees received an average of 3 percent each year, as the Consumer Price Index continued to climb.

I hope the pay raise I've recommended for the 1994-1995 budget will help balance the scales. My budget recommendation to the General Assembly includes a 4 percent pay raise—twice the pay raise I recommended last year—and a 1 percent performance pay bonus for state employees. This pay raise would follow the Comprehensive Pay Plan passed into law last year, with a 2 percent cost-of-living adjustment, a 2 percent career-growth increase, and a one-time performance bonus averaging 1 percent that would be given to employees who are rated "very good" or "outstanding" in their annual performance appraisal. The performance bonus should go to our very best to encourage them to do their very best.

Every budget requires us to get our priorities in order. As I said during the crime session, we can afford to do what we need to do in our priority areas—like education, children's programs, economic development, and crime prevention—and to give our state employees and teachers a fair pay raise. I think the budget proposal I've made does just that.

But our resources are not boundless. We can afford to do this without raising taxes, because revenues look good, and because we are shifting available resources to our highest-priority areas. My budget recommends $150 million in budget reductions and adjustments. Much of these adjustments reflect lower than expected costs, next year, in areas like Medicaid and education enrollment. But we also expect managers in state government to achieve greater efficiencies, and we are giving them the flexibility to find a certain level of savings.

I am proposing that each department in state government eliminate roughly 1 percent of their nonteacher jobs or find equivalent savings from other areas. This means we can find more than $16 million in savings, and we can shift those dollars to higher-priority areas, like education or pay raises. The State Budget Office says that state government now has some 3,300 vacant, but funded, positions. This means departments are getting those dollars, but using them for other areas or turning them back at the end of the fiscal year. Why not shift those resources to higher-priority areas? Permanently eliminating some 500 of these vacant positions from the budget would let departments reach that 1 percent goal without eliminating any filled positions.

We can do much more when it comes to doing business more efficiently and shifting dollars to higher priorities. Next year I will be looking to frontline state employees and managers to help us find even more savings. I want you to be creative and innovative about saving money in every department and every division! That's happening in many state government offices now. At DOT [N.C. Department of Transportation], for example, chemistry supervisor William M. Medford and transportation engineering supervisor Robert J. Downes III came up with an idea to distill spent methyl chloroform, which will save the state $20,000.[1] These two state employees were rewarded financially for their good ideas, under DOT's suggestion system. [This] is the kind of innovative thinking that we want to encourage—and this is the kind of creativity that we want to build upon to make more fundamental changes in how state government services are delivered. We'll talk more about these efforts in future columns, as I detail the efforts under way in many departments to change the way we do business. But meanwhile, State Employee Ombudsman Blanche Critcher and I would welcome your suggestions about other ways to encourage creative cost savings. What kind of incentives should we look at in addition to the state employees' and department suggestion system? Please let us know!

---

[1] All fourteen divisions of the state Transportation Department used 1-1-1 tricholoroethane, or trico, "to conduct asphalt extraction tests on bituminous concrete (asphalt)," wrote NCDOT resident engineer R. J. Downes III. Division 5's Durham site alone generated twelve 55-gallon drums of asphalt-trico waste a year, according to Downes; he and W. M. Medford "constructed a low-cost still using a glass-lined, propane hot water heater," in Durham, and "recycled twelve 55-gallon drums of spent trico this past year. The savings from this recycling effort have already netted $2,345, plus the costs of transportation and handling associated with twenty-four drums of material have been eliminated. Several other highway divisions are constructing similar stills, and if all spent materials were distilled statewide, DOT could save $20,000+ the first year."

Each still would pay for itself after processing just two drums of used trico. Besides saving the state money by "drastically minimizing the need for purchasing new trico," the procedure also reduced "the handling and public exposure to a potentially hazardous material." R. J. Downes III, letter to Sandra P. Washington, community relations coordinator, Governor's Waste Management Board, February 26, 1990.

William M. Medford (1946-   ), born in Asheville; resident of Raleigh; B.S., Western Carolina University. Career with Chemical Testing Sub-Unit, Materials and Tests Unit, N.C. Dept. of Transportation, included assistant chemical testing engineer, 1972-1979, management engineer, 1979-1983, chemical testing engineer, from 1983, and sub-unit head, from 1984; member, Society of Protective Coatings Committees; helped develop national containment guidelines for hazardous paint removal. William M. Medford, letter to Jan-Michael Poff, April 12, 1999.

Robert John Downes III (1947-   ), born in Maple Shade, N.J.; resident of Durham; B.S., N.C. State University, 1976. Assistant resident engineer, 1978-1980, resident engineer, from 1980, N.C. Dept. of Transportation. Robert John Downes III, letter to Jan-Michael Poff, June 14, 1999.

NORTH CAROLINA CITIZENS
FOR BUSINESS AND INDUSTRY

RALEIGH, MAY 12, 1994

[Governor Hunt's May 12 address to North Carolina Citizens for Business and Industry was nearly identical to his remarks for the North Carolina Bankers Association, Pinehurst, May 20, 1994.]

I met with my cabinet earlier this week at a retreat. It was a chance to look back at what we had accomplished in the past sixteen months— and forward, to where we go from here. As I looked back, I was impressed that we have made some real fundamental changes in the way government does business. We've taken a different approach to problem solving. We've understood that government cannot do it alone. Business cannot do it alone. Together, we can make a real difference. Let's look at what we have done together.

Smart Start

Now we have eighteen counties in North Carolina where kids are getting the quality childhood education and health care they need to come to school ready to learn. In Jones County, Smart Start money is being used to make sure children get a healthy start. There are no pediatricians in Jones County, so one day a week, those funds are used to bring a doctor to those children so they can have a chance to be healthy.

In the western counties that have joined together to form a partnership, Smart Start funding has been pooled with DOT [Department of Transportation] funds to purchase nineteen vans—and make sure that children get to quality child-care programs. In all of our Smart Start counties, it is moving children off of waiting lists and into quality child-care centers; in Orange County, they've totally gotten rid of the waiting list!

You helped make this happen. You testified before the Appropriations Committee to get Smart Start off the ground. You reminded legislators of the importance of being proactive, not reactive; of investing in the front end so you won't have to pay more on the back end. The North Carolina Bankers Association endorsed our efforts. Since then, you have provided critical input to the statewide effort, from the leadership of Jim Goodmon—CEO of Capitol Broadcasting, as chairman of the Partnership for Children—to your support of your local Smart Start programs. And we need your help to keep Smart Start growing in all 100 counties.

Today I want to announce another example of creative business leadership that is helping our children. Duke Power is making a tremendous gift of time and talent by loaning us one of their top executives. Bob Allen is district manager of Duke's Charlotte operation.[1] He is also committed to child advocacy issues. He knows business, and he knows what role business can play in helping our children, and he is committed to making it happen. Now for the next two years, he is combining his commitment to children with his business savvy and putting them together to help Mecklenburg County's children. He will be working full time on the county's Smart Start effort and will be encouraging members of the business community to get behind the effort.

Not every company could do what Duke Power has done, but their generosity shows how seriously they take the future of our children and how partnership between businesses and government can change our state. It is a tribute to them and a challenge to all of us.

SOS

We're in the process of setting up SOS [Support Our Students], an after-school program designed to make sure that at-risk children in our state have a safe, supportive, interesting place to go in the afternoons. You helped us pass it, along with my proposals to keep dangerous criminals behind bars longer and deter at-risk children from crime, during the recent special session. Now we need the leadership, and energy, and creativity of business leaders across the state to support these programs, to really make them work, so that we can turn these students around.

Standards

This summer our Standards and Accountability Commission will be recommending rigorous new standards for our students. These standards will require fundamental change in the way our schools operate. You and I know we need to make real, substantive changes in our educational system, and I know we can't do that without you.

From the start, business leaders have been serving on the commission and helping to set those standards. In meetings all across the state, business leaders have told us what they need, but aren't getting, from our schools—and that is a real difference. The CEO of Freightliner, Jim Hebe, told me at a meeting of CEOs and governors in Washington that, in all of his years of doing business across the nation and around the world, no government leader had ever asked him what he needed from schools! We've asked, and we will follow up with action.

In short, with your help we've begun a sea change of reform here in the past sixteen months. We have more to do in the short legislative session that begins later this month—and in next year's long session.

Last week, as many of you know, I unveiled my budget priorities for the next fiscal year. As you know, our fiscal picture is good. Our revenues are up substantially, and we have asked departments to find efficiencies so that we can restructure our priorities.

Those priorities are clear. In my office, I have a chart with my mission statement on it. It says, "Education is our future—it's everything."

Some 47 percent of my proposed expansion budget would go to education by improving teacher and faculty salaries, investing in equipment, encouraging excellence in teaching, and addressing technology needs. I'm proposing more than $1 million for Tech Prep, to develop courses, revamp curriculum, and boost equipment needs at high schools across the state; and I'm proposing $1 million for our new JobReady initiative, to encourage school-business partnerships to develop apprenticeships and other school-to-work transition efforts. I've proposed that we build on the success of Smart Start, by adding twelve new partnerships next year, and I want to continue to build this program until we achieve our goal: that every child in this state who wants it can afford quality child care.

Through your work on the Economic Development Commission, and in hearings, you've helped us develop a comprehensive state economic development plan. We're asking for funding to begin marketing the state by regions, bringing together the combined resources of the state, the regions, and local economic development councils. And we're asking for more money to use in the Governor's Competitive Fund, which last year helped us bring in some 4,300 new jobs, almost half in economically distressed counties.

There is much talk, these days, about tax cuts. I've recommended, as part of our economic development plan, that the state conduct an audit of all state business taxes, so that we can determine where tax cuts would be most helpful. And as you know, I have recommended two cuts already in the unemployment insurance tax. Those cuts will save you $310 million over the next two years alone.

The key word in all of our work together in the past year is *partnership*. You have played a critical role in this administration so far, and we are depending on your insights and experience in the future. We are both committed to the same things. We want our children, all children, to grow up and come to school ready to learn. We want to reform our educational system, so that our students graduate from school, ready to get good jobs and succeed; and we all want our state to be better— better positioned in every way to meet the challenges of the twenty-first century.

I was in Charlotte, earlier this year, at a meeting of the Standards and Accountability [Commission] when I heard the testimony of Jim Bavis, vice-president of Human Resources for Duke Power. He started out by noting that North Carolina was in "pretty good" shape as a state, and then he reminded us that "pretty good" isn't good enough when you are competing with the rest of the world. And then he read a poem that provided a glimpse of the future of our state. He applied it to our students. I've adapted it to apply to all of our people:

There once was a pretty good state
    That had a pretty big task
To ensure that its pretty good students
    Would never again come in last.
They established some very good standards
    Putting their schools to the test
And now North Carolina's students
    Are not pretty good—they're the best.

We can't be content to be "pretty good." Working together, we can make this state the best. I look forward to our continued work together, as partners.

---

[1] Bob Allen, graduate of Wake Forest University; former assistant Mecklenburg County manager and fundraising director, United Way of Central Carolinas; employed by Duke Power since 1984, company's Charlotte area district manager since 1991. Allen's task in the Mecklenburg County area was to "cultivate corporate and other private support for the Partnership [for Children] and Smart Start in an effort to offset state dollars with private-sector dollars and to boost business involvement in Smart Start." Press release, Smart Start Receives Major Corporate Support, Raleigh, May 12, 1994, Governors Papers, James Baxter Hunt Jr.

BUILDING SUCCESSFUL BUSINESS-EDUCATION
PARTNERSHIPS TO ACHIEVE WORLD-CLASS STANDARDS

Chapel Hill, May 13, 1994

[The following is a transcript of Governor Hunt's speech at the fifth in a series
of education reform conferences mounted by the National Alliance of Business.
A much abbreviated version of his text was released to the press as "National
Alliance for Business, May 13, 1994." See also press release, Governor Hunt Says
New Standards Will Drive Education Reform, Chapel Hill, May 13, 1994,
Governors Papers, James Baxter Hunt Jr.]

I slipped up to New York this week [to] the National Center [on]
Education and the Economy, which set the standards for education under
Goals 2000.[1] It struck me that this is the first time in the history of America
that we're beginning to see the whole picture and focus on all of its
important parts, like school reform, and to have an explicit policy set
out at the national level for our nation to get it right. And by the way,
Bill,[2] we in North Carolina also talk about preschool. We have a program,
called Smart Start, which is designed to provide quality day care and
health care to every child in North Carolina.

We believe you have to give children the right things in the first five
years, which is the best investment we can make for their future. We
are working on school-to-work transition, and then we're working to
set standards higher for our schools to expect more from our kids. It's
all aimed at one thing: a world-class workforce. America never did have
that before, because we didn't have to have a world-class workforce.
But we do today, and I am delighted that our nation is focusing on it
and that the National Alliance of Business, under Bill Kolberg's wonderful
leadership, has come here to help us focus on it.

Let me share with you our mission statement. If you come to the
Governor's Office in the State Capitol, you will see a mission statement
that has four statements. The first says: "Education is our future. It's
everything." In the full sense of that word, I believe that is true, and it
really is what we have to be about much more seriously and much more
effectively. We have not done it well enough in the past. We appreciate
Bill Kolberg saying nice things about us, but we know how far we have
to go.

Today, we are not meeting our educational challenge in North Carolina,
despite the hard work of so many people in this room. The math problem
I've given you today is an eighth-grade problem, but employers tell us
that many of our high school graduates in North Carolina are barely
able to master this kind of real-life problem. I said high school graduates.

We are sending youngsters into the workplace today without the ability to think and without the practical and technical skills they need for entry-level jobs. We are failing to produce the workers that businesses need, and we are failing to produce the workforce that North Carolina needs to build a prosperous future.

It's really easy for us to criticize our schools, and we do it a lot, because they are our schools. Bill Kolberg, this is the number-one public education state in America! And I'll just tell you that we are about public schools. The people in North Carolina care deeply about public education in this state.

The truth is, we are dumping many of society's toughest problems into our classrooms. We're sending our children to school without quality day care, without health care, without parental involvement, without teaching them values—all of these things are necessary for a good start in life. We're asking our teachers to deal with drugs, weapons, and teenage pregnancy, and I can go on and on, and we're asking them to deal with kids who don't think there's any purpose in their life.

We're expecting a lot, but we have not spelled out the expectations of them. Educators tell me that they need to know what we, as the customers, want. We've not given our schools a clear mission. We've not laid out clear, measurable goals. We've not set specific standards for achievement until recently. Then this wave of involvement came along, starting with *A Nation at Risk*.[3] We didn't even have the people who keep the records out there involved in this—thank goodness, we do now.

Our mission ought to be educating students—producing graduates, if you want to use a manufacturing term—graduates who can work, and think, and succeed in the modern workplace, as well as, of course, to be good citizens, and good parents, graduates who can get a good job, and hold a good job, in that real world of work that is changing so fast. That puts such great demands on us.

That's where we need to take education reform in North Carolina. That's why I appointed an Education Standards and Accountability Commission last fall, after it was set up through legislation by our General Assembly. It's made up of business people, parents, and educators. It is charting the course for this mission. Very simply, I think that this commission is taking a giant leap for North Carolina, tying educational standards to the demands [in] the workplace for the first time in our history. We've talked about it in the past, but we have never really set those standards with employers, and parents, and teachers involved.

I want to report to you, today, that the standards commission has traveled to every region of this state, giving our people input into this.

These are our schools; these are our children; this is going to be our workforce. The people need to be involved in it. I went to most of those hearings, myself; and they invited people to come, particularly employers, and they asked real people what kinds of things graduates ought to know, and be able to do, to get and hold a good job. And let me tell you, they heard it: They heard from business people all over this state, they heard from educators, they heard from parents, they heard from students—all kinds of folks.

Let me tell you what I heard at one of these hearings. A businessman told me that he decided to set up a button-making shop in Warren County. Warren County is probably one of the bottom five of our counties in per-capita income. Six years before he came here, he'd started up similar companies in Hong Kong, and in China, where he hired high school graduates to analyze and repair circuit boards. Here in North Carolina, he had to hire an electrical engineer, a college graduate, to do the same work, at $40,000 a year—and the engineer required a secretary.

Across the state, employers, and teachers, and parents are telling us what they need, but aren't getting, from our schools. In many cases, this is the first time they've been asked. Jim Hebe, the chairman of Freightliner, a company that's doing great things in our state, and has the largest share of the largest truck market in the world, and in this country—he told a group of governors and corporate executives a few months ago that in all his years of doing business across the nation and across the world, no one had ever asked him what his company needed from the local schools. Well, now we're asking. And we're going to act on it.

This summer, the standards commission will present a set of essential skills they think our students ought to master before graduation. This is the first step in a dialogue about what we should teach our kids, and what we should do, to make sure that they learn these skills from the earliest grades. It's going to mean a recommitment to the basics, what I call the new basics: the basics for the twenty-first century. These, of course, include the three Rs, which are still the most fundamental things, but also technology, problem-solving, analytical thinking, and even teamwork. Just as importantly, students must know how to apply these new basics.

Now, this math problem that you have on your table is just an exercise, but it ought to be a requirement. That's the kind of thing students must be able to do to work in the factories, and the labs, and the offices of tomorrow. They've got to be able to solve this math problem, and they need to know how to use the problem-solving technique, to program a computer on the factory floor or any one of thousands of jobs that you have in your places of business. We will be spending the next year determining what those standards ought to be.

Once we have rigorous new standards in place, then we've got to decide, as a state, how we're going to help all children reach those high standards. We're going to have to dramatically change the way our schools are organized, so that teachers can teach and students can learn more effectively. If we do not give teachers and parents a greater voice, we cannot hold our schools accountable to higher standards, and we will not have the best ideas in helping to reach them. So in a real sense, standards can help drive school reform and also the kind of resources that we're going to need.

Make no mistake about it, these standards will help us chart the course of real education reform that we need in North Carolina. John Dornan, the head of the Public School Forum, says that if our standards commission can build broad public support, that will be the engine that drives reform.[4] With that support, and your support, and with the support of business and industry in this state, we can make the fundamental changes in our schools that you and I know we need to make.

But North Carolina is doing more than raising standards. We're also raising skill levels, as Bill Kolberg mentioned. We're targeting the 75 percent of our high school graduates, who go straight from high school into the workplace without getting further education—or at least, a formal program. The Governor's Workforce Preparedness Commission, chaired by one of our top CEOs—Bill Burkhardt, of Austin Foods—has designed a comprehensive state workforce development system. The centerpiece of this system is our JobReady initiative, which will draw businesses into partnerships with schools to create all kinds of programs, especially apprenticeship programs that will improve technical education and enrich the career development program that must start in the earliest grades.

Let me tell you about a success story I saw in this area just a couple of weeks ago. Out in east Wake County, the Siemens Energy and Automation Company, in Wendell, is working in partnership with the East Wake High School. They're going to launch their apprenticeship program this fall, which will train sixteen juniors. They will daily take two hours of training, in addition to their other courses, at a special center on the campus that the company has equipped, and will spend the summer working in the Siemens plant. After two years, each student will get an apprenticeship-training skills certificate and a chance at a good job. The company will get first crack at sixteen well-trained, entry-level workers who can help that company compete in the world economy.

Siemens, a German company, thinks it's a good deal, and I think it is, too. That is truly a win-win situation at a time when the youngsters need to win, and the companies need to win, and that's the kind of business-school partnership that I hope will take root in every community in North Carolina. I'm asking the General Assembly to provide $1 million to finance grants for these kinds of transition programs.

And finally, I want to issue a little warning. I want to say to all of you that education reform will not be easy. We talked a lot about it, we've started some things, but we have a lot of work ahead. Change is always hard. It's harder in the public sector than it is in the private sector, and it's tough enough there. And education reform is about change, fundamental change in the way we do business in our schools; fundamental change in what we expect from our schools, from our students, from our teachers, and from parents, and in how we hold schools accountable.

Education reform will not be painless, and it will not be without controversy; and when it gets controversial, that's when the schools, administrators with vision and courage, and the teachers who will work at it, must make it work. That's when they really need the business community behind them—and incidentally, if I haven't made it clear, reformed schools must always be educating better. Scores must be going up. Ability to work must be getting better. You don't reform just for the sake of reform; you reform so you can do a great job of teaching and helping children learn.

So I just want to say to you that I intend to make next year, the long [legislative] session that begins next January, a time that we really focus on education reform—deep-seated, thorough reform of our schools, so that they work better, and our students learn a lot more and are able to come out and be much better workers. I want to ask you to be prepared to support us. Bill Burkhardt, chairman of the Workforce Preparedness Commission, will be in particular need of the business community.

But it's about our future. It's about our children's future. We can do this job. We've got to get involved in it. We've got to reclaim our schools. Too many of us have left it up to the educators. We can't do that. They don't want us to do that. They want our partnership, and if they don't, they need it anyhow.

President Clinton came right down here and stayed with us as we celebrated the 200th anniversary of this, the oldest, finest, public university in America. This is where the idea started. That's the kind of people we have here in this state. Think about it: This was a little, poor, southern state. But we had the vision, the courage, and the will to put our tax money into doing it first for our people. What we need is that same kind of vision and energy in our lives so we can make our workforce the best and help our children learn the most. We can do it.

We've got to have high standards, and we can have them because our kids can do it! We've all got to work together at it. We've got to work hard, harder than we've ever worked before.

But I want to tell you, I am excited about world-class competition. I worked hard to help pass NAFTA [North American Free Trade Agreement], and I encourage the passage of GATT [General Agreement on Tariffs and Trade]. I welcome competition against the world, because we in America, and I hope we in North Carolina, can do it. It's all going to turn on the workforce. It's all going to depend on our schools, our families, on what happens to these young people—all the way through. I believe people in North Carolina are on the right track. I want all of you to know how much I appreciate the leadership you've given, and I want North Carolina to lead in America.

I want to call Bill Kolberg to come back here in five years and be able to give us proof that we're doing the best job. I think we can. I thank all of you for the work you're doing, and together, let's make North Carolina all it can be, all it should be, all it must be.

---

[1] Hunt attended the May 11 trustees' meeting of the National Center on Education and the Economy. Governor Hunt's Schedule for May 8-14, 1994, Governors Papers, James Baxter Hunt Jr.

[2] William H. Kolberg (d. 1996), born in Nome, N.D.; resident of Washington, D.C.; B.A., M.S., University of Denver; U.S. Army, 1944-1946. Associate manpower administrator, deputy U.S. assistant secretary of labor for administration, 1968-1971; assistant director, U.S. Office of Management and Budget, Executive Office of the President, 1971-1973; assistant U.S. secretary of labor, Employment and Training Administration administrator, 1973-1977; vice-president for public affairs, Union Camp Corp.; president, CEO, National Alliance of Business, 1980-1996; board member, 1991-1995, and chair, Malcolm Baldridge National Quality Award; adjunct lecturer, John F. Kennedy School of Government, Harvard University; author; commentator; consultant. *New York Times,* July 8, 1996; Richard M. Rodero Jr., Corporate Development, National Alliance of Business, letter to Jan-Michael Poff, September 9, 1999; *Washington* (D.C.) *Post,* July 6, 1996; *Washington* (D.C.) *Times,* July 8, 1996.

[3] National Commission on Excellence in Education, *A Nation at Risk: The Imperative for Educational Reform* (Washington, D.C.: U.S. Government Printing Office, [1983]).

[4] John Neill Dornan (1944-   ), born in Canonsburg, Pa.; resident of Raleigh; B.A., Indiana University of Pennsylvania, 1966. High school English teacher, Moon Twp., Pa., 1966-1969; field representative, 1969-1970, communications specialist, 1970-1971, National Education Assn.; assistant executive secretary, Illinois Education Assn., 1971-1974; associate executive director, Coalition of American Public Employees, 1974-1976; associate executive director, N.Y. Educators Assn., 1976-1982; executive director, N.C. Assn. of Educators, 1982-1986; executive director, Public School Forum of North Carolina, from 1986. *News and Observer,* October 30, 1988.

MOUNT OLIVE COLLEGE COMMENCEMENT

MOUNT OLIVE, MAY 14, 1994

I am proud to be here with you at Mount Olive College, a college I love and have deep connections with. My father served as chairman of the board of trustees here for fifteen years.

As I look out at you today, I see a glow on the face of you graduating seniors out there. I don't think it's just the sunlight. There's a glow that's the result of the work of dozens of people who have loved you and cared about you.

The glow is there because of the concern of your families, who have fed you full of values and watered you with love. They have sacrificed and struggled to help you get where you are today. This is your day, and this is their day. I hope you can feel them walking beside you as you walk toward the stage to get your diplomas today, and I would like to ask all parents and guardians here today to please stand.

The glow is there because of your friends. They have counseled you through the tough times and laughed with you through the good times. They have argued with you about ethics, collaborated with you on projects, and supported you through all-nighters. As you climb the stairs today, I want you to feel them walking on the same step.

The glow is also there because of this school's faculty and staff. This is a wonderful school. They have broadened your minds, challenged your assumptions, and polished and refined your rough ideas. As you shake hands and accept your diploma today, I hope you can feel their hands linked in yours.

Your family, friends, and faculty have been helping to sculpt your values, and polish your thoughts, and make your ideas shine. Today that shine reflects not just your work, but theirs. The question now is what you do with that shine. How long will it last when you leave here and go out into the world?

You can let the shine get dulled, or you can keep it fresh and share it with others. That's not an easy thing to do, but the people I've seen who do it successfully seem to me to have a few things in common. First, they have principles. They know what they believe in. They have an ability to look inside themselves and ask themselves what matters. Many of them spend regular time on their knees or in meditation identifying what is truly important for them. They are faithful church members, receiving nourishment regularly.

You can start that process today, while you're waiting for your name to be called. Take a few moments, today, to look inside and think about your principles. Then, next week, make a point of spending more time thinking and putting those principles into your own words. If you take the exercise seriously, you can keep those as a guide to you for a long period of time.

The second thing successful people have in common is an understanding of their talents. They know what they can do, and do well. They take an honest look at themselves and understand what they can and can't do. They have a facility for taking complicated ideas and stating them simply, so they make teaching or writing the focus of much of their work. They have a love of being around other people, and understanding their needs, so they make sales the focus of their work. They have a knack for getting the big picture and organizing priorities, so they become managers of people.

You may need to find a few minutes today to take a clear look at your talents and to think how you can truly use them as you emerge from here. And then you need to set goals for yourself as to how you can follow your principles and use your talents daily—and over time. The Reverend Dr. Martin Luther King Jr. said: "You ought to believe in something in life, believe that thing so fervently that you will stand up with it till the end of your days." You need to set goals about what you want to be, and believe, and do.

You don't need to think small. You can dream. Senator Robert Kennedy said about his brother, President Kennedy: "Some men see things as they are and ask why; he dreamed things that never were and said, 'Why not?'" Today is a day to dream big dreams; think big thoughts; set ambitious goals.

In my daily work as governor, I keep a chart in my office that sets some big goals for my administration: making sure every student comes to school ready to learn; setting higher standards in our schools; deterring young people from crime; developing a world-class workforce. Then there are a series of steps my administration is taking to achieve each of those goals. That's the kind of plan you should think about making for your life—in any line of work that you choose.

But thinking, and planning, and formulating doesn't make it happen. To keep your shine bright, you have to get started doing it. Sometimes that's the hardest part. But it's also the most important part.

There's a lot that needs to be done in this world that isn't getting done right now. You can do it through your work. All across our state every year, thousands of college graduates are choosing to provide for other people by raising crops, or livestock, or bringing in new jobs. They're seeking to protect other people by serving in law enforcement, monitoring our water quality, or serving in elected office. They're seeking to inspire others by teaching in the classroom or operating a child-care center.

You graduates today can do what needs to be done—show your shine, and share it—in your volunteer time. Each of you can be a volunteer. You can help a family trying to move off welfare through your church's outreach program. You can help students with their homework in an after-school program. You can lead a Boy or Girl Scout troop. You can be a mentor to a child who has lost a parent. You can volunteer to deliver meals to senior adults.

When you own your own businesses, you can free up employees to volunteer in their children's schools, or help supply the schools with computers, or serve on a local board looking at the best ways to help children. And you can do what needs to be done—show your shine, and share it—by being a good parent, loving your child, and loving other children who need a hand. Put them first. Your love and time is the best thing that you can give them, not your money.

It is up to us, whether we are in public service or in the private sector, to keep our glow alive and let our inner light, Jesus Christ's light, shine before others. I think that is what Jesus would be doing if he were here today. Mother Teresa of India reminded us of this when she wrote:

Christ has no body now on earth but yours—
No hands but yours,
No feet but yours.
Yours are the eyes through which Christ is to look out
In compassion for the world;
Yours are the feet with which He is to go about doing good;
Yours are the hands with which He is to bless now.

Mount Olive College has helped you to learn and develop your eyes, and hands, and feet, and heart for a lifetime of service. It has helped you to develop your shine and get ready to share it. Today, this morning, you begin a lifetime of work sharing that shine with everyone around you. I am proud of you. I know this college is proud of you. I wish every one of you good luck and God's richest blessings.

GOVERNOR'S ENTREPRENEURIAL TOWN MEETING

Raleigh, May 23, 1994

It's good to see the members of my Entrepreneurial Development Board here—and so many other people interested in the work that entrepreneurs are doing to move the state forward. I want to listen closely to what you have to say.

North Carolina needs entrepreneurs! Small and growing businesses create 80 percent of the new jobs in our state. A lot of people talk about the great buffalo hunt, and we care about bringing larger, new businesses to this state. But we need to [do] all we can to boost the new job development in small and growing businesses, and North Carolina needs entrepreneurs' ideas. You understand what it takes to make business work in this state, what we can do, what we can do better, and how we can help. That's why I created the North Carolina Entrepreneurial Development Board last year, the first board of its kind in this state; and that's why I named Bob Luddy to head it up. Bob describes entrepreneurs as "free thinkers often in conflict with conventional wisdom and the establishment."

I didn't expect that group to come up with conventional ideas. I didn't want them to rubber-stamp the establishment. I wanted to hear what they really thought we needed to do to help them grow. They've told us, and they've started changing things already!

The board has worked with the Council for Entrepreneurial Development to create entrepreneurial roundtables to assist entrepreneurs in the southeast region of the state—the Entrepreneurial Roundtable, in Fayetteville, and the Northeastern Entrepreneurial Roundtable, in Rocky Mount. Other roundtables are already planned for Wilmington, Asheville, Hickory, Ahoskie, and Roanoke Rapids.

This past January, the board submitted a report to me and the General Assembly on how we can make North Carolina the entrepreneurial incubator it should be.[1] We've already started to work on implementing some of those ideas. We're looking at speeding up some permitting and finding ways to make more venture capital available in our state, and our Economic Development Board is proposing taking a close look at taxation in the state.

This year I am taking their recommendation and asking the General Assembly to authorize an audit of business taxes and tax credits in our state. Not just some taxes: I want them to look at every one of them. That includes corporate taxes, intangibles taxes, unemployment insurance taxes, workers' compensation, special sales taxes, existing business tax credits, and proposed tax credits to find out if any of them need to be changed. As you know, over the past year I've already proposed two separate cuts in the state's unemployment insurance tax, which will save businesses about $310 million.

Now, some people may ask why we need to make changes to our state's small business environment. *Entrepreneur* magazine already describes North Carolina as a hot spot for economic development. We already have all the right ingredients for success: a strong, diverse manufacturing base; excellent colleges and universities; a strong position in the global export market; an excellent workforce; and a history of entrepreneurial development. We're already doing pretty well.

The reason is, we don't want to be a good place to start and grow companies. We want to be a great place to start and grow companies. You are showing us the way to do that. I commend you for your work and your desire to make North Carolina all that it can be, should be, and must be. Now I'd be glad to take any questions you may have.

---

[1] North Carolina Entrepreneurial Development Board, *A Report to the Governor and the North Carolina State Legislature* ([Raleigh, N.C.: The Board], January 31, 1994).

UMSTEAD STATE PARK

WAKE COUNTY, MAY 25, 1994

Look around Umstead [State] Park. This is why we're here: this beautiful meadow, our stately pine forests down east, and our spectacular mountains in the west. This is what we're working to preserve, for our families and for their families. Improving our parks is a quality-of-life issue, an environmental issue—even a business issue.

I'm glad to see so many of you here, today, united for our parks. Companies like CP&L, Duke Power, and SAS Institute have joined together with the environmental coalition and this administration to demonstrate concern for our park system and commitment to Senate Bill 733.[1] The state's League of Municipalities, along with the County Commissioners' Association, have also joined in, as have North Carolina Citizens for Business and Industry and many, many others. They know that funding for our state parks system has not kept pace with the state's growth. It has not kept pace with usage of our parks, which last year topped 12 million visitors.

Many of our busiest park facilities, buildings, picnic areas, and parking lots were built more than fifty years ago. But we have not done a good enough job maintaining them. For years, our state has ranked at the bottom, nationally, in per-capita spending on its parks—spending only $1.50 per citizen, compared to the national average of $5.00. Now we're beginning to see the results of this neglect. Our parks are deteriorating, and we must act now to preserve them for our children, their children, and their children.

The parks bond issue passed last fall will help us address this backlog of need. [It] showed us people's perspectives. But we need to make sure that our parks are protected, preserved, and maintained down the road, just as we do with other infrastructure. This bill could help us do that. This bill will set up a steady source of funding to maintain parks, acquire new park land, and renovate existing parks that have fallen into disrepair. Every time property changes hands, part of the transfer tax will go toward preserving our parks, and for the first time in our history, our parks will have a consistent source of funds that will save our natural resources, repair aging facilities, and provide our citizens with better service. It's about time that we take action on this front.

Like these young people here today, our parks are a precious resource that we cannot afford to squander. These young people from Ravenscroft,[2] who volunteer to help maintain the trails here, are learning the importance of stewardship, and the preschoolers visiting with the snake and the possum will always remember their experiences here. We owe it to them to preserve what you see here. We owe them a healthy environment, and along with that, a sound economy and the same quality of life their parents now enjoy. We owe them passage of Senate Bill 733!

---

[1] Senate Bill 733 was ratified July 16, 1994, as c. 772, *N.C. Session Laws, 1993, Extra and Regular Sessions, 1994*: "An Act to Establish a Parks and Recreation Trust Fund."

[2] Ravenscroft was a private school, in Raleigh, offering primary and secondary education.

RDU BUSINESS EXCHANGE MEETING

LONDON, ENGLAND, MAY 27, 1994

[Hunt boarded American Airlines' inaugural flight from Raleigh-Durham International Airport to London, England, May 26, 1994, as the prelude to a very brief visit to the British capital. He addressed the International Advisory Council of the Children's Museum about the World, and the RDU Business Exchange meeting, on May 27, and returned to North Carolina the following day. Governor Hunt's Weekly Schedule for May 22-28, 1994, Governors Papers, James Baxter Hunt Jr.]

I'm proud to be in the United Kingdom today, leading this outstanding group of North Carolina business and community leaders and attending this historic weekend of events. As governor of North Carolina, I want to express my appreciation to our friends in the United Kingdom [for] making all of us feel so welcome and for giving us this important opportunity to expand and strengthen our economic, educational, and cultural ties.

The United Kingdom is one of our state's top foreign investors and trading partners, with more than 125 companies and more than 40,000 employees. Since 1978, the UK's business investment in North Carolina has grown $1.6 billion—and now totals $3.8 billion. I want to reaffirm North Carolina's strong support of our British friends. We will continue to look for ways to open new market opportunities, between the UK and North Carolina, and improve the two-way flow of trade, investment, and communication.

Some of you may not know this, but a North Carolina firm was involved in the construction of the "Chunnel" that was recently completed. Power Curbers, Incorporated, based in Salisbury, North Carolina, was honored recently with the Governor's New Product Award for its rail-tunnel invert concrete paving machine.

The new London flight from Raleigh, along with our existing international passenger routes from RDU and Charlotte, is opening up new opportunities for our state and will showcase North Carolina's economic appeal and our great economic potential. This will go a long way toward making us more competitive in the global marketplace. North Carolina's business climate will become even more attractive, both for American companies doing business with the U.K. and Europe, and for foreign companies seeking to set up operations in the U.S.

Companies are coming to our state for a number of reasons: the quality of our workforce and our commitment to workforce development, higher standards in our schools, and early childhood education to help make sure every child comes to school ready to learn. We in North Carolina are working hard to build a world-class workforce for a world-class economy, producing graduates who can work, and think, and succeed in the modern workplace—graduates who can get a good job, and hold a good job, in the real world of work. We're setting rigorous new standards for high school graduates. We are developing a comprehensive school-to-work transition system to make sure graduates enter the workforce with practical work skills.

We in North Carolina know that education is economic development. So at the same time, we've launched an aggressive new economic development strategy. As part of that, we are preparing to build the North Carolina Global TransPark, bringing together the infrastructure and services that companies will need to compete and win in the twenty-first century. The Global TransPark is the first-of-its-kind facility that will enable companies to manufacture and distribute goods from one location. It is designed to serve [the] needs of the businesses of the future, where global goods can move from truck to train or from plane to plant.

And by building this project in North Carolina, we are ensuring that our state has a competitive edge, creating an engine for business progress that will bring new, high-quality, high-paying jobs to our citizens.

We are proud of the things we are doing in North Carolina to attract good jobs and to make life better for our people, and we want to make sure that the United Kingdom and the rest of the world knows [sic], too! We want people to see North Carolina as a great vacation spot, a great business climate, and a great place to live. We've just launched a $5 million international marketing program to promote travel, and tourism, and international air services between North Carolina and the U.K. Our goal is to strengthen North Carolina's position as an international gateway to America and to showcase North Carolina for European vacationers. As part of this program, we've developed an International Marketing Task Force of travel and tourism-related professionals who will come up with the best plan for marketing our state.[1]

While our task force is getting started, our Travel and Tourism Division is already making plans to bring in travel agents, from the United Kingdom, to tell them about our state so they can tell vacationers about North Carolina. And we have a story to tell—about a state with natural scenic beauty, from the mountains to the coast; where the first English colony was founded; and the latest technological and medical research is done. We're proud of North Carolina and want to do all we can to improve and expand business opportunities between North Carolina, the United States, and the United Kingdom.

Today we're delighted to have two widely respected business leaders with us who can help us build a stronger partnership between North Carolina and the U.K. They have a unique insight into the global marketplace and will tell us about successful strategies for business expansion and economic opportunities that exist for us.[2]

---

[1] "Highway funds appropriated in a reserve by the General Assembly, for developing and promoting international air services and increasing our gateways," supported the International Tourism Marketing Program and a three-year campaign to promote North Carolina in the United Kingdom. Hunt announced the program at a May 18, 1994, news conference in Charlotte. Press Announcement on International Gateways, Governors Papers, James Baxter Hunt Jr.

[2] The governor concluded his remarks by introducing two British speakers with North Carolina connections: Anita Roddick, founder of the Body Shop, Britain's largest international retailer; and John Grimond, foreign editor of the *Economist*. The U.S. headquarters of the Body Shop was in Wake County. Grimond's favorite vacation place, according to Hunt, was "the mountains of North Carolina."

PUBLIC SCHOOL ADMINISTRATOR TASK FORCE

Raleigh, May 31, 1994

[For related press release, see Hunt Gives Charge to School Administrator Task Force, Raleigh, June 1, 1994, Governors Papers, James Baxter Hunt Jr. The task force was established May 7, 1993. Executive Order Number 12, N.C. *Session Laws, 1993,* 2:3225-3227.]

There is a chart in my office that sums up the challenge before you today. It's the mission statement of this administration. The first line says, "Education is our future—it's everything."

North Carolina's future depends on world-class schools, and a world-class workforce, to help us compete in a global marketplace. We face some critical challenges ahead in our schools and in the workplace, and all of you—teachers, administrators, business leaders—must help us face them.

This task force brings together some of our state's best minds from business and industry, education, and government. It includes Superintendent Bob Etheridge; our state's fiscal watchdog, Auditor Ralph Campbell;[1] teachers and principals; and community leaders, like Vernon Malone, chairman of the Wake County commissioners.[2] Each one of you has a stake in making sure that we can give our students the kind of education they need to face the next century. That means we must have higher standards and hold schools, including administrators, accountable for achieving those standards.

That's why I created the Education Standards and Accountability Commission, last year, to set rigorous new standards for high-school graduation. This group of educators, parents, [and] community and business leaders will make North Carolina the first state that ties what we're doing in the classroom to what employers need in the workplace. This group has spent the last six months conducting hearings around the state, finding out from top business leaders, employers, parents, and educators exactly what our children need to know [and] be able to do to become world-class workers, and citizens, of the twenty-first century.

We are helping teachers improve their skills with our National Board for Professional Teaching Standards, a rigorous system that encourages excellence in teaching by encouraging teachers to seek voluntary board certification; and we hope to soon begin our Teacher Academy to train teachers in critical skills, like site-based decision making, and to allow teachers to pass their skills on to others.

We must have higher expectations for our administrators, as well. The task force on which you serve was created to make sure the dollars we spend on education are spent for the classroom, rather than unnecessary administrative costs. This group faces an important challenge. It is your job to look at our schools' administrative costs and make sure that those dollars are being spent wisely. It may not be an easy task, but it is one that we must do.

This task force must analyze the existing ratio of administrators to students and teachers. How many administrators do we now have per pupil? How many should we have? This group must determine the most effective and efficient ratios needed to administer quality education at the local level. We must have guidelines to help us know what is best for our students. We need your skills and your knowledge to help us find these answers and set new goals for improving the quality of education.

The last line of my mission statement sums up your final challenge: "The status quo is unacceptable." We cannot afford to conduct business as usual. Today's global economy and the needs of today's businesses demand change, not the status quo. Our schools must be able to produce graduates who can succeed in tomorrow's workplace. That is why I have asked business and industry leaders to help us face the challenge of making our schools better, on this task force and in other arenas. They have a great stake in this, and their experience in increasing productivity in their own organizations can help guide us.

Each one of you knows how important this is for the future of our state, and each one of you knows this will be difficult work. Change is never easy, and it is never achieved without some struggles. But as you begin your work, remember that your job—our job—is to make North Carolina's schools the best they can be. If we meet that challenge, then we can make North Carolina all that it can be; all that it should be; all that it must be.

---

[1] Ralph Campbell Jr. (1946-   ), born in Raleigh; B.S., St. Augustine's College, 1968; U.S. Army Reserve, 1971-1977. Field auditor, N.C. Dept. of Revenue, 1977-1986; plan auditor, State Health Benefits Office, 1986-1990; administrative officer, N.C. Dept. of Insurance, 1990-1992; was elected state auditor, 1992, re-elected 1996; member, 1985-1992, mayor pro tem, 1989-1991, Raleigh City Council; Democrat. *North Carolina Manual, 1997-1998*, 183-184.

[2] Vernon Malone (1931-   ), born in Wake County; B.A., Shaw University; U.S. Army. Classroom teacher, 1957-1968; federal programs director, appointed 1968, Governor Morehead School for the Blind; member, from 1972, chairman, Wake County Board of Education; member, chairman, Wake County Board of Commissioners. *News and Observer*, August 1, 1976; Linda Wise, comp., *Directory of the State and Local Officials of North Carolina, 1993* (Raleigh: Rufus L. Edmisten, Secretary of State, 1993), 210.

NATIONAL BOARD FOR PROFESSIONAL TEACHING STANDARDS PRESS CONFERENCE

Raleigh, June 13, 1994

[For related press releases, see Hunt Pushes for Excellence in Teaching with Certification, Raleigh, June 1, 1994, and Governor Hunt Urges House to Support Higher Standards for Teachers, Raleigh, June 13, 1994, Governors Papers, James Baxter Hunt Jr.]

There's no secret to what makes excellent schools. It's excellent teachers, and we have plenty of them in North Carolina.

I'm standing here, today, with teachers who are striving for excellence. We need more teachers like them, and we can do something about that in this [legislative] session.

Meghan Lawson, an English teacher at Blowing Rock School; Scott Muri, an Avery County middle-school teacher; and Claire Middleton, a middle-school teacher at Coulwood Middle School, in Charlotte, have spent the last year undergoing a rigorous test of their teaching skills. Each has spent more than 125 hours demonstrating talent, skill, and knowledge in teaching, lesson planning, student learning, and professional growth. They are among fifty-one pioneer teachers across North Carolina who are working to meet voluntary national standards and be recognized nationally as highly accomplished teachers. The standards are set by the National Board for Professional Teaching Standards, a group largely of classroom teachers that I have chaired since 1987.[1]

I'm convinced that one of the most important things we can do for education is to raise standards and expectations—for schools, students, and teachers. That's the driving goal of my administration. So I have asked the legislature, this year, to appropriate $500,000 that will help North Carolina teachers who seek national board certification and reward those who do. This will help 200 teachers achieve national recognition for excellence. It will help pay their board assessment fees, fund up to five days of release time, and give national board-certified teachers a $5,000 one-time bonus.

Unfortunately, that request has been given a low priority in preliminary discussions by the House Appropriations Subcommittee on Education. Last week I talked with members of the subcommittee, with the Appropriations Committee leadership, and with Speaker Blue to let them know how important I think this is. I am hopeful that it will be approved and included in the House budget this week.

The focus of this session is education. Part of what we have to do is pass a fair salary increase for all teachers, and we're making good progress toward that in this session. But money by itself will not do all we need to do in North Carolina schools. We have to clearly define what we expect of our schools, our students, and our teachers. That's what we're doing with the national board certification; and that's what we're doing with the Standards and Accountability Commission, which will recommend rigorous new standards for students next month. Higher standards will require fundamental changes in the way our schools are organized and operated. We'll be expecting more, and we'll be holding schools, students, and teachers accountable.

If we're going to expect more from teachers, then we ought to reward those who strive for excellence. Now I want to introduce you to some of these teachers and let them tell you why this effort is important. You'll hear from classroom teachers and national board certification candidates Meghan Lawson, Scott Muri, and Claire Middleton—and you'll also hear from Rose Marie Lowry, NCAE [North Carolina Association of Educators] president, and Eddie Davis, a Durham teacher and member of the State Board of Education.[2]

---

[1] The National Board for Professional Teaching Standards, which Hunt cofounded, was one of at least four nationwide education advocacy boards on which the governor served during his third term. He also chaired the National Commission on Teaching and America's Future, was vice-chairman of the board of the National Center on Education and the Economy, and was appointed to the NGA's National Education Goals Panel. Press releases, Hunt Named to National Governors' Association's Education Goals Panel, Boston, August 1, 1994, and Hunt to Chair National Education Study Panel, Raleigh, November 10, 1994, Governors Papers, James Baxter Hunt Jr.

[2] Rose Marie Lowry-Townsend, native, resident of Pembroke; B.S., Pembroke State University (later University of North Carolina at Pembroke), 1975; M.Ed., University of North Carolina at Greensboro, 1979; doctorate in education administration, Campbell University. Career with Robeson County School System, since 1975, included fifth-grade teacher, 1975-1980; director, health career awareness, Robeson Board of Education, 1980-1984; principal, Union Elementary School, 1984-1990; and principal, Pembroke Middle School, from 1996. Chair, N.C. Task Force on American Indian Educators, and of National American Indian/Alaskan Native Caucus; president, N.C. Assn. of Educators, 1991-1992, 1993-1994, 1995-1996; Democrat. Rose Marie Lowry-Townsend, letter to Jan-Michael Poff, June 24, 1999.

The appointment of Durham resident Eddie Davis III, to the State Board of Education, was effective May 6, 1993, and expired March 31, 2001. Letters of Appointment to Boards and Commissions, Governors Papers, James Baxter Hunt Jr.

FUTURE FARMERS OF AMERICA STATE CONVENTION

RALEIGH, JUNE 14, 1994

Seeing that picture takes me back a long way, to a time in my life when I learned a lot: about agriculture, about leadership, and about service to the state of North Carolina. Thirty-eight years ago, I was sitting out there in the audience where you are now, proud to be wearing the blue and gold, and listening to speakers at this convention. Today I want you to think about what you can learn through this organization, about agriculture, about leadership, and about service, and I hope at least one of you will set a goal: of coming back to speak to this convention, as governor, in a few years, and talking about the knowledge and experience you have gained through this organization and building on it.

This is what I learned from my years in the Future Farmers of America. First, I learned about agriculture, not just the part I knew from growing up on a tobacco farm in Wilson County. I learned about all the crops, all the livestock, all the poultry and dairy products we raise in this great state; and I learned the complexity of raising all of those crops, the science behind successful agriculture. All the while, I was learning the theory in the classrooms of Wilson County and at N.C. State, but the people I came in contact with through F.F.A. helped me to appreciate the reality, as well.

Second, I learned about leadership. Today as I look back on my life, I can tell you honestly that if it weren't for this organization, I wouldn't be here today as governor of North Carolina. The F.F.A. helps develop leaders a step at a time, through local chapters, then on a regional level, then on a state level. Your adult leaders know how to help you, and encourage you, and bring out your best, and you know how to respond: working cooperatively with each other and learning what you need to learn. For those who work hardest, there are scholarships and titles of office, but for everyone there are rewards of experience that will serve you for the rest of your life.

The third thing I learned through F.F.A. is about service, service to my community, to my region, and to my state. People who grow up in agriculture are familiar with hard work, honesty, and the role we have in protecting our land. F.F.A. nurtures those values and adds to them, working with you and your families, your schools, and your communities to encourage you to help other people.

We need you, your good ideas, and your desire to serve—now, more than ever. We need you to serve in helping to make this state safer. We are spending millions of dollars, every year, to fight crime: by beefing up law enforcement and keeping dangerous criminals behind bars. But if we are to really make our state safer, we need to go to work on the next generation of young people. That means we need thousands of volunteers, all across the state, who are interested in working on solutions to those problems.

You may know what the needs are in your community already, but I'd like to suggest that you get involved in a new program that will be starting up this fall in communities across our state: SOS, or Support Our Students. The Cooperative Extension Service, through the 4-H youth development program, will be helping us with this on a local level, using their community-building skills to get programs off the ground, focusing particularly on the needs of middle-school students. But the real success of this program will be determined by the thousands of volunteers who help youngsters with their homework, design fun and interesting activities, and serve as role models. It's one thing to have adults involved, and we will need them, but in many ways, our young teenagers will learn best from you, the people they know can really understand their needs. I hope you will consider getting involved.

With the kind of grass-roots support that this program can give to volunteer programs across the state, we can truly make our streets safer and make our futures brighter. You can help our country achieve what is truly its destiny: excellence. And the people in my generation are counting on you to do just that.

John Gardner, who wrote a book called *Excellence*, once said, "A nation is never finished. You can't build it and then leave it standing like the pyramids. It has to be built and rebuilt. It has to be re-created in each generation by believing, caring, men and women. It is our turn now. If we don't believe or don't care, nothing can save this nation. If we believe and care, nothing can stop us." I know you believe and care for this state and this country enough to keep building them. I hope you will continue to serve through this organization and throughout the rest of your lives. We're counting on you.

PRESS RELEASE: GOVERNOR HUNT'S PROPOSALS WOULD BOOST FOSTER CARE SERVICES IN NORTH CAROLINA

RALEIGH, JUNE 22, 1994

North Carolina's 11,000 foster children will get better foster care, including more caseworkers and more financial support, if Governor Jim Hunt's foster care proposals are approved by the North Carolina General Assembly. Hunt has included $5 million in his budget request to the legislature to provide for foster-care programs in the state, including eighty-five more caseworkers, better training and more assistance for foster parents, and a new effort to recruit foster families. The senate cut

Hunt's proposals to $1.1 million, but the measures passed the House. Both houses are now reconciling differences between their budgets.[1]

The number of children in foster care has nearly doubled over the past six years. More than half are in foster homes or in child-caring institutions. Nearly three-fourths have learning disabilities, emotional or physical problems that require special care or attention.

"We have a responsibility to protect North Carolina's foster children and to provide them with safe, nurturing homes," Hunt said. "Many of these children have been victims of abuse or neglect. That's why it is so important that we make sure they have good foster-care programs and homes available, and that we do all we can to give them a better start in life."

Hunt has also directed the North Carolina Division of Social Services to mandate criminal background checks and ban convicted felons from foster parenting. Hunt's legislative proposals to help improve the state's foster-care programs include:

—Increasing the monthly payment to foster parents and families adopting children from a flat subsidy of $265.00 per month, per child, to a sliding scale based on the age of the child. Hunt proposes a monthly payment to families at $315.00 for children 0-5 years old; $365.00 for children 6-12 years old; and $415.00 for children 13-18 years old. North Carolina now ranks forty-third in the nation in the amount reimbursed to foster families for caring for these children, and is one of only seven states that does not recognize the higher cost of raising older children and teenagers. If the General Assembly passes Hunt's proposal, North Carolina will climb to nineteenth out of fifty states in the amount of money it pays monthly to foster families.

—Providing eighty-five additional foster-care licensing and placement workers in social services offices to recruit, train, and support foster families.

—Providing two professional positions and one clerical support staff to develop a new training program for foster families and social workers. Foster parents would be required to complete a new comprehensive training program to help them meet the challenges of providing care. The funding would also increase training for social workers at the county level to help them better support foster children and families.

—Launching a recruitment effort of foster-care parents to help place the growing number of North Carolina children needing foster care.

More than 5,000 of North Carolina's foster children are in mental hospitals, group homes, training schools, or in their natural family homes under supervision of local social services offices. The other 6,000 are in foster family homes or in child-caring institutions.

"We're on the right track with these proposals, but we have a long way to go to make sure that our foster children have every chance to succeed," Hunt said. "We need to do more for these children, making the fundamental changes necessary to ensuring a brighter future for them and our state."

---

[1] The $4.6 million foster-care package ultimately approved by the General Assembly included three of the governor's major proposals: the graduated payment scale to foster parents; funding for mandatory training for foster parents and social workers attached to foster-child agencies; and funds to recruit more foster parents. Legislators did not fund the eighty-five new foster-care staff positions Hunt requested. Press release, Governor Hunt Sees Foster Care Legislation as Step in the Right Direction, Raleigh, July 22, 1994, Governors Papers, James Baxter Hunt Jr.; see also "An Act to Modify the Current Operations Appropriations Act of 1993, to Make Appropriations for Capital Improvements for the 1994-1995 Fiscal Year, and to Make Other Changes in the Budget Operation of the State," *N.C. Session Laws, 1993, Extra and Regular Sessions, 1994*, c. 769, secs. 25.40-25.41, ratified July 1, 1994.

PRESS RELEASE: GOVERNOR HUNT PUSHES FOR HIGH-TECH RESEARCH AT BLACK COLLEGES

RALEIGH, JUNE 23, 1994

Five state-supported historically black colleges and universities could get nearly $2 million to help them keep pace with advances in biotechnology research and education if the legislature approves Governor Jim Hunt's budget request.[1] Without more money, the state's historically black colleges and their students are in danger of being left behind in the competitive and growing field of biotechnology, Hunt said.

"Historically black colleges and universities have educated some of North Carolina's best minds, and these students deserve access to the most up-to-date training we can offer," he said. "Today's students are tomorrow's workforce, and they need the specialized training in science and technology this initiative will provide."

The money will be divided among the five state-supported historically black colleges and universities—Elizabeth City State, Fayetteville State, North Carolina A&T State, North Carolina Central, and Winston-Salem State Universities—to help the schools buy equipment and supplies for students and train instructors. Pembroke State University also would get a share of the funds.[2]

The North Carolina Biotechnology Center has helped the state's historically black colleges and universities design their biotechnology programs. The center estimates that the number of students majoring in the sciences and technology will grow as the demand for workers continues to rise. Over the next several years, experts say, the number of jobs created in biotechnology fields will range from 800 to 1,000 each year.

Biotechnology includes a wide range of scientific techniques that use living cells to make new products and improve existing ones, from genetic research that offers new treatment for diseases to producing better crops at harvest time. With its reputation for quality medical institutions and universities and its solid agricultural base, North Carolina already has attracted sixty-five companies specializing in biotechnology research. In his first eighteen months, the governor has launched an intensive effort to recruit more biotechnology companies.

"Helping our universities train young people for jobs in these industries will help make our state's economy stronger," Hunt said. "Supporting biotechnology research and education will prepare our students for the jobs of the future."

---

[1] The General Assembly approved $2 million in biotechnology funds, for the five historically black colleges and universities of the University of North Carolina system and Pembroke State University, under *N.C. Session Laws, 1993, Extra and Regular Sessions, 1994,* c. 769, s. 28.2.
[2] Effective July 1, 1996, Pembroke State University was renamed as the University of North Carolina at Pembroke. *North Carolina Manual, 1997-1998,* 881.

NORTH CAROLINA COMMISSION ON BUSINESS LAWS AND THE ECONOMY

RALEIGH, JUNE 28, 1994

I want to thank all of you for taking time from your busy schedules to serve on this commission and help the state deal with these issues. This commission is important to me. I see it as an innovative way to bring together an outstanding group of business leaders, professionals, and legislators who can join with my administration to build bridges between major employers and the state of North Carolina.

All of you know that North Carolina has a lot to offer corporate employers, large and small. We have a great work environment, a favorable tax structure, a well-trained pool of employees, and an administration committed to helping businesses prosper. In the past eighteen months, we have done a good job attracting new businesses and jobs to our state. But as U.S. attorney general Janet Reno said yesterday, "Good isn't good enough." We have to keep doing better.

I am convinced that we need to do more to make sure we have business laws that are responsive to the needs of large corporations. This commission is a major step in that direction. Just having a commission like this sends a strong message to the business world that our state is committed to building corporate relationships, but we want to do more: We want to create the best business climate in the United States. Nothing is more important to the people of this state and to their future than creating a strong, vital economy. The best way to do that is to create an environment that encourages businesses to create jobs and invest in North Carolina.

We've already started that process. Russell Robinson,[1] Peggy Glass, and many of you here today helped revise and modernize our state's Business Corporation Act in 1989. As a result of that work, at least two large, successful corporations decided to re-incorporate here: Federal Paper Board and Rayonier Corporation, a paper company recently spun off by ITT with over $1 billion in annual sales. And recently I have had discussions with the CEO of a large, successful, Fortune 500 company concerning its possible re-incorporation here. He is enthusiastic about what North Carolina has to offer and our level of interest, but I'm afraid that company is holding back on making the change because of one of the antiquated provisions in our law dealing with shareholders' lawsuits, which I believe is behind the times. I know that Mike Easley will be asking this group to consider our shareholders' derivative suit statute.

As we undertake this effort, some may wonder if simply changing the legal environment—building a strong, legal bridge with corporations—will have any tangible benefit for the citizens of North Carolina. I think it will, if we build on those relationships. In 1986, I helped convince Wayne Calloway and PepsiCo to move their corporate charter from Delaware to North Carolina.[2] It has paid off for both sides. We've gotten a great new employer for hundreds of our citizens, and PepsiCo is impressed with North Carolina, spreading the word that our state has a responsive corporate environment.

No one should mistake our objective, here. We are not in a contest with Delaware or any other state to see who can enact the most favorable corporate laws, regulations, or tax structures. What we want, here in North Carolina, is an environment that will allow corporations to operate efficiently in today's global economy and help our state prosper and grow. This group must see to it that we keep these goals in mind as we start on this task.

---

[1] Russell M. Robinson II (1932-   ), born in, resident of Charlotte; was educated at Princeton University, 1950-1952, Duke University, 1952-1953, and Duke University School of Law, 1953-1956. Attorney; chairman, Business Corporation Act Drafting Committee, N.C. General Statutes Commission, 1968-1973, 1985-1991; director, 1971-1974, 1986-1989,

Legal Services of Southern Piedmont; member, from 1987, chairman, 1989-1997, Board of Trustees, University of North Carolina at Charlotte; chairman, from 1994, Committee on Civil Justice, Commission for the Future of Justice and the Courts in North Carolina; author. Tim Gray, "Clout: Ranking the State's Most Powerful People," *Business North Carolina* (July 1999): 28-31, 40; Janice Mauney, assistant to Russell M. Robinson II, letter to Jan-Michael Poff, March 15, 1999.

   [2] D. Wayne Calloway; born in Winston-Salem; resident of Greenwich, Conn.; was graduated from Wake Forest University, 1959; employee of Vicks Chemical Co., 1959-1965, and of ITT Corp., 1965-1967, before being hired as a strategic planner by PepsiCo, in 1967. Career with PepsiCo included controller of Frito-Lay; chief of Pepsi-Cola and Frito-Lay divisions in Canada; president of Frito-Lay, from 1976; PepsiCo president, from 1985, chairman and chief executive officer, from May 1986. "The Quiet Numbers Man Headed for the Top at Pepsi," *BusinessWeek*, February 10, 1986, 56-57.

MEDIA ADOPTION SUMMIT

RALEIGH, JUNE 30, 1994

I was reading a story about a couple of great foster children last night. Michelle is a nine-year-old girl with bright eyes and a beautiful smile. She gets good grades in school. Her sister, Tequita, is seven, energetic, and loves to hug people; she just won her school's Terrific Kid award.

They're the kind of kids a lot of families would love to permanently adopt, but no one would know about them if they hadn't been featured in a "Sunday's Child" article and on a "Wednesday's Child" TV story.[1] That's why we are gathered here today. Through your papers and television stations, you can literally help change the lives of some of our children. Those children can change the future of our state.

My administration is committed to improving our foster-care system and to increasing our adoption rates. In my budget, I've proposed $5 million to improve the lives of the 6,000 children in foster care here. We ought to increase payments and improve training for foster parents, expand the Foster Parent Association, and increase the number of foster-care workers that we have. But the best thing we can do for our children is to find them safe, permanent, adoptive homes. Kids who get placed early are less likely to have emotional problems, they're less likely to get involved in crime, and we owe it to them to do all we can to help them now.

Through the grant we've received from the U.S. Department of Social Services, we will be setting up a licensed African American adoption agency and adding ten new county councils of Friends of Black Children. These councils have been extremely successful in helping our county DSS [departments of social services] officials place African American children.

But none of these programs can be truly effective if no one knows about them. That's why you are so important. There are 500 Michelles and Tequitas right now who are in foster care, looking for safe, permanent homes. You can help them by deciding today to run "Wednesday's Child" and "Sunday's Child" features.

You won't be working alone. You will have the support of hundreds of caring, loving, committed people in state government. The Department of Administration, through the Youth Advocacy and Involvement Office, will be administering the program, and there is no more committed person in the state to this program than Secretary Katie Dorsett. She has devoted her life to children as a mother and public servant, has volunteered with the Friends of Black Children in Guilford County, has served on the board of the Children's Home Society, and has worked closely with the Black Child Development Institute.

The Department of Human Services, through the Adoption Unit of the Department of Social Services, will be helping link up stations with foster children and will also screen prospective parents. Secretary Robin Britt has shown his commitment to children through a lifetime of service in the halls of Congress and on the streets of Greensboro; and he knows in a deeply personal way the needs of children who lose their birth families: He lost both of his parents by the time he was four years old. And I have heard about the needs of foster-care children in this state at the dinner table from my daughter, who did her graduate school social-work practice in the foster-care unit of the [Wake] County Department of Social Services.[2]

We have the commitment, and we ask you today to share it with us. Find the children. Tell their stories in the print and on the air. Help these children find parents, and help prospective parents see how these children can be a part of their families. Then watch the program work and be reminded of what your newspapers and television stations can do to change our future in the state.

---

[1] "Wednesday's Child" and "Sunday's Child" human-interest stories featured children available for adoption. Press release, Governor Urges Media to Join Adoption Effort, Raleigh, June 30, 1994, Governors Papers, James Baxter Hunt Jr.

[2] Elizabeth Brame Hunt Amigh (1968-   ), born in Wilson; bachelor's degree in sociology, minor in women's studies, Wake Forest University, 1990; master's degree in social work, University of North Carolina at Chapel Hill, 1994; assistant counselor, Angeline's (YWCA day shelter for homeless women), Seattle, Wash., 1990-1991; social worker, Wake County Public School System, since 1994; was married to Kevin Mark Amigh. Shearin correspondence.

HIGHER EDUCATION STANDARDS

RALEIGH, JULY 6, 1994

For the last ten months, the North Carolina Education Standards and Accountability Commission has been listening and learning. Educators, parents, legislators, and business leaders on the standards commission have gone across the state, listening to employers, and teachers, and parents, and students—and learning from them. The commission has posed a critical question: What should North Carolina graduates know and be able to do to succeed in the workplace and in college; how can we prepare our young people for the offices, labs, and factories of the future?

Here's what the commission heard at six public hearings across the state: Teach the basics, and a whole lot more. Teach essential skills, like reading, writing, and math. Teach our youngsters how to use those skills and how to apply them in the real world of work.

I attended all but one of the commission's hearings, and I heard story after story illustrating that North Carolina's students are not coming out of school equipped to face the challenges of work. We must expect a lot more from all students. All students must reach higher standards if they are going to be successful in college or in the workplace. Our schools must offer a more rigorous academic curriculum, especially in the basic core subjects such as English, math, science, and language arts, and the schools must offer incentives for effort and achievement.

Based on its hearings and a year of intensive research, the commission has come up with ten basic skills that it believes students must know, and be able to apply, in order to graduate from high school. These are real-life skills, like reading, writing, and math—skills that the commission believes will help students think and succeed in real life.[1] Some of these skills may spur questions or debate. That's exactly what we want to happen, because today is just the first step.

Now parents, and teachers, and business leaders must come together to assess these basic skills. Are they the right skills? How can we develop standards to help teach those skills. For example, if reading is an essential skill, what level of reading skills ought to be mastered by which grade?

I want parents, and teachers, and business leaders in every local community to help us answer these questions and help us decide what higher standards our children should achieve. I want North Carolina to engage in a statewide dialogue about improving our schools. Over the next year, I will challenge parents, and teachers, and business leaders in every community, at every school, to sit down and discuss these skills.

Are they the right skills for your child or employees? What should the standards be for your school, in your community? What kinds of changes do we need to make in your school to help your children meet higher standards?

Next year, the State Board of Education is scheduled to adopt rigorous new standards for our schools, higher standards for all students. But higher standards cannot be imposed from above. Instead, higher standards must be developed with real involvement by teachers and parents. Employers must also be involved, to make sure that students are learning the skills they will need on the job.

That means that the state's leaders—the governor, legislators, superintendent of public instruction, the State Board of Education, the standards commission, and appointed and elected public school leaders— have a tremendous responsibility. We have a responsibility to listen to people in the schools and communities across North Carolina, not just to talk. We must be responsive to their needs, concerns, and questions, and we must be committed to insisting on standards that are rigorous, real, and measurable. We have a responsibility to help teachers as they make significant changes in order to ensure that our children meet these higher standards; and we have a responsibility to the taxpayers, who are paying a lot for public education, but aren't getting their money's worth: That must change.

All of us in North Carolina must recognize that making our schools work better and helping our children achieve higher standards requires a serious, long-term commitment. Higher standards is [sic] not a quick fix, but part of a deeper commitment to reform that is continual and flexible. Make no mistake about it: Our children's future is at stake. Our responsibility is to expect more of them and help them to achieve more.

Now I'll turn to E. K. Fretwell, chairman of the standards commission and former chancellor of UNC-Charlotte, to outline the commission's draft report for you.

---

[1] The Education Standards and Accountability Commission proposed "that all high-school graduates be required to master six tasks: using numbers, solving problems, processing information, working as part of a team, and using technology. None of those is required for graduation now." Furthermore, the commission recommended "that graduates be able to demonstrate essential skills required for those tasks, including reading, writing, speaking, listening, using numbers, analytical and creative thinking, solving problems, and teamwork. Again, none of those skills is now required for graduation." Press release, Governor Hunt Challenges State to Help Set Higher Standards in Schools, Raleigh, July 6, 1994, Governors Papers, James Baxter Hunt Jr.

DEDICATION, ALCATEL FIBER-OPTIC
MANUFACTURING FACILITY

Claremont, July 12, 1994

I'm glad to be here today to help celebrate the growth of one of North Carolina's finest industries. Governor Martin, I'm glad you could be part of this celebration, today. You played a vital role in bringing this company to Catawba County. You worked hard for North Carolina's economic development, and I'd like to thank you, on behalf of the people of North Carolina, for your service.

John Peterson, C. J. Phillips, and everyone at Alcatel know what corporate citizenship is all about. They have reminded us of the critical role business leaders play in helping to improve our schools, and they know the importance of building school-business partnerships. Alcatel's generous contribution of $50,000 in cable to Catawba Valley Community College is an example of Alcatel's commitment to that partnership. That $50,000 in cable will interconnect the campus, building a technology network to benefit Catawba Valley students and Catawba County employers.

Alcatel is setting an example for every company in North Carolina, and I want to thank Alcatel for its commitment to excellence in education. At the same time, I want to commend Catawba Valley Community College for coming to the rescue when Alcatel needed 250 workers trained quickly in a high-tech, high-quality work environment and in basic and special skills. I'm sure John Peterson and C. J. Phillips are grateful, but Dr. Dunbar,[1] I am grateful, too.

Most of all, I want to commend the workers at Alcatel. You worked hard to learn the skills taught you by the community college. Your dedication exemplifies the workforce this state has to offer high-tech companies, and we're proud of you. The people here today represent the best of North Carolina, working together as partners to boost our schools, our universities, our quality of life, and the business climate in North Carolina—and you all have shown, here in Catawba County, what we can do statewide.

In the last eighteen months, we've laid the groundwork for an energetic new economic development effort that invests in our workers and our industries. We are working to build a world-class workforce for a world-class economy, producing graduates who can work, and think, and succeed in the modern workplace—graduates who can get a good job, and hold a good job, in the real world of work. For the last year, my Education Standards and Accountability Commission has been working to set rigorous new standards in our schools, making sure that the skills students learn in school are the skills they need in the workforce. The commission held six hearings across the state, asking teachers, and employers, and parents what high-school graduates ought to know and be able to do.

Based on its hearings and a year of intensive research, the commission issued a draft report last week recommending that all high school graduates be required to master six tasks: communicating, using numbers, solving problems, processing information, working as a team, and using technology. None of that is required for graduation now! And the commission has come up with ten basic skills that it believes students must have to master those tasks. These are real-life skills, like reading, writing, and math, skills that the commission believes will help students think and succeed in real life. Now we need to hear from employers, business leaders, teachers, and parents in every community across North Carolina to determine how to set standards in North Carolina schools that measure those skills.

At the same time, my Commission on Workforce Preparedness has been working to boost workforce training efforts. Under the direction of Executive Director Sandy Babb and Chairman Bill Burkhardt, CEO of Austin Foods, the commission has mapped out a long-range blueprint for school-to-work transition called JobReady. It's a comprehensive plan designed to give every youngster an accessible path from school to work. The goal is to help every student, especially those students not going on to college, get good work with good wages in the global economy. JobReady also encourages school-business partnerships by helping businesses and schools set up apprenticeships, cooperative education, internships, and mentoring programs.

We've taken some important steps toward building a brighter future in North Carolina, and we're looking every day for ways to make our state an even better place to do business. We have put together a strategic economic development plan to help us recruit industries, and we have a Transportation 2001 plan that will improve our roads, highways, and public transportation, making it easier to transport products; and we're building the North Carolina Information Highway, linking workers with community colleges, universities, and other training facilities statewide. The Information Highway will use state of the art communications technology to link schools, hospitals, law-enforcement agencies, and other facilities across the state.

I think we're on the right track. We are proud of the things we are doing to attract good jobs and to make life better for our people, and we want to do all we can to help Alcatel and other businesses improve and expand their opportunities in North Carolina.

---

[1] Cuyler Dunbar was president of Catawba Valley Community College, Hickory. *Directory of State and County Officials of North Carolina, 1993,* 84.

COMMISSION FOR A COMPETITIVE NORTH CAROLINA

Asheville, July 21, 1994

In my office in the Capitol, I keep a chart that lays out my mission statement. It keeps me focused and helps keep our administration focused.

[Hunt reads mission statement.]

This mission statement drives our legislative agenda. It drives our budget. It drives our agency policies. It drives the work that I do, [and I] want it to guide the work you do.

We share a charge, one delivered to us by the people of North Carolina back in November 1992. As I listen to you this morning, I'm reminded again that we share a mission. All of us in this room are working to build a brighter North Carolina. We are working to make government work better and to galvanize our people to be part of a positive solution.

Every benchmark that this commission sets is part of that mission. Every goal you lay out to improve schools, keep our neighborhoods safe, strengthen our families, help our children, and create good jobs is part of that mission. We've begun to set some benchmarks in our legislative initiatives: providing every child with quality health care and child care as part of Smart Start; immunizing 90 percent of all two-year-olds by the year 2000 as part of Healthy Start; requiring every high school graduate to have the basic skills for success in work and life. These efforts are under way.

But we need your leadership and your dedication. Reinventing government and education reform will be the focus of my '95 legislative agenda. I'm looking to you, along with my policy office and my budget office, to lay out specific ways we can make government work better for our people. Your challenge is a great one. You must not only set these benchmarks, and help us come up with ways to hold ourselves accountable, you must involve the people of the state in this effort. Let them know what you're doing. Ask for their input. Make them part of the positive solution.

The public has lost faith in government and lost faith in government's ability to respond to the everyday needs of their families. They don't think government can be held accountable, so they throw up their hands in disgust. Once they learn about your benchmarking efforts, I believe they will be surprised. Benchmarking is about running government more like a business. It's a commonsense approach: If you don't meet your quota, your departmental budget gets docked. Most folks would say it's too commonsense for government!

You are going to prove them wrong. You are going to show that government can respond to pressing needs in a way that sets out rewards for success and consequences for failure.

Your work is critical to our efforts. Your committees are already tackling the fundamentals of North Carolina's quality of life, setting goals that are fundamental to our state's future. We need your leadership in mapping out a blueprint for North Carolina, and we need your leadership in setting benchmarks to help us interpret that blueprint to determine if we're building the machine the right way.

Your benchmarks can help make government more efficient, and more effective, and more accountable. By setting a specific goal for reducing teenage pregnancy or high school dropouts, and by holding government agencies' feet to the fire, you can truly help reinvent government. Nothing is more important.

ADVISORY COMMISSION ON MILITARY AFFAIRS

RALEIGH, JULY 25, 1994

I want to thank you for coming today and for agreeing to serve on this important commission. I especially want to thank our base commanders for coming today, and I want to thank all of you for working on behalf of the active duty and retired military in North Carolina.

I have asked you to serve on the Governor's Advisory Commission on Military Affairs to look at ways we can improve relations among our military on the state level and our surrounding communities. We must do all we can to improve the lives of military families who serve at these bases or who have chosen to retire here. North Carolina has a strong military tradition. We have always taken seriously our duty to protect and defend our country. In the revolution, our soldiers fought so hard they earned the nickname "Tar Heels." Today, our soldiers are leading our armed forces around the world: in Grenada, Panama, and the Persian Gulf. They have played a critical role in military and humanitarian efforts, and this nation owes them a great debt.

Our bases are vital to the defense and security of our nation, but they also have a tremendous impact on our economy, and building our economy and bringing good jobs to our state has been a cornerstone of this administration. We have over 700,000 veterans and over 57,000 military retirees in North Carolina. The number of military personnel in North Carolina is on the rise, while the number nationwide has dropped. The military provides good jobs for many people in our state. The economic impact of our state's military installations are [sic] vital to our economy, generating more than $6.5 billion per year and approximately 135,000 military and civilian jobs that would otherwise not be here.

I'm looking to you to play a special role in keeping our bases strong. We must work to form closer partnerships between state government, our local governments, our business community, and our military commands. Together, we can continue to improve our relationship, better enabling us to meet challenges that lie ahead. That's why Senator Beverly Perdue, Representative William Wainwright,[1] Senator John Kerr, and so many others in the General Assembly have taken strong steps during this year's short session to recognize the importance of our military. The General Assembly appropriated $200,000 to provide for research to enhance North Carolina's position as we prepare for BRAC [base realignment and closure] '95. The money will also provide for a military liaison office to strengthen communication between local, state, and federal government actions related to the BRAC and other Department of Defense actions that may affect North Carolina. The liaison office will also raise awareness of the economic impact of the military and its potential for growth in North Carolina.

Our legislators are also taking leadership roles as we move forward on the Global TransPark. The TransPark presents tremendous opportunities for the Department of Defense, and I've had many discussions with interested D.O.D. officials about that—including Secretary Perry, in Washington. The interest was demonstrated a couple of weeks ago when Vice-Admiral Edward Straw, the commander of the Defense Logistics Agency, came to Kinston to visit the TransPark. The DLA is facing many of the same transportation and distribution challenges, and Admiral Straw thinks the GTP can play an important role in meeting the military's needs in the future.

There are a lot of other things our administration is doing to help our active duty and retired military personnel:

—We've reestablished the Jobs for Veterans Committee. Jimmy Woodard is the chairman of that group and will tell you about that later.[2]

—Our Division of Veterans Affairs offers assistance to veterans and their dependents with claims for federal, state, and local benefits.

—The Veterans Affairs Commission oversees the state's veterans programs and the state's scholarship program for children of war veterans.

—Fort Bragg and Pope Air Force Base conducted a study, led by the North Carolina Department of Commerce's Division of Community Assistance, to find ways to build the economy and protect the environment without threatening the military's mission. Some of the recommendations from that study are being implemented today, and the Pentagon has called it a model land use study for other U.S. military installations.

I have told Department of Defense officials about how important our military bases are in North Carolina, and I'll continue the fight to keep our bases strong. I traveled to Norfolk last year to testify at the Base Realignment and Closure Commission hearing on the naval aviation depot at Cherry Point. As a result of our efforts, an estimated 5,000 military and civilian jobs will come to Cherry Point from BRAC '93. We believe it is in the nation's best interest, as well as North Carolina's, to do all we can to ensure that our bases remain healthy through the BRAC '95 process. My staff is monitoring this situation, working closely with our congressional delegation, including Representatives Hefner[3] and Lancaster, to build good relations between our state and the Department of Defense.

It will be up to you to guide our state's efforts to build on our relationship with our active military personnel, retirees, and their families, and to provide a forum to discuss issues important to them. I look forward to working with you to achieve a new spirit and commitment to cooperation and friendship between our state and the military personnel who live here.

---

[1] William L. Wainwright (1947-), born in Somerville, Tenn.; resident of Craven County; B.S., Memphis State University, 1970. Presiding elder, New Bern District, N.C. Conference, A.M.E. Zion Church; pastor, Piney Grove A.M.E. Zion church, 1985-1993; member, N.C. House of Representatives, from 1991; Democrat. *North Carolina Manual, 1995-1996,* 667.

[2] James A. Woodard (1943-), born in Roanoke Rapids; resident of Conway; B.S., N.C. State University, 1967; U.S. Navy, 1967-1973; U.S. Naval Reserve, 1973-1993. Retired navy captain; administrative officer, State Veterans Nursing Home Program, from November 1996. James A. Woodard, letter to Jan-Michael Poff, March 3, 1999.

[3] Willie Gathrel Hefner (1930-), born in Elora, Tenn.; resident of Concord; president, WRKB Radio, Kannapolis; member, U.S. House of Representatives, 1975-1998, and chairman, Subcommittee on Military Construction; Democrat. *Biographical Directory of Congress,* s.v. "Hefner, Willie Gathrel (Bill)"; *North Carolina Manual, 1993-1994,* 950, *1997-1998,* 1069.

NOTES, SMART START ANNOUNCEMENT LUNCHEON

RALEIGH, AUGUST 11, 1994

A year ago, we came together in the Research Triangle to talk about Smart Start and our vision for North Carolina's children. We said then that Smart Start had the potential to change the future of our state— by lifting up our children. Today, thanks to the efforts of Robin Britt, and Jim Goodmon, and Walter Shepherd,[1] and all of you, we are making those changes; and we are making North Carolina the first state in the country truly committed to providing quality, affordable child care and health care for all of our children.

Smart Start's first eighteen pioneer counties have made remarkable changes in their communities:

—More than 1,500 children have been taken off waiting lists to receive child-care subsidies. In Orange County, they don't have a waiting list anymore.

—In Jones County, they didn't have a pediatrician before. Now they have one, once a week, to treat their children.

—In the western consortium, Smart Start and DOT [Department of Transportation] funds have been pooled to buy nineteen vans to link families with services.

—In Cumberland County, librarians are providing daily storytelling sessions at thirty-two different child-care centers.

But remarkable changes are taking place across North Carolina, in your communities. That's because in all your communities, in all 100 counties, people have joined hands to work together for our children. You understand, better than anyone else, what our children need and want. They need love. They need to be held. They need to be encouraged. They need to have their minds stimulated. You know that, and other people in our state are beginning to share our dream. The General Assembly knows that. That's why they've committed to starting twelve new partnerships this year, and why we will ask them to add more next year, and more the year after that, until we reach our goal: that every child in this state who needs child care and health care gets child care and health care.

But when the new Smart Start partnerships are announced in September, there are no winners or losers.[2] The only way your county will lose will be if you don't do anything at all. If you work together, we win. In fact, some of the most impressive work in the past year in this state has been done by counties that didn't make the first round of funding. Two examples:

—Catawba County ranked very high on the list, but because of the classification system, they couldn't be selected. They could have been devastated. Instead, they went home and had a celebration to recognize that they have, for the first time, put together a truly countywide effort! They said they had so much momentum from the planning process that they were unstoppable, and they have been! They have gotten the county commissioners to create a children's committee and have worked on a state-of-the-child conference there. And just two weeks ago, they sponsored a western regional Smart Start conference for thirty-one counties and have emerged as a leader in our Smart Start efforts.

—Yadkin County ranked near the bottom of the criteria used for selection last year. They could have grumbled about not getting a state grant. Instead, they put their heads together to find out what else they could do. Since then they have kept working, have set up their own partnership, have hired a part-time staff person, and have found other funds to help their children.

These communities have embraced the spirit of Smart Start, the spirit that has lifted up North Carolina and its children. Smart Start isn't about new staff. It's about mobilizing people at the grass roots. It isn't ultimately about hiring staff people. It's about mobilizing a grass-roots effort to reach out to and love our children at the most important time in their lives.

Smart Start is about spreading the truth that you already know: that our children are truly our future. It's about our shared commitment to North Carolina's children [dropped text] that everybody in this state shares your commitment. It's about helping people to see that if we give our children the start they need, we won't have as many school dropouts. We won't have as much crime. Our families will be stronger, and our state will have a brighter future—a future we can all be proud of.

---

[1] Walter L. Shepherd, former hospital administrator; former assistant dean, East Carolina University School of Medicine; resigned as executive director of both the Governor's Commission on Reduction of Infant Mortality and the N.C. Healthy Start Foundation to become executive director, N.C. Partnership for Children, on January 1, 1994. Governor Jim Martin appointed Shepherd, in 1990, to direct the effort to cut the state's staggering infant mortality rate; by the time he left the post, the number of infant deaths had been reduced by 14 percent, to the lowest level in North Carolina history. *News and Observer*, June 26, 1990, November 21, 1993, July 11, 1995.

[2] The twelve additional Smart Start partnerships for 1994 were based in Ashe, Avery, Catawba, Chatham, Duplin, Durham, Forsyth, Lenoir-Greene, Nash-Edgecombe, Pasquotank, Person, and Wilkes Counties. Smart Start Announcement, Raleigh, September 21, 1994, Governors Papers, James Baxter Hunt Jr.

NOTES, TEACHERS' TOWN MEETINGS

Asheville, August 15; Franklin, August 16; and Marshall, August 17, 1994

[Compare these notes for the teachers' town meetings with the North Carolina Business Roundtable text, October 31, 1994, reprinted elsewhere in this volume.]

What do teachers need to be able to do their job? I want to hear from you.

That's why my Teacher Advisory Committee, a group of fifteen classroom teachers who advise me—and Karen Garr, my teacher adviser—have been holding more than thirty teachers' town meetings around the state.

Here's what we're hearing from people:

—First, teachers need to be able to teach in safety. We must restore discipline and make our schools safe places to learn.

We have new safe-school laws in place, which makes [sic] it a felony to bring guns to campus; and crime session provided money for new school social workers and guidance counselors. What about automatically expelling any student who brings weapons or drugs to school, or who assaults someone there? Would need to provide better alternative school settings at same time.

—Second, we have to do more to make sure our children come to school healthy and ready to learn. Smart Start is under way in eighteen pioneer counties, and we'll be launching the program in twelve additional counties next month. Our goal is to make sure every child who needs it gets the quality affordable day care, health care, and other critical services they'll need to succeed in school and in life.

—Third, we have to set higher standards for what students should know and be able to do, for both basic skills and higher academic subjects. That's the goal of the Standards and Accountability Commission, which has recommended that we require the mastery of ten essential skills—like reading, writing, using math, analytical thinking—in order to graduate. And that we make sure kids graduate able to apply those skills to the real world of work. If we are going to expect more from our students, we need to do more to help them achieve higher standards.

—Fourth, we have to do more for the 50 percent of North Carolina students who go straight from school into the workforce without any additional training.

JobReady would encourage businesses to work with schools to form apprenticeship programs, so students get hands-on experience while still in school. JobReady would also bring job brokers into schools to help students get jobs and work with students earlier, in primary grades, to find out more about the kinds of jobs that are available and the skills they will need to get good jobs.

—To do all of these things, we have to do more for teachers, including better pay, better training, more time to plan lessons, more voice in education policy, and more accountability. The 7 percent pay raise, which I supported, is a step in the right direction.

And we need to do all we can to encourage excellence in teaching. The GA's [General Assembly's] action in the short session to provide $500,000 for NBPTS [National Board for Professional Teaching Standards] will help North Carolina encourage our teachers to be the best in the nation.

Teacher academies.

I think we have a responsibility to do more to help our teachers help our students achieve these higher standards.

HEALTH CHECK KICKOFF

RESEARCH TRIANGLE PARK, AUGUST 25, 1994

Nothing can warm your heart more than seeing a healthy child out playing and enjoying life. But nothing can break your heart more than seeing a sick child who didn't get appropriate medical care.

Across North Carolina, we're fortunate to have some of the best doctors and health care available to our citizens. However, some of our children aren't getting the health care they so desperately need to grow up healthy, happy, and strong—and it's not because our health-care system is failing them. It's because we've failed to educate parents and help them realize the importance of preventive health care for their children. That's why we're here today.

We have a plan to reach out to parents and help them make sure their children grow up happy and healthy. Today I join with you in celebrating an event that bridges another gap in our service-delivery system. This one has the potential of bringing regular health care to hundreds of thousands of youngsters. We call it Health Check.

Of 380,000 low-income children eligible for free Medicaid health services in our state, only about 160,000 receive any services. Health Check's goal is to serve all these children. It will provide local coordinators to help children who are not getting the health-care services they need, like medical and dental checkups, and every parent will get a "Health Check Record" to help them keep track of their children's medical records. This program will also locate and bring in physicians across the state to serve these children. The Health Check toll-free hotline that we'll be touring [sic] today will give parents the information they're seeking when they need help.

This program isn't just a good idea—it can literally save lives. I want you to meet Lonnie Holden and his mother, Karen. Lonnie is an eight-year-old Wake County youngster with a future, thanks to regular health checks.

Lonnie is fortunate that his parents were insured and diligent about his checkups. It was during his eighteen-month checkup that a tumor was detected in one of Lonnie's kidneys. He had surgery and chemotherapy to treat his condition. Now he enjoys karate, baseball, and basketball. Because he was checked in time, he was given a chance at a healthy, successful life.

That is what we want for every youngster in North Carolina, and that is what this program will help do. Health Check can make a difference for the youngsters in every county who need these vital services—when a child is sick and a mother doesn't know where to go for help, or when a child is injured, or becomes ill—Health Check will help parents locate the services their children need.

Meeting the needs of North Carolina's children and families is a top focus of this administration. We are doing all we can to see that children across North Carolina have every opportunity to succeed. We've already begun to meet those needs with Smart Start, SOS, and family resource centers. We have also launched an effort to improve chances for adoption of our foster children by using the help of the media to place foster children in loving, nurturing homes.

I want to commend Secretaries Robin Britt and Jonathan Howes, and all of you here today. We couldn't have done all of these things for children without you, and we couldn't have launched Health Check without you. I am grateful, and I know that families across North Carolina are also grateful.

We have the opportunity to make a tremendous difference in the quality of life for our state's children. We're very fortunate to have support from the health-care community in the public-private partnership that has come together to provide these services to children across the state. I urge and challenge your leadership in all counties to work together in this effort to make sure good health care is available to all of our children. They deserve nothing less.

Champagne splattered Governor Hunt and Mayor Margaret Kluttz as she christened the Piedmont during its visit to Salisbury, one of a number of ceremonial first stops the train made on its inaugural run, May 25, 1995. The following day it joined the popular Carolinian in regular Raleigh-Charlotte rail passenger service. Although the trip between the capital and queen cities was scheduled to take 3 hours, 45 minutes, Hunt wanted equipment and track upgrades that would cut the commute to two hours. Both the Piedmont and Carolinian were a joint effort between the state and Amtrak, and both trains were key elements in the Hunt administration's plans to provide North Carolinians with a more comprehensive transportation system. (Photograph by Gary Allen, Raleigh *News and Observer*.)

The wedding of the Hunts' daughter, Elizabeth, to Kevin Mark Amigh, September 9, 1995, provided the perfect opportunity for a family photograph. Gathered in the Grand Hallway of the Executive Mansion were: *first row* (l-r), Joseph Thornton Hawley, Hannah Streeter Hawley, Stephanie Davies Hunt, James Baxter Hunt IV, Lindsey Derrick Hunt; *second row*, Rebecca Joyce Hunt Hawley, Jimmy Lee Hawley, Rachel Henderson Hunt Nilender, Olav Nilender, Governor Hunt, Kevin Mark Amigh, Elizabeth Brame Hunt Amigh, First Lady Carolyn Leonard Hunt, Deborah Lynn Derrick, James Baxter Hunt III. (Photograph courtesy of the Office of the Governor, James Baxter Hunt Jr.)

NORTH CAROLINA RURAL
ECONOMIC DEVELOPMENT COUNCIL

RALEIGH, AUGUST 31, 1994

Partners are those who reach out to us when we need a hand; who give us a boost when we are down; who smooth out the bumps in the road when we need help. Without partners, the road would be a lot bumpier!

The North Carolina Rural Economic Development Council has demonstrated over the last year just what it means to be a good partner. You all are working hard [to] smooth out the bumps in the road, so to speak, for rural North Carolinians. You are building public-private partnerships, bringing the resources of local, state, and federal governments together with the private sector to improve the lives of our state's rural residents—and you're doing it in new and innovative ways: working to ease regulatory burdens that hamstring the delivery of public services to rural areas; working to develop a rapid response team that can help rural communities in crisis; working to encourage North Carolina's communities to apply for the Clinton administration's new empowerment zones and enterprise community grants. Some fifteen of our state's communities are applying for these grants, thanks in part to your efforts.[1]

You've shown what partnership really means, and what we can achieve for our people if we work together. All of us in this room are committed to making the good life—good schools, healthy children, good jobs—a reality for rural North Carolina. That's why we've worked so hard to launch Smart Start in eighteen counties, including rural counties down east and out west. We know that giving rural preschoolers quality child care and health care will help them come to school ready to learn and help them build a brighter future.

That's why we're working to improve our schools, making sure our students graduate with the real skills they need to compete for good jobs. We know that without a well-educated, well-trained workforce, rural communities cannot compete for the high-paying jobs they so desperately need. That's why we're working to build the Information Highway, linking every school in every corner of our state. We know that a student in Swain or Tyrrell County should have a chance to take the same advanced science class as a student in Charlotte, Raleigh, or Durham.

That's why I've directed my Commerce Department to step up its efforts to promote rural North Carolina and to recruit good companies to rural communities. In fact, my top industrial recruiter is in western

North Carolina, right now, with a team of his best economic developers! We know that without high-skill, high-wage jobs, rural economies cannot grow—and that's why I'm proud to announce that the Rural Economic Development Council, the Rural Economic Development Center, and the Governor's Office are working together to create a national demonstration project to help rural communities solve critical water and sewer problems.

Our new project, called the Rural North Carolina Water/Sewer Resource Group, brings together technical and funding agencies from all levels of government and the nonprofit community. This ground-breaking effort will build a new partnership to assess the water and sewer needs in rural areas, track how the resources are now being spent, target regulatory problems, and look for ways to boost water and sewer services in rural communities. We know water and sewer services are the lifeblood of a rural community. We know that the improvements we can make with this new demonstration project can help us bring new jobs, and new energy, to rural areas. This is what North Carolinians can do when we work as partners!

Each of you, here today, has helped build this partnership and has helped open the door of opportunity to residents in rural North Carolina. I'm proud of your energy, your efforts, and your accomplishments. On behalf of the people of this state, I want to thank you. Because of you, rural North Carolina will be a better place tomorrow.

---

[1] Applicants for federal grants under the Enterprise Community and Empowerment Zone program included cities, counties, and partnerships thereof: Anson County; Asheville; Bertie, Hertford, Pasquotank, and Tyrrell Counties; city of Boone, and Watauga and Madison Counties; Charlotte; Columbus County; Durham; city of Fayetteville and Cumberland County; Greensboro; Raleigh; Robeson County; cities of Rocky Mount, Wilson, and Edgecombe, Wilson, and Halifax Counties; Warren, Halifax, and Northampton Counties; Wilmington; and Winston-Salem. Press release, Governor Hunt Supports Fifteen Communities Seeking Federal Grants, Raleigh, July 6, 1994; see also press release, Governor Hunt's Budget Proposal Targets Rural Community Development, Raleigh, July 28, 1994, Governors Papers, James Baxter Hunt Jr.

NOTES, SUPPORT OUR STUDENTS VOLUNTEER MEETING

RALEIGH, SEPTEMBER 7, 1994

SOS is unique—the first statewide program driven by volunteers

This is the first time I have ever called so many volunteer leaders together. But this is [also] the first time we've ever designed a statewide public-private partnership that so depends on volunteer support.

SOS [Support Our Students] is an after-school program that can have a tremendous impact on our school-age children: keeping them away from crime and showing them a better way to live their lives.

There is tremendous support for the program across the state

People across our state know the need for it. They told me in a series of meetings last fall. This summer, they have applied to be a part of it: 163 YMCAs, Boys' and Girls' Clubs, churches, and nonprofits from seventy-six counties have looked at their communities and proposed solutions to the local needs of their local children.

SOS is not a big-government program

Next week we'll be announcing the sites. It won't be a big-government program. The state will be contributing seed money and logistical support to enhance existing programs and get new programs up and running for three years. The programs will be locally designed to meet local needs.

My dream with SOS is that children all across our state will see a whole new world open up to them. My dream is that, rather than learning about drugs and violence after school, they'll learn about computers and sports; that they'll get to know high school kids who have decided to reject violence as a way out of a problem; that they'll see people from their communities who've found meaningful jobs, not just menial jobs; that they'll learn that team projects are a lot more fun than teen pregnancies.

The program hinges on community and volunteer support—you can help

So today we would like your best ideas about how to involve the greatest number of volunteers. Each of you has information about, and insight into, important volunteer resources across the state; and every program in this state will be needing consistent volunteer support, from high school and college students, church members, retired adults, and young professionals—people willing to commit a couple of hours a week to make a real difference in our children's lives. I'll be volunteering, myself. I'd like you to volunteer. I'd like you to consider asking those you represent and work with to volunteer, as well.

We need to find new volunteers—particularly those with minority backgrounds

And I also want you to think of ways we can reach a whole new group of volunteers: people who haven't thought of volunteering before, or who thought they had nothing to offer. In particular, I'd like your ideas about how to enlist good role models in minority communities who may have volunteered in the past and gotten away from it, or who haven't thought about how important their help can be to their community.

Here are the people you need to know

Before we begin talking about that, I'd like to introduce you to two people you need to know.[1]

Once the sites are selected, we will be bringing together the coordinators of each of the selected programs to conduct volunteer training workshops. Those workshops are designed to make sure that the people who work with volunteers have a good plan for working with them.[2]

Now I want to hear from you. You are the experts, the ones who know who and where the volunteers are. I want to hear your ideas about how we can link hands with the people running these programs all over the state and involve your church members, young professionals, high school students, fraternity brothers and [sorority] sisters in SOS.

Today we want your advice about how to make them successful. We know it is a good idea. We know that quality after-school programs make a tremendous difference in the lives of the children they serve.

---

[1] At this point in his remarks, Hunt actually introduced three people: Don Willis, acting director, SOS; Leslie Boney, governor's director of community involvement; and Barry Stanback, deputy secretary, Department of Human Resources, who "has been taking a leadership role in developing the SOS program."

[2] Hunt introduced Judith Bell, director, Governor's Office of Citizen Affairs, to speak about the workshops.

COASTAL FUTURES CONFERENCE

WILMINGTON, SEPTEMBER 7, 1994

Thank you, Rich: I knew when I appointed you as chairman of the Coastal Futures Committee that you would bring the level of commitment and concern needed to undertake such a tough job and show results so quickly! I know the long hours, dedication, and hard work that you and all the members of this committee have put into this report.[1] I thank you on behalf of all of us who hold North Carolina's coast dear.

Twenty years ago, we nearly lost the fragile beauty of our coast. I was lieutenant governor then, and I remember the battles we fought to see the Coastal Area Management Act passed. But it did pass, and it was one of the earliest and most progressive programs of its type in the country. The Coastal Area Management Act has given our coast a great legacy, a legacy of protecting and safeguarding one of our most beautiful natural gifts. Sea walls and other beach-destroying structures have been banned, important ecological systems have been improved and protected, and public access to our beaches and sounds have [sic] been preserved.

My family and I have spent many hours enjoying our beaches. But only if we act now can we make sure it will still be here, and still be just as beautiful, when my grandchildren have grandchildren of their own.

Two decades after we passed the original Coastal Area Management Act, we stand at a crossroads. In the last decade, population along our coast has grown almost twice as fast as our entire state. By the turn of the century, in just six short years, many of our coastal counties will boom with growth rates reaching up to 20 percent.

While we welcome economic development, we must realize that unchecked growth can burden our infrastructure and stress our fragile coastal environment. So we must act now to chart a new course for our coast. That's what I asked the Coastal Futures Committee to do, and that's what they've done. We have an excellent framework for balancing coastal development and preserving the breathtaking beauty of our coast.

The coast belongs to all of us. The fisherman and his family in Wanchese have a stake in its future, but so does the family from Asheville who spend their annual vacation here. We must make certain we protect the coast, now, for them and their grandchildren. The committee's recommendations will help us do that.

But we need stronger land-use planning, too. Right now, planning for many coastal communities is little more than an exercise in bureaucratic paper work. We need to look at big coastal development decisions in light of what they will do to our coast now, and what kind of impact they will have years down the road. Our water, sewer, and road systems also must catch up with development.

We must take a regional approach to coastal issues. By approaching water quality protection and improvement, economic development, transportation, and waste disposal on a regional basis—not with a piecemeal, community-by-community approach—we can make sure our beautiful beaches, sounds, and estuaries will still be here when our great-grandchildren reach our age. We must also be creative in developing our delicate coastal region. We must encourage environmentally friendly development like eco-tourism and aquaculture.

During the first twenty years of environmental management on the coast, we've done a good job of controlling pollution in the traditional way: from the end of the pipe. Now we must work to control pollution from nonpoint sources. For example, we can't afford, economically or environmentally, to let our oyster beds continue to fall victim to storm-water runoff.

Finally, we've got to educate our residents about the environment. We can't expect them to preserve and protect the world around them, unless we make sure they understand that world and how they affect it.

Balancing economic growth with environmental protection in North Carolina is an immediate and pressing challenge for all of us, whether we live along the coast or in the mountains. But folks, we've got to do it now. I, for one, am tired of hearing about dwindling fish stocks, closed shellfish beds, dying wetlands, and contaminated wells!

We've all got to work together. Enacting your recommendations will require a strong commitment and strong leadership from public officials, private citizens, and all of us who enjoy and depend on our North Carolina coastal resources. We must act now, or write the future off. But I'm not about to do that. Help me win this battle. Help me make sure that our great-grandchildren, and their grandchildren, can enjoy the same beauty we enjoy today!

---

[1] See North Carolina Coastal Futures Committee, *Charting a Course for Our Coast* ([Raleigh, N.C.: The Committee], 1994). L. Richardson Preyer, identified earlier in this volume, was committee chairman.

STATE EMPLOYEES ASSOCIATION ANNUAL CONVENTION

Charlotte, September 9, 1994

Unity means joining together for a common goal. As state employees, all of us share a common goal: serving our 8 million customers, the people of this state. Unity means relying on one another, working as a team, with a common spirit and resolve. In many ways, that's how state government works. As state employees, we rely on one another. We are a team.

I rely on you and the fine work you do, every day, to give our 8 million customers the quality service and products they need; and you rely on your governor to chart a course for our state that includes safe neighborhoods, good schools, and prosperous communities. You rely on me to fight for our common goals. I take that responsibility seriously, and I intend to keep on fighting. I intend to keep on fighting for things that are important to state employees, like a fair pay raise next year.

You know I recommended a fair pay raise, the same pay raise, for state employees and teachers this year, twice the raise you all got last year. You know that I pushed for that raise to follow the Comprehensive Pay Plan. You know I fought to protect your retirement funds and health insurance, making sure they weren't used to balance the state's budget. State employees have worked hard for those benefits, and they ought not to be up for grabs.

You all know how hard Blanche Critcher, my state employee ombudsman, has worked to keep me informed every day about the issues and problems that concern you. Blanche has talked personally with hundreds of state employees over the last year, and she's let me know just what's on your mind.

A very important part of my job is to listen, to you and to other people across North Carolina. As I've traveled across our state in the last twenty months, I've listened and I've learned. I've heard one common concern from our people, from Murphy to Manteo: How can we build a better future for our children—a future with safe neighborhoods [and] safe classrooms where our children can learn?

I have five grandchildren. Many of you are parents, grandparents, aunts, and uncles. As governor and as a grandfather, I'm committed to doing everything I can to help our children. I challenge you to do the same.

We must come together as a community, in unity, to help our children resist drugs and alcohol, crime, violence, and unwelcomed pregnancies.

Next week, North Carolina will launch our new SOS [Support Our Students] program in dozens of communities across the state. Born in the crime session, SOS is our new effort to make a difference in the lives of many young people. I believe it can help us reach them before they have lost hope, before exposure to crime and violence changes them forever.

SOS is an after-school program that relies on local volunteers to give youngsters enriching, positive activities to fill the after-school hours. It relies on people, like you, to be role models, someone to look up to, someone to learn from. SOS isn't a "big government" program, and we aren't creating a new division in state government! It's just a way for the state to encourage local people, people like you, to decide what works best to reach out to youngsters in their community.

That's just one of the things we're doing to build our children's future. Smart Start is now in place in eighteen counties, helping preschoolers get the quality day care and health care they need to succeed in life, and it's working. Down in Jones County, there is now a pediatrician, thanks to Smart Start. In a few weeks, we'll be expanding Smart Start to twelve more counties, and the day isn't far off when we'll be reaching out to every child in North Carolina who needs it.

But building a better future for our children takes more than programs, folks. It takes unity. It takes all of us.

I know what a formidable force state employees can be, and I know what that force can do if we put it to work for our children. Last year, we put a new policy in place that provides eight hours of leave time for state employees to get involved in their children's schools. Take those eight hours of child involvement leave, and get involved.

Right now almost half the parents of our nation's high schoolers don't come to PTA meetings, don't volunteer at their child's school, don't come to plays or football games, or get involved in any way in their child's education. Just imagine what a positive force we could create if every parent did get involved. Just imagine how our children would thrive.

Business leaders know it. That's why a CEO friend of mine requires his employees to attend PTA meetings and fires those who don't. In his mind, an employee who doesn't care about his child's future doesn't care about the right things. Just imagine what a positive force we could create if every manager in state government encouraged his or her employees to do the same. Imagine what a positive force we could create if every state employee without kids decided to use those eight hours of leave time to help someone else's child, by volunteering in a SOS program.

I'm going to be volunteering in Wake County's SOS Program. I challenge you all to do the same in your communities. Just imagine what we could do, folks. Isn't that the definition of unity?

Together, I know we can build a better future for our children. We can do it if we start with the children. I challenge each of you, and each and every state employee, to join me. Let's show the rest of North Carolina what unity is all about.

AMERICORPS ANNOUNCEMENT

CHAPEL HILL, SEPTEMBER 12, 1994

[The speech to the North Carolina Child Care Corps, Greensboro, November 9, 1994, echoes much of Hunt's AmeriCorps text, below. For related press release, see Governor Hunt Kicks Off State AmeriCorps Programs, Raleigh, September 12, 1994, Governors Papers, James Baxter Hunt Jr.]

About thirty years ago, I heard President John F. Kennedy speak at Reynolds Coliseum. I was an undergrad at N.C. State, sitting way up in the rafters. I remember President Kennedy's enthusiasm and his charisma. But most of all, I remember his challenge. He challenged us to embrace community service. He challenged us to demand more of ourselves; to give more to our country; to be part of something larger and better. His challenge was part of the reason I went into politics, to try to make a difference.

John F. Kennedy left us a great legacy. He gave his best to our country, and he urged all of us to give our best. He inspired generations of Americans and shaped a tradition of community service. That's what

AmeriCorps is all about. President Clinton's national community service effort is a domestic Peace Corps, challenging America's young people to give their best to their country by working here at home to solve community problems.

North Carolinians are living up to that challenge. Today I'm proud to announce that North Carolina will get $2.2 million in AmeriCorps grants to launch fourteen new community service programs. I want to thank Congressman David Price for his efforts to secure federal funds for this effort. Within one year, North Carolina will have almost 500 AmeriCorps volunteers helping day-care teachers get additional training, tutoring middle-school students, teaching adults how to read, boosting affordable housing, and mentoring at-risk youngsters. Here at this day-care center, AmeriCorps volunteers will serve as substitute teachers so that day-care workers can get the training and education they need to provide even higher-quality care for our children. In Warren County, AmeriCorps volunteers will help middle-school students with reading and math. In Charlotte, they'll work to educate at-risk teenagers about teenage pregnancy. In Wilmington, they'll work with the police department to make neighborhoods safer. Across the state, AmeriCorps volunteers will be building a better future for North Carolina. Volunteers like Nancy Washburn, of VISTA [Volunteers in Service to America], will be making a difference, and I commend her and all of our VISTA volunteers for rising to President Kennedy's challenge.

There is great excitement in North Carolina about what we can do to build up our communities. I've seen it with Smart Start, our day-care and health-care initiative; and I'm seeing it now with SOS [Support Our Students], our new after-school program for troubled youngsters. Smart Start and SOS can help us give our children a better start in life and help deter them from crime. When North Carolinians work together and put our communities first, there's no limit to what we can do!

I want to say a special word of thanks to the community leaders who serve on our state Commission on National and Community Service and its chair, Jim Van Hecke; and I want to thank the hardworking folks in the Governor's Office of Citizen Affairs, headed by Judith Bell, who've helped make this happen.[1] With their leadership and encouragement, North Carolina communities have gotten excited about AmeriCorps. Because of their leadership, a whopping seventy-five North Carolina communities applied for AmeriCorps grants, developing specific plans to target community problems with community service. We'll be working to do whatever we can to support these efforts and to encourage them to apply for AmeriCorps grants next year.

Because of their leadership, North Carolina has distinguished itself as the state with the highest number of AmeriCorps programs per capita! Now that tells you how committed North Carolinians are to their communities. North Carolinians helping North Carolinians: That's the definition of community service. AmeriCorps will help us do just that.

---

[1] James M. Van Hecke Jr. (1947-   ), born in Greensboro; resident of Tryon; A.B., University of North Carolina at Chapel Hill, 1969; graduate study at Princeton University Theological Seminary and University of North Carolina law and business schools. Chairman, N.C. Democratic Party, 1986-1988; member, 1993-1998, and chairman, N.C. Commission on National and Community Service; administrator, Pavillon International, Mill Spring, N.C. Letters of Appointment of Boards and Commissions, Governors Papers, James Baxter Hunt Jr.; James M. Van Hecke Jr., letter to Jan-Michael Poff, September 1, 1999.

Judith Bell; resident of Durham; former CETA program director, Baton Rouge, La.; former economics professor; former member, U.S. Department of Labor Manpower Advisory Committee; worked in computer-based education for IBM, 1981-1992; diversity training instructor, Equal Opportunity Services Division, N.C. Office of State Personnel, 1992-1993; was appointed director, Governor's Office of Citizen Affairs, 1994. Press release, Hunt Names Two to Lead State's Citizen Involvement Efforts, Raleigh, June 16, 1994, Governors Papers, James Baxter Hunt Jr.

SUPPORT OUR STUDENTS ANNOUNCEMENT

RALEIGH, SEPTEMBER 14, 1994

[The following text is almost identical to one Hunt used in Charlotte later that day.]

In Halifax County, a Baptist church is working with the school system to develop after-school programs in the district's four middle schools, sharing space between the schools and church fellowship halls.

In Davidson, Montgomery, and Rowan Counties, leaders will work together to find ways of helping motivate fourteen-year-olds to do better in school, using everything from speakers, to sports, to satellite technology.

Here at Daniels Middle School, a partnership of families, students, and youth agencies will be developing a pilot after-school program with the aim of replicating it in schools and neighborhoods throughout Wake County.

All of these programs, and good programs in forty-nine other counties, are pioneer SOS [Support Our Students] sites. All together, they are receiving $4.6 million in grants to develop enriching after-school activities for students who need structured activities and good role models.

Six months ago, the General Assembly, under the leadership of House Speaker Dan Blue and Senate president pro-tem Marc Basnight, approved funding for the SOS program. You know why we need this program. The lives of our children are fundamentally different, these days. Up to 80 percent of our children come home to empty houses. In many cases they get into trouble—drugs, violence, teenage pregnancies—in other cases, trouble gets them. That's just not right.

But we also know what works. A recent study by the Cooperative Extension Service in sixteen states shows that getting children involved in quality after-school programs gives them something positive to look forward to in the afternoon. We know the programs can help them do a better job completing their homework. They can reduce bad behavior in school. By putting kids face to face with good volunteer role models, the programs encourage students to become good, productive citizens.

The pilot programs we're announcing today will pioneer this initiative—to bring together a wide range of volunteers who can reach out to our children in the afternoon. The state will serve as a catalyst, with three-year grants ranging from $46,000 to $200,000 to serve our students, particularly those in the middle years of school. Local communities will contribute the rest in donations, in-kind contributions, and volunteer support. I'll be volunteering in this program, and in other programs, as I travel the state.

SOS depends on communities to embrace their children and to get involved to make their lives better. That's why SOS is a community program, put together by community leaders to help community children. Let me give you an example of how this can work, of what can happen when communities work together.

In 1991 a retired IBM employee, named Eva Lee, who had experience in the school system, decided her community needed an after-school program to help the children of Sanford. She convinced some other teachers to volunteer. The program got started and grew.

One of the girls touched by the program had just been caught shoplifting. Her grades were near failing. Since she got involved in the program, and came in contact with a group of caring people who are there for her every afternoon, she's stayed out of trouble and gotten serious about school. Her attitude, and her grades, have soared.

The SOS grant will help provide transportation for the program and get on board someone to run it full-time. But the community is doing its part, too. The city of Sanford is making land available for a building. A broad-based committee is raising money to build a building. A local brick company is donating 30,000 bricks. Volunteers want to get involved.

Two children who've been involved in the program will serve as student teachers for younger children.

There are fifty-two different programs, and the proposals selected are as different as the geography of the regions of our state. But they all are built on a common resource, the people of our state: people who believe we can turn around our children; people who believe that, working together, we can make a real difference in the lives of our children; people who believe that we can give our students something to hope for and dream about. SOS can succeed—and must succeed. Our children deserve nothing less, and if we all work together on it, it will succeed.

DEMOCRATIC PARTY RALLY: INTRODUCTION OF VICE-PRESIDENT AL GORE

RALEIGH, SEPTEMBER 21, 1994

[Although this document is dated September 21, the event was held the preceding day; see Governor Hunt's Schedule for September 18-24, 1994, Governors Papers, James Baxter Hunt Jr. The governor used an edited version of this text, also misdated, to introduce Vice-President Al Gore at a fund-raising dinner on September 20.]

I've heard a lot and read a lot in the papers about how tough this year is going to be for the Democratic Party. Well, those people just haven't seen all of you!

Let me tell you about tough elections. This summer, I was at a National Governors Association meeting in Boston, and I had a chance to visit the John F. Kennedy Library. It reminded me of why I got into politics—and why a lot of Americans got inspired to go into politics and public service—and there's nothing at that library about how politics is supposed to be easy.[1]

John Kennedy never promised us it would be easy. He promised us it would be difficult, and he made us realize it would be worth it. That's the legacy and the lesson that we ought to remember, this year. Because the future of our state and our nation is at stake, this year, and we're not going to let the doomsayers and the naysayers keep us from fighting for that future.

This is an important election. It's important for our party, for our state, and for our nation. It's important for the direction we've set in North Carolina these past two years.

Look at what we've done these two years, Democratic leaders and a Democratic legislature, and ask yourself whether North Carolina can afford to go back:

—Look at Smart Start and free immunizations for children.

—Look at what the legislature did, this year, for the public schools, and the university system, and the community colleges.

—Look at what the legislature did, this year, to keep dangerous criminals in prison.

—Look at what we did to keep kids from going into crime.

—Look at what we did to keep guns and drugs out of schools.

—Look at what we've done to bring new industry and new jobs to North Carolina, and look at the record number of jobs that came to our state last year.

—And look at one more thing: Look at how we did it without raising taxes!

That's the Democratic record in North Carolina. I'm proud of it. We ought to talk about it, and we can win on it—and we ought to be proud of President Clinton and Vice-President Gore. Yes, they've taken their licks, and they'll tell you they've made their share of mistakes. But the mistake we haven't made is to forget what got us here. It was putting people first: investing in education and job training, looking out for the middle class, getting tough on crime, and making government work better.

The Republicans are riding high, but they're forgetting something. The American people did not vote for more of the same in 1992. They did not vote for keeping the status quo and keeping gridlock in Washington. The Republicans may think gridlock and "more of the same" is something to brag about, but I don't, and I don't think we Democrats ought to let them get away with it.

Bill Clinton and Al Gore are working and fighting, every day, to bring change to Washington, and they're making headway. They fought for a crime bill that's going to mean more police officers, more prisons, and more prevention programs in North Carolina, and that's a record to be proud of!

They fought for an economic plan that, for the first time since 1980, is bringing the deficit down. Unemployment is down. Interest rates are low. Inflation is low. Jobs are up, trade is up, and the economy is growing. That's a record to be proud of. And while Republicans talk about cutting government spending, Democrats are doing it: Vice-President Gore has led the reinventing-government initiative, and that's going to cut the federal payroll by 250,000 positions.[2] That's a record to be proud of!

So yes, it's tough, and it's difficult. But it was difficult for John Kennedy to stake his political career on equal rights for all Americans. It was difficult, but it was right.

What we're about is difficult, but it's right, and it's worth fighting for in this election. So I challenge you, tonight. I challenge you, and all Democrats, to stand up and be proud of what we're doing and what we've already done. And I challenge you to work, and fight, and sacrifice, and do everything you can the next seven weeks so that our party can get our state and our nation headed in the right direction.

Thank you. I'll be counting on you. Now let me present some important people to you.

[Hunt introduced congressional candidates.]

Now let me present our very special guest: Al Gore is one of us. He's from right next door. He's been here before, and he's won here before. In 1988 he won our state's presidential primary, and I'm sure he thinks he won because I endorsed him.

This is a man of courage and real conviction. He wrote a great book that tells a lot about him. Not just that he cares deeply about the environment and about our planet, but that he's a man who cares deeply about his family and his children—and a man who has thought deeply about all of our families and our children.[3]

He and his wife, Tipper, have been an important part of this administration. As vice-president, he has been a quiet but forceful voice in the deliberations and decisions that take place in the White House, and he has had the courage to stand out front on difficult and controversial issues. He's shown leadership in taking on the difficult challenge of reinventing government and making it work better and more efficiently, and he's been a real friend of North Carolina when we've needed a voice in Washington.

Now, you know that not long ago, he suffered a little injury on the basketball court in Washington. He was playing with some members of Congress, and you can guess how dangerous that is. But you may not know that some people describe Al Gore as a "raging bull" on the basketball court.[4]

Ladies and gentlemen, it's time we had some raging bulls in the Democratic Party, and it's time we got charged up for this campaign! So it is with great pride and honor that I present to you the vice-president of the United States, the Honorable Al Gore.

---

[1] A more dramatic description of the Kennedy Library visit appears in the governor's remarks to the Democratic Party Executive Committee. "A few weeks ago, I had the chance to visit the John F. Kennedy Library. It is a place that evokes deep emotions and leaves deep

impressions," Hunt said. "It sits on a point of land in Boston Harbor, with the wind sweeping over and the waves lapping up on the shore. Standing out there, I could feel John Kennedy's energy, and boldness, and vision. His vision has inspired generations of Democrats, shaping our history, and our tradition, and our party. John Kennedy gave his best to the people of this country, and he urged all of us to give our best." Democratic Party Executive Committee, Raleigh, August 13, 1994, Governors Papers, James Baxter Hunt Jr.

[2] See U.S. National Performance Review, *From Red Tape to Results, Creating a Government That Works Better and Costs Less: Report of the National Performance Review/Vice-President Al Gore* (Washington, D.C.: U.S. Office of the Vice-President/U.S. Government Printing Office Superintendent of Documents, [1993]).

[3] Albert Gore, *Earth in the Balance: Ecology and the Human Spirit* (Boston: Houghton Mifflin, 1992).

[4] Playing basketball, Gore severed his Achilles tendon. He was on crutches during his Raleigh visit. *News and Observer*, September 21, 22, 1994.

PRESS BRIEFING NOTES, SOUTH AFRICA TRIP

RALEIGH, SEPTEMBER 22, 1994

[Hunt's thirty-nine-member trade delegation visited South Africa and Zimbabwe from September 28-October 6, 1994. For the governor's itinerary, see N.C. Dept. of Commerce press release, Governor Hunt Leads Trade Mission to Southern Africa, Raleigh, September 22, 1994, Governor's Papers, James Baxter Hunt Jr.]

Once again, North Carolina is ahead of the curve. Next week, North Carolina will be the first state, and I will be the first governor, to lead a trade mission to South Africa since the historic elections that dismantled apartheid this spring. I hope North Carolina will be the first state to build an economic bridge with South Africa and bring export dollars to our state.

During my trip to Cape Town, Johannesburg, and Zimbabwe, I'll be meeting with dozens of government, business, and economic development officials to lay that groundwork for investment in North Carolina.

South Africa is emerging as one of the ten major markets in the world, according to the U.S. Commerce Department, and has been targeted by the Clinton administration for significant trade and investment activity. With democracy and a stable currency, the country's needs are great, and I think North Carolina can meet those needs. So I'm going over there to make my case—and make some contacts.

President [Nelson] Mandela has made housing, infrastructure, and technological improvements a priority, authorizing major government initiatives. Why can't those houses be built with North Carolina lumber, building materials, and construction company expertise? Why can't those roads be built by North Carolina companies, using North Carolina equipment?

South Africa may not be ready for the Information Highway, since they only got TV about twenty years ago. But they certainly need telecommunications equipment and expertise, and North Carolina can certainly give it to them.

There are dozens of potential markets for our state, like textiles or banking. We're home to some of the nation's largest banks. Zimbabwe has no banks. That's one of the topics on my agenda, and that's why representatives of First Union, BB&T, and First Citizens Bancshares are part of this trade mission.

This is an historic opportunity, and North Carolina is the first to take it. There's a reason North Carolina has been number one in recruiting international companies for the last four years. It's because we're aggressive. We're going to stay aggressive, and this trip will help us do that.

I'll send you all a postcard.

UNIVERSITY OF WITWATERSRAND

JOHANNESBURG, SOUTH AFRICA, OCTOBER 5, 1994

[This address is largely identical to one the governor delivered to an audience at the University of Western Cape, Cape Town, South Africa, September 29, 1994.]

I'm honored to be here, today, and to have the opportunity to address one of the issues closest to my heart—education—in a time and place of such historical opportunity.

When he became the first of four South Africans to win the Nobel Peace Prize some thirty-three years ago, Albert Luthuli described his people as "living testimony to the unconquerable spirit of mankind."[1]

"Down the years," he said, "they have sought the goal of a fuller life and liberty, striving with incredible determination and fortitude." It is that determination and fortitude that brought about the new South Africa we see today. That triumph of human dignity was aided by this university, and the others across South Africa, that were opposition institutions, rejecting racial discrimination and fighting for academic excellence.

It is that determination and fortitude that fueled the students and faculty of South Africa and helped to topple apartheid. The courage and strength of the children of Soweto, who left their secondary schools in protest, recalls the courage and strength of North Carolina's black college students, whose sit-ins at a local Woolworth's lunch counter helped spark our own Civil Rights movement.

It is that determination and fortitude that will enable the citizens of South Africa—all citizens—to reach their individual potential, their economic potential, and to help this new South Africa reach its global potential.

* * *

As the great American educator, John Dewey, once said, there can be no democracy without an educated population.[2] Universities have a vital role to play in this effort. As you well know, universities cannot be ivory academic towers. Universities are laboratories of ideas, nurturing thinkers, and citizens, and leaders. Universities are catalysts for change.

Your efforts here at Wits to eliminate apartheid are evidence of that great power. I commend you for having the vision to develop outreach activities that made a difference. Your campus law clinics, your rural activities, and your voluntary service work helped empower black South Africans, and I commend you for your leadership.

Now more than ever, South African universities must continue to provide leadership. The challenge of building a prosperous nation requires even greater leadership, and is an even greater challenge, than dismantling apartheid.

South Africa's educational and economic needs are so great: a 60 percent black illiteracy rate; a tragically high infant mortality rate in the townships and homelands; 7 million homeless; 40 percent black unemployment and a massive shortage of skilled labor; an education system for black South Africans that must catch up from years of government neglect.

The challenge is formidable, but so is the determination and fortitude of South Africa. I've seen it in the faces of the educators, [and] business, community, and government leaders I've encountered on North Carolina's trade, education, and cultural mission.

* * *

And the commitment of the United States is just as strong. I am proud of the strong and swift action President Clinton has taken to strengthen the education sector in South Africa. He has boosted support for South Africa's historically black institutions; aided in the development of model methods, practices, and materials to improve the quality of education; developed new programs to provide job skills training for unemployed township youth. These efforts are targeted to help black South Africans prepare themselves for leadership roles alongside white South Africans in a post-apartheid society.

But no government—neither the South African government nor the United States government—can do it all. The challenge to build the new South Africa into all it can be is a challenge facing the people. It is a challenge facing educators, business and community leaders, of your nation and mine. It is up to us to build the public-private partnerships that can fuel your development; partnerships for educational excellence; partnerships that will serve to educate all South Africans, creating a world-class workforce and a world-class citizenry.

* * *

That is one of the reasons we are here today. As the North Carolina delegation explores new relationships here in South Africa, it is appropriate to spend time here at Wits. It is, in fact, partially a return for the visit of your vice-principal, June Sinclair, and her colleagues from Afrikaner colleges to North Carolina this past summer. Her visit to some of North Carolina's historically black colleges and universities— Winston-Salem State, Bennett College, St. Augustine's, North Carolina A&T and Shaw Universities—has helped us to establish relationships and spurred us to action in rebuilding South Africa's post-apartheid society.

Your efforts as one of the leaders of post-apartheid education [are] critical. Wits' proposed focus on science and engineering, your efforts to equip your classrooms and to link up with the information technology available are to be commended. North Carolina stands ready to serve as your partner in these efforts. We stand ready to be your partner in educational excellence. Through traditional linkages and new relationships, North Carolina's historically black colleges and universities and our historically white institutions stand ready to help reconstruct education at all levels.

In North Carolina, we have the largest number of historically black colleges [of] any state in the country. Our eleven schools include five public [and] six private institutions. They are diverse: One is all-female; ten are coeducational. They range in size from 500 to 8,500 students. Their programs range from liberal arts and sciences to comprehensive, specialized engineering. They've produced great leaders, from presidential candidates like Jesse Jackson to astronauts like the late Ron McNair.[3] As Vice-Principal Sinclair knows, these schools, and our historically white institutions, are ready to build bridges across continents. And I stand ready to help them.

The North Carolina Intercultural and International Education Consortium—made up of Bennett College, Johnson C. Smith, Winston-Salem State, St. Augustine's, and North Carolina Central University—has already established exchange programs with Russian universities and schools in other West and East African countries. A&T University, a historically black university founded as North Carolina's black land-grant college, has formed such a partnership with Fort Hare. The two universities are working together to develop a master's program, along with community development and leadership programs. A&T's "Ways to Grow" program is designed to help small farmers in that region increase productivity of crops and animals, and faculty and student internships between the two schools are providing even more ways to grow. Such exchanges build up education and also build up leaders and communities.

North Carolina's universities are seeking new and innovative ways to participate in the building of the new South Africa. Representatives of A&T University and Western Carolina, a historically white school, are meeting on this mission with South African officials overseeing President [Nelson] Mandela's housing construction program. It is our hope to work with NGO's (nonprofits) here to launch a community-based program modeled after our own Habitat for Humanity. We envision bringing American students, and faculty, and community leaders to South Africa to help build the new homes so desperately needed. That's the kind of idea that North Carolinians have and the kind of energy and spirit that we can bring to partnerships with you.

* * *

The North Carolina Consortium wants to form similar partnerships with South African universities. In fact, the consortium chair, Bennett College president Gloria Scott, spent Election Day here on your campus, exploring joint ventures with Vice-Principal Sinclair and other leaders of Wits.[4] North Carolina's education leaders participating on this mission, including Dr. Prezell Robinson,[5] president of St. Augustine's College and vice-chairman of our state's Board of Education, stand ready to help as well. Under the leadership of Dr. Scott, Dr. Robinson, and others in historically black and white institutions of North Carolina, my state stands ready to be your partner in educational excellence.

Friends, let us be partners! Looking to the consortium for guidance, let us develop sister schools, exchanging expertise and ideas as well as students and faculty.

Let us work together to boost teacher training in South Africa. That could mean bringing teachers to our country for training and degrees, or it could mean a more ambitious effort to encourage teachers to achieve higher standards. As chairman of the National Board for Professional Teaching Standards, I have spent the last eight years working to raise teaching standards in my own country. We are developing a voluntary certification system that encourages teachers to become board-certified. So far, some fifty-one teachers in North Carolina have applied for this certification, spending 100 hours or more documenting, analyzing, and striving to improve their classroom teaching. North Carolina's legislature has agreed to reward those who become certified by raising their salaries. I urge you to investigate this program to encourage excellent teaching and offer the board's help in adapting our efforts to South Africa's needs.

Let us work together to improve math and science curricula, an area that deserves special attention in this country. I urge South African schools to work with North Carolina's colleges and universities to build departments, and faculty, and programs. We must do all we can to nurture future scientists and engineers, leaders who will pioneer medical and infrastructure improvements in South Africa. In my previous administration, I founded North Carolina's School of Science and Math, the nation's first state-supported, residential high school for science and math. We've reaped the dividends of this investment many times over, as those students have become scientists, researchers, engineers, policy makers, and leaders of every stripe. The school has been a model for other states, and it can be a model for South Africa as well. I invite you to visit the school and to pursue exchange programs for South African youngsters and faculty.

Let us work together to give South African schools the technology you need to level the playing field across this nation. In North Carolina, most of our universities and colleges are creating on-line libraries, which allow access beyond the boundaries of the campus, and they're using video and satellite signals to deliver educational programming across the state. This offers great promise in the vast regions of South Africa.

In North Carolina, we are making strides as the first state to build an Information Highway, a high-tech partnership between the state and telephone companies that will allow information to be transmitted instantly between high schools, community colleges, and universities, as well as hospitals, law-enforcement agencies, and other facilities. Soon a student in the poorer mountain region of our state will be able to take an advanced science class at the School of Science and Math, using the high-tech interactive video that the Information Highway provides. That high-tech global link can be extended to South Africa as a way to share our resources and expertise with you.

* * *

Your commitment to academic excellence and your willingness to provide educational leadership [are] so critical. As we have learned in North Carolina, you cannot build a strong economy without a strong education system, and that strength must come from the roots, beginning in the earliest grades. To ensure that South African children have the opportunities that education can afford, well-trained teachers in every school must encourage every child to achieve; and the public and private sectors must work together to equip them with the tools for success, so every teacher can teach, and every child can learn. As South Africa emerges as one of the world's ten major markets, the demand for an educated citizenry and workforce will increase. Your hard-won political freedom must be matched by growing economic opportunities, and those can only be sustained by a well-educated, well-trained workforce.

* * *

I want to leave you with another thought from Albert Luthuli, the winner of the Nobel Peace Prize so many years ago. His comments ring as true now as they did then. He said, "The task is not yet finished. South Africa is not yet home for all her sons and daughters. . . . There remains before us the building of a new land, a home for all who are black, white, brown, from the ruins of the old narrow groups, a synthesis of the rich cultural strains that we have inherited."

Together, we can now realize that vision, using education as a catalyst. It will require hard work and persistence. It will require determination and fortitude. Together, I know we can do it.

---

[1] Albert John Mvumbi Luthuli (1898?-1967), born in Rhodesia (later Zimbabwe); died in South Africa; teacher, Adam's Mission Station College, 1921-1936; chief, Abasemakholweni tribe, South Africa, 1936-1953; president-general, African National Congress, 1953-1967; first black African to win a Nobel prize (peace, 1960); winner of United Nations Human Rights Prize, 1968; author, *Let My People Go* (autobiography, 1962), and *African Freedom* (1964). *Nobel Prize Winners*, s.v. "Luthuli, Albert"; *Who's Who of Nobel Prize Winners, 1901-1990*, s.v. "Luthuli, Albert John." Besides Luthuli, the other three South African Nobel Prize winners were Max Theiler, medicine and physiology, 1951; Aaron Klug, chemistry, 1982; and Desmond Mpilo Tutu, peace, 1984. *Who's Who of Nobel Prize Winners, 1901-1990*, 230.

[2] John Dewey (1859-1952), born in Burlington, Vt.; A.B., 1879, University of Vermont; Ph.D., Johns Hopkins University, 1884; honorary degrees. University professor; philosophy professor, University of Minnesota, 1888-1889, University of Michigan, 1889-1894; philosophy professor, dept. head, 1894-1904, School of Education director, 1902-1904, University of Chicago; philosophy professor, from 1904, Columbia University; author. *Who Was Who in America, 1951-1960*, s.v. "Dewey, John."

[3] Civil-rights leader Jesse Jackson and astronaut Ronald McNair were both graduates of North Carolina A&T State University. Jackson got his B.A. in 1964. *Who's Who in America, 1982-1983*, s.v. "Jackson, Jesse Louis."

Ronald E. McNair (1950-1986), born in Lake City, S.C.; B.S., North Carolina A&T State University, 1971; Ph.D., Mass. Institute of Technology, 1976. Physicist; in 1978, became one of first three black Americans chosen as NASA astronaut; second black American in space, *Challenger* space shuttle mission, February 1984; died in 1986 explosion of *Challenger*. *American National Biography*, s.v. "*Challenger* Shuttle Crew."

[4] Gloria Dean Randle Scott (1938-   ), born in Houston, Tex.; B.A., 1959, M.A., 1960, Ph.D., 1965, Indiana University; honorary degrees. Educator; college administrator; director, Office of Institutional Research and Planning, 1968-1973, North Carolina A&T State University; assistant to the president for educational planning and evaluation, Texas Southern University; vice-president of Clark College, Atlanta, nine years; taught at Bryn Mawr, Atlanta University, and Grambling State University, 1978-1987; president, Bennett College, from 1987; member, from 1969, and first black president, 1975, Girl Scouts of America; member, National Commission on International Women's Year, 1976-1978, National Commission on International Year of the Child, 1978-1980, and of President's Board of Advisers on Historically Black Colleges, from 1990. *Black Women in America: An Historical Encyclopedia*, s.v. "Scott, Gloria Dean Randle."

[5] Prezell Russell Robinson (1922-   ), born in Batesburg, S.C.; resident of Raleigh; A.B., St. Augustine's College, 1946; M.A., 1951, Ed.D., 1956, Cornell University; honorary degrees; U.S. Army, 1942-1944. Professor of sociology and dean of instruction, 1956-1964, executive dean, 1974-1966, acting president, 1966-1967, president, 1967-1995, and Charles A. Mott Endowed Distinguished Professor of the Social Sciences, St. Augustine's College, Raleigh; president, United Negro College Fund, 1978-1981; appointed to U.S./Liberian Commission by President Jimmy Carter, 1980; alternate U.S. representative to U.N., 1992, 1996; project manager, Developmental Technologies, Pretoria, South Africa, 1996. *News and Observer*, August 1, 1971, October 11, 1996; *Who's Who in America, 1998*, s.v. "Robinson, Prezell Russell."

SOUTH AFRICAN ENTREPRENEURS

Johannesburg, South Africa, October 5, 1994

I'm honored to be here, today, and to have the opportunity to address this fine group of South African business leaders. In South Africa and in North Carolina, the entrepreneurial spirit is thriving. In South Africa and in North Carolina, the entrepreneurial spirit is creating jobs, building businesses, and boosting communities. In South Africa and North Carolina, small and emerging businesses are the backbone of a vibrant economy. Your presence in such large numbers, here today, is testimony to your willingness to build a strong and sustaining economy, and testimony to the entrepreneurial spirit of South Africa. Your spirit survived despite the obstacles of apartheid, and I commend you for your determination and fortitude.

Now more than ever, South African entrepreneurs must continue to provide leadership. The challenge of building a prosperous nation requires even greater leadership, and is an even greater challenge, than dismantling apartheid. South Africa's educational and economic needs are so great: a 60 percent black illiteracy rate; a tragically high infant mortality rate in the townships and homelands; 7 million homeless; 40 percent black unemployment and a massive shortage of skilled labor; an education system for black and colored South Africans that must catch up from years of government neglect.

The challenge is formidable, but so is the determination and fortitude of South Africa. I challenge you, today, to demonstrate your determination and fortitude anew. Take a leadership role. Form the public-private partnerships necessary to improve your schools. Galvanize your community to look for innovative ways to build a prosperous future for every South African.

The determination and fortitude of North Carolina's small business leaders is [sic] just as important to my state's future. Some 80 percent of our new jobs created come from small- and medium-sized businesses, in high-tech fields such as computers, telecommunications, medical services, and biotechnology, and in services and traditional manufacturing. More than half of North Carolina's workforce is employed by small businesses, and the work they perform accounts for more than half of our state's gross domestic product.

Just as one of North Carolina's strongest assets is its vigorous and rapidly growing small-business sector, the men and women who make up that sector face special challenges. Entrepreneurs have charted out a new course, with a new vision, new ideas, and new energy. But they can also encounter new difficulties with bureaucratic red tape, elusive venture capital, export assistance, and other start-up support systems.

We in North Carolina have taken steps to recognize the increasing importance of homegrown businesses, because we know this: What's good for our small businesses is good for our economy. I believe the same is true for South Africa.

Small businesses in North Carolina benefit from good schools and universities, transportation, technology, and government and private-sector support. But in order to grow our own business, I believe entrepreneurs need even more support. The challenge for my administration is to create an atmosphere where small firms can be nurtured into thriving businesses. That includes black-owned businesses: North Carolina ranks seventh among the fifty states in the number of black-owned businesses. These small businesses will continue to create new jobs to employ our citizens, especially in rural communities.

What are we doing, under my administration, to achieve this result? First, we asked for input and advice from the real experts: businessmen and -women just like you. We put together an Entrepreneurial Development Board to speak for small businesses, and we have traveled across the state to gather input from entrepreneurs as part of our economic development planning process.

Under the leadership of my secretary of commerce, Dave Phillips—working closely with my special assistant, Carolyn Coleman, who is a key member of this trade delegation—my administration has developed the state's first five-year plan for minority economic development. Secretary Phillips hosted a series of meetings to listen to the views of North Carolina's minority business leaders about the future of minority economic progress in our state, then targeted those areas of concern in our minority economic development plan.

We know that smaller entrepreneurial firms, especially those that are black-owned, must struggle to find capital. Just this month, we have set up the North Carolina Capital Access Program, which should provide $60 million worth of loans to some 1,300 small businesses, mostly women and minorities. These are entrepreneurial firms that may lack the necessary collateral or résumé to qualify for conventional loans. This special low-loss reserve will be created to back higher-risk business loans, giving them a boost and providing even greater protection than traditional loan guarantees.

My administration is also exploring a viable, cost-effective means of increasing minority-owned and entrepreneurial participation in state contracting activities. We're looking at [an] integrated financing and bonding program that would make small companies eligible for a line of credit, based primarily upon their total volume of awarded state contracts. Our goal is to help minority-owned companies comply more easily with the requirements of these state contracts.

North Carolina wants to encourage entrepreneurs, and we are actively seeking ways to nurture our homegrown businesses. My secretary of commerce, Dave Phillips, and my special assistant, Carolyn Coleman, want to share our ideas and successes with you and with representatives of the South African government.

North Carolina wants to foster ties with you, and with other business leaders who will become the economic leaders of the new South Africa, and the commitment of the United States is just as strong. I am proud of the strong and swift action President Clinton has taken to strengthen the education and economic sector in South Africa. We have boosted support for South Africa's historically black institutions; aided in the development of model methods, practices, and materials to improve the quality of education; and developed new programs to provide job skills training for unemployed township youth. Our administration has provided American experience, expertise, technology, and capital in key areas of private-sector development, including the development of a small and micro-enterprise industry. We have targeted key housing and electrification needs and have targeted capital needs with the new Enterprise Fund. These efforts are targeted to help black and colored South Africans grow their own jobs and build a vibrant economy in this post-apartheid society.

But no government, neither the South African government nor the United States government, can do it all. The challenge to build the new South Africa into all it can be is a challenge facing the people. It is a challenge facing educators, business, and community leaders of your nation and mine. It is up to us to build the public-private partnerships that can fuel your development; partnerships for educational excellence; partnerships that will serve to educate all South Africans, creating a world-class workforce and a world-class citizenry.

In North Carolina, small businesses have taken an active role in boosting education. Some have "adopted" schools. Others have donated computer equipment. Still others have given their employees time off to volunteer in the schools, mentoring and tutoring troubled youngsters who might otherwise drop out.

Some businesses have formed partnerships with local schools, setting up apprenticeship programs that provide hands-on training during the school year and summer for high-school students. Students graduate with the technical and practical job skills needed for the modern work world, and sponsoring companies get first crack at the best entry-level workers around. That, my friends, is a win-win proposition!

The impact of North Carolina's strategies is stimulating the economic viability of the African American and other minority communities in North Carolina. But it's a slow process, and it's one that requires solid public-private partnerships. Just as the entrepreneurial spirit lies with you, so does the power to build a more prosperous future for your new nation. I challenge you to join hands with your government and educators to build that foundation, brick by brick, starting today.

PRESS RELEASE: GOVERNOR HUNT'S TAX AUDIT TO
EXAMINE BUSINESS, PERSONAL TAX CUTS

RALEIGH, OCTOBER 6, 1994

One of the nation's Big Eight accounting firms will conduct a tax audit next month at the request of Governor Jim Hunt, analyzing the state's tax climate as it affects businesses, working families, and children.

KPMG Peat Marwick was awarded a contract this week to assess North Carolina's tax structure, including business and individual taxes, exemptions, and tax credits. The Peat Marwick study will include corporate income and franchise taxes; personal income tax; consumption, sales, and use taxes, including food tax; and property taxes, including intangibles tax. The accounting firm will compare North Carolina's tax policy with that of nineteen competing states, constructing computer models to gauge the impact of tax policies on large and small businesses and families of varying income levels.

After the month-and-a-half-long study, Peat Marwick will prepare a report for Governor Hunt, assessing North Carolina's tax strengths and weaknesses and making broad recommendations for change. The firm will also deliver computer models capable of containing analysis. Specifically, Hunt has asked the auditors to determine how the tax structure can boost the state's competitiveness and how it can reward working families and families with children.

Hunt has said he wants to propose tax cuts, for businesses and families, in the 1995 legislative session. But he has maintained that a thorough analysis of the state's tax climate and its revenue forecasts must be conducted first.

"I believe this is the time to look hard at tax relief, for families and for businesses," Hunt said. "I intend to propose tax relief policies to the General Assembly next year. But first I want to put North Carolina's current tax picture in sharper focus, to make sure we move forward with sound and fiscally responsible policies that will improve the quality of life in our state. I'm hopeful that the tax audit can help us do just that."

The tax audit was recommended by the North Carolina Economic Development Board as part of a strategic plan to boost North Carolina's competitiveness and was funded by the General Assembly this summer. The audit is designed to:

—Review North Carolina's tax structure and determine how our business and personal taxes compare with those in nineteen competing states, such as Virginia, South Carolina, Tennessee, and Alabama;

—Compare North Carolina's personal income taxes with other states, assessing how effective they are in rewarding work and supporting families and children;

—Assess the state's tax system's impact on economic development and recommend ways to increase that impact;

—Review the state's business tax credits;

—Examine personal income taxes and gauge how they influence the decisions of businesses. Some small companies are taxed under personal income tax as opposed to corporate income tax.

[Attachment]

Economic Development Tax Audit:
Impact of the Tax Structure on
Economic Development in North Carolina

Overview of Proposed Study, Issues, and Method of Analysis

October 1994

Economic Development Tax Audit: Background

Public perception regarding the personal and business tax burden is a key element in defining the attractiveness of a state's business climate.

North Carolina has a relatively low overall business tax burden, however, the mix of taxes and burdens created by specific taxes were issues often brought before the Economic Development Board in public hearings—such as the corporate income tax and intangibles tax.

There is also strong interest in rewarding work and supporting families and children through tax policy. The tax system should also encourage entrepreneurship and small business growth.

Objectives: What Are We Trying to Accomplish?

A tax system that is healthy and fairly distributes the tax burden while keeping tax rates competitive.

A tax system that rewards work and supports families and children.

A tax system which creates a favorable business climate for existing firms and encourages the attraction and retention of high-impact firms, and industries, and entrepreneurs.

A tax system that targets tax incentives and credits on achieving strategic objectives.

Proposed Scope of the Study

Develop a clear understanding of the structure of North Carolina's taxes and how they compare to selected business and personal taxes in competing states.

Identify impacts of the tax system on economic development and develop recommendations for tax modifications.

Examine personal income taxes relative to other states and for effects towards rewarding work and supporting families and children.

Review the state's business tax credits.

Examine personal income taxes and determine how they influence the decisions of businesses.

Study Approach

A series of balance sheets and household budgets will be prepared, representing a cross section of businesses and households.

The state and local tax burden for each representative business and household will be calculated for North Carolina and approximately nineteen competitor states.

North Carolina's overall business tax "burden" will be compared to competing states. The impacts of "red flag" taxes, i.e., corporate income, will be assessed as will differential impacts by type of business, i.e., small entrepreneurial companies, will also be assessed. The personal tax burden for different-income households will also be compared to states in the audit.

Alternatives will be developed which seek to meet objectives for change in North Carolina's business and personal tax system.

The revenue impacts of proposed changes will be examined using existing revenue-forecasting models.

Policy options will be prepared to provide the governor with a range of strategies to achieve desired strategic changes in [the] tax system.

Study Participants

An interagency staff group is being formed to staff the study. Principal staff will include representatives from the following organizations: Governor's Policy Office; Department of Revenue; Office of Budget and Management.

A major accounting firm or other experienced and recognized consultant will be retained to provide specialized services. (KPMG Peat Marwick, Policy Economics Group, has been selected.)

The General Assembly, the Office of the Treasurer, the Department of Commerce, and other state agencies will be involved, as will business, interest groups, and other appropriate parties that will be consulted during the process.

Themes

Recommendations of the tax audit will focus on four key themes:
—Maintain a healthy revenue base;
—Ensure fair and competitive business taxes;
—Promote entrepreneurship;
—Reward work and support families and children.

Goal is to provide governor with several options for action consistent with the above themes.

Sources of North Carolina General Fund Tax Revenues, 1992-1993
Personal Income: 50 percent
Sales and Use: 30 percent

Corporate Income: 5 percent
Franchise: 5 percent
Insurance: 3 percent
Intangible: 2 percent
Other: 5 percent
Total revenue collected: $7.9 billion

Preliminary List of Study Issues
The following list of issues has been suggested as preliminary candidates for inclusion in the study:
Business Taxes (Large to Medium Companies)
—Corporate income tax
—Corporate franchise tax
—Sales and use tax
—Intangibles tax
—Property tax
Business Taxes (Small/Entrepreneurial Companies)
—Investment tax credit
—Depreciation of capital assets
—Personal income tax marginal rates
Household Taxes
—Property taxes
—Intangibles tax
—Sales and use tax, includes sales tax on food
—Standard deduction/personal exemptions
—Existing and potential tax credits, such as Earned Income Tax Credit or Child Tax Credit

Preliminary Schedule
Finalize workplan; determine what can reasonably be accomplished:
August 12
Initiate study through interagency staff group: August 15
Consultant retained: October 3
Initiate revenue impact estimates: September 15
Develop business and household balance sheets: September 30
Complete analysis: November 15
Preliminary recommendations to governor: November 23
Note: Briefings with the governor and other briefings and
consultation with interested parties will be held
throughout the period of the audit. The consultant will
present interim results as available.

EUROPEAN-AMERICAN YOUTH
APPRENTICESHIP SYMPOSIUM

CHAPEL HILL, OCTOBER 12, 1994

[For related press release, see Governor Hunt Hosts European Youth Appren-
ticeship Delegation, October 7, 1994, Governors Papers, James Baxter Hunt Jr.
The symposium remarks are similar to Hunt's text for the Andrew Johnson
Memorial Apprenticeship Forum, Raleigh, May 4, 1995.]

You and I know that education is our future. It's everything. Education
has made North Carolina what we are today, and it will shape the North
Carolina of our tomorrow. It is the foundation of a prosperous future
for each and every North Carolinian.

But sometimes it is difficult for students to make the connection
between learning and earning. As parents, we know that our children
sometimes struggle to understand the connection between what they
learn in school and how they'll earn a living. Too many students can't
make that connection. They tune out. Sometimes, they drop out. Too
often, they graduate without the real skills they need to work and think
in the modern workplace. Too often, they can't get or hold a good job
in the real world of work.

But let me tell you about one young man who has made that
connection. Let me tell you about Matt Baker, a student at East Wake
High School, in Wendell, who I met this spring. Matt joined an innovative
youth apprenticeship program, a partnership between East Wake High
School and Siemens Energy and Automation, Incorporated. Matt spends
two hours a day, five days a week at a training center built by Siemens
right on [the] school grounds, learning the skills he needs to become
an electronics technician. During the summer, he will actually work
on the factory floor.

When Matt graduates from East Wake, he will already have the skills
he needs for a good, high-paying job. He'll also have an apprenticeship
training certificate, and Siemens will have first crack at a top-notch,
well-trained worker. It's a win-win situation. That's what successful
partnerships are all about, and that's the kind of business-school
partnership I'd like to see take root in every community.

If North Carolina is going to be a leader in the global economy, we
must produce a well-trained, well-educated workforce. If we want high-
skill, high-wage jobs, then we must produce high school graduates
equipped with the skills they need to get those jobs. [We] must link the
words *high school* with the words *high skill*.

It's a fact that half of our high school graduates go straight from high school to the workplace without the technical or practical experience that Matt is getting. Employers tell me that many of our high school graduates are barely able to master eighth-grade math problems. We are sending youngsters into the workplace without the practical and technical skills they need for entry-level jobs. We are failing to produce the workers that businesses need, and we are failing to produce the workforce that North Carolina needs to build a prosperous future. We need to do better by our students and by our employers. We need to do better in producing the kind of workforce our state needs.

We're making some progress:

—Under the strong leadership of Commissioner Harry Payne[1] and Superintendent [of Public Instruction] Bobby Etheridge, those two departments have set up a fine apprenticeship program just down the road in Durham. The program is giving students classroom instruction, job training, and a paycheck through a partnership between Southern High School and Vaughn Electric.

—Our Education Standards and Accountability Commission, made up of business leaders, parents, and educators, is charting a course for our mission. Very simply, the commission is taking a giant leap for North Carolina, tying educational standards to the demands of the workplace.

—Our Workforce Preparedness Commission, chaired by one of our top CEOs, Bill Burkhardt of Austin Foods, and guided by Executive Director Sandy Babb, has designed a comprehensive state workforce development system. The centerpiece of this system is our JobReady initiative, which will draw businesses into partnership with schools to create youth apprenticeship programs, improve technical education, and enrich the career development program that must start in the earliest grades.

—I co-chair a National Governors Association task force on workforce preparedness, bringing together other governors and top CEOs to lead states' efforts to graduate all of America's students "job ready."[2] This fall, I hope to lead a group of governors to Europe to see their apprenticeship programs in action.

The National Alliance of Business recognized North Carolina as "State of the Year" for our efforts at workforce preparedness, but we have a long, long way to go. I think we can show the nation how school-business partnerships can equip thousands of students, like Matt Baker, with the real skills he needs for the real world. But we can't do it alone. We need advice and input from experts like our European friends, and we need your help.

When you hear these European experts on vocational training and apprenticeship programs at tomorrow's symposium, they'll tell you that business support has been the key to the success of the programs in their countries. Listen to them. Learn from them—and talk to them. Then, talk to me—and talk to Sandy Babb, who's worked so hard to set up this fine symposium.

I want to hear your suggestions and your ideas. Your views are critical to the success of our statewide apprenticeship effort, and your support is just as critical. That's why I'll be setting up a business advisory council to advise me and the Workforce Preparedness Commission about setting up youth apprenticeship programs. If our success depends on business support, then we need to get the perspective of business leaders. I urge each of you to help us in this effort; to encourage business leaders in your communities to do the same; to give our children a brighter future; to give us all a brighter future. Don't miss the chance to make a difference.

---

[1] Harry Eugene Payne Jr. (1952-   ), born in Wilmington; A.B., University of North Carolina at Chapel Hill, 1974; J.D., Wake Forest University, 1977. Attorney, 1977-1992; member, N.C. House of Representatives, 1981-1992; was elected N.C. labor secretary, 1992, reelected in 1996; winner, numerous honors and awards; Democrat. *North Carolina Manual, 1991-1992*, 426, *1997-1998*, 258-259.

[2] Hunt co-chaired the NGA School-to-Work Roundtable. BellSouth Leadership Conference on Workforce Preparedness, April 15, 1994, Governors Papers, James Baxter Hunt Jr.

CAMPAIGN TALKING POINTS
DEMOCRATIC PARTY RALLY

SOUTHERN PINES, OCTOBER 12, 1994

This is an important election. It will decide the direction of our state and our nation for the next two years—and for many years to come.

You are here because you care about that future, and you are working to make it better. Thank you for caring and for working.

This year, we Democrats must remember what got us here. Remember how we won two years ago. Remember what we were elected to do.

In 1992, we told North Carolina that there is a new Democratic Party, and we are proving it.

We called a special legislative session on crime. We passed tough laws that will keep dangerous criminals in prison longer. We're going to put first-degree murderers and repeat violent felons behind bars for life. We're going to put them where they can't prey on law-abiding citizens!

But we weren't just tough. We were smart, too. We passed prevention programs to keep young people out of crime. Because if we don't do something about the way young people are growing up today, we'll never be safe from violent crime!

Then we had a legislative session on the budget, and we passed the most progressive education program ever seen in this state. It will mean better teaching, and smaller class sizes, and more emphasis on the basics, and higher standards, and it was Democrats who passed it.

This is a clear difference between Democrats and Republicans. Republicans oppose the education program, and Democrats support it. That's what's at stake the next two years!

So this is the Democratic record in North Carolina: better education; a tougher and smarter war against crime; innovations, like Smart Start, to give children in North Carolina a better chance to learn and succeed; better job training.

Our economy is growing. North Carolina created more new jobs last year than any year for the past decade. We're known around the world as the best place to live and do business.

And don't forget this: We've done it all without raising taxes in North Carolina!

This is a record we can be proud of, this is a record we can run on, and this is a program we can win on, this year!

I know it is a difficult year for our party, but politics is never easy. It is difficult and challenging. It can be mean, and negative, and vicious. But it's important, because our state is important, and our children's and grandchildren's future is important.

We're fighting for their future, this year. We're fighting for the people who make this state what it is: the people who work hard, and pay the bills, and pay their taxes, and go to church, and raise their families.

We care about the things that worry them: Are their families safe from crime? Are their kids safe at school? Are their kids learning? Will they be able to get a good job when they graduate? Is there going to be any money left at the end of the month?

These are the questions the people of North Carolina ask every day and every night. They are the questions that should concern us, and motivate us, and inspire us in this campaign.

They are what this election is about, and they are what the Democratic Party ought to be about. If we put them first, we will be successful this year, we will do what we promise to do, and we will keep North Carolina moving forward.

FORESTRY CONFERENCE

RALEIGH, OCTOBER 18, 1994

Thanks, Jonathan.[1] As you said, my father was a soil conservationist, and one thing he always taught me was to love this earth. Foresters, like soil conservationists, have that same deep love for the earth. I'm pleased to be with you, today, as we celebrate one of our most beautiful and valuable resources: the forests that blanket two-thirds of North Carolina.

As I travel across North Carolina, I'm always struck by its beauty and diversity, especially now when the trees, like the ones along our beautiful Blue Ridge Parkway, are alive with the red and gold colors of fall. Our forests—this rich, renewable, and diverse resource—gives [sic] us an enormous array of products and job opportunities, and it's a critically important part of the environment we all depend on for our quality of life. Balancing those economic and environmental needs is critical to our state's survival. Jonathan's department recently finished a long-term plan, and one of the main goals was figuring out how to maintain both a sound economy and a healthy environment. That should be our goal, and one that we all work together to reach. It will take a partnership between government, universities, industry, environmental groups, and citizens to ensure the future of our state's forests and the forestry industry, and I'm extremely proud of the way we're going about it in North Carolina.

Despite the impression that we are running out of forests, that they are being cut down faster than they are growing—that simply isn't the case here in North Carolina. Over the past thirty years, in spite of unprecedented population growth, we've lost just 9 percent of our forests—just a small amount in comparison to other states—and we're replanting 90 percent of the areas we harvest each year. Now that's a fact worth celebrating!

Thousands of North Carolina citizens own their land and value what it provides. The majority of our forests, 76 percent, are owned by more than 330,000 North Carolinians. With their large share of this valuable resource, private landowners are the ones who will determine much of what happens to our forests. We depend on them to be responsible stewards of our forests.

It is the state's responsibility to help educate landowners about the value of their forests and consider incentives to encourage better stewardship. I welcome ideas from you about incentives. My administration has just launched a study of North Carolina's tax code and may consider asking the 1995 General Assembly to create incentives that will encourage responsible care of our forests.

Our forests provide products, jobs, and economic opportunities for our citizens. North Carolina ranks first among all southern states in terms of value added to the economy through the manufacturing of wood products. The pulp and paper sector is currently investing over $1 billion in new plants and equipment, more than any other industrial sector, and this sector ranks second in terms of hourly wage rates paid to its workers.

No one can dispute the importance of our forest resources to our way of life. But we have to recognize that the world, and our state, are changing rapidly and that many of those changes will affect North Carolina's forests. The demand for houses, furniture, and paper continues to increase. Much of the wood to meet these demands will come from the privately owned forests of North Carolina, putting unprecedented pressures on our forests as a source of raw materials. As our population grows, the demand for wood products increases while available land for producing new forests decreases. Our citizens are growing more and more concerned about the environment, increasingly demanding that we manage our forests in environmentally responsible ways.

We all care about protecting both the environmental and economic integrity of North Carolina's forests, but we've got to do more than just provide lip service. We've got to act. I ask all of you—private industry, universities, state government, and environmental organizations—to work together to develop a new, broad-based, forest management initiative that will help us provide an adequate supply of new and recycled wood fiber for our forest products industry and help maintain the diversity and health of our forests.

In North Carolina we have a tradition of rolling up our sleeves and working together to solve problems. In 1989 the forestry industry worked together with the Division of Forest Resources, the Sierra Club, and the Wildlife Federation to pass a law requiring loggers to follow the best management practices to protect water quality.[2] Today that program is working well, and it's working well because everyone is behind it. I know we can do it again. The American Forest and Paper Association has drafted guidelines for sustainable forest principles, and I commend the industry for taking the initiative. I want Secretary Howes to convene a meeting of industry, universities, government, and environmental organizations to begin discussing a sustainable forestry initiative here in North Carolina.

If we take an aggressive approach now, our children and grandchildren will be the beneficiaries. I look forward to working with you to meet this critically important challenge. This is an exciting time and a challenging time. Together we can rise to meet the challenge.

<hr />

[1] Jonathan B. Howes, secretary of environment, health, and natural resources, was identified earlier in this documentary.

[2] See *N.C Session Laws, 1989*, c. 179, "An Act to Limit the Forestry Exemption under Sedimentation Pollution Control Laws to Forestry Activities Using Best Management Practices," s. 2, ratified June 1, 1989.

CENTENNIAL CAMPUS CELEBRATION
NORTH CAROLINA STATE UNIVERSITY

RALEIGH, OCTOBER 19, 1994

Ten years ago, this campus came into being out of a vision for the future.[1] We envisioned this premier research university, working in partnership with private industries and public agencies, to develop new high-tech materials, production techniques, and product lines. We envisioned these partnerships leading to world-class, state-of-the-art research and technology facilities that would attract the greatest minds, the brightest students, and cutting-edge companies to North Carolina. We envisioned North Carolina leading the nation with its knowledgeable workers, high-tech investment, and high-skill, high-wage jobs. We envisioned North Carolina competing with other countries, not just states, for those industries.

This vision grew out of 350 beautiful acres out here. You and I helped plant the seeds. Together we nurtured our dream, and now we are beginning to reap the harvest. It's grown into a complex where 1,700 people now work, teach, and study. Ten corporate and government partners have signed on as tenants. Eight hundred more people will come here when the latest projects are completed.

Today, our vision is becoming a reality. But our vision is more than new buildings and new roads. It's ideas: ideas that lead to exciting new developments, like recycled blue jeans; and rocket nozzles that may one day help put a man on Mars; like models that will help us predict long-term global climate change; and software that will help pave our new Information Highway; ideas that improve the quality of life for North Carolinians and all Americans.

These are ideas sewn in partnerships, ideas nurtured by partnership between this public university, private companies, and government— a government that makes wise public [investments]. Just look in the program at the list of hundreds of partners that are working with North Carolina State. We are raising the concept of team-based research to new heights here, and companies are taking notice. More and more businesses are moving to North Carolina just to be near the world-class research and the talented [faculty and] graduates that these partnerships produce.

Because of these partnerships, this new campus pays for itself every five years in research dollars alone.

In return, the school's partners get help from brilliant scientific minds working in top-notch research facilities. The technological breakthroughs that result can help business partners increase production and improve quality, and they can help government partners save money and sometimes even save lives. Like any true partnership, it's a win-win. Money for research projects helps fund faculty and graduate assistants. Students get hands-on experience with high-tech equipment and manufacturing techniques; many are hired by company partners in cooperative education programs in college and, later, as full-time employees after they graduate. Ninety-five percent of the graduates from this College of Textiles walk right into jobs after graduation. That's because they have the skills [and] have already mastered the equipment that will run the textile mills of the future, equipment that N.C. State's private partners in the textile industry helped furnish. Trained and knowledgeable workers are part of the return those textile partners are getting on their investment in the future.

Public partners like the National Weather Service have also learned the value of working in partnership with this university. The Weather Service takes up the third floor of the Research III Building behind me. N.C. State graduate Kermit Keeter works there.[2] Using a model developed by the Marine Fisheries Division, Kermit helped predict that flooding on the Outer Banks during Hurricane Emily would come from the sound side, not the ocean side, saving property damage and probably lives. That's part of the return the National Weather Service and taxpayers are getting on their investment in the future.

The National Science Foundation saw a good investment in the Engineering Graduate Research Center here at the Centennial Campus. It just awarded N.C. State $1.45 million to buy equipment for the Department of Civil Engineering that will be housed in the new center. Even though the center is still under construction, the National Science Foundation saw an investment in the future that could bring a big return for us all.

An investment in the future: That's what we envisioned ten years ago. We knew that the future of our state and our role as a global competitor depended on N.C. State developing state-of-the-art research and teaching facilities. Too often, education and research efforts get shortchanged. But we in North Carolina are committed to supporting those efforts through public-private partnerships. We are committed to seeing that the Centennial Campus fulfills its potential and helps North Carolina fulfill its potential through innovative investments for the future.

The nation knows we're committed. *Fortune* says the Triangle is the best place in the country to do business, and *Money* magazine says it's the best place to live, but such recognition doesn't come by accident.[3] The recognition we receive and the progress we make happen because we all have a vision. We are committed to our vision. We are committed to the vision of the Centennial Campus.

A decade ago, all we had was 350 acres and a dream. Now look around you, and see how far our commitment has taken us. We must keep our commitment strong. We must go the rest of the way. We must see our vision through.

---

[1] Hunt announced the transfer of 355 acres from Dorothea Dix state mental hospital to establish the N.C. State University Centennial Campus, on December 17, 1984. Poff and Crow, *Addresses of Hunt, 1981-1985*, 517-518.

[2] Kermit Keeter (1946-   ), born in Shelby; resident of Cary; bachelor's degree in psychology, graduate work in psychology and statistics, East Carolina University; bachelor's degree in meteorology, N.C. State University. Meteorologist; nineteen-year career with federal weather service included postings at National Climatic Center, Asheville, and National Weather Service offices in Ft. Worth, Texas, and Raleigh. *News and Observer*, January 14, 1996.

[3] Kenneth Labich, "The Best Cities for Knowledge Workers," *Fortune*, November 15, 1993, 50-78, picked Raleigh-Durham number one; the cover of the magazine announced "Best Cities for Business" and showed Hunt and five technical workers against a backdrop featuring the Executive Mansion. Marguerite T. Smith and Sherry Nance-Nash, "The Best Places to Live in America," *Money* (September 1994): 126-144, put the Raleigh-Durham-Chapel Hill area at the top of the magazine's eighth-annual livability ranking of the 300 largest metropolitan areas in the country.

NORTH CAROLINA BUSINESS ROUNDTABLE

GREENSBORO, OCTOBER 31, 1994

[Addresses delivered before the Education—Everybody's Business Coalition, September 12 and December 9, 1994, are very similar to the text prepared for the N.C. Business Roundtable, below; for related press releases, see Governor Hunt to Outline Education Agenda to Business Leaders, Greensboro, October 28, 1994, and Governor Hunt Asks for Business Leaders' Help in Improving North Carolina Schools, Greensboro, October 31, 1994, Governors Papers, James Baxter Hunt Jr.

Hunt's notes for the August 1994 teacher town meetings, reprinted earlier in this volume, seem to outline this speech, but emphasize different details.]

I wanted this meeting of the Business Roundtable to focus on education, because nothing is more important to our future than what happens in our public schools today. As I travel around the state, I hear a lot from people about our schools. I hear a great deal of concern, frustration, and even disillusionment.

For over a decade, there's been a lot of talk about, quote, education reform. But people don't think there's been real progress. Business people worry about whether high-school graduates are ready to work in the modern economy. Parents worry about whether schools are safe and whether their children are learning the basics. Taxpayers worry about whether they're getting their money's worth.

Teachers and educators are concerned, too. They say students are coming to school with more problems than ever before. They say they aren't getting the kind of help and support they need from parents and families. Teachers even worry about whether North Carolinians still support the public schools.

As I listen, two things become very clear: First, North Carolinians are committed to making their public schools work. But second, we haven't had a real plan to make them work. There have been too many different reform plans going in too many different directions. Too much stop and start. Too many promises and too many disappointments.

We need a different approach to improving our schools—a bigger, more comprehensive, more focused approach. An approach that gets us all working together, instead of pulling apart; an approach that sets clear goals; an approach that is based on common sense; an approach, above all, that works: This is the kind of approach that I want to offer today. These are the goals that I propose we set.

Number 1. Every school must be a safe place for students to learn and teachers to teach. There is too much violence, too many guns, too many knives, too many fights, and too many drugs in our schools today. There is too much fear, and it's time to expel fear from our schools. Every superintendent and every principal must make it clear that they will not tolerate guns, and drugs, and violence, and discipline problems— zero tolerance—and if they need more authority or more resources to do it, they'll get it.

Number 2. We must improve the teaching profession in North Carolina. The secret to a good education is simple: It's good teachers. We've got great teachers in North Carolina, and you'll hear from one today. We've got some poor teachers, and they should be taken out of the classroom.

We can make the quality of teaching what it needs to be, and we can recruit, and train, and keep good teachers. Here's how we can do it: Train teachers as professionals, treat them as professionals, hold them to professional standards, and pay them like professionals. That's what it takes.

Number 3. We need more emphasis on teaching the basics, and we need higher standards for what students should know and be able to do. In 1993, we established the North Carolina Standards and Accountability

Commission. Business people told the commission they were concerned about whether a high-school diploma means anything in North Carolina. So the commission identified the basic skills that our students must master. They start with reading, writing, and math in the early years. For graduates, they include communication—that is, reading, writing, and speaking—using numbers, solving problems, processing information, teamwork, and using technology. These are the skills you need to get a good job and be successful in the world today, and a high-school diploma should guarantee that a student has mastered these skills.

Number 4. We should do more to get young children ready for school. This is why we began Smart Start, and Smart Start is something different for state government. It's not a big bureaucratic program that hires a lot of people in Raleigh. Smart Start gets local people working together, looking at their needs, and coming up with solutions. It uses state money as seed money, so creative ideas and approaches can take root.

The fact is, too many children start school with a handicap. They have never seen a book. They don't have a good, loving family. They don't have the kind of support and encouragement they need. These kids deserve a better chance, and our state needs for them to have it.

And Number 5. We need to get more for our tax dollars. Taxpayers spend a lot of money on the schools, and they deserve to get their money's worth. The schools do need more resources: new buildings and facilities, more teachers, better teacher pay, more textbooks, more school buses, more computers, and more instructional supplies and equipment. But the schools also need to put more resources into the classroom instead of administration. They need better training for teachers, and managers, and superintendents, and principals. They need more flexibility and freedom from rules set in Raleigh, and they need teachers and parents to have more voice in what happens.

So these are the goals I believe we should set, and they are goals I believe we can achieve. Some of it must happen in Raleigh, but not all of it can happen in Raleigh. As Ed Shelton said, this Business Roundtable was formed not just to elect a governor, but to bring a new direction and new leadership to our state.[1] The people in this room, today, have the ability to bring about a fundamental change in North Carolina's schools—and in our future.

It's easy to talk about what's wrong. It's tempting to look for something, or somebody else, to blame. But I'm not interested in what caused the problems. I'm not interested in fixing blame. I'm interested in fixing the schools, and fixing the schools is a lot like raising kids. This really hit me, last week, when I had my son Baxter's three children on the farm.

I hadn't seen them for a year because they've been overseas. I was amazed at how much bigger and smarter they've gotten, and I want nothing more than for them to grow up to be smart, and successful, and honest citizens. But there's not one magic thing you can do to make that happen. It takes a lot of things, and all the parts have to work together for the whole to succeed.

---

[1] Builder Ed Shelton, with his brother Charlie, owned The Shelton Companies and Shelco, Inc., Charlotte. An adviser to Governor Hunt said of the pair, "'They built everything Winston-Salem could hold and had to move to Charlotte to have something else to build.'" The Sheltons were also extremely effective fund-raisers. Ed was finance chairman of Hunt's 1992 campaign for governor and later generated $7.8 million for the Charlotte-Mecklenburg Arts and Science Council. Brother Charlie raised money for Republican gubernatorial candidates Jim Martin (1988) and Leo Daughtry (2000). Tim Gray, "Clout: Ranking the State's Most Powerful People," *Business North Carolina* (July 1999): 28-31.

IMPACT-WEST BOOT CAMP DEDICATION

MORGANTON, NOVEMBER 4, 1994

Franklin Freeman just told you about one of the graduates from a boot camp like this who left feeling like a new man—with a new attitude, a new spirit, and a new confidence that he could turn his life around. We can do the same thing for almost all the young men who walk through these gates. We can help turn their lives around, and they need that help.

Too many kids are growing up without learning values and discipline. They have no respect for other people's property; no sense of responsibility; no respect for authority; no fear of punishment. Too many kids are growing up in troubled families, without fathers or role models. They're growing up around drugs, gangs, and violence. They have no education; no job skills; no opportunity; no hope. I believe we can keep a lot of these youngsters on the right track, but it's a tough job, and it takes a lot of tough love.

Here, [at] this boot camp, first-time, nonviolent offenders can benefit from military-style discipline and rigor. They can learn the value of a hard day's work. They can learn what they didn't learn at home. But it won't be an easy lesson. For ninety days, they'll have to work, and work hard: work to improve themselves; work to change their lives; work to get back on the right path.

As you'll see on our tour, the first group of trainees is already hard at work, clearing brush with bush axes. A new class of thirty will come every month. All told, North Carolina will be putting 720 young people through the rigors of boot camp every year. They get up [at] 5:00 A.M., start every single day with one hour [of] calisthenics, and they do hard, physical labor for seven hours a day: community projects, like clearing trees, planting crops, and pruning trees. They dig holes, put in irrigation pipes, and put up fences. They go through a ropes course to train them in team working and to build their self-confidence. At night, they study. [They're] in bed at 9:00 [P.M.].

It's tough, but it's tough love. It's what they need to get back on the right track and to help them become productive citizens.

It's leaders like Senator Sandy Sands and Representatives Bobby Hunter and Walt Church who made this boot camp a reality.[1] They helped me get the funds in the General Assembly last year to build this boot camp and to expand the boot camp we have down east; and they've been tough on crime, passing laws in our special session to keep violent criminals behind bars longer. They abolished parole for first-degree murder. They toughened sentences for rapists. They passed "three strikes and you're out." They added almost 4,000 new prison beds, and they took steps to put victims first in the criminal justice system.

We have a lot more work to do. I need Bobby Hunter and Walt Church [to] continue [to] pass tough laws and fund prisons—and [I] need good, strong, local law enforcement [officers like] Sheriff Ralph Johnson to help me keep even more dangerous criminals off the streets.[2]

We need more boot camps, but we need more than that. We need more efforts to reach troubled kids early to deter them from crime. We need to make sure they get the right kind of help, the right education, the right guidance early in life. That's what SOS [Support Our Students] is all about, helping at-risk youngsters stay out of trouble with after-school programs created by local communities. That's what Smart Start is about, making sure our children have quality child care, health care, and other basic health services [so that they] come to school healthy, and ready to learn, [and] not drop out.

We need to reach out to our youngsters and give them the tough love they need. That's what this IMPACT [Intensive Motivational Program of Alternative Correctional Treatment] boot camp is all about, and I'm proud to be part of this great effort.

---

[1] Alexander P. Sands III (1945-   ), born in Reidsville; A.B., Duke University, 1967; J.D., University of North Carolina at Chapel Hill, 1971; N.C. National Guard, 1968-1974. Attorney; member, N.C. Senate, 1987-1990, 1993-1994; Democratic nominee for U.S. House, Fifth District, 1994. *News and Observer*, November 6, 9, 1994; *North Carolina Manual, 1993-1994*, 417.

Robert Carl Hunter (1944-   ), native of McDowell County; B.A., 1966, J.D., 1969, University of North Carolina at Chapel Hill. Attorney; former assistant district attorney, Twenty-ninth N.C. Judicial District; member, N.C. House of Representatives, from 1983; Democrat. *North Carolina Manual, 1995-1996,* 606.

Walter Greene Church Sr. (1927-   ), born in Caldwell Co.; resident of Burke Co.; attended Amherst College, 1945-1946, and University of Wisconsin, 1962-1964; U.S. Army, 1952-1955. CEO, Western Carolina Savings and Loan; member, 1977-1985, former chairman, N.C. Savings and Loan Commission; member, N.C. House of Representatives, from 1993; Democrat. *North Carolina Manual, 1995-1996,* 565.

[2] Ralph Johnson was sheriff of Burke County. *Directory of State and County Officials of North Carolina, 1993,* 129.

LUMBERTON CORRECTIONAL INSTITUTION DEDICATION

LUMBERTON, NOVEMBER 5, 1994

[The remarks the governor delivered in Lumberton were almost identical to his text for the Neuse Correctional Institution Dedication, Goldsboro, September 8, 1994. Governors Papers, James Baxter Hunt Jr.]

As governor, one of my primary responsibilities is to do all I can to ensure the safety of the people of our state. I'm committed to that. I'm committed to doing everything I can to put dangerous criminals behind bars, and I'm committed to making sure there's enough prison space to keep them there. This prison demonstrates that commitment. Eventually, it will hold 624 criminals.

I've been pushing Correction Secretary Franklin Freeman to help us keep criminals off the street by doing everything in his power to continue to open up more new prison beds as quickly as possible. We may not be able to eliminate crime from our society, but we can keep more dangerous criminals off our streets, and we're making headway. This is already the fourth prison to open up this year. Just yesterday I dedicated the third one, the IMPACT-West boot camp, near Morganton.[1]

Today we're housing 3,600 more inmates than we were just a year ago. For the first time in ten years, the number of violent criminals being paroled from prison has actually dropped, and more prisons are on the way. By the end of the year, more than 1,000 new beds will be added; and next year, we'll have 4,000 new beds, with the opening of the Marion Correctional Institution and expansions at other existing prisons.

I've pushed Correction officials to put every prisoner to work. So I'm proud to report that the inmates here will be put to work on Department of Transportation [DOT] road crews; and when they're not doing that hard road work, they won't just be sitting around back here at the prison, watching TV. They'll be working to keep this place clean and working in the kitchen.

In fact, across the state, 2,000 inmates are working for the DOT; and another 2,000 are in prison industries, growing food and making furniture, license plates, soap, and other things used by government agencies. Many inmates are working for local governments, cutting grass, clearing brush, and sweeping streets. You'll know who they are, because they wear vests that have the word *INMATE* in block letters on the back. They worked to make those vests, too.

While we have been waiting for the rest of our prisons to be built, we have been doing all we can to find every available bed. We have gone to court to press our case for relief, and we have worked with North Carolina's sheriffs and county commissioners, and other states, to lease space while we're increasing capacity in our own state.

The Department of Correction can put inmates to work and build prisons, but that's still not going to be enough. We must also work together to raise our children right and deter them from a life of crime. It begins early on. That's why we have Smart Start, to make sure our preschoolers have affordable, quality day care to make sure our kids go to school healthy and ready to learn.

Once we've got them on the right track, we want to keep them there. So, our SOS [Support Our Students] program will give kids something to do after school to keep them out of trouble and deter them from a life of crime.

These are good government initiatives, but government isn't what will make them work. You must make them work. Each of you here, today, must get involved to fight crime in Robeson County. You must reach out to at-risk children. You must do things, like volunteer in SOS programs. I'm going to do it myself.

The people of our state are tired of crime. They're tired of being frightened. They're tired of worrying about their safety and their children's safety.

We're doing something about it. We're burning the candle at both ends. On one end we're building prisons, like this one, to put dangerous criminals behind bars. On the other end, we're trying to keep our children from growing up to become criminals in the first place. For that, we need your help. We need all of you working together. We need to do it for our children. We need to do it, because they are our future.

---

[1] Hunt also broke ground for one prison, the Caswell County Work Farm, and dedicated another, the Neuse Correctional Institution, in 1994. See Groundbreaking, Caswell County Prison Work Farm, Yanceyville, April 25, 1994, and Neuse Correctional Institution Dedication, Goldsboro, September 8, 1994, Governors Papers, James Baxter Hunt Jr.

As Hunt pointed out to his Yanceyville audience, April 25, prisons provided benefits beyond keeping criminals off the streets: "This prison means good news for this county. It provides jobs for 126 people. Its $8 million construction cost will help support the local economy while it is being built, and its $4.2 million annual payroll will ensure that Caswell County will benefit from this prison for years to come."

ALBEMARLE-PAMLICO ESTUARINE STUDY SIGNING

WASHINGTON, NOVEMBER 11, 1994

Introduction

Today has been a long time in the making. It was here in Washington, more than seven years ago, that the Albemarle-Pamlico Estuarine Study [APES] was born. I'm proud to be here, today, to sign the study's Comprehensive Conservation Management Plan on behalf of everyone who holds North Carolina's coast dear.

This plan makes recommendations that are critical to the future of North Carolina's coast. Along with the recommendations of my Coastal Futures Committee, it lays out an important framework for protecting our coast, a framework that I'm committed to building upon. Over 100 research projects were funded by this study between 1988 and 1992. Many of those researchers found problems in the estuary, like the "phantom algae" discovered by Dr. JoAnn Burkholder of N.C. State.[1] We now know that phantom algae is responsible for at least a quarter of the fish kills in the Pamlico and Neuse Rivers in recent years.

To fix these kinds of problems, we must start now. My administration's coastal agenda lays out four broad goals for protecting North Carolina's coast. First, we must protect and improve water quality; second, we must protect natural areas and vital habitats; third, we must protect and restore marine fisheries; and fourth, we must promote better stewardship of our coastal resources.

Water Quality

To protect and improve water quality, we must strengthen our basinwide approach to water-quality planning. A comprehensive basinwide approach is essential to cleaning up coastal rivers, and doing so in a cost-effective way that allows for future economic development. North Carolina has led the nation in shifting from piecemeal environmental protection to comprehensive planning for each river basin. Following through on the APES recommendations, and continuing the hard work of our Division of Environmental Management, will help us realize the full potential of basinwide planning.

We also must work to reduce nonpoint source pollution. The Albemarle-Pamlico study has shown us that nonpoint sources, like agriculture and forestry, also contribute to our water-quality problems. We've got to do a better job of providing technical assistance to reduce pollution from those sources, as well—and we've got to do more to restore degraded waters to the conditions we enjoyed during the 1930s and 1940s. We've closed too many shellfishing waters over the years, shutting down people's livelihood and depriving our state of a valuable economic resource.

Natural Areas

To protect natural areas and vital habitats, we have to purchase more of these valuable resources—some of which are too important to leave in the hands of hope. We must also work to protect, restore, and create wetlands. I have asked Secretary Jonathan Howes to appoint a wetlands task force to help us design a comprehensive wetlands policy for North Carolina that ensures these resources are protected, but in a way that balances environmental protection with economic development.

Fisheries

Next, we must work to protect and restore our marine fisheries. Our measures to improve water quality and protect vital habitats will go a long way toward helping our depressed fisheries. But, at the same time, we must enhance fisheries management and strengthen enforcement activities.

Stewardship

Finally, we all have to be better stewards of our coastal resources. The coast is ours. It's ours to destroy, and that's already happened in other places. But it's also ours to save. Every North Carolinian—from the family in Asheville that comes to Wrightsville Beach to vacation to the fisherman in Ocracoke—must understand that to save the coast, we've got to be good stewards of it.

Good stewardship means educating the next generation. We must strengthen environmental education. The site we stand on today will soon be an estuarine education center, part of our Partnership for the Sounds project. I hope my grandchildren will come here to learn about the estuary and what an important role it plays in their lives.[2]

Good stewardship means improving our coastal land-use planning process and streamlining permitting. We need to do more to help business, industry, and local governments balance economic development with environmental protection. That means we must provide local government with the resources to create, and follow through on, their land-use plans. We owe it to the coast. We owe it to local governments. We owe it to the people of North Carolina.

Conclusion

Our coastal problems are complex, and they require complex solutions. Those solutions will only come with everyone—farmers, businesses, fishermen, tourists, local governments, landowners—working together to save our coast. It will require strong commitment and strong leadership from public officials, private citizens, and all of us who enjoy and depend on our coastal resources.

I am committed to preserving coastal North Carolina. As I work in the weeks ahead to put together my budget and legislative package for the 1995 session of the General Assembly, I intend to put forward detailed proposals for getting that job done. My family and I have spent many hours enjoying our beautiful beaches. I want to make sure they will still be here, and still be just as beautiful, when my grandchildren have children of their own. That's my commitment to you today, and I want you to make a commitment: to doing all you can to build a brighter future on North Carolina's coast, and the entire state, as well.

---

[1] JoAnn Burkholder (1953-   ), native of Rockford, Ill.; B.S., Iowa State University; M.S., University of Rhode Island; Ph.D., Michigan State University. Associate professor of aquatic botany and marine sciences, N.C. State University; discoverer of fish-killing dinoflagellate, *Pfisteria piscicida*; member, N.C. Marine Fisheries Commission. *News and Observer*, August 6, 1995, May 18, 1997.

[2] Begun in 1993, Partnership for the Sounds was a not-for-profit, primarily state-funded organization whose purpose was to promote eco-tourism on the Albemarle-Pamlico peninsula. Concerned parties in Beaufort, Bertie, Hyde, and Tyrrell Counties, four of the state's poorest, sought to compensate for diminishing jobs in farming, forestry, and fishing—the backbone of the peninsula's economy—by bundling the region's natural assets into a tourist destination. The partnership was headquartered in Columbia; the "estuarine education center" to which Hunt referred opened in Washington as the North Carolina Estuarium. "This group's plan is to sell swampland," *Business North Carolina* (January 1999): 16-18.

NORTH CAROLINA JUDICIAL CONFERENCE

RALEIGH, NOVEMBER 18, 1994

[This conference was "the first convocation of the state's entire judiciary," according to the *News and Observer*, November 19, 1994.]

Let me tell you a story that illustrates why so many people have lost confidence in our judicial system, especially our criminal justice system.[1]

Three years ago, a Winston-Salem man named Jeffrey Gary got a six-year sentence for sexual assault. He was paroled in March of 1993 after serving less than eighteen months. A month later, he violated parole and went on a crime spree. Gary was eventually arrested again and got another six-year sentence for breaking into someone's home. He was sent to prison but was released after only a month. That's because the Parole Commission's records only showed the parole violation, not the new robbery conviction.

This mistake caused Gary to walk free. Just five days later, police say he broke into a woman's home, beat and raped her. When Gary was arrested for that crime, he literally laughed at police. He thought the system was a joke. A lot of people think he was right.

Gary's case illustrates everything that's wrong with our judicial system. Look at [it] from [the] perspective of victims, family, all the "rank and file" who hear about it—and feel threatened because their government cannot or does not protect them. Here [was] a career criminal who couldn't be kept behind bars where he belonged, a prison system too crowded to hold him, and a paper trail that couldn't keep up with the crimes he was committing. But worst of all, we have a victim who was victimized by the system as much as she was victimized by her attacker.

There are many more stories like this. That's why we need to reform our judicial system. That's why we need the Commission [for] the Future of Justice and the Courts, which Chief Justice Exum has established, to chart a course for judicial reform. I commend him for taking this initiative and John Medlin leading it with other distinguished members.[2]

This is a time for fundamental change. [It's] needed: People are demanding it.

The first thing we need to do is to institute merit selection for judges. Judges should be on the bench based on their qualifications—and not their political party. Partisanship has no place in the cause of justice, and judges shouldn't have to run campaigns requiring large expen[diture]s and often financed by those with business before the court. As my own hometown newspaper in Wilson said in a recent editorial, "Merit selection would end voting out of ignorance and the potential for large contributors 'buying' judgeships."

But I believe we must still provide a mechanism, like [a] retention vote, so the people can remove bad judges. [We] must change [the] system in [a] way so people approve [the changes] in [a] referendum.

Second, we must make our judicial system more efficient, so that thugs like Jeffrey Gary don't walk out the door. That means applying information technology to our court system. That means a communication link between our law enforcement agencies, our county courthouses, prisons, and the Parole Commission. Our Criminal Justice Information Network Study Committee, created during this year's [legislative] crime session, is already working on that. Places like Mecklenburg County are showing us the way. Progress in this information technology field is so important because it can help us cut costs, reduce volumes of paperwork, and save time. As incidents show, it can save lives, too.

Third, we must keep dangerous criminals behind bars longer. That means tougher sentences and more room in prisons. During the crime session, we abolished parole for first-degree murderers, toughened sentences for most violent rapists with bad records, passed the "three strikes and you're out" law, and lengthened the sentences of criminals who use guns. But we still have work to do, and I'm going to continue to push to toughen sentences next year—and I'm going to push for more prisons, as well.

We know that longer sentences don't mean much without prison beds. You've got to be able to put away dangerous criminals without having your hands tied by a lack of prison space. We're building prisons just as fast as we can. We've opened up 2,500 new beds this year and will open up another 4,000 next year, and we need to do more. And, as you at this judicial conference know, we must also give our courts the resources they need to handle those who break our laws. Prosecutors tell me that we need more DA's, more judges, and more professional training, especially family court judges, and I hope this is something at which the Commission [for] the Future of Justice and the Courts will take a close look.

Finally, I want all of us to refocus our priorities. Victims must come first. During the crime session, we put more resources into victims' compensation and victims' assistance. But we need to do more to make sure victims are well served by their system and that their rights are protected. I'll be proposing measures in the '95 session to do just that.

As you know better than I, our courts are seriously overloaded today. And not just criminal justice—our civil courts need to expand the beginning we have made into arbitration and mediation, instead of litigation. The picture is a far different one from that which the Bell Commission faced thirty years ago when it tackled judicial reform.[3] Now we have more people, more crime, more violence, more drugs, and a serious breakdown of family that all too often lands in your laps.

In summary, we have a criminal justice system that is broken. It just doesn't work in the way that North Carolina needs. Our people know it. Victims know it. And criminals know it.[4]

What they may not know is how committed we are to fixing it. All of us must be committed to making it work. We owe it to the people of our state, to help them feel safe, to give them hope for the future, to restore their confidence in justice, and to enable you in the judiciary to do the good job you are trying so hard to do.[5]

---

[1] "Speak candidly," Hunt wrote next to this paragraph.

[2] James Gooden Exum Jr. (1935-   ), native of Snow Hill; A.B., University of North Carolina at Chapel Hill, 1957; LL.B., New York University; U.S. Army Reserve, 1961-1967. Attorney; resident superior court judge, Eighteenth Judicial District, 1967-1974; associate justice, 1975-1986, chief justice, 1986-1994, N.C. Supreme Court; Democrat. *News and Observer*, July 28, August 5, 1994, December 5, 1995; *North Carolina Manual, 1993-1994*, 619-620.

John Grimes Medlin Jr. (1933-   ), born in Benson; B.S., business administration, University of North Carolina at Chapel Hill, 1956; was graduated from Executive Program, University of Virginia, 1965; U.S. Naval Reserve, 1956-1959. Banker; career with Wachovia Bank and Trust Co., Winston-Salem, 1959-1993, included president, 1974; president, CEO, Wachovia Bank and Wachovia Corp., 1977-1993; board chairman, Wachovia Corp., from 1987; chairman, Commission for the Future of Justice and the Courts in North Carolina; member, numerous civic and service organizations. *News and Observer*, January 25, August 5, 1994; *Who's Who in America, 1998*, s.v. "Medlin, John Grimes, Jr."

[3] During the mid 1950s, state senator J. Spencer Bell chaired the Committee on Improving and Expediting the Administration of Justice. James W. Patton, ed., *Messages, Addresses and Public Papers of Luther Hartwell Hodges, Governor of North Carolina, 1954-1961* (Raleigh: Council of State, State of North Carolina, 1962), 1:177, 390; 2:524, 624; for a brief summary on the need for court reform and the Bell Commission, see *North Carolina Manual, 1997-1998*, 733-734.

[4] Hunt instructed himself to "Pause" at this point in his text.

[5] The governor jotted these notes at the end of his text: "Close: 1) Do what people want: Medlin commission; you as judges and leaders of the system in your communities; system that serves the people; don't get it too [illegible]; Don't ignore man in street['s] concerns; 2) We can do it—figure out; get legislative support; get people['s] support; be bold (we did the right thing)."

WILSON COUNTY GLOBAL TRANSPARK FOUNDATION FUND-RAISING CAMPAIGN KICKOFF

Wilson, November 28, 1994

I feel like I've just spent a long weekend in heaven! Since Wednesday, I've been back in Wilson County with my family at the farm in Rock Ridge for the Thanksgiving holiday, and now I'm here with so many of my friends and neighbors. Like many of you, my family and I gave thanks for all the wonderful things in our lives. We all have a lot to be thankful for—our families, our friends, our future in North Carolina, especially here in Wilson County—and we have a lot to be proud of, too: our quality of life, our skilled workforce, our world-class universities, and our long tradition of generating progressive and innovative ideas to make life better for our people.

The Global TransPark [GTP] is one more progressive and innovative idea in that long tradition. We were first in state-supported universities. We were first in flight. Now we are the first to recognize that our constantly changing world requires an entirely new type of high-tech manufacturing and transportation system. That system is the North Carolina Global TransPark, and it's going to be a breakthrough in economic growth, business development, and job opportunities for us here in Wilson County and for the entire state.

The GTP has already won worldwide recognition. Thailand and Germany are working on facilities modeled after our idea, and there's a reason for that. The GTP will open up whole new markets for goods made and grown in Wilson and throughout North Carolina. By putting airplanes at the back door of manufacturing plants, companies will save time and money, and their customers all over the world [will] get goods more quickly.

The GTP means improving our business climate. We lead the nation in attracting new investment, and our state is home to some of America's finest and most progressive corporations. Progressive ideas like the GTP will keep them coming.

The GTP means new and exciting opportunities for our people. The best estimates are that it will create nearly 100,000 jobs that are either on-site or tied directly to it. The GTP means an incredible opportunity for our farmers when we need it most. We are just beginning to enter a new era of world trade. North Carolina's farmers and agriculture are in line to be big winners when new markets open up.

The GTP means that Wilson County is in position to be a beacon for defense manufacturers and their suppliers. The United States military is excited about the Global TransPark, and the Defense Logistics Agency has asked to be involved in our planning. Defense manufacturers and suppliers know the value of eastern North Carolina as home to some of our nation's most important military bases. They are going to want direct links with this huge and stable market. With I-95 and the planned improvements for U.S. 264 and U.S. 117, Wilson County is at a strategic crossroads to benefit from that advantage.

The Global TransPark will attract more high-wage, high-tech industry, and the companies that service or supply them will follow. We've seen that kind of growth happen in other parts of the state, and it can happen here, too—and we're moving quickly toward that day. It was just four years ago that the Global TransPark concept was first introduced by Dr. Jack Kasarda. Since then, we've selected the site, completed our master plan, and attracted our first tenant.[1]

We're also working to make sure that Global TransPark strikes a healthy balance between industrial development and environmental protection. We've made a commitment to protecting the environment, and we plan to live up to that commitment.

The state supported the GTP, and we're counting on support from the federal government. But the GTP also needs support from the private sector. The GTP Foundation is well on its way to raising $30 million in private funds to help develop the Global TransPark. That much-needed $30 million will go a long way. A portion of those funds will build a $6 million facility for Mountain Air Cargo that will be the first GTP tenant to distribute North Carolina products all over the world.

The funds raised by the foundation will show the world that North Carolina businesses are committed to this project, and I can tell you that's very important. The federal government and potential TransPark tenants need to know that we have the support of the business community. Businesses in other counties are already showing their support. Lenoir has raised $3 million. Wayne County has raised $1 million. Pitt County just started and is already over $500,000. Duplin County added $600,000 and Greene County, $100,000. The GTP Foundation has raised more than $17 million in less than a year.

Wilson's own BB&T has been instrumental in the success of the foundation, giving $1 million and working hard to raise additional money. I want to urge all of you to pitch in and help, too. You'll get great returns on your investment. Eastern North Carolina's economy will flourish, and that's good for all businesses, not just tenants of the GTP. This project is one of the best things we can do for the future of eastern North Carolina, and that's why I've devoted so much attention to it.

With your help, we can make it happen. We can add to the list of things North Carolina is first at. We can make North Carolina the first state to use twenty-first century transportation and manufacturing technology to capture the lead in the global economy.

---

[1] The Global TransPark's first tenant was Mountain Air Cargo, Inc., founded by former state legislator David Clark and his brother, Walter. The company planned to move its Anderson, South Carolina, and Miami, Florida, maintenance operations to a new GTP facility that would employ from 100 to 300 people. Mountain Air Cargo Announcement, Raleigh, April 15, 1994, Governors Papers, James Baxter Hunt Jr.

COUNCIL OF STATE GOVERNMENTS

PINEHURST, DECEMBER 5, 1994

I want to welcome all of you, especially my fellow governors, to the beautiful state of North Carolina. I hope you all get a chance to explore Pinehurst and enjoy our beautiful scenery, some of the world's finest golf courses, and of course, our famous North Carolina barbecue. I want to thank North Carolina representative Bobby Hunter, who has served as an outstanding chairman of this group, and our state senator Richard Conder for working so hard to organize this event.

This is an important time to gather and reflect on the nature of state government. All of us face new challenges as we work to deliver services more efficiently and effectively—and as we respond to the very clear message the voters sent last month. People have let us know that government needs to work better. They don't want partisan bickering. They don't want big government.

They want government that works—and works better. They want us [in] government [to] do a better job keeping their families safe and keeping their economies strong. They want government to get by on less—and maybe to give folks a little more at the end of the day.

Folks, this is a time of opportunity. It's an opportunity to do what states have wanted the federal government to let us do for years. It's a time for the new Congress and a president, who's been a governor, to give us fewer mandates; more flexibility; more chance[s] to be creative and innovative. It's a time to reshape government; a time to reshape the relationship between the federal and state governments; and a time for those of us in state government to reshape ourselves, as well, looking for new ways to solve some old problems.

The effort to solve problems from Washington hasn't worked. The problems are still there. It's the states that are coming up with solutions. It's the states that are laboratories of change in health care, and welfare reform, and education, and a host of other areas. We're rolling up our sleeves and looking for new approaches and new partnerships to reduce crime, boost educational opportunities, and create jobs.

What we need is more flexibility to do even more. Instead of reacting to Washington's every move, let us work together to figure out new ways to solve old problems. That means Democrats and Republicans working together; governors and legislators working together; government and business working together. We can do that. We're already doing it in many states, including North Carolina.

Here in North Carolina, we've used state government as a catalyst. We've brought businesses together with local governments and nonprofit agencies. With our Smart Start early childhood initiative, we're bringing together public and private sectors to provide every child in North Carolina with access to quality, affordable day care and health care, in the earliest years, so they'll come to school healthy and ready to learn. With our SOS [Support Our Students] crime prevention program, we're bringing communities together to provide constructive after-school activities for troubled youngsters. In neighboring Richmond County, our SOS program has brought bankers, teachers, social workers, and retired people together to set up an after-school program for at-risk kids. This is the kind of new approach that can help us reduce crime down the road.

Across the state, we're galvanizing local communities to come together for their children, bringing local leaders, local ideas, and local resources together to decide how best to serve local children. I challenge you all to go back home and look for new way[s] to seize this opportunity we have now. Think big. Think bold. Look for new partners in this effort, and let us challenge the status quo together.

STATEMENT ON TAX RELIEF

RALEIGH, DECEMBER 8, 1994

[For related press release, see Governor Hunt Proposes $483 Million Tax Cut, Raleigh, December 8, 1994, Governors Papers, James Baxter Hunt Jr.]

North Carolina is enjoying strong economic growth, with one of the lowest unemployment rates in the nation. But national economic numbers don't mean much to families who are working harder just to stay ahead— to pay their bills, to educate their children, and to pay their taxes. The average North Carolina family of four, earning $30,000 a year, pays more than $2,300 in state and local taxes alone, almost $200 every month.

The people of North Carolina deserve better. They deserve to keep more of their hard-earned money, and state government can get by with less. Today, I'm proposing we do just that.

When the General Assembly convenes, I will propose that we cut taxes by $483 million a year. This will be the largest tax cut in North Carolina's history. More than $373 million of that will be in individual tax relief, including:

—An increase in the standard exemption for each person in a household, from $2,000 to $2,500 a year;

—Creation of a $50.00 per child tax credit;

—Repeal of the intangibles tax on stocks and bonds;

—An increase in the homestead exemption for low-income taxpayers over sixty-five and making more of them eligible for the exemption.

In addition, I will propose reducing the corporate income tax rate for North Carolina businesses from 7.75 percent to 7 percent. Businesses will also benefit from the intangibles tax repeal.

These tax cuts would take effect over the next eighteen months. If enacted, this will mean lower taxes for every North Carolina taxpayer, and it means we're giving families a break. A family of four earning $30,000 will see its taxes cut by one-third. A single mother of two who earns $20,000 a year will see her taxes cut by two-thirds. The increase in the personal exemption and the new child tax credit means [sic] that a family of four, making $17,000 or less, will pay no income taxes. That ceiling would be raised from $13,000.

Six months ago, I expressed my hope that the 1995 legislature would be able to provide tax relief for individuals and for businesses; and as you know, the 1994 legislature set aside $28 million for tax cuts. In developing my proposal, I have relied upon a comprehensive tax audit by Peat Marwick. The audit found that for families of all income levels, North Carolina income taxes are higher than average, compared to twenty-one competitor states; and while our overall business tax burden is average, Peat Marwick found that the corporate income tax rate is higher than that of competitor states and that our intangibles tax sticks out like a sore thumb. These taxes hurt North Carolina's ability to compete.

Back in 1991, the state faced a very difficult budget shortfall, and the legislature took courageous action to restore our fiscal health. The General Assembly cut spending and raised corporate and personal taxes, asking people and businesses to share the burden because times were tough. Now that times are better, they deserve to share the benefits as well. We can afford to do this, and we can afford to meet our state's most important needs, including early childhood education, public education, and prisons.

We are having good revenue growth, but we cannot rely on that to finance this tax relief package. Instead, we must cut the size and cost of government. This means state government must change. We need to set priorities, reallocate resources, and downsize. Every major corporation in the United States is bringing this kind of discipline and accountability to its operations. It's time that state government did the same.

For the last few months, I have been meeting with key people in my administration to identify savings and efficiencies. We're looking hard at GPAC [Government Performance Audit Committee] and every major efficiency study in the last twenty years; and we're working hard to streamline, reorganize, and serve our citizens more efficiently. But we cannot accomplish all this without the tools that businesses use for downsizing: budget and personnel flexibility, new technology, and new ways of managing. I've talked with legislative leaders about the need for budget flexibility, and they've indicated their willingness to give us the tools we need to cut the cost of government.

Earlier today, I talked with a number of legislative leaders of both parties in both houses. While they have not had time to review my tax relief proposal in detail, I am optimistic that we can work together in a cooperative and constructive way. I believe our first task in the 1995 legislative session ought to be easing the tax burden of working families. North Carolina families need all the help they can get. I believe government can get by with less, and I believe that people ought to have a little more at the end of the day.

NORTH CAROLINA FOUNDATION
FOR RESEARCH AND ECONOMIC EDUCATION

RESEARCH TRIANGLE PARK, DECEMBER 15, 1994

[Although similar to the "Statement on Tax Relief," December 8, 1994, the December 15 address to N.C. FREE more strongly emphasized the benefits of Hunt's tax-cut plan to businesses. The latter text also advocated gubernatorial veto. The governor's N.C. FREE speech is almost identical to that which he delivered to the N.C. Business Roundtable, January 9, 1995.]

John Medlin put it well a few months ago. As he told 400 business leaders at the North Carolina Business Roundtable, "North Carolina must reassess public policies and take action to make itself more attractive in the new global marketplace for investment and jobs."[1]

It's a fact that our competitors are countries, not states. Our workers are compared to knowledge workers of Germany and Japan. Even our students are held to international standards.

It's a competitive world out there. North Carolina has to do everything in its power to stay ahead of the pack—and to beat the competition. We're in pretty good shape, with a low unemployment rate and a strong forecast of economic growth. We had a record number of new jobs in 1993, accolades from *Fortune* and *Money* magazines this year, and we've got a forecast of continued growth next year. But we cannot be complacent. The national economic outlook is uncertain, and our state is not immune to layoffs, relocations, and shutdowns.

I believe that 1995 is the time to take bold action that will keep North Carolina ahead of our competitors. We should move on two fronts. First, we should expand our commitment to developing a well-educated and highly skilled workforce. Education is economic development, and we cannot give that short shrift. Second, we should seize the opportunity to cut taxes for businesses and individuals, to enhance our strong business climate and sharpen our competitive edge. We need a competitive tax structure to help us keep and attract capital and to create good jobs. That was borne out by the tax audit I commissioned last year. Peat Marwick says North Carolina's tax policies are out of line with twenty competitor states across the country. Our corporate income tax and intangibles taxes are red flags and potential barriers to economic development.

North Carolina's corporate tax rate is the fourth-highest of the twelve southeast states, after West Virginia, Kentucky, and Louisiana. The General Assembly raised that tax during the lean times. Now we owe it to the business community to roll that tax back to 7 percent, and we owe it to the business community—especially small businessmen like Jim Blanchard—to repeal the intangibles tax. Only seven of our competitor states have an intangibles tax, and ours is the second highest! It's hurting entrepreneurs and small business owners who own their own stock. It's hurting individual savings and investment, and it's hurting investment in North Carolina.

I believe that one of the best ways North Carolina can keep our economy strong is to cut taxes for businesses and individuals. That's why the half-billion-dollar tax-relief package I proposed last week includes $110 million worth of business tax cuts, including an intangibles repeal and a corporate income tax cut. My tax-relief package also includes increasing the personal exemption for each member of a household, from $2,000 to $2,500, and creates a new tax credit of $50 per child. This means a family of four, earning $50,000, would see its state taxes cut by 13 percent. That same family, earning $75,000, would get a 7 percent tax cut. There's been a lot of talk about cutting other taxes, including eliminating the food tax. But we found that cutting the food tax in half would only produce a savings of $100 for a family of four earning $30,000. Under my tax-relief plan, that family would save $220. Now, I haven't figured out what it would mean for John Davis, with his five children. John, I think the state may end up owing you![2]

I'm convinced this tax-relief package will help existing industries grow, help us recruit business without having to resort to give-aways, and will increase buying power for individuals; and I'm convinced that we can finance the tax cuts largely by downsizing government. Some people in government think we can't afford not to have this money, and that's part of the problem. Too many people in government think like that. But we have to realize that it's not the government's money, it's the people's money. This means state government must change. We must set priorities, reallocate resources, and make tough decisions. Every major corporation in the United States is bringing this kind of discipline and accountability to its operations. It's high time that state government did the same.

As I've told my cabinet, in plain language, it's time to cut the cost and size of government. We're looking at every program, in every division, in every department, to see if it's needed and if it can be done more efficiently. We're cutting out fat. We're focusing on quality, cost, and results.

As every state agency works to reorganize and streamline, I'm taking a hard look at GPAC [Government Performance Audit Committee] and every major government efficiency study of the last twenty-five years. Let me tell you, there are no sacred cows. We've already shut down our Canadian and California trade offices, although we're not shutting down our recruiting efforts. We're going to flatten the organizational chart and cut middle management. We're going to reduce medical expenses for prisoners. We're going to reduce operating budgets of all state agencies by 10 percent, and at least one department is on the table.[3] We've already identified close to $200 million worth of savings, and we'll be making detailed recommendations to the General Assembly next month.

Folks, I think we can make state government leaner, more efficient, and more accountable, but we can't do it without the tools businesses use to downsize. I'll be asking the General Assembly for those tools, including veto, budget and personnel flexibility. I'm hopeful that legislative leaders of both parties will work together in a cooperative and constructive way to provide those tools—so we can provide tax relief to businesses and families.

But I would urge the business community not to take this tax-relief package for granted. Let your voices be heard in the General Assembly. Let your legislators know that cutting taxes is good for your business and good for your family. Let them know that North Carolina families and businesses need all the help they can get, and let them know that government can get by with less, and that people deserve a little more at the end of the day.

---

[1] Accuracy of quotation attributed to Medlin could not be verified.

[2] John N. Davis was executive director of the North Carolina Foundation for Research and Economic Education. John N. Davis, letter to Jan-Michael Poff, June 29, 1990; see also *News and Observer*, February 10, 1992.

[3] Hunt was referring to the Department of Crime Control and Public Safety.

WELFARE REFORM TASK FORCE PUBLIC HEARING

CHARLOTTE, DECEMBER 14, 1994

Our society is based on work. Work helps us reach our goals, like owning a home and raising a family. Work helps define us and ties us to our community. Work builds a sense of responsibility, a sense of pride.

But too many people don't have that sense of pride that comes from working hard and supporting themselves. They don't know the pride of providing for their families or standing on their own two feet. They've become dependent on today's welfare system, a system that takes away pride and self-esteem, takes away independence and self-sufficiency, and takes away the drive to build a better life. We've got to change that. That's why I created this task force, and that's what this hearing is all about.

It is a big job, but I've got capable people to serve on the Welfare Reform Task Force—and a fine chairman in Dr. Bertha Maxwell-Roddey. They've been looking at ways to change our welfare system to move people from welfare to work. The members of this task force include employers, social workers, teachers, and former welfare clients. They understand how the system is broken and how hard it is to break free from that system.

They know that the best way to help support families is to help them work. I believe strongly that welfare recipients should be required to work. They should work for their benefits, and while they're working and learning real job skills, they should have opportunities for job training and education so they can get even better jobs to support their families.

I believe the tax-relief package I proposed last week, the biggest in North Carolina's history, will help, as well. It will mean a family of four, earning up to $17,000, will pay no taxes, taking thousands of working poor off the tax rolls so they can use that money to support their families. It will mean a single mother, with two kids, who earns $20,000, will see her taxes cut by two-thirds.

Tonight, we're holding the first of six public hearings across North Carolina to hear your ideas on how to make the system work and how to help our people work. Next month, I expect a list of specific recommendations from the task force to help accomplish those goals. I will propose welfare-reform legislation to the General Assembly shortly thereafter and will push for action in the upcoming legislative session.

There is no time to waste. The sooner we start moving families off welfare rolls and into the workforce, the better off they, and their children, will be. So we need to hear from you. We need to hear what's wrong with the welfare system and how to change it. We need your help to make the system work better for families, for children, and for North Carolina taxpayers.

We want to change the welfare system so that it builds responsibility instead of dependence; so that it builds pride instead of hopelessness; so that it encourages families to stay together instead of tearing them apart; so that it discourages our teenagers from having children when they are still children, themselves. Tell us how. Tell us how to help people get the skills, education, and job training they need to work and support their families. Tell us how to help people find the transportation and child care that will allow them to work.

Government doesn't have the answers, folks. You do! Now I'll turn the hearing over to our task force chairman, Dr. Bertha Maxwell-Roddey.

ENVIRONMENTAL EDUCATION CONFERENCE

Research Triangle Park, December 15, 1994

My five grandchildren are growing up in a different environment than I did. They're growing up in a more fragile environment, an environment that is increasingly being damaged. Pollution, disappearing natural resources, and an increasing number of endangered species are all facts of life now. But my grandchildren are also growing up in a social environment that is more concerned and more aware, an environment that fosters a sense of stewardship of our earth.

Our children and grandchildren are learning that they have a responsibility to be good citizens of the earth—and you know what those children are doing? They're turning around and teaching their parents and their grandparents. They're educating the rest of us about protecting our environment, and you all can take some of the credit for that. As educators, you're teaching our children the basic skills they will need to learn, like reading, writing, and using numbers; and you know that environmental education can be used to teach the three R's and more. Environmental education can increase awareness, knowledge, and skills, and it can broaden understanding, help develop commitment, and encourage informed decisions and constructive action to ensure stewardship of our earth.

We've got to instill a conservation ethic in North Carolina. To do that, we've got to have a strategy to provide a basic understanding of the cause and effect relationship between human behavior and the environment and the economics of that relationship. In other words, we've got to have a plan. That's why you're here: to help develop the State Environmental Education Plan.[1]

We're already doing a lot here in North Carolina. We've got wonderful programs across the state that touch the lives of all our children, helping them understand the environment and their place in the world. Almost a million schoolchildren took part in environmental programs at places like our Museum of Natural Sciences, our marvelous North Carolina Zoo, and our state forests, and in programs like our Wildlife Resources Commission's wildlife workshops and the soil and water [conservation] districts' annual poster, speech, and essay contest. Folks, that's what we were able to do piecemeal—without a comprehensive plan. Can you imagine what we could do with a plan of action?

Our children are our leaders. They're our future business people, farmers, teachers, parents, and elected officials. They must have a better understanding of our environment if they're going to lead us into the twenty-first century. They've got to understand that we must have both a healthy environment and a sound economy. They've got to understand that you can't have one without the other.

Regulation has been the primary focus of our efforts to protect our environment, but the real solution lies in education. We must make sure everyone, especially our future generations, have [sic] a better understanding of our environment. It is the only way we can protect it.

We talk a lot about North Carolina's beauty and abundant natural resources, from our mountains to our coast. But from our mountains to our coast, we've got big environmental problems. The names "the Smokies" and "Blue Ridge" are taking on whole new meanings thanks to pollution that is cutting visibility at our highest altitudes; and trees along those peaks have been stripped bare by acid rain. Across the state, leaking underground storage tanks threaten our water supply, and on our coast, overfishing and pollution are wiping out our marine fishery resources.

Those problems are also threatening our state's second-largest industry: tourism. Just look at how important tourism is to our state. Last year, tourists visiting the Great Smoky Mountains and the Nantahala River brought $60 million to Swain County. The white-water season on the Nantahala River generated $42 million alone in tourism dollars. But it's far more than money: Our environment is the air we breathe, the water we drink, the soil in which we grow our food. Our very lives depend on it. So do the lives of our children. That's why it's so important to teach them all about our environment. That's why your jobs are so important. We must make sure you have all the tools you need to do the best job you can do—the best teaching materials, the best training, and most importantly, the best long-range environmental education plan—to teach our children what is perhaps the most important lesson they will ever learn: how to nurture and protect their earth.

---

[1] The fourteen-objective North Carolina Environmental Education Plan was presented to Governor Hunt in April 1995. For a description of the plan, see "*Environmental Education: Providing a World of Opportunities*," supplement to the *News and Observer*, April 20, 1995.

COMMISSION FOR A COMPETITIVE NORTH CAROLINA STATEWIDE ELECTRONIC TOWN MEETING

Raleigh, January 5, 1995

[Spread among Raleigh, Asheville, Greenville, Boone, Manteo, Charlotte, Greensboro, and Wilmington, a thousand participants joined Governor Hunt and the Commission for a Competitive North Carolina to discuss the state's future. The January 5 meeting, coordinated via the North Carolina Information Highway, was to help determine goals in economic development, education, environmental protection, public safety, and quality-of-life issues that the state should attain by 2015. Participants were asked how business, citizens, and government could collaborate to meet those goals. Press release, Governor Hunt to Host Statewide Town Meeting on North Carolina's Future, Raleigh, December 22, 1994, Governors Papers, James Baxter Hunt Jr.]

I'd like to welcome all of you to this statewide town meeting. Hello to all of you at the sites across the length and breadth of our [illegible] state.

I commend the members of the Commission for a Competitive North Carolina and the hundreds of you who are taking the time to participate today. Today we're really seeing democracy in action—citizens taking part in setting the direction of their state. By helping this commission set goals, you all are helping to make sure state government is focusing on the things that are important to you and your neighbors; and you are helping, in a novel way, to make government more accountable.

North Carolina citizens want government to do a better job, especially when it comes to protecting their families; and they want government to be more efficient, to use tax dollars more wisely. They want a more accountable government.

Nearly [a] year ago, I set up this commission to help us reach those same goals. I charged this bipartisan group of business, industry, education, civic, and nonprofit leaders with mapping out a blueprint for North Carolina's future and constructing a framework for translating that blueprint into action.

As parents, we use report cards to help measure our children's success in school. As citizens, we need a report card for North Carolina. We need clear, measurable goals for specific areas of need, such as decreasing teenage pregnancy—and we need specific benchmarks, such as a lower level of births to teen mothers by a certain year, so we can measure the state's progress in meeting those goals.

For the last year, the commission has been gathering research and data to help it set benchmarks. Now we're asking for your advice. What should North Carolina's high-priority areas be? Where should we target our limited resources?

With your help, the commission will propose specific benchmarks in eight key areas—the ones listed there in your workbooks—and the commission will also propose a process for monitoring those benchmarks and for holding government accountable for meeting them.[1] Ultimately, I want to ask the legislature to incorporate those benchmarks into the state budgeting and appropriations process. This will ensure that available resources are redirected from low- to high-priority areas. That way, benchmarks can guide our state's budget allocation process and make it more strategic—for us to do [a] better job.

[North Carolina is] not [the] first [state to measure governmental efficiency against benchmarks]. In Oregon, Texas, and Florida, benchmarking has meant that agencies meeting their goals have been rewarded, while agencies that have failed to reach their goals have seen their budgets cut. As I said to the commission a year ago, benchmarks can put pressure on state government to show results. Vague promises and projections have to be replaced with clear goals and progress checks. That's what people want from their government, and we want people involved in their government. In this town meeting and in subsequent public hearings, North Carolinians have a voice in setting the benchmarks, and down the road that means a voice in the budget process. You can tell the General Assembly how it ought to spend your tax dollars and where not to spend them.

So let us know what you think. The Commission for a Competitive North Carolina is really about you, and about the kind of North Carolina you want to leave for your children. Together, I think we can make government work better for you. Now I'd like to introduce the members of the commission serving as moderators at each of the eight sites.

[Hunt introduced moderators Bob Mauldin, chairman and CEO of Centura Bank, and Senator Beverly Perdue, Raleigh; Mack Pearsall, Asheville businessman and co-chair of the Commission for a Competitive North Carolina, and Morganton attorney Juleigh Sitton, Asheville; Secretary of Revenue Janice Faulkner and Representative Gene Arnold, Greenville; Mary Mountcastle, president of the Z. Smith Reynolds

Foundation, Boone; Representative Howard Hunter and Sandy Babb, director, Workforce Preparedness Commission, Manteo; Norman Cohen and House minority leader James Black, Charlotte; Julianne Still Thrift, Salem College president, and Vic Hackley, community college system president, Greensboro; and Jim Leutze, UNC-Wilmington chancellor, and Representative Thomas Wright, Wilmington.]

Now we'd like to hear from those of you at each of our sites. What are your thoughts as to what our state's goals ought to be in the eight key areas listed in your workbooks? Let's start with "Healthy Children and Families," the first goal listed in your workbook. That's the number-one goal in my mind, because I think the best way to build a brighter future for North Carolina is to start with the children, and I'd like to start with Boone, where I know that's an area close to the heart of Mary Mountcastle.

---

[1] "A Workbook for Our Future" was a first-draft outline of problems, goals, and progress measurements to enable the competitiveness commission to create performance benchmarks. The "eight key areas" to be evaluated were: "Healthy Children and Families"; "Quality Education for All"; "A High-Performance Workforce"; "A Prosperous Economy"; "A Sustainable Environment"; "Competitive Technology and Infrastructure"; "Safe and Vibrant Communities"; and "Active Citizenship and Accountable Government." Press release, Hunt's Commission for a Competitive North Carolina to Hold Public Workshops, Raleigh, January 25, 1995, Governors Papers, James Baxter Hunt Jr.

PRESS CONFERENCE, NATIONAL BOARD FOR PROFESSIONAL TEACHING STANDARDS

WASHINGTON, D.C., JANUARY 5, 1995

National Board certification marks a revolution in education, and the eighty-one teachers who have earned this first-ever certification can call themselves revolutionaries. These teachers have spent every day in their classrooms encouraging our children to do their best and be their best. On top of that, they've spent hundreds of hours demonstrating their talent, skill, and knowledge in teaching, lesson planning, student learning, and professional growth. They've given an entire year to this process, compiling portfolios of student work, videotaping their teaching, and spending long hours writing essays—all without a guarantee of success. Yet, they took that risk because they believed that the National Board certification process would make them better teachers, regardless of the outcome.

From California to New York, Washington to Georgia, inner-city Detroit to rural Idaho, these eighty-one teachers from twenty-three states have met tough and rigorous standards developed by their peers. This was no personality contest. It was an exacting test of their knowledge and skills, with each teacher's performance individually evaluated by expert teachers and judged against the strictest standards for teaching ever designed.

In the end, these teachers have taught us well. They've taught us how dedicated America's teachers are, and they've reminded us again how quality teaching can change a child's life. When I look at Scott Muri and Janice Ward, two of North Carolina's eight National Board certified teachers,[1] I know that they instill the kind of excitement and creativity in their students that they brought to the certification process; and I know that they inspire their students as much as they've inspired me. In the best sense of the word, they are revolutionaries, bringing about change in the lives of their students.

Today is only the beginning of this revolution. Today's first group of National Board certified teachers will be followed by many more, as certification becomes available in more subjects and in more grade levels every year, and I'm hopeful this revolution will take seed across our nation. Already, more and more states and cities are beginning to understand the importance of National Board certification, and they are beginning to encourage their teachers to seek certification. Iowa, Mississippi, New Mexico, and my own state of North Carolina have led the way, along with school districts like Boston; Rochester; Vancouver, Washington; and Fairfax, Virginia; and visionary leaders like Governor George Voinovich, of Ohio, and Governor Terry Branstad, of Iowa, have played a large role in making this effort a success, through their work on this board and in their states.[2]

In North Carolina, we're supporting the NBPTS [National Board for Professional Teaching Standards] with a 4 percent raise for teachers who achieve National Board certification, full reimbursement for the certification fee, and up to three days of release time for teachers to prepare their portfolios. I pushed hard for this action, and encourage all other policymakers to do the same, because I believe we've got to do all we can to support our teachers. At the end of the day, we're only as smart as our schools and as accomplished as our teachers.

I applaud Scott, and Janice, and the seventy-nine other teachers being honored today. I rejoice in their achievement and success, because I know it will mean achievement and success for our children in their classrooms across America. I am proud of them, and I'm proud of every single teacher who underwent the rigorous National Board certification process. Just as you are better for it, so are we. With that, let me turn the podium over to our real stars: Scott Muri, of Avery County, North Carolina; and Janice Ward, of Charlotte, North Carolina.

[1] North Carolina's first eight National Board certified teachers were Marsha Brigman, social studies and language arts teacher, Carmel Middle School, Charlotte; Deborah Camp, fifth-grade teacher, Lake Wylie Elementary School, Charlotte; Hilda Hamilton, math and science teacher, Mabel Elementary School, Watauga County; Denise Huff, special program teacher, Smith Middle School, Charlotte; Scott Muri, sixth-grade math and science teacher, Avery County Middle School, Newland; Susan Patterson, fourth-grade teacher, Starmount Elementary School, Charlotte; Gloria Smith Wansley, academically gifted and talented program teacher, Matthews Elementary School, Matthews; Janice Ward, seventh-grade science, math, and health teacher, South Charlotte Middle School. North Carolina Standards and Accountability Conference, Research Triangle Park, January 12, 1995; press release, Governor Hunt Announces State's First National Board Certified Teachers, Raleigh, January 5, 1995, Governors Papers, James Baxter Hunt Jr.

[2] George V. Voinovich (1936-), born in Cleveland, Ohio; B.A., Ohio University, 1958; J.D., Ohio State University, 1961. Attorney; Ohio assistant attorney general, 1963-1964; member, Ohio House of Representatives, 1967-1971; auditor, 1971-1976, county commissioner, 1977-1978, Cuyahoga County, Ohio; Ohio lieutenant governor, 1979; Cleveland mayor, 1979-1989; was elected Ohio governor, 1990, re-elected in 1994; Republican. Barone and Ujifusa, *Almanac of American Politics, 1996*, 1035.

Terry E. Branstad (1946-), born in Leland, Iowa; B.A., University of Iowa, 1969; J.D., Drake University, 1974; U.S. Army. Attorney; farmer; member, Iowa House of Representatives, 1972-1978; Iowa lieutenant governor, 1978-1982; was elected Iowa governor, 1982, re-elected in 1986, 1990, and 1994; Republican. Barone and Ujifusa, *Almanac of American Politics, 1996*, 502, 506.

ROBERT WOOD JOHNSON FOUNDATION MENTAL HEALTH SERVICES PROGRAM FOR YOUTH

Asheville, January 18, 1995

Thank you for the opportunity to join you, today, as you celebrate the success of the Mental Health Services Program for Youth. The Robert Wood Johnson Foundation[1] is to be commended for providing funding for this national initiative and for helping us find ways to better care for our most cherished resource: our children.

The most serious responsibilities that today's parents, communities, and political leaders face revolve around our children. Those responsibilities become even greater when the children we are nurturing suffer from serious mental illness. You and I know that in today's world of tight fiscal constraints, it's often difficult to meet those responsibilities adequately. And in today's world, although we want to help all children achieve success, sometimes children with mental health problems are overlooked. We don't recognize their need or see their pain—or the pain of their families. We don't realize that it is poor fiscal policy to allow their needs to go unaddressed.

The Robert Wood Johnson Foundation, through the Mental Health Services Program for Youth, has brought these issues into sharp focus. You have brought national attention to the needs of these children and their families. By joining forces with the Washington Business Group on Health, together you have placed the need for services to children with mental problems squarely on the agenda of this country. Leaders in state governments have participated in training events you have sponsored and have read the materials you produced. The congressional briefing in October of 1993 was one of the best-attended briefings, packing the Senate Caucus Room to overflowing.

As the corporations of this country have designed their health benefit packages, you have reminded them of the importance of mental health coverage, especially for children. You have told state governments, the federal government, and corporations that children with emotional problems can be helped, and you have talked of the toll that not helping them takes on their schools, their communities, their parents' workplaces, and on the costs of services provided too late to avoid expensive, long-term treatments.

I am very proud to have been a part of this initiative from the very beginning. As chair of the Mental Health Services Program for Youth Advisory Committee, I helped select the sites across the country for these very special projects. When I made site visits several years ago with the other members of the advisory committee, I was impressed with the creativity and commitment of the competing states, and I am proud to see that you who were selected have done so well.

You have helped children. Children like Jim, an abused preschooler, abandoned before he even started kindergarten. His problems, over the next ten years, earned him the label of an impossible case. But he wasn't impossible to the Robert Wood Johnson project staff. Thanks to the combined efforts of therapists, a caring foster family, case managers, and caring teachers, Jim today is a happy sixteen-year-old planning for a bright future. You turned a—quote—impossible case—into a future productive member of our society.

I want to take a few minutes to tell you what we're doing in North Carolina. My administration has been dedicated to children from day one. We have made it our top priority to improve the quality of life for children and families, and that philosophy has been the foundation of every initiative of the past two years of this administration.

In North Carolina we know that investing in our children is investing in our future. Our early childhood initiative, known as Smart Start, provides our children with quality child care, health care, and critical family services in the first five years of their lives, ensuring a brighter future for them and for North Carolina. Through Smart Start, local communities make the decisions about how best to serve their children. The state is the catalyst, bringing together the public and private sectors to build a better life for our children.

Over the past two years, twenty-four local partnerships serving thirty-two counties have made a difference in the lives of tens of thousands of young children and their parents. Smart Start has meant working families have more access to better child care. Poor families are getting more affordable child care, which frees them up to work. Children are getting preventive health care, and families are getting better access to information about available services.

However, we also recognize children who haven't had the benefit of a Smart Start, or those whose lives have been later complicated or compromised, need help, too. We have made spectacular progress in organizing and delivering services to these children with serious mental health problems and their families. This progress is based, in large part, on our mental health program for children, called the Children's Initiative. The Robert Wood Johnson Foundation deserves praise, because the Children's Initiative program has made such a substantial impact in North Carolina.

Our program is based in the Smoky Mountain-Blue Ridge area. It is a very rural area which has a strong history of close cooperation among the agencies working to help children. As a result of this program, services have been improved and costs lowered by tearing down the barriers between agencies and bringing everyone together to look at the total needs of each child. The program has expanded services to include all of those available in a community, both public and private, and a strong case management system has been put into place to organize this wide array of services for the child and his family. Our efforts are paying off: An independent evaluation shows that the program is getting children the services they need in their communities.

For dramatic changes to be successful, we had to change the way our professionals provide those services. Now case managers are being trained differently, and with the help of a federal grant, curriculums are being redesigned in one of our major universities. East Carolina University is working with three eastern North Carolina counties, testing our new ideas and new ways of doing business. The end result will be a new, more effective way of training graduate students to work with children with serious mental problems and their families. Our hope is this effort will become a model for other universities to follow.

Another facet of our efforts to help these children is called Carolina Alternatives. Carolina Alternatives is our Medicaid waiver program for children, and it is showing spectacular success. I am very proud of the fact that North Carolina is at the forefront of national Medicaid reform.

Let me tell you how Carolina Alternatives came about and what it has done. In 1991 we saw a dramatic increase in Medicaid costs for psychiatric inpatient treatment of children under age eighteen. Costs reached $34 million, having doubled over the previous three years. We found that children were hospitalized who did not need to be, and that children received longer treatment than necessary, because community-based alternatives were unavailable.

Through a Medicaid waiver, the state began a prepaid, capitated, managed-care program named Carolina Alternatives. Its goal is to contain inpatient costs and develop community-based, family-focused treatment alternatives for children eligible for Medicaid. The program creates a comprehensive system of care while saving the state money.

Carolina Alternatives is designed to increase access to services and family involvement in treatment planning while reducing costs and unnecessary hospitalizations. As a result:

—Expanded services allow children to be helped in community-based programs;

—Parents are now part of the treatment-planning process;

—Parents can access the program through mental health programs which have organized networks of public and private providers, including school and child-welfare agencies.

Carolina Alternatives is slowing the increase in costs while improving access to care for Medicaid-eligible children who need it. The program now serves more than 6,000 children in ten pilot areas and has already lowered hospital costs more than 30 percent. Thanks to this program, we have accomplished a great deal in a short time, and I know that each of you have [sic] similar success stories to tell.

But the sand is shifting. We run serious risk that the national agenda will change, and we will lose ground. We have come so far, but we have much further to go to help our children and their families.

Our message remains clear: Children come first. We must show that our approaches are sound, that they benefit children and families, and that the cost of providing services is far less than the cost of doing nothing. The Robert Wood Johnson Foundation has a key role to play. The foundation's positive attention to the issues of children and the issues of health care will be very important in keeping decision makers focused on these issues. We have established a strong base on which to build the future for our children. We have gained knowledge and experience, thanks to you. I am so proud to be a part of this work and so pleased to share the successes with you today.

---

[1] Based in Princeton, N.J., the Robert Wood Johnson Foundation was the country's largest health and health-care philanthropy. *News and Observer*, March 1, 2000.

NORTH CAROLINA INFORMATION HIGHWAY SHOWCASE
NATIONAL INFORMATION INFRASTRUCTURE
ADVISORY COUNCIL

CARY, JANUARY 26, 1995

[This final script for the state's information highway presentation to the National Information Infrastructure Advisory Council was dated January 25, 1995. The showcase itself was presented the twenty-sixth, the second day of the council's three-day meeting at SAS Institute, Cary. President Clinton and Vice-President Gore established NII to devise communications policy and make recommendations to Congress. Some saw the council's decision to hold a monthly meeting in North Carolina, rather than Washington, D.C., or the usual Silicon Valley locations, as adding further luster to the Research Triangle Park's reputation as a technology center—and the perfect opportunity to promote the capabilities of and generate support for the state's information highway. Governor Hunt's Schedule for January 22-28, 1995, Governors Papers, James Baxter Hunt Jr.; *News and Observer*, December 28, 1994, January 24, 27, 1995, September 6, 1998.]

JANE PATTERSON[1] (8:00 A.M.): Good morning to all—fellow National Information Infrastructure Council members; members of the media, particularly those viewing this meeting from the ComNet Convention in Washington, D.C.; corporate partners in the North Carolina Information Highway; ladies and gentlemen:

As both a council member and a representative of North Carolina government, I've been very involved with the conception, development, and implementation of the North Carolina Information Highway. I can say, without qualification, that it's the most exciting and advanced high-speed, multimedia information exchange system literally anywhere on the planet. North Carolina boasts a long history of technological firsts, from the Wright brothers to the Research Triangle's recent designation in *Fortune* magazine as the number-one location in America for "knowledge workers."

North Carolina has emerged as a national leader because of its natural and human resources. We've also risen to the top because of the cooperative relationship between leaders from the public and private sectors. On the one hand, the leadership of North Carolina has demonstrated the vision and foresight necessary to propel the state ahead in business, industry, technology, and a great many other arenas. On the other hand, our business and government leaders have known how to transform vision into reality, how to turn ideas into tangible benefits for our citizens—in short, how to make things happen. At this point, I'd like to introduce one of these leaders, North Carolina's governor, Jim Hunt.

For nearly a decade, now, his vision and pragmatism have been helping to move the concept of an information superhighway from the computer lab to schoolrooms, government offices, corporate boardrooms, medical centers, and innumerable other locations across the state. He is here today to show you how. Please join me in welcoming Governor Hunt.

GOVERNOR HUNT (8:02 A.M.): Thank you Jane, for your remarks. I'd like to extend my warmest welcome to everyone here in this room, today— and let me say to the members of the National Information Infrastructure Council that I've rarely had the opportunity to meet two dozen such distinguished people twice in less than twelve hours![2]

In the next forty minutes we will have the chance to see, firsthand, how some of the most advanced telecommunications technology works. I'd like to ask the council members to extend my thanks to the national leadership, especially Vice-President Gore, for placing such high priority on this kind of technological initiative.

Before we move to the demonstrations, I want to make one key point: The North Carolina Information Highway is not theoretical. It is actual. It is real. In many ways, it is usable today and will quickly become a valuable, irreplaceable tool in education, health care, economic development, business, public safety, criminal justice, and other aspects of everyday life in this state. For example, those of you who've had a chance to look through our showcase materials will have seen a listing of some one hundred interactive courses and sessions currently offered over the highway. These offerings raise the quality of education for students and teachers across the state. They disperse expert knowledge to some of the state's most remote and rural classrooms from our top-notch universities, our community colleges, and nationally recognized secondary schools, such as the North Carolina School of Science and Math.

In its ability to create equal access to education, health care, and many other critical services, the North Carolina Information Highway expands the meaning of the word *democracy*. Technologically, socially, and economically, it provides an information infrastructure model for other states to follow. It points the direction to a national information infrastructure that will enable the United States to maintain and increase our competitive edge in the global arena.

Jane set the stage for me by emphasizing that the combined talent of North Carolina's business and government leaders has shaped the North Carolina Information Highway. Let me take a minute to expand on that point. In 1982, the North Carolina General Assembly created the

State Information Processing Services, or SIPS, to control what was then the country's first statewide digital computer network. SIPS currently links all the state's school systems, community colleges, and universities. In 1983, MCNC [Microelectronics Center of North Carolina], a private, nonprofit corporation in nearby Research Triangle Park, launched an interactive microwave and fiber-optic network for video and data. The network links universities, colleges, and government agencies. It operates today under the name NC-REN.

In 1989, BellSouth, GTE, Fujitsu, MCNC, and the University of North Carolina at Chapel Hill worked to create VISTAnet, one of five gigabit test-beds in the United States. Two years later, Southern Bell, a BellSouth company, and Northern Telecom launched Vision Carolina, a public-private project that linked sixteen educational sites on a fiber-optic network. Vision Carolina provided more than 100 distance learning classes per week over a DS-3 network.[3]

With this long-standing and well-tested history of public-private collaboration in the background, in 1992 former governor Jim Martin took a momentous step toward the creation of today's information highway. We asked the private sector to develop a design for a publicly switched, ATM/SONET[4] broadband network to help us meet statewide telecommunications needs. Southern Bell, Sprint-Carolina Telephone, and GTE developed this plan, joined by the state's eighteen independent telcos,[5] including Access One. AT&T became the SONET interexchange carrier. This plan provided the foundation on which today's applications are built.

Critically important to the development of the North Carolina Information Highway has been the willingness of the private sector to bear the financial and other risks associated with pioneering an ATM/SONET network. Essentially, the private sector has agreed to fund the infrastructure development of the North Carolina Information Highway, and the state has agreed to be the highway's first customer—its anchor tenant, if you will. With the first tariff for commercial use already approved by the Utilities Commission, we anticipate that the state's first business customers will be using our broadband highway shortly.

The combined expertise, resources, and long-range planning of the private and public sectors have been indispensable to the launch of the highway. They provide a model for similar cooperation among state governments and businesses across the country. Now let me turn from how the North Carolina Information Highway was developed and focus on how it works and its benefits to our citizens.

Through the University of North Carolina's sixteen campuses, our community colleges, Duke University, and our science and math high school, we have centers of educational excellence peppered across the state. As in all states, however, educational instruction, facilities, and services can lag behind in rural areas. One of the great promises of the North Carolina Information Highway is to make top-notch instruction available to literally any student, anywhere in the state.

The highway is already helping North Carolina students share the state's cultural resources, and a national infrastructure will bring treasures to students across the country. For example, as we've been talking, students at two North Carolina high schools have been on a video field trip. They're touring the Information Age Exhibit at the Smithsonian's Museum of American History. High Point Central High School is in one of our urban areas. Manteo High School is in a small coastal town near Kitty Hawk, on our Outer Banks. They are about 300 miles apart, and many of the students have never been to the Smithsonian—until today. Let's drop in on them.

(Visual [8:08 a.m.]: Smithsonian, Manteo High School, and High Point Central High School come on line.)

Hunt: Good morning, this is Governor Hunt. I'm in Cary, North Carolina, at a meeting of the National Information Infrastructure Advisory Council. Please carry on with your museum tour. We may have some questions for you in a few minutes.

(Visual [8:08 a.m.]: Schools, Smithsonian remain on screen and tour proceeds.)

Dr. Allison: Good morning, Governor Hunt. We're glad you could join us. *(Continues tour.)*

Hunt (8:16 a.m.): Dr. Allison, may I break in with a question or two at this point? *(Governor Hunt for a Manteo student):* What has today's tour added to your education? Does anyone from the council have a question?

Hunt (8:18 a.m.): Thank you for allowing us to be with you, today. We'll let you get back to your "regularly scheduled programming."

What we've witnessed here is literally history in the making. The doors of education have been opened almost as widely as the mind can imagine. As networks like the North Carolina Information Highway are developed across the United States and around the globe, education exchanges like today's will occur nationally and internationally. But let me remind you: What we've seen here is not futuristic. Distance learning takes place in North Carolina every day. The highway supports up to thirty-two educational sessions per day and 700 hours of interactive video instruction per month. As the system's capabilities expand, we will see the educational value of the information highway increase and the costs of using the service decline. It is hardly surprising that this kind of educational innovation should spring from a state which boasts the first state university in America.[6]

As everyone in this room knows, the issue of education, particularly lifetime education, is critically important to the industrial and commercial success of this country. Remote professional training is one of the highway's commercial benefits, along with high-speed data exchange. Our second application, the North Carolina Economic Development Information System, EDIS, demonstrates the tremendous potential for economic development that the highway holds.

EDIS has been under development for about two years and continues to grow. The objective of the system is to enable commercial, industrial, and other developers to identify, tour, and obtain data on any site in North Carolina from a single personal computer or work station. Seven regional economic development offices in the state are building databases about the land within their boundaries. These databases contain information on the state's geography, topography, demographics, infrastructure, environmental characteristics, and other details. By this fall, EDIS information will be available over the Internet, and video teleconferences will be available among regional economic development offices in the state.

Once fully operational, the system will allow a developer to access this information for any area of the state, build a model of any promising site, and hold a video teleconference with site experts and economic development officers. Developers will be able to compile this information from a single workstation in North Carolina. Eventually, interested parties will access the EDIS from personal computers anywhere in the world.

At this point, I'd like to invite North Carolina's secretary of commerce, Dave Phillips, to take the microphone and lead us through this exciting application.

(Secretary Phillips takes the podium.)

SECRETARY PHILLIPS (8:21 A.M.): Thank you, governor. Let me add my welcome to the NII Council and the other members of the audience here today. Now let's imagine a theoretical situation. I'm going to ask Ken Atkins, the economic development director of Catawba County, and Tim

Johnson, technical services manager of the Center for Geographic Information and Analysis, to join me at the work station and bring this scenario to life.

Ken, the North Carolina Department of Commerce has developed interest from a multinational firm in expanding their operations in North Carolina. They're looking for a site here that meets the following parameters.

(Visual: Overlay N.C. map, county boundaries shown.)

PHILLIPS: It should be no more than ten miles from an interstate or four-lane road and should have easy access to an ample number of telecommunications or electronics workers.

(Visual: Overlay, roads.)

PHILLIPS: The site should be within one hour of a port or an intermodal service.

(Visual: Overlay/clip coverage, ports/intermodals.)

PHILLIPS: Average land costs should be below $20,000 per acre, and the site should be within a one-hour drive of a major airport.

(Visual: Overlay/clip coverage, airports.)
(Visual: Final coverage, six counties remaining.)

PHILLIPS: Based on this information, there are six North Carolina counties that meet our client's needs.

KEN ATKINS: In Catawba County, one area that meets your client's requirements is the Conover West Business Park in Catawba County. Let's connect with Scott Millar from my office and take a look at information there.

(Atkins-Millar general greeting.)

ATKINS: Scott, can you call up some information on the Conover West parcel?

SCOTT MILLAR: Here is the cadastral, or property line, information on the park. What other information do you need?

(Visual: Millar to corner of screen, Conover West parcel coverage fills remainder.)

ATKINS: Scott, show us the general topography in the park. Is there enough flat land for Secretary Phillips's project?

(Visual: Overlay, topo.)

MILLAR: I think the best remaining site is the Lail Site. *(Moves mouse to site.)*

PHILLIPS: Scott, the client is very interested in a park-like environment—corporate neighborhood, trees, sort of a high-tech setting. Does this work with that vision?

(Visual: Remove topo, add vegetation layer, add structures layer, remove property lines.)

MILLAR: Yes, as a matter of fact, the site is wooded, and we have helped three corporate headquarters move into this section of the park recently.

(Visual: Add infrastructure water-sewer layer.)

MILLAR: I'm also bringing up information on water lines in blue, sewer lines in black, and fiber-optic telecommunications lines in orange.

(Visual: Add fiber-optic layer.)

PHILLIPS: This is a very interesting site, Ken. I know the client will have a keen interest in watershed areas, nearby Superfund sites, and critical wildlife habitat areas. Do you have any information on those?

ATKINS: We don't keep that information in our office, but over the North Carolina Information Highway we do have access to environment, health, and natural resources databases through the North Carolina Center for Geographic Information and Analysis. Scott, can you get that information and overlay it on our model?

(Visual: Superfund sites coverage.)

ATKINS: There are no protected watersheds or protected habitats in the vicinity. As you can see, there does happen to be a contaminated site relatively nearby. Scott, can you check on its status?

MILLAR: Of course. It's current. We updated the database on December 15, about a month ago.

ATKINS: Just to finish off, Scott please bring up an aerial photo of the site to show the secretary.

PHILLIPS: Thank you all. It seems this site will certainly meet the client's needs. I'll be back in touch, but first I need to travel across the state to see five more sites in the next hour. *(Turns to NII Council members.)* As you've just seen, the North Carolina Information Highway will provide developers instant access to almost any location in the state. From a single workstation, they will be able to conduct virtual-reality inspections of all potential sites. These statewide capabilities are unique to the North Carolina network. Economists estimate that the highway will add $2.7 billion to the state economy and create 44,000 jobs by the year 2003. Approximately $892 million will be added to the state economy by 1999.

HUNT (8:27 A.M.): Dave, that's fascinating technology. I'd like to invite members of the NII Council to ask one or two questions at this point.

HUNT (8:29 A.M.): Gentlemen, thank you for that excellent demonstration, and thank you for being with us here today.

(Visual: Millar goes off line; Phillips, Atkins leave podium.)

HUNT: I'm excited and delighted to see North Carolina tying technology into solid, innovative, practical approaches to economic development. As with the educational exchange we watched, this system clearly provides a model which could be replicated either statewide or nationally as ATM/SONET networks emerge across the country.

Now I'd like to turn to our final application of the morning. It is an ATM- and computer-based medical image management system developed by the Department of Radiology at Duke University Medical Center, in Durham, North Carolina. North Carolina is renowned for its exceptionally high levels of medical achievement. Our four major medical centers—Duke University Medical Center, the University of North Carolina School of Medicine, East Carolina University School of Medicine, and the Bowman Gray School of Medicine at Wake Forest University—are national leaders in medical research and practice. In the same way that the North Carolina Information Highway will give students access to educational opportunities previously unavailable, the highway will spread expertise from these highly sophisticated centers to the most remote hospitals and health-care providers.

Developments at Duke Medical Center provide a leading-edge foundation for expanding medical information exchange across the state. I'd like to introduce Dr. Carl Ravin, chairman of the Duke Medical Center Department of Radiology, who will highlight some of the technology in place at Duke.

(Dr. Ravin takes the microphone.)

Dr. Carl Ravin (8:31 a.m.): Thank you for that introduction. I'm pleased to be able to present some of our technology to the members of the NII Council today. Assisting me with this demonstration will be Minh DoVan, who has taken a lead in developing the technology, and Dr. Allan Johnson, a professor of radiology at Duke. Dr. Johnson, are you with us?

(Dr. Johnson comes on line.)

Dr. Allan Johnson (8:31:30 a.m.): I'm with you, Dr. Ravin. Members of the council, I'd like to take a minute to discuss some of the technology we have on site here at Duke Medical Center and what it means to radiologists. Fully digital computer image generation and storage represent a transformation in radiology. Computer storage of medical images will do for radiology departments what the personal computer has done for business offices.

Duke's system operates on three ATM switches that transmit medical images internally. A fourth ATM switch connects Duke Medical Center with the North Carolina Information Highway. Medical images that work best on the system include CT scans, MRI scans, and X-rays, such as the one I have on my screen here. Dr. Ravin, let me turn the demonstration back over to you at this point.

Ravin (8:34 a.m.): Thanks. *(Turns to Minh.)* Minh, would you please retrieve a copy of the image Dr. Johnson is looking at and bring it up here on our screen? *(To the audience:)* Minh is retrieving the image from our database at Duke. Stored on disk, it represents about 80 megabits of information. It would take several hours to transmit this information to a distant site by telephone and modem.

(Visual [8:35 a.m.]: Minh retrieves the image. It is transmitted to the projection screen. Drs. Johnson and Ravin consult briefly [30 seconds] about the image.)

RAVIN: This is an X-ray taken following cardiac surgery. Dr. Johnson, I'd like you to take a look at the left ventricle.

JOHNSON: Sure. Let me enhance the image through the window and level controls on my system. That's better. I can see the ventricle clearly. It looks as though it has been repaired carefully.

RAVIN: The image suggests to me that this patient may need further surgery if any blockages occur at the scar tissue sites. Do you see any potential for this?

JOHNSON: I would recommend follow-up X-rays at three and six months to monitor for such blockages.

(Visual [8:36-8:39 A.M.]: Minh retrieves subsequent images—contrast injection into coronary arteries, MR exam of the knee for evaluation of ligaments, CT of the abdomen—and keeps each image on screen for approximately 30 seconds.)

RAVIN (8:35:30 A.M.): You've just seen the future of medical image management in action. Computerized image storage allows radiologists and physicians to enhance specific anatomical structures for improved diagnosis. ATM networks enable instantaneous remote transmission of medical images and simultaneous voice communication between consulting specialists. Thanks to a grant from the National Telecommunication and Information Administration, we anticipate that North Carolina's four major medical centers will begin testing this technology in the field and establishing critical links to remote hospitals and health-care facilities that rely on specialized medical center expertise.

In the near future, the North Carolina Information Highway will allow for remote diagnosis and consultation. In situations requiring patient transfers between medical centers, it will allow medical information to be rushed to physicians at the receiving hospital so they can preview the case. The day is coming when practitioners or students at remote sites will be able to watch medical procedures using laparoscopy and other imaging devices.

HUNT (8:39 A.M.): Thank you both for that fascinating look at medicine over the North Carolina Information Highway. Both Dr. Ravin and Dr. Johnson would be happy to answer one or two questions from NII members at this point. *(Governor moderates questions.)*

Hunt (8:41 a.m.): Thank you all for your participation.

(Visual: Duke Medical Center camera goes off line.)

Hunt (8:41 a.m.): What we've seen here is one of the health care applications the North Carolina Information Highway holds forth. But there are more. For example, since August 1994, East Carolina University's School of Medicine, in Greenville, has been setting telemedicine "firsts." According to the National Institute of Telemedicine, East Carolina University leads the country's medical schools in the number of telemedicine conferences. The school is linked with two distant hospitals, one in Belhaven, North Carolina, and one at Camp Lejeune. The link provides emergency-room staff with instant specialist consultations and allows the institutions to share MRI images, CT scans, and other radiological pictures in seconds.

In July of last summer, we created the North Carolina Health Care Information and Communications Alliance. The alliance provides a broadband test-bed for telemedicine, and its mission is to accelerate the development of health-care information and treatment systems like the one we've just seen. It is the only organization of its kind in the United States. The alliance brings together North Carolina's brightest minds in medicine and technology. Following the public-private sector model I spoke about earlier, organizations participating in the Health Care Alliance include the state's three publicly funded major medical centers, Duke University Medical Center, IBM, AT&T, GTE, BellSouth, Blue Cross/Blue Shield, Unisys, Northern Telecom, and several other companies.

As we've seen in the last forty minutes, in the fields of health care, economic development, and education, the North Carolina Information Highway is breaking important new ground. In these and other arenas, including business applications, public safety, and criminal justice, we are providing an operational superhighway prototype—a model that other states can, and I predict will, follow as they develop and deploy their own advanced telecommunications networks.

In the same way that Orville and Wilbur Wright pioneered the skies, the North Carolina Information Highway is mapping new ground for a national superhighway information infrastructure. We are proud to be in the vanguard of twenty-first century telecommunications. I'm delighted to have had the chance to demonstrate some of our current capabilities—and speaking on behalf of everyone involved in this trend-setting project, we in North Carolina will be pleased to assist other states and officials at the national level as a national information infrastructure takes shape across the country.

PATTERSON (8:45 A.M.): Governor, thank you for walking the council through these highlights of the North Carolina Information Highway. *(To the council:)* You've just seen the governor of North Carolina demonstrate our state motto, *Esse quam videri,* or "To be, rather than to seem." Now let me turn [the] floor over to the council.

---

[1] Besides being the governor's senior adviser on policy, budget, and technology, Jane Patterson was also a NII Advisory Council member. *News and Observer,* December 28, 1994.

[2] NII members met at the Executive Mansion for dinner with the governor on January 25. Governor Hunt's Schedule for January 22-28, 1995, Governors Papers, James Baxter Hunt Jr.; *News and Observer,* December 28, 1994.

[3] For more on the creation of the Vision Carolina network, see Poff, *Addresses of Martin, 1989-1993,* 339-340.

[4] Asynchronous transfer mode/synchronous optical network.

[5] Telcos: telephone companies.

[6] The University of North Carolina at Chapel Hill was the first state-supported university in the country to open its doors to students.

TOBACCO GROWERS ASSOCIATION OF NORTH CAROLINA

RALEIGH, FEBRUARY 3, 1995

We have a lot to be proud of in North Carolina. We are home to some of the best places to live in America. We have one of the lowest unemployment rates. We are known for our top-notch universities and our Research Triangle Park, where some of the world's brightest minds go to work every day.

But North Carolina's roots lie in agriculture and tobacco. Over the years, tobacco has helped make North Carolina what it is today. We are the number-one producer of tobacco in the nation, and we grow the best quality tobacco anywhere in the world. All of you in this room are responsible for that, and I want to thank you for your hard-earned efforts.

Most of you know that I grew up on a tobacco farm in Wilson County. Tobacco bought our clothes, our groceries, paid our bills, and helped me get a good education. And so many of us rely on tobacco. We rely on it to provide good homes for our families and to build a brighter future for our children.

Our state's number-one cash crop reaches far more than the 280,000 people whose livelihood depends on the tobacco industry. Tobacco plays a vital role in the overall well-being of our state's economic health.

Tobacco employs roughly one out of every eleven workers in our state. From field to final market, that's worth more than $1 billion to our state's gross product.

But it hasn't been all that. In 1994, tobacco farmers faced some pretty tough obstacles. Early in the season there were numerous threats of large tax increases to finance the health plan.[1] There was much discussion about an allotment buyout and possibly a complete dismantling of the program as we know it. By late summer, fear struck all our producers as we heard more and more about the 700-plus million pounds of surplus tobacco and very likely a 45 percent quota reduction for 1995. This would have been absolutely devastating to all of you in this room. It could have meant nearly half of our growers being forced out of business, millions of dollars in lost revenues to our state, and many thousands of jobs lost.

Fortunately, we cleared those hurdles. Our '94 leaf sold strong in the close of the market. Tobacco companies agreed to buy the Stabilization pounds.[2] The secretary of agriculture granted a 16 percent quota increase for 1995.[3]

Throughout that period, I spoke to President Clinton several times about how important tobacco is to our economy, and I have worked with our congressional delegation to stay informed and involved in making sure your concerns were represented and protected.[4] Last November I hosted a meeting with your president, Keith Parrish, and executive vice-president, Charles Harvey, and several other key organizations in an effort to make certain we all work together to come up with positive solutions to the issues facing our tobacco farmers. That means all of us, working hard to protect our right to grow tobacco, in 1995 and for generations to come.

We may have cleared some tough hurdles, but the job is not done. Tobacco will likely come under attack again. But together, we can do some things to protect our crop.

As growers, you must stay informed of regulatory issues related to your commodity. You must take your involvement in the Tobacco Growers Association to a new level, one of legislative awareness. That means letting your representatives in Raleigh and in Washington know how you feel on issues affecting you and your farming. You must work together to secure a larger world market share and protect the domestic content here at home. You must work hard, as producers, to regain any lost appreciation for the contributions tobacco has made in our state. As independents, you must unify your efforts and take the lead in promoting your cause and your industry.

I look forward to working with you to keep North Carolina's tobacco production strong. You are the most productive and efficient farmers in the world. Your presence here today sends a strong message about where tobacco stands in North Carolina. That's why I feel good about tobacco in this state, and I feel good about the future of North Carolina.

---

[1] To help fund its ill-fated plan for national health-care reform, the Clinton administration proposed increases, ranging from $.75 to $2.00, in the federal excise tax on each pack of cigarettes. Press release, Hunt to Meet with Congressional Leaders on Tobacco Tax, Raleigh, December 22, 1993, Governors Papers, James Baxter Hunt Jr.

[2] Hunt was referring to 300 million pounds of surplus tobacco warehoused by the Flue-Cured Tobacco Cooperative Stabilization Corporation. Flue-Cured Tobacco Cooperative Stabilization Corporation, Raleigh, May 26, 1995, Governors Papers, James Baxter Hunt Jr.

[3] Albert Michael Espy (1953-   ), born in Yazoo City, Miss.; B.A., Howard University, 1975; law degree from University of Santa Clara, 1978. Career with state of Mississippi included assistant secretary of state, 1978-1980, assistant secretary of state for Public Lands Division, 1980-1984, and assistant attorney general, 1984-1985; elected to U.S. House from Mississippi's Second Congressional District, 1986, re-elected in 1988, 1990, 1992, and was the first black to represent the state in Congress since Reconstruction; member, House Agriculture Committee; U.S. secretary of agriculture, from 1993; Democrat. *Current Biography Yearbook, 1993*, 183-187.

[4] For related press releases, see Governor Hunt Writes President to Protest Tobacco Tax, Raleigh, April 23, 1993; Hunt to Meet with Congressional Leaders on Tobacco Tax, Raleigh, December 22, 1993; and Governor Hunt Lobbying Congressional Leaders Against Tobacco Tax, Raleigh, July 24, 1994, Governors Papers, James Baxter Hunt Jr.

DEMOCRATIC PARTY EXECUTIVE COMMITTEE

RALEIGH, FEBRUARY 11, 1995

First, I want to thank Tom Hendrickson for his service as our chairman these past two years. He's worked hard to modernize our party and strengthen our finances and our organization. He didn't flinch when we went through a difficult election cycle. He deserves our thanks, and I ask you to join me in thanking him and his family.

Now I want to address some things I've been reading in the media, lately. A lot of people in politics and journalism are obsessed with labels. They want to put everybody and every idea into little boxes labeled *liberal* or *conservative, left* or *right, Democrat* or *Republican*. Well, I don't care about boxes or labels. I care about people.

I care about North Carolina, and I care about the leadership that the Democratic Party gives North Carolina. That's why I invited six families to my State of the State speech this week. The Democratic Party is about those people. Throughout our history, we have stood and fought for working people, and families with children, and retired people, and single mothers, and that's what we are about today. Some people say it's Republican to talk about tax cuts, but I think about one of those families: Brent and Sheila Gerald. He's a fire fighter in Greensboro, and she stays at home with their daughter, Alexandria. He wants a tax cut so they can save more money for their daughter's college education. That's what the Democratic Party is about.

I remember when, thirty years ago, John Kennedy cut taxes. That put an end to a recession and led to the longest peacetime economic expansion ever in this country. That's what the Democratic Party is about.

For a long time a lot of Democrats, and a lot of Democrats here today, have campaigned for cutting the food tax. I looked at doing that this year. But you know what I found? I found that my tax cut would mean even more tax relief for middle-class people and low-income people. That's what the Democratic Party is about.

When I was governor before, I cut personal income taxes. That's what the Democratic Party is about.

The fact is, we can have new ideas and, at the same time, be true to our historic principles as a party. That's what we've been doing as Democrats.

It was Democrats like Dan Blue who rescued this state during the 1991 budget crisis. The Executive Branch of state government had hit the snooze switch. It was Democrats who made the tough decisions that cut spending and still kept our commitments to education, and children, and health care, and economic development. That's what the Democratic Party is about.

It was Democrats, last year, who came up with a crime-fighting plan that is both tough and smart. We know that you can be for tough sentences for criminals and for programs that keep kids out of crime. We know that people deserve to live in safe communities. That's what the Democratic Party is about, and it will be Democrats this year who fight to give North Carolina's children a better start and a Smart Start. We ought to put children first this year in North Carolina, and that's what the Democratic Party is about.

I set out three goals in my State of the State speech: cut taxes, fight crime, and help children. That's what's good for the people of North Carolina, and that's what the Democratic Party ought to be about. When I hear a new idea for our state, I don't ask whether it's liberal, or conservative, or left, or right. I just want to know whether it moves North Carolina forward. That's the only difference I care about, and that's what the Democratic Party is about.

So let's stop worrying about labels. We Democrats know what it's like to be labeled, and we've fought against that kind of politics. Let's focus on people, not labels. Let's stop worrying about what happened last November. We got caught up in a national tide. I know what that's like. I've been there. And I know that we can come back. After I lost in 1984, Terry Sanford won the United States Senate race in 1986, and we will come back in 1996![1]

In fact, we can start our comeback before next year. There's a new election on March 28 for Elaine Marshall's state senate seat, and I want everybody here to either write her a check or find out what else you can do to help her win that election and keep that senate seat on the Democratic side.[2]

What we've got to do is put people first, and we've got to rebuild our party from the bottom up, from the precinct all the way up to the state headquarters. That's why I'm recommending that you elect Wayne McDevitt as our state party chairman. Wayne McDevitt has come up through the North Carolina Democratic Party. He started out as president of the Madison County Teen Dems, and if you know anything about mountain politics, you know what that means. He's been state president of the Young Democrats. He was statewide director of the party's coordinated campaign in 1982, and you know what a good year that was.[3]

He's been named one of the ten most outstanding young Democrats in America. He's been a precinct chair and a delegate to county, district, state, and national conventions. He's served on committees at every level, and he's worked for candidates at every level.

He's got the energy, and determination, and vision we need. He'll go to every county and work to revitalize every precinct. He'll be a listener, and he's already done a lot of listening to a lot of you around the state. He'll be a vigorous and outspoken leader. He'll speak up for our party and our principles. Wayne McDevitt is the kind of leader our party needs these next two years.

I know what the 1996 election means for the Democratic Party and for North Carolina, and I know that if we stand for the right principles; if we stand up for the people who work hard, and pay their taxes, and obey the law, and raise their families; and if we come together and build from the bottom up, and get people excited and involved, we will have a great year in 1996, and we will give North Carolina the leadership it deserves. So I ask you today to choose a chairman who will build our party and help us build our state's future. I ask you to elect Wayne McDevitt as the next chairman of the North Carolina Democratic Party.

---

[1] Seen by many as the Democrats' best hope to wrest from conservative Republican Jesse Helms the U.S. Senate seat he held since 1973, Hunt lost a close, brutal election campaign in 1984 by a 51 percent to 49 percent margin. Two years later, former governor Terry Sanford defeated incumbent senator Jim Broyhill to win an upper-house seat for the

Democrats. Luebke, *Tar Heel Politics 2000*, 37; *News and Observer*, November 5, 1986; see also William D. Snider, *Helms and Hunt: The North Carolina Senate Race, 1984* (Chapel Hill: University of North Carolina Press, 1985).

Terry Sanford (1917-1998), governor, 1961-1965; president, 1969-1985, and president emeritus, from 1985, Duke University; U.S. senator, 1986-1992; Democrat. Previously identified in Mitchell, *Addresses of Hunt*, I, 149n; see also *News and Observer*, April 19, 20, 21, 22, 23, 26, 1998.

[2] Incumbent Elaine Marshall lost her Fifteenth District senate seat to Republican challenger Dan Page by a mere seven votes in November 1994. His victory in the special election, the following March, narrowed the Democratic majority in the upper house to two.

Marshall's loss to Page did not signal the end of her political career, however. In 1996 she became the first woman elected to the North Carolina Council of State by defeating NASCAR driving legend Richard Petty in the race for secretary of state. That same year, Page was re-elected to the state senate; in 1998, he challenged incumbent Democrat Bob Etheridge to represent North Carolina's Second Congressional District. Page aired the first television advertisement in the country that attempted to saddle a political opponent with the Clinton-Lewinsky sex scandal—and lost heavily to Etheridge. *News and Observer*, March 27, 29, 30, 1995, November 4, 1998.

Elaine F. Marshall (1945-   ), born in Lineboro, Md.; resident of Harnett County; B.S., University of Maryland, 1968; J.D., Campbell University, 1981. Lenoir County schoolteacher, 1969-1970; instructor, Lenoir Community College and Johnston Technical Community College, 1970-1977; book and gift store co-owner, 1969-1974; owner-decorator, The Custom House, Dunn, 1975-1979; attorney in private practice, from 1981; member, state senate, 1993-1994; was elected secretary of state, 1996; Democrat. *North Carolina Manual, 1997-1998*, 171-172.

[3] Wayne McDevitt (1953-   ), native of Marshall; B.A., University of North Carolina at Asheville, 1975. Teacher, coach; regional manager, N.C. Dept. of Natural Resources and Community Development, 1977-1980; was attached to Western Governors Office, 1980-1984; special assistant to the chancellor, UNC-Asheville, 1984-1985; general manager, assoc. director, N.C. Arboretum, Asheville, 1986-1993; senior adviser to Gov. Hunt, 1993-1997; secretary, N.C. Dept. of Environment and Natural Resources, from 1997. Involvement with Democratic Party included president, N.C. Young Democrats, 1980-1981; director, N.C. Democratic Party Statewide Campaign, 1982; director, N.C. Campaign Fund, 1982-1983; chairman, CEO, N.C. Democratic Party, 1995-1996. *News and Observer*, March 5, 1995; *North Carolina Manual, 1997-1998*, 338-339.

BUDGET STATEMENT

RALEIGH, FEBRUARY 13, 1995

[For related press release, see Governor Hunt's Budget Holds Line on Spending, Saves $200 Million, Raleigh, February 13, 1995, Governors Papers, James Baxter Hunt Jr.]

Last week I set three goals for the General Assembly: cutting taxes, fighting crime, and, most importantly, helping children. Today I'm sending a budget to the legislature that shows we can afford to give working families tax relief, to build new prisons to protect our people, and to do more for children, especially with Smart Start. But it will require tough choices and new priorities.

This budget is my blueprint for those choices and priorities. First, we are holding the line on state spending. This budget virtually eliminates growth in state government—less than 1 percent growth from 1994-1995, down from 9 percent the year before and 12 percent the year before that.

Second, we are changing state government's priorities: cutting bureaucracy and middle management and putting our money in schools, early childhood, and other direct services. We can afford to cut taxes without hurting schools and children because revenue growth is strong, and because we've found $200 million in permanent savings, including $59 million in GPAC [Government Performance Audit Committee] recommendations. Every state agency will see an average 2 percent cut, including the Governor's Office. Some departments will cut mostly jobs, and some will cut virtually none. The agencies themselves have made these recommendations, involving front-line managers to help us find new ways to do a better job delivering services.

We're cutting $79 million by eliminating almost 2,000 state jobs and downsizing agencies. Of the 1,927 jobs to be cut, 565 are filled. Another 762 are vacant jobs, and 600 are from retirement and attrition. We've eliminated more than 400 middle management jobs and entire layers of management in our effort to flatten the organization.

Of course, we want to help good state employees find other jobs, when we can, in the private and public sector. The Office of State Personnel, the Employment Security Commission, and our Division of Employment and Training [have] formed a special partnership to offer more transitional services than ever before, and they'll be working closely with the state employees' association to help people find new jobs if they're available. I've directed my cabinet to give priority consideration to these employees for any vacant jobs.

You have a list of 171 specific savings we've found. We've cut $46 million by streamlining operations. We've eliminated another $5 million in programs. We've privatized and reduced costs to find another $12 million, and we've found other sources of revenue besides the General Fund, as GPAC recommends. We've found $17 million in federal funds, and we've shifted $7 million to the Highway Fund. All told, we've picked up $59 million in GPAC and state auditor recommendations. With the $31 million in GPAC savings from our last biennial budget, our GPAC total is $90 million now. Since the original GPAC savings estimate of $275 million was revised down to about $94 million, it looks like we've pretty much picked GPAC clean.

Here are some of the things we're doing to make state government work better:

—We're cutting $14 million from administrative overhead at DPI [Department of Public Instruction], recommending things like decentralizing textbook storage, consolidating regional technical assistance centers, and consolidating school planning. At the local level, we're cutting $2.5 million by recommending that school systems collapse funding categories for administrative positions and cut that by 5 percent.

—We're saving $2 million closing and consolidating regional offices as GPAC recommended.

—We're closing trade offices and shutting down the Energy Division in Commerce, and we're saving $90,000 by eliminating a marketing position at the Global TransPark.

—We're following the state auditor's recommendation to reduce medical costs for prisoners and following GPAC's recommendations to close down two prisons.

—We're streamlining Medicaid claims at the Department of Human Resources, working towards a "paperless" system to cut red tape.

—We're privatizing some child support collection to make sure we track down those deadbeat parents.

—In the Department of Administration, we're consolidating federal and state surplus property warehouses. We're consolidating mailrooms as GPAC recommended, consolidating office storage centers, and combining Motor Fleet and Auxiliary Services Divisions. Doing this can save us about $3 million.

—And we're doing commonsense things like reducing the flow of paper in state government. The budget office will review all internal and external forms and reports to save even more money by making sure we produce less paper in state government.

This is a good start, but we need to keep looking for ways to continue this effort to change the way state government works and to deliver services more efficiently.

Because of these cuts, savings, and efficiencies, we can achieve the goals I set out last week. We can provide a $483 million tax cut that helps working families and makes us more economically competitive. We can build the new prison beds we need to protect our people against dangerous criminals. We can cut class size in the first grade, put more teachers in public schools, boost workforce training in community colleges and support for enrollment and buildings at universities. We can provide a 2 percent salary increase for teachers and state employees, and we can expand Smart Start to twelve counties this year. Yes, this is an ambitious agenda, but if we make the cuts this budget proposes, we can achieve it.

ASSOCIATION OF CHAMBER OF COMMERCE EXECUTIVES

CHARLOTTE, FEBRUARY 20, 1995

[The following address is similar to those the governor delivered to a Leadership North Carolina class, February 23; business roundtables in Wilmington, February 27, Greenville, March 6, and Hickory, March 20; and the Mt. Airy Chamber of Commerce, April 7, 1995.]

I'm honored to be here, today, with so many of North Carolina's finest leaders. You represent the best of North Carolina—business, community, and volunteer leaders—and your work represents the best spirit of North Carolina. When I look around here, I see people working together for their communities. I see people from different regions, with different views, sharing a sense of optimism, can-do spirit, and community pride. I see partnerships being strengthened here, today, that will strengthen every community in our state tomorrow. Business, community, and volunteer leaders working as partners in every community will help us build a better economy, a better place to raise families, and a better future in North Carolina.

[I] want to tell you, as governor I take great heart in your work and in your optimism. I'm optimistic that we can build just as strong a partnership in Raleigh. Despite some predictions, I'm optimistic that Democrats and Republicans can work together as partners in the legislature to build a better future. I'm optimistic that we can develop a new approach for a new century.

There are three goals I believe the legislature should focus on this year: cutting taxes, fighting crime, and most importantly, helping children.

First, we ought to cut taxes because it's the right thing to do. It's the right thing to do for all the people who work hard, and raise families, and pay taxes in your communities. These families deserve to keep more of their money, and state government ought to get by with less.[1]

I've proposed a tax cut of nearly a half-billion dollars, the largest tax cut in our state's history. Three-fourths of it would go to individuals and families. Every individual that works [would] get [a] tax cut. We should raise the personal exemption for every member of a household by $500. We should create a tax credit of $50 per child.

This tax cut will give the most relief to the working people who deserve it the most. I'm happy to say that the state House, which has a Republican majority, has already passed it.

Cutting taxes is also the right thing to do for our economic future. That's why I've proposed cutting the corporate income tax to 7 percent and repealing the intangibles tax. Doing both this year will help business, and create jobs in your communities, and make our state even more attractive and competitive. I'm happy to say that the senate, with a Democratic majority, has already passed the intangibles tax repeal.

I do have to report to you today that a lot of legislators, Democrats and Republicans alike, are not convinced that we ought to cut the corporate income tax. They need to hear from you. They need to know what Peat Marwick's tax audit found and what you all know—that North Carolina's high corporate income tax rate hurts our competitive standing—and they need to remember the promise made to them [the business community] when the tax was raised [in] '91 during the budget crisis. Now that times are better, it's time to roll that tax back.[2]

The second goal the legislature should focus on this year is fighting crime, and fighting crime starts with tougher sentences for violent criminals. When a criminal is locked up behind bars, every North Carolinian is safer. So I'm asking the legislature to increase sentences for violent felonies, like second-degree murder, rape, [and] armed robbery, by 30 percent.[3] That means we'll need more prison space, so I'm proposing repealing the prison cap and building 2,000 new prison beds over the next two years—part of a plan to build 4,000 new beds in four years.[4]

I'm also proposing that we enact a victim's rights amendment to our state constitution. I believe if criminals have rights, victims of crime should have rights, too. I'm pleased that this is moving quickly through the General Assembly.

The third goal the legislature should focus on is helping children. We've got a big job to do there. We need to scrap the present welfare system and replace it with a system that requires work, protects children from poverty, and rewards personal responsibility. We need tougher child-support enforcement measures. We need to let deadbeat dads and moms know that, in North Carolina, we will insist that parents support their children.

We need to make fundamental changes in our schools. I've set out a comprehensive, commonsense plan that starts with restoring discipline in our schools, improving the quality of teaching, getting back to basics, setting higher standards, and improving job-training programs.[5] And we need to start earlier. We can't wait until children get to school, when too many of them are already programmed to fail.[6] That's why I'm pushing hard to expand Smart Start, our innovative early-childhood effort run by local public-private partnerships. Smart Start lets local people decide what their children need and lets local communities decide how to provide it. It's time Raleigh did a lot more listening and a lot less dictating to local communities.

This is an ambitious agenda for our state's future, but we can do it. We can do it if we've got the courage to change the way we do things, especially in state government.[7]

A week ago, I proposed a budget that includes the $483 million tax break. It includes more prisons and tougher prison sentences. It includes smaller classes and more local Smart Start partnerships, and it includes something you don't see in many government budgets. It includes a list of 171 specific cuts, savings, and efficiencies: $200 million worth of savings. It proposes abolishing nearly 2,000 state jobs that aren't needed, cutting out layers of middle management, doing away with programs that aren't needed, and even eliminating entire departmental bureaucracies that aren't needed.[8]

You all know that in businesses, cutbacks are never popular. But you also know that someone has to look at the bottom line to make sure we're doing what's right for our customers. Those are the tough choices that business makes every day. It's about time that state government did the same! This is not something we should do just one time and forget about it. This new way of doing business ought to replace business-as-usual in Raleigh!

But it won't be easy, because there are a lot of people in Raleigh who don't want change. They don't want us to cut taxes. They don't want us to build more prisons. They don't want us to change public education, and they don't want anything cut. They'll be in the legislature every day, and they'll put a lot of pressure on legislators who want to do the right thing.

Unfortunately the taxpayers, and the victims of crime, and the children won't be in the legislature every day. They don't have many lobbyists walking the halls for them. You and I have to be their lobbyists.

So this is the message I want to leave with you today: Change will not happen unless you help make it happen. You can be part of changing North Carolina. I urge you to do it. I urge you to make yourselves heard. I urge you to look hard at these issues, make up your own mind, and let your legislators know how you feel, and I hope you'll do it regardless of your political party. I hope you'll urge your legislators to do the same—to put people first and politics last, to debate important issues on their merits, to listen to each other, to learn from each other, and to find common ground.

Folks, I believe we can put politics and partisanship aside in this legislature, Democrats and Republicans together. We can change the way state government works, Democrats and Republicans together. We can build a better future for North Carolina, Democrats and Republicans together, and I urge you as chamber leaders throughout our state to help make it happen.[9]

---

[1] Hunt made a similar statement almost three weeks earlier: "Some people say we can't afford to cut taxes. They forget that it's the people's money, not the government's. I think the people need it more than the government does." N.C. Citizens for Business and Industry Legislative Forum, February 2, 1995, Governors Papers, James Baxter Hunt Jr.

[2] "Now, some people don't think we need a business tax cut. They say business taxes are low enough, and we don't need to do anything else," said Hunt at the N.C. Citizens for Business and Industry Legislative Forum. "They ought to do their homework, starting with the tax audit I commissioned last spring at the recommendation of the North Carolina Economic Development Board. Peat Marwick found our tax policies out of line with twenty competitor states. It called our corporate income and intangibles taxes 'red flags,' barriers for existing companies looking to expand and out-of-state companies looking to relocate. North Carolina's corporate tax rate is the fourth-highest in the Southeast. When the General Assembly raised that tax during tough economic times, business leaders believed it would be rolled back once times got better. That time is now."

Revisiting the topic minutes later, he said: "Finally, some people say we don't need to cut business taxes now. We can wait to pass tax cut legislation, they say. But they miss the point: North Carolina must send a signal now. We must take down those red flags and signal to business across the nation, and around the world, that North Carolina is doing everything we can to boost our business climate." N.C. Citizens for Business and Industry Legislative Forum, February 2, 1995, Governors Papers, James Baxter Hunt Jr.

[3] At this point in his text, Hunt jotted "Comes after special session: 3 strikes [you're] out; life w/o parole."

[4] "Prevention. I volunteer in SOS," the governor added in the space following this paragraph. He also wrote, "One [of] 3 states already elig[ible] to get fed[eral] matching funds."

[5] Near these lines, Hunt wrote in the righthand margin: "alter[native] schools, ed[ucation] boot camps, cut class size in ele[mentary] school. . . ."

[6] "Abuse—neglect," scribbled Hunt.

[7] "Emphasize," the governor noted next to this sentence.

[8] Here he added, "All areas but Corr[ections] and Schools—fewer number [of] employees. Cutting out one of nine cabinet dep[artmen]ts—$3 million. Inc[rease] in growth [of] gov[ernmen]t—less than 1 percent (from 9 percent to 12 percent)."

[9] In the left-hand margin next to this paragraph, Hunt gave himself delivery instructions: "slow" and "punch."

MILITARY BASE REALIGNMENT AND CLOSURE:
LETTER TO WILLIAM PERRY,
UNITED STATES SECRETARY OF DEFENSE

RALEIGH, FEBRUARY 22, 1995

[The decision of the Defense Base Closure and Realignment Commission (BRACC), in 1993, to transfer 160 F/A-18 Hornet jet fighter planes to Cherry Point Marine Corps Air Station, in Havelock, promised a tonic for a region of the state plagued by low per capita income and high unemployment. The aircraft reassignment would generate an estimated 5,000 military and civilian jobs and an annual payroll of $150 million. But as Havelock-area businesses, schools, and real estate developers joined with local and state officials to prepare a welcome for the Hornets, trouble brewed in neighboring Virginia.

F-14 Tomcat and A-6 Intruder aircraft stationed at Oceana Naval Air Station, Virginia Beach, were being phased out of operation. Tidewater Virginians believed the eventual departure of the planes made the military installation a vulnerable target during the 1995 round of BRACC deliberations. In 1994, they launched a concerted lobbying campaign to divert the Hornets from Havelock to save Oceana.

The Virginians' effort captured the attention of the Department of Defense: The transfer of the Hornets to Oceana made the list of proposed realignments and closures that Secretary William Perry announced on February 28, 1995. But it was the responsibility of BRACC, which began its final round of hearings on March 1, to determine where the F/A-18s would land. *Congressional Quarterly Almanac, 1995*, 9/19-22; *News and Observer*, February 23, 25, 28, March 1, 1995.]

Dear Mr. Secretary:

As your department finalizes its recommendations to the Base Realignment [and Closure] Commission, I want to emphasize the importance of North Carolina's military installations to our national defense. I urge you to follow the course set by the 1993 BRACC and to assure that any BRACC decisions be based on the military value of bases.

You will recall that the 1993 BRACC determined that when Cecil Field, Florida, closes, the navy wing should relocate to Cherry Point Marine Air Station, in Havelock, North Carolina. Since that time, North Carolina, Cherry Point, and the local governments in the area have been aggressively planning for that move. More than $25,000,000 has been spent in that effort. Though other states have tried to convince the Department of Defense that North Carolina is not and cannot be prepared for the receiving of these military personnel, their families, and the attendant population growth, that is not the case. North Carolina is fully prepared to give these fine citizens the same welcome that each of our military communities gives on a daily basis to men, women, and their families stationed at our military installations.

I am disturbed to read from press reports that Navy secretary John Dalton may have recommended to you that F/A-18 jets currently scheduled to go to Cherry Point may instead be transferred to Oceana Naval Air Station, in Virginia. This would be especially unfortunate if such a move was based solely on the recommendation of Virginia senator John Warner, as reported in the press, instead of on military value.[1]

The Marine Corps has done a fine job in planning for the improvements necessary on base at Cherry Point and at an outlying field. Everything is complete except the final environmental impact statement, but I am informed that it is only a matter of time before the statement is satisfactorily completed.

The local governments in a four-county area surrounding Havelock have been hard at work in planning the necessary infrastructure improvements to accommodate this most welcomed infusion of new people to that region. Bond issues for new schools were passed in the recent election; local realtors and builders are in the process of making the plans to add the housing necessary to accommodate these people, so that on-base housing will not be needed as a part of your investment.

Our state has allocated the necessary funds to do a massive and comprehensive water and sewer study, not only for those counties directly involved by the Cherry Point expansion, but also Onslow County, the home of Camp Lejeune. That study is well under way, and we believe that the fruits of that study will be beneficial, not only to the military families coming to the area, but also all citizens.

The North Carolina Department of Transportation has already done extensive transportation studies in the area, and we will expedite the completion of projects essential to adequately serve the transportation needs of Cherry Point and the surrounding area. The Aviation Division of that department is prepared to address air-space problems if they arise.

I am not aware of any weakness in the planning or implementation process which should cause you, the navy, or the Marine Corps any concern. If other states have raised questions that should be addressed, please contact me immediately so that we might address them before action is taken to change the 1993 BRACC action.

Thank you again for your continued support of the military installations in North Carolina and the families which make them the pride of our nation.

My warmest personal regards.

> Sincerely,
> Jim Hunt [signed]
> James B. Hunt Jr.

---

[1] John Howard Dalton (1941-   ), born in New Orleans, La.; resident of Washington, D.C.; B.S., U.S. Naval Academy, 1964; M.B.A., University of Pennsylvania, 1971; U.S. Navy, 1964-1969. Banker; president, Government National Mortgage Assn., 1977-1979; national treasurer, Carter/Mondale campaign, 1979; chair, member, Federal Home Loan Bank Board, 1979-1981; president, real estate division, Gill Cos., San Antonio, Texas, 1981-1984; chair, CEO, Freedom Capital Corp., and chair, president, Seguin Savings Assn., San Antonio, 1984-1988; secretary of the navy, from 1993; Democrat. *Who's Who in America, 1999*, s.v. "Dalton, John Howard."

John W. Warner (1927-), born in Washington, D.C.; resident of Middleburg, Va.; B.S., Washington and Lee University, 1949; LL.B., University of Virginia, 1953; U.S. Navy, 1944-1946; U.S. Marine Corps, 1950-1952. Attorney in private practice, 1954-1956, 1960-1969; assistant U.S. attorney, 1956-1960; undersecretary, 1969-1972, secretary, 1972-1974, U.S. Navy; director, American Revolution Bicentennial Commission, 1974-1976; elected to U.S. Senate from Virginia, 1978, returned in subsequent elections; was ranking Republican on Senate Armed Services Committee. Barone and Ujifusa, *Almanac of American Politics, 2000*, 1636-1637.

INDIAN UNITY CONFERENCE

FAYETTEVILLE, MARCH 17, 1995

For twenty years, the Indian citizens of our state have come together for the annual Indian Unity Conference to talk about issues affecting the Indian community, such as economic development, health, education, and political concerns. But the Indian Unity Conference provides an opportunity for all citizens to recognize the important contributions Native Americans have made to this state and this nation. Long before our industrial parks, our developed housing communities, our tourist attractions, and our commercial business districts, the Indians were here tending the land.

I am proud of the contributions Native Americans have made, especially to this state. Today, North Carolina has the largest Indian population east of the Mississippi River. There are over 80,000 Indians living in North Carolina in all 100 counties—six state-recognized tribes and one federally recognized tribe. And we have numerous community and business organizations working hard to improve the lives of Native Americans, such as the United Tribes of North Carolina and the North Carolina Commission of Indian Affairs.

The theme for this year's conference is especially fitting: "Our Past Guides Our Future." Because of the contributions Native Americans have made in the past, we are benefiting today and in the days ahead. People like David McCoy, Bruce Jones, Greg Richardson, Ronnie Sutton, Glenn Maynor, Jo Ann Locklear, Sammy Jacobs, and Ogletree Richardson have worked hard to improve the economy, the schools, and the quality of life for our Native American citizens.[1]

Our past is also guiding our future in the number of jobs, housing, and educational opportunities for Native Americans. There are many exciting things under way! Robeson County, Halifax County, and the city of Charlotte have been federally designated as rural enterprise communities. That means these areas will be getting several million dollars to help implement economic development strategies to benefit the Indian population in these regions.

The Indian Cultural Center, under planning and further development in Robeson County, will provide our state with a unique opportunity to showcase our rich Native American heritage and provide an economic boost for Indian citizens in Robeson County and the entire state. The Indian Housing Authority continues to provide affordable, low-income housing for Native Americans in our state, with plans to build twenty housing units each [in] Columbus and Warren Counties.

The Incentive Scholarship Program for Native Americans, passed by the General Assembly last year, will help finance the cost of a college education for more American Indians at our sixteen campuses within the UNC system.[2] Waccamaw-Siouan students in Columbus County schools are showing all of us what can be done with a little hard work: For the third straight year, these students have led all other races in reading test scores in the county. Our thanks to the county's Title V Indian Education program that provides full-time tutors and a highly involved Parent Committee.

And the North Carolina Commission of Indian Affairs will be using funding from an AmeriCorps planning grant to help us better utilize current resources among our state tribes and organizations for volunteer efforts in the community.

Native Americans are making some significant contributions that all of us are benefiting from in this state. You are using your strength in numbers, working together and working in unity. Together we can accomplish even greater things for the Native American community in North Carolina. Together let us pledge to continue these efforts and to find new ways to work as partners.

---

[1] David Timothy McCoy; enrolled member, Turtle Mountain Band of Chippewa Indians, Belcourt, N.D.; B.S., 1976, M.Ed., 1979, University of Georgia; master of public health, 1982, J.D., 1985, University of North Carolina at Chapel Hill. Director, Master of Public Health Program for American Indians, School of Public Health, University of North Carolina at Chapel Hill, 1985-1987; deputy director, N.C. Commission of Indian Affairs, 1987-1989; general counsel, 1989-1994, chief deputy secretary, 1995-1997, N.C. Dept. of Administration; deputy chief of staff, Office of the Governor, 1997-1999; acting secretary, May-June, 1999, secretary, from June 22, 1999, N.C. Department of Transportation; author. David Timothy McCoy, letter to Jan-Michael Poff, April 7, 1999; *News and Observer*, June 13, 22, 1999.

A. Bruce Jones (1929-   ), born in Buffalo, N.Y.; resident of Raleigh; B.S., Pembroke State University (later University of North Carolina at Pembroke), 1957; M.A., George Peabody College, 1964; U.S. Army, 1949-1952. Teacher, principal, Robeson County schools, 1957-1965; project field supervisor, 1965-1966, project director, 1966-1968, N.C. Fund Manpower Program; assistant operations director, 1968-1969, operations director, 1969-1973, N.C. Manpower Development Corp.; owner, operator, Western Auto Store, Hillsborough, 1973-1975; executive director, state Commission of Indian Affairs, 1976-1994. A. Bruce Jones, letter to Jan-Michael Poff, October 18, 1988; *News and Observer*, December 4, 1994.

Gregory A. Richardson (1951-), born in Halifax County; resident of Raleigh; A.A.S., King's Business College, 1978; B.S., St. Augustine's College, 1980; U.S. Army, 1971-1972. Career with N.C. Commission of Indian Affairs, N.C. Dept. of Administration, included assistant dir. of employment and training, 1975-1982; dir., Section 8 housing assistance program, 1982-1989; and executive director of the commission, from 1995. Executive director, N.C. Indian Housing Authority, 1989-1994; special assistant to the assistant secretary for public and Indian housing, U.S. Dept. of Housing and Urban Development, 1994-1995. Gregory A. Richardson, letter to Jan-Michael Poff, June 24, 1999.

Ronnie Neal Sutton; B.A., M.S., University of West Florida Naval War College; M.A., Central Michigan University, 1979; J.D., University of North Carolina, 1985; U.S. Air Force, 4 years; U.S. Navy, 22 years. Retired navy aviator; attorney; chairman, Robeson County Democratic Party, 1991; was elected to N.C. House, 1992, re-elected in 1994, 1996; member, House Subcommittee on Military, Veterans, and Indian Affairs. *North Carolina Manual, 1997-1998*, 700.

Glenn Allen Maynor (1946-), born in, resident of Lumberton; was educated at Fayetteville Technical College and UNC-Pembroke. Member, Lumberton City Council, 1975-1994; executive director, Robeson County Housing Authority, 1976-1994; Robeson County sheriff, from 1994. Glenn Allen Maynor, letter to Jan-Michael Poff, March 10, 1999.

Jo Ann Locklear (1945-), native of Lumberton; was educated in Robeson County public schools. Deputy clerk, 1966-1975, assistant clerk, 1975-1994, and clerk, from 1994, of Superior Court; chair, Robeson County Democratic Party, 1992-1993. Jo Ann Locklear, letter to Jan-Michael Poff, April 23, 1999.

Sammy Jacobs could not be identified.

Brucie Ogletree Richardson (1943-), born in Halifax County; resident of Warrenton; B.S., N.C. Wesleyan College, 1986; M.Ed., N.C. Central University, 1989; Ed.D., NOVA Southeastern University, 1999. Educator; counselor; supervisor, Franklin-Vance-Warren Opportunities, 1970-1973. Career with Warren County Schools included: K-12 librarian, 1964-1966; first-grade teacher, 1967-1968; Indian education home-school coordinator, 1974-1986; Title V Indian Education dir., 1986-1996; third-grade teacher, 1986-1991; preschool coordinator, 1989-1991, and from 1998; high school assistant principal, 1991-1996; and elementary school assistant principal, 1996-1998. Brucie Ogletree Richardson, letter to Jan-Michael Poff, April 23, 1999.

[2] *N.C. Session Laws, 1993, Extra and Regular Sessions, 1994*, c. 769, s. 17.3.

NORTH CAROLINA ASSOCIATION OF EDUCATORS

RALEIGH, MARCH 24, 1995

I'm happy to be here, today, with North Carolina teachers, the hardest-working people in our society today; and I'm happy to see a line from my own mission statement hanging in this hall: "Education is our future—it's everything." I've got it on a chart in my office in the Capitol, and I carry it on a little card in my pocket. I believe that with all my heart, and I know that you do, too.

You and I forged a partnership in 1992—a partnership for teaching; a partnership for better schools; a partnership for a better future for our children; a partnership for a better North Carolina. That partnership helped me get here, today. It's helped us make great progress for teachers and students in the last two years. Because of that partnership, I feel a sense of optimism and confidence about the future of our schools, and that partnership is vital in this legislative session.

Just this week, your representatives have been fighting a very tough battle against people who want to repeal the teacher tenure law.[1] I want to say to you, very clearly and very strongly, I oppose repealing that law! It's not about protecting bad teachers. As Jay Robinson says, a good principal and a good superintendent can fire a bad teacher today.[2] It's about protecting good teachers—protecting good teachers against political, arbitrary, and capricious firings and personnel actions. The way to build better schools is not to punish teachers, but to give teachers the support you need to do your job.

I'm committed to fighting with you and the NCAE [North Carolina Association of Educators] leaders to make sure teachers get that support. In the last two years, I've spent a lot of time in classrooms, and I've spent a lot of time listening to teachers; to your leaders, to Cecil Banks,[3] Rose Marie Lowry-Townsend, and your lobbyist, John Wilson;[4] to the classroom teachers who make up my Teacher Advisory Committee, including eleven NCAE members; to my teacher adviser, Karen Garr; and to hundreds of classroom teachers at teacher town meetings across the state. There's no doubt in my mind, North Carolinians are committed to their public schools. What they want, and what we need, is a commonsense plan that sets clear goals—a plan that works. That's the approach teachers tell me they want, and that's the approach we're taking in this administration.

With teachers' help, I've developed a five-part agenda for change in the public schools. It's a commonsense plan that works, an approach that teachers tell me they want. It doesn't rely on gimmicks or silver bullets. It requires steady work and sustained commitment, not quick fixes. It's not teacher bashing and public-school bashing.

The first thing we must do is give teachers the tools they need to do their jobs. You and I know the secret to good schools: It's good teachers. We've got great teachers in North Carolina. We can make the quality of teaching what it needs to be, and we can recruit, and train, and keep good teachers. But we've got to train teachers as professionals, treat them as professionals, and pay them like professionals.

Teachers tell me they need better training, more time for planning, and more voice in how schools are run. That's why we need the Teachers' Academy; real duty-free periods; site-based decision making; National Board[5] certification, and financial rewards for teachers who meet this strenuous challenge. We've made great progress in these areas. We must not let that progress be eroded.

Teachers need better pay. I know salaries aren't where they need to be. Despite the great gains we've made in the last two years, we have a long ways to go. I've proposed what amounts to a 3 percent salary increase. We need to keep working at it, and we will.

Second, we must restore discipline and make our schools safe places to learn and teach. You can't teach in schools that are unsafe and [in] classrooms that are disruptive. You need more support to keep schools safe, more school resource officers on campuses—it means zero tolerance for guns, drugs, and weapons, and zero tolerance for students who put others in danger. We should automatically expel those students for up to a full year. But don't put them on the streets. Put them in alternative schools, or even in education boot camps, where they learn to read, and write, and do math, and do what they're told.

Third, we must go back to basics, emphasizing reading, writing, and math. That means cutting class size, and I propose doing that in my budget.

Fourth, we must set higher standards for what our students should know, and be able to do, so they graduate with the skills they need to be good workers and good citizens. The Education Standards and Accountability Commission [that] I set up two years ago is doing just that. Teachers are part of this effort, serving on the commission and working through my Teacher Advisory Committee, and there are 120 teachers working in the pilot projects. We've identified the basic skills that students must master, and by the year 2000, a high-school diploma will guarantee that a student has mastered these skills.

Fifth, we must do more to get young children ready for school. You know what happens when kids start school and they're not ready to learn, or they're behind because they haven't had the kind of love, and help, and care they need. You inherit those problems, and you're somehow expected to fix them.

That's what Smart Start is about. The NCAE has been a strong supporter of Smart Start, and I appreciate that support. Your entire board was at the legislative hearing, this week. Smart Start needs your help now, more than ever before. Its future is at stake. Its opponents do not want it to move forward. But I am determined, and people all over this state are determined, that we've got to make a commitment in this legislature to do more, not less, for North Carolina's children and North Carolina's future.

We need to build an even stronger partnership to fight for Smart Start, and public schools, and children, and changing the future of North Carolina! We've got to get our priorities right in North Carolina. We've got to get our priorities right in our schools. We need to give teachers more voice and more say. We need to give you more support. Parents and families need to get more involved. Principals, superintendents, school board members, legislators, and yes, governors need to do more.

I learned a lot in the eight years I was out of office. I learned a lot about why education reforms haven't worked. I learned a lot about what it takes to be a good teacher. I learned to listen to teachers, and that's something I try to keep doing.

You all have taught me a lot, and I'm going to keep on listening to you and learning from you, and I'm going to keep on working with you—working for public schools and teachers; working for fair treatment, and high standards, and professional respect for teachers. Make no mistake about it, you have a governor who believes in teachers, who believes in public schools, and who will fight for both! You and I are working together to build our state and build a better future. I thank you for what you do, and I'm proud to stand, and work, and fight alongside you.

---

[1] Although it did not pass the House, H.B. 210, "A Bill to be Entitled an Act to Phase Out Teacher Tenure," was folded into a legislative study of "teacher tenure, performance evaluation, and incentives." *N.C. House Journal, 1995,* 124, 6730, 722; *N.C. Session Laws, 1995,* c. 542, s. 2.1(7e).

[2] Jay M. Robinson (1928-   ), native of Mitchell County; B.S., Appalachian State University, 1950; M.A., University of North Carolina at Chapel Hill, 1957; Ed.D., Duke University, 1976; U.S. Army Air Force, 1946-1948. Educator; superintendent, Cabarrus County Schools, 1965-1977, and of Charlotte-Mecklenburg Schools, 1977-1986; served as vice-president for public affairs and as vice-president for special projects, University of North Carolina General Administration, 1986-1993; as chairman, State Board of Education, 1993-1997, he played a major role in reorganizing the Department of Public Instruction, 1995, and in creating and implementing the ABCs of Public Education school reform program. *News and Observer,* September 24, 1993, March 15, October 3, 1997, August 20, 1999; Poff and Crow, *Addresses of Hunt, 1981-1985,* 431n.

[3] Cecil Banks was president, North Carolina Association of Educators, in 1995. *News and Observer,* January 25, 1995.

[4] John Wilson; former teacher, Daniels Middle School, Raleigh; president, in early 1980s, chief lobbyist, and executive director, from July 1, 1995, North Carolina Association of Educators. *News and Observer,* February 17, May 27, 1995.

[5] National Board for Professional Teaching Standards.

GREATER RALEIGH CHAMBER OF COMMERCE

RALEIGH, MARCH 27, 1995

[Hunt delivered a speech, similar to the one reprinted below, to the N.C. Restaurant Association, June 26, 1995. For related press release, see Governor Hunt Unveils Welfare Reform Plan, Raleigh, March 27, 1995, Governors Papers, James Baxter Hunt Jr.]

I'm happy to be here and talk to you today about my proposal to reform our state's welfare system. I can sum it up in a few words: work and personal responsibility. Work is the foundation of our society. It builds our economy, but it builds much more than that. Work builds our self-esteem, self-confidence, and our skills. Work helps us provide for our families. Work connects us to our communities. Most of all, work builds responsibility and a sense of pride.

Work should be the foundation of our welfare system, as well. We need a system that encourages people to move from welfare to work; a system that helps people get the skill training they need to get decent jobs; a system that rewards work and encourages families to stay together; a system that encourages independence and self-sufficiency. But what we have is a welfare system that's broken: a system that penalizes welfare recipients for saving money, for holding a job that pays decent wages, and even for encouraging their children to save money for college; a system that traps people into a cycle of dependency. Welfare was meant to be a way to help families get back on their feet, not a way of life.

Back in September, I appointed a welfare reform task force, with employers, educators, social workers, state legislators, a noted economist, and a number of welfare clients. I charged this group with developing a blueprint for change, focusing on the principles of work and personal responsibility. As the task force found at public hearings across the state, many welfare recipients want to stand on their own. They want to work and feel the pride of self-sufficiency. That's what Work First is all about.

Work First will revamp North Carolina's welfare system and replace the JOBS [Job Opportunities and Basic Skills] program. It will put people to work, require personal responsibility, and protect children from poverty. Work First will demand and reward work, not punish those who go to work. If people need child care or job skills in order to work, we'll help them get it. But within two years, anyone who can work must get a job.

We'll require welfare recipients with school-aged children to work at least thirty hours a week. Within twelve weeks of getting your first AFDC [Aid to Families with Dependent Children] check, you must find work. If you can't find a private-sector job, you must be in job training and work in the public sector without pay. You must earn welfare benefits, even if you don't earn a salary.

Work First sets limits: off welfare within two years. It also sets limits on the number of children served—no additional cash benefits for any child born ten months after the mother has gone on welfare. The biggest barrier to work for most welfare mothers is child care and job training, so Work First will help provide that.

But Work First requires more than work. It also requires personal responsibility. Every single person on welfare in this state will have to sign a personal responsibility contract. Every single person will have to live up to that contract or be cut off welfare. Signing this contract is a promise: a promise not to have more children while on welfare; a promise to immunize your children; a promise to stay in school and live at home, if you're a teen parent; a promise to make a plan to get off welfare, and to stick to that plan. If you break your contract, we cut off your welfare. That's a promise.

Welfare reform should also discourage teen pregnancy and promote responsible parenting. We must discourage irresponsible behavior that lands people on welfare in the first place, with a concerted effort against teen pregnancy that lets young people know it is wrong to have a child outside marriage. At the same time, we must discourage teen mothers from having more children. We know that a teen mother who puts off that second child and graduates from high school has a better chance to succeed on her own and to escape the trap of welfare dependency. That's why I've asked the legislature to provide $1.5 million to expand our Adolescent Parenting Program. In twenty-four counties, this program is working with teens who've had one child so they don't have another, counseling them about abstinence and encouraging them to stay in school. We've decreased dramatically the number of teens with second pregnancies, and we've increased dramatically the number of teen mothers who graduate from high school. I want to see these kinds of results in every county across this state.

Personal responsibility also means taking responsibility for your children, but there are thousands of deadbeat parents out there who refuse to support their children. Too often, taxpayers are forced to pick up the tab for a parent's neglect. It's not just welfare families that need help with child support. Too many families can't get the child support the courts have awarded them—like the housekeeper in northeastern North Carolina who's been trying for seven years to collect back child-support for her young son. The boy's father, a lawyer who's moved from state to state, owes almost $10,000.

We've got to go after deadbeat dads—and moms. We owe it to single mothers to see that fathers meet their obligations, and we'll do whatever it takes. We are going to see that parents support their children in North Carolina.

We're now drafting a tough child-support enforcement bill, one of the toughest in the country. I will urge the legislature to pass it. This will let us take away deadbeat parents' driver's licenses, their hunting and fishing licenses, their professional and business licenses. We'll go after deadbeat doctors, dentists, lawyers, and other professionals. We'll deny them new vehicle permits. We'll track them down across state lines. We'll track them down in ways they've never dreamed of. We'll even put their faces on wanted posters! I want posters like this all over the state. I want the names and faces of the "Ten Most Wanted" deadbeat parents posted in every store, library, and public place in the state. In Georgia, this poster helped track down seven of their ten worst deadbeat parents. More importantly, it helped Georgia collect more than $32,000 in child support. I want to send a clear signal: We demand that parents in North Carolina take responsibility for their children.

Putting work first, requiring personal responsibility, preventing teen pregnancy, cracking down on deadbeat parents: These are the kinds of things we need to do in North Carolina if we want to reform our welfare system. It won't be easy. It won't be a quick fix, and it won't be without some costs, but we cannot afford the status quo.

We cannot afford partisan politicking, either. Welfare reform is not a partisan issue. I believe there is a great deal of common ground between Republicans and Democrats on welfare reform, and I am working with legislators of both parties to craft a compromise approach. Together, we can hammer out a welfare reform plan that is tough but compassionate. Together, we can move people from welfare to work without hurting children. Together, we can make the welfare system work again.

Attachment/Handout: North Carolina Work First[1]

Work First is Governor Jim Hunt's welfare reform effort, revamping the state's welfare system to require work and personal responsibility— moving people from welfare to work. The governor's plan puts people to work, imposes strict time limits on benefits and tough sanctions on those who refuse to participate in the Work First program. It eases re-entry to the job market through job training and temporary help with child-care and health-care costs. It streamlines the welfare system through a shorter, simpler application.

Work First is the centerpiece of Governor Hunt's welfare reform package, which also includes cracking down on parents who refuse to support their children, expanding the state's teenage pregnancy prevention programs, and encouraging abstinence.

Work First will impact an estimated 120,000 parents who qualify annually for Aid to Families with Dependent Children (AFDC) in North Carolina. All welfare recipients will be required to develop a detailed plan for how they will move off the welfare rolls. They must sign a contract agreeing to stick to the plan before receiving benefits. Benefits end if they break the contract.

Work First gets people into the workforce early, then motivates them to move toward self-sufficiency. It replaces the JOBS [Job Opportunities and Basic Skills] program, which put more emphasis on training and less on work. Work First requires results, commitment, and sets a time limit for benefits.

The work and training requirements of Work First will be phased in. Because of fiscal constraints, about 30 percent of AFDC recipients will be included in the work requirement the first year. In this first phase, 35,000 parents of school-aged children will be required to get a job within two years (8,000 more than are currently enrolled in the JOBS program). Parents will get help with child-care and health-care expenses if they need it. County department of social services directors will choose the parents to be included in the first phase.

As parents in the first phase find jobs, resources will be freed up to include the remaining 29,000 parents with school-aged children in Work First's work requirement. Work First ultimately will require all AFDC recipients to work, except older adults over 65 and people with significant disabilities. Mothers of preschool children will move into jobs as funding becomes available or their children start school, whichever comes first. They will be required to participate in family literacy programs until they begin the program's work requirement.

No new dollars are required for Work First. Funds from the JOBS program ($50 million) will be redirected to Work First. Another $109 million will be used for child-care and other program costs. These funds are already available in federal, state, and county budgets.

Key Provisions

Work First means work first! Within twelve weeks after people begin receiving AFDC, they must have a job or perform community service work while in job training. Following are the program's key provisions:

Personal Responsibility Contract: Welfare recipients must sign contracts detailing how they will move off welfare rolls. Parents of preschoolers must agree to keep their children properly immunized. Teen parents must agree to stay in school and graduate. Teen parents under 16 must live with their parents or under approved supervision. *(Waiver required from federal government.)*

Emergency Grants: A one-time emergency grant of up to three months' cash benefits will be available to help see families through a temporary emergency that threatens their ability to be self-sufficient. The goal is to keep people off the welfare rolls from the beginning. The grant must be repaid if the parent goes on AFDC. *(Waiver required from federal government.)*

Sanctions: Benefits will be denied to any AFDC applicant or current recipient who fails to sign a personal responsibility contract. An initial contract violation will result in terminating the parent's AFDC and Medicaid benefits, but will not affect food stamps. A subsequent sanction will result in ending the entire family's AFDC benefits. Parents whose benefits end because of contract violations cannot reapply for assistance for six months. *(Waivers required from federal government.)*

Time Limit: AFDC benefits are limited to two years from the time recipients enter the work program. People who have exhausted their time limit cannot reapply for assistance for three years. *(Waivers required from federal government.)*

Family Cap: No additional AFDC cash benefits will be provided for children born after the parent has been on welfare for ten months. *(Waiver required from federal government.)*

Teen Pregnancy Prevention: Expand the state's teenage pregnancy prevention program. Increase efforts to prevent subsequent pregnancies and encourage teen mothers to finish high school. Conduct statewide pregnancy prevention campaigns.

Child Care and Health Care: Help with child-care and health-care expenses will be available for parents in Work First's work and training component. Temporary help will be available for up to eighteen months once welfare recipients earn enough income to move them off AFDC benefits. Temporary help for eighteen months will also be available for those who gain full-time work by the end of their two-year time limit.

Assets: The cap on savings will be raised to $3,000 and on the cash value of a car to $4,500, so participants can have reasonable savings and dependable transportation. *(Waivers required from federal government.)*[2]

Marriage: Families with both parents living together will no longer be penalized. They will be eligible for the same benefits as single parents. *(Waiver required from federal government.)*

---

[1] Most of the proposed Work First provisions listed in this handout required federal waivers to be enacted. They were granted early in 1996. Press release, Governor Hunt Gets Federal Waivers for Work First, Washington, D.C., February 5, 1996, and attachment thereto, Work First: Federal Waivers Approved, Governors Papers, James Baxter Hunt Jr.

[2] The proposed motor vehicle cash value had increased to $5,000 by September 1995 and was approved at that level the following February. Attachment to press release, Governor Hunt Launches Work First Welfare Program, Raleigh, September 14, 1995; attachment to press release, Governor Hunt Gets Federal Waivers for Work First, Washington, February 5, 1996, Governors Papers, James Baxter Hunt Jr.

NORTH CAROLINA LAW ENFORCEMENT ASSOCIATION

RALEIGH, MARCH 27, 1995

I'm proud to be here with some of North Carolina's finest law enforcement officers. The citizens of this state owe you a great debt—for our peace of mind, for the safety of our families, and for the safety of our communities. Your job is to protect the people of this state, and **you do an outstanding job.** You and your officers put yourselves on the line every day, and I want you to know how much we appreciate your hard work and dedication. On behalf of the citizens of this state, I want to thank you.

My job is to help you do your job and to give you the tools you need for your daily fight against crime. We made a good start in last year's crime session. With your help, we convinced the General Assembly to lengthen sentences for dangerous criminals, toughen gun laws, and increase prison capacity. We launched new efforts to deter youngsters from crime and began looking at tougher punishment for young criminals. We boosted support for crime victims and drug and alcohol treatment, and we began developing a statewide criminal justice information system.

But we have more to do in this legislative session. First, we need to make sure that when you arrest a criminal, he stays behind bars. That's why I'm proposing that we increase, by 30 percent, sentences for violent crimes, like second-degree murder, rape, armed robbery, and other felonies; and we must make sure that those who assault law enforcement officers get the punishment they deserve. I'm proposing that assault on a law enforcement officer with a deadly weapon be upgraded to a violent felony.[1] That means our Three Strikes law will apply—and that anyone who assaults a law enforcement officer will pay the price.

To stop the revolving door, we need more prison space, and we need to repeal the prison cap. My plan is to build 4,000 prison beds over the next four years and to find faster and cheaper ways to do it.

I believe we need a law requiring registration of sex offenders and notifying communities where they live—and I believe we should pass a Victims Rights Amendment to our state constitution. If criminals have rights, victims of crime should have rights, too.

All of these measures are moving quickly through the General Assembly, and I'm confident that they'll be passed into law this year.

Tougher laws are a first step, but my administration has worked just as hard to help law enforcement officers through the Governor's Crime Commission. In our first two years, my crime commission has awarded nearly $10 million in federal grant money to law enforcement agencies for things like multi-county drug task forces and major-crime investigative units. This week, we're awarding some $7 million more in grants to local law enforcement agencies, including support for school resource officers, community-oriented policing projects, and automated fingerprint identification systems.[2] Safe schools and community policing are priorities in this administration. We've provided more than $5 million for SRO's so far, we've created a community-oriented policing center, and we've set up a Center for Prevention of School Violence to help your communities make their classrooms safer.

I'm especially proud of the crime commission's support for automated fingerprint ID systems. There are now such systems in every urban area of the state, and we have plans to ensure every department access to the system in their area. You know how critical this is for computerized records and reporting systems, for child abuse and gang investigators, for dangerous offender units that target violent criminals and put offenders on a fast track for prosecution and prison.

The Governor's Crime Commission's job is to help you. That means we need to hear from you. The police chiefs and sheriffs on the commission are a vital link to frontline law enforcement. But we want to know what every law enforcement officer in this state thinks. Bill Pittman, the new director of the crime commission and a former DA, is going to be setting up law enforcement forums across the state to find out what we can do to help police officers, sheriff's deputies, and other law enforcement officers. We need your input, so please call Bill at [number] to share your thoughts.[3]

One of the things we are doing is eliminating an entire layer of bureaucracy in our state's crime-fighting effort. As part of my plan to reorganize the Department of Crime Control and Public Safety, we're abolishing thirty-seven administrative jobs here in Raleigh—and bringing the individual law enforcement officer closer to the governor. My goal in reorganizing [the] department is to cut bureaucracy, putting the money where it counts: in the frontline fight against crime. We would cut no services or law enforcement manpower. But we would save $3 million, $1 million more [than] the Government Performance Audit Committee thought when it recommended this move a few years ago.[4]

My reorganization plan would shift public safety and crime prevention agencies to four other state agencies, keeping those services intact:

—The Highway Patrol, Emergency Management, the National Guard, Civil Air Patrol, and the crime commission would report directly to me.

—ALE [Division of Alcohol Law Enforcement] and the Crime Prevention Division would be moved to the Department of Justice, under Attorney General Easley.

—Victim and Justice Services would be moved to the Department of Correction, under Secretary Franklin Freeman.[5]

Our goal is to fight crime with fewer bureaucrats, with more support for frontline law enforcement officers. I hope you'll support this effort and that you'll let your legislators know that you support it.

The fight against crime is not a partisan one. I'm optimistic that there is a great deal of common ground between Democrats and Republicans in the legislature for providing you with the tools you need in your frontline fight against crime. Together, we can build a safer North Carolina.

---

[1] *N.C. Session Laws, 1995*, II, c. 507, sec. 19.5.

[2] See press releases, Hunt Announces Grants for Local Crime Prevention Efforts, Raleigh, March 28, 1995, and North Carolina's Crime Commission to Focus on Safe Schools, Helping Cops, Raleigh, May 22, 1995, Governors Papers, James Baxter Hunt Jr.

[3] Bill Pittman; B.S., University of North Carolina at Chapel Hill; law degree from N.C. Central University; U.S. Air Force veteran. Attorney; newspaper reporter; magazine editor; founder, Southern Strategies political consulting and lobbying firm; special assistant, N.C. Dept. of Crime Control and Public Safety, 1979-1981; administrator, Wake County District Attorney's Office, assistant district attorney for Wake County, 1987-1993; was partner in Bass, Bryant and Moore law firm, Raleigh, before joining the Hunt administration in 1994 as associate general counsel to the governor; executive director, Governor's Crime Commission, February-November 1995; became legal counsel to Hunt on January 1, 1996. Press release, Governor Hunt Announces Staff Changes, Raleigh, December 27, 1995, Governors Papers, James Baxter Hunt Jr.

[4] Hunt initially opposed the 1993 GPAC recommendation to abolish the Department of Crime Control and Public Safety, an agency established during his first administration. But by 1995, he "became convinced that the GPAC proposal would cut unnecessary bureaucracy and provide millions more for prisons, to keep criminals behind bars." Defending the governor's plan to eliminate the agency, Press Secretary Rachel Perry observed, "'The last time I checked, none of the thirty-seven bureaucrats who are losing their jobs caught any criminals in the last two years. The reorganization does away with a layer of bureaucracy and streamlines the communication between the public safety agencies and the governor.'" Press release, Governor Hunt's Reorganization Cuts Costs, Not Services, Raleigh, February 16, 1995, Governors Papers, James Baxter Hunt Jr.; see also *Our State, Our Future: Report of the North Carolina Government Performance Audit Committee*, 16-17.

Democratic and Republican lawmakers naturally differed over the fate of Crime Control and Public Safety. The budget plan adopted by the Democrat-held senate proposed eliminating the agency, while that approved by the GOP-led House retained it. The compromise budget reached by House and senate negotiators, and ultimately passed by the General Assembly, kept the agency intact.

Republicans defended CC&PS for two reasons. Eliminating the agency, first, would give the impression they had "gone soft on crime by cutting a department named Crime Control." Second, the proposal placed the National Guard and Highway Patrol under the governor; senate minority leader Betsy Cochrane spoke for many GOP legislators when she said, "'We are very concerned about politicizing what is supposed to be law enforcement.'" *News and Observer*, March 10, April 27, May 19, June 23, 25, August 12, 1995.

[5] The reorganization plan proposed melding the Division of Victim and Justice Services with the Division of Adult Probation and Parole, within the Correction Department, thus "eliminating a layer of middle management and saving another $1 million." Press release, Governor Hunt's Crime Control and Public Safety Reorganization Cuts Costs, Not Services, February 16, 1995.

COASTAL AGENDA

Jacksonville, March 31, 1995

Our coast is important to all of us. Whether you live here, work here, or just visit, North Carolina's coast is truly special. Today we must act to preserve this special area for future generations.

Last September I accepted the report from the Coastal Futures Committee on ways we can improve coastal management. At that time, I made a personal commitment to do everything I could to move ahead on accepting the CFC's recommendations. In November I made a similar commitment when I accepted and signed the management plan produced by the Albemarle-Pamlico Estuarine Study. Today I'm here to make good on those commitments—to endorse a comprehensive action agenda that will preserve, protect, and restore North Carolina's precious coastal resources—and I'm asking you to commit to this cause, as well.

I expect this agenda to become the backbone of our coastal protection efforts. Many people—folks like Rich Preyer who care deeply about North Carolina's environment—spent a great deal of time and energy studying our coast and making sound recommendations. The studies are done. It's time to quit studying. It's time to move beyond rhetoric into action. It's time to roll up our sleeves and get to work on bettering our coast.

You will be [the] workhorses in that effort. The Coastal Resources, Marine Fisheries, and Environmental Management Commissions all play critical roles in protecting our coastal resources and will all be called upon to provide leadership in developing new programs and improving existing ones—and all of us here today are going to have to be fully committed to this cause. I'm counting on all of you.

There are four basic goals of my coastal agenda that I want to talk with you about today: protecting and improving water quality, protecting and restoring natural areas and vital habitats, strengthening the state and local partnership to improve coastal management, and protecting and restoring marine fisheries.

First, we must protect and improve water quality—and we must realize that coastal water problems don't begin here. They may originate well upstream. We must take a comprehensive approach to all sources of pollution. To do that, we must strengthen basinwide planning. We must also reduce nonpoint source pollution and restore degraded waters. My budget underlines that commitment by providing $1.3 million to improve DEM's [Division of Environmental Management] basinwide planning database and adding eighteen new positions to deal with nonpoint pollution.

To improve water quality, we must adopt a new supplemental classification for the restoration of degraded waters. Today I'm recommending that the Environmental Management Commission move quickly to establish a classification called use restoration water, or URW, and that the South River in Carteret County be the first URW river in the state.

We must also strengthen our enforcement program for nonpoint pollution—the runoff from fields, roads, development, and other areas. I've provided substantial funding in my proposed budget to begin that effort in a major way. If all of these studies have shown one thing, it is that nonpoint source pollution is a major problem that has not been addressed in our coastal region. I know that farmers and foresters want to do the right thing. I want to help them do the right thing, in the right way.

Second, we must protect and restore natural areas and vital habitats. We've already lost a great deal of our coastal natural heritage. We can't afford to lose any more, and we will if we don't move quickly.

We must make a concerted effort to protect and acquire critical natural areas. That means expanding the coastal and estuarine reserves, amending the conservation tax credit to provide greater incentives for private conservation efforts, and developing policies that make it easier for the state to accept donations of special lands.

We must also realize the vital role that wetlands play in protecting water quality, providing wildlife habitat, and supporting our marine fisheries. We know that we've already lost more than a third of our wetlands, much of that in the last half of this century. Today we've got to commit to restore and enhance wetlands like never before. That's why I want us to establish a wetlands bank that receives funds from parties who are permitted to fill wetlands but must offset that damage. Money from that fund would be used by DEM to carry out wetlands mitigation. We talk about improving efficiency and effectiveness in state government, while at the same time promoting a good environment. A wetlands banking program embodies that rhetoric.

Third, we must strengthen the state and local partnership to improve coastal management. That means improving CAMA [Coastal Area Management Act] land-use planning so that it is relevant. To do that, we've got to provide technical assistance to local governments as they embark on the land-use planning process. My budget recommends seven new division positions to assist local governments and another $500,000 in pass-through grants to local governments for this type of assistance.

Finally, we must protect and restore marine fisheries. We don't currently have a lot of bragging rights where marine fisheries are concerned. Of the twenty-nine major fisheries stocks in North Carolina, seventeen are in trouble. I see Bruce Freeman here today.[1] Bruce has only been on the job about ten days, but I'm counting on him to spearhead this effort. I've committed $4 million in my budget to improving marine fisheries operations, but we've got to go beyond that commitment.

We've got to develop policies that address the myriad of problems facing our marine fisheries resource. I'm counting on the Marine Fisheries Commission to use the time we've gained by instituting a commercial licensing moratorium to develop a comprehensive fisheries management program. We cannot continue to bicker and whine about fisheries. We've got to do something constructive, and we've got to work together.

I've talked a lot about commitment today—commitment to our coast. I'm asking every one of you to commit to making a difference on the North Carolina coast. It's going to take backbone. Nowhere is that more evident than in the case of marine fisheries. For too long we've chosen to take the expedient path when it came to our marine fisheries resource. We've gone where there was the least resistance rather than making the right decisions.

I'm here this morning to tell you that I expect you to make the right decisions. You should be listening to the citizens of this state who view a healthy coastal environment as their birthright. We're just five years away from a new century. We want the citizens of the twenty-first century, our grandchildren and their children, to enjoy the coast that we've taken for granted. This coastal agenda is the blueprint for achieving that goal. We must act now to preserve, protect, and restore our coast. We can afford to do no less.

---

[1] Bruce Freeman, former fisheries manager, state of New Jersey; director, N.C. Division of Marine Fisheries, from 1995. *News and Observer*, February 26, 1995.

MEDIA ADVISORY:
LAKE GASTON PIPELINE SETTLEMENT PROPOSAL

Raleigh, April 6, 1995

[Straddling the North Carolina-Virginia border, Lake Gaston was completed in 1962 as part of a Virginia Electric Power Company hydroelectric project that dammed the Roanoke River. The lake presented a tempting target to rapidly growing but water-starved Virginia Beach. In January 1984, the city received a permit from the U.S. Army Corps of Engineers to build an 85-mile-long pipeline across southeastern Virginia to the lake, from which it wanted to draw 60 million gallons of water a day.

Opponents from northeastern North Carolina and southside Virginia warned that the drawdown of water by the pipeline would damage the environment and siphon away economic opportunity. The state of North Carolina and the Roanoke River Basin Association quickly went to court to block the project. During the ensuing decade, as the city of Virginia Beach prevailed in one lawsuit after another, North Carolina officials found new legal challenges to delay the pipeline's completion.

North Carolina seemed unable to land a knockout punch in its war of attrition against Virginia Beach. The city, which instituted strict water usage policies in 1992, had spent large sums of money defending itself in court and was anxious to stop litigating and start laying pipe. In December 1994, the two sides began meeting with federal mediators to find a solution.

The proposed pipeline settlement, announced April 6, 1995 (and reprinted below), did not please everyone. Cities and towns in the Roanoke River basin feared it would negatively affect economic development. The city of Norfolk opposed the ban on its future sale of pipeline water outside southeastern Virginia. Negotiators amended the settlement by extending the deadline for legislative approval to June 30; allowing Norfolk to sell Lake Gaston water to Newport News, beginning in 2010; and charging Virginia Beach 10 cents per each 1,000 gallons of water it withdrew from Lake Gaston. Virginia and North Carolina were to divide the money equally, with most of North Carolina's $1.1 million annual share slated to fund economic development in the northeastern counties.

Before it could go into effect, the settlement required approval by the Virginia legislature, then the North Carolina General Assembly, and finally Congress. Governor George Allen agreed to call Virginia lawmakers into special session for that purpose—if they promised to limit the session to the pipeline and gave him a firm adjournment date. They did not, and the June 30 deadline passed without any action taken by the Old Dominion. An irritated Hunt declared, "We've worked hard to draft a compact that would have guaranteed the protection of Lake Gaston and the Roanoke River basin, and protected communities in North Carolina and Virginia. But it looks like political bickering won out. Virginia's failure to act has left us no alternative but to go back to court." Although approval of the pipeline by the Federal Energy Regulatory Commission, in late July 1995, lifted the last regulatory barrier to the project, the legal battle to block the removal of water from Lake Gaston continued into Hunt's fourth term. James W. Clay et al., eds., *North Carolina Atlas: Portrait of a Changing State* (Chapel Hill: University of North Carolina Press, 1975), 157; *News and Observer*, March 21,

April 7, 25, 29, June 20, 21, 27, 29, July 3, 27, 1995, October 27, December 25, 1996; press release, Governor Hunt: Virginia Politics Will Mean a Fight on Lake Gaston Pipeline, Raleigh, July 6, 1995, Governors Papers, James Baxter Hunt Jr.]

Attention News Editors/Reporters:

Attached is a summary of court-appointed mediator John Bickerman's settlement proposal concerning the Lake Gaston pipeline. This proposal is the result of four months of court-ordered mediation between North Carolina and the city of Virginia Beach over the city's proposal to withdraw up to 60 million gallons of water daily from the Roanoke River basin.

"Senator Helms and I have reviewed this court-ordered proposal by the federal mediator, and we've discussed the matter," said Governor Jim Hunt. "We agree that this proposal has advantages for North Carolina. We will review the proposal very carefully before we make any decisions for North Carolina."

Summary of Mediator's Settlement Proposal
April 6, 1995

1. Interstate Compact
    —An interstate compact between North Carolina and Virginia would permanently prohibit withdrawals by Virginia from the Roanoke River basin above the permitted 60 mgd [million gallons per day] from the Lake Gaston pipeline.
2. Striped Bass Spawning Protection
    —Virginia Beach would use its Kerr Reservoir water storage to assure that river flows are not reduced during the striped bass spawning season.
3. Bi-state Water Advisory Commission/Regional Water Authority
    —A bi-state commission to study and monitor use, conservation, and coordination of water resources would be created to make recommendations concerning such resources and for the protection of the Roanoke River basin. The commission would have an equal number of members from North Carolina and Virginia, to be appointed by their respective governors.
    —Virginia Beach will pay $100,000-$200,000 per year to a fund to control hydrilla, a highly destructive weed infestation in Lake Gaston, and other environmental purposes to benefit North Carolina communities in the Roanoke basin.

4. No Water Sales Outside Southeastern Virginia
    —Norfolk and communities receiving Lake Gaston pipeline water
    would agree not to resell Gaston pipeline or any other water outside
    southeastern Virginia.
5. Northeastern North Carolina Connection to Pipeline
    —Northeastern North Carolina communities could connect to the
    pipeline at any time for their long-term water needs, upon obtaining
    standard federal and state permits.
6. Commitment to Water Conservation Programs
    —Virginia communities taking water from the pipeline would be
    required to implement long-term water conservation programs.
7. Reductions During Drought
    —All communities attached to the pipeline would be required to
    first use all local water supplies, including emergency wells, and
    to adopt mandatory water use restrictions. During the most severe
    droughts (example: 1981 drought), water withdrawals from the Lake
    Gaston pipeline would be reduced or terminated.
8. Highway Improvements
    —Routes [U.S.] 17 and 168 in Virginia would be improved expedi-
    tiously to the same standard as in North Carolina to facilitate both
    tourist and other transportation to North Carolina.

NORTH CAROLINA SCHOOL BOARDS ASSOCIATION

RALEIGH, APRIL 27, 1995

[The text delivered to the North Carolina Association of Teacher Assistants,
May 5, 1995, is similar to the following address to the state School Boards
Association.]

This is a group that is committed to improving education. You know
how important education is to our future. You see the challenges we
face up close, in your own schools.

Education is the key to North Carolina's future—the key to our future
workforce and the key to our future economy. To make our schools the
best they can be, I believe we must do five things.

First, we must make every school a safe place for students to learn
and teachers to teach. In this legislative session, I pushed for a program
of zero tolerance in our schools—zero tolerance for drugs, or guns, or
any weapons and zero tolerance for any student who puts others at risk.
That means automatic expulsion of up to one year for any student who
brings a weapon to school, alternative schools where those students

[incomplete], and education boot camps for students who need an even tougher lesson in discipline. I'm happy to say that Senator Roy Cooper has introduced zero-tolerance legislation, and Representatives Jim Black and Jean Preston are pushing funding for alternative schools through the House.[1] I'd like you to call your local representatives and encourage them to support those efforts. I'm also happy to say that our Department of Human Resources has already contracted with the Eckerd Foundation to set up an educational boot camp.[2]

Second, we must improve the teaching profession in North Carolina. We need to recruit good teachers, train good teachers, and keep good teachers. We can do that if we train teachers as professionals, treat them as professionals, and pay them as professionals. I've proposed continued funding of the National Board for Professional Teaching Standards, and I'm hopeful that the General Assembly will support that.

Third, we need more emphasis on teaching the basics and higher standards for what students should know and be able to do. That's why we established the North Carolina Standards and Accountability Commission. The commission has come up with ten basic skills that it believes students should know and be able to apply in order to graduate from high school. The standards commission is now monitoring the work of more than a hundred teachers, who are applying those skills in ten pilot school systems across the state, to develop new standards that will be tested next year. By the year 2000, we'll have one simple rule for all of our students: If you don't meet the standards, you don't graduate from high school. And I want to offer an unconditional guarantee to employers: If our students don't meet your standards, then we'll take them back and work with them until they do, at our expense!

Raising standards in our schools is critical if we are to produce a well-educated workforce. I am deeply disappointed to see the majority in the House Appropriations Committee gut the state's standards efforts in their budget-slashing zeal. What is their alternative to ensure that a high-school diploma has value? [I've] seen none.

The business and education communit[ies] have been strong supporters of higher standards in the schools. You have been a strong voice. I urge you to let your voice be heard now. It's important that your legislators hear from you how important the standards effort is to better schools.

I support local flexibility. But we need strong standards in place. Flexibility without accountability won't produce the kind of schools we need.

Fourth, we need to help our children get ready for school. No education reform plan will work if our children don't come to school ready to learn. Already, Smart Start has helped tens of thousands of children, in nearly a third of our counties, get day care, health care, and other critical services. But our needs are so great. That's why we need to expand Smart Start to twelve more counties this year, and I'm working with legislative leaders to find a way that we can do that and boost private support at the same time.

Fifth, we need to get more value for our tax dollars, and I'm glad to see Jay Robinson providing leadership on education reforms that cut bureaucracy, increase school flexibility, and improve accountability. Taxpayers spend a lot of money on the schools, and they deserve to get their money's worth.

If we can accomplish these things, we'll be taking a big step forward in education in North Carolina. What we can't afford to do right now is take two steps back. But that's the risk the House leadership is taking by undercutting efforts to expand Smart Start and to raise standards.

I've laid out my goals, and I believe we have a good education reform plan in place. I feel good about the path North Carolina is taking to meet those goals, a path that's based on common sense. We've come a long way. We can't afford to falter. We can't afford to let politics get in the way of progress. We can't afford to let our children down. I want us all to work together to keep our state moving forward, for our future and for our children's future.

---

[1] Roy A. Cooper III (1957-   ), born in Nashville; resident of Nash County; B.A., 1979, J.D., 1982, University of North Carolina at Chapel Hill. Attorney; member, state House, 1987-1991, and senate, from 1991, senate majority leader, from 1997; Democrat. *North Carolina Manual, 1995-1996*, 465, *1997-1998*, 424-425.

James Boyce Black (1935-   ), born in Matthews; resident of Mecklenburg County; A.B., Lenoir-Rhyne College, 1959; doctor of optometry, Southern College of Optometry, 1962; U.S. Naval Reserve, 1955-1961. Optometrist; former president, N.C. State Optometric Society; member, 1981-1984, and from 1991, minority leader, 1995-1998, state House of Representatives; member, Matthews Town Council, 1988; Democrat. *North Carolina Manual, 1995-1996*, 533, *1997-1998*, 526.

Jean Rouse Preston; resident of Carteret County; B.S., 1957, M.A., 1973, East Carolina University. Educator; special education teacher, 1968-1974; director of reading, K-12, 1975-1978; program administrator, children with special needs, Greene County Schools, 1978-1979; member, state House, from 1993, and co-chair, Appropriations Committee-Subcommittee on Education; Republican. *North Carolina Manual, 1995-1996*, 643, *1997-1998*, 679-680.

[2] Two new Eckerd Wilderness Camps, one in Bladen County and the other near Kerr Lake, joined four others already operating in North Carolina in 1996. "Building strong citizens and strong futures is what Eckerd Wilderness Camps are all about," Hunt said at the opening of the Bladen County camp. "You all may not know this," he recalled, "but the very first official meeting I ever had as governor, on Inauguration Day in 1977, was

with Jack Eckerd to talk about bringing the Eckerd Wilderness Camping program to North Carolina to help our young people. Since then . . . the four camps we put in place have helped almost 4,000 young men get on the right track. Almost three-quarters of the graduates from our wilderness camps are still in school one year later, almost 90 percent see their standardized test scores improve, and only 16 percent of those who finished the program in the first half of 1994 had gotten in trouble with the law again a year after leaving camp. That's why I pushed for money to build two new camps during the special crime session in 1994, and I am glad the General Assembly also recognized the value of this program and approved the funding. This is one of the camps they approved." Bladen County Wilderness Camp Tour/Roundtable, Elizabethtown, April 1, 1996, Governors Papers, James Baxter Hunt Jr.

SMART START LUNCHEON

ASHEVILLE, APRIL 28, 1995

[Often called the centerpiece of Governor Hunt's third administration, Smart Start faced an uncertain future as the General Assembly convened in 1995. Hunt wanted to add twelve new counties to the program during each year of the 1995-1997 biennium. But the results of an Associated Press poll released in January revealed that a majority of state lawmakers preferred to delay expansion until they saw how well existing programs performed. The leadership of the GOP-controlled House opposed any expansion of Smart Start.

Hunt was unwilling to see his early childhood initiative die from a loss of momentum and vowed to fight for it "'with every breath I've got.'" Armed with progress reports from Smart Start projects across North Carolina, and bolstered by a statewide poll that found a 71 percent approval rating for the program, the governor appealed to business, civic, religious, and education groups for support—and asked them to lobby their legislators on behalf of "the children." Smart Start's backers were heartened further when the program passed its first state financial audit in early March.

But amid the favorable reports emanating from Smart Start counties also came news of questionable spending priorities by local partnerships, and an overall lack of accountability within the program, that caused House Republicans to wonder if the state was getting its money's worth. There were calls for budget cuts. Conservative critics argued that Smart Start was not living up to its billing as a private-public partnership, citing as proof a report that corporate sponsors had given just $5,000 to the $48 million program by June 30, 1994.

On May 31, 1995, a bipartisan group of lawmakers released a proposal to revise Smart Start. It would have increased state oversight, required a 20 percent match of private funds to tax dollars, and spread to all 100 counties the $58 million Hunt wanted for the thirty-two existing Smart Start programs. The governor quickly scuttled the plan, saying local control was the key to Smart Start's flexibility and effectiveness; that Smart Start programs already under way would suffer funding cuts harmful to participating families; and that the 20 percent match was unacceptable. But Hunt also backed away from his initial opposition to any matching funds provision and signaled his approval of a 15 percent match: 5 percent cash, 10 percent in donated goods and services. *News and Observer,* January 4, 15, 19, February 21, March 1, 9, 23, 26, 31, April 6, 12, 20, 27, May 14, 20, 25, 28, 31, June 1, 1995. Hunt's comments on negotiations over the program include Smart Start Media Availability, Raleigh, May 31, and Smart Start Statement, Raleigh, June 7, 1995; see also press release and attachments, Governor Hunt Urges Legislators to Resolve Smart Start, Raleigh, June 7, 1995, Governors Papers, James Baxter Hunt Jr.

The governor explained the need for Smart Start, and reviewed its successes, before a variety of audiences in 1995: National Governors Association, Plenary Session, Governors Campaign for Children, Washington, D.C., January 29; Sir Walter Cabinet, Raleigh, February 7; Business Roundtable, Wilmington, February 27; Enterprise Community Designation Announcement, Lumberton, February 28; Business Roundtable, Greenville, March 6; Cleveland County Chamber of Commerce, Raleigh, March 15; Highland United Methodist Church, Raleigh, March 28; Chambers of Commerce of Eastern North Carolina, Raleigh, April 5; Education Commission of the States, Durham, April 19; Rotary International Annual District Meeting, Winston-Salem, May 16; North Carolina Association of Broadcasters, Greensboro, October 25; and Baptist State Convention President's Luncheon, Winston-Salem, November 13. Governors Papers, James Baxter Hunt Jr.]

I'm happy to be in Asheville and to have the chance to talk with you about one of the issues closest to my heart: children. I ran for governor because I believe we can build a brighter future for our state if we start with our children. If we can provide quality child care, health care, and other critical services in their earliest years, we can make North Carolina a better place for years to come.

Smart Start is helping us do just that. It is helping children come to school healthy and ready to learn. It is helping us build a strong workforce and economy, and it will mean fewer dollars spent on prisons, welfare, and dropouts down the road. In less than two years, Smart Start has helped tens of thousands of children and their families. Working families have more access to better child care. Poor families are getting day care, so they can work. Children are getting preventive health care, some for the first time. Families are getting practical help, like parent education, to support stronger families.[1]

Here in western North Carolina, Smart Start has taken more than 250 children off [day-care] waiting lists so their parents can work and stay off welfare; purchased vans to help get children and families to the child care, health care, and other family services they need; and provided critical training for more than 600 child-care teachers so they can provide even better care for your children. Smart Start is doing all of this in a new way. It's bringing together businesses, churches, nonprofits, and government. It's not Raleigh calling the shots; it's communities galvanizing around their children. It's local people deciding how to serve local children.

The state provides seed money: $68 million, so far. A statewide public-private partnership, headed by a CEO, sets goals for our children.

The state offers training and technical support. But then we stand back and let the people of North Carolina go to work—and it is truly the people of North Carolina who are supporting Smart Start. Last week, First Union, Wachovia, NationsBank, and Glaxo announced $7 million in gifts to Smart Start, the largest gifts some of these companies have ever given.[2] Business, nonprofit, and church leaders have given millions in in-kind services, furniture, equipment, toys, and supplies; and they've given their time, spending hundreds of hours making Smart Start work in their community.

Here in western North Carolina, volunteers in the Region A counties have already given some 16,000 hours of service to our children, and I know the people of Buncombe County are supporting Smart Start, too. It's your friends and neighbors who are working so hard with Children First and with the new family resource center in West Asheville. This afternoon, I'll be hearing from many of them when I visit First Presbyterian Church and its day-care center. I'll be hearing about the needs of children here, including the long waiting list for child-care subsidies.

Your legislators will soon decide whether to expand Smart Start to twelve more counties next year. If they do, Buncombe County could get almost $2 million to help launch Smart Start. If they don't, Smart Start will lose momentum, here and across the state.

You need to let your legislators know that you support Smart Start, and that you want it expanded. Some of your legislators are here, today. I wish every member of your delegation would have been able to join us, today. I hope you'll let every one of them hear from you, instead. Let them know how important Smart Start is to Buncombe County. Let them know how important it is to keep the momentum going. Let them know how important it is to build up children and families in this community.

At the same time, the legislature must expand Smart Start in a way that fulfills the state's obligation to our children, without passing the buck to business. The House leadership is moving ahead with a so-called deal for Smart Start that is, in fact, a raw deal. It would require a 20 percent cash quota to be raised every year by local partnerships. If any Smart Start partnership fails to meet that quota, the House wants to withhold that amount in Smart Start funding.

The impact on Buncombe County is dramatic. If you raised a pro-rata share, you all would have to raise almost $350,000 in cash, this year, before you get one dime of Smart Start money. You'd have to raise nearly double that, next year, and continue at that level year in and year out.

Private-sector support is critical to Smart Start's success, and we want to boost that support—here in Asheville and across the state. I'm talking every day with Smart Start folks and legislative leaders about how we can do that. But it is wrong to make the future of Smart Start dependent on an arbitrary cash quota, at [an] unrealistic level, that you must raise from businesses in your county—and it is wrong to play political games with our children's future like that. You need to let your legislators know how you feel about this proposal! Let them know that you expect them to put your children first—and politics second.

---

[1] "Parents as first teachers," Hunt jotted at this point in his text.
[2] For press releases on corporate financial support of Smart Start, see N.C. Companies Give $7 Million to Smart Start, Governor Hunt Announces, Raleigh, April 19, 1995; Governor Hunt Announces $1 Million Gift from BB&T to Smart Start, Raleigh, May 11, 1995; Winston-Salem Rotary Club Makes Donation to Smart Start, Winston-Salem, May 19, 1995; Governor Hunt Announces $1 Million Gift to Smart Start from Food Lion, Raleigh, May 24, 1995; and N.C. Company [Sea-Land] Gives $10,000 to Smart Start, Governor Hunt Announces, December 22, 1995, Governors Papers, James Baxter Hunt Jr.

YEAR OF THE MOUNTAINS COMMISSION

ASHEVILLE, APRIL 28, 1995

This region is one of North Carolina's greatest natural treasures. Its heritage, its people, and its beauty should be cherished and celebrated. That's what I hope this commission will help us do. I want you to help us celebrate the beauty of North Carolina's mountains, spread the word about your unique culture, and encourage the kind of responsible development that your children and grandchildren will be proud of.[1]

There are so many good things happening here already, good things that you can build upon to create a better future, and good things that should be shared with the rest of our state and throughout the Southeast. Our Department of Cultural Resources and Department of Commerce are working hard, with people from seventeen counties in this area, to create a national center for your craft industry through Handmade in America. Mountain artisans are known for the beauty of their work, and I'm proud of what many of them have accomplished through guilds and schools like the Penland School, the John C. Campbell School of Folk Arts, and the Sawtooth Center. You must find new ways to encourage and preserve the work of mountain artists and craftsmen so that it can be shared.

I hope this commission will also encourage responsible stewardship of our environment so that we can preserve the precious natural beauty of this area. You have the opportunity, now, to make sure these mountains, recognized around the world for their unique plant and animal life, will be just as beautiful for our grandchildren and their children.

I have something to announce, today, that I believe will help you reach all of these goals and provide a boost for this region as well as our entire state. Next Thursday, in Raleigh, the Department of Transportation will unveil its draft Transportation Improvement Program. It will include an additional $20 million for the Asheville Connector. The board is expected to adopt the plan in June, and I assure you they know [where] I stand on this project: that $20 million belongs to Asheville!

As many of you know, the Asheville Connector is part of the urban loops program in the Highway Trust Fund.[2] This new multi-lane freeway is vital to the economic development and overall progress of this area, one of the very things this commission hopes to promote. This highway will extend existing I-26 at I-40, west of Asheville, to U.S. 19/23/70, the future I-26 north of Asheville, giving folks coming from Tennessee a more direct route. And there's more exciting news: An additional $4.1 million will be added to our transportation plan for an access road from N.C. 191 to the North Carolina Arboretum in Asheville. That will give visitors even more reason to come to this area and appreciate western North Carolina's beauty.

There will be other projects announced for this area, of course, but I wanted to personally tell you about these today. We're proud of what we've accomplished in transportation for the Asheville area, since January 1993, including $200 million to push ahead the completion of I-26 between Asheville and the Tennessee line at Sam's Gap by the year 2001. We've also spent $32 million, total, for highway projects in Buncombe County, and we have paved more than 310 miles of secondary roads at a cost of $48.7 million. We'll continue to do more for this area, with the fine leadership of your Department of Transportation Board member Gordon Myers,[3] and we'll continue to support you and help you find new ways to stimulate the region's economy, preserve your unique heritage, and share it with the rest of North Carolina—and the entire country.

---

[1] Executive Order Number 74 established the Year of the Mountains Commission. Hunt set aside July 1, 1995-June 30, 1996 as the Year of the Mountains. *N.C. Session Laws, 1995,* 2:2131-2134.

[2] "An Act to Establish the North Carolina Highway Trust Fund, to Provide Revenue for the Fund, to Designate How Revenue in the Fund is to Be Used, and to Raise Revenue for the General Fund," was ratified July 27, 1989. *N.C. Session Laws, 1989,* II, c. 692.

[3] The governor appointed Gordon S. Myers, of Fairview, to two terms on the state Board of Transportation: March 5, 1993-January 15, 1997, and April 1, 1997-January 15, 2001. Letters of Appointment to Boards and Commissions, Governors Papers, James Baxter Hunt Jr.

TRANSPORTATION 2001

RALEIGH, MAY 4, 1995

I want to thank the members of our state Board of Transportation for all your hard work. You are vital, not only for what you do for your own communities, but also for what you do to help build our entire state. You are a good team, working together to make our Department of Transportation more efficient while providing our state with one of the best transportation systems in the country.

This is our third TIP [Transportation Improvement Program] update since the beginning of this administration.[1] Last year at this time, we talked about the new Transportation 2001 plan, a plan unlike any other transportation program our state has put together in its history. It takes a comprehensive look at the transportation needs of our entire state. It goes beyond highways to include public transportation. It goes beyond piecemeal road projects to look at North Carolina's future economic development needs and how we can develop the transportation system we need to address those needs.

It's a plan that has kept us focused. In it, we promised to speed up highway construction, completing highways that are vital to economic development. We promised to eliminate the maintenance backlog and develop and implement a master plan for [getting a] public transit system up and running.

We're making a lot of progress. In just the last three years, we've spent $2.6 billion on construction. We plan to spend another billion dollars this year to speed up critical projects and start new ones, and over the next seven years we plan to spend $7.4 billion on needed construction projects.

To help clear up the maintenance backlog, we plan to spend another $32 million in the coming year. That makes $64 million we've spent, since 1993, to help us take care of those crumbling bridges, and those potholes I'm sure you're all too familiar with, and make our existing highways safer. And to help develop and get our public transit system running, I signed an executive order yesterday to create the Transit 2001 Commission to develop and implement a master transit plan.[2] Later this month, May 25, we'll see the inaugural run of the new

Piedmont train, providing an alternative way to get to Greensboro, Charlotte, and other cities west of Raleigh. Secretary Hunt will join me for [the] kickoff. [I] hope you can be there, too.

We're also working to accelerate secondary road paving to get our citizens out of the dust and mud. In the last year, we've spent $108 million to pave 863 miles of secondary roads across the state, and we'll be spending another $115 million in the next year to pave another 875 miles. And because we know how hard it is to keep track of all the various secondary road projects, especially when they are usually referred to only as numbers, we are, for [the] first time, publishing a list of secondary roads to be paved by name. That'll help you, and the people in your communities that you serve, keep track of what has been done and what will be done.

Everywhere I go, people are talking about transportation. They want to know when roads will be paved or widened. They are glad to be getting out of the mud and grateful for better access to get where they need to go. That goes for the businesses that keep this state's economy going, too.

I remember, as a boy growing up in Wilson County, when the road to our farm was paved. That taught me how important roads were to our family and business. Governor Kerr Scott changed the lives of thousands of rural citizens. When I became governor, I wanted to continue that commitment to good transportation, so I proposed a $300 million bond issue, which I'm happy to say was overwhelmingly approved by voters.[3] Passage of the Highway Trust Fund also was critical. That plan helped us fund current projects and put us in position to develop Transportation 2001.

Again this year, more money has been added to construct and finish corridors and highways sooner. We are keeping our commitment to the people of North Carolina. They can count on the priorities we've set to remain priorities:

—We're staying on schedule on the U.S. 74 corridor, adding $15 million to build the Monroe Bypass Connector and another $10 million to build the U.S. 74 Shelby Bypass. Ninety-five percent of the corridor is now built or funded.

—Along the U.S. 64 corridor, we're adding $10 million for [the] U.S. 264/64 Manteo Bypass. That's on top of $113 million that was added to construction on the corridor last year. Ninety percent of the corridor is now built or funded.

—On the U.S. 17 corridor, the contract for the Neuse River bridge will be let this September. Seventy-five percent of the corridor is now built or funded.

—Last year, we added $53 million for construction along the U.S. 421 corridor. That corridor is now fully funded and construction is on schedule.

—Completion of the U.S. 1 corridor has been accelerated by two years, and it should be finished by 1999, just in time for the U.S. Open.

This year's TIP update includes many more important projects:

—We're adding $38 million to fully fund the Smith Creek Parkway, in Wilmington.

—We're adding $31 million to the Northern Wake Expressway, which represents 6 percent of the total project. Seventy-three million [dollars have] been added since 1993.

—We're adding $25 million to the Fayetteville Loop, which is 23 percent of the total project cost.

—We're adding $20 million to the Greensboro Western Loop, an amount that represents 4 percent of the total project cost. Construction is to begin next year.

—We're adding $113 million to the Charlotte Outer Loop, which is 12 percent of the total project cost.

—We're adding $20 million to Asheville's loop, which is the I-26 connector. That represents 17 percent of the total project. We've added $34 million to that project since 1993.

—We're adding $10 million to U.S. 19/74/129, also known as Corridor K, in Cherokee, Swain, and Graham Counties. We've spent or added $56 million to that project since 1993.

You're going to get your own copy of the new TIP update in just a moment, and you'll see that it contains much, much more. I've just hit some of the highlights. We've got lots of projects under way all across the state.

Two years ago, I appointed you to the Board of Transportation. If you didn't know it then, you certainly know now that it is a mammoth job to oversee our comprehensive transportation system. But you have met the challenge. You have provided strong leadership. You've done it by working together on a common vision to move our state forward.

Thanks to your help, we've come a long way. But we still have a long way to go. We must keep our promise and maintain our commitment to develop a comprehensive transportation system that will be second to none, a system that will lead to a stronger economy, safer highways, and a brighter future for our state.

---

[1] *Transportation 2001: Setting a New Pace for a New Century; Governor Hunt's Plan to Accelerate Improvements in Our Transportation System; 1995-1996 Update; Transportation Improvement Program* ([Raleigh: N.C. Dept. of Transportation, 1995]).

[2] The Transit 2001 Commission was created under Executive Order Number 77, signed May 2, 1995. *N.C. Session Laws, 1995*, 2:2146-2147.

[3] Legislators paved the way for a referendum on a $300 million highway bond package under *N.C. Session Laws, 1977*, c. 643, ratified June 21, 1977. North Carolina voters approved the measure by a 2:1 margin. "A $300 Million Decision," and "The Month in State Government," *We the People of North Carolina* (December 1977): 6.

BASE REALIGNMENT AND CLOSURE
COMMISSION HEARING

Baltimore, Maryland, May 4, 1995

[The Base Realignment and Closure Commission (BRACC) gave a bipartisan delegation from North Carolina twenty minutes, during hearings on May 4, 1995, to defend the proposed deployment of F/A-18 Hornet aircraft from Florida to Cherry Point Marine Corps Air Station, Havelock. The 1993 BRACC process had assigned the jets to Cherry Point, but subsequent political pressure from the Old Dominion caused the Department of Defense to recommend the Hornets' posting to Oceana Naval Air Station, Virginia Beach. Governor Hunt, U.S. senators Jesse Helms and Lauch Faircloth, and U.S. representatives Eva Clayton and Walter Jones went to Baltimore to convince the commission of the validity of the original plan. Hunt's testimony is reprinted, below.

Less than a month after the hearings ended, a BRACC member visited Cherry Point to review the base's capacity to handle the new aircraft. The governor also hoped to strengthen North Carolina's position during a mid-June meeting with commission chairman Alan Dixon. But the state's best efforts could not overcome the Defense Department's belief—mistaken, in Hunt's view—that it was cheaper to send the Hornets to Oceana than to base them at Cherry Point. The final list of base closings and realignments, released June 23, supported DOD's position. *Congressional Quarterly Almanac, 1995*, 9/21; *News and Observer*, April 10, May 5, 6, 26, June 17, 24, 1995; press releases, Governor Hunt Fighting to Keep North Carolina's Military Bases Strong, Raleigh, February 28, 1995, State Hires Consultants to Work on BRACC Recommendations, Raleigh, March 16, 1995, Governor Takes Fight for F/A-18 Squadrons to Baltimore May 4, Raleigh, April 25, 1995, BRACC Agrees to Governor Hunt's Request for New Cost Analysis on F/A-18s, Raleigh, May 25, 1995, and Governor Hunt Criticizes BRACC Decision to Move F/A-18s to Oceana, Washington, June 23, 1995, Governors Papers, James Baxter Hunt Jr.]

In 1993, the Base Closure and Realignment Commission, on the basis of military value determinations, concluded that the aircraft at Cecil Field should be "redistributed from NAS Cecil Field to two MCAS [Marine Corps air stations] on the East Coast, Cherry Point and Beaufort." The commission's rationale was that such a realignment would "dovetail with the recent determination for joint military operation of Navy and Marine Corps aircraft. . . ." The BRAC Commission in 1993 understood that inter-service, joint military operations were necessary in order to achieve the most efficient, cost-effective utilization of our military resources. In addition to the inter-service rationale, the '93 commission also concluded that the realignment of the F-18 aircraft to Cherry Point "alleviated concerns with regard to future environmental and land use problems. . . ." As a result of the BRAC '93 directives, the navy has spent approximately $25 million in preparation for receiving the aircraft at Cherry Point. This expenditure was entirely reasonable in light of the unassailable rationale provided for the decision by the '93 commission. It made sense then, and it makes sense now.

The Department of Defense now proposes to ignore the BRAC '93 commission decision and its underlying rationale. It recommends redirecting the F-18 aircraft from Cecil Field to NAS [Naval Air Station] Oceana rather than to Cherry Point. A few F-18 aircraft also will be assigned to MCAS Beaufort, South Carolina, and Atlanta, Georgia. We respectfully suggest that this commission consider the Department of Defense recommendation to be a substantial deviation from the BRAC criteria, a deviation, as we will make clear today, which will not stand scrutiny.

What happened between 1993 and 1995, and why did it happen? To answer these questions, it is important to understand that Oceana was considered by the '93 commission as a potential receiver for the F-18 aircraft. The commission concluded that "the movement of Cecil Field F-18 aircraft and personnel to NAS Oceana defeats the increase in military value achieved by the integration of Navy carrier-based aviation with the Marine Corps carrier aviation at Cherry Point and Beaufort. . . ." Oceana was not overlooked; it was specifically considered and rejected as an appropriate receiver site for these airplanes. We contend the rationale which supported that conclusion in 1993 is still fully applicable in 1995, and in light of new budget considerations, possibly more relevant.

To justify ignoring the directive of the '93 commission, it was necessary to change the playing field. Accordingly, the 1995 navy recommendation to the Department of Defense [DOD] included a so-called rule that ". . . the introduction of aircraft types not currently aboard a station is not allowed." This rule would eliminate Cherry Point as a receiver for F-18s but would qualify Oceana as a receiver site because of the existence of only one reserve squadron of F-18s at Oceana. Adherence to this rule would more than eliminate Cherry Point as a potential receiver; it would destroy the inter-service synergy dictated by the '93 commission decision. The rule is designed to direct the F-18s to Oceana.

A review of the cost-avoidance and related numbers attributed to the '93 decision and the 1995 DOD recommendation provides another example of the navy's efforts to justify ignoring the 1993 decision. In 1993, after a thorough study, the commission determined that it would cost $228 million to move the F-18s to Oceana and $147 million to move the aircraft to Cherry Point. These numbers were based on the relocation of thirteen, twelve-plane squadrons and a training squadron. The navy's recommendation to DOD, and DOD's recommendation to this commission in 1995, now includes an estimate of $28,370,000 as the cost of moving the aircraft to Oceana and $332,340,000 as the cost to move the aircraft to Cherry Point. How is this $385 million flip-flop possible? Is there any basis in logic for it? The answer is clearly no.

The navy's explanation for the dramatic difference in the commission's 1993 cost determination and the navy's 1995 numbers includes the reduction of squadrons from thirteen to eight. It is important, however, to note that the navy's 1995 cost figures at Cherry Point are still premised on the original planning numbers. Only Oceana's cost estimates benefit from the reduction in number of squadrons. In addition, the navy contends that the cost attributed to Oceana will be offset by phasing out fifty-six A-6 aircraft and the redirection of the S-3 aircraft to NAS Jacksonville in lieu of Oceana—a violation of the navy's new so-called rule. These factors simply cannot account for the difference in the 1993 commission cost determination of $228 million and the $28 million navy estimate in 1995.

In addition, the navy's 1995 cost estimate for Cherry Point includes $42,800,000 for additional family housing units, even though the navy's own housing study at Cherry Point indicates that these units are not required; $39,500,000 for additional enlisted quarters, despite existing excess capacity; and $25,000,000 for an unnecessary and counter-productive parallel taxiway. At this point, I am pleased to turn over the presentation of our case to North Carolina's senior senator, Jesse Helms.

[Testimony from North Carolina's junior United States senator, Lauch Faircloth, followed Helms's. Hunt then offered closing remarks.]

We believe that we have presented a case that establishes that the navy/DOD recommendation to this commission represents an unsupported rejection by the navy and DOD of the 1993 commission decision and a substantial deviation from the BRAC criteria. This recommendation ignores the joint service operations decision and the environmental and land use determinations of the '93 commission. It appears that the navy has concluded that Oceana is at risk of closure if it does not receive these airplanes, and the navy wants to keep Oceana open at all costs. We have established today that the "at all costs" standard is very high, and a cost being paid with taxpayers' dollars. The Honorable Owen Pickett, the member from the district in which

Oceana is located, explained the navy's logic and its efforts in this matter best when he said: "When the military wants to do something and it is expensive, they underestimate the cost, and when they don't want to do something, they overestimate the cost."[1]

Because of the demonstrated deviation, we request the commission to reject the DOD recommendation and uphold the '93 commission decision to locate the F-18s at Cherry Point. Thank you very much for the opportunity to appear before you today. We will be happy to entertain any questions you have concerning our presentation.

---

[1] Owen Bradford Pickett (1930-   ), born in Richmond; resident of Virginia Beach; B.S., Virginia Polytechnic Institute, 1952; LL.B., University of Richmond, 1955. Attorney; member, Virginia House of Delegates, 1972-1986; was elected to U.S. House of Representatives, 1986, and was returned in subsequent elections; Democrat. *Biographical Directory of Congress, 1774-1989*, s.v. "Pickett, Owen Bradford."

NORTH CAROLINA ECONOMIC DEVELOPMENT BOARD

HIGH POINT, MAY 5, 1995

[Hunt delivered speeches, similar to the one prepared for the Economic Development Board, to Forsyth County elected officials, May 5, and the Davidson County chambers of commerce, May 31, 1995. Governors Papers, James Baxter Hunt Jr.]

I have enjoyed the time I have spent with my economic development team last night and this morning. This is a winning team, and I'm grateful for your dedication and hard work. I want to thank Bob Jordan for his leadership, and I want to thank each one of you. You all have brought your enthusiasm, experience, and expertise to the table to help build North Carolina's economy and improve the quality of life for our people.

You all know, better than most, how important it is for North Carolina to stay ahead of the curve. You know that it takes better schools, a better start for children, safer neighborhoods, and a leaner state government to stay ahead of the curve; and you know that all of us must put partisan politics aside to work together to build the kind of state our children deserve.

Back in February, I laid out three priorities for the General Assembly this year: cut taxes, fight crime, and, most importantly, help children. And I proposed a budget that saves $200 million, abolishes nearly 2,000 state jobs, cuts out layers of middle management, does away with programs, and even eliminates entire departmental bureaucracies that aren't needed. The budget passed by the House this week doesn't go as far in downsizing, but it's a good start in the right direction.

I am pleased that the General Assembly has passed a [$363] million tax cut. Cutting taxes is the right thing to do for all the taxpayers who work hard and raise families in this community. Our people deserve to keep more of their money, and state government can certainly get by with less.

It was about this time, last year, that you all recommended a tax audit as part of your strategic plan for economic development. I followed your advice, and the tax audit conducted by Peat Marwick this fall was an invaluable tool in putting together my tax-cut package. Based on that tax audit, I recommended a tax cut of nearly a half-billion dollars, the largest tax cut in our state's history. I proposed repealing the intangibles tax on stocks and bonds, raising the personal exemption for every member of a household by $500, and creating a tax credit of $50 per child. I'm pleased that the General Assembly has enacted these cuts into law.

But I'm disappointed that we're not moving ahead with the corporate tax cut. I recommended cutting the corporate tax rate to 7 percent, this year, to make sure our economy continues to grow. As you know, North Carolina has the fourth-highest corporate income tax rate among our competitor states. I hope we can move quickly to roll back that tax next year so we can do an even better job recruiting new industry into the state, increasing bottom-line profits, and helping businesses invest, expand, and create jobs. We need to keep working on that one.

The second goal I wanted the legislature to focus on, this year, is fighting crime, starting with tougher sentences for violent criminals. We're building on what we did in last year's crime session, repealing the prison cap, and increasing sentences for violent felonies, and building 2,000 new, no-frills, prison beds.

The third goal the legislature should focus on is helping children. We've got a big job to do there. We must make fundamental changes in our schools. I've set out a commonsense plan that starts with restoring discipline in our schools, improving the quality of teaching, getting back to basics, setting higher standards, and getting a better value for our education dollar. I want to cut class size this year, make classrooms safer, and cut bureaucracy in Raleigh and at the local level. The school reorganization plan that Jay Robinson and the state school board is [sic] mapping out will help us achieve some of those goals, and I'm optimistic that we can make real progress in giving local schools the flexibility they need while holding them accountable for results.

To make school reform work, we need to start earlier. That's what Smart Start is all about. Smart Start is providing quality child care, health care, and other critical services to children under six who need it. It's making a difference for tens of thousands of children and their families in thirty-two counties, and I hope we can convince the legislature to expand it.

In the end, good schools are the key to our economic future. A good workforce is what we need to attract good jobs. But there are some other things we can do to make sure we bring more high-skill, high-wage jobs to North Carolina.

Our Competitive Fund has been a critical tool in that effort. The $12 million that the General Assembly has provided for the fund in the past two years has helped create more than 9,000 new jobs and brought three-quarters of a billion dollars in investment into our state. In my book, that's a good return on our investment!

But we can do even better. That's why we're developing new guidelines, based on recommendations from academic and economic experts on the Business Incentives Task Force, to use the fund more strategically. This year, I'm asking the legislature for $10 million for the Competitive Fund, and I need your help in fighting for this as legislators begin deliberating on the expansion budget in the coming days.

Let me outline other items in our economic development legislative package:

—We should expand the Targeted Jobs Tax Credit to distressed areas of our fifty most affluent counties. Currently, businesses in the fifty most distressed counties are eligible for a $2,800 per-job tax credit. We should expand the credit to areas of high poverty in the top fifty counties at $1,000 per job. This would let us use the tax credit in all 100 counties and help us create new jobs in areas of the state where they're most needed.

—We should expand small business incubator programs, with $1.5 million for the Technological Development Authority.

—We should modify the Investment Tax Credit so businesses can use it to stimulate private venture capital for existing and emerging companies.

—I've earmarked $290,000 for the Research Triangle World Trade Center so that small businesses can get timely and accurate information on the global economy.

—And to help small businesses, I've recommended an additional $1 million to expand training in biotechnology at the state's historically black universities and Pembroke State University.

The General Assembly will be making some critical decisions about economic development in coming weeks. I appreciate the leadership of Representative Owens, Senator Conder, Representative Hunt, and Senator Hobbs, and I appreciate your support on economic development issues.[1] As the legislature considers our economic development package, it's important that they hear from this development team. Secretary Phillips and his staff will be fighting hard for our package, but we need your support as well. I'm counting on my team!

---

[1] William Clarence Owens Jr. (1947-   ), born in Elizabeth City; attended College of the Albemarle, 1966-1967; National Guard, 1967-1992. Vice-president, W. W. Owens and Sons Moving and Storage, Inc.; manager, Albemarle Mini-Warehouses, Inc.; director, Consolidated Development Corp.; general partner in Owens and Robertson, real estate development; member, Pasquotank County Board of Commissioners, 1976-1995; president, 1991-1992, N.C. Association of County Commissioners; vice-chairman, from 1993, Executive Committee chairman, N.C. Economic Development Board; member, N.C. House of Representatives, from 1995; Democrat. *North Carolina Manual, 1995-1996*, 640-641.

Senator James Richard Conder was identified earlier in this volume.

John Jackson Hunt (1922-   ), born in Lattamore; B.S., Wake Forest University, 1943; D.D.S., Emory University, 1946; U.S. Army, 1950-1952. Dentist; building materials retailer and wholesaler; farmer; member, state House, 1973-1976, and from 1989; Democrat. *North Carolina Manual, 1995-1996*, 604.

Fred M. Hobbs (1953-   ), born in Erwin; resident of Orange County; B.S., N.C. State University, 1975. Consulting civil engineer; founder, Hobbs Engineering, 1982; president, Hobbs, Upchurch and Associates, 1983; member, N.C. Senate, from 1995; was appointed by Governor Hunt to N.C. Economic Development Board; Democrat. *North Carolina Manual, 1995-1996*, 477.

HIGHWAY PATROL GRADUATION

RALEIGH, MAY 12, 1995

[The following address is similar to Hunt's May 19, 1995, text for a meeting of the Governor's Crime Commission.]

I'm proud to be here, today, to help you celebrate the completion of twenty-six weeks of intensive training. I'm also proud to be here to commend you for your commitment to building a safer North Carolina. North Carolinians rely on our Highway Patrol for our peace of mind, for the safety of our families, and for the safety of our communities. As governor, protecting the safety of our people is my top priority, and I want you to know that this administration is equally committed to fighting crime and helping you in our efforts to build a safer North Carolina.

With the help of Colonel Barefoot[1] and the Highway Patrol, we've worked hard over the last two years to fight crime and keep dangerous criminals off our streets. During last year's crime session, we took

important steps in the right direction by convincing the General
Assembly to lengthen sentences for dangerous criminals, toughen gun
laws, and increase prison capacity. We launched new efforts to deter
youngsters from crime and began looking at tougher punishment for
young criminals. We boosted support for crime victims and drug and
alcohol treatment, and we began developing a statewide criminal justice
information system.

This year, we are working even harder to build on the progress made
during the crime session. I'm asking lawmakers to toughen sentences
for violent criminals by 30 percent, including second-degree murder,
rape, and armed robbery. Repealing the state's prison cap will help make
sure criminals serve their complete sentences.

But to keep more dangerous criminals locked up, we must have more
space for them. That's why I'm proposing to build almost 4,000 new
prison beds, over the next four years, in no-frills prisons and boot camps.
At the same time, we should cut costs, and use existing prison space
more efficiently, by allowing for the privatization of prisons and double-
bunking inmates in single cells.[2]

To protect families and victims of crime, I've proposed a victims rights
amendment to the North Carolina Constitution. We're also pushing for
mandatory impact statements, so judges will know exactly what victims
have gone through before they hand down a sentence, and we're pushing
to increase our victim restitution efforts to make sure more victims are
reimbursed for their losses. I also want legislators to pass a law requiring
criminal background checks for day-care providers and foster parents
and will push for a law requiring registration of sex offenders and
notifying communities where they live.[3] I'm proud that these measures
are moving quickly through the General Assembly. I'm especially pleased
that my proposal to lengthen sentences for those who assault law-
enforcement officers has passed the state House this week.

Tougher laws are the first step, but we've also got to make our crime-
fighting efforts easier, more efficient, and safer, especially for the Highway
Patrol. You may know about my plans to abolish the Department of Crime
Control and Public Safety. You should know that it will in no way cut
into the manpower or the good work of our crime prevention and public
safety agencies. The elimination would only do away with thirty-seven
administrative jobs in that department.

My goal in reorganizing [that] department is to cut bureaucracy and
put the $3 million in savings where it counts: in the front line against
crime. These savings can then be redirected to support more law
enforcement officers and build more prisons, keeping more dangerous
criminals off our streets where they can't hurt our people.

These proposals will go a long way in our efforts to build a safer state, but we're doing things to help make North Carolina safer right now. The Governor's Crime Commission has awarded some $17 million in federal grant money to law-enforcement agencies for drug task forces, major crime units, and community-oriented policing projects. We've funded school resource officers and established the Center for the Prevention of School Violence to help the communities where you live and work make their classrooms, and communities, safer.

My crime commission has been supportive of the Highway Patrol's helicopter program and drug-fighting efforts. We funded the use of the patrol's helicopters for aerial support in marijuana eradication, and we provided funds for equipping military surplus helicopters for use in drug interdiction. Most recently, we funded Operation Eagle Eye to allow the patrol to provide aerial support to other law-enforcement agencies throughout the state. We want to help the patrol meet its goal of having a helicopter in each troop to help respond quickly to local agency requests for assistance.

We are also going to fund an asset forfeiture program, to be set up in the Department of Justice, to help all law-enforcement agencies, including the patrol, to take the profit out of crime.

My crime commission has been involved in the effort to upgrade computer and identification technology for the entire criminal justice system. We have led the effort to get automated fingerprint identification systems in every urban area in the state and have plans to ensure that every department has access to a system in their area. We will work hard with Secretary of State Rufus Edmisten to implement the recommendations of the state Criminal Justice Information Network study.[4] We want to tie the DMV [Division of Motor Vehicles] computer, and the SBI [State Bureau of Investigation] computer, and the computers of other agencies into one statewide system. We want to set uniform standards and lower the identification times so that, when you make an arrest, you know who you're dealing with and won't just write somebody a ticket and let them go without knowing whether or not they're wanted for murder in another state.

We also want to work toward a unified statewide radio system, allowing all agencies to work together more closely and to have a more coordinated response to emergencies. In addition, I have asked Colonel Barefoot to serve on the crime commission's law-enforcement committee to make sure the needs and views of the patrol are considered in the commission's deliberations. I want the commission to hold law-enforcement forums across the state to find out what we can do to help law-enforcement officers. I hope you will get involved in those forums and share your thoughts and ideas about how we can help you do your jobs.

But the fight against crime isn't just your fight or my fight. It's everyone's fight. I want us all to work together— in our neighborhoods, our schools, everywhere—to build a safer North Carolina and a brighter future for our children. It's our obligation to the people of North Carolina [unintelligible], and looking at your faces today, I know it's an obligation we can meet.

---

[1] A thirty-four-year veteran of the Highway Patrol, Holly Springs resident Robert A. Barefoot became its commander on March 1, 1993. Governor Hunt's Schedule for February 28-March 6, 1993; Swearing-in of State Highway Patrol Commander Robert Barefoot and Executive Officer Cecil Williams, Raleigh, March 1, 1993, Governors Papers, James Baxter Hunt Jr.

[2] The General Assembly authorized private confinement facilities under *N.C. Session Laws, 1995,* II, c. 507, s. 19. Section 19.2 created a $250,000 "reserve for bunking inmates in shifts," a practice also known as "hot bunking." A pilot program at Lincoln Correctional Center was to schedule "inmates' daily activities in such a manner that at least two different groups of inmates may occupy the same dormitory space during different portions of each twenty-four-hour day."

[3] Lawmakers approved the following measures to protect the unaware and defenseless from being victimized: "An Act to Authorize the Department of Justice to Provide Criminal Record Checks to Domiciliary Care Facilities, Home Care Agencies, Hospices, Licensed Child-Placing Agencies, Residential Child Care Facilities, and Other Providers of Treatment for or Services to Children, the Elderly, and the Sick and Disabled," *N.C. Session Laws, 1995,* I, c. 453, ratified July 18, 1995; *N.C. Session Laws, 1995,* II, c. 507, sec. 23.25, required "Criminal History Checks of Child Day Care Providers and Study Use of Central Registry on Child Abuse and Neglect," and sec. 23.26 mandated "Criminal History Checks of All Foster Parents in Licensed Family Foster Homes." See also press release, Governor Hunt Outlines Crime Proposals to Help Victims, Raleigh, January 19, 1995, Governors Papers, James Baxter Hunt Jr. The statute on sex-offender registration is identified earlier in this volume.

[4] Rufus L. Edmisten (1941-   ), born in Boone; B.A., University of North Carolina at Chapel Hill, 1963; J.D., George Washington University, 1967. Attorney; aide to U.S. senator Sam J. Ervin Jr., and deputy chief counsel, Senate Select Committee on Presidential Campaign Activities—Watergate Committee; N.C. attorney general, 1974-1984; Democratic nominee for governor, 1984; was elected N.C. secretary of state, 1988, re-elected in 1992, resigned in 1996. *North Carolina Manual, 1995-1996,* 231-232, *1997-1998,* 174, 178.

ADOLESCENT PREGNANCY PREVENTION COALITION OF NORTH CAROLINA

RALEIGH, MAY 23, 1995

I'm honored to receive this award, and I want to thank the Adolescent Pregnancy Prevention Coalition for all you have done in the last decade to prevent teen pregnancy in our state.[1]

Teen pregnancy is a fact. It's a fact that seventy-two teenagers in North Carolina will become pregnant today. It's a fact that many of those young girls will drop out of high school and go on welfare. It's a fact that many will never hold a job or pay taxes, and they will be trapped in a cycle of welfare dependency—along with their children. But we don't have to accept that fact. We can change it, and we must change it.

We must join forces to prevent teen pregnancy. Families, and churches, and communities must step up their efforts. Business leaders must join our public education campaign to promote teen abstinence, and government must do more to prevent teen pregnancy. That's why teen pregnancy prevention is a key component of our Work First welfare reform plan. We know teenage pregnancy locks thousands of young mothers into the welfare system with little hope of breaking free.

We must discourage teen pregnancy and promote responsible parenting. We must discourage irresponsible behavior that lands people on welfare in the first place. We must launch a concerted effort against teen pregnancy that lets young people know it is wrong to have a child outside marriage.

Today we're launching an all-out attack against teen pregnancy. I'm proud to stand here, today, with Howard Hunter and Shawn Lemmond,[2] two prominent young leaders in the state House. While they may differ in politics, they agree in principle that children must stop having children. They know teen pregnancy is not a partisan issue or a political one. They know that Democrats and Republicans must work together to stop teen pregnancy, and I commend them for their leadership in the House— and in their own communities.

With their help, the General Assembly last year provided $100,000 to help finance the Adolescent Pregnancy Prevention Coalition's statewide public education campaign on teenage abstinence.[3] Starting this month, radio ads will air across the state, focusing on teen abstinence and greater responsibility on the part of young males. With support from the private sector, the coalition is hoping to run TV ads as well. When school starts back, we'll see these posters in schools, churches, health clinics, youth agencies, and social service offices.

We've got to keep working to get the message out to our young people. This is an effort that I support strongly, and I intend to do everything I can to help get that message out. I hope the private and nonprofit sectors will step forward, as well. With their support, this campaign can reach millions of young people across our state. And I hope the General Assembly will provide support as well, with $1.5 million in the expansion budget to boost our Adolescent Parenting Program. This parenting program run by the Department of Human Resources, targets teens, who've had one child, to prevent the second pregnancy, counseling them about abstinence and encouraging them to stay in school.

This is part of what we're doing to discourage teen mothers from having more children. Teen mothers who put off having another child so that they can graduate from high school have a much better chance of succeeding on their own and staying out of the welfare trap, and it's working. In the twenty-four counties where it's operating, this program has cut in half the number of second pregnancies. Ninety percent of the teens involved have graduated from high school. We need this in every single county, and I urge Representatives Hunter and Lemmond to advocate for this in the expansion budget.

---

[1] The Adolescent Pregnancy Prevention Coalition presented its Nick Jeralds Advocacy Award to the governor in recognition of his "leadership in preventing teen pregnancy." State representative Luther R. "Nick" Jeralds (1938-1992; D-Cumberland) chaired the House Human Resources Committee and worked to curtail youth pregnancy in North Carolina. *News and Observer*, December 15, 1992; *North Carolina Manual, 1991-1992*, 393; press release, Governor Hunt Pushes Teen Abstinence Public Education Campaign, Raleigh, May 23, 1995, Governors Papers, James Baxter Hunt Jr.

[2] Joseph Shawn Lemmond (1958-   ), born in Lexington, Ky.; resident of Mecklenburg County; was educated at University of North Carolina at Charlotte; U.S. Navy, 1976-1982. Insurance agent; member, Mecklenburg Board of Commissioners, 1983-1987; police commissioner, 1983-1987, town council member, 1983-1987, and mayor, 1987-1991, of Matthews; member, N.C. House, from 1993; Republican. *North Carolina Manual, 1995-1996*, 615.

[3] *N.C. Session Laws, 1993, Regular and Extra Sessions, 1994*, c. 769, s. 27.10.

PIEDMONT INAUGURAL

CARY, MAY 25, 1995

[Seeking to duplicate the success of the Carolinian, the state officially introduced its second passenger train, the Piedmont, on May 25, 1995. Both trains traveled daily between Raleigh and Charlotte, and stopped in Cary, Durham, Burlington, Greensboro, High Point, Salisbury, and Kannapolis. Like the Carolinian, the Piedmont also was a cooperative effort between the state and Amtrak Corporation, the federal passenger rail operator: North Carolina covered 75 percent of the new train's costs, while Amtrak paid the remainder and supplied operating crews. The Piedmont entered daily round-trip service on May 26, 1995. The Carolinian began plying the rails in 1990 and carried 189,000 passengers during 1994, making it the country's best-performing passenger train supported jointly by any state and Amtrak. *News and Observer*, May 22, 26, 27, 1995.]

It's great to be here with all of you in Cary, one of our state's fastest-growing communities. Thank you all for coming out, and I am so happy to be a part of the kicking-off ceremony for the Piedmont: North Carolina's passenger train. I am especially pleased to be able to dedicate your stop here in Cary, because the Piedmont is the first passenger rail service to Cary in more than thirty years.

When I took office in 1993, I announced that improving rail service transportation was one of my main priorities. I am so proud to be here today and see that promise made into a reality. I want to commend my secretary of transportation, Sam Hunt, and David King,[1] my deputy secretary for transit, rail, and aviation, for their leadership in making the Piedmont happen. They made rail service a priority in the Transportation 2001 program and have worked hard to see that necessary upgrades were made to improve rail service and reduce travel time.

Today's dedication represents North Carolina's national leadership in developing a state-sponsored rail service. Few other states in the country have taken the initiative to purchase equipment and begin a new service. Today is certainly cause for celebration. We're not only making history, we're making a statement that our "Variety Vacationland" includes more than one good way to see our beautiful state.

I look forward to great progress as we approach 2001. In fact, by the year 2000 we want to have the service between Raleigh and Charlotte down to two hours. That would mean the Piedmont would average more than 90 miles an hour. Eventually we want to establish true high-speed rail, 90 to 125 miles per hour, which requires an investment of $100 million or more. That costs less than building an interstate!

The folks in the Department of Transportation are working hard, and we should soon have service extended to the new stadium in Charlotte— so you can board the Piedmont from your hometown, sit back, relax, and step off the train at the front door of the Carolina Panthers' stadium![2]

And we're working with other states to implement high-speed rail service in the future. We want to next turn our attention to the Southeast corridor, which links the South through Atlanta, then to Florida—and also would link us to the Northeast corridor, through Richmond, Washington, and New York.

Now I would like to present Mayor Koka Booth with a replica of North Carolina's newest passenger train, the Piedmont.[3]

Again, thank you all for coming out to see your new passenger train. So without any further delay: All aboard!

---

[1] David Dewitt King (1946-   ), born in Daytona Beach, Fla.; B.S., Davidson College, 1968; M.B.A., University of North Carolina at Chapel Hill, 1970; U.S. Army, 1970-1972. Career with N.C. Dept. of Transportation included: special assistant to the assistant

452 PAPERS OF JAMES BAXTER HUNT JR.

secretary for management, 1973-1975; administrative coordinator, 1975-1979, director, 1979-1990, Public Transportation Division; director, Public Transportation and Rail Division, 1990-1993; deputy secretary, Department of Transportation, from 1993. David King, letter to Jan-Michael Poff, March 10, 1999; *News and Observer*, March 8, 1998.

² The Carolina Panthers of the National Football League played their home games in Ericsson Stadium, Charlotte.

³ Koka E. Booth (1932-   ), born in Kenova, W.Va.; resident of Cary; was educated at N.C. State University. Worked in coal mining, metal fabrication industries before joining public affairs staff, SAS Institute, Cary; Cary mayor, 5-term town council member as of March 1999; winner, several civic and occupational awards; Republican. Koka E. Booth, letter to Jan-Michael Poff, March 19, 1999; *News and Observer*, December 9, 1999.

NORTH CAROLINA VICTIM ASSISTANCE NETWORK ANNUAL CONFERENCE

RALEIGH, JUNE 8, 1995

In my office I have a very special picture that was given to me by the North Carolina Victim Assistance Network [VAN]. It includes the faces of ten very special people—people who were loved and cared for; people who were victims of a terrible crime; people who are no longer with us. The picture is on a table next to my door, so that everyone who comes to see me at the Capitol sees the faces of these crime victims. I hope they also see the pain their families suffer to this day, and I hope they see the need to always remember that victims come first.

But no one has made North Carolinians see the light more than all of you here, today. You all have worked, harder than anyone, to make us see the plight of crime victims and their families and to make us see how much work still has to be done. You have turned your grief and your pain into action. You have fought back. You have helped other victims and families work through their tragic experiences, started Neighborhood Watch programs, and volunteered in dozens of other ways to help create a safer North Carolina.

You've put yourselves on the line in the fight against crime. Brenda Howerton and Hilda Griffin braved the TV lights during our special session on crime, telling their stories as a way to push for our efforts to eliminate parole for first-degree murder. I know everyone at that press conference was truly touched hearing Brenda detail how her son was murdered at a Virginia college three years ago, and Hilda Griffin describe how her husband, Gene, a Charlotte police officer, was gunned down by two teenagers in 1991. They made a difference: The bill was passed into law.

Each of you has been an inspiration. I'm proud to have worked alongside you over the last two years, joined in our fight to help make our communities safer. In the special crime session I called last year, we convinced the General Assembly to make sentences longer for dangerous criminals, to toughen gun laws, and to increase prison capacity. We launched new efforts to steer our youngsters away from crime and began looking at tougher punishment for young criminals. We convinced the legislature to start putting victims first. We increased funding for N.C. VAN to help you continue your outstanding work. We boosted the Victims' Compensation Fund to help crime victims pay medical bills and get compensation for lost wages following a crime, and we changed the law so that criminals injured while committing a crime no longer have rights to money from that fund. In my administration, I've also taken steps to make sure victims of violent crimes are notified when their assailant is eligible for parole. I've directed the Parole Commission to be more responsive to victims, so I want you all to let me know if you have problems.

Last year I heard a lot from you all, and other victims' rights advocates, about the need for a victims' rights amendment. You all helped me think it through and helped me realize that statutes aren't enough. We do need a constitutional guarantee for victims. If our constitution gives criminals basic rights, victims should have rights, too.

I announced my support of the amendment, last year, and urged the General Assembly to support it in my State of the State address. But you all are the ones who got it passed in the House yesterday! You'll get it passed at the polls in 1996, as well, and you know I'll be right there with you to ensure its passage.

When it passes, I want to work with you to make sure we are doing the best we can to guarantee victims the right to be heard in court—and the right to be informed of and involved in all court proceedings related to their case.

But there's more that needs to be done to make North Carolina safer. I've asked the General Assembly to toughen sentences for violent criminals by 30 percent, including second-degree murder, rape, and armed robbery. That means we need to repeal the prison cap, and we need to make sure we have enough prison beds. We've asked the General Assembly to fund 4,000 new prison beds over the next four years, using no-frills prisons and boot camps, and to cut costs by using existing prison space more efficiently.

I've asked the General Assembly to require criminal background checks for day-care providers and foster parents; and to pass a law, that's called Megan's law, to require registration of sex offenders and notifying communities where they live, so residents will know if a sex offender has moved in down the street.[1] I'm pushing for mandatory impact statements, so judges will know exactly what victims have gone through before they hand down a sentence; and we're pushing to increase our victim restitution efforts to make sure more victims are reimbursed for their losses.[2]

But I can't do it alone, folks. I need you by my side! I need your help to make sure all of these measures are passed by the General Assembly this year. Your legislators need to know how you feel about the governor's crime-fighting package, and I urge you to contact them to voice your support.

One of the things I've learned, over the years, is that government doesn't have all the answers. Government, alone, can't make our streets safe. Our law-enforcement officers, as hard as they work, can't do it alone—and you all can't do it alone. But together, we can make our communities safer.

Together, North Carolinians can do amazing things. We can make a difference. You've shown how, and I salute you for it. Together, we can make our children safer and their futures brighter.

---

[1] "Megan's law" resulted from a murder that riveted national attention on the crime of pedophilia and the broader debate over convicts' rights versus victims' rights. Jesse Timmendaquas was arrested for the July 29, 1994, rape and strangulation of seven-year-old Megan Kanda. He was one of three convicted child abusers living in a house, across the street from the Kanda family, in Hamilton Township, New Jersey. Until Megan died, no one in the neighborhood knew of the criminal backgrounds of the three men.

Public outrage pressed New Jersey legislators to draft Megan's law, which required authorities "to notify neighbors, schools, churches, youth groups, and the media within 45 days of an ex-[child sex] offender's moving into a neighborhood." Critics called it the "scarlet-letter law" and claimed it would hamper the reintegration of ex-prisoners into society and dissuade convicted pedophiles from seeking or continuing therapy. Victims' advocates argued that the measure was a badly needed weapon in the struggle against child abuse.

Megan's law became law in late October 1994, when New Jersey governor Christine Todd Whitman signed nine bills aimed at sex offenders. The little girl's fate also prompted the inclusion of a community notification provision in the 1994 federal crime bill. "Natural Born Predators," *U.S. News & World Report*, September 12, 1994, 66; *New York Times*, August 3, 4, 6, 21, 23, 30, October 4, 21, November 1, 1994; "Not in My Backyard!" *Time*, September 5, 1994, 59; P.L. 103-322, "Violent Crime Control and Law Enforcement Act of 1994," *United States Statutes at Large*, Act of September 13, 1994, 108 Stat. 2038-2042.

[2] Neither the proposed impact statement, nor the requests for increasing victims' restitution collections and allowing more victims to be reimbursed, were approved during the 1995 legislative session. Press release, Governor Hunt: Legislators Should Have Done More for Victims this Session, Raleigh, August 1, 1995, Governors Papers, James Baxter Hunt Jr.

3C ALLIANCE GROUNDBREAKING

Mebane, June 12, 1995

For two years, I've wanted to announce jobs at this site in Mebane. The state and this community poured a lot of time and energy into making this site a good home for a good company. Today, we couldn't be happier to help celebrate 3C Alliance's plans to invest $100 million in this community and put more than 500 of our people to work.

This is a very special occasion for me and a unique opportunity to meet with the chief executive officers of three of the world's largest battery manufacturers. But 3C Alliance is a unique company that has provided a unique opportunity for Alamance County and North Carolina. Toshiba, Varta, and Duracell have joined together for the first time to make rechargeable batteries in the United States. This joint venture was billed as one of the top ten economic development deals in the world, last year, by *Site Selection* magazine. It represents three companies, from three countries, forming a partnership to make their companies stronger. That's exactly what we do here in North Carolina, and this project is a perfect example.[1]

The state Commerce Department, the Alamance Chamber of Commerce, the Alamance county commissioners, and the city of Mebane built a partnership to bring 3C Alliance to this site. The state of North Carolina made a commitment of $150,000 from the current Competitive Fund—and [an] additional $375,000 if the General Assembly provides more money for the fund. The state agreed to improve roads and to create a tailor-made worker-training program at Alamance Community College. The city and county agreed to get the site ready for construction of a 240,000-square-foot facility.

We've made a wise investment in 3C Alliance. This company is a prime example of the kinds of industry we [are] working to recruit with the Competitive Fund, and this company is one of the reasons I've asked the legislature for another $10 million for our Competitive Fund. The fund has made our state competitive in our efforts to bring in good companies and good jobs. In this case, Mebane and North Carolina won out over locations in twelve other states—and we're counting on our legislature to help us remain competitive, so we can continue to bring good jobs and good companies like these to North Carolina.

We welcome all of you to North Carolina. I want to extend a special welcome to Varta, who is making its first investment in our state. Duracell and Toshiba are no strangers to North Carolina. Duracell employs 550 North Carolinians in a battery-manufacturing facility in Lexington, and Toshiba maintains a sales and marketing office in Durham. Now I want all three of you to know that if you need to build battery manufacturing facilities here, near this operation, Secretary Phillips, Gary Carlton,[2] who is our chief recruiter, and I will work very hard to help you in any way we can! We want you to be at home here, and we want to help you grow. We value your commitment to us and your confidence in the state of North Carolina.

---

[1] The countries represented by the 3C partners were Germany (Varta Batterie AG), Japan (Toshiba Battery Co., Ltd.), and the United States (Duracell International). "Site Selection's 1994 Top Deals: Gobs of Global Jobs," *Site Selection*, April 1995, 314-315.

[2] Gary E. Carlton (1940-   ), born in Kannapolis; resident of Raleigh; B.S., University of North Carolina at Chapel Hill; was also graduated from Stonier Graduate School of Banking at Rutgers University, Carolina School of Banking at University of North Carolina at Chapel Hill, and Duke University Executive Management Program. Career in finance included 16 years with First Union National Bank, 1963-1979; joined Southern National Bank as regional and city executive, Raleigh, 1979, later served as branch coordinator for Southern National Bank of N.C.; executive vice-president, chief operating officer, from 1986, Southern National Corp.; president and vice-chairman, from 1987, Southern National Bank of S.C.; president, SNB Savings Bank, SSB, from 1993. Director, Business and Industry Development, N.C. Dept. of Commerce, 1995-1997; retired. Gary E. Carlton, letter to Jan-Michael Poff, March 20, 2000.

TAR HEEL GIRLS' STATE

Greensboro, June 12, 1995

Thank you for having me here today. It's great to see all of these bright young faces, the faces of the future and the faces of North Carolina's future leaders. North Carolina has always been a state of pioneers, sending women to Raleigh and Washington before many other states. When I took office in 1993, we had more women legislators in the General Assembly than ever before. Their leadership forced change—laws that make it a crime for a husband to rape his wife[1] and increased funding for domestic violence centers, among other things. Unfortunately, there are fewer women [legislators] in Raleigh today. I hope you all can help change that.

Later this week, I'll be speaking to a group of 400 women legislators from around the country.[2] They are today's leaders. But today I'm with tomorrow's leaders, women who will no doubt be the legislators, lawyers, and CEOs of tomorrow.

You all are not just the leaders of tomorrow; you're going to push people like me to be better leaders today. You are here, this week, to learn how government works, how everyone can play a part, and how anyone can make a difference. But I also want you to challenge government, to challenge authority, to challenge the status quo. It is your ideas, energy, and enthusiasm that will fuel change and help us do a better job improving the quality of life for our people—and it sounds like some of you are already pushing that envelope. I understand that Kyrin Ward, next year's senior-class president at Ragsdale High School, in Jamestown, says government should get the solutions started, but it's up to people to carry them the rest of the way.

She's exactly right! And I wish she could help spread that word in Raleigh. Government doesn't have all the answers, and certainly all wisdom doesn't come from Raleigh. For the last two-and-a-half years, we've tried to take a new approach. Rather than looking to government to solve all the problems, we're trying to use government as a catalyst that brings people together to solve problems in their own communities. That's what we're doing with Smart Start, our early childhood initiative that helps preschoolers get the day care and health care they need to come to school healthy and ready to learn. And that's what we're doing with SOS [Support Our Students], our after-school mentoring effort for middle-school students.

SOS helps steer elementary and middle-school students away from drugs and crime by giving them a safe place to go after school, where they can do homework or get involved in interesting activities or athletics. I proposed SOS, and the General Assembly funded it during last year's special crime session. But what really makes SOS work are the 1,700-plus SOS volunteers who serve as mentors for students across the state. I volunteer once a week, and some of our SOS volunteers are high-school students like yourselves. I know many of you volunteer in community service projects through your school organizations or your church. I commend you for all you're doing to make a difference, and I invite you to get involved with our SOS program.

We have volunteers in Smart Start, as well. They've donated more than 300,000 hours so far. In fact, it seems like just about everyone is pitching in to help. Volunteers are donating time. Businesses are donating supplies. Corporations are donating money. That's the beauty of Smart Start. It brings people together to help children—business people and social workers, ministers and local elected officials, Democrats and Republicans. The state provides seed money, but it's the local people, not Raleigh, who decide how best to help the children in their own communities. And it's working.

Thanks to Smart Start, almost 9,000 children are getting child-care subsidies; 55,000 children are getting better-quality day care; 25,000 children are getting better health care; and 150,000 children have gotten immunizations. But despite its tangible results, there are people in Raleigh who don't want to continue the momentum, who want to cut the successful programs we have in thirty-two counties, and who don't want to expand Smart Start to twelve more counties. I believe we can improve Smart Start, and I've welcomed suggestions by legislative leaders in both houses to make it stronger. I think we should improve accountability, increase support from the private and nonprofit sectors, and eliminate day-care waiting lists in all counties. But we need to preserve the local control and flexibility that's [sic] essential to Smart Start's success. It seems to me that if Kyrin Ward understands why local control is important, then her legislators should understand, too.

The House and senate are now in a standoff over Smart Start. I've presented a plan that I hope can be the basis for consensus. I urge you to call and write your legislators and tell them to support our proposal for Smart Start. Tell them that it's time to come together, work this out, and agree on an approach that expands and improves Smart Start. Tell them that we need to keep working to help children now, so that we spend less money on dropouts, welfare, and prisons down the road. And tell them that it's the local folks, not Raleigh, who should decide how best to help children in their own communities.

I urge you to voice your opinion, to get involved—to make a difference. As your generation of leaders steps up, we will be looking to you for new ideas and new strategies to deal with the challenges that lie ahead. Now I want to take time to let you challenge me with your questions.

---

[1] "An Act to Abolish the Spousal Defense to a Prosecution for Rape or Sexual Offense," *N.C. Session Laws, 1993*, I, c. 274, was ratified July 5, 1993.

[2] Hunt addressed a meeting of the National Order of Women Legislators, Raleigh, June 14, 1995. Governor Hunt's Schedule for June 10-17, 1995, Governors Papers, James Baxter Hunt Jr.

BIPARTISAN LETTER OPPOSING TUITION TAX CREDITS

RALEIGH, JUNE 19, 1995

[H.B. 954, "A Bill to be Entitled an Act to Permit Parents to Choose the Educational Setting that Best Helps Their Child Learn," proposed awarding tuition tax credits to families with children in private schools. Hunt and six bipartisan supporters of public education argued against such credits in a letter, to 300,000 members of business, education, and professional organizations, and asked them to lobby in opposition to the legislation. Dated June 19, 1995, the letter bore the signatures of four Democrats—Hunt; Jay M. Robinson, State Board of Education chairman; Bob Etheridge, state superintendent of public instruction; William R. Friday, UNC system president emeritus—and three Republicans: former governor James G. Martin; Howard Haworth, chairman emeritus, State Board of Education; and William S. Lee, Duke Power Co. chairman emeritus. Press release, Governors Hunt and Martin Join Bipartisan

Opposition to Tuition Tax Credits, Raleigh, June 19, 1995, Governors Papers, James Baxter Hunt Jr.

The text of the letter fleshes out Hunt's notes for remarks to the Education Cabinet, Raleigh, June 19. The governor also spoke against the credits in appearances at the Teacher Town Meeting, Raleigh, June 20; and the Teacher of the Year Conference, Raleigh, June 26, 1995.

Although the General Assembly did not adopt tuition tax credits, it felt them worthy of further investigation; see "Studies Act of 1995," *N.C. Session Laws, 1995,* II, c. 542, s. 2.1(7)f, ratified July 29, 1995; and *N.C. House Journal, 1995,* 496, 925, 1036, 1075.]

Dear Friend of Education:

We have signed this letter because we believe all North Carolina children deserve a good education. And we believe our state faces a crucial decision this year on the future of the public schools.

The 1995 General Assembly is taking a number of positive steps that hold great promise for improving the public schools. These steps include:

—Passing a plan to reorganize our public schools and give local communities unprecedented authority.

—Considering the reduction of class size in the early elementary grades.

—Requiring the expulsion of any student who brings a dangerous weapon to school.

—Working with the State Board of Education to raise standards in reading, writing, and mathematics, and boosting accountability.

We believe the legislature is on the right track with these actions. But we are concerned that this progress would be undermined by enactment of another bill being considered by the legislature, House Bill 954.

H.B. 954 would radically change our state's approach to education funding:

—It would permit, for the first time in our state's history, the use of state tax dollars for nonpublic schools.

—It would provide a $1,000 tax credit, or a direct tax-paid grant to families who pay less than $1,000 in taxes, to families with children in private schools, out-of-state schools, or even home schools.

—It would permit county commissioners to appropriate tax money to nonpublic schools and to let nonpublic schools use public school facilities. In addition, private school students would be permitted to participate in band, athletics, and special interest programs offered by the public schools.

The bill would cost the taxpayers $15 million in 1996 and $77 million in 1997. Because of the potential impact on our state budget, the expenditure of such sums of money need [*sic*] careful consideration:

—The bill, in effect, would create a new entitlement program; the federal deficit shows how costly such entitlements can become.

—The bill provides for no standards and no accountability in exchange for this tax-paid subsidy.

—If that much money is available in the budget, we believe it should be used to (1) reduce class size, (2) raise teachers' pay, or (3) provide other performance incentives for educators.

We appreciate the concerns that the bill's supporters have about the quality of the public schools. After all, we have devoted our lives to working for better education. But we believe that North Carolina's schools deserve a chance to use the new tools this legislature has given them.

For too many years in North Carolina, we have taken a stop-and-start approach to education reform. We have not had a sustained commitment to a commonsense approach that can work. Now that we have that kind of approach, we should give it a chance to work.

North Carolina's educators understand that if real improvements are not made, our people will demand radical action like tuition tax credits. And the taxpayers deserve to get their money's worth from the schools.

We cannot afford to have second-class schools in North Carolina. That would cripple our ability to compete in an information-dependent economy.

But we believe North Carolina should focus on improving the public schools, and we believe the legislature has taken historic action to do that. For the first time, school systems and individual schools will have the authority they need to meet their obligations to taxpayers and be held accountable for the results. That clear authority and accountability could be undermined if H.B. 954, or any tuition tax-credit/voucher bill, is enacted.

The members of North Carolina's General Assembly need to know how you feel about this issue. They need to hear from people who are committed to improving the public schools.

These decisions, with all they will mean for the schools' future, will be made during the next few weeks. It is urgent that you contact your senators and representatives today and discuss these issues.

North Carolina's public schools need your help. They deserve a chance to meet the challenge and the opportunity that the legislature has given them.

Thank you.[1]

---

[1] Below the signatures a line stated, "Letter not printed or mailed at government expense."

Smart Start, the early childhood education and health program Governor Hunt launched in 1993, was the centerpiece of his third administration. Despite widespread popularity, however, it faced the threat of funding cuts by the General Assembly two years later. Hunt, who declared that he would fight "with every breath I've got" to preserve the program, is shown passionately addressing hundreds of supporters attending a Smart Start rally, June 14, 1995, across from the Legislative Building. (Photograph by Harry Lynch, Raleigh *News and Observer*.)

Governor Hunt's expressive storytelling entertains Vice-President Albert Gore Jr. and the children at the Community School for People Under Six, in Chapel Hill. The visit to the school, April 15, 1996, allowed Gore a firsthand look at the benefits of Smart Start. "North Carolina, by far, is the leader among all fifty states in helping the nation understand the importance of focusing on the first years of a child's life," the vice-president said. (Photograph by Jim Bounds, Raleigh *News and Observer*.)

PRESS RELEASE: GOVERNOR HUNT PRAISES HOUSE AND SENATE FOR SMART START AGREEMENT

RALEIGH, JUNE 21, 1995

[Lengthy negotiations between House and senate leaders, with considerable input from Governor Hunt, culminated in the Smart Start funding agreement announced on June 21, 1995. Although Hunt did not win further expansion of the program, the agreement continued the existing level of funding for projects already in place and made planning monies available for twelve new counties. The matching funds requirement Republicans wanted initially was revised in a manner Hunt found acceptable.

House Republicans began the session opposed to any expansion of Smart Start, and some talked of cutting funding for existing programs. But they, too, were pleased with the agreement. "'We won. We wanted three things: account-ability, a match, and no expansion. We got what we wanted,'" said House majority leader Leo Daughtry.

With the House in GOP hands, Hunt and other supporters of Smart Start likely fared as well as they could. Aaron Plyler, a Democrat and co-chairman of the Senate Appropriations Committee, said of the agreement: "'It's not what I wanted, it's probably not what the governor wanted, and I bet it's not exactly what the House leadership wanted. But I'd still say it's a pretty good deal.'" *News and Observer*, May 31, June 1, 2, 8, 11, 15, 18, 22, July 2, 1995.]

House and senate leaders today announced a compromise that would continue, expand, and improve Smart Start, North Carolina's public-private day-care initiative for children. The agreement, which continues funding at current levels for the state's thirty-two Smart Start counties and provides for plans to expand to twelve additional counties, also steps up accountability measures and preserves the program's local control.

Governor Jim Hunt praised legislative leaders for putting politics aside to work together for North Carolina's children. "The House and senate have shown today that Democrats and Republicans can work together to put children first," he said. "I'm especially pleased that this agreement provides planning money for the twelve expansion counties and provides for full funding in the second year, pending a satisfactory independent performance audit. The agreement provides for greater accountability, but without robbing the program of the local control that is central to Smart Start's success. I believe this will help us respond to the pressing need to provide better day care, better health care, and a better start for children and families of North Carolina," he said.

The agreement, which should mean imminent passage of the state's continuation budget,[1] would:

—Provide planning money for the twelve Smart Start counties next year, taken out of the continuation budget, with a commitment to fund the expansion counties in the second year if an independent performance audit is satisfactory. The twelve expansion counties would operate under new ground rules that require a full year of planning time.

—Provide for more accountability over local partnerships' spending, with direct legislative oversight, a strict cap on administrative costs, and an increased role for the North Carolina Partnership for Children.

—Require a 10 percent cash match from the private sector and a match of up to 10 percent in in-kind contributions, donated services, and volunteer hours. This would mean that about $3 million in cash and $3 million in in-kind contributions, donated services, and volunteer hours would have to be raised statewide next year. The independent auditing firm will study the match and make recommendations for revision if it determines that the current formula is unreasonable.

Smart Start, a public-private effort that's designed to provide quality child care, health care, and other critical services to every child under six, is a new approach. Across the state, it has brought together businesses, churches, nonprofits, and government, and it has left the decision-making up to the community. In each Smart Start county, local business people, ministers, civic leaders, educators, community activists, and local officials determine how to best serve local children and who are responsible for raising other funds.

So far, Smart Start has had tangible results. More than 8,600 children are getting the child-care subsidies their families need so they can work and hold down a good job. More than 55,000 children are receiving higher quality child care thanks to better trained teachers and quality incentives to child-care centers. More than 25,000 children have gotten early intervention and preventive health screenings, and more than 150,000 children have gotten immunizations so they can get a healthy start in life.

---

[1] The continuation budget was ratified June 26, 1995. *N.C. Session Laws, 1995*, c. 324.

REACTION TO FDA'S EFFORT TO REGULATE TOBACCO

RALEIGH, JULY 13, 1995

["'Smoking begins as a pediatric disease. Each day, 3,000 children become regular smokers, and almost 1,000 of them will eventually die'" from it, said David A. Kessler, commissioner of the United States Food and Drug Administration. To prevent more children from joining the swelling numbers of young tobacco users, Kessler announced on July 13, 1995, that the FDA had the authority to designate nicotine a drug and to regulate cigarettes as nicotine delivery devices.

President Clinton supported restrictions against cigarette sales to minors and appeared to back the FDA proposal in general; he opted to withhold his unqualified endorsement of Kessler's plan, however, until he had seen specific details. While they agreed upon the need to reduce youth smoking, critics of the proposal protested that the FDA lacked the legal authority to regulate tobacco. They also warned that Kessler's decision, if enacted, would give the FDA "broad controls" over the manufacturing and sale of cigarettes—including the power to shut down the industry entirely. *News and Observer*, July 14, 15, 1995.

Hunt was quick to criticize the FDA's regulatory proposal (see below). He further expressed his steadfast opposition to the plan in remarks delivered in Kinston, July 19, 1995, during ceremonies commemorating the one-hundredth anniversary of the opening of tobacco market season in Lenoir County; notes for a meeting with tobacco growers, September 13, 1995; an address to the North Carolina Tobacco Growers Association, February 2, 1996; and his speech at the opening of the Old Belt Tobacco Market, August 1, 1996. For related press release, see Governor Hunt Takes Case for Tobacco Farmers to White House, Raleigh, July 21, 1995, Governors Papers, James Baxter Hunt Jr.]

I am deeply concerned by the Food and Drug Administration's attempt to impose federal controls on tobacco. I have urged President Clinton, in person and in the strongest possible terms, to reject FDA regulation of tobacco products. I have reiterated my concern to the White House today and am placing a call to the president, as well.

Clearly, FDA does not have statutory authority to take this step. It is using the youth-access issue to justify a regulatory power grab. The matter of youth access to tobacco products can be addressed without giving FDA this sweeping authority.

I will insist that the White House give serious consideration to the economic impact that FDA regulation would have on the people of North Carolina. Thousands of people in our state—people who work hard on farms, in factories, and throughout our economy—depend on tobacco for their families' livelihood. Their financial future should not be jeopardized by overzealous regulators.

The FDA's effort to use regulation to restrict tobacco is "big government" in action. Whether to smoke is a decision adults ought to make, not government.

GOVERNING MAGAZINE CONFERENCE ON CRIME

RESEARCH TRIANGLE PARK, JULY 21, 1995

[Hunt's address to the *Governing* conference was nearly identical to his speech for the North Carolina Sheriffs Association, August 7, 1995.]

Welcome to North Carolina. I want to thank *Governing* magazine for holding its conference in our wonderful state. We're glad to help you host this conference and to foster thoughtful discussion about how public officials can combat crime.

I don't have to tell you how concerned Americans are about crime. Across this nation, people are afraid. People don't feel safe. They're afraid to go to the mall; afraid to walk down the street; afraid to send their kids to school. My own daughter was a victim of crime a few years ago.[1] Her apartment was broken into during Christmas vacation, ransacked, and torn apart. She was afraid. As her father, I was angry—and as governor of a state that's seen violent crime increase 65 percent in the last decade, I want to make sure my daughter, and your daughters, are safe.

Across America, people are looking to government to do a better job protecting them. They want dangerous criminals behind bars. They want prisoners working. They want victims to be put first. They want classrooms without violence. They want to be safe.

In North Carolina, we're taking that directive seriously. Last year, I spent three months researching ways to fight crime before I called a special [legislative] session on crime. I talked with police chiefs, sheriffs, judges, DAs, victims' advocates, and criminal justice experts. I came away believing that an effective crime-fighting strategy must have two components: tough punishment and strong prevention.

Just building prisons isn't enough. Just focusing on crime prevention isn't enough. We need both. That's not an easy concept for many folks, as I learned in our crime session. I spent much of that session working to bring the two sides together to agree on a comprehensive approach.

But we held true to that principle: At my urging, our General Assembly passed a thirty-four-point, crime-fighting plan to make our communities safer and to keep dangerous criminals off our streets. We lengthened sentences for violent criminals, toughened gun laws, and increased prison capacity. We launched ambitious new efforts to deter youngsters from crime and began looking at tougher punishment for young criminals. We boosted support for crime victims, and drug and alcohol treatment, and we began developing a statewide criminal justice information system.

This year, I hope we will build on those efforts. I've asked lawmakers to increase sentences for violent criminals by another 30 percent. We've repealed the state's prison cap to help make sure criminals serve their complete sentences. The General Assembly agreed to put a victims' rights amendment on the ballot next year.

We're building more prisons, and we're building them faster than ever before. Some 12,800 beds have been built or authorized since I took office in 1993, and we're putting more prisoners to work than ever before. We've launched a Community Work Program that has put 12,000 prisoners to work, almost 3,000 more than when I took office in 1993. Prisoners are learning the value of hard work, discipline, and teamwork, and they are doing work that needs to be done.

Two weeks ago, I went out to Jordan Lake with my secretary of correction, Franklin Freeman, to observe prisoners working along a family beach and recreation area. They were clearing brush and logs that had washed up on the shore as a result of recent flooding. Thanks to their work, families were able to spend the next weekend at the lake.

As part of our Community Work Program, a total of 16,000 prisoners are working or training for jobs. They are cleaning up trash along the highways; clearing brush; helping maintain public buildings; working inside prisons, cooking, cleaning, and doing maintenance work—whatever needs to be done. Some work on farms. Some work in soap and paint manufacturing plants, printing plants, laundries, and sewing plants; and some skilled inmates are doing construction jobs, building prisons, and installing security fences.

North Carolina has one prison work farm, and prisoners are helping build two new prison work farms in Caswell and Tyrrell Counties. Right now, inmates grow about 50 percent of the food they consume. When these two new facilities open, prisoners will grow 80 percent of their own food.

We're also working to instill discipline with military-style boot camps for nonviolent offenders. Boot camps combine tough punishment with a ninety-day rigorous program that gives offenders a sense of responsibility, respect for others, and the value of hard work and discipline. In the last two-and-a-half years, we've quadrupled the number of boot camp beds at our facilities in Burke and Richmond Counties. This year, I've asked the General Assembly to provide funding for even more boot camp beds, and we are seeking federal funds for a female boot camp; and legislators have passed a law that allows judges to sentence more offenders to our boot camps.

I believe keeping prisoners behind bars longer and making them work, and work hard, is important. But at the same time, we've got to do more to prevent crime. As part of North Carolina's comprehensive effort to prevent crime, I've directed the Governor's Crime Commission to implement community-oriented policing programs, and we've put more school resource officers on campuses. Our safe schools effort is working to create weapons-free school zones by making it a felony to bring a weapon to school. At my urging, the General Assembly passed a zero-tolerance policy [that] will automatically suspend any student for up to one year who brings a weapon to school.

But in the long run, there's no more important effort than deterring youngsters from crime. That's what SOS [Support Our Students] is all about. SOS is a volunteer-driven program that brings adults and teens into schools to mentor middle school students. In its first year, almost 6,000 students, in fifty-two North Carolina counties, have gotten a new chance at success because volunteers are encouraging them, building their self-esteem, and helping them discover their own potential. My wife, Carolyn, and I volunteer with the SOS program each week, here in Wake County.

We're also investing in our children through Smart Start, our early childhood initiative. Smart Start is helping kids get off to the right start and giving preschoolers a better chance to succeed in school and in life. We know it is the best investment we can make in the future of our state— in education, economic development, and especially crime prevention. If we reach these children early on, they'll start school ready to learn and with a bright outlook for future success.

Smart Start, SOS, and North Carolina's other prevention programs are examples of innovative public-private partnerships to fight crime, efforts that will pay off with a better workforce, a better quality of life, and fewer dollars spent on prisons, welfare, and other social programs down the road. In North Carolina, we have shown that punishment and prevention can go hand in hand. I believe that we must have such a balanced approach, and I hope you all will come away with a sense of what works and what doesn't in our state.

---

[1] A kicked-in door greeted Elizabeth Hunt, a graduate student in social work at the University of North Carolina, upon her return to her Chapel Hill duplex apartment on January 6, 1993. During her weeklong absence, one or more burglars stole $1,400 in personal property, including her car. "'We're thankful that she was away when it happened, but the sense of violation is one that will be with our family forever,'" Governor-elect Hunt said of the incident. "'As a father and as an elected official, I feel very strongly that we've got to make our state a safer place. I owe it to my daughter, and I owe it to all of the six-and-a-half million people in the state.'" *News and Observer,* January 8, 9, 1993.

END-OF-SESSION STATEMENT

Raleigh, July 29, 1995

[The governor delivered similar retrospective addresses on the 1995 legislative session in New Bern, August 21, and Whiteville, August 22, 1995. For related press releases, see Governor Hunt Says 1995 Session a Start, But Not Enough, Raleigh, July 31, 1995, and Governor Hunt: Legislators Should Have Done More For Victims This Session, August 1, 1995, Governors Papers, James Baxter Hunt Jr.]

In my State of the State address almost six months ago, I issued two challenges to the legislature. I challenged them to cut taxes, fight crime, and help children; and I challenged them to put people first and politics second.

Democrats and Republicans in the legislature have worked together to cut taxes, mostly for working families. I wish more had been done, however, and that my proposals to expand the homestead exemption and cut corporate taxes had been enacted.

They haven't done enough to keep violent criminals behind bars. I proposed increasing sentences for violent felonies by 30 percent, exactly what the Structured Sentencing Commission initially proposed. It looks like the senate has prevailed on a 16 percent increase in sentences. I commend the senate for that start but wish more had been done.

They haven't done enough to help children come to school ready to learn. Although the senate leadership was willing to move Smart Start ahead, partisan politicking slowed Smart Start down—and slowed down our efforts to help our state's children.

The legislature has done better on public schools by reducing class size; giving parents, and teachers, and principals more say; passing my "zero tolerance" safe school law; and continuing our efforts to raise standards for the three Rs. This should give local schools more flexibility to improve education, while holding them more accountable for results. I hope legislators will give these reforms a chance to work before they try again to divert tax dollars from public schools. But I had hoped that teachers would have gotten better pay raises and that universities would have gotten the faculty salaries and graduate tuition help that I proposed.[1]

I'm concerned that the General Assembly didn't do enough for state employees with the bonuses. I supported the senate special provision that would have given state employees a bonus, but the House leadership apparently would not go along.[2]

I regret that a welfare reform bill was not passed, and we're looking at ways to put Work First into action without legislation.

I'm glad that legislators did the right thing for environmental protection: protecting public health with more animal waste oversight and protecting the coastal areas.

In the coming months, my administration will focus on what we can do in the Executive Branch. We'll be putting more prisoners to work. We'll be putting more welfare recipients to work, and we'll work with local communities to make Smart Start a success despite new administrative burdens and fewer administrative resources.

We have a challenge ahead of us. This legislature has a challenge ahead, as well: to do better at putting people over politics. This session was an historic one, a chance to show the people of this state that a divided legislature can find common ground—discussing important issues on their merits, listening to each other, and learning from each other. The legislature had a chance to show the people that they could move beyond campaign rhetoric and partisan turf fighting and work together to do the right thing for North Carolina.

They could have done better. I'm hopeful that if they work at it, they can get it right in the next session. We need to work harder to work together. We need to work harder to debate policy instead of campaign slogans. We need to work harder to put the people before politics. We need to work harder to do more for the people of this state. While this session is a start, it isn't good enough, and we can do better.

---

[1] Legislators provided public primary and secondary schoolteachers, with less than thirty years' experience, with a 4 percent increase in base pay for F.Y. 1995-1996. Faculty pay raises at the state's university and community college systems averaged 2 percent. *N.C. Session Laws, 1995*, c. 507, secs. 7.12-13, 17.18-19.

[2] State employees received a 2 percent pay increase effective July 1, 1995. *N.C. Session Laws, 1995*, c. 507, sec. 7.14.

PRESS RELEASE: GOVERNOR HUNT'S PROPOSAL WILL PUT OVER 400 MORE PRISONERS TO WORK

RALEIGH, AUGUST 3, 1995

Governor Jim Hunt's proposal to provide funds to expand the Department of Correction's Community Work Program will put over 400 more prisoners to work in North Carolina. The General Assembly provided $1.5 million this year, and $1.1 million in recurring funds, for 33 inmate work crew supervisors to oversee 420 minimum-custody prisoners working on local projects. Hunt's effort to put more prisoners to work has brought the number of state inmates working or training for jobs to 16,000. Since Hunt took office in 1993, more than 2,600 inmate jobs have been added to the correction workforce.

"One of the issues I ran on in 1992 was putting more prisoners to work, and that's what the Community Work Program is all about," Hunt said. "We all work hard to make a living and support our families; prisoners should be working, too. We're going to do whatever it takes to make sure that every able-bodied inmate in North Carolina's prison system is working—and working hard."

At Hunt's urging, the Department of Correction started the Community Work Program in January. During the first five months of 1995, inmates in the Community Work Program worked several hundred thousand hours on 700 projects in 50 communities across the state, including cutting brush and picking up trash, clearing tire dumps, and maintaining public buildings. In June, an inmate crew cut scrub pines and cleared out grass and weeds around a threatened earthen dam at the North Carolina Zoological Park in Asheboro, and another crew cleared storm debris from June flooding around a family recreation area at Jordan Lake in Chatham County. Last week, a crew stripped and waxed floors and painted walls to get an elementary school in Caswell County ready for students returning later this month.

In addition to the Community Work Program, nine prisons are either expanding their highway cleanup crews or beginning new ones, which will add another 420 inmates to the 2,000-inmate highway labor force in existence. Correction Enterprises employs nearly 2,000 inmates in their operations, which include printing plants, farms, soap and paint manufacturing, laundries, and sewing plants. About 5,000 inmates work inside prisons, cooking, cleaning, and doing maintenance work. More than 100 inmates are on construction jobs, building prisons and installing security fences. In fact, an inmate crew has begun constructing a new, 650-bed prison work farm in Caswell County.

"By having inmates working in our communities, we're not only saving taxpayers money, we're building a better quality of life for our people," Hunt said. "Whether they're clearing brush or repairing public buildings, our Community Work Program is teaching criminals the value of hard work and discipline."

PRESS RELEASE: STATE BOARD OF EDUCATION APPROVES
KEY PART OF GOVERNOR JIM HUNT'S
EDUCATION REFORM EFFORTS

RALEIGH, AUGUST 4, 1995

The State Board of Education today accepted a set of guidelines recommended by the North Carolina Education Standards and Accountability Commission for raising standards that high-school students must meet in order to graduate, a key component of Governor Jim Hunt's education reform efforts.

"This is a critical first step in making sure our students will be able to compete and succeed in the modern workplace," Hunt said. "I applaud the State Board of Education for working to raise standards and improve performance for our students."

The commission's guidelines include:

—Requiring students to master six skills in order to graduate, including communicating, using numbers and data, solving problems, processing information, working in teams, and using technology;

—Developing a new curriculum designed to help students master essential skills, particularly in math, science, and language arts;

—Using grades 4, 8, 10, and 12 as benchmark years to test student performance. Students not performing at acceptable levels will have individual study plans and other strategies to help them catch up;

—Offering Tech Prep in addition to the traditional college-bound paths of study.

The recommendations emphasize student performance as the number-one factor in determining when a student will move on to the next grade level instead of age, maturity level, or other factors.

Hunt created the Standards and Accountability Commission, a bipartisan panel of twenty-five educators, business leaders, parents, legislators, and community leaders, in 1993. The commission held a series of public hearings around the state to get input about what students need to know and be able to do to compete in the modern workplace. The commission is now conducting pilot tests of the essential skills students must know and be able to do before they receive a diploma. The 1995 General Assembly approved Hunt's budget request to continue the pilot testing of standards now under way in ten school districts around the state. Hunt has said that, by the year 2000, every high-school student must perform skills like reading, writing, and using numbers in a real-life setting in order to get a diploma.

REACTION TO PRESIDENT CLINTON'S SPEECH

RALEIGH, AUGUST 9, 1995

["'One of the greatest threats to the health of our children is teenage smoking, and it's rising,'" President Clinton told the Progressive National Baptist Convention at its annual meeting, August 9, 1995, in Charlotte. "'If you wanted to do something to reduce the cost of health care, help over the long run to balance the budget, and increase the health of America, having no teenagers smoke would be the cheapest, easiest, quickest thing you could do.'" *News and Observer*, August 10, 1995.

Hunt accompanied the president while in Charlotte. After he returned to his Capitol office, the governor held a teleconference with newspaper and radio reporters to discuss the day's events. He opened with the following statement.]

Today I made another plea to the president to oppose FDA [U.S. Food and Drug Administration] regulation of tobacco. I spoke with him privately on the way to the Charlotte Convention Center. I reminded him, once again, of the 264,000 jobs at stake in North Carolina.

I was glad to hear him say, during his speech to the Progressive National Baptist Convention, that he recognized the importance of tobacco to our state and that he recognizes that tobacco farmers and their families are good people, working hard, to make a living.

The president was correct when he said that we must deal with health threats to our young people today. I share his concern about the growing number of teens who are smoking. I told the president, today, that North Carolina is ready to join in on an aggressive campaign to curb teen smoking. The best way to do that is to get state and local governments, along with the tobacco industry, working together to prevent young people from having access to cigarettes and to launch a massive public awareness campaign on the dangers of youthful smoking. The success of North Carolina's "Booze It and Lose It" and "Click It or Ticket" campaigns show [sic] it can be done. I was glad to hear the president say that parents must also have a role in preventing their children from smoking.

All of these things—stepping up enforcement of existing rules, public awareness campaigns, and parental responsibility—will help us achieve our goal. We don't need more big-government regulations. It will only guarantee a legal battle that will prevent the kind of immediate, aggressive campaign we need, right now. I urge the president, in the strongest words, to join in a cooperative approach that can reduce teen smoking dramatically and quickly.

REACTION TO PRESIDENT CLINTON'S DECISION ON FDA REGULATION OF TOBACCO

RALEIGH, AUGUST 10, 1995

[President Clinton announced, at a White House press conference on August 10, 1995, that he was "authorizing the Food and Drug Administration to initiate a broad series of steps all designed to stop the sale and marketing of cigarettes and smokeless tobacco to children." Those measures included requiring an ID to buy cigarettes; a prohibition on vending machines; a ban on tobacco advertising on billboards near schools and playgrounds; "images," like the Joe Camel cartoon character, "will not appear on billboards or in ads in publications that reach substantial numbers of children and teens"; the sale of individual cigarettes, T-shirts, gym bags, event sponsorship, and other marketing gimmicks were not to be aimed at teenagers; and the implementation of an annual, $150 million anti-smoking campaign funded by the tobacco industry. Transcript, "Clinton Announces Action to Combat Teen Smoking," *Congressional Quarterly Almanac, 1995*, D-26.]

I'm very disappointed with the president's decision. It's the wrong way to go. We do not need additional regulation and more bureaucracy to enforce what is already the law. It is against the law, today, to sell cigarettes to teenagers. We need to do a better job enforcing that law. We do not need more big government from the FDA [U.S. Food and Drug Administration] to do it. I've been telling the president that for two months and made my case again in our ride to the speech, yesterday afternoon.[1] He told me then he had still not made up his mind.

I knew he was leaning toward more regulation. But I still hoped I could change his mind, up until the last minute. In the limousine, I was arguing with him to enforce existing law against underage smoking rather than turning to more regulation. I thought there was still an opportunity to influence the decision in the right way. But the president called me late last night to tell me of his decision.

As I told him, all of us in North Carolina agree that we ought to do more to stop teenage smoking. But we fundamentally disagree about how to do it.

This is the usual, Washington, big-government way. I'm disappointed that the president has chosen that course.

---

[1] Clinton addressed the Progressive National Baptist Convention in Charlotte. *Charlotte Observer*, August 10, 1995.

CHILD SUPPORT ENFORCEMENT PRESS CONFERENCE

CHARLOTTE, AUGUST 10, 1995

[For related press release, see Governor Hunt's Proposal Will Make North Carolina Amoung Toughest on Deadbeat Parents, Charlotte, August 10, 1995, Governors Papers, James Baxter Hunt Jr.]

A young woman I know in Raleigh broke down in tears last week because she bought a $10.00 pair of shoes for her young daughter. It was $10.00 she would have spent on groceries, but she believed her ex-husband when he told her he'd already mailed his child-support check. The check never came. It hadn't come the month before, or the month before that.

This week, my friend, who works as a day-care center director in Raleigh, went down to the Wake County Courthouse to find out how to force her "ex" to pay the back child support his two-year-old daughter is entitled to. I'm proud to be able to tell my young friend that North Carolina is about to take a tough stance against her ex-husband—one of the toughest in the nation.

At my urging, the General Assembly passed one of the nation's toughest child-support enforcement laws last month. North Carolina's new deadbeat parents law means business. We're going after deadbeat parents where it hurts: their pocketbook, their livelihood, and their recreation. Starting next year, a parent who's more than ninety days behind in child support will lose his or her driver's license; hunting license; fishing license; professional and business license. That means we're going to go after deadbeat doctors, dentists, lawyers, and other professionals. We'll deny deadbeats new vehicle permits. We'll track them down across state lines in ways we never could before, and we'll use new ways, like insurance settlements, to collect unpaid support.

We're even going to put their faces on wanted posters. We'll have posters, like this one, all over the state. The names and faces of North Carolina's "Ten Most Wanted" deadbeat parents will be plastered in every store, library, and public place we can think of in the state. Posters like this work. Ask Sheriff Jim Pendergraph, who has worked with the local child support enforcement office to do in Mecklenburg County what I want us to do statewide.[1] Since March, the sheriff has been able to track down dozens of deadbeat parents who owe more than $400,000 in back child support. We're working to collect that money now.

In North Carolina, there are half a million single parents, like my friend, who are struggling to support their children because deadbeat dads and moms are shirking their responsibilities. I want these people tracked down, and I want them to support their children. Because many of these single mothers rely on welfare to put food on the table, deadbeat parents are costing taxpayers money. But many deadbeats are like my friend's "ex": professionals who simply refuse to support their children unless they're forced to.

Well, we're going to force them like they've never been forced before. We will go after deadbeat dads—and moms. We will do whatever it takes to see that parents support their children in North Carolina. This is more than a new law. It's a clear message to parents in North Carolina: You'd better take responsibility for your children. If you don't, you will be caught and you will face the consequences.

Now I'd like to call on Sheriff Pendergraph to tell us more about how his "Top Ten" list is working here in Mecklenburg County.

[1] James I. Pendergraph (1950-   ), born in Charlotte; A.A. in criminal justice, 1976; was graduated from FBI National Academy, Quantico, Va.; military police, U.S. Army, 1970-1972. Attained rank of deputy chief during twenty-three-year career with Charlotte-Mecklenburg Police; was elected Mecklenburg County sheriff, 1994. Lori Lauer, office of Jim Pendergraph, letter to Jan-Michael Poff, March 8, 1999.

CABINET MEETING: HOG AGENDA

NEW BERN, AUGUST 21, 1995

[The proliferation of factory-style hog farms in the eastern third of North Carolina turned the state into the nation's number-two swine producer by 1994. The industry raised a billion dollars in revenue that year and was poised to turn pork into the state's top agricultural commodity.

However, not everyone believed the near-term economic benefits that the pork industry brought to eastern North Carolina—the jobs, the money—justified transforming the region into hog heaven. People who lived near factory farms complained of the pervasive smell. Some local government officials worried that intensive swine farming was a detriment to economic growth and diversification.

There also was growing concern over groundwater quality and the pollution of area streams and rivers. A hog generates two to four times as much waste as a human, and there were seven million hogs on farms east of Interstate 95. Millions of tons of manure were pumped into lagoons, clay-lined pits in which it decomposed and was stored for spraying onto farmland. Critics of factory pork farming accused government officials and the General Assembly of turning a blind eye to the leaking lagoons and runoff from spraying operations that threatened public health, fisheries, and tourism.

But neither the protests of the aggrieved neighbors of hog farms nor the warnings of environmentalists succeeded in focusing attention on the hog-waste issue the way an event in Onslow County did. On June 21, 1995, as lawmakers were gutting proposed legislation to enact tougher swine industry regulations, a waste lagoon ruptured at Oceanview Farms, near Richlands, sending a 25-million-gallon torrent of fecal soup "surging across roads and crops and into the headwaters of the New River."

The spill at Oceanview Farms was the worst in state history and one of four major hog-waste discharges that summer. One million gallons (June 21, Sampson County) and another 2 million gallons (August 8, Brunswick County) flowed into tributaries of the Cape Fear River, and a million gallons contaminated a tributary of the Black River (July 6, Sampson County). By comparison, 11 million gallons of oil escaped the broken hull of the *Exxon Valdez* in 1989.

The hog-waste spills, and the breaching of a poultry-waste lagoon in Duplin County (July 1995) brought national and international notoriety to North Carolina. The incidents also pointed out the state's need to improve its scrutiny of large-scale agricultural operations. *News and Observer*, February 19, 21-24, 26, March 3, 4, 16-18, 22, 23, 28, 1995, April 5, 17-20, 25, 26, 30, May 8, 10, 13, 23-27, 30, June 11, 22-27, 29, July 1-9, 11, 13-15, 23, 25, 26, 28, 30, August 5, 6, 9, 11-13, 15, 16, 19, 22, 23, 25, 30, 31, September 2, 9, 14, 15, 16, 21, 27, 30, October 8, 10, 12, 14, 15, 21, 26, November 15, 24, 29, 30, December 1, 2, 8, 12, 15, 17, 20, 22, 1995.]

This has not been a good summer for the environment in eastern North Carolina. It has become increasingly apparent that we've got to get a handle on the problems posed by large animal-waste operations. I'm committed to getting this problem under control. We cannot allow these large hog operations to endanger the public health and safety of our citizens.

When I called on DEHNR [Department of Environment, Health, and Natural Resources] to undertake a massive investigation of all animal-waste operations in this state, I wanted to get an overall picture of what was out there. Now that picture is becoming increasingly clear. While most operators are seriously committed to preserving and protecting the environment, a disturbing number have ignored environmental safeguards. We cannot continue to let them blatantly disregard our rules.

Last week, I appointed my members to the blue ribbon study commission on animal waste. Speaker Brubaker and Senator Basnight will also be making appointments to that commission. The commission is going to have its work cut out for it. There are a number of long-term issues they're going to have to grapple with.[1]

In the interim, though, I realize that there are some things that can't wait until the commission completes its work. The recent waste spills, especially the one in Onslow County, point to some weaknesses that we must address now. Today I'm issuing an order requiring that we undertake a number of initiatives immediately.[2] I'd like to call on DEHNR secretary Jonathan Howes for details.

[Howes speaks.]

Folks, I want to send a clear message to the operators of these systems: Shape up or ship out. It's that simple. We will not let you use our rivers and streams as cesspools.

The waters of this state belong to all of us. No one person can presume to take their use away from the rest of us. That's what some operators have done. It's certainly what happened up in Onslow County. Fishermen, marinas, motels, and restaurants have all felt the repercussions from the June 21 spill. They continue to feel it, as a portion of that river remains posted. Folks who once swam and played in the river haven't been able to do so because of the spill.

I want to send a clear message to the operators of these facilities: That's not the way we do business in North Carolina. And, I want to send a clear message to the folks who value North Carolina's environment: We will not let anyone pollute the waters of this state. We will not let anyone take away all of our rights to swim, fish—and yes, drink—from our rivers and streams.

I have long been a supporter of North Carolina's farmers. I continue to support our farmers, and I'm convinced that most farmers share the ideal drilled into me by my daddy: Farmers must be environmentalists. Without a clean environment, farmers can't exist. There's no water or soil for them to glean their living from. I'm not going to let a few bad actors spoil our environment—for farmers, fishermen, for all of us.

---

[1] The Blue Ribbon Commission on Agricultural Waste was established under "The Studies Act of 1995," *N.C. Session Laws, 1995*, II, c. 542, secs. 4.1-4.7, ratified July 29, 1995. The governor, president pro tem of the senate, and Speaker of the House each appointed six members to the commission.

[2] Hunt announced short-term initiatives that the executive branch could undertake to address immediate waste-contamination problems. For example, each new farm needed to pass a site inspection and have an approved waste-management system in place before animals were brought onto the property. Farmers who discharged livestock waste directly into streams or rivers faced increased regulatory scrutiny and were required to have special operating permits. The governor also called upon the Division of Environmental Management to conclude, by December 1, 1995, its follow-up inspections to ensure that corrective action had been taken by hog farms that an earlier survey revealed were in serious violation of the state's water-quality regulations. *News and Observer*, August 22, 1995.

SOS NEWS CONFERENCE

RALEIGH, AUGUST 31, 1995

Two years ago I went to a housing community, in Durham, and met a young man, in sixth grade, who told me something that shook me. He told me how unsafe he felt in his neighborhood when he went home after school.

For the next three months, I talked with people all over the state who told me that, if we really want to keep our young people from getting involved in drugs and crime, we need to give them a safe place to go after school. That's the reason I proposed, and the General Assembly approved, the SOS, or Support Our Students initiative—to give kids a safe place to go in the afternoon where they can participate in constructive activities with older mentors.

We hoped that, at the end of three years, we would be able to recruit enough volunteers and raise enough private money to serve 6,000 students in our fifty-two SOS initiatives. Well, I'm here to announce today, that after just one year, we have exceeded our goal. Our SOS initiatives are already serving more than 6,000 students. More than 2,000 people have volunteered more than 42,000 hours to SOS, and local SOS initiatives have raised more than $2 million in cash and in-kind contributions from businesses, schools, local governments, churches, and thousands of people who believe in SOS.[1]

Today I want to announce another important contribution from a business that believes in SOS: Bruegger's Bagels. One day a week, Bruegger's is donating enough bagels to give 1,400 students in Durham, Mecklenburg, Wake, and Orange Counties their afternoon snack—a donation worth $25,000. And it'll help those SOS initiatives free up money to spend on other things, like a part-time teacher or a new activity.

In making this gift, Bruegger's is issuing the "Great Bagel Challenge," a challenge to other businesses to donate afternoon snacks or other supplies to SOS kids. I want to thank Bruegger's for its support of SOS. I'd also like to thank Rick Wrigglesworth, of Arby's, for funding scholarships to reward outstanding high school seniors who volunteer for SOS; and P. D. Williams, of Cal-Tone Paint, for sponsoring our statewide volunteer recognition ceremony and agreeing to supply paint for SOS facilities statewide.

We need businesses to answer the Bruegger's challenge. We need more of them to follow the examples set by Bruegger's, Arby's, Cal-Tone Paint, and so many other SOS supporters—and we need more volunteers. I'd like to see one volunteer for every student we serve. Across the state, our local SOS initiatives are trying to serve more students. Opening this site at Carnage Middle School will double the number of students being served in Wake County.

We need to keep expanding SOS, because SOS is a public-private partnership that works. We're still gathering the data, but local initiatives are already reporting promising results for SOS students. School performance is going up. Juvenile crime is going down.

SOS is literally changing young people's lives. I've seen it in the young people Carolyn and I work with every week, and I've heard about it from other teachers, and students, and parents across the state. But why don't I let you hear it for yourselves, from two students who are in the SOS program: Michael Robinson and Candace Morgan.[2]

---

[1] The number of volunteer hours donated to SOS between the program's implementation and the fourth quarter of 1996 exceeded 100,000. SOS Expansion Announcement, Charlotte, October 31, 1996; for more on SOS volunteers, see press release, Radio Talk Show Brings Volunteers to Classroom, Raleigh, May 26, 1995. Governors Papers, James Baxter Hunt Jr.

[2] According to Hunt's notation, Michael Robinson and Candace Morgan were students at Daniels Middle School, Raleigh.

STATE EMPLOYEES ASSOCIATION
OF NORTH CAROLINA CONVENTION

GREENSBORO, SEPTEMBER 8, 1995

I'm proud to be here, today, with some of the hardest-working, most creative, and innovative people in North Carolina; and I'm honored to have a chance to talk with you about the progress we're making together and issues of concern to you as we work to build a better North Carolina. We've made much progress this year. We passed the largest tax cut in state history to help working families. It means that a family of four, making $30,000, will see their taxes cut by one-third. A single mother of two will see her taxes cut by two-thirds.

We've done more to protect our communities and our families against crime. We've put tougher sentences in place for violent crimes, and violent criminals are staying behind bars longer. More prisoners are working than ever before, and we're building no-frills prisons, work farms, and boot camps.

We're changing the welfare system. We're requiring welfare recipients to sign personal responsibility contracts. As part of that contract, we're telling them to get a job, paid or unpaid, and to get on a path to work and self-reliance.

We're making commonsense changes in the public schools. We passed a zero-tolerance law to automatically suspend, for up to a year, any student who brings a gun to school. We cut class size in kindergarten and first grade. We're putting more emphasis on the basics and raising standards for what students need to know and be able to do to get a good job. We're giving teachers and parents more say in their schools; and we're helping more children come to school ready to learn through Smart Start, which operates in thirty-two counties in the state and twelve more in the planning stages. Because of Smart Start, more than 60,000 children and their families are getting better child care, and 25,000 young children are getting health care and preventive health screenings, and more than 150,000 kids are getting free childhood vaccinations now, all because of Smart Start.

I know that you are concerned parents, grandparents, aunts and uncles who really care about our children. That's why I created child involvement leave, in 1994, that gives each state employee eight hours of paid leave a year to participate in a child's school activities. I encourage each of you to get involved and make a difference in a child's education.

But, I know state employees didn't get all you'd hoped for in the 1995 legislative session. The General Assembly failed to give you the $300 bonus recommended by the senate. I strongly supported that bonus plan, and I was deeply disappointed when it failed. You should know that since I took office in 1993, state employees' salaries have increased by 8 percent, plus a one-time 1 percent bonus.

Legislators again considered using your retirement and health fund reserves for other things in the budget. That's wrong, and I've fought any attempt to raid that fund. State employees have worked hard for that money. It belongs to you, and it shouldn't be used for anything else.

I urge you to push the General Assembly for full funding of your pay plan. We know pay for performance is what state workers deserve.

I was especially disappointed that legislators eliminated the ombudsman's position, your direct link with my office. During her two years as ombudsman, Blanche Critcher helped more than 1,000 state employees—finding solutions to your problems and keeping me informed of the issues important to state employees. I have now put her to work on other projects serving constituents, but I will continue to seek her advice on issues that are important to you; and as always, I welcome your continued contact with my office.

As many of you know, we have eliminated a number of positions in state government this year, including the cuts at DPI [Department of Public Instruction].[1] According to the Office of State Personnel, we have seventy-seven employees in DPI without jobs. Many of those will be retiring, and those seeking jobs will be given priority in the fifty-two vacancies that exist in that department. In other areas of state government, we have almost 200 who have been "RIF-ed,"[2] but three-fourths of those employees have been placed in other jobs, and we're working hard to place the others. In fact, we have launched an unprecedented effort to assist those employees with our PHASE (Partnership to Help Assist State Employees) program, which is a partnership between OSP, ESC [Employment Security Commission], and the Division of Employ[ment] and Training in the Department of Commerce.

I respect you and the hard work you do. But I believe the work you do, day in and day out, should be free of political pressure. I simply will not tolerate any state employee being subjected to any kind of political pressure. That's why I've asked my campaign not to accept [funds] from rank-and-file state employees. But that doesn't mean that state employees shouldn't take part in the political process. That is your right, and I encourage you to get involved in any way you wish.[3]

I want to continue to work with you to look for ways to give state employees more choices when it comes to supplemental insurance coverage. Every state employee should have a fair, consistent set of insurance choices offered at a reasonable price. My staff is working with leaders of SEANC to make sure that you do. You should know that I have asked State Treasurer Harlan Boyles to head up a study committee to look at this issue and come up with recommendations.[4]

If we want to build the right kind of future for North Carolina, we've got to do more—and do it together. But we can't do it without state employees. State employees are the key to making state government work better. I want to thank you, and I look forward to working with all of you to help find more ways to make our state everything that it can be.

---

[1] Legislative pressure forced the State Board of Education to cut the Department of Public Instruction bureaucracy in 1995. The board's downsizing and reorganization plan, unprecedented in North Carolina state government history, cut the department's workforce of more than 700 employees to 485. *News and Observer*, January 15, February 2, 5, 12, 17, 21, March 2, 3, 9, 23, 26, April 14, 26, 28, May 4, 9, 14, June 14, September 7, 8, 1995.

[2] RIF: reduction in force, a euphemism for *layoff*.

[3] See related press release, Governor Hunt Directs Campaign Not to Solicit State Employees, Raleigh, April 5, 1995, Governors Papers, James Baxter Hunt Jr.

[4] Harlan Edward Boyles (1929-   ), born in Vale; B.S., University of North Carolina at Chapel Hill, 1951. Certified public accountant; was first elected state treasurer in 1976 and was reelected in 1980, 1984, 1988, 1992, and 1996; author; Democrat. *News and Observer*, August 27, 30, September 22, 25, 28, October 11, 1995; *North Carolina Manual, 1997-1998*, 195-196.

"FAMILIES FOR KIDS" PRESS CONFERENCE

RALEIGH, SEPTEMBER 13, 1995

I spent this weekend with my four children and five grandchildren celebrating a family milestone and the joy of my family.[1] It's easy to take family for granted. But for too many children, a stable home is only a dream. The number of children in foster care in North Carolina is soaring, up 200 percent in the past ten years. Much of that increase has come in the last five years. At the same time, the number of families willing to become foster parents, or willing to adopt, is shrinking. Today we're launching an exciting effort to reverse that trend.

Families for Kids will help us find permanent adoptive families for more than 700 children who have been in foster care for more than a year. And we'll reduce the number of children coming into the foster care system by working to strengthen families and keep them together.

The W. K. Kellogg Foundation, of Michigan, is providing a $3 million grant to make sure Families for Kids succeeds. This will be a public-private partnership, joining the Kellogg Foundation with the North Carolina Department of Human Resources, the North Carolina Child Advocacy Institute, the UNC School of Social Work, and families and community leaders in eight pilot counties. Like North Carolina's other public-private partnerships to help children—Smart Start and SOS [Support Our Students]—this effort will bring communities together to make a difference in the lives of young people.

Families for Kids is a major step in our statewide effort to reform the entire child welfare system, and it shows that North Carolinians can do great things when they work together. Families for Kids will:

—Help families stay together by making sure they know where to get the help they need;

—Place foster children who do enter the system in a permanent home within one year;

—It will assign each child to one caseworker;

—Send each child to only one foster home;

—And it will give each family one professional to do their assessment so they only have to tell their story one time.

This effort will begin in eight counties: Buncombe, Catawba, Cleveland, Edgecombe, Guilford, Iredell, Richmond, and Wayne. Together these counties have more than 700 children who have been in foster care for over a year. Some of those children and their foster families are here with us today. In just a minute, you will hear from Dontressa Haley, who will tell you what a difference a caring foster family has made in her life; and you'll hear from Sandra Johnson, who has opened her home, and her heart, to young people in need. But first, I'd like to thank the Kellogg Foundation for helping us make a real difference in the lives of these very special children and families. And thanks to these eight pilot counties for pioneering this crucial effort and making a commitment to Families for Kids through your efforts. Your hard work with this program will help guarantee its success.

---

[1] Governor Hunt was referring to the wedding of his youngest daughter, Elizabeth, which was held September 9, 1995, in the South Garden of the Executive Mansion. Telephone conversation with Janice Shearin, executive assistant to First Lady Carolyn Hunt, October 18, 1999.

WORK FIRST NEWS CONFERENCE

RALEIGH, SEPTEMBER 14, 1995

[For related press release, see Governor Hunt Launches Work First Welfare Reform, Raleigh, September 14, 1995, and attachment thereto, Work First: Reforming North Carolina's Welfare System, Governors Papers, James Baxter Hunt Jr.]

There's a real change going on in North Carolina. While the politicians are continuing to debate welfare reform in Washington, we're doing it here. Today I'm signing and putting in the mail North Carolina's request for federal waivers to implement our Work First plan. With these waivers, we will require 35,000 AFDC recipients to get a job, paid or unpaid, within twelve weeks. If they don't get a job or get into short-term job training, they don't get welfare benefits.

With these waivers, we will require every AFDC applicant to sign a personal responsibility contract. This contract is a promise: a promise to immunize their children; a promise for teen parents to stay in school and live at home; a promise to seek and accept a job; a promise to make a plan to get off welfare—and stick to it. If Work First participants refuse to sign, or break, their contracts, they don't get welfare benefits.

With waivers, we will impose a two-year time limit for benefits, one of the toughest in the nation. After two years on Work First, they're off. And waivers will let us impose a family cap, a signal to Work First participants that they need to take responsibility for their family planning. If they have a child ten months after entering Work First, we will not pay cash benefits for that child. But we don't want to punish the children, so food stamps and Medicaid health care coverage for children would not be affected.

The Clinton administration has committed to speeding up the waiver process, so we expect to have an OK from the federal government in sixty days for some of the waivers we need. Meanwhile, we're taking other steps to get Work First under way. We're already moving JOBS [Job Opportunities and Basic Skills program] participants into Work First, and we're phasing in the first 35,000 people who will be required to work. That's nearly one-third of all adults on welfare. Ultimately, all able-bodied welfare recipients will have to get a job.

True welfare reform means a reform in attitude as well. Training has already begun for social services staff in all 100 counties. And we're launching an education effort in ten pilot counties to get the word out to welfare recipients that work pays, and pays better than welfare, and that their families will be better off if they have a job.[1]

We're working with local governments to make sure they can implement Work First. By October 1, local governments should have an action plan in place that lays out how they'll be moving welfare parents into the workforce. And we'll be working with local employers, and chambers of commerce, and employment officials in state agencies to identify jobs. If there are no jobs in the private sector, Work First participants will work, unpaid, in the public or non-profit sector, earning their benefits that way.

In short, North Carolina is moving ahead. We're not waiting. We're taking action to get people off welfare and into the workforce.

When Congress acts, we'll adjust accordingly. In any case, we can assume that fewer federal dollars will be coming our way. We've got to start now to change our approach, because no one can afford to conduct business as usual.

Welfare was meant to be a way to help families get back on their feet, not a way of life. But it has become a system that traps people into a cycle of dependency—a system that penalizes people for saving money, for holding a job that pays decent wages, and penalizes families for staying together. North Carolina is taking action to fix the system, to put people to work, to require personal responsibility.

We've got a lot of work to do to make Work First a reality, and we've got a real education effort, with employers and with welfare recipients, to make it work. We all must shoulder some of the responsibility— churches, civic groups, business leaders, the community. It won't be easy, and it won't be fast, but I'm confident that Work First will work.

---

[1] The ten pilot counties were Cleveland, Macon, Mecklenburg, Pasquotank, Pender, Person, Stanly, Stokes, Wake, and Wilson. Press release, Governor Hunt Launches Work First Welfare Reform, Raleigh, September 14, 1995, Governors Papers, James Baxter Hunt Jr.

1999 SPECIAL OLYMPICS WORLD GAMES ANNOUNCEMENT

RALEIGH, SEPTEMBER 15, 1995

And the winner is: North Carolina!

Eunice Shriver, founder of Special Olympics International, and Sargent Shriver, chairman and CEO, have come here, today, to join us in announcing that North Carolina will host the 1999 Special Olympics World Games. This is a great day for North Carolina and a great day for the Triangle.[1]

Special Olympics has a special place in our history. Just two years after the first International Games were held in Chicago in 1968, North Carolina held its first Special Olympics Games in Burlington. With us, today, are Mike Stone and Marty Sheets, both athletes from Greensboro who participated in the very first Special Olympics International Games in Chicago. Mike's parents, Robert and Alice Stone, and Marty's parents, David and Iris Sheets—would all of you stand? We have some other athletes from the Triangle here today, and I want to recognize them and their families: Jeremy Williams, of Raleigh; Carl Hibbert, of Raleigh; Paulette Moore, of Chapel Hill, and her fiancé, Michael Brown; and Stephanie Speh, of Durham. I'd like all these athletes and their families here to stand up.

Since our first games, North Carolina Special Olympics has grown to include 23,000 athletes in ninety-seven local programs. I want to share with you the mission of North Carolina Special Olympics: to provide year-round sports training and athletic competition, in a variety of Olympic-style sports, for people with mental retardation, giving them continuing opportunities to develop physical fitness, demonstrate courage, experience joy, and participate in the sharing of gifts, skills, and friendship with their families, other Special Olympics athletes, and the community.

I can't think of anything that has generated more excitement and team spirit in our state in a long time!

I want to share with you a little about how we came to make a bid for these games. Last spring, my commerce secretary, Dave Phillips, came to me and said, "Governor, we have a wonderful opportunity to do something very special for North Carolina." Now, when Dave Phillips tells me we have a chance to do something for North Carolina, I listen—because he's usually right. He told me that this was not just a major economic development issue, but an event that would touch the hearts of all North Carolinians. Then he said it would be the largest sporting event ever held in North Carolina, and it would require enormous support from the public and private sectors.

I chose Dave Phillips as my commerce secretary because he is a salesman—and Dave, I and the people of North Carolina are very grateful for the effort you've made to bring this event here. I am naming Secretary Phillips as chairman of the Games Organizing Committee.

I'm also grateful to many others who have been part of our team to recruit this event. As we have called on our universities and local government and community leaders for support, they have rallied to the cause. I want to recognize Chancellor Michael Hooker, from the University of North Carolina at Chapel Hill; Chancellor Larry Monteith, from North Carolina State University; and President Nan Keohane, from Duke University, who could not be with us today.[2] They have committed their campuses and support for the Games, and we are so grateful for that.

I want to commend Dr. Leroy Walker, president of the U.S. Olympic Committee, for his very significant role in getting this event to our state.[3] It helps to have friends in high places!

[The governor also thanked Dave Lennox, director, North Carolina Special Olympics; Al Baldy and David Heinl, Greater Raleigh Convention and Visitors Bureau; Joel Smith and Sam Sloan, of NationsBank, founding sponsor of the event; and "many other people, including our local mayors and government leaders, without whom we would not be here today."]

It's just another way this community works together when it decides it wants something. No wonder *Fortune* magazine said this was the best place to do business. No wonder *Money* magazine said this was the best place to live.

We have a lot to look forward to in 1999. This event will bring an estimated $100 million boost to the Triangle economy, as athletes, and their families, and coaches from all over the world come to our state and our community. And Eunice, Sargent, I give you my personal assurance that the 1999 Special Olympics World Games will be the best Games ever. We look forward to the challenge and to showcasing our great state and your fine athletes to the world.

---

[1] The Special Olympics World Summer Games were scheduled to be held in the Triangle area, June 26-July 4, 1999. Special Olympics Press Conference, Raleigh, October 1, 1996, Governors Papers, James Baxter Hunt Jr.

Eunice Kennedy Shriver (1921-), born in Brookline, Mass.; B.S., Stanford University, 1943. Social activist; social worker; founder, Special Olympics, 1968; wife of Robert Sargent Shriver Jr. From the time of her appointment, in the mid-1950s, as executive vice-president of the Joseph P. Kennedy Jr. Foundation, Shriver was a world leader in the "struggle to improve the lives" of the mentally retarded and helped launch a "revolution in research on the causes of mental retardation, the care of the retarded, and the acceptance of the retarded by the community" at large; won Presidential Medal of Freedom, 1984, for her work. *Current Biography Yearbook, 1996*, 508-512.

Robert Sargent Shriver Jr. (1915-), born in Westminster, Md.; B.A., 1938, LL.B., 1941, Yale University; honorary degrees; U.S. Naval Reserve, 1940-1945. Attorney; assistant general manager, Chicago Merchandise Mart, 1948-1961; director, Peace Corps, 1961-1966; special assistant to President Lyndon Johnson, 1965-1968; U.S. ambassador to France, 1968-1970; president, 1986-1990, chairman and CEO, 1990-1996, and board chairman, from 1996, Special Olympics; husband of Eunice Kennedy Shriver. *Who's Who in America, 1999*, s.v. "Shriver, Robert Sargent, Jr."

[2] Michael Kenneth Hooker (1945-1999), born in Richlands, Va.; B.A., University of North Carolina at Chapel Hill, 1969; M.A., 1972, Ph.D., 1973, University of Massachusetts at Amherst. Assistant professor, Dept. of Philosophy, Harvard University, 1973-1975; assistant professor of philosophy, 1975-1977, assistant dean, 1975-1977, associate dean, 1978-1980,

and dean of undergraduate and graduate studies, Johns Hopkins University; president, Bennington College, 1982-1986; president, University of Maryland-Baltimore County, 1986-1992; president, University of Massachusetts, 1992-1995; chancellor, University of North Carolina at Chapel Hill, 1995-1999. *News and Observer,* June 30, 1999; *North Carolina Manual, 1997-1998,* 840-841.

Larry Monteith, chancellor of N.C. State University, was identified earlier in this volume.

Nannerl Overholser Keohane (1940-   ), born in Blytheville, Ark.; B.A., Wellesley College, 1961, Oxford University, 1963; Ph.D., Yale University, 1967. Political scientist; faculty of Swarthmore College, 1967-1973, and of Stanford University, 1973-1981; fellow, Center for Advanced Study in the Behavioral Sciences, Stanford University, 1978-1979, 1987-1988; president, political science professor, Wellesley College, 1981-1993; president, Duke University, from 1993; author; Democrat. *News and Observer,* June 20, 1993; *Who's Who in America, 1999,* s.v. "Keohane, Nannerl Overholser."

[3] Leroy Tashreau Walker (1918-   ), born in Atlanta; resident of Durham; B.S., Benedict College, 1940; M.A., Columbia University, 1941; Ph.D., New York University, 1957; honorary degrees. Physical education dept. chair, football, basketball, and track and field coach at Benedict College, 1941-1942, Bishop College, 1942-1943, Prairie View Agricultural and Mechanical College, 1943-1945, and N.C. Central University, 1945-1973; Cultural Exchange Program specialist, U.S. Dept. of State, 1959, 1960, 1962; coach, Ethiopian and Israeli teams, Rome Olympics, 1960; director, program planning and training, Peace Corps, Africa, 1966-1968; vice-chancellor for university relations, 1974-1983, chancellor, 1983-1986, chancellor emeritus, from 1986, N.C. Central University; head coach, U.S. track and field teams, Montreal Olympics, 1976; treasurer, 1988-1992, president, from 1992, U.S. Olympic Committee; author. *Notable Black American Men,* s.v. "Leroy T. Walker"; *Who's Who in America, 1999,* s.v. "Walker, Leroy Tashreau."

NORTH CAROLINA MANUFACTURING EXTENSION PARTNERSHIP OFFICE

CHARLOTTE, OCTOBER 9, 1995

I am proud to be a part of this important gathering of industry, government, and education leaders. This is an exciting time for North Carolina businesses and industries. It is a time of cooperation and collaboration. It is a time of partnership, partnership that will give our existing businesses and industries the edge they need to compete in the twenty-first century.

That edge has a name: the North Carolina Manufacturing Extension Partnership. Here at UNC-Charlotte, this partnership of industry, government, university, and community colleges will mean hands-on engineering help, training, and technical assistance for small and medium-sized businesses.

Today, as we celebrate this partnership, I am reminded of what great things North Carolinians can do when we work together. In 1992 I called for a technology extension plan that would bring together government, industry, universities, and community colleges.[1] Since then, we've worked hard with North Carolina State, our largest engineering college, to help secure funding to make this partnership a reality. Today we have a technology extension service, and North Carolina's small and medium-sized businesses have a new edge.

Our state is already an industrial leader. We lead the nation in the percentage of our workforce employed in manufacturing. The number of jobs has been growing here, while nationally the number of jobs has declined, and our overall wages are rising. But we need to do more. Too many of our small and medium-sized manufacturers have not been able to keep pace with new technology and new management practices. The major reason is cost. These companies, which together employ 856,000 workers and help create almost 75 percent of our new jobs, need help accessing the new technology they need to stay competitive. That's why this partnership is so important!

Under the guidance of the Industrial Extension Service at North Carolina State, three other partnership offices will open this year to provide hands-on technical help, and technological expertise, to businesses. In addition to [this] center, with [its] special focus on polymers and plastics, the Piedmont Triad Center for Advanced Manufacturing at North Carolina A&T State University, in Greensboro, will target the electronics industry. Catawba Valley Community College, in Hickory, will focus on furniture and hosiery. [The] Regional High-Technology Center at Haywood Community College, in Waynesville, will serve western North Carolina with a special emphasis on metals and machinery.

When these centers are up and running, almost 70 percent of North Carolina's companies will be within an hour's drive of a partnership office. That percentage will increase as the partnership grows. We hope to open another office east of Raleigh, next year.

We hope these centers will help North Carolina manufacturers to compete by giving them the tools to design and manufacture better products—and do it more efficiently. But we need your help to help North Carolina businesses. This partnership is driven by your needs—you, the businesses and manufacturers. It is committed to improving your bottom line. So we need your help to make it work. Let us know what works, and what doesn't, and how we can make this partnership even more productive.

---

[1] Hunt, "A North Carolina Agenda for Action, 1992," 20.

VANCE-AYCOCK DINNER:
INTRODUCTION OF GOVERNOR ZELL MILLER

ASHEVILLE, OCTOBER 14, 1995

I want to begin by thanking everyone who has worked so hard to make this Vance-Aycock weekend such a success—and everyone who has done so much to renew, and revitalize, and reinvigorate the North Carolina Democratic Party this year.[1]

Nineteen ninety-six will be a critical year, and I want you to know that I am excited, and optimistic, and enthusiastic about what's ahead next year. I'm going to be making an announcement about my plans in a few months. You probably know what it is, and I want you to know how I'm approaching it.

Nineteen ninety-six will be my last campaign, and I'm going to run it the same way I ran my first: running as a proud Democrat, working hard with other Democrats, standing with Democrats, and fighting alongside Democrats! And we're going to win next year, because we're going to talk about the kind of future North Carolina ought to have, and we're going to talk about what the people of North Carolina can do when they work together, and we're going to talk about the kind of leadership North Carolina ought to have for the next four years!

Our goal should be to give every child in North Carolina a Smart Start.

Our goal should be to give every child in North Carolina an education that prepares them for the twenty-first century.

Our goal should be to build the strongest, and most vibrant, and most innovative economy in the world—not just in the South, not just in the nation, but in the world.

Our goal should be to assure every single person, and especially every older adult, decent health care that doesn't take away every single cent they've saved.

Our goal should be for every North Carolinian to live and work in a place that's safe from violent criminals and drug dealers.

Our goal should be for every North Carolinian to get their money's worth out of every dollar they pay in taxes.

Our goal should be for every North Carolinian to be all they can be and want to be. That's what's at stake next year, that's what Democrats ought to be working on, and that's what we'll be winning on when we meet here next year![2]

Now, our speaker tonight can tell us something about Democrats working and winning. Sam Nunn once described Zell Miller as being "tough as nails."[3] That's high praise coming from Sam Nunn.

But you have to be tough as nails to do what Zell Miller's done. You have to be tough and smart to win re-election in a year like 1994, and Zell Miller did it. You have to be tough and smart to pass the kind of program he's passed in Georgia: sentencing-reform laws that keep violent criminals behind bars; a landmark pre-kindergarten program for every four-year-old in Georgia; a statewide lottery that's built classrooms and put computers into classrooms and universities across his state; and then there's Zell Miller's pride and joy, the HOPE scholarships that have helped more than 100,000 high school graduates go on to higher education.[4]

This man is a builder. This man is a leader. He is the kind of leader that our party and our nation need, and he's the kind of fellow we like having visit us in North Carolina. In fact, he's up here so much I may just declare him an honorary Tar Heel. Please join me in welcoming to North Carolina, and to the Democratic Party's Vance-Aycock Dinner, a great Democrat, a great governor, and a great leader, the governor of Georgia, the Honorable Zell Miller.

---

[1] At this point in his address, Hunt expressed appreciation to the Vance-Aycock Committee; Buncombe County Democratic Women; the Young Democrats, of whom he said, "My hair may be white, but my heart's still in the Young Democrats"; U.S. Senate hopefuls Harvey Gantt and Charlie Sanders; the elected leaders present; the Executive Committee and Executive Council of the state Democratic Party; and Wayne McDevitt, state Democratic Party chairman.

[2] To achieve the listed goals, "We need to appeal to a different kind of voter today, a voter who cares less about party," Hunt told a 1995 meeting of the state Democratic Party Executive Committee. "Just this week I read that 27 percent of all the newly registered voters in Forsyth County registered neither as Democrats, nor Republicans, but as independents. Twenty-seven percent! One in every four new voters! Those voters care about the future we're fighting for and about the goals we're standing for. That's why I strongly believe we ought to let those independent voters vote in Democratic primaries. We ought to make it easier for them to get involved in our party, not harder." Governors Papers, James Baxter Hunt Jr.

[3] United States senator Samuel Augustus Nunn (D-Georgia) was identified earlier in this volume.

Zell Bryan Miller (1932-   ), born in Young Harris, Ga.; A.B., 1957, M.A., 1958, University of Georgia; U.S. Marine Corps, 1953-1956. Former political science and history professor; member, Ga. state senate, 1961-1965; director, Ga. Board of Probation, 1965-1966; deputy director, Ga. Dept. of Corrections, 1967-1968; executive secretary, 1968-1971, to Lester G. Maddox, Ga. governor; member, Ga. State Board of Pardons and Paroles, 1973-1975; Ga. lieutenant governor, 1975-1990, and governor, 1991-1999; author; Democrat. *Current Biography Yearbook, 1996*, 377-381; *Who's Who in America, 1999*, s.v., "Miller, Zell Bryan."

[4] HOPE—Helping Outstanding Pupils Educationally—was a scholarship program, funded by lottery revenues, that furnished grants and loans to students attending Georgia state colleges. The program was limited initially to participation by freshmen and sophomores who maintained a B average and had an annual family income of less than $66,000. Miller proposed HOPE in 1992, and it passed the Georgia legislature in 1993. *Current Biography Yearbook, 1996*, 380.

"CHARACTER COUNTS" COALITION

Research Triangle Park, October 16, 1995

I'd like to thank Michael Josephson and the Josephson Institute for creating this program, and I appreciate the leadership of legislators in helping with our efforts to build character in our young people.

You're in the building business, building up our state and building knowledge and skill. But [I] believe we've missed the boat in many of the things we've been doing. We have dealt with the academics, the extracurricular activities, and a ton of other things we want our young people to be involved in, but we haven't been involved in character development. We have left that to chance. We have assumed that everyone was involved in their church, synagogue, or mosque, and that it would get done. But it isn't.

We cannot leave this to chance, and we cannot *not* do it. I've been in public service twenty-two or twenty-three years now. We've been a part of character education, and we're still working on it with efforts like Smart Start. But we haven't gotten to the best part. Government can't do it. It can only encourage and facilitate.

I've just been to a meeting of the League of Municipalities, in Durham. It started with a group of kids singing the anthems of our military, and they had the veterans in the crowd stand—those people who protected our freedom and saved the world for all of us. It made me think of the radio show I do every month. Last week a seventy-nine-year-old lady called. She asked about those kids who sit slouched in their chairs with their caps on backward and who show no respect for anyone.

We have a lot of people today—adults, too—who do not have respect for themselves. You can see it in the way they dress and in the way they act. They're dressed sloppily; they behave disrespectfully; they slouch in their seats.

They have no respect for themselves or others, for their teachers or custodians in school; they don't have it for the flag or for our nation. In the high school gym, when the national anthem is played, they don't stand or take off their caps. They don't sing. They don't know the words. They don't respect their country. They don't have much respect, or knowledge, of God. We've made a mistake to leave God out. I believe we need prayer in school, if we could find a way to make it fair and to give everyone a chance.

That's where we've got to start if we want to fight crime: The best way to do it is to work with these young people. We're seeing the juvenile crime rate skyrocket. We've got a serious problem that threatens us as a nation.

I'll be doing my volunteer work this afternoon, and my wife will, too. We're doing it in my church: Our men's Sunday school class organized a 4-H camp for kids; we're working with the SOS [Support Our Students] program, and we've started a Boy Scout troop.

Kids aren't going to learn just by being preached at. You learn by getting involved with the right kind of folks.

Every youngster in America should be in these activities. I was amazed at how good it is to be a grandparent. In Wilson County, we've got 109 Little League teams, maybe more; but less than 5 percent of the kids on those teams are black. I want it to be 30 percent. I want every kid to have the opportunity to be involved.

We've got to set examples through government. That's what we're doing with Smart Start. More than 25,000 children are getting health screenings, and 150,000 children are getting immunizations for a better start in life, thanks to Smart Start.

I want to suggest that we develop an approach—I'm not going to call it a program; that sounds too much like someone made a law—an approach to help build character.

I have many differences with Louis Farrakhan, but he is making something happen. They're going to Washington, D.C.[1]

Now we've got to go to our kids and make something happen. I want you all to make something happen. I want you to reach out to our young people and help them become all they can be.

---

[1] Hundreds of thousands of African American men answered the call of Nation of Islam leader Louis H. Farrakhan to attend "A Holy Day of Atonement, Reconciliation, and Responsibility," in Washington, D.C., October 16, 1995. Popularly known as the "Million Man March," the event stressed such themes as economic self-sufficiency, racial pride, the breakdown of the family, crime, and "social pathologies" in the African American community. A controversial figure, Farrakhan was denounced by his opponents as a "race-baiter and anti-Semite." *New York Times*, October 8, 9, 10, 13, 14, 15, 16, 17, 18, 20, 22, 1995.

NATIONAL BOARD CERTIFIED TEACHERS AND NATIONAL BOARD FOR PROFESSIONAL TEACHING STANDARDS BOARD OF DIRECTORS

WASHINGTON, D.C., OCTOBER 19, 1995

[For related press releases, see Hunt Praises Legislators for Expanding Teacher Certification, Raleigh, August 3, 1995; Eight North Carolina Teachers Earn National Board Certification, Raleigh, August 21, 1995; and North Carolina

Leads Nation in Teacher Certification, Raleigh, November 20, 1995, Governors Papers, James Baxter Hunt Jr.]

What an honor and a pleasure it is to be here with all of you board-certified teachers. It has been a long road we have traveled to reach this point, and the journey is by no means over. When I think of being a member of the Carnegie Forum's Task Force on Teaching as a Profession, ten years ago, and now looking at you teachers who have truly made that vision a reality, I can't help but feel such a sense of pride and accomplishment.

While the landmark 1983 *A Nation at Risk* report focused the national spotlight on the troubled state of American education and provoked a wave of reform efforts, most of these initiatives left out a critical element of the education equation: the classroom teacher. Teaching is at the heart of education, and the single most important action we as a nation can take to improve our children's learning is to strengthen the ability, knowledge, and professionalism of our teachers. Knowing this, the task force called for the establishment of a National Board for Professional Teaching Standards, and there has not been a time since then that I have wavered in my commitment to see this idea turn into reality.

Every effort in education, geared to improve student learning, depends on one thing to start with: a quality teacher. The national board and national board certification is [*sic*] a link to quality. Teachers who are national board certified are true professionals, at the top of their field, who deserve the highest prestige in their communities.

The founding members of [the] NBPTS Board of Directors overcame so many hurdles. Never had so many people with a stake in teaching been all together at one table. Never had the profession established standards for performance measuring what highly accomplished teachers should know and be able to do. Never had an assessment been developed that accurately and fairly measured how well a teacher meets those standards. It took the commitment of the founding director to create the vision for every board member since to carry out. Our first national board-certified teachers have the board members to thank for carrying this out.

I remain committed to this process, because there is nothing more important than preparing our children for the future by ensuring they receive the best possible education. Knowing their children are being taught by the best in the profession will give parents a great sense of security.

Throughout history, great changes have required brave people willing to innovate, take risks, and lead the way for others. You, as the first national board-certified teachers, are pioneering this nationwide movement to raise standards and truly professionalize teaching. You took these risks, knowing the only certain reward would be your belief that this certification process would make you better teachers. Your example will inspire other teachers to strive to reach the highest levels of quality in their classrooms.

In 1910 another pioneer educator, Abraham Flexner, transformed medical practice in America by insisting on rigorous professional preparation of physicians.[1] His work laid the groundwork for the development of a medical delivery system unmatched elsewhere in the world. I am confident you, as board-certified teachers, and the others who will follow in your footsteps, will have as significant an effect on our nation's education system and our children.

---

[1] Abraham Flexner (1866-1959), born in Louisville, Ky.; A.B., Johns Hopkins University, 1886; A.M., Harvard University, 1906; honorary degrees. Educator; assistant secretary, 1913-1917, secretary, 1917-1925, director, division of studies and medical education, 1925-1928, General Education Board; director, 1930-1939, director emeritus, from 1940, Institute for Advanced Study; author. *Who Was Who in America, 1951-1960,* s.v. "Flexner, Abraham."

NORTH CAROLINA GANG AWARENESS TRAINING CONFERENCE

FAYETTEVILLE, OCTOBER 25, 1995

[For related press release, see Governor Hunt Pushes Punishment and Prevention to Fight Juvenile Crime, Fayetteville, October 25, 1995, Governors Papers, James Baxter Hunt Jr.]

It's not just New York or L.A. anymore: Even in North Carolina, we're seeing gangs, and drive-by shootings, and young men gunning each other down in our neighborhoods. Violent crime among juveniles is on the rise, jumping an alarming 33 percent in the last five years and almost 200 percent in the last decade.

North Carolina is not yet suffering a gang epidemic, but it's critical that all of us—policy makers, community leaders, law-enforcement officers, prosecutors—take this seriously. I'm glad North Carolina's law-enforcement leaders, including Sheriff Butler and Chief Hansen,[1] the SBI [State Bureau of Investigation], the ATF [federal Alcohol, Tobacco, and Firearms Bureau], the U.S. attorney's office, Fayetteville Tech, the

[N.C.] Justice Academy, and the Governor's Crime Commission are sponsoring this first-ever conference on gang violence. I'm glad to see so many frontline law-enforcement officers here. I hope we can all come away wiser and better able to protect North Carolina's communities.

We already have two innovative projects under way: gang interdiction units funded by my crime commission with the Fayetteville Police and Forsyth Sheriff's Department. These law-enforcement agencies are setting examples for other communities as we work together to tackle the emerging problem of gang violence.

The larger problem of youth crime is one that concerns all of us, and it will take all of us, working together, to solve it. Last year, when I called a special session on crime, I spent months talking with law-enforcement officials to find out what approach we should take, especially to crime. They told me one thing, over and over again: It takes both punishment and prevention.

In the short term, we must make sure we punish criminals. That's why I've pushed hard in the legislature for tougher sentences for violent criminals and for more prison beds to hold those prisoners longer. As a result, we're keeping violent criminals behind bars longer, and we've built or authorized almost 13,000 new prison beds in the last three years.

I believe we should hold criminals accountable, despite their age. A 13-year-old charged with first-degree murder in the brutal beating death of an elderly neighbor is a dangerous criminal—and should be treated as such. During the special crime session last year, the legislature passed my proposal to automatically try that 13-year-old as an adult and to give judges discretion to try juveniles as young as 13, as adults, if they commit violent felonies. At the same time, we're building more detention centers and training-school beds to make sure we have the capacity to handle the violent youths referred to us by the courts.

Too often, violence starts in the schools and ends up in the streets. So we've put a new emphasis on safe schools in the last three years. We're adding school resource officers across the state, with crime commission grants. We've made it a felony to bring a gun to campus, and we're enforcing the new zero-tolerance law I proposed, automatically suspending students for up to one year for bringing that gun to school. We're putting those students in alternative schools, and if they can't make it there, we'll send them to an educational boot camp where they can learn discipline and responsibility as well as academics.

But we've got to get just as serious about preventing a new generation of criminals. That means starting early, with things like Smart Start. We have a wonderful Smart Start effort under way in Cumberland County, giving children the day care, and health care, and family services they need to get on the right track.

That means getting involved, with things like SOS [Support Our Students]. The after-school crime-prevention program that I launched in our crime session is giving 6,000 children in half our counties a safe place to go after school. SOS is giving troubled youth someone to learn from, by matching them up with volunteer mentors who help them [with] schoolwork and other things. I've seen the results in the SOS program that Carolyn and I volunteer in back in Raleigh. As these kids develop self-esteem and self-respect, they develop respect for others, and they're less likely to get involved in drugs, crime, and gangs. If everyone in this room could spend a few hours a week with a troubled young man, North Carolina would never develop a gang problem!

When youngsters do go astray, we need to provide innovative ways to help them turn their lives around. So we're building more wilderness camps, and military-style boot camps—and we're providing more resources for the Governor's One-on-One Program that I started before, which matches juveniles in the court system with adult mentors.

But it's not just tougher laws or more prisons. It's not just law enforcement. It's got to be community involvement. It's got to be churches, and educators, and business leaders, and community leaders from all walks of life working together to reach out to our youngsters. If we work together, I think we can save the next generation from a life of crime. We can help steer them down the path to success, away from drugs, and crime, and gangs.

If we work together, we can do great things in North Carolina. I challenge you all to go home and get your friends, neighbors, and colleagues involved. Together, we can make a difference.

---

[1] Earl R. "Moose" Butler; resident of Fayetteville; A.B., University of North Carolina at Chapel Hill, 1960; adjuster, Associates Discount Corp., Fayetteville, 1960-1963; guidance counselor, teacher, school social worker, Cumberland County School System, 1964-1967; employee from 1967, branch manager, 1974-1994, probation-parole office, N.C. Department of Correction; was elected sheriff of Cumberland County, 1994, re-elected, 1998; Democrat. Sheriff Earl R. Butler, letter to Jan-Michael Poff, October 21, 1999.

Ronald E. Hansen (1939-   ), born in Racine, Wis.; resident of Fayetteville; B.A., Metropolitan State University, 1976; M.A., Sangamon State University, 1980; U.S. Air Force, 1957-1960. Lieutenant of police, Racine, Wis., 1971-1974; chief of police, Menomonie, Wis., 1974-1977, Rock Island, Ill., 1977-1984, and of Fayetteville, N.C., from July 1984. Lori O. Farley, assistant to Chief Ronald E. Hansen, letter to Jan-Michael Poff, November 8, 1999.

SENIOR CITIZENS TOWN MEETING

GREENVILLE, OCTOBER 30, 1995

[This speech is similar to those Hunt delivered to the Senior Tar Heel Legislature, March 22, 1995, and the senior citizens town meeting in Charlotte, October 26, 1995; see also the press release, Governor Hunt to Hold Seniors Town Meetings in Charlotte and Greenville, Raleigh, October 24, 1995, Governors Papers, James Baxter Hunt Jr.]

I'm honored to join all of you here to talk about ways we can improve the lives of North Carolina's older residents. First I want to thank the people who helped make this seniors' town meeting possible.[1] And thanks to all of you for coming here, today, to share your ideas about these important issues. We're going to be facing some tough decisions ahead.

We're hearing a lot of talk from Washington about the cuts in Medicare, and Medicaid, and how that will affect you. That's why it's so important that we all work together to make sure our older citizens, the ones who built this state and made it a place we can all be proud of, get the services you deserve. You are a precious resource.

You have helped make our state great, and I know you have much more to give. That's why I believe all of us must work to do everything we can to make sure that every older citizen of North Carolina has every opportunity to live life to the fullest. Already we've made tremendous progress. This year I urged the legislature to repeal the intangibles tax on stocks and bonds. Now older North Carolinians who have saved for retirement by buying stocks and bonds will have a little more money to see them through.

I had also asked the legislature to increase the homestead exemption for low-income older adults from $11,000 to $15,000, and to raise the property tax exemption from $15,000 to $18,000. They didn't act on my recommendation, but you can be sure that I will continue to push for these changes, which will make such a difference in the lives of so many senior citizens.

We did succeed in increasing the amount of state funding for transportation services for the elderly and disabled by $500,000. This extra money is letting us reach more than 6,000 more, older adults.

Under the leadership of Robin Britt, our fine secretary of human resources, we're taking steps to protect our 32,000 older residents who live in rest homes and nursing homes to make sure they get the best possible care. By the beginning of next year, we'll have more inspectors in the field to monitor the state's rest homes and conduct annual inspections. We'll have better systems in place to train rest home workers to make sure they know how to meet the needs of older residents, and we'll be able to provide better quality care for those residents who need mental health care.

Those are just the first steps toward helping older citizens who need extra care. But we can't stop there. I've created the Long-Term Care Roundtable to give me advice on the best ways to meet the needs of older North Carolinians, whether they need rest home or nursing home care, or whether they're able to keep living at home.

We're also working to protect older adults who rely on others, including family members, for their care. For the first time, we can now impose criminal penalties for the abuse, neglect, or exploitation of older adults who live at home with a relative. A relative has no more right to hurt an older adult than a stranger does.[2]

These are just some of the things we've accomplished. I know we've got more to do. That's why it's so important that we all come together to do everything we can to preserve the legacy you've created and make sure that your needs are never forgotten. Now I want to hear from you. Tell me what we can do to make a difference in your lives.

---

[1] Hunt recognized Louisa Cox, chair, N.C. Association of Agencies on Aging; Charles Byrd, executive director, Pitt County Council on Aging; Dell Hagwood, chair, Pitt Aging Coalition; Bonnie Cramer, director, N.C. Division of Aging; and Lynne Perrin, assistant secretary for aging and special needs, N.C. Dept. of Human Resources.

[2] "An Act to Impose Criminal Penalties for the Abuse, Neglect, or Exploitation of Disabled or Elder Adults Living in a Domestic Setting" was ratified June 14, 1995. *N.C. Session Laws, 1995*, I, c. 246.

FRIENDS OF BLACK CHILDREN

RESEARCH TRIANGLE PARK, NOVEMBER 3, 1995

When I took office almost three years ago, I dedicated my administration to North Carolina's children. I did that because I know, as you know, that the future of our state depends on the future of our children.

Most of us in this room are blessed. We were blessed with loving, supportive families, parents, or grandparents who instilled confidence, self-esteem, respect, integrity, and the other values that build good citizens. We can thank our families for helping us become all we could be—and we can give something back by helping North Carolina's children become all they can be.

I want to commend everyone in this room for all you are doing to make this state a brighter place for our children. Over the last year, the Friends of Black Children has worked with my administration as we've launched an ambitious effort to place foster children in permanent homes—and look what we've done together! We've created the state's first licensed adoption agency specializing in the placement of African American children. We've formed a partnership with North Carolina media outlets and social service agencies to showcase foster children in weekly feature stories. We've provided additional resources for the Friends of Black Children to do their important work.

Because of what we've done together, seventy children now have a family and a home to call their own, and twenty-eight more children are going through the adoption process right now. You've heard some heartwarming stories, here today, that tell the story better than any statistic can. What you've heard and seen today is how you're making a difference. That's something to be proud of. I want to thank you for all you're doing, and I want to work with you to do even more, because we do have more work to do.

There are still more than 600 children who desperately need loving families and permanent homes. We need to keep working together to find adoptive families and to match them up with our neediest children. We need to keep working together to find resources and to galvanize communities and churches around this important cause.

Today I'm proud to announce that the state Department of Administration will provide $50,000 to the Friends of Black Children to help you continue your wonderful work, and I'm pleased to announce that our new Families for Kids initiative is getting a federal grant of $100,000 to step up adoption efforts. The grant will help eight counties provide financial incentives to public and private adoption agencies to work together to place children more quickly.

Now, this money is a good start in the right direction, but it's not enough. I'll be working my head off to find even more resources, and I hope the General Assembly will support us in our effort. Today is a day to celebrate—to celebrate children, and families, and the mission that you all are pursuing. Together we can build a brighter future for our children, and there is no greater good that we can do. Thank you, and God bless you.

NORTH CAROLINA WORKFORCE DEVELOPMENT PARTNERSHIP CONFERENCE

GREENSBORO, NOVEMBER 8, 1995

[For related press releases, see Commission on Workforce Preparedness Awards Almost $200,000 in Grants, Raleigh, June 2, 1995; N.C. School-to-Work Programs to Get Nearly $30 Million in Grants, Raleigh, October 6, 1995; and Hunt and JobReady Students Break Ground on Habitat for Humanity House, Raleigh, February 27, 1996, Governors Papers, James Baxter Hunt Jr.]

Thank you, Senator Martin, and thank you for all you've done to move our state forward by investing in our most precious natural resource: our people. Your leadership in the senate has helped us become the leader that we are in workforce development, and we owe you a great deal.[1]

I am happy to be here with so many people who are working to prepare North Carolina's workforce for the twenty-first century. I'd like to commend Sandy Babb, director of our Workforce Preparedness Commission, for her vision and knowledge in this area and [her] hard work in putting this conference together.

You've heard from many people who know a lot about the challenges we will face in developing our workforce in the coming years. People like George Autry, of MDC, a renowned expert on workforce issues; Marc Tucker, of the Center for Education and the Economy; and former Mississippi governor William Winter.[2] They've spelled out, in very stark terms, the challenge we face in developing our workforce. As they've indicated, our rapidly changing global economy demands more from our workforce than ever before. Technology is the engine that drives today's economy, and it will require a highly trained, highly skilled workforce to fuel that engine.

To keep pace and to compete in the twenty-first century, we must focus on creating high-skill, high-wage jobs; and we must make sure that we have the best system in place to train, and retrain, our workers for those new jobs. We cannot recruit high-quality jobs to our state without a high-skilled workforce, and our existing industries cannot compete. But North Carolina is not content to keep pace. We want to set the pace.

That's what all of us in this room have been doing in workforce development for the last three years: setting the pace. North Carolina has been recognized as a national innovator in workforce development and training, honored by the National Alliance of Business as "State of the Year" two years ago—and we're still leading the way, under the leadership of Workforce Commission chairman Buster Humphreys and Executive Director Sandy Babb. We're creating new partnerships at the state and local level. We're pushing for new accountability. We're designing creative efforts, like JobReady and One-Stop Career Centers, and we're doing it together: All of you in this room are playing a vital role in making sure that our workers have the training they need for tomorrow's workplace.

Folks, we're breaking the mold. JobReady, our school-to-work initiative, is truly changing how we prepare our state's young people to enter the workforce or continue their education. Through partnerships with businesses, JobReady is providing students hands-on experience in the real world of work, with job shadowing, internships, cooperative education, and apprenticeships. JobReady is also teaching teachers about business and industry so that they can help students make better career choices.

Buster Humphreys, our fine Workforce Commission chairman, is showing folks how it can be done at National Spinning. I hope every business person in the state will get a chance to see or learn about his efforts firsthand. He's got high-school students and welfare recipients working on his factory floor, learning the skills they need to become good workers. Welfare recipients are moving from welfare to work. High-school graduates are entering the workforce with apprenticeship credentials and a better shot at a good job, and [the] payoff for Buster [is], he gets good workers. That's a win-win!

JobReady is now getting started in sixteen communities, with the help of a $5 million federal grant. This money will be spread to local communities, where local folks—teachers and administrators, community college faculty and staff, university personnel, parents, students, and local employers—will help them design new JobReady efforts that work for their communities. At the same time, we need to streamline our workforce training efforts at the state level and in the community. North Carolina is on the cutting edge of that with our One-Stop Career Centers, which bring under one roof the services that workers and employers need.[3]

One-Stop Career Centers will help employers find workers faster and help workers find job training and education information faster. We're using technology in new ways, as I saw when I visited a One-Stop Career Center at Southeastern Community College, in Whiteville, this summer.[4] Working with local workforce agencies and with the help of a $3.8 million federal grant, we're building a system of career centers. By next year, we hope to have seven such centers up and running, one of only eight states to get this federal support.

These one-stop centers will be critical to the success of our welfare reform efforts. Last year, the Commission's Welfare Reform Task Force, chaired by Dr. Bertha Maxwell-Roddey, recommended what is now Work First. We're now moving ahead to move North Carolinians from welfare to work and have asked the Clinton administration for waivers so that we can get started as soon as possible.

Work First requires work and personal responsibility. It will require 35,000 AFDC [Aid to Families with Dependent Children] recipients— one-third of the adult welfare population—to get a job, paid or unpaid, right away. It will require them to sign a personal responsibility contract, to make a plan for getting off welfare, and to stick to that plan. It will set a two-year time [limit] for welfare benefits.

For Work First to succeed, the entire workforce system must play a role. Workers from these families will need help finding jobs, they will need short-term basic skills, and they will need job training. The state's workforce development system will be vital to this effort. All of you— business leaders, educators, and job-training specialists—can help these families as they move from dependence on welfare to work and self-sufficiency.

As North Carolina pushes to improve our workforce training efforts, we must keep three questions in mind: Does it work? Is every tax dollar being spent wisely? Is it the most efficient and effective way to deliver services?

Those questions are critical as we monitor congressional action on workforce issues. As you know, federal workforce legislation has passed both houses of Congress and is now in conference. As you heard in your panel discussions this morning, it is likely that block grants will consolidate almost 100 separate workforce programs. For North Carolina, this is an opportunity; an opportunity to make it work; an opportunity to make decisions here, instead of having Washington tell us what to do; an opportunity to come up with innovative ways to target federal and state dollars more efficiently to more effectively serve our citizens.

But this is also a challenge for North Carolina, a challenge of fewer dollars. Our state is likely to see 30 percent fewer federal dollars for workforce programs on top of the cuts we've already seen in the current year. That's why it's so important that we all work together to make sure we use our resources wisely to prepare our workforce for the challenges of tomorrow.

The legislature has put together a special committee to study job-training programs and make recommendations about workforce development programs in the state. The state auditor is conducting a program audit of workforce programs, and my budget office will be evaluating job-training programs as well. But all this scrutiny has a purpose. I want us to come out with a more streamlined, more effective system that gives our workers the training and retraining they need.

Although there are a lot of players in this game, we share a common goal: to build an effective, comprehensive, workforce development system, to build on what we have—and we have so much. We have a wonderful community college system, one of the best in the nation, offering almost 2,000 programs to North Carolinians in every community. We have a strong Employment Security Commission, with more than one in six individuals in North Carolina's civilian labor force using the local job service offices each year. We have public schools, with dedicated teachers and administrators, who are working to graduate our students with diplomas that mean something and skills that are marketable; our effort to raise standards in schools and return to the basics will help in that effort. We have skilled workforce professionals from the JTPA [Job Training Partnership Act] system; you; the vocational rehabilitation system; the Labor Department; social service agencies, who are working their heads off every day to boost workforce development; and we have so many dedicated volunteers. We have businessmen and –women, and community leaders, and ministers, and senior citizens, and high-school students, and hundreds of others who are working in their community to support our education and training efforts.

We have so much, yet we still have much to do. We have to strengthen our community colleges, making them even more responsive to adults in the workforce. We have to make our public schools stronger and make them an integral part of the school-to-work effort. We have to streamline fragmented employment and training efforts into one cohesive system. We have to make sure that our workforce development system is on track to give North Carolina's workers the tools they need to compete and succeed in the next century. We have to hammer out a workforce development blueprint that will make North Carolina's workers the best in the nation, and we must meet that challenge. The future of our economy depends on it.

We are blessed in North Carolina. We have a strong economy, a low unemployment rate, and a vibrant business climate. We are creating record numbers of new jobs, and we are at the top of industrial recruitment lists all over the globe. But we cannot take those blessings for granted. You and I know that our workforce sustains our economy. I was reminded of that during my recent trade mission to Japan.[5] We cannot recruit world-class companies to North Carolina without a world-class workforce. That's why it's vital that all of us keep working together and keep looking for new ways to make sure our workforce stays ahead as we enter the next century. North Carolina's workers and North Carolina's economy depend on it, and I am depending on you, [and I] pledge to work with you, to make it come about.

---

[1] Senator William Nelson Martin (D-Guilford) was identified earlier in this volume.

[2] George Bailey Autry (1937-1999), born in Wilmington; A.B., 1958, J.D., 1961, Duke University. Attorney; chief counsel, staff director, U.S. Senate Subcommittee on Constitutional Rights, chaired by Sen. Sam J. Ervin; campaign aide to President Lyndon Baines Johnson and Vice-President Hubert Humphrey; campaign manager, Luther Hodges Jr. for U.S. Senate, 1978. As president, N.C. Manpower Development Corp. (later MDC), 1967-1999, Autry was widely recognized as "a creative champion" of education and workforce training initiatives "to improve the prospects of poor people and poor places" in North Carolina and throughout the South. *News and Observer*, April 27, 1975, April 26, 1999.

Marc Stephen Tucker (1939-   ), born in Boston, Mass.; A.B., Brown University, 1961; M.S.S., George Washington University, 1982. Director, Project on Information Technology and Education, 1981-1984; executive director, Carnegie Forum on Education and the Economy, 1985-1987; president, National Center on Education and the Economy, from 1988; professor of education, University of Rochester, from 1988; Democrat. *Who's Who in America, 1999*, s.v. "Tucker, Marc Stephen."

William Forrest Winter (1923-   ), born in Grenada, Miss.; B.A., 1943, LL.B., 1949, University of Mississippi; honorary degrees; U.S. Army, 1943-45, 1951. Attorney; member, Mississippi House of Representatives, 1948-56; Mississippi state tax collector, 1956-1964, state treasurer, 1964-1968, lieutenant governor, 1972-1976, and governor, 1980-1984; chair, Southern Growth Policies Board, 1981, Southern Regional Education Board, 1982, Advisory Commission on Intergovernmental Regulations, 1993-1997, and of MDC. *Who's Who in America, 1999*, s.v. "Winter, William Forrest."

[3] For related press releases, see Hunt Announces Grants to Streamline Job Training and Placement Services, Raleigh, August 11, 1995; and Hunt's Workforce Commission Awards Grants for One-Stop Career Centers, Raleigh, February 6, 1996, Governors Papers, James Baxter Hunt Jr.

[4] Hunt visited Southeastern Community College on August 22, 1995. Governor Jim Hunt's Schedule for August 21-23, 1995, Governors Papers, James Baxter Hunt Jr.

[5] The governor mounted a three-week cultural, educational, and trade mission to Israel and Japan, September 17-October 4, 1995. Press releases, Hunt Signs Economic Development Agreement with Israel, Raleigh, April 28, 1994, and Governor Hunt to Lead Mission to Israel and Japan, Raleigh, September 14, 1995, Governors Papers, James Baxter Hunt Jr.

BAPTIST STATE CONVENTION

WINSTON-SALEM, NOVEMBER 13, 1995

I'd like to thank all of you for inviting me here, today, as you prepare for your annual meeting.

You are helping the needy at home and abroad. Your missionary efforts, partnering with churches in the Ukraine and helping the youngest victims of Chernobyl, are heartwarming examples of what people of faith can do to truly make a difference—and you are making a difference here at home, in each of your communities. You're doing it in your churches, in your local mission work, and you're doing it through your leadership. You're leading by example.

Baptists are doing so many wonderful things in North Carolina. You are educating our young people at fine schools, like Wake Forest, Campbell, and Gardner-Webb Universities, and Meredith, Mars Hill, Wingate, and Chowan Colleges. You are healing our sick and training some of the nation's finest doctors at Bowman Gray School of Medicine and North Carolina Baptist Hospital. Your commitment to education and your dedication to making North Carolina a better place have given our state some of its best doctors, lawyers, ministers, and teachers. You're leading by showing your commitment to making life better for all North Carolinians.

We need your leadership now more than ever. You know that Congress is looking at making significant changes in welfare, Medicare, and Medicaid. People want change. They want government to work better. That means finding new ways to do things, but we must do it without pulling the rug out from under our most vulnerable citizens: our children and our elderly.

Here in North Carolina, we're making changes, too. We're cutting government, cutting taxes, reforming welfare, and we're doing it in new ways—ways that aren't big government, but [through] public-private partnerships, like Smart Start, SOS [Support Our Students], and Work First—and we're getting churches involved.

Hundreds of church leaders are involved in Smart Start, where local parents, ministers, business people, and others decide how best to help local children come to school healthy and ready to learn. Much of [the] child care that Smart Start funds provide is provided by church day-care centers. In some rural counties, churches are the only day-care providers around! If every church adopted a day-care center or expanded its own, think what we could do.

Many people of faith are taking leadership roles in Smart Start—people like Malbert Smith, pastor of Greystone Baptist Church in Durham, who serves on the North Carolina Partnership for Children, the public-private, nonprofit corporation that oversees Smart Start.[1] Smart Start is working, folks. In thirty-two counties, Smart Start is providing child care for 10,000 children so their parents can work. It means 35,000 children are getting preventive health care. More than 150,000 children are getting immunizations.

As Malbert knows, government can't do it alone; neither can churches. But when we work together, we can do so much—and so much needs to be done.[2] [There is] SOS, the after-school crime-prevention program that we launched in the crime session.[3] In fifty-two communities, thousands of volunteers are working with young people to guide them and help keep them on the right track. These volunteers are giving those youngsters the love, care, and attention they need to succeed later in life. You and I know youngsters who learn the right values—what Christ taught, how He lived—early in life have a better chance staying out of prison and off welfare later on. If every church sponsored an SOS program or encouraged its congregation to volunteer, think what we could do.

Churches can help reform welfare, too. Work First will move families from welfare to work. In the next year, we want to move 35,000 AFDC [Aid to Families with Dependent Children] recipients, one-third of the adult welfare population in North Carolina, into work. They'll have to get a job, paid or unpaid, in twelve weeks or lose their benefits. They'll have to sign personal responsibility contracts, and fulfill them, or lose their benefits.

It's a tough, but compassionate, approach, but it won't work without the community. We're working with chambers of commerce and employers, matching up jobs with Work First participants, but churches can help, too. Let me tell you what my Sunday school class [in] Wilson is doing [incomplete]. If a Sunday school class in every church sponsored a welfare family like that, think what we could do.

I've seen what North Carolinians can do when we work together, and I know what our churches can do. That's why I'm talking with church leaders from other denominations about how we can join hands to find new ways to make a difference for the people of our state. Helping our fellow man, helping our elderly, our sick, and our poor, is the true spirit of Christian brotherhood. I know that spirit is in every Baptist congregation across this state.

Finally, the longer I serve in public office, trying to change things, dealing with people who are problems, the more I appreciate the work of [the] church in teaching people to do right—teaching them the example of Jesus and the will of God, bringing [them] to Christ [to] live in [a] different way. Please continue to bring in the young people. Keep reaching out and finding them. This state, this country, has come a long way. But you and I know what our real potential is. Help [us be] all [that we] can be.[4]

---

[1] Malbert Smith Jr., of Durham, served two terms on the North Carolina Partnership for Children Board of Directors: September 17, 1993-August 31, 1996, and March 5, 1998-August 31, 1999. Letters of Appointment to Boards and Commissions, Governors Papers, James Baxter Hunt Jr.

[2] "Goal: Safe commun[ities]," Hunt jotted. "Juvenile Crime. (Other crime down). Not juvenile crime. Kids go home at 3:00 to empty home—dangerous neighborhoods."

[3] At this point, Hunt wrote the notation, "13,000 prison beds. Can't build enough prisons to keep us safe, unless [we] prevent crime."

[4] Hunt added the final paragraph in ink. In the margin, he also jotted: "Have thine own way, Lord. Thou art the potter, I am the clay. We work with clay. If [we] don't share basic values—have some character" [illegible].

TRANSIT 2001 COMMISSION

RALEIGH, NOVEMBER 21, 1995

This is an exciting day for transportation in North Carolina. I am delighted we have such a dynamic and talented group of people from the General Assembly, Board of Transportation, university system, human services, local government, and the business community to help us set a new direction for public transportation in our state.

I am grateful to Dr. Thomas Hearn, who has agreed to chair this commission. He is a strong leader and a visionary. I'm glad to see Senator James Speed, Senator David Hoyle, Senator Wib Gulley, Representatives David Miner, Joni Bowie, and Howard Hunter here today. I appreciate your support and leadership on this issue. I want all of you to know how committed I am to this project and its implementation. I will follow your work closely over the next year, and I look forward to your recommendations about how public transportation can strengthen our entire transportation system.[1]

Transportation is vital to the quality of life and economic prosperity of our state. It affects every North Carolinian, every day. Parents need to take their children to school. People need to get to work. Businesses need to transport their products. Families need to go to church. That's why we've embarked on a $11.3 billion, seven-year transportation program, called Transportation 2001, which provides the safest, most efficient, and unified transportation system possible for North Carolina. Highway projects have been accelerated, our maintenance backlog will be eliminated, and public transportation will be made a top priority.

While the highways are the backbone of our transportation system, we must explore and implement alternative forms of transportation. But our challenge will be to make sure those alternative forms of transportation are competitive with traditional modes of transportation. To demonstrate our commitment to that challenge, we appointed a deputy secretary of transit, rail, and aviation, David King, to step up the state's public transportation efforts. David has been a strong leader over the last two-and-a-half years in this area, and I want to thank him for all that he has done.

We have tripled the available funding, to $16 million, for public transportation as part of the Transportation 2001 plan. We provided $6 million for the state's eighteen fixed-route and regional urban transit systems. An additional $3.3 million was set aside for rural, general public, and human services transportation programs, and the public transportation grant program was increased by $1.5 million. We've pushed for improved rail service, between Raleigh and Charlotte, with the Carolinian and the Piedmont, and we dedicated funds to make track improvements to cut travel time; and we've fought hard to protect North Carolina's airport hubs.

But we still have much work to do. We need new transportation alternatives to reduce air pollution, save energy, avoid traffic congestion, and preserve the qualities that make North Carolina such a wonderful place to live; and we need a public transportation system that will work for our people well into the next century. I want you to keep some things in mind as you search for recommendations:

—How do we use technology to make transit more effective and efficient?

—How can we make transit more customer-service oriented?

—How can we provide better mobility to the elderly and disabled, particularly in rural areas where access to medical services is made more difficult by distance?

—How can we provide the proper mix of land development so that North Carolinians have transit choices?

—How can we achieve two-hour rail service in the Raleigh/Greensboro/Charlotte corridor?

—How should these initiatives be funded?

Your work on this commission comes at a crucial time in North Carolina. We have a rare opportunity to plan ahead for North Carolina's public transportation needs, and we have the responsibility to make the most of it. I am grateful to each of you for being part of this effort and for helping build a better North Carolina. Let's get to work.

---

[1] See Transit 2001 Commission, *Transit 2001 Executive Summary and Technical Report* ([Raleigh]: North Carolina Department of Transportation, January 1997).

Thomas K. Hearn Jr. (1937-   ), born in Opp, Ala.; resident of Winston-Salem; B.A., Birmingham Southern College, 1959; B.D., Baptist Theological Seminary, 1963; Ph.D., Vanderbilt University, 1965. Philosophy professor, 1974-1983, dept. chair, 1974-1976, School of Humanities dean, 1976-1978, University College vice-president, 1978-1983, University of Alabama-Birmingham; president, Wake Forest University, from 1983; chair, Transit 2001 Commission. *Who's Who in the South and Southwest, 1997-1998*, s.v. "Hearn, Thomas K., Jr."

Speed, Hoyle, Gulley, Miner, Bowie, and Hunter were members of the Transit 2001 Commission.

James Davis Speed (1915-   ), born in, resident of Louisburg; attended N.C. State University. Farmer; tobacco warehouseman; member, N.C. House, 1961-1971, N.C. Senate, 1977-1996, and chairman, Senate Transportation Committee; Democrat. *News and Observer*, July 28, 29, August 4, 1996; *North Carolina Manual, 1995-1996*, 509.

David William Hoyle (1939-   ), born in Gastonia; B.A., Lenoir-Rhyne College, 1960. Founder, in 1960, president, CEO, Summey Building Systems; founder, SBS, Inc., manufactured housing, construction, and real estate development; mayor of Dallas, N.C., 1967-1971; member, N.C. Senate, from 1993, and chairman, Senate Appropriations-DOT Committee; Democrat. *North Carolina Manual, 1995-1996*, 479.

Wilbur (Wib) Paul Gulley (1948-   ); born in Little Rock, Ark.; resident of Durham; B.A., Duke University, 1970; J.D., Northeastern University, 1981. Attorney; Durham mayor, 1985-1989; member, N.C. Senate, from 1993, and chairman, Senate Judiciary II/Election Laws Committee; Democrat. *North Carolina Manual, 1995-1996*, 475.

David Morris Miner (1962-   ), born in Johnson City, Tenn.; resident of Wake County; B.B.A., Campbell Univeresity, 1989. Textile sales with The Management Group; state director, Jack Kemp for President, 1987-1988; chairman, Americans for a Balanced Budget, from 1989; member, N.C. House, from 1993, and chairman, House Transportation Committee; Republican. *North Carolina Manual, 1995-1996*, 631.

Joanne (Joni) W. Bowie, born in Terre Haute, Ind.; resident of Guilford County; B.A., M.S., West Virginia University. Former schoolteacher; public relations specialist; communications specialist; member, Greensboro City Council, 1977-1988; member, N.C. House, from 1989, and co-chair, Appropriations Subcommittee on Transportation; member, numerous boards and commissions; Republican. *North Carolina Manual, 1995-1996*, 552-553.

Howard J. Hunter Jr. was identified earlier in this volume.

NEUSE RIVER COUNCIL

NEW BERN, NOVEMBER 27, 1995

[Polluted, stagnant water and summer heat caused frequent, large, and widely publicized fish kills in eastern North Carolina waterways during 1995. The Neuse River suffered worst of all. Discharges from factories and sewage treatment plants, mixed with runoff from farms, lawns, and parking lots, heightened nitrogen and phosphorus levels in the river. The nutrient-overloaded waters were prime hunting grounds for pfisteria, a toxic dinoflagellate blamed for killing 10 million fish in the Neuse alone. Humans experiencing prolonged exposure to the microorganism fell ill, and the state temporarily banned commercial fishing in a ten-mile stretch of the lower Neuse, near New Bern, after a massive fish kill in September 1995. *News and Observer*, July 27, 28, August 9, 12, 15, 17, 19, September 10, 22, 23, 30, October 5, 7, 9, 10, 11, 12, 13, 16, 19, 22, 24, November 28, December 16, 1995. Hunt focused on the troubled waterway in his address, reprinted below, to the Neuse River Council and briefly discussed the problem in remarks to the Noon Rotary Club, New Bern, November 27, 1995.]

Thank you, Jonathan,[1] and my special thanks to the Neuse River Council members. I hope you all had a good and restful holiday, and I hope you're ready to roll up your sleeves and get to work on cleaning up the Neuse River.

I don't need to tell you that the Neuse River is at a crossroads. Anyone who has read a newspaper or watched the news on television lately knows we've got a problem. In some ways, the problem is simple: There are too many nutrients flowing into the river. But finding a solution won't be easy.

We have all contributed to the decline of the Neuse— agriculture, forestry, cities, industry, and individuals—and now we must all work together to save it. But I don't think the solution is for bureaucrats in Raleigh to tell the farmers, the business community, local governments, and citizens of the Neuse basin what to do. What we need is for this council, which represents all the interests of the Neuse basin, to design a strategy that will save the Neuse.

We know we can't continue on our current path, and we know that cleaning up the Neuse is going to require tough decisions. As the first basin-wide council in North Carolina, you are being given an unprecedented chance to develop a solution tailored to the Neuse's problems. You will serve as a model for our other councils in their efforts to follow through on the recommendations of the Albemarle-Pamlico Estuarine Study and our coastal agenda.

Now folks, we can't afford to kid ourselves as we start this process today. It will require a change in the way many folks, including some of you, now operate in the Neuse basin. We have to figure out who is responsible for each percentage of nutrients going into the basin. We must require source reduction and caps on nutrients. And we must find a way to pay for these changes.

In the last few months, I've heard from many people about the Neuse: fishermen, local officials, community leaders, and concerned citizens. A lot of folks are depending on us to do the right thing. Today, as your governor, I urge you to do the right thing, and [I] want you to know that my administration will support you in your efforts. Just last week, this administration underlined its commitment to protecting our environment. Our Division of Environmental Management took the unprecedented step of looking at secondary impacts from a proposed expansion of a hog-processing facility in Bladen County.[2] In the coming months, we will continue this vigilance.

The lower Neuse didn't get this way overnight, and it isn't going to get better overnight. But today we're beginning the process that will bring the river back. I look forward to joining together to do this with all of you and with everyone who cares about preserving the Neuse for future generations.

This river belongs to all of us, from the fisherman whose livelihood depends [on] it to the family who vacations here because of it, to the people who love it and love to live along it. It's up to all of us to save this treasure. It will be tough. It will take some time. But we can do it. Let's get to work!

---

[1] Jonathan Howes, secretary of the Department of Environment, Health, and Natural Resources, was identified earlier in this volume.

[2] Carolina Food Processors wanted to expand the slaughter capacity of its Bladen County plant, from 24,000 to 32,000 hogs per day, and required a state permit to increase the amount of waste water it was allowed to dump into the Cape Fear River. Concern for the Cape Fear and the number of new hog farms needed to feed an expanded plant caused environmentalists to press state officials to review CFP's request. *News and Observer*, November 18, 23, 1995.

NORTH CAROLINA FARM BUREAU

GREENSBORO, DECEMBER 4, 1995

[The Farm Bureau speech, below, appears to have been based on Hunt's opening and closing remarks at the Governor's Summit on Agriculture, November 28-29, 1995. For related press releases, see Governor Hunt to Hold State's First Agricultural Summit, Raleigh, November 13; Governor Hunt Concludes First Statewide Summit on Agriculture, Raleigh, November 29; Governor Hunt Pledges Support for North Carolina Farmers, Greensboro, December 5; Governor's Agricultural Summit Provides Gifts to Needy Children, December 21, 1995, Governors Papers, James Baxter Hunt Jr.]

I am proud today to be among my fellow farmers and Farm Bureau members. I've been a member of this organization most of my life, and I know how important the Farm Bureau is to North Carolina. Under the fine leadership of your president, Bob Jenkins, the Farm Bureau has been the voice for our state's farmers and ranchers in Raleigh and in Washington.[1] You have helped keep our agricultural industry strong.

I'm proud of North Carolina agriculture. You should be proud, too. Our agricultural industry employs 28 percent of our workforce. It pumps $42 billion a year into our state's economy. It is the third most diverse agricultural economy in the nation, and it ranks third in net farm income.[2]

Agriculture is not just our largest industry; it is also our most important. It not only supports our state's economy; it also feeds families here and around the world. But as we head into the next century, our agricultural industry faces many challenges. I heard about many of those challenges at our very first Governor's Summit on Agriculture, last week. I know that many of you were there, and I want to thank you for being there. I heard about how the increasing world population is creating unprecedented demand for agricultural products.

I heard about the financial obstacles young farmers face trying to get started, and I heard about the challenges farmers face trying to keep their operations environmentally safe.

But I also heard about opportunities. I heard about new technologies to increase production and new markets opening up around the world for North Carolina farm products. I heard innovative ideas about how to help new farmers overcome the obstacles of high start-up costs. I heard how biotechnology may help us breed highly resistant plants which could help us cut back on the pesticides and chemicals that threaten our environment.[3]

To meet the challenges, we must take advantage of the opportunities. I'm excited about the opportunities I heard about last week. I'm optimistic about the future of farming in North Carolina, and I am committed to doing all I can to make sure it's a bright future.

We must continue to support research and extension at our two land-grant universities in North Carolina. They help inspire young people to pursue careers in agriculture. They give them the education they need, and they help provide our current generation of farmers with the new technology they need to increase production and make farming more profitable.

We must continue to develop the Global TransPark. It will give our farmers a gateway to those expanding markets around the world. U.S. trade representative Mickey Kantor was right, last week at our summit, when he said the Global TransPark is the right thing to do, not only for North Carolina, but for the entire eastern United States; and I'm glad he's offering his support to help us make the project a success.[4] I'm also glad Ambassador Kantor pledged to help keep foreign markets open to North Carolina tobacco. Here at home, I want you to know that I pledge to continue my effort to fight FDA regulation of tobacco. Washington is right to want to curb teen smoking, but they are going about it in the wrong way. We don't need more government regulation of tobacco.

I also want you to know that I'm committed to helping you as we work to deal with the problems of animal waste and agricultural runoff. We're spending $1 million to study alternatives to waste lagoons and $5 million for new wastewater treatment facilities. We've added nineteen new positions to help farmers comply with animal waste regulations and help develop strategies for reducing pollution sources, and I will continue to support our Agriculture Cost-Share program that helps farmers control erosion, runoff, and animal waste.

I also know many of you are concerned over the uncertainty of the 1995 Farm Bill. I share your concern, and I want lawmakers on Capitol Hill to remember that they're not just haggling over money in the budget.

They're making decisions that affect families. I want them to remember one thing: that farm families must make a living, and to make a living their farms must make a profit.

I have a vision for the future of agriculture in our state: a vision of agriculture made stronger by new technology; a vision of agriculture that balances higher production with environmental protection; a vision of agriculture where North Carolina is a leader in the world marketplace. I want you to share that vision. I want you to work together to help make it happen. I want you to use your collective voice to spread the word about all the good things that farmers are doing for North Carolina.

Send the message that you care about the environment, that you work hard to raise your families and send your kids to college, and that you also work hard to feed all of our families—in North Carolina, across the nation, and around the world. You are vitally important to our future, and all of us in North Carolina owe you a debt of gratitude.

---

[1] W. B. (Bob) Jenkins (1932-   ), born in Franklinton; B.S., North Carolina State College (later University), 1954; U.S. Army, 1954-1956. Assistant agricultural extension agent, 1956-1961; field representative, 1961-1962, 1964-1972, field services director, 1972-1975, assistant to president, 1975-1985, president, since 1985, N.C. Farm Bureau Federation; Hookerton postmaster, 1962-1963. W. B. Jenkins, letter to Jan-Michael Poff, January 15, 1990.

[2] "Today less than 2 percent of our population is actively engaged in farming," said Hunt. "Farms are becoming fewer and larger. Forecasters predict that by the year 2000, we could assemble every individual farmer in this state, all in one audience, in one sports arena. However alarming that trend may be to you, it is very unlikely to be reversed." Closing Remarks, Governor's Summit on Agriculture, Greensboro, November 29, 1995, Governors Papers, James Baxter Hunt Jr.

[3] As a farmer, Hunt saw how the use of new and rare technology could become agriculturally commonplace. "Agriculture/agribusiness is more complex and diversified than ever before. Animal agriculture is becoming more and more genetically engineered with regards to breeding and feeding practices. Do you remember when artificial insemination was considered experimental—and only the vet knew how to do it? Nowadays, Carolyn and I cannot imagine breeding our cattle without that practice.

"Ten years ago, the home personal computer was considered a luxury on the farm. Today it is standard equipment, and most of you in this room hedge your grain daily using market reports that are only a few minutes old.

"These are trends that keep us moving forward in agriculture. As I have heard many times, 'It is not possible to plow a straight furrow if you are constantly looking behind.'" Closing Remarks, Governor's Summit on Agriculture.

[4] Michael (Mickey) Kantor (1939-   ), born in Nashville, Tenn.; bachelor's degree, Vanderbilt University, 1961; J.D., Georgetown University, 1968; U.S. Navy, 1961-1965. Attorney; lobbyist; Democratic political activist; campaign chairman, Bill Clinton for president, 1992; Congress confirmed his appointment by President Clinton as U.S. trade representative, 1993. *Current Biography Yearbook, 1994*, 289-293.

ACCEPTANCE OF ELEVENTH ANNUAL
GOVERNMENT LEADERSHIP AWARD
NATIONAL COMMISSION AGAINST DRUNK DRIVING

Raleigh, December 7, 1995

I am honored to accept this award, but I want to make sure we recognize all of the others whose hard work and dedication made it possible. We need to thank Lieutenant Governor Dennis Wicker, the members of the Governor's Task Force on Driving While Impaired,[1] and the General Assembly for passing a set of tough, new laws that will boost our efforts to crack down on drunk driving. We also need to thank Insurance Commissioner Jim Long for his leadership, and Mothers Against Drunk Driving for their public awareness campaigns, and we should thank the staff at our Governor's Highway Safety Program for their work with our "Booze It and Lose It" campaign. And most importantly, we need to thank the dedicated law-enforcement officers who put their lives on the line, every day, to help keep our highways and roads safe. They are the foot soldiers in our war against drunk driving.

I'm proud of all the progress we've made to combat drunk driving in North Carolina. The Safe Roads Act in 1983 laid the foundation for our campaign against drunk driving. In 1993, the General Assembly reduced the legal blood alcohol level from .10 to .08, and last year we kicked off our Booze It and Lose It campaign.[2]

Booze It and Lose It utilizes our most powerful weapon against drunk drivers: sobriety checkpoints. Booze It and Lose It has cut the number of drunk drivers passing through our checkpoints in half and has made North Carolina a model for the nation in the battle against drunk driving. Since we cut the legal blood alcohol level and launched Booze It and Lose It, alcohol-related fatalities have dropped 20 percent, and the work of our Governor's Task Force on Driving While Impaired, under the leadership of Lieutenant Governor Dennis Wicker, should help us reduce fatalities even more. The task force recommended, and the General Assembly passed, some tough new laws that just took effect, including zero tolerance for drivers under twenty-one and an open-container law that bans alcohol when the driver has been drinking.[3]

These tough new measures are not only saving lives, they are preventing injuries and saving our citizens millions of dollars in medical costs and insurance premiums every year. But we still have much work to do. We must continue our fight to keep drunk drivers off of our highways, especially as we approach this holiday season. I want everyone to have a safe and joyous holiday, and I want to send a clear message to anyone who's thinking of drinking and driving this holiday season in North Carolina: You will be caught, and you will pay the consequences. You will lose your license on the spot. You will face fines, court appearances, increased insurance premiums, and jail time. We are not going to tolerate the tragedy caused by drunk driving on our highways.

---

[1] Executive Order Number 59, signed July 26, 1994, established the Governor's Task Force on Driving While Impaired. *N.C. Session Laws, 1995*, 2:2089-2091.

[2] See "Safe Roads Act of 1983" (short title), *N.C. Session Laws, 1983*, c. 435; and "An Act to Reduce the Blood Alcohol Content for Driving While Impaired and Related Offenses from 0.10 to 0.08; to Reduce the Minimum Blood Alcohol Content Necessary for an Immediate Ten-Day Revocation of Driving Privileges from 0.10 to 0.08; to Make the Results of a First Breath Test Admissible Under Certain Circumstances; to Establish that the Revocation of a Provisional Licensee's License for Driving after Consuming Alcohol Shall be until the Licensee's Eighteenth Birthday or Forty-five Days, Whichever is Longer; to Provide Clarification about when an Earlier Conviction for Driving While Impaired can be Used for Aggravation Purposes; to Add a New Grossly Aggravating Factor to Impaired Driving; to Amend the Felony Death by Vehicle Statute; and to Require that there be No Insurance Consequences for a Revocation under G.S. 20-16.5 when there is a Dismissal or Acquittal of the Impaired Driving Offense," *N.C. Session Laws, 1993*, I, c. 285, ratified July 5, 1993.

[3] "An Act to Implement the Recommendations of the Governor's Task Force on Driving While Impaired," *N.C. Session Laws, 1995*, II, c. 506, was ratified July 28 and became effective September 15, 1995.

GOVERNOR'S TASK FORCE ON FOREST SUSTAINABILITY

RALEIGH, DECEMBER 15, 1995

Just over a year ago, I challenged North Carolina's forestry community to develop a plan to keep our forests alive and healthy. Today I'm pleased to be here as you work through the final stages of meeting that challenge. You've managed to bring everyone with a stake in North Carolina's forests to the table, and I want to thank all of you for your extraordinary efforts.

As we move toward a new century, we must look around us and realize just how important our forests are to North Carolina's economic growth, and prosperity, and to its quality of life. We're expecting more from our forests than ever before. They help clean our water. They provide a home for wildlife. They support our tourism industry and give us recreational opportunities. But these competing forces can lead to problems. Our goal must be to manage these forces so that forests are productive for all of us.

People I respect tell me we can meet our needs from our forests for a long time to come. They tell me we can have both sustainable forests and a strong forest industry, and I believe we can. That's why I asked all of the groups concerned about forests—private industry, universities, state government, private landowners, and environmental groups—to work together. I asked them to develop a new plan to make sure we have enough wood and recycled wood fiber to make forest products, while at the same time keeping our forests healthy and diverse.

My family and I have always been committed to good forest management and to stewardship of the land. I believe we all have a responsibility to use our natural resources wisely, so that all of us can enjoy a better life. I thought I knew quite a bit about forests, but I must say I have learned some new things from this report. Perhaps most importantly, I have been reminded, again, how important they are to all of us and how great the forces are that are affecting them. We cannot take our forests for granted. We must take some bold actions, now, to preserve them.

To that end, I want to add my support to the creation of a "Southern Center for Forest Sustainability" here at N.C. State University.[1] We can do that by using some existing resources already committed to sustainability, and I understand the university has already made this recommendation to the Board of Governors. I believe the center should have an advisory panel, similar to this task force, that includes representatives of both industry and environmental groups. I would also ask you to look to other public and private universities for additional resources.

I'm proud of the forest products industry for developing, adopting, and complying with the principles published by the American Forest Products Association, last year, and I'm proud of all the environmental groups that endorsed the industry's sustainable forestry principles. I know it's not always easy for industry and environmental organizations to trust each other and work together, but we're North Carolinians. We're leaders. We work together to solve our problems.

It was in that spirit that Weyerhaeuser and the Environmental Defense Fund, both represented here on this council, announced an agreement this month that settles a five-year-old lawsuit over wetlands. It's an agreement that will serve as a national model for resolving similar conflicts about conservation. That's the kind of thinking that will ensure that North Carolina remains a leader in protecting our environment, while at the same time protecting our economic growth.[2]

When I asked you to work together to develop a sustainable forestry initiative, I was expecting great things. Your report delivers! I know it is still in draft form, and that you are asking for additional comment through mid-January. I look forward to accepting the final version sometime this winter. But today I would like to say a few words about a couple of your recommendations.

First, I support your efforts to have the U.S. Forest Service provide us with up-to-date information. Without that data, we can't make good choices about managing our forests. Ten-year-old information is not good enough. I plan to ask other southern governors to join me in this effort.

Second, we must reinvigorate and expand the Forest Council so that it can continue this discussion of sustaining our forests; and finally, we must target state incentives to those landowners who work to preserve our forests. Government can't, and shouldn't, do everything. We must put our limited resources toward rewarding landowners who are doing it right.

To keep our forests healthy, we've got to work hard at it. With 20 to 30 percent of our forest land already part of our extended urban sprawl, this is one of the greatest challenges we face in maintaining the economic contributions of the forest industry. We must increase production on those lands where we are already doing a good job, while at the same time learning to use new, ecologically sound methods on the bulk of our forest lands—particularly those smaller parcels owned by private citizens.

Finally, today I want to ask your help in my administration's ongoing efforts to clean up the Neuse River. [Last] month I spoke to the Neuse River Council, a group of local government officials, business and industry representatives, and environmentalists. I told them that there are too many nutrients in the Neuse. I told them that I supported a cap, followed by a reduction in nutrients, in the Neuse and in other rivers. I asked them for their help in cleaning up the Neuse.

I want to ask for your help, today, in cleaning up the Neuse. Forestry can play a key role in protecting our waterways. We need to identify soils in the Neuse River basin that erode easily and plant trees on them. We need to establish buffer zones of trees along all our major rivers and streams. We need to restore and enhance forested wetlands along streams to help keep our rivers, lakes, and streams clean.

Forestry can play a key part in the cleanup of our waterways. Your report talked a great deal about forestry best-management practices. We must work together to put those practices in place along the Neuse and along our other precious rivers and streams.

I know you'll heed this call, just as you did when you heeded my call to create this task force. I know you will make sure that our grandchildren and their grandchildren will have the majestic forests that help make our state so beautiful. Once again, thank you for your efforts. I look forward to their fruition.

---

[1] The Southern Center for Sustainable Forestry had been established at North Carolina State University by the summer of 1996. *Report of the Governor's Task Force on Forest Sustainability* ([Raleigh: The Task Force], June 1996), 49.

[2] Five environmental organizations sued Weyerhaeuser Corporation, in 1991, over the draining of wetlands to create tree farms on its 11,000-acre Parker Tract in Washington County. The plaintiffs—the Environmental Defense Fund, National Audubon Society, North Carolina Coastal Federation, North Carolina Wildlife Federation, and Sierra Club—contended that the federal Clean Water Act required the forest-products giant to obtain a permit to drain wetlands. Weyerhaeuser replied that the CWA did not mandate government approval for the company to undertake the scale of operations in which it was engaged on the Parker Tract. Announced on December 5, 1995, the settlement pledged both sides in the lawsuit to "develop plans to protect wildlife habitat, water quality, unique wetland sites, and rare plants" on the tract. *News and Observer*, December 6, 1995.

LETTER TO DAVID A. KESSLER
COMMISSIONER, U.S. FOOD AND DRUG ADMINISTRATION

RALEIGH, DECEMBER 21, 1995

Dear Commissioner Kessler:

I am submitting written comments on the proposed regulations by the Food and Drug Administration, "Restricting the Sale and Distribution of Cigarettes and Smokeless Tobacco Products to Protect Children and Adolescents."

I am strongly in favor of limiting smoking by those under the legal age. I believe that all North Carolinians, in and out of the tobacco industry, would support a strong program to reduce access to tobacco products by those under eighteen. However, more big government is not the way to do it. This is one more example of Washington starting with good intentions but piling on more regulation and bureaucracy to do the job. Instead, the focus should be on supporting states and local communities in their efforts to enforce the law and educate young people.

In these proposed regulations, the FDA subverts basic principles of federalism. In 1992, Congress affirmed the traditional role of the states through the Alcohol, Drug Abuse, and Mental Health Amendments (ADAMHA) Reorganization Act. In addition, the Congressional Research Service has warned that sweeping tobacco regulations of this nature may exceed the federal government's powers under the commerce clause of the United States Constitution. Congress also has withheld jurisdiction over tobacco from the FDA for over eighty years, choosing to regulate tobacco directly or by delegating responsibility to agencies other than the FDA.

There is no need to waste months and taxpayers' dollars fighting in Congress and the courts over whether the FDA should have jurisdiction over tobacco products. States can act now to reduce the use of tobacco products by those under eighteen. The most effective way to do this is for state and local governments to work with merchants, parents, and communities to enforce existing laws and to educate the public about the risks associated with those under the legal age using tobacco.

North Carolina is a good example of a state that has acted in this area. The state of North Carolina prohibits anyone from knowingly selling or furnishing cigarettes, tobacco for cigarettes, smokeless tobacco, or cigarette papers to minors under the age of eighteen (Chapter 628, G.S. 14-313, H.B. 852, 1991).

In addition, a new law effective December 1, 1995, tightens existing restrictions by making it illegal to distribute, or knowingly aid, assist, or abet any other person in distributing tobacco products to minors. This new law also makes it illegal for minors to attempt to purchase tobacco in North Carolina and requires clerks to demand proof of age from a prospective purchaser if the person has reasonable grounds to believe that the prospective purchaser is under eighteen years of age. With an increasing emphasis on enforcement of these laws by state and local agencies, additional federal laws or oversight by federal agencies is unnecessary to prevent those under eighteen from obtaining these products.

North Carolina has not stopped with passage of tough laws. Our state, through the Department of Human Resources, also conducts an annual, random, unannounced inspection of both over-the-counter and vending-machine outlets which distribute tobacco products. These inspections measure the overall level of compliance with the state law regarding youth access to tobacco products, as required by Section 1926 of the Public Health Service Act, commonly referred to as the Synar Amendment.

North Carolina also is emphasizing merchant education. The Department of Human Resources works with local organizations to develop and distribute materials to help merchants understand and carry out their responsibilities under the law.

It is my position that the intent of these regulations, reducing teenage smoking and eliminating underage smoking, can be accomplished without intruding on the rights of adults who choose to smoke and without imposing unnecessary costs on growers, manufacturers, and distributors of tobacco products.

The costs that these regulations would impose on North Carolina are substantial. The FDA has estimated that complying with these regulations on a national level will cost manufacturers $15 million one time, and $150 million annually. Retail sellers will have an additional $67 million in costs annually. These do not include costs to advertisers, vending-machine operators, and organizers of popular sporting events.

If we attribute these costs within North Carolina on the basis of our share of these sectors, based on a 1992 study from Price Waterhouse on the national economic impact of the tobacco industry, complying with these regulations will cost manufacturers in North Carolina $6.3 million one time, and $73.1 million annually. Retail sellers in North Carolina will have an additional $2.01 million in costs annually. These costs do not include the disproportionately large impact on those small merchants who operate in poorer neighborhoods.

The proposed tobacco regulations by the FDA represent the first step toward overall regulation of tobacco, which is an important part of North Carolina's economy and community fabric. According to the North Carolina Department of Agriculture, there are 10,000 growers in North Carolina who produce crops valued at $942.9 million in 1994. Furthermore, there are 47,837 allotment holders, many of whom no longer grow tobacco, but are the widows or children of growers and who derive important income supplements from these allotments.

According to the Employment Security Commission, another 15,229 North Carolinians work in the production end of tobacco, with earnings valued at $749.8 million in 1994. Thousands of other North Carolinians depend in part on earnings from tobacco through employment in wholesale distribution, retail stores, advertising, and other sectors that derive part of their revenues from sales of tobacco products. Price Waterhouse estimated total effects of tobacco on employment from growers, auction warehousing, wholesale and retail trade, and suppliers at 102,663 in 1990. When the induced effects of expenditures on the economy are included, Price Waterhouse estimated total employment effects of 260,346.

The 1992 study by Price Waterhouse estimated the economic impact of tobacco in North Carolina for 1990, based on earnings to growers, auction warehousing, manufacturing, wholesale and retail trade, at $1.6 billion. If the earnings of suppliers to these sectors are included, the total impact of tobacco on the state economy was over $2 billion in 1990. These direct effects do not capture the full impact of tobacco on the economy, however. Price Waterhouse estimated the total direct and indirect impacts on the economy to be $3.7 billion in 1990.

Tobacco also pays state and local taxes. Price Waterhouse estimated state and local tax revenues at $215.6 million in 1990, based on compensation to growers, producers, sellers, and their suppliers. If the indirect impacts of tobacco on the state economy are included, then tobacco was responsible for $366 million in state and local tax revenues in 1990.

While North Carolina's economy is strong, there unfortunately remain poorer rural counties in our state that have not fully participated in our economic growth. For many of these counties, growing tobacco is a fundamental part of their farm economy; loss of tobacco income would be devastating to economies already under stress. For the top-ten counties in per-capita tobacco cash receipts, loss of farm income from tobacco would have a per-capita impact equal to from 5 percent to 10 percent of per-capita income.

These counties, in general, have unemployment rates and poverty rates above the state average and fiscal capacity below the state average. In the twenty counties with the highest per-capita tobacco receipts, cash receipts exceed $500 per capita for eighteen of these counties. Six of these counties have poverty rates at or above 20 percent, and thirteen have poverty rates above 15 percent. Loss of tobacco income would have dramatic effects [on] these poor rural counties.

These economic impacts are important, but they fail to capture the full importance of tobacco in our state. Tobacco helped sustain the family farm and small rural communities long after they had disappeared in other states. Tobacco helped build our public and private universities, our much-admired foundation and nonprofit institutions, and many of the public facilities across our state. The world-renowned research universities and high-technology research parks that epitomize the new North Carolina would not exist without the contributions tobacco has made to the development of our state.

In summary, there is no need to waste months and taxpayers' dollars fighting in Congress and the courts over whether the FDA should have jurisdiction over tobacco products. States can act now to reduce the use of tobacco products by those under the legal age. The most effective way to do this is for government to work with merchants, parents, and communities to enforce existing laws and to educate the public about the risks associated with those under eighteen using tobacco. I respectfully ask the Food and Drug Administration to reconsider its position and yield to states their proper authority to reduce use of tobacco products by those under the legal age to purchase tobacco.

My warmest personal regards.

Sincerely,
Jim Hunt [signed]
James B. Hunt Jr.

GOVERNOR'S CRACKDOWN FOR CHILDREN

RALEIGH, JANUARY 3, 1996

["The goal of the Crackdown for Children is to make parents live up to their obligations to pay child support for their children," Hunt told a Greenville audience on August 28, 1996. "Last year alone, more than $90 million in child support owed to our state's children went unpaid. Deadbeat parents owe North Carolina's children more than $800 million. Almost 74,000 of those parents who are under court order to pay child support simply don't. We can, and we must, do better." Governor's Crackdown for Children, Greenville, August 28, 1996; for related press releases, see Governor Hunt Launches Crackdown on Deadbeat Parents, Raleigh, January 3, and Governor's Crackdown for Children Yields First Arrest, January 5, 1996, Governors Papers, James Baxter Hunt Jr.]

It's because of Kathy and her daughter, Maggie, that we are here today.[1] It's because of the day-care director here in Raleigh, whose ex-husband has ducked and dodged the courts in his refusal to support his two-year-old daughter. It's because of the housekeeper up in northeastern North Carolina, who's been trying for seven years to collect back child support for her young son: The boy's father, a lawyer who's moved from state to state, owes almost $10,000.

These women are struggling to provide a good home and a good future for their children. We owe it to them to see that fathers meet their obligations, too. In North Carolina, we're going to do whatever it takes.

During my State of the State address about a year ago, I vowed that we would go after deadbeat dads—and moms. Now we have one of the toughest child support enforcement laws in the country. Senator Tony Rand and Representatives Bill Culpepper and Charlotte Gardner helped pass our package in the legislature, and I appreciate their leadership.[2]

Today we're launching the Governor's Crackdown for Kids. It's an intensive, comprehensive effort to track down deadbeat parents and make them pay up. And we have a message for deadbeat parents: Your time just ran out, and we're going to see to it that you take responsibility for your children.

Starting this week, we're putting photos of deadbeat parents on "Ten Most Wanted" posters. These posters will be put up all over the state, in libraries, courthouses, convenience stores, and other public places. I urge North Carolinians to use the toll-free number to turn these deadbeats in.

[Hunt stepped over to the poster and pointed out the picture of Thomas Sherin in the lower righthand corner.]

Thomas Sherin, Maggie's father, has the dubious honor of appearing on our first Ten Most Wanted poster. He owes more than $30,000 in child support. All told, these top ten owe their children more than $330,000. That's money that should have been used for food, clothes, shelter, and school[ing] for their children.

Too often, taxpayers are forced to pick up the tab for a parent's neglect, with food stamps and welfare benefits.[3] But it's not just welfare families that need help with child support. Too many families, struggling on [their] own, can't get the child support the courts have awarded them. That's why we're going to be using bank and utility company records to track down deadbeat parents, and we'll be garnishing the wages of parents in twenty-five other states. This summer, we'll start suspending or revoking occupational, professional, or business licenses of deadbeat parents, and we'll be able to seize any insurance settlements of $3,000 or more that they receive, to pay past-due child support. And by the year's end, we'll be suspending, revoking, or restricting drivers' licenses, hunting, fishing, and trapping licenses, and preventing deadbeat parents from registering motor vehicles.

So we've got tough new laws in place, and we've got tough enforcers at the Department of Human Resources who will make sure the laws are enforced. I want to commend Secretary of Human Resources Robin Britt, and Mike Adams[4] and his staff over in the Child Support Enforcement Section, who are working hard to track these deadbeats down. But we've also got to get the message out, letting parents everywhere know that we're cracking down in North Carolina. We have TV and radio public service announcements [that] will be airing across the state next week. Let's take a look at the TV spot right now. Then we'll take any questions you might have.

---

[1] Kathy Sholes, a Mecklenburg County public safety officer, and her twelve-year-old daughter Maggie, reappeared in another of Hunt's speeches; see N.C. Child Support Council Conference, Charlotte, April 17, 1996, reprinted elsewhere in this volume. Press release, Governor Hunt Launches Crackdown on Deadbeat Parents, Raleigh, January 3, 1996, Governors Papers, James Baxter Hunt Jr.

[2] Anthony E. Rand (1939-   ), born in Garner; resident of Fayetteville; A.B., 1961, J.D., 1964, University of North Carolina at Chapel Hill. Attorney; member, 1981-1987, and since 1995, majority leader, 1986-1988, N.C. Senate; Democratic candidate for lieutenant governor, 1988; chairman, Fayetteville State University Foundation; chairman-elect, University of North Carolina General Alumni Assn. North *Carolina Manual, 1995-1996*, 501.

William T. Culpepper III (1947-   ), born in Elizabeth City; resident of Chowan County; B.S., Hampden-Sydney College, 1968; J.D., Wake Forest University, 1973. Attorney; attorney for Chowan County, from 1979; president, Edenton Rotary Club, 1986-1987; chair, Chowan County Democratic Party, 1987-1991; member, Edenton Historical Commission; member, N.C. House of Representatives, from 1993. *North Carolina Manual, 1995-1996*, 572.

Charlotte A. Gardner (1931-   ), born in Baltimore, Md.; resident of Rowan County; A.B., Catawba College, 1952. Former high school educator; member, N.C. House of Representatives, from 1985, and co-chair, Appropriations Committee Subcommittee on

Human Resources; member, numerous civic and public health organizations; Republican. *North Carolina Manual, 1995-1996*, 591.

[3] If deadbeat parents of children on welfare paid the child support they owed, North Carolina could cut its welfare rolls by 20 percent. Press release, Governor's Crackdown for Children Yields First Arrest, Raleigh, January 5, 1996, Governors Papers, James Baxter Hunt Jr.

[4] Michael L. Adams (1948-   ), born in Wake Co.; resident of Garner; B.A., Wake Forest University, 1970; U.S. Army Reserve. Employed by N.C. Division of Social Services, from 1971, and chief, Child Support Enforcement Section, from 1990. Michael L. Adams, letter to Jan-Michael Poff, July 1, 1998.

NORTH CAROLINA ASSOCIATION OF SOIL AND WATER CONSERVATION DISTRICTS

Asheville, January 8, 1996

This is a good time of year to reflect on the past and look forward to the challenges of the future, and it is a good time to thank you for your years of fine work and [to] talk about taking North Carolina's soil and water districts to a new level.

[I] wanted to be with you this year, more than any other time. I don't need to tell you about one of the biggest challenges we faced in 1995: the problems we had with animal waste. You all really helped us deal with that situation. Last July I asked Dewey Botts and Dick Gallo to join forces to inspect every animal waste lagoon in the state.[1] In less than three weeks, the task was done. I'm sure most of you were involved in that effort, and on behalf of the citizens of this state, I thank you.

This new year brings new challenges. Our number-one challenge is protecting and restoring our water. The soil and water conservation districts, and the entire agricultural community, must help us meet that challenge. All of us know the importance of agriculture. Farmers feed and clothe the world. But we also know that, along with municipal and industrial waste, some farms pollute our water. We must learn to balance agricultural prosperity with environmental quality.

Later this year, I will propose increased funding for the agricultural cost-share program. We know cost-share works. We need to expand it. But if we are going to show a real difference with cost-share, then we also need to do more planning and better targeting of the money. We need to put the money where we can get the most bang for our buck— where we can see measurable results.

We must use innovative, incentive-based programs that encourage participation by farmers. [At the] same time, [we must] ensure that "bad actors" are not allowed to pollute indefinitely. We cannot let a few farmers damage our environment and give agriculture a black eye. The farmer who is plowing highly erodible land, who does not have grassed waterways, who is grossly over-applying fertilizer, is going to have to change. He's not only hurting the environment, he is hurting himself.

I also plan to propose at least $5 million to target restoration efforts in the Neuse River basin. Because agriculture plays such a large part in the problem, the majority of that money will go to agriculture, to help farmers do the right thing.

The soil and water conservation districts are vital in our efforts to restore and protect North Carolina's water. Who better to be on the front lines of our battle against water pollution than the soil and water conservation districts, who are there in our rural communities and work one-on-one with farmers to help reduce agricultural runoff. I want [you] to work especially hard to protect our water by reducing nonpoint source pollution. Be aggressive. I don't want you to wait for farmers to come to you for help. I want you to go to the farmers who need your help. I want you to be the solution to many of our water quality problems— and I want you to look beyond district and county lines. Water pollution doesn't obey those boundaries. Your planning efforts shouldn't, either; and I want you to look beyond farms to see how you might be able to apply some of the same pollution control practices to urban runoff and other nonpoint pollution.

You can do the job better than we can in Raleigh. You can do the job if we get you the resources, and I'm going to fight for those resources— the cost-share funds, the technical support, additional operating funds, and computer equipment.

I want to thank you and our partners in the Natural Resources Conservation Service for what you did last year. You worked hard for conservation. You continued your efforts to save our soil and water, just like my daddy did during his years with the SCS [Soil Conservation Service]. You've continued the vision of our own Hugh Hammond Bennett: stewardship of our God-given land.[2]

Now we see a new and greater challenge, but we can do it.[3]

---

[1] C. Dewey Botts was director of the Soil and Water Conservation Division, North Carolina Department of Environment and Natural Resources. Richard Gallo headed the North Carolina districts of the federal Natural Resources Conservation Service. *News and Observer*, April 21, 1996.

[2] Hugh Hammond Bennett (1881-1960), native of Wadesboro; B.S., University of North Carolina at Chapel Hill, 1903; honorary degrees. Soil conservationist; Soil Erosion Service director, U.S. Interior Dept., 1933-1935; Soil Conservation Service director, U.S. Agriculture Dept., 1935-1951; author. *Dictionary of North Carolina Biography*, s.v. "Bennett, Hugh Hammond."

[3] Deleting the final paragraph of his prepared text, Hunt jotted brief but largely illegible notes for a new closing that began with this line.

CRIME PREVENTION IN PUBLIC HOUSING

WINSTON-SALEM, JANUARY 17, 1996

This conference is the only one of its kind in the nation. I'm proud to be a part of it, just as I was proud to be a part of the very first Crime Prevention in Public Housing Conference in 1983.

This year's theme, "Optimizing Resources," is a good one. We have many resources available to us in our effort to make our public housing communities safer, and we must make sure we are taking advantage of them and using them to the fullest. The people who live in those communities, and the people who run them, know firsthand what the needs are, and I hope this conference helps them find new resources, develop new ideas, and create new ways to meet those needs.

I've seen how people here in Winston-Salem are taking advantage of their resources to make their public housing communities better places to live. People in public housing communities have every bit as much [of a] right to a safe community as you and I.

I just got back from the Happy Hill Gardens public housing community near Old Salem. I saw how residents there have transformed an old store from a hang-out for drug dealers into a safe, clean place where people can pick up a loaf of bread, a jug of milk, or other necessities. They were able to do it by pooling resources—getting help from the United Way, the housing authority, local donations, and a grant from the Winston-Salem Foundation. I saw how the housing authority found additional resources to put up more lighting. Police now say that "the sun never sets in Happy Hill," and residents say they feel safer.

I heard about the city's Community Safety Program. That program utilizes off-duty policemen for additional security in Happy Hill and other public housing communities. Since they are hired by the landlords, they don't need search warrants. That means they can go into apartments, catch drug dealers, and have them evicted.

I heard about how many public housing residents in Winston-Salem are getting to know police as friends and neighbors through the city's Community Policing program. Thanks to additional resources from the 1994 federal Crime Bill, the city has eleven of these officers on foot patrol in many of the city's public housing communities. And I also heard how this city is targeting young people, helping them avoid trouble in the first place. The housing authority has set up an after-school tutorial program, in Happy Hill and four other public housing communities, with the help of a grant from the R. J. Reynolds Tobacco Company, and the Winston-Salem Housing Authority is sponsoring a state public-housing basketball league.

Helping steer our young people clear of drugs and crime is one of the most important things we can do to fight crime. That's why I pushed for the creation of SOS [Support Our Students]. SOS matches at-risk middle school students with older mentors in after-school activities in fifty-two counties, [from] 3:00-6:00 [P.M.]. Here in Forsyth County, a $200,000 SOS grant is helping 135 students participate in arts and athletics and helping them with their homework.

We're doing some other things all across North Carolina to help fight crime and make our public housing communities safer. During the 1995 legislative session, I pushed for two laws that will make it easier for housing authorities to kick real troublemakers out of their communities. As a result, landlords can now evict drug dealers and other troublemakers, and they can kick out people living with them who may also be involved. And housing authorities can now make rules about guest and visitor access, helping keep troublemakers out. If someone breaks this rule and the housing authority doesn't know about it when they accept rent, they can still penalize the tenant later. Before last August, the authority couldn't penalize the tenant after rent was accepted.[1]

We've also awarded more than $3 million in grants, through our Governor's Crime Commission, to more than thirty-five local law enforcement agencies for community policing programs. In Asheville, Raleigh, and Fayetteville, police sub-stations have been set up in high-risk areas.

Our North Carolina Housing Finance Authority is sponsoring drug-prevention workshops for apartment owners and managers. Now they will be more alert to drug paraphernalia and better prevent and combat drug trafficking in their neighborhoods.

I'm proud of all we're doing to fight crime and to keep our public housing communities and all of our neighborhoods safer, and I'm proud of what I've seen here in Winston-Salem. You've made good use of all available resources. You've come up [with] new ideas and found new ways to meet your needs. You've shown that by getting people to work together, you can make a difference. You cut crime in your public housing communities here by more than 50 percent.

I'd like to see us cut crime by 50 percent in all of our public housing communities, and all of our neighborhoods, across the state. We can do it by optimizing the most valuable resource we have: people. All of us—government leaders, business leaders, directors of nonprofit agencies, teachers, ministers, the people who live in public housing communities themselves—all of us can and must play a part. We can help our young people develop the values they need to steer clear of crime. We can make our neighborhoods safer, so families don't live in fear. We can give our children hope for a brighter future; provide positive alternatives for all of them. We can do these things if we all work together.

I commend this conference and all of you who lead public housing author[ities] and who live within them. This is the front line of our fight against crime and for people. We must do it together. You are on the line. We must provide you the supplies and the help so that our side wins. I pledge to you my help and that of our state government—every way we can.

---

[1] "An Act to Provide for Expedited Eviction of Persons Engaged in Drug-Related Criminal Activity and Other Criminal Activity that Threatens the Health, Safety, or Peaceful Enjoyment of Rental Property," *N.C. Session Laws, 1995*, c. 419, was ratified July 11, and became effective October 1, 1995. "An Act to Provide that Acceptance of Rent by a Housing Authority is Not a Waiver of Default and to Authorize Housing Authorities to Govern Entry upon Housing Authority Property by Guests and Visitors," *N.C. Session Laws, 1995*, II, c. 520, was ratified July 29 and became effective August 1, 1995.

JOHN LOCKE FOUNDATION

RALEIGH, JANUARY 18, 1996

[Governor Hunt reached across political boundaries to rally support for Smart Start, as the following remarks, delivered before the John Locke Foundation, a conservative think tank headquartered in Raleigh, demonstrate. He also spoke of the early childhood program to other audiences, in 1996, that included the Children's Defense Fund National Conference, Charlotte, February 8; Assemblies of God, Winston-Salem, May 7; North Carolina Federation of Business and Professional Women's Clubs, Raleigh, June 21; NAACP National Convention, Charlotte, July 8; and Buncombe County Partnership Meeting, Asheville, August 16; for related press release, see Smart Start Raises Quality of Child Care in North Carolina, Charlotte, February 8. The speech to the Leadership Raleigh Alumni Association, dated February 7 but delivered February 9, 1996, is similar to Hunt's text for the John Locke Foundation. Governors Papers, James Baxter Hunt Jr.]

I'm happy to be here among my friends and supporters, especially those from Charlotte and Cabarrus County. It looks like we've found one thing we all agree on: lunch!

I commend the John Locke Foundation and everyone here today for coming together to ponder some serious issues. *Rightsizing* government is more than a buzzword. It's a topic that poses fundamental questions: what government should do, and how government should do it.

North Carolina is leading the way in finding new ways to do things, and we're doing it with the cooperation of government, business, and nonprofits. Sometimes we get a little partisan, but at least we're not as bad as Washington. Up there, they can't even agree on what to do to keep the government open, let alone make it work better!

In Raleigh, we're making things happen, and we're doing things differently. We're cutting taxes, although not quite as much as I'd wanted. We need to cut more taxes. I hope we can start with the corporate income tax and look hard at the food tax. We're cutting unemployment taxes for employers, but we can do more. In the last three years, the legislature has enacted three unemployment tax cuts that I proposed. This year, we need to do it again.

Today I'm announcing that I will call a special session of the legislature to cut unemployment taxes by $140 million. This will save employers $50 million in the first quarter of tax year 1996. In fact, two-thirds of our employers will not have to pay a single dime in unemployment taxes this year, and North Carolina will become the state with the lowest average unemployment rate in the nation.[1]

I'd hoped we could provide this tax relief without making taxpayers finance a special session at $50,000 a day. We've looked at it and decided this is the best way to give employers a tax cut this year. But I will urge the legislature to do it efficiently, with a one-day session that doesn't waste tax dollars.

We're cutting spending, although not quite as much as I'd wanted. As the John Locke Foundation has pointed out, I recommended abolishing 2,000 state jobs last year. The legislature only cut 600. It's a good start, but not quite good enough.

A lot of people are talking about welfare reform. In Washington, talking is all they're doing. In North Carolina, we've got a plan called Work First that will put welfare recipients to work. If the bureaucrats in Washington could dig out of the snow and give us our waivers, we could get to work putting 35,000 welfare recipients to work in the first phase alone.

Two weeks ago, we announced a new approach to tracking down deadbeat parents. The legislature has passed some new laws, and I want to thank them—especially Charlotte Gardner—for that. I'm happy to tell you that as of today, two of the "Top Ten" deadbeat dads have been arrested. Another one has turned himself in, and we have leads on two more. All told, deadbeat parents in North Carolina owe $750 million for support for their children, much of it to taxpayers who have provided welfare, food stamps, and other benefits.

Our crackdown is working. So are prisoners, and they're working harder than ever before. Last week, hundreds of prisoners across the state were clearing away snow and busting ice. That's what they ought to be doing everyday.

DOT is doing what every state agency ought to be doing: doing more with less. By the end of this year, DOT will have cut $25 million and 500 positions since January 1993. But they're doing more, 20 percent more, in road construction.

We are moving to privatize some government functions in North Carolina. In the crime session, the legislature enacted my call to provide 500 new drug- and alcohol-treatment beds through privatization. Last year, the legislature agreed to allow privatization of prisons, and we're moving towards that now.

But I think the most important thing we're doing differently in North Carolina is Smart Start. I'm disappointed that some people have turned Smart Start into a partisan issue. It shouldn't be.

Smart Start is something Republicans and Democrats alike should support. It's built on local control and local decision making. Dozens and dozens of churches are involved, and so are nonprofits like the United Way.

Businesses are supporting it. They're giving volunteer hours. They've given $14 million to help run it. Some people think businesses ought to give more, and I welcome their help to achieve that.

Lamar Alexander said the other day that he thought nonprofit corporations, with local boards of directors, should get more involved in delivering human services.[2] When I read that, I thought, "That sounds exactly like Smart Start."

And then, there are the results. Because of Smart Start, almost 10,000 children are getting the child-care subsidies their families need so they can work and hold down a good job. Ten thousand new child-care slots have been created in communities with day-care shortages. Sixty thousand children are receiving higher quality child care, thanks to better-trained teachers and quality incentives to child-care centers. Some 35,000 children have gotten early intervention and preventive health screenings, and more than 150,000 children have gotten immunizations so they can get a healthy start in life.

We need more of these results. We need more of the things I've talked about. What we don't need is more partisanship and more politics as usual. Look at Washington: See what happens when two parties burn bridges instead of building them.

Here in North Carolina, we're making real progress. But the twenty-first century demands new approaches. Let's work together to find them, and let's work together to build the future we want in North Carolina.

---

[1] One week after his appearance before the Locke Foundation, Hunt sought the advice of the Council of State on calling a special legislative session to reduce unemployment insurance tax rates. However, this paragraph indicates he had already decided to proceed. Council of State Meeting, Raleigh, January 25, 1996, Governors Papers, James Baxter Hunt Jr.

[2] Andrew Lamar Alexander (1940-   ), born in Knoxville, Tenn.; B.A., Vanderbilt University, 1962; J.D., New York University, 1965. Newspaper reporter; attorney; television commentator; campaign coordinator, 1966, legislative assistant, 1967-1969, and special counsel, 1977, to Howard Baker, U.S. senator from Tennessee; governor of Tennessee, 1979-1987; chairman, Leadership Institute, Belmont College, 1987-1988; president, University of Tennessee, 1988-1991; U.S. education secretary, 1991-1993; Republican. Barone and Ujifusa, *Almanac of American Politics, 1986,* 1251; *Who's Who in America, 1994,* s.v. "Alexander, Andrew Lamar."

MARTIN LUTHER KING JR. HOLIDAY SERVICE

RALEIGH, JANUARY 19, 1996

Martin Luther King Jr. taught us about right and wrong—and possibilities. He taught us to see beyond the differences of black, white, or Hispanic. He taught us to see beyond the differences of male or female, of Christian, Moslem, or Jew. He taught us to see beyond the differences of rich and poor and the differences of nationality. He did more than anyone in our lifetime to change the way we think about race, the way we think about each other, and the way we think about ourselves. But just as Jesus of Nazareth taught on the hillside at [the] Sea of Galilee but then lived a life of love, and righteousness, and helping for which He was crucified, so Martin Luther King Jr. lived his teachings and showed us the possibilities [for] our lives [and] our society.

We have done much, but [we have] so far to go. It hurts me to know there are still people, even right here in North Carolina, who would kill another person simply because of the color of their skin. The tragic, senseless murders of two people in Fayetteville last year proved just how far we do have to go to reach Dr. King's dream, but I believe we can do it.[1] I believe that one day we can live in the world Martin Luther King Jr. dreamed about, a world where everyone is truly equal.

Dr. King once said, "The doors of opportunity are opening now that were not open to your mothers and fathers. The challenge you face is to be ready to enter those doors." And open the next ones you come to.

Today our challenge is to make sure those doors of opportunity, the doors Dr. King himself helped unlock, remain open for all of our young people. Our challenge is to make sure that our young people are ready to step through those doors of opportunity. We must teach them to work together despite differences of race or color. We must teach them a sense of pride in who they are. We must teach them to respect each other, to understand each other, and to tolerate each other's differences.

I believe that one day we will live in the world Martin Luther King Jr. dreamed of, a world where everyone is truly equal. If we can make that happen, if we are committed to making our world a place where everyone is truly equal, if we just work for it, we will succeed in making King's dream for us and for our children a reality. But we must start, as Dr. King started, in our own homes, in our own communities, in our own churches. [We] must begin a statewide dialogue—one that was going strongly for several years, here in North Carolina, but that has lagged.

Dr. Martin Luther King Jr. died fighting for equality—for all of us. Today we must do more than honor his memory. We must pledge to continue his fight. We must pledge to do everything we can to make his dreams a reality—for us, for our children, [and] for all children throughout [this] state and this nation.

---

[1] Army privates and white supremacists James Norman Burmeister II and Malcolm Wright were charged with first-degree murder in the racially motivated slaying of two African Americans, Michael James and Jackie Burden, of Fayetteville. *News and Observer*, December 9, 10, 11, 17, 1995.

"WORK FIRST" NEWS CONFERENCE

RALEIGH, JANUARY 25, 1996

[For related press releases, see Governor Hunt Gets Federal Waivers for Work First, Washington, D.C., February 5, 1996, and Tough Rules Take Effect July 1 for Work First, Raleigh, June 27, 1996, Governors Papers, James Baxter Hunt Jr.]

Back in September, North Carolina took the Clinton administration up on its offer to let states experiment with welfare reform. We said then that North Carolina wasn't going to wait for Washington when it came to welfare reform. We said North Carolina was going to get going and put welfare recipients to work.

The bad news is, we're still waiting. The good news is, we're putting welfare recipients to work anyway.

Work First is already working. Compared to a year ago, more people are getting jobs, more people are getting off welfare, more people are getting job training and education. In county after county, welfare recipients are getting the Work First message: get a job, and take personal responsibility.

But to make Work First even more effective, we need the waivers. So yesterday I sent DHR [Department of Human Resources] assistant secretary Peter Leousis and a team of social service officials to Washington to state our case. Today I'm sending a letter to President Clinton.[1] Next week, when I travel to Washington for the National Governors' Association meeting, I plan to meet with Donna Shalala[2] at Health and Human Services, and I'll talk to President Clinton about it when the governors meet with him at the White House.

I'm pleased with what we've been able to do while waiting for Congress to act on welfare reform. Thanks in part to a strong economy, and thanks to the dedication of social service workers across the state, we're seeing results with Work First:

—From July through November, more than twice as many Work First participants got jobs, or 9,239 AFDC [Aid to Families with Dependent Children] recipients, compared to 4,022 during the same period in 1994 under the JOBS [Job Opportunities and Basic Skills] program.

—Last month, the percentage of all welfare recipients who were working was at the highest level in four years: 15.5 percent.

—From July through November, 11,200 families got jobs and got off of welfare through Work First. Fewer families are coming into the welfare system, thus reducing AFDC rolls even further. As a result, state AFDC rolls have dropped 6 percent, compared to 2 percent the previous year.

—More than half the people in job training programs under Work First are actually getting paid for their work: about 21 percent more than under the JOBS program.

—Thanks to more people working and fewer families on welfare, we expect to save more than $25 million this year alone.

All this is happening without the tough sanctions that our waivers will allow us to impose. With the waivers, we'll make even more progress. Our Work First personal responsibility agreements will become binding contracts. That means those people will be required to get a job—paid or unpaid, in the public or private sector—in twelve weeks, and they'll have to honor all the conditions of those contracts. And if they don't, they'll lose their welfare benefits.

I know the General Assembly will focus on Work First when they return to town in May, and we welcome that. There is some common ground between Work First and the House welfare reform proposals, as anyone who compares the two will see. I trust the legislature's goal is the same as ours: to put welfare recipients to work, without punishing children. If there's a better way to do it than Work First, let's look at it, together.

I also hope state legislators will take note of what county social service directors across the state are doing to make Work First work, even without waivers. In Guilford County, they've doubled the number of AFDC recipients who've gotten a job since last year. In Alamance County, employers are coming to social services with job openings. In Catawba County, social service and ESC [Employment Security Commission] staff are working side by side to get welfare recipients into jobs. And in the last five months, Cumberland County social workers have tripled the number of welfare recipients who've gotten jobs under Work First, compared to the old JOBS program. Last year, about 300 welfare recipients in Cumberland [County] got work under the JOBS program; under Work First, 900 welfare recipients have gotten jobs already, more in five months than all of last year.

---

[1] James B. Hunt Jr., letter to President William J. Clinton, January 25, 1996, copy attached to press release, Hunt's Work First Program Putting Thousands into Jobs, Raleigh, January 25, 1996, Governors Papers, James Baxter Hunt Jr.

[2] Donna Edna Shalala (1941-   ), born in Cleveland, Ohio; A.B., Western College, 1962; M.S.S.C., 1965, Ph.D., 1970, Syracuse University; honorary degrees; Peace Corps, 1962-1964. Political scientist; assistant secretary for policy development and research, U.S. Dept. of Housing and Urban Development, 1977-1980; political science professor and president, Hunter College-CUNY, 1980-1988; political science professor and chancellor, University of Wisconsin-Madison, 1988-1993; secretary, U.S. Dept. of Health and Human Services, from 1993; Democrat. *Who's Who in America, 1999*, s.v. "Shalala, Donna Edna."

PRESS RELEASE: GOVERNOR HUNT SIGNS PROCLAMATION FOR SPECIAL SESSION

RALEIGH, JANUARY 24, 1996

[For related press releases, see Tax Cut to Save Employers $73 Million in State's Largest Counties, Raleigh, February 19, 1996, and Hunt Seeks Proposals to Improve Jobless Benefits, Raleigh, February 29, 1996, Governors Papers, James Baxter Hunt Jr. The text of the January 24 press release appears to be an expanded version of the governor's notes for the Council of State meeting, January 25, 1996.]

Governor Jim Hunt today signed a proclamation convening a special one-day session of the General Assembly, February 21, to consider a cut in the unemployment insurance tax rate that would eliminate unemployment taxes for nearly 80 percent of North Carolina employers during 1996 and give North Carolina the lowest rate in the country. If passed, before the end of the first quarter of this year, the cut would reduce unemployment insurance paid by businesses $140 million this year.[1]

"By acting now instead of waiting until the session scheduled later this year, we can save employers $50 million," Hunt said. "But I want legislators to keep the cost of this session to a minimum by limiting it to one day, one issue."

Revenue from unemployment insurance taxes is paid into the state trust fund from which unemployment benefits are paid. The Employment Security Law is designed to build the trust fund balance during good economic times and provide enough funds to lessen the impact on the unemployed and on the economy during economic downturns. Because of North Carolina's economic growth and interest earned on its balance, the trust fund is now more than $1.5 billion, far more than the amount required by law.

Hunt's proposal calls for the following three adjustments to the Employment Security Law:

—Implement a zero tax rate for all employers with a positive unemployment insurance tax rate. Employers achieve a positive rate when the unemployment insurance taxes they pay exceed the amount of their unemployment insurance claims. Positive rates range from 0.1 percent to 2.7 percent. Under Hunt's proposal, employers paying this rate, 78.4 percent of the state's employers, would see their rate cut to zero in 1996.

—Allow employers with negative tax rates, 5.4 percent of the state's employers, to prepay taxes so they can qualify for the zero tax rate. Employers receive a negative rate when the unemployment taxes they pay fall short of the amount of their unemployment claims. Negative rates range from 2.8 percent to 5.7 percent.

—Reduce the assigned rate for new employers, 16.2 percent of the state's employers, from 1.8 percent to 1.2 percent, and let those employers qualify sooner for a lower rate. Currently new employers must wait three years before qualifying.

This will be the fourth straight cut in unemployment insurance taxes called for by the Hunt administration.[2]

---

[1] "An Act to Implement a Zero Unemployment Insurance Tax Rate for 1996 for All Employers with a Positive Experience Rating, Allow Employers with a Negative Rating to Qualify for the Zero Rate by Prepaying Taxes, Reduce the Rate for New Employers from One and Eight-Tenths Percent to One and Two-Tenths Percent, Allow New Employers to Qualify Sooner for Reduced Rates, and Authorize a Legislative Research Commission Study" was ratified February 21, 1996. N.C. Session Laws, 1995, Extra and Regular Sessions, 1996, c. 1.

[2] On Hunt's recommendations, the General Assembly approved unemployment insurance tax cuts of 30 percent in 1993, 39 percent in 1994, and 23 percent in 1995. See *N.C. Session Laws, 1993*, c. 85; "An Act to Reduce the Unemployment Insurance Tax Rate," *N.C. Session Laws, 1993, Extra and Regular Sessions, 1994*, c. 10, ratified March 10, 1994; "An Act to Further Reduce Employers' Unemployment Insurance Taxes," *N.C. Session Laws, 1995*, c. 4, ratified February 27, 1995; and press releases, Hunt, Basnight, Blue Announce Business Tax Cut, Raleigh, March 10, 1994; Hunt Proposes Cut in Unemployment Insurance Tax, Raleigh, December 20, 1994; and Tax Cut to Save Employers $73 Million in State's Largest Counties, Raleigh, February 19, 1996, Governors Papers, James Baxter Hunt Jr.

NORTH CAROLINA PRESS ASSOCIATION

CHAPEL HILL, JANUARY 25, 1996

I want to commend the press association for encouraging and challenging North Carolina journalists to do their best, and I want to commend each and every one of you here tonight for the hard work you do, day in and day out. One of the things I like about the Fourth Estate is your willingness to hold the mirror up to your own face, as well as mine. For all your criticism of public officials and public institutions, newspapers in this state have always been willing to take an equally hard look at themselves.

I was reminded of that the other morning when I heard James Fallows being interviewed about his new book, *Breaking the News*.[1] Fallows, the Washington editor of the *Atlantic Monthly*, says that Americans are alienated from the political process and even more alienated from the media. What people care about in politics isn't what the media covers, he says. The solution, according to Fallows, is a new "public-spirited" approach to news coverage.

As we head into an election year, I think it's important for all of us in this room to keep that in mind. Let's keep in mind that we can have a political debate based on principles, and policy, and the future of our state. We can have a political debate that engages North Carolinians in a positive way; that educates them; that details issues they care about, not just the attack of the day. Politics at its best is a process that lets people participate in their government. At its worst—well, we in North Carolina have already seen it at its worst.

In North Carolina this year, we can have a debate that is politics at its best, because you all are doing exactly what James Fallows recommends. I'm heartened by "Your Voice, Your Vote." This new partnership among newspapers, TV, and radio is a new way to cover campaigns. Papers from across the state are taking part in this—from Wilmington, and Asheville, and Winston-Salem, and Fayetteville, and

Greensboro, and Raleigh—[and] will join together to focus [on] voters' concerns and candidates' answers. The *Charlotte Observer* is the driving force behind this project, and I want to commend editor Jennie Buckner for her leadership.[2] That's the kind of thing that can engage the state in a thoughtful discussion about our problems and possible solutions. That's the kind of thing James Fallows was talking about, and that's the kind of thing I hope all newspapers will do as you cover local and state elections this year.

I commend North Carolina's newspapers for looking for new ways to do things. Just as you're willing to look for new ways to do things, government has to look for new ways to do things, too—like Smart Start. Smart Start is a new way to make sure our children can come to school healthy and ready to learn. I'm disappointed that some people have turned Smart Start into a partisan issue. It shouldn't be.

Smart Start is something Republicans and Democrats alike should support. It's built on local control and local decision making. Dozens and dozens of churches are involved, and so are nonprofits like the United Way.

Businesses are supporting it. They're giving volunteer hours. They've given $14 million to help run it. Some people think businesses ought to give more, and I welcome their help to achieve that.

Republican presidential candidate Lamar Alexander was quoted in the *N&O* the other day that he thought nonprofit corporations, with local boards of directors, should get more involved in delivering human services. When I read that, I thought, "That sounds exactly like Smart Start."

And then there are the results: Because of Smart Start, almost 10,000 children are getting the child-care subsidies their families need so they can work and hold down a good job. Ten thousand new child-care slots have been created in communities with day-care shortages. Sixty thousand children are receiving higher quality child care, thanks to better-trained teachers and quality incentives to child-care centers. Some 35,000 children have gotten early intervention and preventive health screenings, and more than 150,000 children have gotten immunizations so they can get a healthy start in life.

We need more of these results, and we need more bipartisan cooperation to bring about even more results. What we don't need is more partisan politicking at the cost of our children's well-being. Sure, there are some things we need to improve with Smart Start. Like anything new and different, we've learned as we've gone along—and I appreciate the help the Republicans have provided. With their help, we've increased oversight and auditing. We've capped administrative costs. We've set ambitious goals for even more private support.

The bottom line is, Smart Start is about children, not politics. I believe that most of North Carolina's elected officials want to do whatever we can to build a better future for our children and grandchildren. I hope that we can work constructively in the upcoming legislative session to do just that, and I hope the newspapers of this state will hold our feet to the fire.

We've seen what happens when two parties burn bridges instead of building them. Just look at Washington. Here in North Carolina, we're making real progress. But the twenty-first century demands new approaches in politics and in political coverage. Let's work together to find them, and let's work together to build the future we want in North Carolina.

---

[1] James Mackenzie Fallows, *Breaking the News: How the Media Undermines American Democracy* (New York: Pantheon Books, 1996).

[2] Jennie Buckner; B.S. in journalism, Ohio State University; managing editor, San Jose *Mercury News*; vice-president, news, Knight-Ridder, Inc., 1989-1993; vice-president, editor, *Charlotte Observer*, from 1993. *Who's Who in America, 2000*, s.v. "Buckner, Jennie."

SWEARING-IN OF
BEN TENNILLE AS BUSINESS COURT JUDGE

RALEIGH, JANUARY 30, 1996

[North Carolina's first special Superior Court judge for complex business cases, Ben F. Tennille, described the first statewide Business Court as being "similar to a Federal District Court. I try cases and write opinions designed to create a body of case law involving issues of importance to business and industry in North Carolina. Cases are assigned to my court by the Chief Justice based upon the corporate and business issues involved and the complexity of the litigation. In addition to establishing the court and handling the caseload assigned to me," Tennille said, "I have designed a model business court, which employs an electronic filing system using the Internet."

The North Carolina Commission on Business Laws and the Economy proposed establishing the Business Court, modeled after the Delaware Chancery Court, "to address North Carolina's disadvantage in competing with Delaware as the state for the incorporation of a new business or the location of corporate headquarters," wrote commission member Robert G. Baynes. Perennially, the First State provided fertile ground for the incorporation of many Fortune 500 companies. "There are many reasons companies choose Delaware," Baynes said, "but the significant one is the Delaware Chancery Court, which provides a high level of judicial expertise and has created a large body of legal precedent on coroporate-law questions. As a result, the outcome of corporate-law litigation is viewed as more predictable than in other states." With the chancery court's specific focus on corporate-law issues, "its decisions are rendered relatively quickly." Robert G. Baynes, "New Business Court and Fast-Track Commercial Litigation," *1996 Law Journal: Special Supplement, Business North Carolina* (July 1996): 54-55; Juliet E. Holmes, judicial assistant to the Hon. Ben F. Tennille, letter to Jan-Michael Poff, May 24, 1999.]

I'm proud to be here today to see Ben Tennille sworn in as North Carolina's first Business Court judge.[1] North Carolina's business climate is the envy of many other states. We have one of the lowest unemployment rates in the nation. We have [a] record number of new jobs, and we've collected accolades from *Fortune* and *Money* magazines.

People know North Carolina is a good place to do business. We have a lot to offer: low taxes, good infrastructure, quality universities, research facilities, and a highly skilled workforce. Now we have something else to offer: a Business Court. Our Business Court will resolve complex legal issues involving business and industries, helping to make North Carolina's business climate even better. Up until now, their legal issues are handled in the regular court calendar, which subjects our businesses to long delays—and it will help consumers who are affected by those delays, as well.

The Governor's Commission on Business Laws and the Economy that I created last year recommended the creation of the Business Court after hearing from consumers, corporate officers, and legal experts. My commission compared our statutes with other states and came up with this unique idea of a Business Court. Only one other state in the country, Delaware, even comes close to having something like this. North Carolina, as usual, is ahead of the pack![2]

Thanks to Attorney General Mike Easley for his hard work, as chair of the Commission on Business Laws and the Economy, and his leadership in creating this Business Court. Establishing this Business Court tells prospective and existing businesses that North Carolina recognizes their special needs and that we're willing to do all we can to encourage their growth and prosperity.

We know this new Business Court is right for North Carolina, and we know Ben Tennille is the person to lead this new effort. With Ben's leadership and guidance, this court will become a key part of our efforts to attract businesses to our state, because Ben Tennille knows the corporate world and he knows the law. Ben has an impressive record in both arenas, including fourteen years as an employment, commercial, and general business lawyer with a firm in Greensboro and nearly ten years serving as the associate general counsel of Burlington Industries.

For the past two years, Ben has headed Burlington Industries' Human Resources and Communications Division, overseeing 2,000 employees at manufacturing facilities in three states and sales offices worldwide.

With Ben you're getting the best of both worlds. He understands the needs of businesses in North Carolina and understands the needs of our people. As the state's first Business Court judge, I'm sure his service on the bench will be evenhanded, efficient, and fair. I know Ben Tennille will serve the people of North Carolina well.

---

[1] Ben F. Tennille; born in Winston-Salem; resident of Greensboro; A.B., 1967, J.D., 1971, University of North Carolina at Chapel Hill. Attorney and partner, Smith Moore Smith Schell and Hunter (later Smith Helms Mullis and Moore), Greensboro, 1971-1985; associate general counsel and assistant secretary, 1985-1993, manager for human resources and communications, Denim Division, 1993-1995, Burlington Industries; state's first special Superior Court judge for complex business cases, sworn into office January 10, 1996. Robert G. Baynes, "New Business Court and Fast-Track Commercial Litigation," *1996 Law Journal: Special Supplement, Business North Carolina* (July 1996): 54-55; Juliet E. Holmes, judicial assistant to Judge Ben F. Tennille, letter to Jan-Michael Poff, May 24, 1999; press release, Governor Hunt Names State's First Business Court Judge, Raleigh, January 17, 1996, Governors Papers, James Baxter Hunt Jr.; "When it Wrinkles, Use a Bench Press," *Business North Carolina* (June 1996): 69-70.

[2] Apart from Delaware's long-established chancery court, New Jersey, New York, and Illinois also had business-oriented courts, and at least ten other states were investigating the concept. "When it Wrinkles, Use a Bench Press," *Business North Carolina* (June 1996): 69.

TALKING POINTS

FEBRUARY 9, 1996

[This typewritten text, titled simply "Talking Points," bears a handwritten note: "This is campaign 'stump speech.'" The note was not written by Governor Hunt.]

I ran for governor again in 1992 because I love this state too much to watch it fall behind—and we're moving ahead today. Over the last three years, we've made progress in important areas:

We're putting education first

—We're cracking down on discipline in our schools. We've passed zero-tolerance and weapons-free school zone laws. We've got more SROs [school resource officers], more students involved (SAVE) [Students Against Violence Everywhere], and we're seeing results: Guns brought to schools by students [have] dropped 23 percent in the last year.

—We're steering kids in the right direction with SOS [Support Our Students], bringing 3,000 volunteers together with 6,000 students in half our counties.

—We're cutting class sizes and giving teachers the tools they need to do their job.

—We're setting higher standards for students so they can get good jobs.

—We're rewarding excellence in teaching, but we need to do more.

—We're cutting bureaucracy and putting more resources in the classroom.

We've launched Smart Start, so kids will come to school healthy and ready to learn. In forty-four counties, Smart Start is helping thousands of families and children get good day care, health care, and family services.

We're putting welfare recipients to work. Our Work First effort focuses on work and personal responsibility, and it's already working. In just five months, we've doubled the amount of welfare recipients going to work through [the] Work First program.

We're cracking down on deadbeat parents. In less than three weeks, we've caught seven of the ten deadbeat dads on our Ten Most Wanted poster. We're serious about making parents take responsibility for their children.

We're putting prisoners to work. Our new Community Work Program has helped put 17,000 prisoners, more than ever before, to work cleaning up our roads, our parks, and public buildings, growing their own food, and even building prisons. During the recent snow and ice storm, hundreds of prisoners were shoveling ice in front of schools, hospitals, and police stations in almost half of our counties.

We've got a strong economy. We've created a record number of jobs in 1993-1994—more than 250,000.

We're cutting taxes. We had the largest tax cut in state history for working families and children.

But we have to do more if we want to build the kind of future we want for our children and grandchildren. But I can't do it without you. We can do it if we do it together.

ECONOMIC DEVELOPMENT BOARD

Charlotte, February 14, 1996

The last time I met with all of you, Bill Lee was taking the reins as chairman of this board.[1] Bill, let me say again that I'm very grateful that you're leading this board's efforts. You, Commerce secretary Dave Phillips, and this board make a strong team, and I'm grateful to all of you for the time you put into making our state's business climate competitive.

This Friday, our attorney general's staff will go before our state supreme court to help protect our economic future. They'll be fighting for us to keep the modest incentives we need to be competitive and to provide jobs for our workers.[2]

North Carolina has built its strong economy with many kinds of incentives—the most important, by far, [being the] education and training [of our] workforce—our community college system, world-renowned universities and research parks, the best state-maintained highway system in the nation, a Triple-A bond rating, and infrastructure such as water, sewer, and road improvements.[3]

In the past three years, this administration has made North Carolina more competitive [and] offered some additional, modest, financial incentives, as well, to give us an extra edge as we compete with other states for new jobs. These include the Industrial Recruitment Competitive Fund, which provides modest cash incentives to help close a deal on new or expanding industry. We've spent about $12 million from this fund; the return on our investment is 10,830 new jobs and nearly $1.2 billion in investment by business in our state. Other financial incentives include the Jobs Creation Tax Credit and the Industrial Development Fund. We have also pushed for major changes in the tax code that benefit businesses and industries in North Carolina.

Now the Maready case argues that business incentives are not used for a public purpose. I say they are used for a public purpose: to create jobs for the people of North Carolina. Incentives are investments in our economy and in our workforce. Our strong economy is proof that we have made wise investments. Consider what incentives have brought to Charlotte: Royal Insurance national headquarters and 1,400 jobs; Sea-Land world headquarters and 650 jobs; Continental General Tire national headquarters and 300 jobs; Transamerica and 230 jobs, just to name a few.

The critics should talk to the thousands of North Carolinians who have completed worker-training programs to get good jobs at the companies that came here because of incentives. They should talk to rural North Carolinians who can work in their counties because of water, sewer, and road improvements that helped bring a company there.

This lawsuit seeking to abolish incentives is ironic when our neighboring states, states that compete against us for jobs, are escalating the use of incentives daily. Over the past three years, North Carolina has lost more than thirty major companies and thousands of jobs to Virginia and South Carolina. That has got to stop! Our policy of modest incentives proves that we can be aggressive and competitive without giving away the store. But this competitive situation is constantly changing, and we must compete and get jobs.

I want to thank your Incentives Task Force, and this board, for your hard work on this issue, and I look forward to getting your recommendations on our use of incentives to bring jobs to the people of North Carolina.

Work First

I want to talk with you for a moment about another effort to move people into jobs: Work First. While Washington [has been] talking about welfare [reform,] North Carolina has been acting.[4]

Work First is our welfare reform effort that's moving people from welfare to work. Many of you have read about it, and I hope many of you are already involved. We received waivers from the federal government to put the full plan in action just last week. It requires all welfare recipients to sign personal responsibility contracts. Those contracts require Work First participants to get jobs, paid or unpaid, within twelve weeks or lose their benefits.

The General Assembly may consider welfare reform when they return in May. We welcome that. I'm sure the legislature's goal is the same as ours: to put welfare recipients to work without punishing children. If there's a better way to do it than Work First, I hope we can work together on it.

Chairman Lee, I appreciate the time and advice you've given my Human Resources and Commerce staff on how we can get the state's business community behind Work First. But I need help from all of you. I want you to help spread the word about Work First.[5]

It's already working. In its first five months, Work First has doubled the number of welfare recipients getting a job and cut welfare rolls by 6 percent. This year, it will save taxpayers more than $25 million.

We need every CEO and every business owner in this state to embrace this program. We need the business community to help it succeed. We're working to find a business leader who will help us get the word out around the state. I want all of you to support the person we select.

Help us rally the business community around Work First. Remind them that moving people from welfare to work, and making them productive citizens, is good for business.

---

[1] William States Lee (1929-1996), native of Charlotte; B.S., Princeton University, 1951; U.S. Naval Reserve, 1951-1954. Registered professional engineer; various positions with Duke Power Co., from 1955, included vice-president of engineering, 1965-1971, senior vice-president, 1971-1975, executive vice-president, 1976-1977, president-chief operating officer, 1978-1982, and chairman-chief executive officer, 1982-1994, president, 1989-1994; appointed by Hunt as chairman, N.C. Economic Development Board, 1995. Letters of Appointment to Boards and Commissions, Governors Papers, James Baxter Hunt Jr.; *News and Observer,* January 11, 1994, July 11, 1996; *Who's Who in America, 1988-1989,* s.v. "Lee, William States."

[2] William Maready, a trial lawyer from Winston-Salem, challenged the constitutionality of the state's use of public money as a lure to private industry. Although Maready won his case in August 1995 before a Forsyth County judge, the decision was appealed to the state supreme court, which ruled 5-2 in favor of incentives six months later. "Incensed over Incentives," *Business North Carolina* (November 1995): 15-17; *News and Observer,* August 3, 11, 17, September 5, 9, October 29, November 24, 1995, February 11, 14, 15, 17, March 9, 18, 1996; see also "Press Release: Governor Hunt Praises Court's Decision on Business Incentives," March 8, 1996, reprinted below.

[3] At this point in his text, Hunt inserted the notation "Goal = Jobs. Do whatever it takes (reas.) to help our people have jobs."

[4] "1. Get a job. 2. Personal responsibility," jotted the governor.

[5] Hunt added, "Get your company involved—jobs. Support."

WAKE FOREST UNIVERSITY FOUNDER'S DAY CONVOCATION

WINSTON-SALEM, FEBRUARY 15, 1996

I'm honored to join all of you in celebrating Wake Forest University's Founder's Day, and I'm especially honored to also help kick off your cyberspace symposium. Although some folks say North Carolina is "a vale of humility between two mountains of conceit"—Virginia and South Carolina—we do like to brag a little. When it comes to technology, we have a lot to brag about.

I am a believer in technology. I've seen what it can do for our people. Technology can save lives. It can educate. It can teach. Technology transcends boundaries and opens up possibilities for our people and our state.

We are truly in a technological revolution. The Telecommunications Act that was just passed by Congress is one example.[1] It will be a landmark for cyberspace. We will begin to see many nontraditional partners revolutionize what you can receive over your telephone, your cable television, or your computer. I understand this fall that they will begin to place a television chip into computers for the 1996 Christmas market.

With the Information Highway, North Carolina is leading the pack in using technology to make life better for our people. The North Carolina Information Highway is a state-of-the-art telecommunications network that provides educational, medical, economic, public safety, and governmental benefits to all parts of the state.

North Carolina is at least three years ahead of the rest of the country, and three to five years ahead of the world, in cyberspace technology. But we can't rest on our laurels. We must forge ahead to make sure all North Carolina schools can take advantage of the opportunities that cyberspace technology offers. We must make sure that the Warren County student can get the same advanced calculus class as a Forsyth County student. We must make sure we take every advantage of technology if we care to develop a world-class workforce that can compete. That's why I'm so pleased to see all of you here, focused on the cutting-edge issues like the Information Highway and the role technology can play in education.

Let me tell you how "cutting edge" we are. When speaking of our Information Highway, Bill Gates, Microsoft CEO and cyberspace expert, told England's prime minister, John Major, that there are only two places in the entire world that had laid out their infrastructure for the twenty-first century. They are Singapore and North Carolina, and Singapore got its direction from us. My technology and policy adviser, Jane Patterson, couldn't be here today because she is back in Raleigh, working with the British prime minister's staff, teaching them how to design their own version of our twenty-first-century technology.

North Carolina is not new to the cutting edge. We were first in the 1980s with the statewide digital highway, one that was used so heavily by schools and businesses that the state moved toward a partnership with the private sector to create the North Carolina Information Highway. We now have the power to link schools with each other no matter how far apart—and to link them with homes, businesses, libraries, museums, and community resources. These connections will enable us to extend the time for learning, whether from home or one of the other community resources. Parents should be able to become more involved with schools through connectivity. Connections between school and work will allow students to learn about real life problems, teachers can draw on a vast new array of resources, and employers will be able to benefit from the reality of a truly seamless web of learning. That's something to brag about.

Our Information Highway has 112 sites, which include hospitals, government, and industries operating right now, with another twenty-three expected to come on line soon. All twenty-six campuses of our universities are on the highway, along with half our community colleges and more than fifty-six high schools. Remember that the Information Highway will allow all of the state's data, voice, and video networks to run across it and thus save the state some money. The test of this going on in the Greensboro area is demonstrating a savings rate of more than 40 percent by using this fast-speed network. That's something to brag about.

You should visit one of our fourth-grade classes where the children in rural farming communities are directly linked to classrooms in countries all the way around the world. You've never seen such excitement and enthusiasm for learning. This is vital when it comes to giving our children the access to education they all deserve. With the power of the Information Highway, small rural schools are linked to larger urban schools and share their resources.

In the Guilford County schools, we have the most innovative use of cyberspace technology of any system in the state. Thanks to the Information Highway, students can now take courses previously unavailable because of low enrollment at their school or the lack of a qualified instructor. Guilford students have taken a three-day electronic field trip to Kenya to study African wildlife, and 1,000 fourth graders have learned how to improve their scores on the North Carolina writing exam, all by using the Information Highway. In 1994, Guilford County's school system became the first system in North Carolina to equip and network all high schools for distance learning, and in just over a year, we can see the results: Attendance rates are up, and discipline problems are down. That's something to brag about. That's the kind of cyberspace technology we need to implement in every county. Just think about the education those kids are getting and what kind of energy they'll bring to Wake Forest and the workplace in a few years.

I want to commend President Hearn and the leaders here at Wake Forest for your decision to make sure that all students coming to Wake Forest have a computer of their own from day one. Your trustees understand that your future graduates must be ready to work in a high-tech world, and the state is moving in that direction by pushing teachers and students to master technology. Our board of public instruction has made it a policy that, beginning in '98: New teachers must be able to demonstrate competency in the use of technology as part of the learning curriculum; in-service teachers may use the rectification process to learn new technologies; and by the year 2000, students must demonstrate competency in the use of technology and must meet certain standards in order to graduate.

We must work together, all of us in the education, commerce, and government communities, to make certain that we develop the resources to help all of our citizens to enjoy the benefit of this digital revolution. Just as North Carolina was first in flight with the Wright brothers, so

North Carolina can be first in cyberspace. The world sees North Carolina as the leader in the effort to use technology to benefit all of our citizens. It is up to all of us to make certain that becomes a reality.

---

[1] P.L. 104-104, "Telecommunications Act of 1996," *United States Statutes at Large*, Act of February 8, 1996, 110 Stat. 56.

CITIES/COMMUNITIES IN SCHOOLS CONFERENCE

RESEARCH TRIANGLE PARK, FEBRUARY 21, 1996

I want to commend all of you for making a difference for North Carolina's young people through Cities in Schools. I know that Cities in Schools works, because I've seen it work firsthand. My wife, Carolyn, volunteers with Wake County Communities in Schools each week. She works with a young man, named George, who goes to Hunter Elementary School. She helps him with homework. She tutors him in reading and math. Most importantly, she is helping him learn to believe in himself.

Carolyn and I both believe that working one on one with young people is the best way we can help the children of today become the responsible adults of tomorrow. We must get our young people on the right track early, so that they can get a good education and succeed later in life. That's why I've pushed hard to make our schools safe places to learn—and to teach. That's why we're raising standards in our schools, to make sure our young people learn the basic skills they need to get a good job and succeed in the workplace. That's why we're giving teachers, parents, and principals more say in running their schools.

That's why we're starting early, with Smart Start, so that every child can come to school healthy and ready to learn, and we're already seeing results. Thanks to Smart Start, more children are getting better quality child care, new child-care spaces have been created, and children are getting the preventive health screenings and immunizations they need to get a healthy start in life.

That's why I created SOS—Support Our Students—to give our children a safe place to go after school, where adult mentors can help them with homework and get them involved in constructive activities. That's why I volunteer every week, with SOS, to work with two young men from Daniels Middle School. I believe each and every one of us can make a difference.

SOS is already making a difference. School performance is going up in counties that have SOS, and juvenile crime is going down. We've reached 6,000 students with our fifty-two SOS initiatives in just one year—a goal we thought it would take three years to reach. More than 3,000 people have volunteered with SOS, giving more than 70,000 hours. Local SOS initiatives have raised more than $3.5 million in private contributions from schools, local governments, churches, and thousands of people who believe in SOS. Businesses have helped lead the way.

But the premier volunteers-in-schools effort in our state is CIS. I'm proud to say Cities in Schools is helping us reach our goals by working with us to make SOS succeed. In Lincoln County, Cities in Schools has joined with SOS to make a difference in the lives of more than seventy children. These young people planted flower beds at a local nursing home as part of their community service project. They spend two days working on math and science lessons with help from tutors. They write short stories to improve their writing skills—and it's working. More than 85 percent of these students improved at school by one letter grade in at least two subjects, last year.

That's what we can accomplish for our young people when we all work together. We need more people to support SOS and Cities in Schools. We need more volunteers, people like all of you here today, who are willing to give their time to make a difference for our next generation. We need more people who have learned, as Carolyn and I have learned, and as all of you have learned, that by working together we can truly make a difference in the lives of North Carolina's young people.

CLEVELAND ELEMENTARY SCHOOL

CLEVELAND, FEBRUARY 22, 1996

[The text for events in Richlands, February 1, and Gastonia, February 13 (document was dated February 9), 1995, was similar to that which he delivered at Cleveland Elementary School, Johnston County. Compare the Cleveland text with the governor's campaign speech notes of February 9, 1996, reprinted above.]

As I drove here today, I was thinking about roads—and how important they are. They get us to our jobs, our schools, our homes; they help us recruit new industry. They help us build our economy.

Roads are the lifeblood of a community in many ways. That's why I'm pleased to announce, today, that we are pumping new blood into

Johnston County by speeding up a critical road interchange that will help commuter traffic and will help school buses deliver Johnston County children to this elementary school more safely. I have directed DOT [state Department of Transportation] to build a loop at I-40 [and] N.C. 42 to ease commuter traffic on N.C. 42 and let school buses travel more safely. This should eliminate the traffic backup here at Cleveland School Road, because motorists will be able to get onto the westbound ramp of I-40 more quickly, and I hope this will eliminate those dangerous left turns across westbound traffic.

We're waiting on the Federal Highway Administration to give us the go-ahead to build the loop. I expect we'll start construction this summer, and [it] should be done by Christmas. I told my DOT folks to get it done, and get it done fast—and they are. At the same time, we're widening N.C. 42 from a two- to five-lane highway from Cleveland School Road to the I-40 interchange. We're starting that this summer, too, and [it] will be done in the summer of '97.

In the last three years, we've spent some $50 million to improve roads, in Johnston County, to pump up the lifeblood of this community. But we know that the most important thing for Johnston County's future is education. Education is our future: It's everything.

You all know that. That's why you worked your heads off to pass the $50 million bond issue, last fall. I commend you for that and hope other communities will follow suit. School facilities are critical. Our students can't learn in buildings that are falling down around them. It's unacceptable that prisoners have better buildings than our students!

I know we need to do more to build better schools in Johnston County and across the state. I am a strong supporter of a statewide school bond issue that will help us do that. First we need to know what the price tag is. I'm talking with legislative leaders about our needs and when we can pass such a bond issue. I'll be counting on you all to help.

But buildings are just the first step in building better schools. One of the most important building blocks is safe schools and cracking down on discipline. We need to keep violent kids and guns out of schools. We're doing that with zero-tolerance and weapons-free school-zone laws, more officers on campus, more alternative schools, education boot camps, and after-school programs like SOS [Support Our Students] for troubled kids. I understand Johnston County has a wonderful SOS effort, coordinated by the Johnston County High School Alumni Association. Right now, twenty volunteers work in afternoons with twice as many kids, to give them something to learn and someone to learn from. But we need more volunteers. I hope you all will get involved.

These safe-schools efforts are starting to show some results. There were 23 percent fewer guns in school, last year, according to DPI [state Department of Public Instruction]. But that's not good enough.

We need to attack drugs in our schools, too. I'm glad to hear that the Johnston school board is considering forming a task force to tackle drug use in the schools. I will call my secretary of crime control[1] when I get back to see how the Governor's Crime Commission can help.

We need to make classes smaller, get back to basics, demand more from students, encourage excellent teachers, cut education bureaucracy, and give teachers and parents more say in running schools. We're doing that, but we need to do more.

We need to make welfare recipients work and take personal responsibility. Work First is doing that. We've doubled the number of welfare recipients who've gotten a job in the last five months alone.

We need to make deadbeat parents take responsibility. We've located nine of our top-ten deadbeat parents, and now we're working to make 'em pay up.

We need to make prisoners work more than ever before. Right now, 17,000 prisoners are working, cleaning up roads, clearing away snow and ice—even building new prison work farms. I know that in Johnston County, we've got almost fifty prisoners working on road squads and another seventy working in a paint plant.

At the same time, we need to build the state's economy. We're seeing record numbers of new jobs, and we're bringing new jobs to Johnston County. In the last three years, we've brought more than 400 new jobs to Johnston and more than $80 million in new and expanded investments.

And we can do all this without raising taxes. In fact, we proposed the state's largest tax cut, last year, most of it for working families with children. This year, the average family of four, earning $30,000, will see its taxes cut by one-third—and the unemployment tax cut passed yesterday will mean three-quarters of our employers will not pay a dime in unemployment taxes this year.

But we still have a lot more to do if we want to build the kind of future that our children deserve.

---

[1] Richard Hancock Moore (1960-   ), born in Oxford; B.A., 1982, J.D., 1986, Wake Forest University; graduate degree in accountancy, London School of Economics, 1984. Attorney; assistant U.S. attorney, N.C. Eastern District, 1989-1992; member, N.C. House of Representatives, 1993-1994; secretary, N.C. Department of Crime Control and Public Safety, from December 1, 1995; Democrat. *North Carolina Manual, 1995-1996*, 355; press releases, Governor Hunt Names Moore as New CC&PS Secretary, Raleigh, November 20, 1995, and Governor Hunt's New CC&PS Secretary Sworn In, Raleigh, December 1, 1995, Governors Papers, James Baxter Hunt Jr.

PRESS RELEASE: GOVERNOR HUNT PRAISES
COURT'S DECISION ON BUSINESS INCENTIVES

RALEIGH, MARCH 8, 1996

Governor Jim Hunt today praised the North Carolina Supreme Court for upholding the use of business incentives by state and local governments to attract new business and help existing industries create new jobs.

"North Carolina is back in business," Governor Jim Hunt said. "Now we can get back to the business of going after new jobs for our people. The Maready case has obscured the real crux of the incentives debate: It's all about jobs and the economic future of our state."

The court's opinion said incentives help create a stronger economy. "New and expanded industries in communities within North Carolina provide work and economic opportunity for those who otherwise might not have it," the opinion says. "This, in turn, creates a broader tax base from which the state and its local governments can draw funding for other programs that benefit the general health, safety, and welfare of their citizens. The potential impetus to economic development, which might otherwise be lost to other states, likewise serves the public interest."[1]

The ruling will allow the city of Winston-Salem and Forsyth County to continue providing financial incentives to companies that create new jobs. The ruling also clears the way for the state to continue using incentives like the Industrial Recruitment Competitive Fund that has brought commitments of 11,000 new jobs and $1.2 billion in investment from fifty-nine companies since 1993.

"Now, with the endorsement of the state Supreme Court, North Carolina can continue to use modest financial incentives as an economic development tool," Hunt said. "This ruling, along with new tax credits being developed by the North Carolina Economic Development Board and our new Business Court, one of three in the nation, brightens North Carolina's job prospects."

Last month, the Economic Development Board recommended to Hunt an aggressive business incentive plan to help existing industries modernize and to help bring new jobs to North Carolina. That plan includes new tax credits to stimulate investment in machinery and equipment by new and expanding industry, to help existing and new employers train workers in new technologies, and to stimulate innovative and product-related research and investment. The board also recommended reducing the state's corporate income tax rate from

7.75 percent to 7 percent or lower and identifying a funding source for an infrastructure trust fund to address economic development-related water and waste water needs.

In January, Hunt designated a former corporate attorney as the state's first business court judge to resolve complex legal issues involving business and industry in the state.[2] This makes North Carolina one of three states in the country with a special court to hear business cases.

The state has held firm in its argument that, in order to compete with other states for new jobs, North Carolina must be able to offer modest financial incentives to companies in addition to [the] state's other incentives: specialized worker training through the community college system, world-renowned universities and research parks, strong financial resources, and an excellent transportation system.

---

[1] *Maready v. City of Winston-Salem, North Carolina Reports* 342 (1996): 727.
[2] See "Swearing-in of Ben Tennille as Business Court Judge," Raleigh, January 30, 1996, reprinted above.

WILMINGTON CHAMBER OF COMMERCE AND ROTARY CLUB

WILMINGTON, MARCH 11, 1996

[Hunt's remarks to the joint meeting of the Wilmington Chamber of Commerce and Rotary Club were almost identical to the text for his March 19 speaking engagement in Southern Pines, and his text for the Glen Raven Mills expansion celebration, Norlina, March 21. The Wilmington address, dated March 11, actually was delivered the next day; see Governor's Schedule for March 9-17, 1996, Governor's Papers, James Baxter Hunt Jr.]

I'm glad to be here in Wilmington, with you, and to have a chance to talk about what we can do together, this year, to build North Carolina's future.

North Carolina is the envy of many other states. We've had low unemployment, record new jobs, national accolades for our quality of life and workforce, and a forecast of continued growth. Here in Wilmington that growth means new jobs, with more than $200 million in new investment and 800 new jobs in the last three years.

But we've got to stay ahead of the curve. We've got to work hard to help companies expand and create new jobs. In Wilmington, that means working hard to boost the tourism and film industries. In the last three years, we've increased funding for travel and tourism marketing by

$7 million, and we've seen more than 5 percent growth in the tourism industry statewide in the last year alone.

We've worked just as hard to boost our film industry, with more feature films produced in the last three years than in the entire twelve years before that. Today I'm pleased to announce that the film industry spent more than a million dollars a day in our state last year; and I'm especially pleased to announce that almost a quarter of that, $240 million, came right from here to Wilmington, where you all had the majority of the state's film production. Our state averaged a new movie every week last year, putting us alongside California and New York as one of the most active film production centers in the country. All told, film makers spent $391 million in our state last year, creating nearly 33,000 new jobs.

But we've had to fight hard for every new job we've gotten in this state, and we've had to fight hard to compete with states like South Carolina or Virginia. Last week's Supreme Court ruling means we can continue our modest use of financial incentives to recruit new jobs. Now North Carolina can get back to the business of aggressively recruiting new jobs. Along with our tax cuts, the new tax credits being developed by the Economic Development Board, and our brand new Business Court, North Carolina's business climate is brighter than ever!

Our aggressive economic development strategies are making a difference, and I'm proud of the progress we've made. But I'm just as proud of the progress we've made in education, in fighting crime, and in strengthening families. In education, we're starting earlier, so kids will come to school healthy and ready to learn. In thirty-two counties, Smart Start is helping thousands of families and children get good, affordable day care and health care—and soon, New Hanover County will be part of that effort.

We're working to make schools safer, with new efforts to keep guns and violent students out of our classrooms. Violent students ought to be in alternative schools or our new education boot camp over in Bladen County, where they can learn the three Rs and respect. We're putting more uniformed officers on campus, and we're seeing results: Guns in schools dropped 23 percent last year. But we have a long way to go.

We've also got to give teachers the tools they need to do their jobs, like smaller classes, and higher salaries tied to higher standards. We've got to get back to the basics, so that students learn the skills they need for the workforce, and we've got to get parents a lot more involved. We're making progress, but we have more to do.

We're keeping violent criminals behind bars longer, and we're putting more prisoners to work than ever before. Almost 17,000 prisoners are working, cleaning up roads, parks, and public buildings; growing food; building prisons; and shoveling ice in recent storms.

We're putting welfare recipients to work and demanding personal and parental responsibility. In just five months, Work First has doubled the number of welfare recipients going to work and will save taxpayers $25 million in its first year. We're demanding responsibility from deadbeat parents, too. With the help of North Carolinians, our Crackdown for Children has located nine of our top-ten deadbeat parents; now we're working to make 'em pay up.

We've done all of this together, with local folks getting involved and making it work. We in North Carolina have much to be proud of, but we have more to do if we want to build the kind of future we want for our children and grandchildren. Together, I know North Carolina can do it.

EDUCATION CABINET AND
EDUCATION GOVERNING BOARDS

RESEARCH TRIANGLE PARK, MARCH 13, 1996

Education, and the education leadership represented in this room, has made North Carolina the state it is today, and it will shape the North Carolina of tomorrow. You all are leaders, and you know what education means to the future of this state. You know North Carolina's economic future is tied to the future of our education system. How well we educate our children and train our workers determines how well we can compete in the global economy.

Now, more than ever, North Carolina must keep its competitive edge in the world marketplace. To do that, we must have the best schools, the best universities, and the best community colleges. We must have the best workers to attract the best jobs, and produce the best citizens, of the twenty-first century.

Last month, I got a letter that illustrates that critical link between education and jobs. A vice-president of Food Lion wrote me explaining what kind of skills it takes to stock shelves and bag groceries today. It's not just heavy lifting anymore: "Today's supermarket is changing," he wrote. "When teenagers come to work in a supermarket, even as baggers, they will need to have basic business and computer skills to be effective."

In Washington, they're talking about jobs and economic security in the presidential race. Here in North Carolina, they're talking about incentives and what the state ought to do to help create good jobs. But we can't debate jobs without debating education. The debate we'll have in North Carolina, this year, about the future of education, is about more than education: It's a debate about our economic future.

We must start the debate at the beginning, with our children. We must start earlier, so every child comes to school ready to learn. That's what Smart Start is about, and that's why we need it in every county.

We must provide our children a safe place to learn, without guns, or violence, or disruptive students. We have new efforts under way, new laws, more officers on campus to do that. We cannot, and we will not, tolerate violence.

But we can't abandon these children. They must continue to learn—the 3 Rs and respect. We're putting more resources into alternative schools, and building the state's first education boot camp, so they can do just that.

We must give our teachers the tools they need to do their jobs. That means smaller classes; that means training teachers like professionals, treating them like professionals, and paying them like professionals—and expecting professional work in return. We must make it a priority, this year, to pay our teachers better and to demand higher standards in return.

We must give teachers, parents, and principals more say. With local control comes accountability. Schools, students, and teachers should be held accountable, with rewards for success and consequences for failure. We must make sure our children are learning the basics, the 3 Rs and more. Today, the basics includes [sic] using technology—like that stock clerk in the grocery store—and problem solving, and teamwork. I commend the State Board of Education for the work it is doing to make this happen and to bring about accountability, more emphasis on basics, and local control.

All of us who care about education must be at the table in this debate, working together and moving forward together. We must make sure our students master those basics and graduate with the skills needed for work or higher education. Our Standards and Accountability Commission is moving ahead to put higher standards in place. By the year 2000, I hope we can offer a guarantee to employers: If North Carolina's high school graduates haven't mastered those basic skills, the state will take them back and retrain them at our own cost!

This is an ambitious agenda, but North Carolina must be ambitious for our children. We must be just as ambitious when it comes to training and retraining our workers and giving our community colleges the support they need to do that. In today's job market, employers must train, and retrain, workers quickly. Helping our community colleges provide that skill training is key to recruiting new industries, creating new jobs, and keeping our state's economy healthy. That's why I worked so hard for the community college bond issue, two years ago.

We've made progress in equipment and training infrastructure, too, but we still need to do more. And we need to work together, as community colleges are doing with my Workforce Preparedness Commission. Together, we're finding a better way to match employers and employees—like our new one-stop career centers, where workers can find the services and the training they need under one roof. Together, we're finding better ways to build a stronger school-to-work transition for students, especially those who will go straight into the workforce from high school. Working with businesses and community colleges, our JobReady effort is helping students get the job training and job skills they need to succeed.

To stay ahead of the curve, we must pay our faculty, at community colleges and universities, better. We must recruit and retain the best, and that means putting our resources into that high-priority area. We must push for a significant salary increase for faculty this year, and we must do it together.

You all know how many companies come and expand here because of the outstanding reputation of our universities. Our colleges and universities are among the best in the nation for their skilled and dedicated faculty and their accomplishments in research and development. As a graduate of both our flagship universities—North Carolina State and Carolina—I understand how important it is to attract top-notch faculty to the UNC system.[1]

I know that North Carolina's universities are part of the reason that our state's economy is strong. Our universities have helped produce a world-class workforce, along with top faculty and graduate students whose research has helped support and recruit jobs to the Research Triangle and across the state. And academic research programs bring in some $1 million a day in other funds to our state. That's why I fought for the university bond issue, two years ago, and have fought to put resources into our universities. I know our universities' link to high-tech research and development has helped make the Research Triangle a world-renowned center of technology, and ideas, and helped push North Carolina onto the cutting edge. We can't afford to lose that edge.

Regardless of the differences we've had in the past, we in this room are united. We know building a strong education system is the most important thing we can do, for education's sake and for the sake of our state's future—and we must be united in making that argument, this year. We must stick with the public schools and stick to the changes we're implementing. We must support our community colleges and their skill training, and we must recruit and retain the best university faculty.

We must work together to make sure the General Assembly understands the issue and the debate. I'm ready and willing to lead the effort, with your help. It is the key to making sure North Carolina stays competitive in the global economy and that our people have the skills they need to get good jobs.

---

[1] Hunt earned degrees in agricultural education (B.S., 1959) and agricultural economics (M.S., 1962) from North Carolina State University. His law degree (J.D., 1964) came from the University of North Carolina at Chapel Hill. *North Carolina Manual, 1995-1996*, 203.

NORTH CAROLINA
ASSOCIATION OF EDUCATORS CONVENTION

CHARLOTTE, MARCH 15, 1996

Never in my lifetime has there been an election that will be more important to the future of the public schools in our state. I believe the most important issue in this election is whether North Carolina is going to make a commitment to have the kind of public schools that our children need, today and tomorrow.

We know our children need a better education, and we know how to do it. We know our children need three things: They need safe schools and orderly classrooms. They need good teachers. They need to graduate with the skills required to succeed in the twenty-first century economy.

I'm here today because I believe that you and I share a commitment and a determination to give them that kind of education, and I believe North Carolinians are just as committed. They want schools to work. They want us to do what it takes to provide their children with the education they need—and so do teachers. I've spent a lot of time in classrooms in the last three years, a lot of time listening to teachers; to your leaders, to Rose Marie [Lowry-Townsend], and Cecil Banks, and John Wilson; to the classroom teachers who make up my Teacher Advisory Committee; to my teacher adviser, Karen Garr; and to thousands of classroom teachers [in] almost 100 teacher town meetings.

We've heard the support, and we've heard the criticism. We know there are people in North Carolina today who would give up on the public schools. We know we'll hear more from them over the next year, in Raleigh and across the state. But let me tell you one thing: I am going to give every last ounce of energy I have to see that we have the kind of public schools our children ought to have. That means safe schools first. Teachers can't teach and students can't learn in an atmosphere of violence and disruption.

We've done a lot in the last three years. We passed a law to expel students who bring guns to school. We're putting more uniformed officers on campus. We're putting more money into alternative programs for kids who are disruptive, so they can learn the 3 Rs and respect. We're building the first education boot camp for kids with serious discipline problems.

We're not going to give up on those kids, but we're not going to let them disrupt the classroom. We're not going to let them keep other students from learning and keep you from doing your jobs, because the second thing our children need is good teachers, and we need to give teachers the tools they need to do their jobs. We've got great teachers in North Carolina. We can make the quality of teaching what it needs to be, and we can recruit, and train, and keep good teachers. But we've got to train teachers as professionals, treat them as professionals, and pay them like professionals.

Teachers tell me they need better training, more time for planning, and more voice in how schools are run. That's why we need the Teacher Academy; real duty-free periods; more staff development; site-based decision making; National Board certification and financial rewards for teachers who meet this strenuous challenge; smaller classes in the early years. We've made great progress in these areas. We must not let that progress be eroded.

Teachers need more voice and more say. We need to give you more support. Parents and families need to get more involved. Principals, superintendents, school board members, legislators, and even governors need to do more listening. But most of all, we need to pay good teachers for good work. That's why the budget I'm preparing now will propose a plan to raise teacher salaries to the national average by 2000. Critics say we can't afford it. I say we can't afford not to. We can't afford not to recruit and retain the best teachers for our children.

But we must also demand the best, from our students and our teachers. We must be willing to set higher standards and to meet those standards. The people of this state want teachers to be rewarded for success and achievement, but they also want consequences for failure.

The third thing our children need is a diploma that guarantees them the skills they need to compete in the workplace of tomorrow. Last month I got a letter that tells the story better than I could. A vice-president of Food Lion wrote me, explaining what kind of skills it takes to stock shelves and bag groceries today. It's not just heavy lifting anymore.

"Today's supermarket is changing," he wrote. "When teenagers come to work in a supermarket, even as baggers, they will need to have basic business and computer skills to be effective."

We must make sure our children are learning the basics. That means focusing on reading, writing, and math, especially in the early years; and that means using technology, like that stock clerk in the grocery store, and problem solving, and teamwork. We must expect more from our students, if we want them to achieve more. That means setting rigorous standards and making sure our students meet them; and that means building better bridges between school and work, with efforts like JobReady. We must have the best workers to attract the best jobs, and produce the best citizens, of the twenty-first century.

We know what we need to do. We just need to stick to it. We've made a good start in the last three years, and I'm proud of what we've done together.

In 1992, we forged a partnership: a partnership for better schools; a partnership for a better future for our children; a partnership for a better North Carolina. This year, and this election, is about the future of our children and of our schools. Are we going to do what we know needs to be done, and stick to it? Or are we going to abandon our public schools?

I know what my answer is, and from what I heard here last night and this morning, I know what your answer is—and I believe I know what the people of North Carolina will say. I know it will be a tough fight, but it's the right fight. It's the most important fight, and it's a fight we'll be in together, side by side. I thank you for everything you do every day. I'm proud to stand with you, and work with you, and fight alongside you.

NORTH CAROLINA MEDICAL SOCIETY

DURHAM, MARCH 15, 1996

You are all heroes. As the debate over health care reform, malpractice reform, and Medicaid funding rages on, people too often forget that. They forget that doctors are on the front lines in our battle to keep our people healthy, fight disease, and save lives. They forget that when it comes to their health and well-being, doctors are the most important advocates they have. That's why we need you to be involved in the debate. That's why your voice needs to be heard. That's why you must play a part in finding the solutions to our health care problems.

You are deeply concerned about people, and you are leaders. That's why, as governor, I have turned to many of you for help during my twenty years of public service. In my first term I named Dr. Sarah Morrow, a highly respected public-health director and pediatrician, to head our Department of Human Resources. I named your president, Dr. David Bruton, known for his strong commitment to education, to head the State Board of Education. As executive director of the Health Planning Commission, I chose a national pioneer in the primary-care field, Dr. Jim Jones, from East Carolina University. Dr. Jones has done an outstanding job working with legislators during the last session to get some major reforms passed, and I commend his efforts.[1]

We in this room share common goals: to help keep our people healthy; to help make sure everyone has access to quality, affordable health care; to help keep health-care costs down; and to make sure doctors can do their jobs.

We're working to keep our people healthy. A healthy North Carolina begins with healthy children. That's why we need to expand Smart Start, our early childhood initiative that provides health care, day care, and other critical services from all walks of life. Thanks to Smart Start, more than 35,000 children have gotten preventive medical screenings.

We have a lot to be proud of in our immunization effort; so do you. We've provided free immunizations to more than 150,000 children. North Carolina now has one of the best immunization rates in the nation. You've been a big part of that, and I'd especially like to thank Dr. David Tayloe for his leadership in the effort.[2]

I also understand that many of you are working on a new campaign to make sure our elderly citizens get the immunizations they need. You're joining in a massive campaign with public-health officials, emergency medical services, and the National Guard to immunize citizens sixty-five and older on November 3. I commend your efforts, and I'm proud of the way private doctors and public-health officials have worked side by side in our efforts to immunize both children and senior citizens.

You've also been a big part of our efforts to decrease our state's infant mortality rate. Thanks to the leadership of the Infant Mortality Commission, we are doing a better job—but as you know, we still have a long way to go. I believe that, working together, we can reduce our infant mortality rate even more, in all segments of our population.

We're working to make sure everyone has access to health care. We have a responsibility to make sure no one is deprived of life-saving health care, whether they live in the city or the country, are working or unemployed, middle class or poverty stricken, elderly or disabled.

For our people living in the more rural, remote areas of our state, access to health care can be a problem. Our system of rural health care is fragile. We need to make it stronger. We're linking doctors in rural hospitals with specialists at our medical research universities through our North Carolina Information Highway. We're working to make it easier for people in rural areas to get to a doctor and get the quality care they deserve, and we're working to make it easier for doctors to have the quality of life they deserve if they choose to work in the rural communities where they are so badly needed. With guidance from Jim Bernstein, in our Office of Rural Health and Resource Development, and pioneers like Dr. Harvey Estes, we're working to increase pay differentials and create incentives like our in-locum tenens program to attract and keep good doctors in the rural and underserved parts of our state.[3]

But access also means making health care more affordable. Almost 1 million North Carolinians have no health insurance, and as you know, everyone else pays the cost of their care. This cost shift accounts for one-third of every hospital bill nationwide and nearly half of every bill in North Carolina. It drives insurance rates up and makes it impossible for many people to afford insurance.

We're working to make our insurance system more fair. The Health Care Planning Commission, which I chaired, recommended some commonsense health insurance reforms that were enacted last year with your help. People no longer have to remain locked into jobs to hold onto their health insurance. We now have a uniform pre-existing conditions exclusion set at twelve months for policies regulated by the state. The pre-existing condition period applies only once, so workers can change jobs without losing coverage, and we've passed guaranteed renewability to guard against unfair policy cancellations.

We're working to keep health-care costs down. Health care is a $21 billion business in North Carolina, and state government is a major payer. One-third of the state budget goes to providing health care. We have an obligation to look for ways to reduce health-care costs, and we have an obligation to make the system work in a way that benefits both the patient and the medical profession.

With your help, I believe we're taking steps in the right direction. We've modified the Collaborative Practice Act to allow physicians and mid-level practitioners to form professional corporations. We've taken steps that allow physicians to obtain certificates of public advantage for cooperative agreements that improve access, control costs, improve quality, and help implement health reform measures. And the [North Carolina] Medical Society is leading the way. We've taken steps in the right direction towards malpractice reform which will help us control costs, protect good doctors from frivolous lawsuits, and still hold bad ones accountable for their actions.

We're working to help doctors do their job. That means health-care reform should never get in the way. Doctors need to be the ones making the medical decisions, and no one should ever interfere with the doctor-patient relationship. I'm proud of the way we fought, together, to overturn the twenty-four-hour-stay rule for new mothers, and we must always fight to preserve the sanctity of the doctor-patient relationship.

More changes are coming in health care, and we need to be realistic. But we should respect the right of a doctor to choose the most effective treatment. We should respect the right of a patient to choose the most effective doctor, and we should protect the right of everyone to have access to quality affordable health care. We can't do it in one sweeping motion, but we can do it right, and we can do it together, working together to iron out our differences.

We've made a good start in the right direction, but we still have a lot more to do. You have played a major role in what we've accomplished so far, and I want you to continue to play a major role as we move forward. I want to hear from you and hear your ideas. Together we can work to provide all North Carolinians with the kind of health care they deserve.

---

[1] Sarah Taylor Morrow (1921-   ), born in Charlotte; B.S., 1942, M.P.H., 1960, University of North Carolina at Chapel Hill; M.D., University of Maryland, 1944. Director, Chester County (S.C.) Health Dept., 1953-1959; associate director, 1960-1968, director, 1968-1977, Guilford County Health Dept.; secretary, N.C. Dept. of Human Resources (later Dept. of Health and Human Services), 1977-1984. *North Carolina Manual, 1983,* 683.

H. David Bruton (1934-   ), born in Candor; A.B., 1957, M.D., 1961, University of North Carolina at Chapel Hill; U.S. Air Force, 1964-1966. Pediatrician, Sandhills Pediatrics, Inc., 1966-1997; chairman, State Board of Education, 1977-1982; secretary, N.C. Dept. of Health and Human Services, from 1997. *North Carolina Manual, 1997-1998,* 359-360.

James G. Jones (1933-   ), native of Pembroke; B.S., Wake Forest University, 1959; M.D., Bowman-Gray School of Medicine (first American Indian to attend the school). General practice-family medicine, in Jacksonville, 1962-1965, and Greenville, since 1975; member, from 1962, vice-president, 1971, and family medicine section chair, 1972, N.C. Medical Society; associate clinic professor, 1971-1982, clinic professor of family medicine, from 1982, University of North Carolina School of Medicine; associate clinical professor, 1972-1975, and professor of family medicine, from 1975, East Carolina University; director, Family Practice Residency Program, ECU. *News and Observer,* November 16, 1986.

[2] David T. Tayloe Jr. (1949-   ), born in Philadelphia; resident of Goldsboro; M.D., University of North Carolina at Chapel Hill, 1974. Pediatrician; vice-president, 1990-1992, president, 1993-1995, N.C. Chapter, American Academy of Pediatrics; member, Immunization Advisory Committee, N.C. Dept. of Health and Human Services, 1995; chairman, Wayne County First Steps Consortium, from 1995, and of Wayne Initiative for School Health, from 1997; was appointed to N.C. Institute of

Medicine, by Governor Hunt, 1999; active in many other civic, legislative, and medical boards and organizations. David T. Tayloe Jr., letter to Jan-Michael Poff, November 9, 1999.

[3] James D. Bernstein (1942-   ), born in New York City; B.A., Johns Hopkins University, 1964; Master of Hospital Administration, University of Michigan, 1968; U.S. Public Health Service, 1968-1970. Service unit administrative officer and hospital administrator, 1968-1970, acting service unit director, 1970, Santa Fe Service Unit, Indian Health Service; fellow, Career Development Program in Global Community Health, U.S. Dept. of Health, Education, and Welfare, 1970-1973; director, Office of Research, Development, and Rural Health, N.C. Dept. of Health and Human Services, from 1973. James D. Bernstein, letter to Jan-Michael Poff, March 16, 1999; *News and Observer*, February 7, 1982.

Edward Harvey Estes Jr. (1925-   ), born in Gay, Ga.; B.S., 1944, M.D., 1947, Emory University; U.S. Navy, 1950-1952. Cardiologist; chief of cardiology, 1953-1954, chief of medical service, 1958-1963, Durham VA Hospital; rose from instructor to associate professor, 1953-1960, professor, from 1961, Duke University School of Medicine; professor and chairman, from 1966, Dept. of Community Health Sciences, Duke medical school; president, 1977-1978, N.C. Medical Society; author. *News and Observer*, December 21, 1975; letter, William N. Hilliard, executive director, N.C. Medical Society, to Memory F. Mitchell, Historical Publications Section administrator, May 24, 1979.

PRESS RELEASE: HUNT CREATES COMMITTEE TO STRENGTHEN REGULATIONS FOR REST HOMES

RALEIGH, MARCH 20, 1996

[Eight wheelchair-bound men died in the smoke and flames of a flash fire, March 17, 1996, ignited by a faulty electrical outlet at Scotch Meadow Rest Home, Laurinburg. It was the worst resident home disaster in North Carolina history. Although Scotch Meadow was in full compliance with state safety guidelines, the age of the building made it exempt from a lifesaving feature required of new nursing facilities: a sprinkler system. At the time of the fire, 364 rest homes and 91 nursing homes in North Carolina operated without sprinklers. *News and Observer*, March 19, 20, 21, April 1, 11, 25, May 1, 2, 15, June 20, 1996.]

Governor Jim Hunt announced today he will name an ad hoc committee to develop an action plan within five weeks designed to beef up the state's standards, penalties, and inspection process for North Carolina's rest homes.[1]

"The tragic fire at a Laurinburg rest home this week shows we must move forward quickly to review and toughen state standards, where needed, for rest homes and nursing homes," Governor Hunt said. "We must ensure that North Carolinians living in these homes are safe, secure, and getting the quality care they deserve to meet their needs."

Committee members, to be named later this week, will include families of rest home and nursing home residents, older adults, advocates, medical professionals, and representatives of the rest home/nursing home industry. The committee will report its recommendations on rest homes to Hunt by April 30, in time for needed changes to be brought before the General Assembly for its short session in May.

Hunt wants the committee to review and make recommendations on the state's standards for safety and quality care in homes, the penalties now assessed for violations, and the state and county inspection process for homes. Specifically, he asks that the committee:

—Consider a mandatory sprinkler law like Virginia now has;

—Review current standards for staff ratios to ensure that sufficient staff is provided to care for and meet the safety needs of the residents. The committee should look closely at the needs of the most vulnerable rest home residents who need help with basic care like eating, bathing, and getting out of bed;

—Increase the state's penalties, last updated by the General Assembly in 1983;

—Determine if the state should continue to rely largely on counties to conduct routine inspections of rest homes or if the state should assume sole responsibility for inspections;

—Determine if an increase in payments to rest homes will be needed to help offset improvement expenses.

Hunt also announced that Human Resources secretary Robin Britt is taking immediate steps to strengthen the state's response to problems in nursing homes. Effective April 1, the North Carolina Division of Facility Services will:

—Use a single inspection system for nursing homes which takes advantage of the tougher federal penalties. Nursing homes have been subject to both state and federal penalty structures, depending on the nature of inspections. Under federal rules, penalties range from $50 to $10,000 per day for violations. State rules cap penalties at $5,000 per violation;

—Shift five state staff members from nursing home licensing duties to complaints investigations to speed up the state's response to complaints.

Hunt's ad hoc committee will also make recommendations for nursing homes. North Carolina licenses more than 1,400 rest homes with more than 27,000 beds, a 22 percent increase since 1990. The state has 357 nursing homes with more than 42,000 beds, a 30 percent increase.

---

[1] Twenty-three committee members were listed in the press release, Hunt Names Panel to Strengthen Rest Home Standards, Raleigh, March 25, 1996, Governors Papers, James Baxter Hunt Jr.

GOVERNOR'S CONFERENCE ON TRAVEL AND TOURISM

HIGH POINT, MARCH 25, 1996

It's great to be in High Point, the "Home Furnishings Capital of the World." It's also headquarters to the nation's largest hosiery and textile manufacturers, and you've got some wonderful tourist attractions here, too, like the Furniture Discovery Center and the Angela Peterson Doll and Miniature Museum!

Tourism is doing well all over North Carolina. It's growing every year, at a rate 3 to 4 percent faster than the rest of the United States! Travel and tourism generated $9.2 billion in North Carolina last year, an increase of more than 8 percent from the year before—the biggest jump in five years—and travel and tourism provides more than a quarter-million jobs with an annual payroll of more than $2 billion. Nearly $700 million in state and local tax revenues can be traced directly back to travel expenditures. That goes a long way to help us pay for education, health care, highways, and other things we need to improve the quality of life in our state.

You all are making that happen. You're not only working hard to keep your own businesses healthy, but you're also working hard to keep the tourism industry healthy across North Carolina; and you're working together, with us, in so many unique ways to promote travel and tourism in our state. We're working together on the North Carolina Golf Marketing Alliance, which promotes North Carolina's outstanding golf in the United Kingdom and Germany. We're working together on the "Year of the Mountains," testing a joint print advertising campaign in two national magazines to build business in the spring. We're working together with CP&L [Carolina Power and Light] and others in the corporate community to explore joint programs to strengthen our tourism base. We even worked together, with private industry, to spruce up our newly renovated I-95-North Welcome Center: The Hickory Furniture Market donated all the furniture.

We're putting our prisoners to work to boost the travel and tourism industry, too. The Travel and Tourism Division has specially trained inmates from the North Carolina Correctional Institution for Women answering our 1-800-VISIT-NC line. Since the program began, more than 2.5 million requests for information have been answered.

Under the creative and dynamic leadership of its new director, Gordon Clapp, I know our Division of Travel and Tourism will continue to work with you to develop more new and innovative ways to make the most of our resources and boost travel and tourism in our state. Gordon hit the ground running. He works well with the industry. His enthusiasm is contagious, and he's already making a difference. He's the one behind our very first statewide conference on heritage tourism, which will be held next January; and he's created an interagency marketing council, made up of five departments, to strengthen our efforts to build the tourism industry.[1]

I'm proud of all that we have accomplished, so far. We've made a good start in the right direction, but we have more to do. We've got a great product to sell—the natural beauty of North Carolina—and we need to protect it. When it comes to pollution, we are all part of the problem, and we all need to work together to find solutions.

We need to do more to market our product. That means state-of-the-art marketing techniques to tell millions of potential visitors from around the world about all that North Carolina has to offer: our natural beauty, our hospitality, and our heritage. We need to develop even more public-private partnerships, between government and the travel industry, to use the resources we have wisely and to develop new ones. You have already been working with us on a long-range plan, and I look forward to seeing it when we meet again at next year's conference at the Grove Park Inn, in Asheville.

We've got a great thing going. We've got a beautiful state, from the mountains to the sea. We've got progressive leadership in our Travel and Tourism Division. We've got aggressive leadership in our travel and tourism industry, and together, we've got a great partnership that will guide us to an even brighter future for the industry and for our state.

---

[1] Gordon W. Clapp (1932-   ), born in Swampscott, Mass.; resident of Dunn; B.A., Duke University, 1954; U.S. Air Force and Air Force Reserve. Owner, president, Clapp Travel Services, Bangor, Portland, and Orono, Maine., 1972-1987; deputy commissioner for tourism, state of Maine, 1987-1989; travel and tourism dir., New England Governors' Conference, Inc., Boston, 1989-1992; founder, N.C. Civil War Tourism Council, Inc., 1994-1995, worked with N.C. Dept. of Cultural Resources and N.C. Assn. of Convention and Visitor Bureaus to educate people about the state's Civil War heritage; executive director, from Dec. 1995, N.C. Tourism, Film and Sports Development Division, N.C. Dept. of Commerce. Gordon W. Clapp, letter to Jan-Michael Poff, March 19, 1999.

PRESS CONFERENCE ON CRIME PREVENTION AND YOUTH

RALEIGH, MARCH 29, 1996

I want to begin by telling you a story about a girl named Sholanda. It's the story of a girl who got into trouble early. By the age of 13 she had been suspended from school three times for fighting. Things got worse. She was arrested for assaulting another student with a weapon and put on probation.

But Sholanda was referred to the Governor's One-on-One Program. For the past six months, a 29-year-old volunteer mentor has been working with her. She hasn't been suspended from school, and this last grading period, she joined the honor roll for the first time. But what's even more important is that Sholanda has learned that someone cares about her. That's the difference volunteers can make in the lives of our children, and that's the difference volunteers have been making in our SOS [Support Our Students] and Governor's One-on-One Program.

Today I'm announcing what may be the largest donation of time and talent ever made by a single group to the children of our state: The Woman's Missionary Union of the Baptist State Convention has pledged the volunteer time of 72,000 women, from 3,000 churches all across our state, to our SOS and Governor's One-on-One programs. Beginning this October, they'll be volunteering to help students with homework, organizing clubs and activities, serving on advisory boards, working as adult mentors, helping send the kids to summer camps or find jobs—and they'll be trying to convince their family members, friends, and neighbors to do the same.[1]

Their help couldn't come at a more critical time. Juvenile crime rates are increasing across our country. While we're making good progress in North Carolina, we know that the best way to stop juvenile crime is to prevent our young people from becoming criminals in the first place. SOS and the Governor's One-on-One Program are helping us do that. Last year, 90 percent of the young people who joined the Governor's One-on-One Program were referred by the police or courts, but 75 percent of them had no further involvement with the courts or police after getting help from their volunteer mentors. We're seeing similar results with SOS. We [are] still working on a comprehensive evaluation of the program, but we already know what's happening in some programs. For example, 86 percent of the students in Lincoln County's SOS initiative have improved their average by at least one letter grade since they started getting help from volunteers.

But numbers don't tell the whole story. The most important things happen one by one, with young people like Sholanda. One by one, we can turn the children of our state away from crime and towards a brighter future.

Good things happen when we work together. I'm glad that churches are working together with us in this important effort to help at-risk children. I hope this gift inspires even more people and groups to help us help our children. They need us all. On behalf of all the people of

North Carolina, I thank the women of the Woman's Missionary Union for making this commitment to our future.

---

[1] The Woman's Missionary Union of the Baptist State Convention was not alone in its commitment to helping children. The North Carolina Jaycees pledged the services of its 6,000 members as volunteers and fundraisers for SOS and Smart Start. They also planned to raise $15,000 and boost in-kind donations for the programs. Jaycees Press Conference, Raleigh, May 29, 1996; press release, N.C. Jaycees Make Major Commitment to Governor Hunt's Smart Start, SOS, Raleigh, May 29, 1996, Governors Papers, James Baxter Hunt Jr.

SWEARING-IN OF JANICE FAULKNER
AS SECRETARY OF STATE

RALEIGH, APRIL 1, 1996

[The Secretary of State's Office became the target of a state audit, in 1995, after a newspaper investigation revealed questionable spending and management practices by Secretary Rufus L. Edmisten. Edmisten resigned, and Hunt appointed Janice Faulkner to complete his term as secretary of state. Faulkner was the first woman in North Carolina history to hold the post. *News and Observer*, December 15, 1995, March 13, March 22, 1996.]

When I named Janice Faulkner to be secretary of revenue more than three years ago, I knew she was smart. I knew she was strong. I knew she was a leader. I knew she had energy, enthusiasm, and spirit. I'd seen it in her work as an English professor at East Carolina, in her stint as Democratic Party executive director, in her leadership of our state's world trade community, in her effort to build up the communities of eastern North Carolina.[1]

Janice Faulkner builds people up and helps them do their very best. Few people can inspire so many to do so much. She believes the best of people, and people do their best for her.

I knew Janice brought those skills to our administration. What I didn't know is how quickly she would build a strong team of dedicated, motivated people, people who helped her build this agency into an international model of efficiency and effectiveness. Today the Department of Revenue collects more taxes, more quickly, than ever before. It is the most cost-efficient department of revenue in the nation. We are number one in the number of tax returns filed electronically because of the ITAS [Integrated Tax Administration System] system Janice helped put in place.

Today, Revenue leads the nation in successful motor fuels and drug tax collections. It's a model for other states and other countries, nominated for and winning the kind of prestigious awards that most agencies only dream of. And this has all happened with a new approach, a team-oriented approach that gives state employees more say. Anyone who questions whether quality management can work in state government ought to spend a day at Revenue, where the team approach has worked to reduce turnaround for critical tax transactions by 70 percent.

Janice Faulkner has shown that good management can serve North Carolina taxpayers well, and she has shown that good employees can become great employees if they have a great leader. I know she can do the same as secretary of state. I've looked hard, in and out of state government, for a strong leader and manager who can do what it takes to fix the problems at hand. Janice Faulkner is good, and she's tough. She can make this department work, and she can restore the public's confidence in the Secretary of State's Office. That's what the taxpayers of this state deserve.

I am proud to appoint Janice to this office and even prouder that she is the first woman ever to serve on the Council of State. I know you all— her friends, family, and colleagues—are proud of all that she has done and all that she will do. Let's wish her well and wish her Godspeed.

---

[1] Janice Faulkner (1932-   ), born in Martin County; B.S. in English and social studies, M.A. in education and English, East Carolina University. Educator; career with East Carolina University included alumni affairs director, 1962-1966, associate professor of English, 1966-1981, Regional Development Institute director, 1983-1992, associate vice-chancellor for Regional Development Institute, 1992-1993. First woman to serve as executive director, N.C. Democratic Party, 1981-1982; N.C. secretary of revenue, 1993-1996; was first woman appointed as N.C. secretary of state, 1996, and first woman to serve on N.C. Council of State; board member, past president, N.C. World Trade Assn. *North Carolina Manual, 1995-1996*, 404; press release, Governor Hunt Appoints First Woman to Council of State, Raleigh, March 21, 1996, Governors Papers, James Baxter Hunt Jr.

SECOND ANNUAL AMERICORPS ISSUES SUMMIT

RALEIGH, APRIL 10, 1996

You have been working hard to change people's lives. They are grateful to you. I am grateful to you, and I am proud of you.

When we launched AmeriCorps here just over a year and a half ago, we had high expectations. You have not let us down. A lot of good things have happened, and they've happened because of you. All of you deserve credit for those accomplishments, and now you're poised to do even more. At this Second Annual Issues Summit, you will listen and learn about things that are working in other places, and you can take it [sic] back to your communities to make your programs even stronger.

I want to thank our State Commission on National and Community Service, especially its chair, Jim Van Hecke; and I want to thank Judith Bell and her folks in my Office of Citizen Affairs, who've coordinated the volunteer effort that is making AmeriCorps work for communities all across North Carolina.

Last year there were more AmeriCorps programs here than any other state in the country. That shows how far you're willing to go to make this state an even better place to live and work. Now there are more than 600 AmeriCorps volunteers working in seventy-five counties across our state. You all are from different communities, different backgrounds, and different age groups, but you have one thing in common: You have spirit that guides you to help those who need it. You are making a difference in their lives, and you are inspiring the next generation of great volunteers.

At the Gaston Literacy Council, AmeriCorps volunteers are teaching people things they never could have dreamed of. Two years ago, there was a middle-aged woman who was working at the Firestone plant who couldn't read or write. But an AmeriCorps volunteer helped her unlock the gifts inside her. She became the gifted poet she always knew she could be.

Just last month, the Durham Housing Authority—AmeriCorps volunteers helped open a store in one of the public housing communities. They helped residents organize a citizens' police force that gets kids on and off of school buses safely. They helped set up baseball leagues for six- to twelve-year-olds that local businesses have sponsored; and thanks to help from AmeriCorps volunteers, this summer, residents will open a day-care center so that parents can go to work and know their children are being taken care of. All of these volunteers came from public housing communities themselves. They shared information, like you all are doing today, and got people involved. Even though these folks aren't as fortunate as many of us, they're helping all of those around them.

That's what all of you are doing. You are working in partnership with schools, churches, nonprofit organizations, and businesses; and you're working in partnership with each other; and all of you are doing it to make our state and our country a better place to live. You are building affordable housing, so families can have a better place to live. You are supporting Smart Start, providing day care, health care, and other critical services to preschoolers so they can come to school healthy and ready to learn. You are volunteering in the SOS [Support Our Students] crime-prevention program, giving middle-school students a safe place to go after school and steering our youngsters away from drugs and crime.

That is the spirit of AmeriCorps, and that's the spirit of Smart Start and SOS: to reach beyond government and into the community for solutions.

AmeriCorps is providing solutions to some of the toughest problems our society faces. We need to build on that, not tear it down. You need to let your elected officials know that. I want you all to keep the spirit alive in yourselves. I want you to bring it to life in others around you, and I want you to keep working to make your communities and our state all that it [sic] can be.

NORTH CAROLINA
HOME FURNISHINGS EXPORT COUNCIL

HIGH POINT, APRIL 17, 1996

I doubt there's any one industry in North Carolina, or in the country, for that matter, that is more united, more committed, or more determined to grow than our furniture industry. I am proud of the furniture industry and the reputation it has given our state. This industry has made North Carolina the furniture capital of the world. We didn't get that reputation overnight. For many years, this industry has been growing.

Furniture is a major part of our international trade efforts. Our Commerce Department's International Trade Division participates in trade shows all around the world and helps our home furnishings industry sell their products in the global marketplace. The top destinations for North Carolina's furniture are Canada, Japan, and Saudi Arabia. Mexico has become the fifth top destination for North Carolina furniture.

I have thought a lot about what we could do to help this industry grow even more. One way we've tried to boost exports is by promoting furniture on our trade missions. In the last three years, I have led missions to Japan, Mexico, and South Africa. These countries offer strong markets to our furniture industry. Last year, while I was in Japan, Secretary Phillips, Bill King,[1] Bill Fenn, and other Commerce staff joined me on a tour of Otsuka, a Japanese company that is the largest single user of North Carolina furniture in Japan. We saw the new Tokyo Fashion Town, a major complex under construction in Tokyo Harbor, that will house the world's largest furniture showroom. We also met with executives of several other major Japanese furniture companies, and I can tell you they are excited about buying our furniture.

Another of our efforts is the creation of the Furniture Export Office that's located here in High Point. Since its creation, we have seen tremendous growth in our home furnishings exports. Last year alone, this industry's exports were nearly $200 million.[2] During 1993, exports totaled $167 million. That's something to be proud of.

But we didn't stop with the Furniture Export Office. Last year, during a lunch at the Executive Mansion, I asked each of you to serve on this council and to help us create new ways to sell more of the products we make. That's a pretty big responsibility because the more products we sell, the more jobs we create.

Once we provide jobs for our workers, we have to keep them competitive. I'm glad to see on your agenda that you're going to talk about setting up a furniture technology symposium. I want you to think of ways we can better use the Furniture Technology Center we created at N.C. State University to equip our workers for all the changes taking place in technology. Our goal should be to train our workers for the competitive jobs. If we do that, we'll keep the companies and keep the workers employed—and let me tell you, jobs is [sic] what we're all about.

---

[1] William T. King was director, International Trade Division, N.C. Commerce Department.

[2] North Carolina was the fourth-largest exporter of furniture in 1994. Press release, Governor Jim Hunt Attends High Point Furniture Market, Raleigh, April 18, 1996, Governors Papers, James Baxter Hunt Jr.

NORTH CAROLINA CHILD SUPPORT CONFERENCE

CHARLOTTE, APRIL 17, 1996

[Hunt delivered speeches similar to this at the District Court Judges Conference, June 17, and at Crackdown for Children events in Greenville, August 28, and Charlotte, October 18, 1996. For related press releases, see Governor Hunt Unveils New "Ten Most Wanted" Poster, Announces Success of Governor's Crackdown for Children, Charlotte, April 17, 1996, Hunt Launches Second Phase of Crackdown for Children, High Point, July 1, 1996, Governor Jim Hunt Unveils New "Ten Most Wanted" Deadbeat Parent Poster, Announces Increase in Child Support Collections, Charlotte, October 18, 1996, and Governor Jim Hunt Announces Tougher Penalties for Deadbeat Parents, Raleigh, December 2, 1996, Governors Papers, James Baxter Hunt Jr.]

Three months ago, I introduced North Carolina to a wonderful young lady named Maggie Sholes. She shared her story of growing up without her father's emotional and financial support. We heard how her father, Thomas Sherin, owed more than $30,000 in back child support for

Maggie. We heard how Maggie's mom has struggled, working long hours to provide for her daughter—and we unveiled our first "Ten Most Wanted" deadbeat parent poster. And there among the ten was a picture of Maggie's dad.

A lot has happened since that day. Maggie has almost $5,000 in her college fund that wasn't there before, and a new computer to help her with her schoolwork, all because someone saw Thomas Sherin on this poster, called our hot line, and turned him in. That was one of almost 900 calls that have been placed to our new hot line since the first of the year, with tips to find deadbeat parents. Those calls were from people who are tired of carrying the load for parents who shirk their responsibilities. They are tired of seeing their tax dollars used for welfare payments to children who should be getting child support, and they are letting deadbeats know they won't stand for it anymore.

We're not going to stand for it anymore, either. We're demanding personal and parental responsibility. That's why we launched the Governor's Crackdown for Children, and I'm proud to say that it's working. Just ask Maggie's father, Thomas Sherin. Or ask Larry Carr and Gary Threadgill: We arrested them in Florida and brought them back to face judges in North Carolina. Or ask Frank Clemmons: We found him in California and started withholding money from his paycheck.

Since we unveiled it in January, we've collected more than $14,000 from the parents on our first "Ten Most Wanted" poster. Statewide, we've collected over $3 million more than we expected in child support payments the first quarter of this year.[1] That's money families can use to buy food and clothes. That's money their children have waited years for. The number of parents having child support withheld from their checks has increased 12 percent and the number of fathers coming forward and admitting their paternity is up 5 percent.

Today we [are] giving deadbeat parents even more reason to live up to their responsibility. We're putting ten more deadbeat parents on the hot seat. This is our newest "Ten Most Wanted" deadbeat parent poster. These parents, nine men and one woman, owe their children $390,000. One of these parents, Johnnie Lee Houston, is from Mecklenburg County and has eight children he has run out on. I hope North Carolinians will respond with information on these ten parents as quickly as they did on the last poster to help us track down these deadbeats.

It's amazing how much of an impact these posters have! A deadbeat parent who hadn't been seen or heard from in two years was so afraid he might end up on our poster that he called the child support office where he used to live, gave them his address in Virginia, and volunteered to start paying more child support. A bank vice-president from the

Midwest, who also feared seeing his face on the poster, paid off his $10,000 back debt and has begun making regular child support payments.

In addition to the posters and income withholding here in North Carolina and across state lines, our new law allows us to use bank and utility records to track deadbeat parents. In July we'll be able to suspend or revoke their occupational, professional, and business licenses and seize their insurance settlements in excess of $3,000.[2] And in December we'll be able to suspend or revoke driver's licenses, keep them from registering a car, and take away their hunting and fishing licenses.

We're still working to get the word out. We're encouraging counties to take advantage of our new law and put out their own local posters. Eleven counties have done that, including Mecklenburg County; the local poster here has been a huge success. We're encouraging businesses to help spread the word in their employee newsletters. We're going to visit high schools to spread the word that no matter how old you are, if you have a child, you have a moral and a financial obligation to support that child. And starting today, this poster, along with information about our tough new law, is available worldwide on the Internet.

We're making progress. You've been a big part of that. I want to thank you for your efforts on behalf of the hundreds of thousands of North Carolina families and children you help every day. I'm glad we've passed the toughest child support law in the nation. I'm glad we've been able to give you the tools you need to track down these parents who dodge their responsibilities, and I'm glad we've been able to create the penalties we need to make them realize that, one way or the other, they must pay.

Our message is simple: We're getting tough. We won't forget, and we won't give up. If you are a deadbeat parent, your time just ran out.

---

[1] Eighteen of the nineteen offenders whose faces appeared on the first two "Ten Most Wanted" posters had been found or arrested, and $40,000 had been collected from them for their children, during the first nine months of Crackdown for Children. From the beginning of January to the middle of October 1996, the state located approximately 132,000 deadbeat parents and corralled an additional $13.8 million in child support. By December, 114 parents who failed to make support payments had professional licenses revoked. Governor's Crackdown for Children, Charlotte, October 18, 1996; press release, Governor Jim Hunt Announces Tougher Penalties for Deadbeat Parents, Raleigh, December 2, 1996, Governors Papers, James Baxter Hunt Jr.

[2] State child-support enforcement agents had uncovered more than 1,100 holders of professional licenses who owed back child support. They were given twenty days "to clear their debt, make arrangements to start paying, or ask for a case review—otherwise, their licenses will be revoked." Press release, Hunt Launches Second Phase of Crackdown for Children, High Point, July 1, 1996, Governors Papers, James Baxter Hunt Jr.

PRESS RELEASE: EVALUATION FINDS
SOS IMPROVING STUDENT GRADES, BEHAVIOR

RALEIGH, APRIL 18, 1996

An independent evaluation of Governor Jim Hunt's Support Our Students after-school initiative concludes that participating students are getting better grades and improving their behavior, and that community groups and schools are providing strong support for the local efforts. The report finds that SOS students' grades in math, science, and language are up by 8.9 percent, the number of students committed to training schools is down 14 percent, and 87 percent of parents whose children had discipline problems report improved behavior by their children since starting SOS.[1]

The study, conducted by evaluators at N.C. Central University between October 1995 and April 1996, recommends continuing SOS, increasing funding to serve more students, and makes recommendations about how the program can operate more effectively. The conclusions are based on an analysis of data from surveys of staff, parents, and students in all fifty-two programs; in-depth interviews; and site visits at twenty-eight of the fifty-two programs and from the School Information Management System (SIMS).

"It's clear to us that SOS is really filling a void for the latchkey students in our state," said Dr. Beverly Jones, director of N.C. Central's Institute for the Study of Minority Issues and principal investigator on the evaluation team.[2] "But SOS is not just keeping them safe. It's using community resources to lift them up academically, emotionally, physically, and socially."

"SOS works because students like it, staff members work hard at it, and communities support it," said Governor Hunt, who volunteers weekly with two students as part of the Wake County SOS program. "This evaluation shows that making a small investment in our young people can pay big benefits for them and for our future."

SOS was proposed by Governor Hunt and approved by the General Assembly with $5 million in funding during the special session on crime in 1994. Fifty-two county programs were selected in September 1994, with grants ranging from $46,000 to $200,000. Most sites have been serving students since January 1995. SOS now serves more than 6,000 students in fifty-two counties.[3]

During its first year of service, more than 2,100 community volunteers worked with students. Last month, the Women's Missionary Union of [the] Baptist State Convention announced its commitment to provide volunteers from as many as 3,000 churches to support SOS students. In addition, during its first fiscal year, local programs received more than $2 million in cash and in-kind contributions. During the first five months of fiscal year 1995-1996, local programs raised more than $1 million.

The evaluation assesses the effectiveness of each of the program[s] in meeting the goals set forth in the legislation. Specifically, it finds that SOS is:

Reducing juvenile crime: A survey done by the Division of Youth Services determined that since SOS began, training-school commitments in SOS counties have decreased by 14 percent, while the number of students committed in non-SOS counties went up 4 percent.

Recruiting community volunteers: The evaluation finds "extensive volunteer support of programs by local teachers, retired people, high school students, and college students." Programs recruit volunteers from an average of more than three different organizations, and the study found that during the first quarter of 1995-1996, the average county program had received more than 430 hours of volunteer service.

Reducing the number of latchkey children: Sixty-five percent of SOS parents report that their children were home alone, or had no place to go, before starting SOS.

Improving academic performance: Students improved their grades in math, science, and language after enrolling in SOS. Math grade point averages increased 14.4 percent once students enrolled in SOS; language scores were up 6.5 percent; science scores were up 6.1 percent. Among parents who said their students had "low" or "poor" grades prior to starting SOS, 78 percent noted improvement.

Meeting other needs of students, improving attitudes and behavior: Students report a "high degree" of satisfaction with programs. Eighty-seven percent of parents who said their children were having disciplinary trouble at home or in school prior to SOS reported improvement.

Improving collaboration with existing community resources: [The r]eport says programs' performance has been "excellent. All directors have worked diligently to obtain as much assistance as possible from other community resources." Programs report having established collaborative relationship[s] with an average of more than three different agencies.

The report also assesses individual county programs based on the counties' self-reported success in recruiting and retaining volunteers, developing collaborations, training and retraining staff members, and the number of days and hours their program operates. In addition, the study recommends that SOS make changes in three key areas:

—Clarifying the definition of who is "at-risk." Currently, individual counties make their own judgments of which students the program should serve.

—Improving local documentation of student enrollment figures, continuing to expand volunteer recruitment and retention, and clarifying instructions to make reporting of in-kind contributions more uniform.

—Continuing the evaluation of the program to develop more long-term data assessing the program's effectiveness.

SOS director Joe Canty said he is addressing those recommendations, including working to standardize and clarify reporting procedures and providing on-site consultation for counties identified as having special needs in particular areas.

---

[1] Beverly W. Jones et al., *Support Our Students Evaluation Project: Final Report* ([Durham]: North Carolina Central University, Institute for the Study of Minority Issues, 1996).

[2] Beverly Washington Jones; resident of Durham; B.A., 1970, M.A., 1972, North Carolina Central University; Ph.D., University of North Carolina at Chapel Hill, 1980. Career with N.C. Central University included: professor of history, 1972-1985; director, Institute on Desegregation, from 1987; assistant dean, 1987, dean, from 2000, University College. Chair, Academic Help Center, Durham, 1990-1996, Durham City Schools Board of Education, 1991-1992, and of Durham Committee on Racial Understanding; vice-chair, N.C. Commission on National and Community Service, 1995-1997; author. Beverly Washington Jones, letter to Jan-Michael Poff, March 16, 2000.

[3] The number of counties served by SOS grew to sixty-four, after state lawmakers approved annual grants of $65,000 to launch new programs in Brunswick, Burke, Cabarrus, Chatham, Granville, Macon, Madison, Northampton, Orange, Pender, Rockingham, and Washington Counties. Programs in Bladen, Forsyth, Lenoir, Lincoln, Mecklenburg, Union, and Wake Counties were awarded expansion funds. Press release, Governor Hunt Announces Help for At-Risk Students, Charlotte, October 31, 1996, Governors Papers, James Baxter Hunt Jr.

BUDGET STATEMENT

Raleigh, May 6, 1996

[For a fuller look at the spending proposals Governor Hunt unveiled on May 6, 1996, see *North Carolina State Budget: Recommended Changes to the 1996-97 State Budget, 1995-97 Biennium, James B. Hunt Jr., Governor* ([Raleigh]: Office of State Budget and Management, May 1996). *Overview: Fiscal and Budgetary Actions, North Carolina General Assembly, 1995 Session and 1996 Session* (Raleigh: Fiscal Research Division, North Carolina General Assembly, [1996]), recaps the state budget as adopted.

Budget-related press releases include: Governor Jim Hunt Recommends $100 Million for Universities, Raleigh, May 6, 1996; Governor Hunt Proposes Education Budget, Raleigh, May 6, 1996; Governor Jim Hunt Proposes 6 Percent Pay Raise for State Employees, May 6, 1996; Governor Hunt's Budget Proposal to Benefit Older Adults, Raleigh, May 7, 1996; Governor Hunt's Budget Recommends Smart Start Expansion, Raleigh, May 7, 1996; Backgrounder: Summary of Key Items of Governor Hunt's Budget Not Funded in the Budget Passed by the House, Raleigh, May 28, 1996; Governor Hunt's Bill to Cut the Tax Burden on Elderly Introduced into House, Raleigh, May 30, 1996, Governors Papers, James Baxter Hunt Jr.]

Today I am presenting a budget to the General Assembly that puts education first. First and foremost, that means giving North Carolina teachers a 7 percent pay raise—a down payment toward raising teacher pay to the national average by the year 2000.[1] We know that good schools start with good teachers. We know that we have to do more to recruit and retain good teachers. Almost half our teachers are leaving the profession within three years, mostly because of low salaries. The average salary for a North Carolina teacher is 16 percent below the national average. We wouldn't stand for 16 percent below average in recruiting good jobs, so why settle for less in recruiting good teachers?

As we raise salaries for teachers, we must raise standards as well. We should raise the bar for entry-level teachers, for teachers seeking a continuing license and seeking tenure. My budget supports the State Board of Education ABC plan, holding schools accountable with rewards for success and sanctions for failure.[2]

Second, we should start earlier, so that children come to school ready to learn. We must expand Smart Start to the eleven counties in which planning has been under way since last year. Smart Start is working well, as the "Big Six" audit mandated by the General Assembly says. Financial accountability is being increased. In thirty-two counties, Smart Start has created more child-care slots, pared down waiting lists for subsidized child care, improved the quality of child care, and helped train day-care teachers. With one of the highest numbers of working mothers in the country, North Carolina has an obligation to support our families by supporting Smart Start.[3]

Third, we should give teachers the tools to do their job, like smaller classes and safer classrooms. We should cut class size in the second grade, as the legislature has already done for kindergarten and first grade; put a sworn law enforcement officer in every high school; make sure every county has an alternative school for discipline problems. I'll be proposing $10 million for alternative schools and will ask every school system for a "safe school plan" that details how disruptive students will be taken out of the classroom.[4]

My budget also proposes a 7 percent pay raise for university and community college teaching faculty, additional resources for university graduate students, increased workforce training and equipment for community colleges, and more technology in public schools.[5] And I'm proposing a 6 percent salary increase for state employees, which will fully fund, for the first time, the Comprehensive Pay Plan. My budget would earmark $10 million for the Salary Adjustment Fund to help the state recruit and retain top-notch state employees.[6]

For the last three years, we have worked hard to make state government more efficient. Every year, my budget has proposed cuts in state agencies. Last year I proposed $200 million in cuts. This year we can save another $117 million by eliminating layers of bureaucracy in state government, streamlining services, maximizing resources, and eliminating 987 state jobs. Of those jobs, 539 are now filled and 448 are vacant, or will come from retirement and attrition. About one-third of the jobs to be cut will be in the Department of Human Resources, which began reorganizing last year. Overall, we're saving $27 million by cutting jobs—without cutting essential services.

We've worked hard to minimize the impact to state employees. We will work to help state employees whose jobs are cut find other jobs—in the private and public sector. The Office of State Personnel, the Employment Security Commission, and our Division of Employment and Training formed a special partnership last year to offer more transitional services than ever before. As a result, the vast majority of displaced employees who wanted re-employment found it, in or out of state government. This year, we'll continue that partnership.

To protect the environment, my budget proposes efforts to clean up the Neuse River, improve animal waste management, restore wetlands, boost water quality monitoring, and support the senate's innovative Clean Water Management Trust Fund.[7]

To help taxpayers keep more of their money, I've proposed a 1 percent cut in the food tax and an increase in the homestead exemption for senior citizens, which the legislature did not enact last year.[8]

To build the economy, I've proposed that we cut the corporate income tax by 1 percent over four years. We should implement the new tax credits proposed by the Economic Development Board to boost investment, new jobs, research and development, and worker training. I will also ask the General Assembly to provide $2 million for the competitive recruitment fund, which has brought commitments of 11,000 new jobs and $1 billion in new investment to our state, and we'll be launching a new effort to build up economically distressed areas.[9]

To continue our crime-fighting effort, the legislature should increase sentences for violent felonies, such as second-degree murder and rape. We should put more prisoners to work by expanding prison work crews.

We should make sure sex offenders cannot get unsupervised probation,[10] and we should require that all inmates test drug-free before release.

We've made a good start in all these areas in the last three years, but we have more work to do this year, in this session. I'm optimistic that this challenge is one we can meet, if North Carolina's leaders work together. I'm optimistic that this session can be a productive one, a session that focuses on the needs of North Carolinians and especially on our public schools.

---

[1] State lawmakers approved raises of 5.5 percent, on average, for public schoolteachers. *N.C. Session Laws, 1995, Regular and Extra Sessions, 1996*, c. 18, s. 28.14.

[2] "An Act to Implement the Recommendation of the Joint Legislative Education Oversight Committee to Implement the State Board of Education's ABC's Plan in Order to Establish an Accountability Model for the Public Schools to Improve Student Performance and Increase Local Flexibility and Control, and to Make Conforming Changes," was ratified June 21, 1996. *N.C. Session Laws, 1995, Regular and Extra Sessions, 1996*, c. 716; c. 18, s. 18.19, set aside initial funding for the ABC's of Public Education Program.

[3] Hunt wanted $21.2 million for Smart Start, but he received less than half of that amount: $10.1 million. *News and Observer*, August 3, 1996; *North Carolina State Budget: Recommended Changes to the 1996-97 State Budget*, 54.

[4] Funds for cutting class size in second grade from 26 to 23 students per teacher were authorized under *N.C. Session Laws, 1995, Regular and Extra Sessions, 1996*, c. 18, s. 18.3. Section 18.28(b) provided for a "uniformed school resource officer" for every high school in the state. Section 18.28(a) directed the State Board of Education to "adopt guidelines for assigning students to alternative learning programs," aid local school districts "in developing and implementing plans for alternative learning programs," and "evaluate the effectiveness" of those programs.

Hunt vowed, on May 9, to "ask the State Board of Education and the Center for the Prevention of School Violence to work" with each school in the state to enact a safe school plan, "detailing exactly how unruly students will be dealt with." Citizens Forum on Education, Raleigh, May 9, 1996, Governors Papers, James Baxter Hunt Jr.

[5] Community college and University of North Carolina system faculty received 4.5 percent pay raises. *N.C. Session Laws, 1995, Regular and Extra Sessions, 1996*, c. 18, secs. 28.10-11. To aid graduate students attending schools within the UNC system, Hunt recommended spending $8.4 million for health insurance for those with assistantships and providing more than $1.6 million in tuition remission for nonresidents. For the community colleges, he requested $6 million for equipment and books and almost $11 million for new industry training, focused industrial training, and occupational extension courses. He also asked for $10 million for the public school technology fund. *North Carolina State Budget: Recommended Changes to the 1996-97 State Budget*, 23, 26-27, 32-33.

[6] Most state employees received salary increases of 4.5 percent. *N.C. Session Laws, 1995, Regular and Extra Sessions, 1996*, c. 18, s. 28.12.

[7] The Wetlands Restoration Program was established under c. 18, s. 27.4, *N.C. Session Laws, 1995, Regular and Extra Sessions, 1996*; s. 27.6 created the Clean Water Management Trust Fund. *North Carolina State Budget: Recommended Changes to the 1996-97 State Budget*, 75-83, describes Hunt's funding proposals for environmental protection projects.

[8] The state sales tax on food was reduced from 4 percent to 3 percent under "An Act to Reduce Taxes for Citizens of North Carolina and to Provide Incentives for High Quality Jobs and Business Expansion in North Carolina." *N.C. Session Laws, 1995, Regular and Extra Sessions, 1996*, c. 13, s. 1.1, ratified August 2, 1996. The homestead exemption was increased from $15,000 to $20,000 for totally and permanently disabled North Carolinians, aged 65

or older, and earning no more than $15,000 per year. *N.C. Session Laws, 1995, Regular and Extra Sessions, 1996,* c. 18, s. 15.1.

[9] Many of the components of the governor's proposed economic development package were included in the "William S. Lee Quality Jobs and Business Expansion Act" (short title), *N.C. Session Laws, 1995, Regular and Extra Sessions, 1996,* c. 13; for example, section 2.1 cut corporate income taxes from 7.5 percent to 6.9 percent over four years. For more details of his jobs and investment plan, see "Press Release: Governor Jim Hunt Pushing Tax Credits To Boost Jobs, Investment," Raleigh, May 24, 1996 (reprinted below) and pages 4-5, *North Carolina State Budget: Recommended Changes to the 1996-97 State Budget.* The "competitive recruitment fund" for which Hunt requested $2 million was the Industrial Recruitment Competitive Fund, according to *North Carolina State Budget: Recommended Changes to the 1996-97 State Budget,* 67.

[10] *N.C. Session Laws, 1995, Regular and Extra Sessions, 1996,* c. 18, s. 20.14.

NOTES, CITIZENS' FORUM ON CRIME

Greensboro, May 7, 1996

[Hunt delivered similar speeches to the North Carolina Police Executives Association, Atlantic Beach, July 15, and the North State Law Enforcement Officers Association, July 17, 1996. For related press release, see Governor Hunt Calls for Tougher Punishment and More Work for Prisoners, Raleigh, October 29, 1996, Governors Papers, James Baxter Hunt Jr.]

The FBI crime report says that crime in some major cities across the country has dropped slightly, but it actually went up in some cities here in North Carolina, including Greensboro and Winston-Salem. We can't eliminate crime, but government has an obligation to do everything it can to keep people safe.

Before I called the special session on crime a few years ago, I spent a lot of time listening to Chief Daughtry[1] and other law-enforcement officers, to prosecutors and victims' advocates, to community leaders and people like you across the state. Here's what I heard: Do more to keep dangerous criminals behind bars where they belong, and do more to deter youngsters from crime.

They also told us to make prisoners earn their keep. To build no-frills prisons, and work farms, and boot camps. To make the criminal justice system work better for victims. And give law-enforcement officers the tools they need to do their job.

We've listened hard, and we've made some progress in those areas. But we have more work to do to keep our neighborhoods safe.

Next week, I'll be presenting a crime-fighting package to the General Assembly for action in this short session. I want to tell you all about it and ask for your help in getting this package passed in the legislature.

First I'll ask the legislature to toughen sentences for violent felonies, like second-degree murder or rape. We've made a good start in the last three years. Now second-degree murderers are serving 110 percent more time in prison than in 1992.

But we need to do more. Last year, I asked the legislature to increase sentences for violent felonies by 30 percent, although sentences were increased only 16 percent. This year I will urge the legislature to toughen sentences by another 14 percent.

Keeping dangerous criminals behind bars means keeping sex offenders off the street, as well. Last year we enacted a law mandating sex offenders to register with local law enforcement. I proposed this because I believe citizens have a right to know who's living in their midst. I've already put a stop to unsupervised probation for sex offenders, but the General Assembly should pass a law to make that change a permanent one.

Second, I'll ask the legislature to put more prisoners to work. More prisoners are working today than ever before. Some 18,000 are cleaning up roads, cutting brush, building prisons, and growing their own food.[2] Our new community work program will be putting more prisoners from the Guilford Correctional Center out on community work crews soon, cleaning up along our highways. But we need to make sure every prisoner is working, so I've asked the General Assembly for funding to supervise more work crews. This will let us put another 700 inmates to work.

Third, we need to increase prison capacity. We've built or authorized 13,000 prison beds in the last three years, but we need more prison space. The reason paroles dropped 40 percent last year was because we had adequate prison beds. We can't fall behind. That's why we're looking for new ways to keep prisoners behind bars, like leasing another 1,000 out-of-state beds this year[3] and launching a "hot bunking" project in Lincoln County that puts prisoners to work in twenty-four-hour shifts.

Fourth, we need to do more to make the system work better—helping law enforcement, doing better by victims, and combating recidivism. I'm a strong supporter of the Victims' Rights Amendment and will be working alongside Catherine Smith and other victims' advocates to ensure its passage this fall.[4]

I've asked [the] General Assembly for more support for the Criminal Justice Information Network to help law-enforcement officers gather data to track down criminals, and I am proposing that we require all prisoners to test drug-free before release, to make sure we're not putting drug users back on the street.

Finally, we need to do more to prevent, and crack down on, youth crime. Juvenile crime continues to rise, and it's something we all should take very seriously. I'm asking the General Assembly to expand our SOS [Support Our Students] after-school crime-prevention program. That's a volunteer-driven effort that's gotten almost 3,000 volunteer mentors together with 6,000 young people in the afternoons, to keep them out of trouble. Here in Guilford, volunteers are helping kids with homework and encouraging them to achieve.

I hope the legislature will also agree to put a sworn law-enforcement officer in every high school, and to put in resources so every county has an alternative school for disciplinary problems.

And we need to deal appropriately with young criminals and those who lure them into crime. I'm asking the General Assembly to require fingerprinting of juveniles charged with violent crimes and to toughen penalties for adults selling drugs or handguns to juveniles.[5]

We've made a good start in fighting crime and making our streets safer, but we have a great deal of work left to do—and we must do it together. Now I want to hear from you. There's still so much we need to do.

---

[1] Sylvester Daughtry Jr. (1945-   ), B.S., North Carolina A&T State University, 1973; was graduated from four law-enforcement programs, including FBI National Academy. Greensboro policeman from 1968, promoted through ranks to assistant chief-Field Operations Bureau commander, 1983, and was appointed chief of police, 1987; vice-president, International Assn. of Chiefs of Police; past president, North State Law Enforcement Officers Assn. Sylvester Daughtry Jr., letter to Jan-Michael Poff, June 30, 1993.

[2] Subsequent texts put the number of working inmates at 17,000. For example, see North Carolina Police Executives Association, Atlantic Beach, July 15, 1996, Guilford Prison Farm, Gibsonville, October 29, 1996, Governors Papers, James Baxter Hunt Jr.

[3] N.C. Session Laws, 1995, Regular and Extra Sessions, 1996, c. 18, s. 20.16, authorized the Department of Correction to spend as much as $10 million during F.Y. 1996-1997 to house 500 more prisoners out of state. The increase brought to 2,367 the number of convicts North Carolina warehoused beyond its borders.

[4] Catherine Gallagher Smith (1955-   ), born in Pittsburgh; bachelor's degree in journalism, Duquesne University. Publicity, advertising assistant, WPXI-TV, Pittsburgh, 1980-1982; member services coordinator, N.C. Academy of Family Physicians, Raleigh, 1982-1985; program development and public relations director, N.C. Council of Community Mental Health, Developmental Disabilities, and Substance Abuse Programs, Raleigh, 1986-1990; executive director, from 1990, and first full-time director, N.C. Victim Assistance Network. News and Observer, March 27, 1994.

[5] For fingerprinting of juveniles, see N.C. Session Laws, 1995, Regular and Extra Sessions, 1996, c. 18, s. 23.2(a-b); s. 20.13 increased the punishment for the sale of guns and drugs to minors.

CITIZENS' FORUM ON
ECONOMIC AND FINANCIAL SECURITY

CHARLOTTE, MAY 8, 1996

This morning I was in Rowan County where Freightliner president Jim Hebe and I announced that American LaFrance, the nation's oldest fire truck company, would locate a manufacturing plant and create 150 new jobs. Freightliner, the parent company, has invested tens of millions of dollars, and created 2,500 new jobs, in our state in the past three years. Just last week, we announced the location of a new corporate headquarters, Coltec Industries, in Charlotte. That's the kind of economic development we need. We need more jobs that pay good wages, and we need more investment in our communities.

We've done well. We've created over 300,000 new jobs in the last three years. We're still rated in the top three states for new investment. We've pushed through the largest tax cut in North Carolina history. But we must do more.

The budget I presented to the General Assembly this week puts education first, because education in the key to a quality workforce. To improve our schools, we need to pay our teachers better, so I've proposed bringing North Carolina teacher pay to the national average. The average salary for a North Carolina teacher is now 16 percent below the national average. We wouldn't stand for 16 percent below average in recruiting good jobs, so why settle for less in recruiting good teachers? I'm also committed to education by making our schools safer and by expanding Smart Start to eleven more counties.

I want to outline for you the jobs and financial security package I'm presenting to the General Assembly. It's designed to keep North Carolina competitive and create more high-quality, high-wage jobs. It's designed to help North Carolina workers get the training and skills they need to get better jobs and wages. It's designed to help our existing industries and small businesses.

First, we want to help taxpayers keep more of their money. The 1 percent cut in the food tax and the increase in the homestead exemption for senior citizens will help us do that.

Second, we need to help North Carolina workers get the training and retraining they need. I want us to enact a worker training tax credit to help companies, especially our existing companies, that create new jobs or invest in new technologies. And we need to boost the resources for our community college job-training programs.

Third, we need to do more to create good jobs, with new and existing companies. Cutting the corporate income tax by 1 percent, during the next four years, will help North Carolina compete with other states and help our industries create new jobs. Our Economic Development Board, chaired by one of Charlotte's finest leaders, Bill Lee, has recommended a package of innovative tax credits to stimulate more jobs and investment: We should enact each and every one. I'm proposing a tax credit for investment in new machinery and equipment, an important tool to help existing companies compete and attract new industry. I'm proposing a research and development tax credit that will encourage both existing and new companies to invest in new and improved products.

Fourth, we need to do more to help our entrepreneurs and small businesses. I'm asking the legislature to expand our incubator program, through the Technological Development Authority, by adding a facility for technology-based businesses. My tax-credit package will also help small- and medium-sized companies add jobs and investment, and our small businesses and existing industries would get an additional boost through expansion of the Technology Extension Service. We unveiled our first manufacturing extension partnership right here in Charlotte, and I want to do more to help existing companies bring new technology to the factory floor.

I'm also targeting some special assistance to our most distressed rural areas, and I would like to see, in the future, that kind of special development assistance extended to poor urban neighborhoods, as well.

I will need your help to pass this aggressive budget to help our economy and all our businesses—both big and small and existing and new companies [sic]. I will need your help this session to make sure all our citizens feel financially secure.

CITIZENS' FORUM

NEW BERN, MAY 10, 1996

[The following address covered the same points as Hunt's Environmental Lobby Day speech, Raleigh, May 21, 1996.]

Last summer's fish kills and hog-waste spills were a wake-up call. It was a wake-up call for the Neuse and New Rivers and for North Carolina's leaders. We need to do more, in government and industry, to protect our waters.

We made some progress last year, with new efforts to crack down on polluters, but we have a long way to go. That's why I'm asking the General Assembly to provide $57 million for environmental programs this year. I want to tell you about our proposals and ask you to help us pass them.

First, we need to clean up the Neuse River. I'm asking the General Assembly for $7 million to reduce nutrient pollution, and I'm asking [for] another $1 million to conduct better research to help us understand and fix the Neuse's problems, and I hope the General Assembly will support that.[1]

Second, we need to clean up this state's animal-waste problems. That means helping farmers comply with tough new rules on animal waste; that means creating and funding an effective animal-waste permitting system; and that means doing more to inform the public about increased setbacks and train operators of huge hog operations. The Blue Ribbon Commission on [Agricultural] Waste has made some good proposals to deal with animal-waste problems, and I'm glad to see that, but we need to do more. I commend Congressman Valentine in particular for his leadership in moving the committee forward.[2]

I support increased setbacks for large hog operations that will separate them from their neighbors. I support more public notice for applicants for large animal-waste operations. I support more training for system operators.

Third, North Carolina needs to do better in protecting and restoring our wetlands. It's part of improving our water quality. I've asked the legislature to create and fund an aggressive wetlands restoration program to reverse our historical heavy loss of wetlands and eliminate bureaucratic red tape in the program.

We need to do more to stop efforts to weaken wetlands protection. My administration worked hard to create a wetlands protection program that worked. Those rules have been in place two months, but opponents are trying to gut them—and trying to destroy valuable wetlands. I will fight that proposal.

Fourth, I strongly support the senate's plan to create a trust fund to ensure a dedicated source of revenue to restore and protect our waters. I applaud Senators Basnight and Perdue for leading the efforts to develop this important and innovative effort.

Finally, we need to do more to monitor water quality. We need a stronger network for monitoring our rivers and streams. We need to collect data in a more effective way. We need to get citizens more involved with a new citizens' monitoring effort. Folks are already calling us to find out how to get involved in this. I salute Senator Perdue for her leadership on this: It was her idea.

We need to do everything we can to keep our rivers clean. It's our obligation. I was here, in August, talking with Rick Dove about that.[3] Now we've got a plan of action, and I need your help to turn that plan into reality.

---

[1] In February 1996, the governor proposed a restoration plan for the Neuse River that was intended to cut nutrient pollution by 30 percent. His administration also recommended "requiring a 50-foot vegetated buffer around all streams, a 25-foot setback from ditches for land application of animal waste," and creating a "coalition" of "municipal and

industrial waste dischargers . . . to enforce caps on nutrient discharges and require a 30 percent nutrient reduction for facilities not in the coalition." Press release, Governor Hunt Receives Praise from Environmental Groups, Raleigh, March 6, 1996, Governors Papers, James Baxter Hunt Jr.; see also *News and Observer*, February 8, 9, 10, 13, March 3, 1996.

Items in Hunt's proposed 1996-1997 budget for the cleanup of the Neuse River included $7 million, to be allocated between the Lower Neuse River Basin Association ($2 million) and the agriculture cost share program ($5 million), to advance the effort to reduce nutrient pollution; and $1 million for monitoring and research. Legislators approved $720,000 for the research and monitoring project, $2 million to the Lower Neuse association, and $1,750,000 to the cost share program. *N.C. Session Laws, 1995, Regular and Extra Sessions, 1996*, c. 18, secs. 27.1, 27.8; *North Carolina State Budget: Recommended Changes to the 1996-97 State Budget*, 75; *Overview: Fiscal and Budgetary Actions, North Carolina General Assembly, 1995 Session and 1996 Session*, J-42.

[2] Itimous T. (Tim) Valentine Jr. (1926-   ), born in Nashville; A.B., The Citadel, 1948; J.D., University of North Carolina, 1967; U.S. Army Air Force, 1944-1946. Attorney; member, state House of Representatives, 1955-1960; legal adviser, 1965, legislative counsel, 1967, to Gov. Dan K. Moore; chairman, state Democratic Executive Committee, 1966-1968; was elected to Congress from North Carolina's Second District, 1982, returned in subsequent elections, and retired in 1994; co-chairman, Blue Ribbon Study Commission on Agricultural Waste. *News and Observer*, April 3, 1994, August 30, December 2, 1995, January 11, 12, 19, 25, February 3, 9, March 7, April 11, 25, May 2, 29, 1996; *North Carolina Manual, 1993-1994*, 944.

[3] Rick Dove was a retired Marine colonel, attorney, and former commercial fisherman. As the Neuse River's keeper, a position funded by the Neuse River Foundation, Dove patrolled the waterway and reported on its condition. *News and Observer*, October 11, 1995.

NORTH CAROLINA
CITIZENS FOR BUSINESS AND INDUSTRY
LEGISLATIVE CONFERENCE

RALEIGH, MAY 14, 1996

[For related press release, see Governor Hunt Urges Business Leaders to Invest in Children, Raleigh, May 14, 1996, Governors Papers, James Baxter Hunt Jr.]

I'm honored to be here for NCCBI's eleventh legislative conference and to have a chance to visit with the best and the brightest of North Carolina's business community. You all have set out a vision for our state that's built on foresight. You all have taken the long view about what it takes to build our state. Anyone who's run a business—whether it's a cattle farm, a bank, a power company, or the business of state government—knows that building a future requires that kind of vision. That kind of vision is critical, this year.

Great things are happening in North Carolina. We've got one of the strongest economies in the nation, record job growth, and one of the nation's lowest unemployment rates. We have an opportunity, in this legislative session, to build on that prosperity, to build on North Carolina's progress and build up our state.

One place we've made real progress is tax reduction. With bipartisan support—Democrats and Republicans, House and senate, legislature and governor working together—we passed the largest tax cut in state history, last year. With bipartisan support, we cut the unemployment tax four years running: We saved employers more than half a million dollars, savings that can create new jobs, and better worker training, and better facilities. With bipartisan support, we have an opportunity to make more tax cuts, this year: to cut the food tax by 1 percent; to boost the homestead exemption for senior citizens; to cut the corporate income tax back 1 percent over the next four years. And we have a chance to enact new tax credits to boost investment, new jobs, research and development, and worker training; to continue our modest financial incentives to create new jobs; and to launch new efforts to build up economically distressed areas.

But the real chance we have, in this session, to build up our future, is building up our children: by doing more for our children in public schools; by doing more for our children who'll be coming to school in the next five years. This is where NCCBI has real vision and courage. You've said tax cuts alone won't build the kind of future our children need. You've said the most important investments we make are in the next generation.

You all know it matters [what] kind of teachers our children have: dedicated professionals who are paid good salaries for good work—not burned-out teachers, those left after the cream of the crop flees the profession.[1]

You all know it matters what kind of classrooms our children have: safe and orderly places where teachers can teach and children can learn—not dominated by disruptive and violent students.

You all know it matters what kind of day care we provide for our young children and young families: quality early childhood education to help kids come to school ready to learn—not inadequate, inferior day care, or worse, none at all.

That's what this session is all about, my friends. That's what NCCBI has been all about. That's why you've been such a strong supporter of education reform, and higher standards, and Smart Start. That's why I hope you'll show the same vision and courage, this year. I hope you will take the long view, looking at what's good for our economy, and our state, and our future; and that's why I hope you'll support my program. Let me tell you what's in it:

—Raising teacher pay to the national average by 2000, and raising teacher standards, too. Some say it can't be done. I say we can't afford not to do it. The average salary for a North Carolina teacher is 16 percent below the national average. You all wouldn't settle for 16 percent below average in recruiting good jobs, so why settle for less when it comes to recruiting good teachers?

—Expanding Smart Start to eleven more counties. The Big Six audit mandated by the General Assembly says that Smart Start is working well, and you've seen it: In thirty-two counties, Smart Start is creating more child-care slots; paring down waiting lists; improving the quality of care; training day-care teachers.

—Reducing class size in the second grade. The General Assembly and I have worked together to cut classes in kindergarten and first grade, and we need to continue that.

—Making schools safer by putting a uniformed law enforcement officer in every high school and making sure that every county has access to an alternative school program.

—Supporting the State Board of Education's ABC plan, holding schools accountable for performance with financial incentives for success and tough sanctions for failure.

We've made a good start in the right direction, in North Carolina, but we've got much more to do. Together, we can get it done. Together, we can build the kind of state our children deserve.

---

[1] "If we want to keep good teachers in the classroom, we've got to have higher standards and pay higher salaries," Hunt said. "New studies show that one-third of our new teachers are leaving the profession within the first five years, and many of those are the very best who leave. North Carolina has dropped to forty-second in the nation in teacher pay. South Carolina has moved up to thirty-eighth, Virginia is twenty-fifth, and Tennessee is twenty-sixth. We wouldn't settle for forty-second in new jobs or college basketball—why should we settle for being forty-second in teacher pay?" Roundtable with Business Leaders, Greensboro, June 12, 1996, Governors Papers, James Baxter Hunt Jr.

SMART START-BLUE CROSS AND BLUE SHIELD PRESS CONFERENCE

RALEIGH, MAY 15, 1996

We've heard a lot of questions, lately, about Smart Start. Is it working? Is it getting the private support that it should? Is it really helping children?

Well, the results are in. Smart Start is working. It's working well, and it's working for children, and the private sector is fully behind it. Look at what Blue Cross is doing today: Under the leadership of Ken Otis, one of North Carolina's major corporate citizens is bringing free health insurance to hundreds of children in Smart Start counties who don't have it now. Robin Lane and the Caring Program for Children will make sure that children whose parents can't afford health insurance will be able to visit a doctor's office for regular checkups or get treated when they break a bone.[1]

I commend the Caring Program for the wonderful work they do to help children, and I commend Blue Cross for taking the long view of a healthy economy and a healthy citizenry. Blue Cross understands that we can build our economy by building up our children. These folks understand that making sure children come to school healthy and ready to learn is part of what we must do to ensure North Carolina's prosperity. But they're not the only ones. That's why groups like NCCBI [North Carolina Citizens for Business and Industry] have supported Smart Start. That's why top corporations like Wachovia, First Union, NationsBank, Glaxo Wellcome, Food Lion, and BB&T support Smart Start. That's why foundations like the Carnegie Foundation,[2] the Z. Smith Reynolds Foundation, and the Broyhill Foundation—of Broyhill Furniture fame, which gave the Caldwell County Smart Start partnership $100,000 just a few weeks ago—support Smart Start. And that's why I can announce, today, that Smart Start has met the private fund-raising challenge set last year by the legislature. With the help of Ashley Thrift,[3] chairman of the North Carolina Partnership for Children, and executive director David Walker, Smart Start has raised the required $2.9 million in cash and $3 million in in-kind contributions.

The Big Six audit that the General Assembly mandated has shown that Smart Start is working well, and the state auditor's report gave local partnerships a solid report card. Financial accountability is already being stepped up, and Columbia University says Smart Start is one of the eight top initiatives of its kind in the country. What reason would there be not to expand Smart Start to the eleven counties in which planning has been under way since last year?

In thirty-two counties, Smart Start has created more child-care slots, pared down waiting lists for subsidized child care, improved the quality of child care, and helped train day-care teachers. With one of the highest numbers of working mothers in the country, North Carolina has an obligation to support our families by supporting Smart Start. We owe it to our children to expand Smart Start and to provide to the twelve counties named by the partnership, yesterday, the help they need to spend the next year planning.

Blue Cross's generosity, today, is evidence that North Carolina's corporations support Smart Start, because it works. I hope our legislature will do the same.

[1] Kenneth C. Otis II, native of Bethesda, Md.; bachelor's degree, political science, Yale University, 1962; M.B.A., Harvard University, 1968. Various marketing positions, including advertising director, American Airlines, 1968-1974; career with Colonial Penn Group, 1974-1987, included executive vice-president for group life and health insurance; vice-president and chief financial officer, executive vice-president of marketing and health care services, Blue Cross and Blue Shield of Florida, 1987-1993; president, chief executive officer, Blue Cross and Blue Shield of North Carolina, from January 1, 1994. *News and Observer*, November 6, 1993.

The North Carolina Council of Churches, the Presbyterian Synod of North Carolina, and Blue Cross-Blue Shield of North Carolina founded the Caring Program for Children in 1986. The private, nonprofit organization made health insurance available to uninsured children from low-income families that were ineligible for Medicaid. Working in conjunction with Blue Cross-Blue Shield and the North Carolina Partnership for Children, the Caring Program planned to provide 500 Smart Start children, and their siblings, with health insurance coverage in 1996. Press release, Hunt, Blue Cross and Blue Shield Announce Gift to Smart Start, Raleigh, May 15, 1996, Governors Papers, James Baxter Hunt Jr.

[2] The Carnegie Corporation, of New York, awarded a $225,000 grant to the North Carolina Partnership for Children. Press release, Hunt Announces Carnegie Grant for Smart Start, Raleigh, January 24, 1996, Governors Papers, James Baxter Hunt Jr.

[3] Ashley Ormand Thrift (1946-   ), born in Charlotte; A.B., University of North Carolina at Chapel Hill, 1968; J.D., University of South Carolina, 1972; U.S. Army Reserve, 1968-1974. Career with University of South Carolina included acting dean for campus relations, 1971-1972; assistant dean, School of Law, 1972-1974; and associate counsel, 1974-1975. Legislative counsel to Congressman James R. Mann (D-S.C.), 1976-1977; associate counsel, U.S. House Judiciary Committee, 1977; legislative director and counsel, 1977-1984, chief of staff and counsel, 1984-1992, to U.S. senator Ernest F. Hollings (D-S.C.); counsel, 1992-1995, member/partner, from 1995, Womble, Carlyle, Sandridge and Rice, PLLC. Ashley Ormand Thrift, letter to Jan-Michael Poff, April 25, 2000.

TALKING POINTS ON ANIMAL WASTE

RALEIGH, MAY 23, 1996

[The Blue Ribbon Study Commission on Agricultural Waste released, in early May 1996, its regulatory proposals for governing the swine industry. Well-financed industry supporters vied with environmentalists and the neighbors of hog farms to influence the legislative debate over how the commission's recommendations would translate into state law. Governor Hunt believed that some of the proposals needed to be tougher (see below). The perennially powerful pork lobby ultimately was unable to counteract the negative publicity resulting from waste spills and contaminated water. The rules, as adopted, signaled a major victory for the environment. "An Act to Implement the Recommendations of the Blue Ribbon Study Commission on Agricultural Waste," *N.C. Session Laws, 1995, Regular and Extra Sessions, 1996,* c. 626, was ratified June 21, 1996; Blue Ribbon Study Commission on Agricultural Waste, Report to the 1995 General Assembly of North Carolina, 1996 Regular Session ([Raleigh: The Commission, 1996]); *News and Observer*, May 9, 26, 29, June 1, 4-9, 11, 13, 19, 21, 1996.

Hunt included much of the following text in his letter to members of the House Agriculture Committee as they prepared to vote on legislation to regulate the swine industry. Media Advisory, June 4, 1996, Governors Papers, James Baxter Hunt Jr.]

The Blue Ribbon Commission [on Agricultural Waste] made some good recommendations, but we need to do more to ensure that the public health and environment are protected. That's my number-one concern. We need to do the right thing for the state and the right thing for eastern North Carolina communities. These are reasonable, commonsense proposals designed to make sure that communities and hog farms can live in harmony and support each other.[1]

Like all major industries, large hog farms have an impact on the surrounding community. If we as a state don't recognize those impacts and deal with them, we will see less and less community support for a viable industry. I'm not talking about a lot of new recommendations. I'm only talking about differences in a couple of key areas: increasing the distance between large farms and their neighbors, increasing public notice, and increasing the amount of time operators spend learning how to run these waste systems.

The issues of public notice and setbacks are community issues. They're good-neighbor issues. Ask yourself: Wouldn't you want to know if one of these huge operations was coming to your neighborhood? Would you want one of these operations locating within 100 feet of your property line? Currently, these large farms can locate within 100 feet of their neighbor's property line. I want to increase setbacks for the largest facilities, increasing the setback for farms with 500,000 to a million pounds of hogs to 500 feet from the property line, and 1,500 feet for those with over a million pounds. I also want to increase public notice and require operators to publish a notice in a local newspaper when they intend to site one of these large facilities in a community.[2]

I want system operators to receive sixteen hours of training. I don't think it is too much to ask that the operators of these systems, which can involve millions of gallons of potentially harmful waste, spend two days learning how to do it right. I'm sure the folks who live along the New River would certainly agree.[3]

I want to increase the Division of Soil and Water Conservation's role in monitoring these operations. Today I am asking that DEM [Division of Environmental Management] and the Division of Soil and Water Conservation work cooperatively on these waste issues. DEM has only a handful of staff to devote to animal waste. Soil and water conservation districts have hundreds of folks. Although DEM will maintain primacy for the time being, we want to increase Soil and Water Conservation's role. At the end of December, DEHNR [Department of Environment, Health, and Natural Resources] would reevaluate this issue and make a recommendation on the future which could include giving the Division of Soil and Water greater permanent responsibilities.

These are reasonable amendments. They don't go too far, but they do close the few gaps left by the blue ribbon study commission. They won't end pork production in North Carolina. In fact, they'll help pork producers by ensuring that they are good neighbors and have a reputation as such.

------

[1] Hunt flanked the body of his letter to the House Agriculture Committee with statements that repeated his belief, indicated early in these talking points, of the need to establish a common ground between environmental protection and economic development. "We are at a crossroads in eastern North Carolina," the letter began. "Communities east of I-95 are worried about their fate if large swine operations are sited nearby. At the same time, the swine industry needs to continue to grow and support the local economy. We need an effective framework of regulations that will ensure communities that large swine operations do not threaten the public health, the environment, or neighboring landowners' use and enjoyment of their land. Effective management of animal waste is a critical issue for North Carolina." In closing, the governor said, "I want a clean environment and excellent public health. I also want pork, beef, dairy, and chicken production to remain a growing, vital part of our economy. My proposals will ensure that is the case. I hope you will look at them carefully and think about them in terms of what you want for your communities, for your families, for your friends. Do the right thing for everyone: Adopt these proposals, and let's make sure that our farm economy in North Carolina continues to prosper." Media Advisory, June 4, 1996.

[2] "Communities need to know what's going on in their backyards," Governor Hunt wrote to House members. "By requiring public notice in a newspaper, we may get information from all of the neighbors that will help our regulators in making sound permit decisions." Media Advisory, June 4, 1996.

Legislators exceeded the governor's recommendation on hog-farm setbacks but did not go far enough on the issue of public notification. As adopted, the law established setbacks for all swine houses and waste lagoons at a minimum of "1,500 feet from any occupied residence; at least 2,500 feet from any school, hospital, or church; and at least 500 feet from any property boundary." But Hunt's call for a regulation requiring farmers to publish locally an announcement of their intention to construct a new hog factory fell upon deaf ears. The General Assembly instead required a farmer to notify nearby property owners by certified mail. *N.C. Session Laws, 1995, Regular and Extra Sessions, 1996*, c. 626, s. 7.

[3] Chapter 626, *N.C. Session Laws, 1995, Regular and Extra Sessions, 1996*, required animal waste system operators to take sixteen hours of classroom instruction—but not during two consecutive days. Section 5 states, "An applicant for initial certification shall complete ten hours of classroom instruction prior to taking the examination. In order to remain certified, an animal waste management system operator in charge shall complete six hours of approved additional training during each three-year period following initial certification." Initially the Blue Ribbon Commission on Agricultural Waste recommended that twelve hours of instruction were sufficient for operator certification; some lawmakers wanted to cut the requirement to eight hours. Blue Ribbon Study Commission on Agricultural Waste, Report to the 1995 General Assembly of North Carolina, 1996 Regular Session ([Raleigh: The Commission, 1996]), 22; *News and Observer*, May 24, June 4, 1996.

Twenty-five million gallons of hog waste spilled into the New River from Oceanview Farms' lagoon on June 21, 1995. See "Cabinet Meeting: Hog Agenda," New Bern, August 21, 1995, reprinted elsewhere in this volume.

PRESS RELEASE: GOVERNOR JIM HUNT PUSHING
TAX CREDITS TO BOOST JOBS, INVESTMENT

RALEIGH, MAY 24, 1996

Governor Jim Hunt has proposed an economic development package, included in his 1996 budget, that provides tax credits to boost worker training, research and development, and incentives to create jobs and investment and boost financial security for North Carolinians, especially in economically distressed counties.

Governor Jim Hunt's economic package, named [the] "Quality Jobs and Business Expansion" bill (H.B. 1343/S.B. 1275) was introduced into the North Carolina House today by Representatives Bill Owens, of Elizabeth City, and Larry Shaw, of Fayetteville, and was referred to the House Finance Committee. The bill was introduced in the North Carolina Senate by Senator John Kerr, of Goldsboro, earlier this week and [was] referred to [the] Senate Finance Committee.[1]

"This economic development package is designed to keep North Carolina competitive and create more high-quality, high-wage jobs," Hunt said. "Our economic record is good, but we have to be aggressive in finding ways to keep good jobs and investment coming to our state and building a business climate that nurtures the companies already here."

Hunt's proposals include:

—Create a 7 percent tax credit to stimulate investment in machinery and equipment by new and expanding industry;

—Create a worker-training tax credit up to $500 per worker for half of the training expenses, so existing and new employers can train workers in new technologies;

—Create a research and development tax credit equal to 5 percent of eligible research and development expenses to stimulate innovation and product-related research and development;

—Create [a] Quality Jobs Standard to ensure that new jobs pay above-average wages and provide health insurance;

—Expand the existing Jobs Creation Tax Credit statewide so that companies creating jobs in the state's most economically distressed counties get a higher credit, while companies locating in the state's most prosperous counties get a lower credit. Currently, the tax credit exists for fifty of the state's most-distressed counties.

—Provide $5 million in loans and grants to improve water and sewer and other infrastructure needs in the ten most economically distressed counties in North Carolina, as well as easier access to existing state programs;

—Create a $20,000 jobs-creation tax credit for each new job created by an eligible new or expanding industry in the ten most-distressed counties. This new plan gives special help to the ten most economically distressed counties: Tyrrell, Swain, Northampton, Graham, Richmond, Hyde, Mitchell, Bertie, Hertford, and Warren.

---

[1] Representative William Clarence Owens Jr. (D-Pasquotank) and Senator John Hosea Kerr III (D-Wayne) were identified earlier in this volume.

Larry Shaw (1949-   ), born in High Point; resident of Cumberland County; B.S., 1972, masters in education, 1974, Alabama State University; honorary degree. Founder, chairman, chief executive officer, Shaw Food Services; member, N.C. House of Representatives, from 1995, and of House Committee on Business and Labor, Subcommittee on Economic Expansion and Growth; Democrat. *North Carolina Manual, 1995-1996,* 657.

RECEPTION, AMERICAN
ASSOCIATION OF RETIRED PERSONS

RALEIGH, JUNE 13, 1996

[Hunt's notes for the Older Americans Month Reception, May 1, 1996, and his text for the Older Workers Symposium, June 14, 1996, contain much of the same information covered in his remarks to the AARP reception. For related press release, see Governor Hunt's Budget Proposal to Benefit Older Adults, Raleigh, May 7, 1996, Governors Papers, James Baxter Hunt Jr.]

A year and a half ago, at the North Carolina White House Conference on Aging, AARP president Gene Lehrmann and I met to discuss the concerns of older workers. Older workers were, as you know, being frozen out of the workforce. Gene asked if I would set a positive example by supporting the hiring of older workers. I did that immediately by creating the Older Workers Task Force under the Division of Aging and the Governor's Commission on Workforce Preparedness. Dr. Sarah Morrow agreed to chair the committee. The task force was asked to look at older workers' employment issues and submit recommendations for addressing those issues. I'll be taking a hard look at the report's recommendations Dr. Morrow is presenting [to] me tomorrow.

I commend the AARP Leadership Council and the national office for your foresight into a real problem. People are living longer—long enough to have two or three jobs after retirement. I won't be governor all my working life, but I will work at something to remain active. I'm not alone: Our state has almost 900,000 AARP volunteers. What a tremendous asset!

That is why I've worked hard to make sure the needs of our state's older citizens are met. We've had some good successes so far, but there's still more to do. Last year's intangibles tax repeal and changes in the tax laws for personal exemptions have helped more than 700,000 older taxpayers reduce their taxes by more than $77 million. We've created a Senior Education Corps of retirees who volunteer in after-school projects, like SOS [Support Our Students] and other tutoring programs, and it's being operated as a pilot program in Northampton County right now. We've also increased state funding so 6,000 more seniors are getting help with transportation services.

I've proposed increasing the homestead tax exemption, which would save seniors another $14 million. It didn't pass last year, but I've recommended the change again this year, and I'm hopeful it will pass. I've also asked the legislature to cut the food tax by one cent, and I've asked for a $5 million increase for home and community-based services, like home-delivered meals and adult day care, so those who need help the most can get the care they need in the comfort of their own homes.[1] I'm recommending putting $7.5 million into the North Carolina Housing Finance Agency, for the Housing Trust Fund, to ensure safe and affordable housing for low- and moderate-income North Carolinians.

We also need to make sure that older adults living in rest homes are safe. That is why I've asked legislators to create a $10 million revolving loan fund to let rest homes and nursing homes borrow money to install and upgrade their safety equipment, like sprinklers and smoke detectors.[2] I want to require that rest homes and nursing homes without sprinklers install high-tech smoke detection systems as well as putting sprinkler systems in newly constructed family care homes and group homes for adults with disabilities.

You need to hit people in the pocketbook to get their attention, so I'm asking lawmakers to double the current fines for serious, life-threatening violations and to replace fines for minor violations with required action plans to correct problems. If they aren't corrected, I want to fine them. I want staffing increased during the night and the current inspection process to be streamlined, reducing red tape and improving efficiency. Finally, I'm asking for a 3.5 percent increase in rates for rest homes that can be used to increase staff ratios and offset inflation.[3]

It's going to be difficult to get many of these recommendations through the General Assembly. I urge you to talk to your legislators and let them know you support these proposals.

---

[1] State lawmakers approved the governor's proposed $5 million increase in home aid and community-based services. *Overview: Fiscal and Budgetary Actions, North Carolina General Assembly, 1995 Session and 1996 Session*, H-20.

² The General Assembly pared Hunt's request, for the sprinkler/smoke detector revolving loan fund, from $10 million to $1 million. The estimated cost to install sprinkler systems in nursing and rest homes without such devices, in North Carolina, exceeded $34 million. *News and Observer*, April 11, 1996; *N.C. Session Laws, 1995, Extra and Regular Sessions, 1996*, c. 18, s. 24.26B; *North Carolina State Budget, Recommended Changes to the 1996-97 State Budget, 1995-97 Biennium*, 56.

³ The 3.5 percent rate increase for rest homes was approved; see *Overview: Fiscal and Budgetary Actions, North Carolina General Assembly, 1995 Session and 1996 Session*, H-22.

AMERICAN LEGION CONVENTION TALKING POINTS

GREENSBORO, JUNE 14, 1996

[This text covers the same points Hunt addressed in his remarks for the Veterans of Foreign Wars Reception, Raleigh, October 6, 1995; Veterans of Foreign Wars Convention, Greensboro, June 28, 1996; and the State Veterans Home groundbreaking, Fayetteville, October 9, 1996.]

I am honored to be here with my friends from the American Legion. Today [is] Flag Day. [I'm] proud to stand with you to honor our flag.

You have done so much to help make North Carolina, to help make your country, a better place for us all. First, you have committed yourselves not only to protecting our freedom, but also to improving our communities and to helping our young people grow up with the best possible chance to succeed.

I am proud of all of your efforts, and I am proud of all 725,000 veterans living in North Carolina. I want you to know that North Carolina is committed to helping our veterans. Our State Division of Veterans Affairs office assisted nearly 600,000 veterans last year, and provided hometown service to veterans in all 100 counties!

These are exciting times for veterans in North Carolina, and I'm proud to tell you about several long-awaited projects now under way across our great state, including construction of the first state veterans' home, in Fayetteville—a peaceful place where our veterans can receive the best long-term care.¹

North Carolina currently operates two state veterans' cemeteries, in Black Mountain and Jacksonville, and we have a third one under construction near Spring Lake scheduled to open next year.

I know my friend, Larry Tetterton, wants me to be sure I mention the Persian Gulf War Memorial. Larry chairs the commission that has worked hard pushing for a monument to our men and women who fought for Kuwait's freedom.² A few weeks ago, we received a $100,000 check from Kuwait that will help fund construction of that memorial. [There's] more to do. [It will be a] monument you will be proud of [and one] our children [will] learn from.

We are also working hard, together, to help children. Through the state scholarship for children of war veterans, some 16,000 young people have received education they otherwise would not be able to afford, including 369 last year.[3] At state-supported schools, these scholarships take care of tuition, room and board, and many school fees—a total of about $5,000 per student, each year.

We must continue our commitment to our children and grandchildren. We must make our schools safer. We must pay our teachers and state employees what they deserve. We must work to give our children the best possible future we can.

And we must take care of our veterans. Together, we can do it.

---

[1] "This home couldn't come at a better time," the governor said in Fayetteville. "Federal funds are being cut. More than 172,000 of our 713,000 veterans are sixty-five and older, and by the year 2005, the number will nearly double." A $6.9 million grant from the federal Department of Veterans Affairs augmented state monies to build the $10.5 million, 150-bed nursing home. Construction of the project was estimated to take eighteen months. Veterans of Foreign Wars Convention, Greensboro, June 28, 1996, and State Veterans Home Groundbreaking, Fayetteville, October 9, 1996, Governors Papers, James Baxter Hunt Jr.

[2] Larry Edward Tetterton (1936-   ), born in Bethel; resident of Louisburg; B.S., 1958, M.Ed., 1966, N.C. State University; diplomas from Command and General Staff College, 1976, U.S. Army War College, 1983; retired as colonel after 33 years of service with U.S. Army. Assistant director, Marketing Division, N.C. Dept. of Agriculture, 1986-1990; was appointed by Hunt to Persian Gulf War Memorial Commission, February 20, 1996. Larry Edward Tetterton, letter to Jan-Michael Poff, March 16, 1999.

The Persian Gulf War Memorial Commission was established initially by Governor James Grubbs Martin in September 1991. Hunt extended the life of the commission under Executive Orders 33, 82, and 91. Executive Order Number 91, December 13, 1995, in *N.C. Session Laws, 1997,* 2:2527-2528; Poff, *Addresses of Martin, 1989-1993,* 538.

[3] The state's annual contribution to the scholarship program exceeded $4 million. Veterans of Foreign Wars Convention, Greensboro, June 28, 1996, Governors Papers, James Baxter Hunt Jr.

NORTH CAROLINA VICTIM ASSISTANCE NETWORK

RALEIGH, JUNE 20, 1996

These stat[istics] are a grim reminder: Domestic violence is a crime we can never forget. Every day, a woman in North Carolina is beaten by her husband or partner. Every day, we get an average of sixty-eight reported cases of domestic violence, and those are just the ones we know about. There are many more we don't know about.

It's the victims advocates, like the folks at the Victim Assistance Network [VAN], or the crisis counselors at Interact, or the Coalition against Domestic Violence who do know about it. You all know that domestic violence is the crime people don't talk about. It's the crime that happens behind closed doors. It happens to women of all ages, of all races, of all economic backgrounds, but it happens—every day.

It happened to Dawn Jolly, and Nancy Williams, and Norma Jean Russell, and so many others who are represented tonight. We, as a society, failed these women. We didn't protect them. We didn't stop their abusers from killing them. But we can vow, every day, to do more to stop it from happening again. It's a vow everyone needs to take. We can all do more. We can support women's shelters. We can provide more resources to victims' services. We can push our courts to get tougher on abusers and encourage law-enforcement officers, magistrates, prosecutors, and judges to take every incident seriously.

We can pass tougher laws, if we put politics aside. Just yesterday, the senate approved new protections for victims of domestic violence. I'm proud of what they've done. Protective orders should be free. Violating a restraining order should be a criminal offense. Judges should consider domestic violence in custody disputes. I hope the House will pass this bill in the final days so we can use these laws to protect women.[1]

The private sector needs to be involved in the fight against domestic violence, too. I'm proud to announce tonight that Polaroid is doing just that, with the help of the Governor's Crime Commission. Together we are providing hundreds of law-enforcement agencies, shelters, and rape-crisis centers across the state with cameras, so victims of domestic violence can document the violence. With these pictures, I hope our prosecutors can do more to put abusers behind bars—where they belong.

I want to commend the Victim Assistance Network for all they've done to bring this issue to the forefront, working with the coalition and other advocates. I'm proud to stand with you against domestic violence, and I'm proud to stand alongside N.C. VAN this fall as we fight for the victims' rights amendment—to help victims of domestic violence and of all crimes. Together, we've got to stop the cycle.

---

[1] "An Act to Make Changes to the General Statutes Pertaining to Domestic Violence," *N.C. Session Laws, 1995, Regular and Extra Sessions, 1996*, c. 591, was ratified June 20 and became effective October 1, 1996.

CHURCH BURNING TASK FORCE

RALEIGH, JUNE 26, 1996

[Arsonists ravaged dozens of African American churches across the South in 1995 and 1996. Six were burned in North Carolina, and minority churches in Durham, Fair Bluff, and Charlotte received bomb threats. Although investigations into each of the fires in North Carolina later revealed that racial hatred was not a factor, the sight of a gutted church "sparked legitimate anxiety and trepidation among many," said a *Charlotte Observer* editorial. "The fires are a harsh reminder of a shameful past when terror and intimidation through firebombings and vandalizing of black churches was commonplace." *News and Observer*, June 16 (reprint of *Charlotte Observer* editorial), 23, July 5, 31, 1996.

Documents focusing on crimes of religious and racial violence against African Americans include Hunt's remarks for the White House Visit to Discuss Church Burnings, Washington, D.C., June 19, 1996, and the Ministers' Meeting/Prayer Service, Raleigh, July 24, 1996; see also the following press releases: Governor Hunt Meets with Local Minority Ministers, June 4, 1996; Governor Hunt Issues Statement Regarding a Fire at a Black Charlotte Church, Raleigh, June 7, 1996; Governor Hunt Will Offer a Reward in Church Fire, Raleigh, June 7, 1996; Governor Hunt Appoints Task Force to Target Racial and Religious Violence, June 14, 1996; Hunt Names Members of Task Force on Racial and Religious Violence, June 20, 1996; and Hunt Speaks to Minority and Religious Leaders about Church Watch, July 26, 1996, Governors Papers, James Baxter Hunt Jr.]

Thank you all for being here today and agreeing to be a part of this very important group. I especially want to thank Attorney General Mike Easley for agreeing to chair this Task Force on Racial or Religious Violence and Intimidation.[1]

Our country was founded on freedom of religion, and that is one of our most precious liberties. Any threat on a place of worship is a threat to every citizen's right to exercise their religion. We cannot, we will not, tolerate religious and racial violence.

Five black churches in North Carolina have been burned since December—three in just the last two months.[2] So far, we have arrested four people in connection with three of those fires. But we've got to do more, not only in capturing those responsible, but also in preventing any more violent acts against our churches. We've got to make the penalties for burning a church tougher than ever before, and we've got to get to the bottom of the religious and racial hatred that would make someone commit such a horrible crime.

Last week I met with President Clinton and governors from six other southern states who are experiencing the same thing that we are here in North Carolina. We exchanged ideas and shared information about ways to combat this violence. I came out of that meeting with an action plan about what we need to do, here in our state, to fight these arsonists;

and now I am looking to each of you to help make this plan a reality and find ways to protect our religious freedom.

First, I want you to establish a uniform statewide system for reporting, recording, and responding to arson, vandalism, and bomb threats against racial or religious groups.

Second, I want you to establish a central location for collecting information about racial or religious violence.

Third, I want you to research policies, procedures, and laws against hate-group activities and racial intimidation.

Next, we must establish a statewide support network for racial or religious groups that have been victims of violence or intimidation; and fifth, we must educate the public and law enforcement officers and provide training to respond to such activity.

I want you to encourage cooperation and streamline law enforcement activities dealing with racial or religious violence and intimidation. I want to be updated at regular intervals on the status of your activities and have a final report submitted to me no later than December 31. We have made some progress: I am proud to say that a bill to stiffen penalties for church burning, developed by my legislative staff while working closely with the Legislative Black Caucus, passed the General Assembly. I want to commend the Black Caucus and Representative Mickey Michaux for their hard work on this important piece of legislation.[3] As North Carolinians, we cannot, we must not, tolerate racial and religious violence. I know I can rely on the hard work of each and every one of you to help us win this fight.

---

[1] Hunt signed Executive Order Number 96, establishing the Task Force on Racial or Religious Violence and Intimidation, on June 14, 1996. *N.C. Session Laws, 1997*, 2:2543-2545.

[2] The number of burned black churches in North Carolina did not stop at five. St. James AME Zion Church, in Maysville, was fire-bombed on June 30, 1996. *News and Observer*, July 1, 2, 1996.

[3] "An Act to Raise the Penalty for Burning of Religious Structures," *N.C. Session Laws, 1995, Extra and Regular Sessions, 1996*, c. 751, was ratified June 21, 1996.

Henry M. (Mickey) Michaux Jr. (1930-   ), native, resident of Durham; B.S., 1952, J.D., 1964, N.C. Central University; U.S. Army, 1952-1954, and Reserve, 1954-1960. Attorney; business executive; member, state House, 1973-1977, and from 1985; U.S. attorney, Middle District of N.C., 1977-1981; Democrat. *North Carolina Manual, 1995-1996*, 628.

STATEMENT ON SPECIAL LEGISLATIVE SESSION

RALEIGH, JUNE 27, 1996

[Negotiations surrounding the state's F.Y. 1996-1997 budget stalled over the allocation of a $700 million surplus. The Republican-controlled House was determined to keep approximately $400 million in the bank. The Democratic majority in the senate believed, just as strongly, that most of the windfall should benefit environmental programs and public education.

As the June 21 deadline for adjourning the 1996 short session approached, the senate urged the House to agree to an extension to work through the budget impasse. The House refused. The session ended.

State representative and Republican gubernatorial candidate Robin Hayes was a solid supporter of the decision to terminate the short session on schedule. Soon after adjournment, he said, "'All things considered, we'd have been better off reaching a settlement. But I'm very comfortable with this. We did the right thing. We're saying let the public decide in November which approach they like best. I think we've positioned ourselves to run very strong campaigns.'"

Governor Hunt called upon the General Assembly to reconvene on July 8. Within four weeks, legislators passed a budget that spent about $415 million of the surplus and gave incumbents from both parties "something to brag about" in time for the fall elections. But Democratic candidates also capitalized on the Republicans' willingness to shut down state government during the summer of 1996. Hunt won a fourth term as governor, having defeated Hayes by a 56 percent-to-43 percent margin. Although the GOP retained control of the House, the party saw its majority cut by seven seats. The Democrats' majority in the senate grew by six. Ferrell, *North Carolina Legislation, 1996*, I-1; Joint Resolution 15, *N.C. Session Laws, 1995*, 2:2068-2070; Luebke, *Tar Heel Politics 2000*, 215-216; *News and Observer*, June 20, 22, 23, 25, 26, 28, 29, August 3, 4, 1996.]

The following statement was distributed, June 27, as both a speaking text and a press release. It also formed the basis of Hunt's opening remarks at citizens' forums on the stalemate over the state budget, held July 2 (Goldsboro) and July 3 (Greensboro and New Bern), 1996.]

Last week, we saw the first budget gridlock in North Carolina history. This week, we've learned just how devastating that gridlock is. We don't have enough teachers, or textbooks, or school buses for students starting school next month. We can't enforce our tough new hog regulations; and as we've heard today, we can't open prisons, or hire enough prosecutors, or give law enforcement officers the tools they need to keep our communities safe.[1]

North Carolina is a state in crisis, and we've got an obligation to fix it. That's why I will call the legislature back to Raleigh for a special session on Monday, July 8, at 1:00 P.M. I will urge them to act as quickly as possible to pass a budget and tax cuts and credits.

I'm talking with legislative leaders from both houses and both parties today and urging them to start working on a new budget, one that gets the job done right. That means doing more than fixing what's broken. Getting the job done right means doing what's right for our state. Leaving our teachers at forty-second in the nation in teacher pay isn't doing the job right. Leaving our community college instructors last in the South in pay isn't doing the job right. Letting our universities lose good faculty isn't doing the job right. Refusing to put uniformed officers in every high school and provide alternative schools in every county isn't doing the job right. Ignoring the pressing need for day care isn't doing the job right. Refusing to provide the resources to keep our water clean isn't doing the job right.

I urge the House leadership to be cooperative in this effort and to work with the senate to do the things I've outlined. We know what to do. We know what it means to do the job right, and the people of this state expect their elected officials to do no less. The people expect their legislators to put aside partisanship to do the job—and do it right.

---

[1] The impasse over the state budget also threatened almost 400 state employees with unemployment after June 30. See press release, Governor Hunt Directs 30-Day Reprieve for State Employees, Raleigh, June 28, 1996, Governors Papers, James Baxter Hunt Jr.

NORTH CAROLINA SCHOOL
RESOURCE OFFICERS ASSOCIATION

WILMINGTON, JULY 15, 1996

School safety has been a focus of the Governor's Crime Commission in the last three years, and we've put seventy-one officers in schools across North Carolina. But we need more.

We need more, because we're seeing more guns, drugs, and violence in our schools. Last year, our schools reported crimes, from weapons possession to rape, committed against more than 1,500 students and 1,300 staff. Almost 600 students were arrested for bringing weapons or drugs to school. That is not acceptable. Teachers can't teach, and children can't learn, in an atmosphere of disruption and violence. That's why you are so important.

I know firsthand how much SROs [school resource officers] are part of the solution. I've visited dozens of schools, talking with teachers, parents, students, and SROs about what we can do to make our schools safer. They've told me what a difference you're making. When I visited Buncombe County a few months ago, students at T. C. Roberson High School told me how much safer they felt knowing Officer Brenda Frasier was there. At first, many of them thought she was there to arrest them or get them in trouble, but she slowly won their trust, their friendship, and their respect. They feel safer. I know all of you are making students at your schools feel safer, too. That's why we need more like you.

I've urged the General Assembly to invest $14 million to put an SRO in every high school in North Carolina and to provide an alternative school for every county. If a high school doesn't need an SRO, let's focus on middle schools. It's never too early to prevent crime.

The state senate agrees with my proposal. I'm disappointed that the House has not put enough resources in its budget to do these things. I want you to let your legislators know how you feel! Why is this so important? Because each of you, every school resource officer, has a success story to tell.

The Center for the Prevention of School Violence [that] we established in 1993 has played a big role in training school resource officers and helping schools tackle violence. They've also tracked the schools' successes, and the results are telling. Last year, we saw a 32 percent drop in guns brought to school campuses. My home county of Wilson saw a 63 percent drop in reported acts of school violence. Buncombe County saw a 33 percent drop. Montgomery and Iredell Counties also saw significant drops, and these school systems all had one thing in common: SROs.

The "Safe Schools Pyramid" has the school resource officer as the foundation for a reason: because you are the most important piece of the puzzle for safer classrooms. You're making a difference, and I commend you. Your motto, "We see. We listen. We care," couldn't be any more accurate.

I'm proud of you. You all are helping North Carolina be all that it can be, must be, and should be. We need to do more, and we can't do it without you. I need to hear from you on what more we can be doing.

TESTIMONY BEFORE U.S. SENATE SUBCOMMITTEE ON NATIONAL PARKS, HISTORIC PRESERVATION, AND RECREATION

WASHINGTON, D.C., JULY 18, 1996

Good morning. Thank you for this opportunity to comment on Senator Helms's bill, Senate Bill 988, the "Oregon Inlet Protection Act."[1] The Oregon Inlet stabilization project is important to the state of North Carolina for two reasons: the safety of fishermen and others who must travel through the inlet, and the economic impact of the inlet on the fishing industry and the coastal economy.[2]

Safety Concerns

Since 1960, twenty-five people have been killed because their boats became trapped in the inlet. I've brought with me a photograph of one of the numerous ships which ran aground in the inlet. The photograph is of the *Coral Breeze*, which was lost in 1982 on New Year's Day. Fortunately, no lives were lost in this accident, but until the Oregon Inlet is stabilized to prevent the frequent shoaling and shifting of the navigation channel, lives are in jeopardy.

Each year, the Coast Guard station at Oregon Inlet answers an average of 140 distress calls from vessels in the inlet or in the waters surrounding the inlet. Those men and women of the U.S. Coast Guard must brave the waters of the Oregon Inlet as well. Today, commercial and recreational fishermen consider the inlet to be one of the most treacherous on the East Coast. Yet, the Oregon Inlet is the only deep-water access along 120 miles of North Carolina's coast to the harbors of the Currituck, Albemarle, Croatan, and portions of the Pamlico Sounds.

Mr. Chairman,[3] if you have ever been out on a fishing vessel or some sort of recreational boat during inclement weather, you know the importance of access to safe harbors. Yet, in order to reach the safety of our harbors, vessels in the area must pass through Oregon Inlet, even though storms can make the trip through the inlet even more dangerous. The inlet and the navigation channel frequently shift. In fact, the inlet has migrated about two miles south since it was created in 1846 by a strong northeastern storm. You can see this migration in the photographs now being displayed. This series of photographs, taken during the last five years, vividly show [sic] the significant changes which have taken place in the inlet. If you look closely, you can see the sand is creeping south underneath the Bonner Bridge, which spans the inlet, at an extraordinary pace.

Because a terminal groin was built to protect the Bonner Bridge, the migration of the southern side of the inlet has been slowed. However, the migration of the northern side continues unabated, thereby shrinking the inlet, making it more treacherous. Mr. Chairman, the issue of safety is paramount. Help us with this so we can save lives.

But we cannot overlook the important impact the project will have on the region's economy.

Economic Concerns

Northeastern North Carolina is primarily rural and is one of the poorest regions of our state. The state funded an economic analysis, completed in January 1995, that clearly shows that if we stabilize this inlet, the positive economic benefits will make a tremendous difference for this depressed region. The study concluded that the Oregon Inlet project would stimulate an expansion of marinas, trigger additional investment in seafood processing plants, and prompt improvements to the basic infrastructure which serves the fishing and tourism industries. These economic activities would result in a significant decrease in the unemployment rates of a ten-county region, from 6.9 percent to 4.7 percent. Remarkably, the decrease in unemployment in Hyde County is projected to decrease from 10.6 percent to 5.0 percent and in Tyrrell County from 11.9 percent to 6.7 percent.

One reason why these unemployment figures are so staggering is because of the Wanchese Seafood Industrial Park. The Wanchese park was built to be one of the nation's premier seafood industrial facilities, offering fishermen a central location where seafood buyers, processors, distributors, and suppliers could be reached. The seafood park was built following Congress's authorization of the stabilization of the Oregon Inlet in 1970. The project description included an expansion of the Wanchese Harbor, and with this knowledge the state contributed over $8 million to the seafood park's construction. [The park] never achieved its goal, because the inlet has not been stabilized.

Mr. Chairman, the stabilization of the Oregon Inlet is important to the state of North Carolina. This Congress authorized it twenty-six years ago. Again, I urge quick consideration and approval of S. 988, the "Oregon Inlet Protection Act." Thank you.

---

[1] "Oregon Inlet Protection Act" was the short title of S. 988, "A Bill to Direct the Secretary of the Interior to Transfer Administrative Jurisdiction Over Certain Land to the Secretary of the Army to Facilitate Construction of a Jetty and Sand Transfer System, and for Other Purposes." The measure, introduced June 19, 1995, by Senator Jesse Helms, ran aground in the Subcommittee on National Parks, Historic Preservation, and Recreation and remained there through the end of the 104th Session of Congress. Library of Congress, Thomas: Legislative Information on the Internet (http://thomas.loc.gov/home/thomas.html).

Jesse Helms (1921-   ), born in Monroe; resident of Raleigh; was educated at Wingate College and Wake Forest College (later University); honorary degrees; U.S. Navy, 1942-1945. Former city editor, *Raleigh Times*; administrative assistant to U.S. senators Willis Smith, 1951-1953, and Alton Lennon, 1953; executive director, N.C. Bankers Assn., 1953-1960; member, Raleigh City Council, 1957-1961; career with Capitol Broadcasting Co., Raleigh, 1960-1972, included executive vice-president, vice-chairman of the board, and assistant CEO; was elected to U.S. Senate in 1972 and was returned in subsequent elections; chairman, Senate Foreign Relations Committee; Republican. *Biographical Directory of Congress*, s.v. "Helms, Jesse"; *North Carolina Manual, 1995-1996*, 1024.

[2] Hunt wrote, next to this paragraph: "Dare Co[unty]—Outer Banks—where Am[erican] Indians met the 1st English settlers in 1584. Wright Bro[ther]s flew 1st airplane. Fishing indus[try] has been a living and 'way of life.' Comm[erce]. Recreation. (Gulf Stream and cold waters of North)."

[3] Ben Nighthorse Campbell (1933-   ), born in Auburn, Ca.; resident of Ignacio, Co.; B.A., University of California at San Jose, 1957; attended Meiji University, Tokyo; U.S. Air Force, 1952-1954. Rancher; jewelry designer; member, Colorado state legislature, 1983-1986; was elected to U.S. Congress in 1986 and was returned in subsequent elections; Democrat. *Biographical Directory of Congress*, s.v. "Campbell, Ben Nighthorse."

NOTES FOR STATEMENT ON BUDGET STALEMATE

RALEIGH, JULY 26, 1996

[Three long weeks after Governor Hunt called the General Assembly back into session, House and senate negotiators finally reported some progress in the attempt to craft a mutually acceptable state budget for F.Y. 1996-1997. Hunt hoped to keep that newfound momentum building and asked legislators to remain in Raleigh the weekend of July 26-28 in case there was a breakthrough. The Republican leadership decided instead to adjourn the House until the following Monday evening. When the governor learned of the decision, he quickly called a press conference; see *News and Observer*, July 27, 1996. His notes follow.]

—In two weeks, August eighth, school starts in Madison County: without enough teachers, textbooks, or school buses. Across North Carolina, principals and superintendents are scrambling to open schools without the resources they need to hire almost 1,400 new teachers.

—The House has done a disservice to the people of North Carolina today.

—The senate was willing to work through the weekend to get it done. I asked Speaker Brubaker yesterday, and again today, to stay and finish the job. There is absolutely no excuse for adjourning.

—The people of North Carolina are fed up. They've seen their elected officials spend nine weeks, and $3 million of their tax dollars, in Raleigh this summer, and there's still no budget!

—This is not right. And the people of this state won't stand for it. They expect their elected officials to put politics aside and do what's right.

—I urge Speaker Brubaker and the House Republicans to listen to their constituents and finish the job Monday. There's no excuse for anything else.

PRESS RELEASE: STATEMENT ON THE BUDGET

RALEIGH, AUGUST 2, 1996

The budget agreement reached by legislative leaders contains some good news for North Carolinians, especially on tax cuts. The tax cuts that our administration proposed and the legislature passed will leave more money in the hands of working families and help create more jobs throughout our state. But a session that lasted this long should have accomplished more, especially for education. While the pay raises in this budget agreement do provide some relief for state workers, they deserve more. The teacher pay raise in particular does not make enough progress toward raising North Carolina out of forty-second place in the nation in teacher pay. Much more remains to be done.

This budget also makes progress by cutting class size in second grade and providing more law enforcement officers for our high schools to help make our classrooms safer. We must continue those efforts.

I want to express sincere appreciation for the leaders of the senate and those members of the House who fought hard for our public schools and for Smart Start. Because they stood strong, eleven more counties will begin providing working families with better day care and other early childhood services in 1997.

Unfortunately, the length of this session will make it hard for schools to get ready to open in just a few weeks. Our administration is committed to working closely with the State Board of Education, the Department of Public Instruction, and local schools to get this money out of Raleigh and into the classrooms as quickly as possible.

NOTES, STATE EMERGENCY RESPONSE TEAM
APPRECIATION DAY

RALEIGH, AUGUST 3, 1996

[The activities of the State Emergency Response Team during the prelude to and aftermath of Hurricane Bertha earned words of praise and thanks from Governor Hunt on August 3, 1996. Bertha had spun ashore between Topsail Island and Wrightsville Beach on the twelfth of the previous month. Before it departed eastern North Carolina, the category-two storm caused two deaths and $1.2 billion in losses.

Near the end of his SERT Appreciation Day notes, Hunt said, "We've got a long hurricane season ahead of us, folks. We may be dealing with as many as four storms in the next month or so." As it happened, there was just one: Its name was Fran. Jay Barnes, *North Carolina's Hurricane History* (Chapel Hill: University of North Carolina Press, 1998), 162-172. For press releases related to Hurricane Bertha, see Governor Hunt Proclaims State of Disaster, Raleigh, July 15, 1996; Governor Hunt Requests Federal Disaster Aid, Raleigh, July 16, 1996; Governor Hunt Asks U.S. Secretary of Agriculture to Help Farmers, Raleigh, July 16, 1996; Governor Hunt Seeks Disaster Relief for Hurricane Victims, Raleigh, July 18, 1996; Six More Counties Added to Federal State of

Disaster List, Raleigh, July 22, 1996; and Governor Hunt Continues Relief Efforts for Farmers Hit by Bertha, Raleigh, July 23, 1996, Governors Papers, James Baxter Hunt Jr.]

—While the rest of the state was busy making plans for the July 4 holiday, you all were watching and waiting for Hurricane Bertha.

—When she crossed our shores, you were ready.

—I've seen how you come together in the Emergency Operations Center. I've been there with you as you make sure our citizens are protected.

—Thousands of workers from more than thirty agencies in state government, the private sector, and volunteer agencies were on duty around the clock during this emergency. As always when danger threatens our state, you were in the field helping those who needed it most.

—The men and women of our National Guard distributed generators and safe drinking water and provided security for homes that the owners couldn't get to themselves.

—Our Highway Patrol and DMV [Division of Motor Vehicles] enforcement officers controlled traffic and kept the public out of dangerous areas.

—The Department of Transportation put up barricades before the storm and worked in the aftermath, clearing streets and repairing our highways.

—The Ferry Division carried people to safety. The Civil Air Patrol surveyed damaged areas through flying missions with volunteer cadets. Forest Resource workers helped clear access to roads by cutting fallen trees.

—Almost 100 Department of Correction crews came out to oversee inmates as they cleaned up debris on the roads and helped farmers salvage their crops. The Department of Human Resources worked with the Red Cross and Salvation Army getting shelters ready for those who had nowhere else to go.

—The Energy Division from our Department of Commerce worked with power companies to get electricity back on, and EMS [emergency medical services], fire, and rescue folks from Human Resources and Insurance did their part, getting the sick and injured to places they could get the attention that's always needed.

—My Office of Citizen Affairs worked in this emergency, with public information officers, to let people know what to do and where to go.

—One Motor Fleet Management employee, who was paged at church, left the service to provide cars to those going down to the coast to help with recovery and survey damage.

—After the crisis passed, our Travel and Tourism office let everyone know when the beaches were open again, so we could get tourist dollars back here during an important vacation time for families.

—The list goes on and on. You all are the ones who make a difference in an emergency. You make things happen. You help save lives.

—I'm proud of the quality work you're doing. On behalf of all North Carolina's citizens, I want to commend all of you for your outstanding service.

—We've got a long hurricane season ahead of us, folks. We may be dealing with as many as four storms in the next month or so.

—I'm counting on you to continue doing your best.

WORK FIRST FORUM

ASHEVILLE, AUGUST 16, 1996

[The Asheville speech of August 16, 1996, is typical of those Hunt delivered during the third and fourth quarters of 1996 that extolled Work First and sought private support for program participants needing jobs. He relied on the same basic text, with portions tailored to reflect local accomplishments, at Work First forums and roundtables in Jamestown, July 17, Raleigh, July 23, Monroe, August 26, Charlotte, September 4, Fayetteville, October 9; the Goodwill Industries Employment Center groundbreaking, Greensboro, October 7; and Host Marriott/Work First, Charlotte, October 10, 1996. See also press release, Hunt Calls on Triangle Businesses, Churches to Boost Work First, Raleigh, July 23, 1996. Governors Papers, James Baxter Hunt Jr.]

I want to thank all of you—ministers, community and business leaders, teachers, and parents—for coming here today to show your support for Work First. To help our neighbors, to break the cycle of welfare dependency, we must change welfare. We must encourage personal responsibility.

We must move people into the workforce and help them learn to earn their keep:

—Teresa McClure of Waynesville, mother of two, hadn't held a job for a year. Work First taught her how to handle a job interview and taught her how to write a résumé. She now is an insurance agent for State Farm.

—Vicky Zuber, mother of two teenagers, was unemployed for six months. Work First helped her in the job search, and she now works in human resources at LEA Industries, a furniture manufacturer in Waynesville.

That's the kind of difference Work First is making for thousands of North Carolina families. We've seen 17,000 families get jobs and leave welfare since Work First began. The number of families on welfare dropped nearly 13 percent in the first year of Work First, and Work First is expected to save taxpayers about $90 million over two years. Clearly our efforts are boosted by the strong economy we've worked so hard to build here in North Carolina, but revamping our approach, shifting the focus from a welfare check right from the start, is having a dramatic impact.

To make this work even better, we need you to get involved and get your neighbors involved. You can be a mentor or a role model. You can give someone a chance to stand on their own by giving them a job. Your church or civic club can help them make the transition from welfare to work by providing clothes, transportation, or child care. Your church or business can offer space for literacy classes, or you can "adopt" a family like my Sunday school class did. We helped a mother of four get to her job until she got her own transportation.

There's already some creative community involvement here in Buncombe County. The American Association of University Women is working with the Henderson County Work First staff to create a life-skills course that churches will be able to teach Work First participants, and the Asheville-Buncombe Community Christian Ministry put on their own Work First forum—this one encouraged local pastors to recruit members of their congregations to hire Work First participants. There are so many local employers who already have recognized that Work First is a good place to look for employees. Big businesses and small: J&S Cafeteria picks up their new employees in a van and drives them to work. The Haywood County Hospital has arranged to give work experience to welfare recipients, and so far they have hired three Work First participants.

These companies are just a sample. Employers across North Carolina are beginning to recognize this untapped labor pool. Folks, this is a new way of thinking. It's a new way of doing business, and it is working!

Work First is about communities coming together to help families in need. All of you here, today, can make a tremendous difference in the lives of those families. Work First is putting people in jobs, cutting welfare rolls, saving money, and helping our economy. Most of all, it's helping families learn to stand on their own.

We're still charting the course, but we're headed in the right direction. With your help, we can continue moving forward. Together, we can do this.

High winds and torrential rains from Hurricane Fran pummeled North Carolina and caused hundreds of millions of dollars in crop losses. Secretary Dan Glickman, of the U.S. Department of Agriculture, Governor Hunt, and Congresswoman Eva Clayton discuss federal aid to storm-stricken farmers, September 9, 1996, at a Raleigh press conference. (Photograph by Mel Nathanson, Raleigh *News and Observer*.)

Top: Hunt escorts Microsoft CEO Bill Gates to the Raleigh Civic and Convention Center, April 11, 1996, where the governor introduced him at a small-business expo. (Photograph by Harry Lynch, Raleigh *News and Observer*.) *Bottom*: Lars von Kantzow, president and CEO of Perstorp Flooring, of Sweden, hands Hunt a sample of the Pergo laminated flooring to be produced at a new, $25 million manufacturing plant in Garner, North Carolina. The factory was dedicated on December 6, 1996. (Photograph by Jim Bounds, Raleigh *News and Observer*.)

FDA/TOBACCO PRESS CONFERENCE

GREENVILLE, AUGUST 28, 1996

[Tobacco product manufacturers, advertisers, and retailers filed a lawsuit, in 1995, aimed at halting the Food and Drug Administration's plans to regulate tobacco as a drug. Both North Carolina and Kentucky submitted friend of the court briefs, in mid-October 1996, on behalf of the plaintiffs. *News and Observer,* August 29, 30, September 1, 21, October 16, December 3, 16, 25, 1996; see also press releases, Statement by Governor Jim Hunt on Clinton's Apparent Decision to Accept the FDA's Recommendation to Classify Tobacco as a Drug, August 21, 1996; Governor Hunt to Fight FDA Regulation of Tobacco, Raleigh, August 22, 1996; Governor Hunt Calls for Legal Action Against FDA Tobacco Rules, Greenville, August 28, 1996; N.C. Joining Lawsuit to Block FDA's Tobacco Regulation, Wilson, September 20, 1996; Clarification of Incorrect Newspaper Article on Tobacco Lawsuit against FDA, October 21, 1996, Governors Papers, James Baxter Hunt Jr.]

I have asked the attorney general[1] to file legal action against the U.S. Food and Drug Administration on behalf of the tobacco farmers and growers in North Carolina. We have a big stake in this decision to regulate tobacco as a drug, and we are going to fight the federal government every step of the way. The attorney general and I have talked at length, and we've decided to pursue legal action by either filing a lawsuit or joining an existing lawsuit, whichever is most effective. We're going to take this to court to keep the FDA out of the tobacco fields.

I believe these new rules amount to nothing more than big government trying to regulate tobacco out of existence. If the FDA is allowed to regulate tobacco as a drug, there's nothing to keep them from declaring it a controlled substance and preventing everyone from smoking. This decision will be devastating to North Carolina, because tobacco is our number-one cash crop. Many North Carolina families depend on this crop to pay their grocery and electric bills and to give their children a good education.

We are not going to sit back and let that happen without a fight. It will hurt our growers. It will hurt the 260,000 North Carolinians who make a living working in tobacco. It will hurt our families by devastating their economy, and it hurts our state by cutting revenue.[2]

It is wrong for the federal government to suggest our tobacco farmers are growing a drug, and it is just as wrong to suggest that our farmers want teenagers to smoke. Tobacco farmers don't want children to smoke. None of us want children to smoke. In fact, we have strongly supported tougher enforcement of laws against teenage smoking. I have repeatedly pressed the Clinton administration to adopt an alternative teenage-smoking initiative developed by the U.S. Department of Health and Human Services. It includes tougher enforcement of laws against teenage smoking and stronger education efforts, rather than FDA regulation.

Tobacco is a great part of our heritage in eastern North Carolina. We are not giving up that heritage. We are fighting for it.

---

[1] Attorney General Michael F. Easley was identified earlier in this volume.

[2] "Every pound of tobacco sold here at the High Dollar Warehouse, and all across the flue-cured producing areas, generates $24 in revenue. When critics tell us we need to find an alternative crop or a substitute source of income for tobacco, I tell them we may never be able to replace the contribution tobacco brings to our economy." Border Belt Tobacco Market Opening, Fairmont, July 25, 1996, Governors Papers, James Baxter Hunt Jr.

BRIEFING, HURRICANE FRAN AFTERMATH

RALEIGH, SEPTEMBER 9, 1996

[Eastern North Carolina was still cleaning up from Hurricane Bertha when Hurricane Fran made landfall near Bald Head Island the night of September 5, 1996. Unlike Bertha, Fran was "a major hurricane, a real category three with all the trimmings." During the eleven hours it swept inland from the coast, roared northwest along Interstate 40, and crossed the Virginia border, Fran unleashed high winds, torrential rains, and flooding that left at least $5 billion in damage in its wake. Twenty-four people died as a result of the storm.

Governor Hunt declared all of North Carolina to be in a state of emergency. Hundreds of thousands of people were without electricity. Disruption of water-sewer, transportation, and telephone services was widespread and lasted for weeks in some areas. The Research Triangle region was especially hard hit; cleanup of storm damage in Raleigh alone cost $33 million. Barnes, *North Carolina's Hurricane History*, 172-204; *News and Observer*, September 7, 1996, March 2, 1997, August 25, 1998.

Hurricane Fran figured in Hunt's speech at the Remington Arms Company Grand Opening, Madison, September 19, 1996. Fran-related press releases include: Governor Hunt Appeals to State Employees to Work in Disaster Relief, Raleigh, September 9; Governor Hunt and FEMA Announce Additional Resources for Cleanup, Raleigh, September 11; Governor Hunt, N.C. Delegation Push to Get Funds to Help State Recover, Raleigh, September 12; Governor Hunt Gets Flood Damage Update from Western Officials, Raleigh, September 16; Governor Hunt Announces Counseling Guide for Students Affected by Fran, Raleigh, October 1; and Governor Hunt's Request for Maximum Federal Aid Granted, Raleigh, December 6, 1996, Governors Papers, James Baxter Hunt Jr.]

North Carolina is a state in crisis. I don't know about all of you, but I've just had four of the longest days of my life. I've worried about our state and our citizens, and I've worried about my neighbors, my family, and my farm in eastern North Carolina.

We have lost lives, and we have lost property. Conditions are still horrible for many of our people—from our coastal communities, through eastern North Carolina, and well into the Piedmont. Many of us have no water. We have no power, and ice and gasoline have become precious commodities. We are dealing with our problems, but we need to think first about those less fortunate than we are. First, we need to help people with medical problems and people with infants and small children.

But the one thing North Carolinians do have is spirit—and nothing, not even the most powerful and destructive hurricane in recent memory, can take that away from us. Today as we pause to get an update on conditions and needs, especially in the thirty-four counties already declared federal disaster areas, I want to pay tribute to the hundreds of thousands of North Carolinians who are helping their neighbors and who are helping people they've never met. I've always known the people in this state were special, but I have never been more moved by the spirit of survival and the spirit of helping others than I have in the past four days. I'm grateful to the many people who have called radio and TV stations and our Emergency Operations Center to volunteer their time, their chain saws, their air conditioned homes, and their showers to anyone—anyone—who needs them.

I'm grateful, also, to other states who [sic] have sent utility crews to restore power to our homes. Governors Lawton Chiles, of Florida, and David Beasley, of South Carolina, are sending help, and I'm going to ask other states to send truckloads of ice and other supplies to us.[1] We are asking the federal government for everything they have to help us get back on our feet. Today, Agriculture secretary Dan Glickman is touring the agricultural damage in our state.[2] I'm meeting with him at 1:00 P.M. today, and I'm going to ask him for every penny we can get for our farmers.

Our state has mobilized all the resources we can find, and we are still looking for more, to get us back to normal. We have 2,300 National Guard soldiers and airmen handling security, cleaning debris, helping with rescue missions, and providing generators. Since the hurricane hit, we've had more than 2,000 inmates removing debris from coastal counties.

Our DOT [Department of Transportation] has more than 3,000 employees working twelve-hour shifts to remove debris and barricade roads that are flooded. DOT says intersections in major urban areas are still without power, so traveling to work will be treacherous with no stoplights. For that reason, we have told state employees in the thirty-four federal disaster counties to stay home unless they work at a hospital, or prison, or are considered emergency personnel.

Our utility companies—CP&L [Carolina Power and Light], Duke Power, and ElectriCities co-op—are represented here today, and I want to thank them for working around the clock to get power restored.

Today I want you to get an update from FEMA [Federal Emergency Management Administration] and our state emergency officials on the aftermath of this storm. Then I want to hear your ideas for mobilizing even more of our resources so our people can get their lives back. We are going to need more patience than we've ever had, and we're going to need to be creative and cooperative to get through this crisis.

---

[1] Lawton Chiles (1930-1998), born in Lakeland, Fla.; B.S., 1952, LL.B., 1955, University of Florida; U.S. Army, 1953-1954. Attorney; member, Florida House of Representatives, 1959-1966, and senate, 1967-1970; U.S. senator from Florida, 1971-1989; director, LeRoy Collins Center for Public Policy, 1989-1990; elected governor of Florida, 1990, re-elected in 1994; Democrat. Barone and Ujifusa, *Almanac of American Politics, 1996*, 295; *New York Times*, December 14, 1998.

David M. Beasley (1957-   ), born in Lamar, S.C.; B.A., 1979, J.D., 1983, University of South Carolina. Attorney; member, South Carolina House of Representatives, 1979-1992; was elected governor of South Carolina, 1994; Republican. Barone and Ujifusa, *Almanac of American Politics, 1996*, 1200.

[2] Daniel Robert Glickman (1944-   ), born in Wichita, Kans.; B.A., University of Michigan, 1966; J.D., Georgetown University, 1969. Attorney; U.S. congressman from Fourth Kansas District, 1977-1995; U.S. agriculture secretary, from 1995; Democrat. *Who's Who in America, 1998*, s.v. "Glickman, Daniel Robert."

NORTH CAROLINA ASSOCIATION OF LONG-TERM CARE FACILITIES

GREENSBORO, SEPTEMBER 17, 1996

North Carolina is fortunate to have a tremendous adult-care home program that meets the needs of thousands of older and disabled residents who can no longer remain in their homes. These are people who are not yet in need of nursing home care, but who do need and deserve the best long-term care available.

I know your industry is far different today than it was ten years ago, and that you have had to make many changes to keep pace. In fact, residents eighty-five and older make up the fastest-growing segment in North Carolina. Your services are critical to helping give them quality care.

North Carolina is committed to giving you the tools you need to provide that quality care. You are already working hard under the new licensure rules to see that your staff receives the finest training. Medicaid now pays for enhanced personal care services for your residents who need extensive or total assistance. Drawing these Medicaid dollars helps free state dollars and allows us to better address the special needs of our older citizens.

This year, my budget included funds to meet many critical needs for you and for our seniors. At my urging and with your persistence, the General Assembly passed many of those items:

—Almost $3.8 million to provide you with a 3.5 percent increase in State/County Special Assistance reimbursement. I know that the cost of business goes up for you like it does for everybody else, and this increase will go a long way to help you meet expenses.

—A $1 million revolving loan fund to enable adult care homes and nursing homes to install smoke detectors, sprinklers, and other safety equipment.

—Requiring criminal history record checks of unlicensed job applicants in adult care homes, nursing homes, and home care agencies. Your association and the North Carolina Health Care Facilities Association worked hard to get this through.[1]

—Expanding the homestead exemption to give low-income seniors a tax break.

—Increasing funding for in-home and community-based services by an additional $5 million per year, allowing us to offer services like home-delivered meals and in-home help to 4,500 older adults who need them but who do not qualify for Medicaid.

—Providing $100,000 to support the four Alzheimer's Association chapters in the state.

—Providing $100,000 for the North Carolina Senior Games program.

—Giving tax relief to seniors and families by reducing the sales tax on food.

I commend seniors across our state for coming together to push for what they need. They communicated with me and with their legislators. They told us what they needed, and they fought hard for it. Folks, that's how to get things done: teamwork.

I encourage you to build relationships with the key senior groups and community aging programs in North Carolina. You may not always agree on issues, but I bet you are not too far apart on most things. You can accomplish so much when parties come to the same table. I encourage you to work in your communities with your long-term care ombudsmen and our community advisory committees.

I am asking all departments of state government to do the same. We must cut the red tape and streamline government. I have asked Secretary

Robin Britt to reduce some of the hurdles that hinder your ability to serve your residents. The Department of Human Resources will be doing an audit of the monitoring process and will look at making necessary changes to streamline this process.

Friends, I'm in your corner. I am committed to working together with you to do everything we can to help the changing needs of our seniors and disabled residents and to provide top-quality care to those who need it.

---

[1] "An Act Requiring Criminal History Record Checks of Unlicensed Applicants for Employment in Nursing Homes, Adult Care Homes, and Home Care Agencies," N.C. Session Laws, 1995, Regular and Extra Sessions, 1996, c. 606, was ratified June 21, 1996.

WELCOMING REMARKS
BILLY GRAHAM'S CAROLINAS CRUSADE

Charlotte, September 26, 1996

God calls us to service in many different ways. We serve Him as pastors and missionaries, as day-care workers, and in senior citizens centers. We serve Him as volunteers with the Red Cross, Boy and Girl Scouts, and the Food Bank. We serve Him as choir members or musicians in churches, while others share the story of Jesus Christ in their daily lives. And then, there's Billy Graham's service.

Jesus told His disciples to "Go into all the world and preach the Gospel to every creature."[1] Billy Graham does that. He is a disciple of Jesus, and he has carried out that commandment like no one I have ever known.

Billy Graham has received many honors and awards. His advice has been sought by countless political and religious leaders around the world, including a number of United States presidents. But if you asked Billy, he would tell you that his greatest accomplishment, his greatest reward, is the countless number of lives he's changed for the better.

I am honored to know Billy Graham. I am honored that he has been my friend for more than two decades. He has inspired me with his rare faith and complete trust in God.

Ruth and Billy Graham have given their lives to God.[2] Because of them, millions have come to the cross and have heard about the love and forgiveness that is found in Christ.

Jesus said, "Let your light so shine before men that they may see your good works."[3] Billy Graham, your light is a beacon to the world. You are God's vessel. You have helped us all understand the simple message of Jesus, and we are closer to Him because of you. I believe I speak for all North Carolinians when I say we've never been more proud of one of our own than we are of you. It is my honor to welcome you to your home state of North Carolina and to pray for God's blessing on this crusade.

---

[1] "Go ye into all the world, and preach the gospel to every creature." Mark 16:15.

[2] William Franklin (Billy) Graham married Ruth McCue Bell on August 13, 1943. Ruth's father was missionary surgeon Dr. Nelson Bell, of Montreat, N.C. *Current Biography Yearbook, 1973*, 152, 154.

[3] "Let your light so shine before men, that they may see your good works, and glorify your Father which is in heaven." Matthew 5:16.

DRUNK DRIVING ROUNDTABLE

WINSTON-SALEM, OCTOBER 16, 1996

[For related documents, see Mothers Against Drunk Driving press conference text, Raleigh, November 26, 1996; and a pair of press releases: Governor Hunt Announces Plan to Toughen Penalties for Drunk Drivers, Raleigh, October 16, 1996, and Governor Hunt Signs Into Law Tough New Drunk Driving Penalties, Raleigh, August 7, 1997. Governors Papers, James Baxter Hunt Jr.]

Just last week, we mourned the deaths of two people killed in a fiery car crash in Charlotte. Three weeks ago today, three students were hit on their way to class at Broughton High School; while two are recovering, another remains in critical condition.[1] The first week of September, two Wake Forest University students were killed in a car wreck and three others injured; one of those who is still in the hospital was her high school's SADD [Students Against Drunk Driving] president. These tragedies have one thing in common: alcohol.

Two of the drivers have each been charged with two counts of second-degree murder. The third has been charged with driving while impaired, felony assault with a deadly weapon inflicting serious injury, and others. Between them, they have seventeen pages of driving records, including convictions for DWI and driving with their license revoked. That is unacceptable. Those drivers should not have been on the road.

North Carolina shouldn't tolerate drinking and driving, and here's what I want us to [do] about it: Get them off the road.

First, we must take some immediate action by speeding up prosecutions. With Chief Justice Mitchell,[2] I am creating a strike force of retired judges to speed up drunk driving trials by clearing the backlog of cases in the counties that need it most. So when you're caught, there will be no delays and no need for continuances. You'll be tried swiftly. I want these special courts to be held all across the state. If we run out of court-room space, we'll set up court in our National Guard armories.

Second, we need even tougher laws.[3] Law enforcement officers need the authority to seize drunk drivers' cars at the time of arrest and hold them pending trial. We do this when people set up drag races—we should do at least that to drunk drivers. I want to require judges to take the cars of convicted drunk drivers who have lost their driving privileges in a previous DWI case and are caught again for the same offense. They ought to know better.

I want repeat offenders to spend more time in jail. Jail time should be mandatory for the second offense and any additional driving with revoked license convictions as a result of DWI. I also want to increase jail time from seven days to sixty days for offenders convicted of a second DWI within three years.

I want to change the definition of a habitual DWI offender to someone convicted of two DWIs within seven years, rather than the current three convictions, and we should put them in jail for a year. Their sentence should include mandatory treatment and require them to go through the Department of Correction's Drug and Alcohol Rehabilitation program. Nine percent of the people in prison are there for DWI. These people are sick, and they need help. That's no excuse, but treatment is part of this solution, and this program is part of the solution.

Together with the legislature, we've put tougher laws on the books—including changing the blood alcohol content level from .10 to .08 to be considered impaired—but we need to do more. I commend Lieutenant Governor Dennis Wicker for his work with my Task Force on Driving while Impaired. I'll continue working side by side with all of you, and the legislature, to make sure that North Carolina's roads are as safe as they can be. These are ideas that I think will work. Now I want to hear from you all.

---

[1] William Bradford Rice III, with a record of four drunken driving charges and one conviction in a seven-year period, drove into three Broughton High School students September 25, 1996, as they waited to cross Peace Street, in Raleigh. He was charged with his fifth DWI, as well as having a fictitious license and no insurance, in the Raleigh incident. *News and Observer*, September 27, 1996.

[2] Burley Bayard Mitchell Jr. (1940-   ), native of Raleigh; B.A., N.C. State University, 1966; J.D., University of North Carolina, 1969; U.S. Navy, 1958-1962. Attorney; assistant attorney general of N.C., 1969-1972; district attorney, Tenth Judicial District, 1972-1977; judge, N.C. Court of Appeals, 1977-1979; secretary, N.C. Dept. of Crime Control and Public

Safety, 1979-1982; associate justice, 1982-1994, chief justice, 1995-1999, N.C. Supreme Court; Democrat. *News and Observer*, July 30, August 1, September 3, 8, 1999; *North Carolina Manual, 1997-1998*, 745-746.

[3] Hunt got his wish for stricter DWI measures in 1997. "An Act to Implement the Governor's Recommendations on Driving While Impaired," *N.C. Session Laws, 1997*, II, c. 379, was ratified August 7 and became effective December 1, 1997.

NOTES, PULL THE PLUG

RALEIGH, OCTOBER 21, 1996

I want to thank you all for helping me kick off the second annual "Pull the Plug on Media Violence Week." Our young people, like the students here today, are the reason we're doing this.[1] As parents and grandparents, we want to make sure you understand that what you watch on TV and play on video games isn't the way real life usually works out.

One year ago, we launched this project to encourage parents to take an active role in what their children watch on TV and play in video games, some of them very violent.

Last year, I issued a challenge to this group to keep this important educational tool alive by working on it year-round. You have done a tremendous job. You've changed the name of this effort to include not just TV and video games, but all forms of media. The North Carolina Coalition for Pulling the Plug on Media Violence has doubled its number of sponsors, doubled its number of financial contributions, and more importantly, doubled the number of materials—bookmarks, bumper stickers, and flyers—for distribution to more than 800,000 kindergarten through fifth-grade students across the state this week.

We all know there's a connection between viewing violence on television and an increase in violent behavior among young people. American children now watch an average of twenty-three hours of TV each week and see more than 12,000 violent acts each year. With numbers like these, there's little wonder why juvenile crime continues to rise. By the time you students graduate from high school, many of you will have spent more time watching TV than you've spent in the classroom.

TV violence isn't the only thing to blame on violent behavior, but it is the easiest thing to fix, and there is something parents can do about it, right now. Know what your children watch. Set reasonable limits. Plan ahead, and participate in their viewing.

Let's all work together and make viewing a family affair by pulling the plug on media violence, this week and every week.

[1] Fifth-grade students from Leesville Road Elementary School, Wake County, were present for Hunt's declaration that October 20-26, 1996, was "Pull the Plug on Media Violence Week" in North Carolina. Press release, Governor Hunt Helps Schools Pull the Plug on Media Violence, Raleigh, October 21, 1996, Governors Papers, James Baxter Hunt Jr.

GOVERNOR'S CONFERENCE ON TEACHING AND NORTH CAROLINA'S FUTURE

Chapel Hill, December 16, 1996

This conference today is a historic one for North Carolina. For the first time that anyone here can remember, or is aware of, we have drawn together representatives of all the people who can make a difference in our schools, and we have spent all our time focused on what matters most for good schools: good teachers.

You've had a chance to hear today about some of the excellent work we are doing in North Carolina to raise standards, in our colleges and in our public schools, and to get and keep good teachers. You've also, I hope, had an opportunity to learn about what still needs to get done to make our schools the envy of the nation.

The National Commission on Teaching and America's Future, which I have had the privilege of chairing, has tackled the core question of how we can ensure that every child, in every classroom, in every community in this country has a competent, caring, and high-quality teacher to help them learn what they need to know to succeed in the twenty-first century. We found in our two years of national research and deliberations a number of disturbing facts:

—Nearly one-fourth of all secondary teachers lack even a minor in the fields in which they teach, a figure that is much higher in low-income schools;

—More than half of all students taking a physical science course are taught by out-of-field teachers;

—And more than a quarter of newly hired teachers, nearly 30,000 per year, are hired without having met state standards.

Unfortunately, some of those problems can be found right here in North Carolina, and we have to change that.

The commission has learned that most schools and teachers have been unable to change, not because they don't want to, but because they don't know how. What this conference, and our work for the next four years, must be about is showing teachers how to teach to new standards, and demands, and giving them the support and resources they need to do that.

The national commission is convinced that what matters most to improving education is the quality of teaching in America's schools. We believe that we must develop ways to give teachers the knowledge they need to succeed and the incentives to stay in the classroom, and we have to make sure our schools of education are equal to the best schools of medicine, law, and engineering.

When I became governor in 1977, I resolved to improve the quality of schools and teaching. I'm pleased to announce that this is the tenth anniversary of the North Carolina Center for the Advancement of Teaching, which provides teachers time to study in depth with master teachers.[1] There are many other examples of excellence in our state as well:

—A teaching fellows program, which provides $20,000 scholarships to highly able students who commit to teaching for at least four years in our state;[2]

—The first state in the nation to establish legislation to support teachers seeking national board certification, the established standard of accomplished teaching, and to reward those who achieve it. As a result of that legislation, North Carolina has ninety-four national board-certified teachers, more than any other state in the nation. Fifty-three of those ninety-four teachers are with us today, as you know. Thanks to them, we are on our way to meeting the national commission's goal of at least one board-certified teacher in every school; and we can thank our good friend, Bill Friday, for his leadership in this area. Thanks to him, just last week the North Carolina Progress Board adopted a new education goal supporting national board certification.[3]

—The North Carolina Teacher Academy that's helping teachers meet the goals of our Standards and Accountability Commission and our ABC plan;

—A new North Carolina Professional Teaching Standards board that will enable teachers to set high standards for entry into their profession;[4]

—Fledgling professional development schools attached to some of our colleges and universities;

—A citizenry that just voted overwhelmingly to support a $1.8 billion bond referendum to build better schools;[5]

—A strong commitment from the people of North Carolina to raise the pay of our teachers to the national average by the year 2000.[6]

We have reason to be proud of all we've done in our state. But I'm not satisfied, and neither are our parents, our taxpayers, and our children. Neither are you. That's why you're here: so you can learn how to help solve problems and make our teaching force the strongest and best in the country.

I know my friend, Linda Darling-Hammond, reviewed all the commission recommendations for you this morning, and I know you've spent time discussing some of them in your breakout sessions.[7] But let me tell you how your governor stands on these recommendations. I want us to look closely at what we have to do, right here in North Carolina, to take this blueprint and build a new and stronger teaching profession.

First, get serious about standards for both students and teachers. Let me say to all you teachers, and principals, and superintendents, if you are not familiar with the work of the Standards and Accountability Commission in this state, you need to get familiar. I'm dead serious about holding the Class of 2000 to higher standards, having them develop portfolios and do senior projects, and prove that they can do something with the material they've mastered. And of course, that means they must have mastered the basics, and we'll measure that as well.

I'm serious about teacher standards, too. I challenge my teacher friends and their organizations, the AFT [American Federation of Teachers] and the NCAE [North Carolina Association of Educators], to look at models in other states and to use their own ingenuity to come up with ways for you to monitor your profession, to support each other in growing as professionals, but also to counsel out those in your ranks who don't meet high standards of practice. And I challenge my friends in the colleges and universities to make your schools of education top-notch and to understand that, if they don't measure up to the highest standards, we will close them. Our eager and idealistic young people should not spend four or five years in a system that doesn't adequately prepare them to teach.

Second, reinvent teacher preparation and professional development. I want to commend those of you who are working toward professional development schools. I encourage that, and I'm committed to them. I also want you to find ways to have good classroom teachers on your college faculties. Wouldn't it be marvelous if every school of education had, as adjunct faculty, some of our national board-certified teachers? I believe you could do that, working together with our superintendents. Find new ways to use staff allocations, at both K-12 schools and colleges, so teachers can have new roles and teacher education majors can benefit from the best role models.

And while I'm talking to school people, I challenge you to find new and creative ways to use personnel and schedules, so that our teachers have time for professional development, planning, collaboration, and reflection during the school day instead of on weekends and late into the night. I refer you to some of our entrepreneurial schools for some models of using time creatively and for the best interests of students.[8]

Third, overhaul teacher recruitment, and put qualified teachers in every classroom. Let me issue a challenge to our new superintendent, Mike Ward, and his staff at the Department of Public Instruction.[9] I hope that one of your goals, in the next year, will be to put in place a system that will let both prospective teachers and school district personnel officers know where the vacancies are and how to apply for the available jobs. I hope you will work with our local superintendents to help them streamline the paperwork they require of applicants and improve their hiring procedures. No young person seeking a job should have to wait months for an acknowledgment to an application or a response to an interview. I encourage the State Board of Education and you, Mr. Superintendent, to continue your push in the area of teacher recruitment. And I urge you teachers in the audience to become teacher recruiters yourselves. I hope you'll seek out your best and brightest students and encourage them to follow your footsteps to a career in teaching.

Fourth, encourage and reward knowledge and skills. It's no secret that I am committed to raising our teachers' salaries to the national average by the year 2000, and it's clear from the vote in November that the public supports me on that. But I don't mean to get there by just doing more of the same. I am looking to all of you for support in making changes in our salary schedule that will raise significantly the beginning teacher's salary but will also hold that beginner accountable when the time comes for her to get tenure. I'm looking for ways to reward teachers who gain new skills that help local school systems meet their goals and that help students learn more, skills like second languages and second areas of licensure in shortage areas. And I want to pay our national board-certified teachers more than we are currently paying them. I hope you will put your minds to work to come up with other ways we can improve our salary plan, as well.

Finally, create schools that are organized for student and teacher success. I know we have many shining examples in this state, schools where teachers and parents have a voice, where time and resources are used to the best possible advantage, and where students are learning more every day. I know, because I've been in schools like that, and I've presented Entrepreneurial Schools Awards to schools like that. But there aren't enough of those schools in North Carolina. Some of our schools are too big and impersonal, and our students are lost in them, they're not safe in them, and the teachers don't communicate with the students or each other well. I want our schools to try "schools within a school" to break down those impersonal mega-schools into student-friendly communities, where every child is known by the principal and the teachers, and every child can be a star at something. I want schools and school systems where the vast majority of the staff in them actually teaches the children, and I want principals who still have their hearts and their hands in the classroom, principals who understand that schools work better when everybody has a say in things and works together.

Now, this isn't going to be easy, folks, and everybody won't like everything we do. But I want the touchstone for everything we do to be what's best for students—not what's easiest, not what's cheapest, not what's politically expeditious, but what's best for the children we teach. I believe we'll find that also will be best for the teaching profession, and best for the parents, and best for our communities.

I believe the conclusions and recommendations of this report speak for themselves.[10] Standards, and accompanying accountability measures, for students and teachers are key to reforming American education. Access to competent teaching must become a new student right. Access to high-quality preparation, induction, and professional development must become a new teacher right. The reform movement of the last decade cannot succeed unless it attends to the improvement of teaching.

Our children cannot wait. They deserve a quality education that cannot wait. They deserve teachers they can rely upon every year in school, and the citizens who support and pay for K-12 education deserve results. Our state's future depends on the strength of efforts to provide better teaching.

This report, *What Matters Most*, tells us how we can make this happen in all our towns and cities, for all our children. And I want and expect North Carolina to lead the nation in implementing these recommendations. I pledge to work as hard as I can, for the next four years, to restore teaching to its rightful place as a highly regarded profession, the one profession that makes all the others possible. If we do that, we will have the kind of schools we want, and we will have the kind of graduates we want. We can do it together.

---

[1] Establishment of the North Carolina Center for the Advancement of Teaching, at Western Carolina University, was authorized under *N.C. Session Laws, 1985*, c. 479, s. 74.

[2] The first teaching fellowships were offered in the mid-1980s by the North Carolina Public School Forum. Poff, *Addresses of Martin, 1985-1989*, 612.

[3] The North Carolina Progress Board was established, and its duties described, under *N.C. Session Laws, 1995*, c. 117, ratified May 29, 1995. William C. Friday, president-emeritus of the University of North Carolina, was a member of the board. Letters of Appointment to Boards and Commissions, Governors Papers, James Baxter Hunt Jr.

[4] See N.C. *Session Laws, 1993, Extra and Regular Sessions, 1994*, c. 740, ratified July 13, 1994.

[5] The $1.8 billion in school bonds was only a down payment on the $6.2 billion a legislative panel determined that the state needed for repairs and renovations to existing schools as well as the construction of new buildings. Better than 70 percent of the votes cast in the November 1996 referendum favored passage of the bond issue. *News and Observer*, October 30, November 1, 6, 1996.

[6] During his 1996 campaign for governor, Hunt declared he would raise teacher salaries to the national average by the year 2000 if reelected. As he stated later in this address, he interpreted his decisive victory at the polls as a popular mandate to accomplish that goal. See also *News and Observer*, December 17, 1996.

[7] Linda Darling-Hammond, of the Teachers College, Columbia University, was executive director of the National Commission on Teaching and America's Future. *What Matters Most: Teaching for America's Future, Report of the National Commission on Teaching and America's Future* (New York, N.Y.: [The Commission], September 1996), v.

[8] Entrepreneurial schools were characterized by "teachers, parents, and students . . . dedicated to 'bold leadership and responsible risk-taking to advance teaching and improve learning.'" The first awards recognizing such schools were announced in 1994. Hunt's Teacher Advisory Committee, consisting of fifteen classroom teachers, which he formed as a conduit between "the state's classrooms and education policymakers in his administration," paid evaluation visits to each school before selecting the winners. Press release, Hunt Praises Buncombe County School for Taking Risks to Improve Education, Raleigh, September 2, 1994, Governors Papers, James Baxter Hunt Jr.

[9] Mike Ward (1953-   ), born in Louisburg; B.S., 1977, M.Ed., 1981, Ed.D., 1993, N.C. State University. Former school principal, superintendent; vice-chairman, N.C. Education Standards and Accountability Commission, from 1993; was elected state superintendent of public instruction, 1996; executive director, N.C. Standards Board for Public School Administration; author. *North Carolina Manual, 1997-1998*, 209-210.

[10] *What Matters Most: Teaching for America's Future, Report of the National Commission on Teaching and America's Future* was cited in footnote 7, above.

OMITTED SPEECHES AND STATEMENTS, 1993-1997

[Speeches and official papers not reprinted in this volume are catalogued, by title, below. Press releases consisting largely of the governor's direct quotations also have been included. An asterisk denotes documents either mentioned or excerpted in annotations accompanying Hunt's published remarks. A dagger identifies a speaking engagement indicated on the governor's weekly agenda for which no prepared address was provided. Existing copies of Governor Hunt's speeches and other public papers are housed at the Division of Archives and History, North Carolina Department of Cultural Resources, Raleigh.]

1993

January 13, GKN-Person County Announcement, Roxboro

January 15, Statement on Correction Secretary [Franklin Freeman], Raleigh*

January 15, Johnson C. Smith University "Campaign for the 90's" Newsletter, Raleigh

January 18, Draft Remarks, Liberty Bell Ringing, Martin Luther King Jr. Commemoration, Raleigh

January 28, Groundbreaking, University of North Carolina School of Social Work, Chapel Hill

January 28, Press Release: Hunt Cabinet Agrees Not to Lobby, Issues Ethics Order, Raleigh

February 4, Swearing-in of Chief Judge Gerald Arnold [Court of Appeals], Raleigh

February 5, Swearing-in of SBI Director Mike Coman, Raleigh

February 8, Cities in Schools Luncheon, Introduction of Bill Milliken, Research Triangle Park

February 9, Sir Walter Cabinet, Raleigh

February 9, North Carolina AFL-CIO Banquet, Raleigh†

February 10, Welcome, Emerging Issues Forum, Raleigh†

February 11, North Carolina Business Committee for Education, Raleigh*

February 17, Governor's Task Force on School Violence, Raleigh

February 24, Principals' Executive Program, Chapel Hill

February 25, Prison Bond Plan, Raleigh*

February 25, Roast of Jonathan Howes, Chapel Hill

February 26, Workshop, North Carolina Association of Educators, Raleigh

March 1, Swearing-in of Highway Patrol Commander Robert Barefoot and Executive Officer Cecil Wilkins, Raleigh

March 1, Partners in Quality, Charlotte

March 3, Democratic Party Gala, Raleigh†

March 4, Partners in Quality, Charlotte [not delivered]

March 4, Education Summit, Charlotte [not delivered]

March 4, Task Force on School Violence [notes], Charlotte

March 9, State Employees of North Carolina Annual Membership Luncheon, Raleight

March 11, State Boards of Education, Raleight

March 15, Press Conference, Pepsi-Cola Announcement, Winston-Salem

March 18, Next Century Schools, Durham

March 22, Jack Tate Roast, Charlotte

March 24, Distinguished Women's Awards Banquet, Raleigh

March 25, Presents "County Government Week" Proclamation, North Carolina Association of County Commissioners Board of Directors, Raleight

March 31, WTVD Neighborhood Heroes/Jefferson Awards Program, Durham

March 31, North Carolina Museum of Life and Science, Durham [delivered April 1]

April 1, Frank Porter Graham Child Development Center, Chapel Hill*

April 1, North Carolina League of Municipalities [draft], Raleigh*

April 2, Appreciation Dinner Honoring Terry Sanford, Laurinburgt

April 5, Global TransPark Conference [interim text], Mt. Olive

April 8, Announcement on Eighth-Grade Math Scores, Press Conference with Superintendent Etheridge, Raleigh

April 8, Glaxo-Wake County Infant and Maternal Clinic Dedication, Zebulon*

April 12, Announcement of Federal Aviation Administration Grant to Kenan Institute, Chapel Hill*

April 13, Press Conference, Tax Cut on Unemployment Insurance, Raleigh

April 15, Kenan-Flagler Business School Board of Visitors, Chapel Hill

April 20, Testimony before Legislature, Joint Appropriations Committee [Smart Start], Raleigh*

April 21, Awards Presentation, Governor's Business Council on the Arts and Humanities, Raleigh

April 22, Governor's Awards for Excellence in Waste Management, Raleigh

April 22, Wake County Communities in Schools, Garner

April 26, Swearing-in of Major General Gerald Alton Rudisill Jr. as Adjutant General, Raleigh

April 28, Charge to Entrepreneurial Development Board, Raleigh*
April 28, "The Naked Soul": Polish Paintings from the National
    Museum, Raleigh
April 29, Dedication, Alice Poe Center for Health Education, Raleigh
April 29, Delta Sigma Theta Sorority, Raleigh*
April 29, State Employees Association of North Carolina Legislative
    Day, Raleigh
May 5, Charge to Small Business Council, Raleigh
May 5, Take Pride in America Award Winners, Raleigh*
May 6, Economic Development Board, Raleigh*
May 6, National Association of Retired Federal Employees State
    Convention, Raleigh
May 7, Columbus County Committee of 100, Whiteville
May 7, Selma Middle School Dedication, Selma
May 10, North Carolina Peace Officers' Memorial Day, Raleigh
May 11, Children's Home Society, Raleigh*
May 11, "Change by Leake" Remarks, Raleigh
May 12, North Carolina Alliance for Public Education, Raleigh*
May 18, 20-Year Anniversary, Sickle-Cell Syndrome Program,
    Raleigh
May 19, National Health and Fitness Day One-Mile Walk, Raleight
May 21, Centennial, Western North Carolina Conference, AME
    Church, Raleigh*
May 24, Press Release: Hunt Urges House to Support Veto
    Referendum, Raleigh
May 24, Small Business Advisory Council, Raleigh
May 26, Themes for Barbara Buchanan Remarks, Raleigh
May 27, X2000 High-Speed Train Demonstration, Raleigh
May 28, Boy Scout Dinner Honoring Smedes York, Raleigh
    [delivered May 27]
June 4, Dedication, Revlon Plant Expansion, Oxford
June 7, Edison Electric Institute, Charlotte
June 9, Jacob Gunnells Bone Marrow Donor Drive, Raleigh
June 11, Testimony before Defense Base Closure and Realignment
    Commission [interim text], Norfolk, Va.
June 14, Apex Bioscience Plant Dedication, Durham
June 15, Economic Development Briefings, Raleigh*
June 15, Discover Wilson, Wilson
June 16, Economic Development Briefing for Legislators and
    Cabinet Members, Raleight
June 17, Economic Development Briefing for the Media, Raleight
June 22, Lee Wing Retirement, Raleigh

June 28, Public School Leadership Meeting, Raleigh
June 29, NFL Ticket Campaign Kickoff, Raleigh
June 29, North Carolina Board of Science and Technology, Raleigh
June 30, Herbert F. Gaye Luncheon, Raleigh†
June 30, Ministers at the Mansion, Raleigh*
July 7, Press Conference on Stricter Drunk Driving Law, Raleigh
July 8, Community College Board of Trustees [notes], Raleigh
July 8, Environmental Management Commission [notes], Raleigh*
July 9, Governor's Luncheon for Children, Charlotte
July 12, Commission on Workforce Preparedness, Raleigh*
July 13, North Carolina Rural Economic Development Council,
     Raleigh [delivered July 14]*
July 19, State Government Summer Intern Reception, Raleigh
July 20, North Carolina Air Cargo Authority Annual Meeting,
     Chapel Hill
July 20, *BusinessWeek* Reception, Raleigh
July 28, Opening of 104th Wilson Tobacco Market, Wilson†
July 28, Smart Start Briefing for County Government Leaders,
     Raleigh*
July 28, Legislative Overview, Raleigh
July 29, Smart Start Conference, Durham
August 9, North Carolina Sheriffs Association [emended text],
     Wilmington*
August 9, North Carolina Sheriffs Association [clear text],
     Wilmington*
August 13, Broadband Technologies Opening, Research Triangle
     Park
August 14, BASS Masters Classic, Birmingham, Alabama
August 18, Roanoke Island Historical Society, Manteo
August 18, Presentation of North Carolina Award to Andy Griffith,
     Manteo
August 19, Reception Honoring Full-Time National Guard
     Employees, Raleigh†
August 19, Schlegel Plant Groundbreaking, Reidsville*
August 23, Siecor Plant Groundbreaking, Winston-Salem
August 24, School Violence Prevention Forum, Charlotte [delivered
     August 26]*
August 25, School Violence Forum, Greenville*
August 26, Governor's Business Committee for Education,
     Asheville†
August 31, Central Carolina Community College Center of
     Excellence, Lillington

August 31, Wake County School Violence Forum [notes], Raleigh*

August 31, Ed Renfrow Swearing-in [as state controller], Raleigh

September 1, Press Conference, Education Standards in Public Schools, Charlotte†

September 1, Economic Development Financing, North Carolina Economic Developers Association, Winston-Salem*

September 2, Hockmeyer Equipment Corp. Ribbon-Cutting, Elizabeth City

September 2, Albemarle Soil and Water Conservation District [notes], Elizabeth City

September 2, Elizabeth City Chamber of Commerce, Elizabeth City*

September 3, North Carolina Education Standards and Accountability Commission, Raleigh, Greensboro, Wilmington [as delivered]*

September 3, North Carolina Education Standards and Accountability Commission, Raleigh, Greensboro, Wilmington*

September 7, Louisiana Pacific OSB Plant Announcement, Person County

September 9, North Carolina Democratic Women, Raleigh

September 13, North Carolina Day Care Association Leadership Conference, Chapel Hill*

September 13, Presentation of World Citizen Award to Dr. Leroy T. Walker, Charlotte

September 13, Smart Start Luncheon, Winston-Salem [delivered September 14]*

September 14, Press Conference, Governor's Open Golf Tournament, Winston-Salem

September 14, Governor's Awards for Excellence [state employees], Raleigh

September 15, Lenoir County Committee of 100, Kinston*

September 16, Governor's Award for Outstanding Volunteer Service, Greenville*

September 17, Merck Manufacturing Co. Tenth Anniversary, Wilson

September 22, Standards and Accountability Commission, Raleigh†

September 22, Mental Health Association/Business and Industry Symposium, Raleigh*

September 23, Breakfast Remarks to Senegalese Delegation, Raleigh

September 23, Sonora Desert Exhibit Opening, North Carolina Zoological Park, Asheboro

September 23, North Carolina Partnership for Children Board, Raleigh*

September 24, AFL-CIO Convention, Fayetteville [delivered September 22]*

September/October [no date], North Carolina Agenda for Action: A Progress Report, Raleigh

October 5, Closing Remarks, Southeast United States-Japan Conference, Osaka

October 10, Tar Heel Farm Credit Office Building Dedication, Raleigh†

[No date], University of North Carolina Essay, Raleigh [printed in *Chapel Hill Newspaper*, October 10]

October 13, Bravery and Heroism Awards Presentation, Raleigh

October 14, Coastal Futures Committee, Raleigh*

October 14, North Carolina Business Committee for Education, Raleigh*

October 15, North Carolina State Fair Opening, Raleigh†

October 16, High Point Furniture Market, High Point*

October 18, Governor's Awards for Outstanding Volunteer Service, Raleigh*

October 19, Press Conference, Crime Statement, Charlotte*

October 19, Chamber of Commerce, Charlotte†

October 20, State Employees Combined Campaign, Raleigh

October 20, Groundbreaking, Bristol Compressors, Sparta*

October 21, Christmas Stamp Dedication, Raleigh

October 21, Press Briefing on National Board for Professional Teaching Standards, Raleigh

October 21, Inauguration of President Nan Keohane [clear text], Duke University, Durham [scheduled for October 23]

October 21, Inauguration of President Nan Keohane, Duke University [emended text], Durham [delivered October 23]

October 22, Installation of Chancellor Julius Chambers, N.C. Central University, Durham

October 24, National Association of Extension 4-H Agents, Winston-Salem

October 25, Acceptance, National Alliance of Business Award, Washington, D.C.*

October 25, Total Quality Education Kickoff, Raleigh*

October 26, *Fortune* Magazine Announcement, Raleigh

October 26, Press Release: Statement on Death of Roy Park, Raleigh

October 27, Smart Start Luncheon, [no location]

October 29, Teacher Advisory Committee, Raleigh*

October 29, Dedication, Pitt County Memorial Hospital, Greenville*

October 29, NFL Parade, Charlotte

November 5, Press Release: London Gateway Statement, Raleigh
November 6, Anti-Crime Rally [notes], Durham
November 6, Presentation, James B. Hunt Young Citizen Awards, Winston-Salem
November 7, Opening Remarks, Korea-Southeast U.S. Conference, Research Triangle Park†
November 10, N.C. Medical Care Commission, Raleigh
November 12, Seymour Johnson Air Force Base, Goldsboro
November 12, Duke Conference, North Carolina SCOPE [Student Conference on Policies in Education], Durham*
November 12, North Carolina Awards, Raleigh
November 15, Day Care Teacher Graduation, Wilmington
November 15, Cape Fear River Assembly, Wilmington*
November 16, Acceptance, Elon Homes for Children Award, Elon College
November 16, Nippon Paint Press Conference, Charlotte
November 17, Awards for Infant Mortality Reduction, Raleigh*
November 18, Opening, VEDCO Cogeneration Plant, Fayetteville
November 18, Student Body Presidents, Raleigh*
November 19, Habitat for Humanity Lending Program, Raleigh
November 19, North Carolina Governor's Cup Billfish Conservation Awards, Raleigh
November 23, State Employees Combined Campaign, Raleigh
November 22, American Institute of Banking, Raleigh [delivered November 24]*
November 30, Economic Development Briefing for International Business Reporters, Raleigh†
December 1, World AIDS Day, Raleigh
December 2, Sheriff John Baker Re-election Kickoff, Raleigh
December 8, Sprint/Mid-Atlantic Telecom Headquarters Ribbon-Cutting, Wake Forest
December 8, Press Release: Statement on Low-Level Waste, Raleigh
December 9, North Carolina Agribusiness Council, Raleigh
December 9, Lighting of Capitol Christmas Tree, Raleigh
December 13, High Point Chamber of Commerce, High Point*
December 15, Merisel Inc. Building Dedication, Cary†
December 17, Announcement of Health Planning Commission Executive Director [Dr. Jim Jones], Raleigh
December 17, Announcement of Health Planning Commission Executive Director [extended version; Dr. Jim Jones], Raleigh
December 20, Click It or Ticket News Conference, Introduction of U.S. Transportation Secretary Federico Pena, Raleigh*

1994

January 3, Fiftieth Anniversary, North Carolina Association of Soil and Water Conservation Districts [clear text], Raleigh

January 3, Fiftieth Anniversary, North Carolina Association of Soil and Water Conservation Districts [emended text], Raleigh

January 4, Talking Points on Crime: Comments to State Senators, Raleigh*

January 5, Indian-American Community of the Triangle, Raleigh

January 5, Bridges II Groundbreaking, Fayetteville

January 5, Rural Teleconference [North Carolina Information Highway], Wilmington

January 6, North Carolina DARE [Drug Abuse Resistance Education] Officers' Association Fifth Annual Conference, Raleigh*

January 7, North Carolina Supreme Court 175th Anniversary, Raleigh†

January 10, Wayne County Plant Opening [Pate-Dawson Co.], Goldsboro

January 10, Global TransPark Foundation Event [kickoff, Wayne County Global TransPark campaign], Goldsboro

January 13, Greensboro Kiwanis Club, Greensboro*

January 13, Piedmont Japanese Business Association, Greensboro

January 14, Substance Abuse Center Groundbreaking [clear text], Greensboro [event scheduled for January 13]*

January 14, Substance Abuse Center Groundbreaking [emended text], Greensboro [delivered January 13]*

January 14, Martin Luther King Jr. Day, Raleigh

January 18, Governor's Teleconference on Crime [draft script], Raleigh*

January 20, North Carolina Commission on National and Community Service, Raleigh [delivered January 21]

January 20, Introduction of John H. Bryan, Raleigh

January 21, African American Ministers, Raleigh*

January 21, African American Ministers [emended text], Raleigh*

January 21, African American Ministers [expanded text], Raleigh*

January 22, Briefing on Special Legislative Session for Legislators and Law Enforcement, Greensboro†

January 22, North Carolina Democratic Party Executive Committee, Greensboro†

January 24, Freightliner Parts Plant Announcement, Gastonia

January 25, Joint Rotary Clubs [notes], Charlotte*

January 25, Charlotte-Area Legislators [notes], Charlotte*
January 25, Teacher Advisory Committee, Charlotte*
January 26, North Carolina Association of Educators Summit on
    School Violence, Raleigh*
January 27, State Education Commission-North Carolina Education
    Governing Boards, Chapel Hill*
January 27, Governor's Educators' Forum on Crime [draft script],
    Raleigh*
January 27, North Carolina Press Association, Chapel Hill*
January 30, National Governors' Association Panel on Education
    Reform and School-to-Work Transition, Washington, D.C.†
February 2, Presentation, Order of the Long Leaf Pine to Dale
    Earnhardt and Richard Childress Racing, Raleigh
February 3, State Board, National Board for Professional Teaching
    Standards, Raleigh†
February 4, Ribbon-Cutting, Burke County Sheriff's Office and
    Detention Center, Morganton*
February 4, Juvenile Crime-SOS Program, Liberty*
February 6, Kress Collection Exhibit Opening, North Carolina
    Museum of Art, Raleigh
February 8, Citizens' Forum, North Carolina Education Standards
    and Accountability Commission, Morrisville*
February 8, North Carolina Leadership Council Forum on Crime,
    Research Triangle Park [delivered February 9]*
February 10, Opening Message, Emerging Issues Forum, Raleigh
February 14, Law Enforcement-Victims' Advocates Press
    Conference, Raleigh*
February 15, Briefing for Chamber of Commerce Representatives,
    Raleigh*
February 15, NandoLand Computer Announcement, Raleigh
February 15, Local Government Partnership Council, Raleigh
February 15, Citizens' Forum, North Carolina Education Standards
    and Accountability Commission, Wilmington*
February 16, Crime Prevention Briefing, Raleigh*
February 16, North Carolina Democratic Chairs Lobbying Day,
    Raleigh*
February 17, Crime Victims Briefing [notes], Raleigh*
February 22, SOS [Support Our Students] Program [notes], Raleigh*
February 24, SAVE [Students Against Violence Everywhere]
    Program News Conference [short text; designated file copy],
    Raleigh

February 24, SAVE [Students Against Violence Everywhere]
Program News Conference [long text], Raleigh
February 24, Association of Furniture Manufacturers, Raleigh
February 24, North Carolina Black History Month, Raleigh†
February 25, Healthy Start Program, Raleigh*
February 28, Press Conference on Crime Session, Raleigh†
March 3, Special Session Update, Raleigh
March 8, Statement on Prison Sentencing, Raleigh*
March 15, Press Release: Letter to State Representatives on Pace of
Special Legislative Session on Crime, Raleigh
March 16, North Carolina Citizens for Business and Industry,
Introduction of Erskine Bowles, Raleigh
March 17, YMCA North Carolina Youth Legislature, Raleigh
March 17, Mallinckrodt Veterinary Co. Announcement, Raleigh
March 18, MCNC Award Forum, Research Triangle Park
March 18, North Carolina Association of Educators Convention,
Winston-Salem
March 18, North Carolina Conference of Superior Court Judges,
Raleigh*
March 22, Local Government Partnership Council, Raleigh†
March 23, Distinguished Women of North Carolina Awards, Raleigh
March 25, Testimony before Senate Subcommittee on Education,
Arts, and Humanities [National Board for Professional Teaching
Standards], Washington, D.C.†
March 25, National Science Foundation Site Visit Team [North
Carolina Science and Mathematics Alliance], Raleigh
March 25, North Carolina Indian Unity Conference, Fayetteville†
April 6, Crime Forum, Winston-Salem [not delivered]
April 7, Crime Forum [emended text], Winston-Salem
April 7, Forsyth County Democratic Party, Winston-Salem
April 8, Tribute to William Craig Campbell, Raleigh
April 11, Comprehensive Strategic Economic Development Plan,
Raleigh
April 11, Business and Children, Chapel Hill [delivered April 12]*
April 12, SCOPE [Student Conference on Policies in Education]
Report, Raleigh
April 12, Legislative Reception Honoring New North Carolina
Museum of History, Raleigh
April 13, Speech to Business and Community Leaders, Havelock
[delivered April 14]
April 14, Question and Answer Session with Youth Leadership,
Havelock

April 14, Ceremony Honoring Governor Hunt, United States Naval Aviation Depot, Cherry Point

April 14, Crime Forum, Havelock

April 14, Crime Forum, [emended text], Havelock*

April 15, BellSouth Leadership Conference on Workforce Preparedness, Raleigh*

April 15, Mountain Air Cargo Announcement, North Carolina Global TransPark, Raleigh*

April 18, Marcellus Waddill Excellence in Teaching Award, Wake Forest University, Winston-Salem

April 18, Dedication of U.S. 220 in Honor of Tom Burton, Rockingham County

April 20, Executive Order on Historically Black Colleges and Universities, Raleigh

April 21, Citizens Forum on Crime [notes], Asheville*

April 21, Citizens Forum on Crime [notes], Sylva*

April 25, Groundbreaking, Prison Work Farm, Yanceyville*

April 25, Wolverine Plant Announcement, Roxboro

April 27, McLeod Addictive Disease Center, Inc., Charlotte

April 27, Crime Forum [notes], Charlotte*

April 27, Wilson County Law Enforcement Association [notes], Wilson [delivered April 29]*

April 28, Youth Summit, Raleigh

April 29, Foster-Forbes Recycling Day, Wilson*

April 29, Environ Products Opening, Wilson

April 29, Ribbon-Cutting, Leslie-Locke, Pender County

May 2, Proclaims May as "Older Americans Month," Raleigh†

May 3, Governor's Business Council on Arts and Humanities, Raleigh

May 4, ASMO Ribbon-Cutting, Statesville

May 9, Fiftieth Anniversary, North Carolina District Council of the Assemblies of God, Winston-Salem

May 13, Governor's Advocacy Council for Persons with Disabilities, Durham

May 13, National Alliance of Business, Chapel Hill

May 13, National Alliance of Business [emended text], Chapel Hill

May 13, National Alliance of Business [edited transcript], Chapel Hill

May 17, North Carolina Local Government Partnership Council, Raleigh*

May 17, Foundation Summit [Smart Start], Raleigh*

May 18, Governor's Council on Physical Fitness Annual Fun Walk, Raleigh†
May 18, Press Announcement on International Gateways, Charlotte*
May 18, Commission for a Competitive North Carolina, Introduction of Governor William F. Winter, Charlotte
May 19, Legislators Meeting, Global TransPark Commission, Kinston
May 20, North Carolina Bankers Association [clear text], Pinehurst
May 20, North Carolina Bankers Association [emended text], Pinehurst*
May 20, Presentation of Boy Scouts Distinguished Citizenship Award to Jim Goodmon, Raleigh [delivered May 25]
May 23, Domestic Violence Conference, Raleigh
May 23, Planned Parenthood Reception, Raleigh
May 25, Press Briefing, Legislative Short Session [notes], Raleigh*
May 25, Reaction to Lawsuit by Low-Wealth Schools, Raleigh
May 25, Democratic Gala, Raleigh
May 25, Tribute to Jim Goodmon, Research Triangle Park
May 26, Consolidated Diesel Co. Luncheon, Rocky Mount
May 26, American Airlines Inaugural Flight to London, Raleigh-Durham International Airport, Wake County
May 27, International Council, Children's Museum About the World, London, England
June 1, Unisphere International Ventures Forum Joint Ventures Conference, Research Triangle Park
June 1, Economic Development Forum, Raleigh
June 2, Eastern North Carolina Chamber Legislative Day, Raleigh
June 3, *Fortune* Magazine-Northwestern Mutual Life Luncheon, Raleigh
June 7, Receives 1994 Distinguished Service Award from North Carolina Association of Directors of Developmental Disability Centers, Raleigh†
June 8, North Carolina Association of County Commissioners, Raleigh†
June 9, State Employees Association of North Carolina Legislative Day Rally, Raleigh
June 9, Receives 1994 Political Action Award from North Carolina Victim Assistance Network, Raleigh
June 9, Youth Leadership Speech, North Carolina Leadership Seminar East, Raleigh [delivered June 10]
June 10, JobReady Conference, Washington, N.C.

June 11, Welcome, North Carolina State Democratic Party
    Convention, Raleigh
June 13, International Radiology Teleconference, Raleigh
June 13, Presentation of Governor's Awards for Bravery and
    Heroism, Raleigh
June 13, Durham Service Corps "Summer of Safety" Program
    Kickoff, Raleigh
June 13, Foster Care Youth Graduation, Raleigh
June 15, Proclamation Commemorating Smokey Bear Day, Raleigh
June 15, Press Release: Statement on House Budget, Raleigh
June 21, Education Resource Center Groundbreaking, Shaw
    University, Raleigh
June 22, Presentation of Cystic Fibrosis Public Service Award to
    Rufus Edmisten, Raleigh
June 23, Indian Cultural Center Lease Signing [notes], Raleigh
June 23, Indian Cultural Center [notes], Raleigh
June 25, Visit by U.S. Attorney General Janet Reno, Raleigh
    [delivered June 27]
June 27, North Carolina Teachers of the Year Conference, Raleigh
June 29, Winston-Salem Youth Meeting [920 Youth Career Club],
    Raleigh
June 29, Retirement Reception Honoring State Representative
    Vernon James, Raleigh
June 29, U.S. Senior Open Business and Industry Dinner, Pinehurst
July 6, Press Conference, Tar Heel Challenge National Guard
    Dropout Prevention Program, Raleigh
July 11, Teachers' Town Meeting, Raleigh†
July 12, Dedication, Alcatel Fiber Optic Manufacturing Facility,
    Claremont
July 12, Project Turnaround, Catawba Middle School, Catawba
    County
July 16, Press Release: Statement on 1994-1995 Budget Passed by
    General Assembly, Raleigh*
July 21, Association of Clerks of Superior Court of North Carolina,
    Asheville
July 21, Quaker Oats Announcement, Asheville
July 25, Health Care Information and Communications Alliance,
    Raleigh
July 25, State Government Summer Intern Reception, Raleigh
July 26, ASMO of North Carolina Announcement, Greenville
July 26, Jim Graham Thirtieth Anniversary, Raleigh
July 27, Tobacco Market Opening, Smithfield†

July 27, Welcome International Students, Summer Institute in American Business, Communications, and Culture [Fuqua School of Business, Duke University], Raleigh

July 27, "Kids Klassic" Fishing Tournament Kickoff, 25th Annual Bass Masters Fishing Competition, Greensboro†

August [no day], State Employees of Association of North Carolina Newsletter Column, Raleigh

August 9, Wake County Bar Association, Raleigh

August 9, Legislative Candidate Reception [Andy Penry, Sen. Linda Gunter, Rep. Jane Moseley], Cary

August 10, Governor's Hurricane Preparedness Conference, Greenville

August 10, Odell Williamson Auditorium Dedication, Brunswick Community College, Supply

August 13, Democratic Party Executive Committee, Raleigh

August 15, North Carolina Business Committee for Education [notes], Asheville

August 16, Jackson County Justice and Administration Center Grand Opening, Sylva

August 16, Mountain Health Care Alliance, Franklin

August 19, Appalachian State University Citizens' Forum on Education [notes], Boone

August 24, Lord Corporation Announcement, Raleigh

August 24, Women's Equality Day, North Carolina Council for Women, Raleigh

August 25, Receives First "Goodness Grows in North Carolina" Visa Credit Card from Agricultural Commissioner Jim Graham, Raleigh†

August 26, North Carolina Association of County Commissioners, Asheville

August 26, Craggy Correctional Center Tour, Asheville

August 26, Swearing-in of Sydnor Thompson, North Carolina Court of Appeals, Charlotte

August 26, Groundbreaking, Interstate 77 Widening Project, Charlotte

August 31, Groundbreaking, Cisco Systems, Inc., Research Triangle Park

September 1, State Board of Education, Raleigh

September 6, Springmoor Retirement Community Tenth Anniversary, Raleigh

September 7, Healthy Mothers, Healthy Babies Coalition of Wake County Networking Fair, Raleigh*

September 7, Storm Drain Stenciling Project, Wilmington

September 8, Corning/BioPro Announcement, Research Triangle Park

September 8, Neuse Correctional Institution Dedication, Goldsboro*

September 9, Rally for Phil Baddour, Goldsboro [delivered September 8]

September 12, Presentation, Governor's Awards for Excellence [state employees], Raleigh

September 12, "Education: Everybody's Business," N.C. Citizens for Business and Industry, Research Triangle Park*

September 13, Governor's Advisory Committee on Agriculture, Forestry, and Seafood Industries, Raleigh

September 13, Fund Raiser, Congressional Candidate Richard Moore, Smithfield

September 14, Support Our Students Announcement, Charlotte*

September 14, Receives Master Builder Award from North Carolina Housing Finance Agency, Raleigh

September 14, Fund Raiser, State Senator Fountain Odom, Charlotte

September 15, New Garden Place Apartments, Greensboro

September 15, Tech Prep Conference, Greensboro

September 15, William R. Kenan Jr. Institute for Engineering, Technology, and Science, Raleigh

September 16, Entrepreneurial Schools Awards, Raleigh

September 18, Wilson Community Health Center [notes], Wilson

September 18, "Alternatives" Open House [notes], Wilson

September 19, Groundbreaking, Ericsson, Inc., Research Triangle Park

September 19, Ketner Awards, Raleigh

September 20, Family Resource Center Grant Announcement, Goldsboro*

September 20, Swearing-in of Linda Hayes, Governor's Crime Commission Chairwoman, Raleigh

September 21, Democratic Party Rally, Introduction of Vice-President Al Gore [short text], Raleigh [delivered September 20]*

September 21, Ribbon-Cutting, MCI Network Management and Customer Service Center, Cary

September 21, Smart Start Announcement, Raleigh*

September 21, Swearing-in of Bill Goldston as Chairman, North Carolina Ports Authority, Raleigh

September 21, Governor's Awards for Excellence in Waste Reduction, Raleigh

September 21, Wake County Young Democrats, Raleigh

September 22, Welfare Reform Task Force, Raleigh

September 22, AFL-CIO Reception, Raleigh

September 23, Meredith College Second Century Challenge Campaign, Raleigh

September 29, University of Western Cape, Cape Town, South Africa*

September 29, South African Olympic Committee, Cape Town, South Africa†

October 4, Keynote Address, "Made in USA" Opening, Johannesburg, South Africa†

October 5, Address to South African Broadcasters, Johannesburg, South Africa†

October 8, Sesquicentennial Celebration, Monroe†

October 8, Vance-Aycock Dinner, Introduction of Maggie Lauterer, Asheville

October 10, Rally for Congressman Martin Lancaster, Goldsboro

October 11, Custom Molders, Inc., Announcement [Vance County], Raleigh

October 11, David Price Luncheon, Raleigh

October 11, Fundraiser, Alamance County Sheriff Richard Fry, Burlington†

October 11, "Investing in Excellence" Capital Campaign Celebration, Elon College

October 12, Leadership North Carolina Press Conference, Raleigh

October 12, AT&T PersonaLink Customer Care Center Ribbon-Cutting, Morrisville

October 12, Head Start Center Ribbon-Cutting, Southern Pines

October 13, North Carolina Awards, Raleigh

October 13, Reception for State Supreme Court Candidate Jim Fuller, Greensboro [delivered October 14]

October 14, Town Meeting, Grimsley High School, Greensboro

October 14, Sandy Sands Reception, Winston-Salem

October 17, Piedmont Triad Visitors Center Dedication, Pelham

October 18, Reception for Larry Townsend, Raleigh†

October 18, Reception for State Court of Appeals Candidate Judge Sydnor Thompson, Raleigh

October 18, Reception for Colon Willoughby [notes], Raleigh [delivered October 19]

October 24, Novopharm Groundbreaking, Wilson

October 27, Sea-Land Announcement, Charlotte

November 1, "State of the Child" Conference, Raleigh*

November 2, SOS [Support Our Students] Talking Points, Ferndale Middle School, High Point*

November 4, IMPACT-West Boot Camp Dedication [clear text], Morganton

November 4, Child Health Advocate Award, Greensboro*

November 4, Western Economic Development Commission [clear text], Asheville

November 4, Western Economic Development Commission [emended text], Asheville

November 4, HandMade in America, Asheville

November 9, Governor's Awards for Outstanding Volunteer Service, Morganton

November 9, North Carolina Child Care Corps, Greensboro*

November 10, North Carolina Science Teachers Association, Raleigh

November 12, James B. Hunt Young Citizen Awards, Wake Forest University, Winston-Salem

November 18, North Carolina Judicial Conference [clear text], Raleigh

November 21, Founders Day Convocation, Warren Wilson College, Asheville

November 21, Reception Honoring Bill Lee, Charlotte†

November 22, Commission on Substance Abuse Treatment and Prevention, Raleigh*

November 22, Governor's Awards for Outstanding Volunteer Service, Sanford

December 2, "Seeing Eye to Eye" Conference, Raleigh

December 2, Dedication, Terry Sanford Public Policy Institute, Duke University, Durham

December 5, Farm Bureau Federation, Winston-Salem†

December 7, North Carolina White House Conference on Aging, Research Triangle Park

December 8, Groundbreaking, Museum of Natural Sciences, Raleigh

December 9, "Education—Everybody's Business" Coalition, Greensboro*

December 12, Press Conference, Chief Justice Announcement [Appointment of Burley B. Mitchell Jr.], Raleigh

December 20, Howard Benton Dinner, Benson [delivered December 21]

December 21, Continental General Tire Announcement, Charlotte

1995

January 3, Swearing-in of Burley B. Mitchell Jr. as Chief Justice, Raleigh

January 9, North Carolina Business Roundtable, Charlotte*

January 9, North Carolina Soil and Water Conservation Districts, Raleigh

January 11, Tim Valentine Reception, Raleigh

January 12, North Carolina Education Commission, Research Triangle Park*

January 12, North Carolina Standards and Accountability Conference, Research Triangle Park

January 13, Martin Luther King Jr. Holiday Service, Raleigh

January 13, Press Release: Gov. Hunt Lays Out Education Goals for '95, Raleigh

January 17, Governor's Awards for Outstanding Volunteer Service, Williamston

January 19, Professional Teaching Standards Commission, Raleigh

January 19, John Locke Foundation, Raleigh*

January 19, Laurinburg-Scotland County Area Chamber of Commerce, Laurinburg*

January 23, North Carolina Business Roundtable, Research Triangle Park*

January 24, Governor's Programs of Excellence in Education, Research Triangle Park

January 26, North Carolina Press Association, Chapel Hill*

January 29, Plenary Session, Governors' Campaign for Children, National Governors' Association, Washington, D.C.*

January 31, Presents Electronic Benefits Transfer Resolution [pilot program for welfare benefit recipients], Southern Governors' Association, Washington, D.C.†

February 1, Charlotte Convention Center Opening, Raleigh [Hunt appears via Information Highway]

February 1, University of North Carolina Center for Public Television Fortieth Anniversary, Raleigh

February 2, North Carolina Citizens for Business and Industry Legislative Forum, Raleigh*

February 6, Governor's Summit on Travel and Tourism, Raleigh

February 7, Sir Walter Cabinet, Raleigh*

February 7, Secretaries of State Annual Conference, Greensboro

February 7, North Carolina Health Care Facilities Association Annual Convention, Greensboro

February 8, Announcement of William C. Friday Fellowships for
Human Relations, Blumenthal Press Conference, Raleigh
February 10, Founders' Day, Wingate College, Wingate
February 10, David Price Talking Points, Raleigh
February 11, North Carolina Democratic Party Executive
Committee, Raleigh*
February 13, Press Conference, Budget Statement, Raleigh
February 20, Leadership Conference, Carolinas Association of
Chamber of Commerce Executives [clear text], Charlotte
February 22, *Fortune* Magazine Luncheon, Raleigh
February 23, Leadership North Carolina, Raleigh*
February 23, YMCA Youth Legislature, Raleigh
February 27, Efson, Inc., Plant Opening, Wilmington
February 27, North Carolina Business Roundtable, Wilmington*
February 29, Robeson County Enterprise Community Grant
Announcements, Lumberton [delivered February 28]*
March 3, Smart Start Executive Directors' Reception, Raleigh
March 6, North Carolina Business Roundtable, Greenville*
March 6, Governor's Advisory Committee on Agriculture, Forestry,
and the Seafood Industry, Kinston
March 10, National Guard Visit, Raleigh
March 15, March of Dimes-CEO Luncheon, Raleigh
March 15, Cleveland County Chamber of Commerce, Raleigh*
March 16, James B. Hunt Literacy Awards Reception, North Carolina
Reading Association, Raleigh
March 16, Banquet Honoring Bill Bell, Durham†
March 17, N.C. Equity, Raleigh
March 18, Tribute to Speaker Dan Blue, Raleigh
March 20, Wilkes County DOT Event, Wilkesboro
March 20, North Carolina Business Roundtable, Hickory*
March 21, North Carolina Restaurant Association, 1995 Carolinas
Foodservice Expo Ribbon-Cutting [clear text], Charlotte
March 21, North Carolina Restaurant Association, 1995 Carolinas
Foodservice Expo Ribbon-Cutting [emended text], Charlotte
March 22, North Carolina Sports Development Commission, Raleigh
March 22, Senior Tar Heel Legislature, Raleigh*
March 23, Commission for a Competitive North Carolina, Raleigh
March 23, Elaine Marshall Rally, Lillington
March 28, Smart Start Meeting, Raleigh*
March 28, Distinguished Women of North Carolina Awards,
Research Triangle Park

March 29, Introduction of John Medlin, North Carolina Citizens for Business and Industry, Raleigh

March 29, Smart Start Business Leaders' Reception, Raleigh [delivered March 30]

March 30, Business Leader Luncheon, Welcome Carolina Panthers Football Coach Dom Capers, Raleigh

March 31, Grand Opening, Welcome Center, Marine Corps Air Station at Cherry Point, Havelock†

March 31, Allies in Defense of Cherry Point, Havelock†

April 3, North Carolina Museum of Art Amphitheater Groundbreaking, Raleigh

April 4, Swearing-in of Hal Lingerfelt as Commissioner of Banks, Raleigh

April 5, Smart Start Press Conference [clear text], Raleigh

April 5, Smart Start Press Conference [emended text], Raleigh

April 5, Eastern North Carolina Chambers of Commerce, Raleigh

April 5, Learning Net/Information Highway, Raleigh

April 5, Democratic Legislative Gala, Raleigh

April 6, Opening, Marion Correction Institution, Marion [delivered April 7]

April 7, North Carolina National Guard Association, Greensboro

April 7, Mt. Airy Chamber of Commerce, Mt. Airy [delivered April 10]

April 12, Congratulates Students from Northampton and Halifax Counties on Winning 1995 National Electric Car Championships, Raleigh†

April 13, Press Release: Statement by Governor Jim Hunt on Governor Beasley's Decision to Keep Barnwell Hazardous Waste Disposal Site Open, Raleigh

April 18, Governor's Business Awards Program, Governor's Business Council on the Arts and Humanities, Raleigh

April 19, Education Commission of the States [clear text], Durham

April 19, Education Commission of the States [emended text], Durham*

April 19, Smart Start Private Support, Raleigh

April 20, Environmental Education, Jordan Lake State Educational Forest, Chatham County

April 20, IBM Thirtieth Anniversary [notes], Research Triangle Park

April 22, North Carolina Reduce, Reuse, Recycle Campaign [notes], Raleigh*

April 24, North Carolina Victim Assistance Network Peace Rose Planting Ceremony, Raleigh

April 24, North Carolina Soft Drink Association, Research Triangle Park†

April 24, Receives Susan Kelly Fontes Award for Volunteerism from Wake Up for Children, Raleigh†

April 25, Transamerica Announcement, Charlotte

April 27, Press Release: Statement from Gov. Hunt on the Death of Joseph Bryan, Raleigh

April 27, Smart Start Luncheon [clear text], Asheville

May 1, SBI [State Bureau of Investigation] National Accreditation Announcement, Raleigh

May 1, Older Americans Month, Raleigh

May 2, BRACC [Base Realignment and Closure Commission] Conference Call Talking Points, Raleigh

May 2, Press Release: Statement from Governor Jim Hunt in Response to the House Vote on Smart Start, Raleigh

May 4, Andrew Johnson Memorial Apprenticeship Forum, Raleigh*

May 5, Forsyth County Elected Officials, Winston-Salem*

May 5, North Carolina Association of Teacher Assistants, Greensboro*

May 6, Young Democrats Swearing-in, Raleigh

May 6, Jefferson-Jackson Day, Introduction of Evan Bayh, Research Triangle Park

May 10, North Carolina Interagency Coordinating Council, Raleigh†

May 10, North Carolina A+ Schools Program Reception, Raleigh

May 11, University Budget Statement, Raleigh

May 11, North Carolina State University "Connecting in North Carolina" Conference, Raleigh

May 11, Smart Start Gift from BB&T, Wilson

May 11, Smart Start Gift from BB&T, Lumberton

May 11, Press Release: Gov. Hunt Recommends $35 Million for UNC Faculty and Research, Raleigh

May 13, Commencement Address, Lees-McRae College, Banner Elk

May 16, Rotary International Annual District Meeting, Winston-Salem*

May 17, North Carolina Education Standards and Accountability Commission, Raleigh

May 17, "Playday for Health" Kickoff, Raleigh†

May 18, Freightliner Training Center Dedication, Cleveland*

May 18, Induction Ceremony, North Carolina Sports Hall of Fame, Raleigh

May 19, Governor's Crime Commission, Raleigh*

May 19, Grantham Rescue Squad Twentieth Anniversary, Grantham

May 22, Travel Council of North Carolina [clear text], Wilson
May 22, Travel Council of North Carolina [emended text], Wilson
May 22, Corning, Inc., Groundbreaking Ceremony, Wilmington
May 22, AmeriCorps Issues Summit, Raleigh
May 22, North Carolina Teaching Fellows, Raleigh†
May 23, Reunion for Retired Prison Superintendents, Raleigh-
    Durham National Guard Armory, Wake County
May 24, Older Workers' Task Force, Raleigh
May 24, Smart Start Gift from Food Lion, Charlotte
May 25, Piedmont Passenger Train Inaugural, Raleigh
May 25, Piedmont Passenger Train Inaugural, Durham
May 25, Japan Metals and Chemicals Company Announcement,
    Durham
May 26, Flue-Cured Tobacco Cooperative Stabilization Corp.,
    Raleigh*
May 31, Smart Start Media Availability, Raleigh*
May 31, Davidson County Council of Chambers of Commerce,
    Raleigh*
June 1, Town Meeting Talking Points, Charlotte*
June 6, Coastal Lobbying Day, Raleigh
June 7, Smart Start Statement, Raleigh*
June 8, Asian-American Hotel Owners Association, Raleigh
June 12, Lowe's Companies, Inc., Iredell County Distribution Center
    Groundbreaking, Statesville
June 13, SOS [Support Our Students] Blue Ribbon Awards Day [clear
    text], Raleigh
June 13, SOS [Support Our Students] Blue Ribbon Awards Day
    [emended text], Raleigh
June 13, 1995 North Carolina Public Service Award: Presentation to
    Chancellor Paul Hardin, Raleigh
June 14, National Order of Women Legislators, Raleigh*
June 15, Community Development Block Grant Announcement,
    Raleigh
June 19, Tar Heel Boys State, Winston-Salem
June 19, Governor's Awards for Bravery and Heroism, Raleigh
June 19, Talking Points for Education Cabinet, Raleigh*
June 20, Teacher Town Meeting, Raleigh*
June 22, Torch Run Ceremony, State Games, Raleigh [delivered June 23]
June 23, Dedication, University of North Carolina School of Social
    Work, Chapel Hill
June 23, Talking Points: Alvah Ward's Retirement Party, Raleigh

June 23, Press Release: Governor Hunt Criticizes BRACC Decision to
    Move F/A 18s to Oceana, Washington, D.C.*
June 26, Teacher of the Year Conference, Raleigh*
June 26, North Carolina Restaurant Association, Raleigh*
June 27, Perstorp Announcement, Raleigh
June 28, Booze It and Lose It, Raleigh
June 29, Marrowthon '95 Kickoff, National Bone Marrow Donor
    Registry, Raleigh†
July 19, Tobacco Talking Points, Kinston*
July 19, Thomas Baum Ferry Dedication, Manteo
July 19, Parks and Recreation Trust Fund, Raleigh
July 20, Press Release: Sex Offender Bill, Raleigh
July 21, Accepts first James and Carolyn Hunt Early Childhood
    Award from Day Care Services Association, Chapel Hill†
July 27, Summer Intern Reception, Raleigh
July 27, Wake County Democratic Women, Raleigh†
July 28, Biogen, Inc., Announcement, Research Triangle Park
August 7, North Carolina Sheriff's Association, Atlantic Beach*
August 7, NASA Signing Ceremony, Raleigh
August 8, Governor's Awards for Excellence in Waste Reduction,
    Raleigh
August 8, Goodyear Tire and Rubber Co. Plant Announcement
    [Statesville], Raleigh
August 8, Progressive National Baptist Convention, Charlotte
    [delivered August 9]
August 9, Women's Suffrage 75th Anniversary, Raleigh
August 11, Yancey County Guardrail Announcement, Burnsville
    [delivered August 14]
August 14, National Association of State Directors of
    Administration, Asheville
August 14, Center for the Prevention of School Violence/PHP Grant
    Announcement, Swannanoa
August 17, Clarence Lightner Reception, Raleigh
August 21, Tryon Palace Commission Fiftieth Anniversary, New
    Bern
August 21, Craven County Community Leaders, 1995 Legislative
    Session, New Bern*
August 22, Southeastern Community College Job Training Center,
    Whiteville
August 22, Columbus County Community Leaders Luncheon,
    Whiteville*
August 22, Boys and Girls Club, Jacksonville

August 23, Pasquotank County Luncheon, Elizabeth City

August 23, National Football Foundation and College Hall of Fame, Raleigh

August 28, Economic Development Board Chairman Announcement: Bill Lee, Charlotte

August 29, Wilson Chamber of Commerce, Wilson*

August 29, Mountain Air Cargo Groundbreaking, Global TransPark, Kinston

August 30, Press Release: Statement from Governor Hunt on the Death of Former Representative Jim Lambeth, Raleigh

August 31, North Carolina Economic Development Board, Goldsboro

August 31, SOS [Support Our Students] Press Conference [clear text], Raleigh

September 2, V-J Day Fiftieth Anniversary, Wilmington

September 5, Swearing-in of Garland Garrett as Secretary, N.C. Department of Transportation, Raleigh

September 5, Press Conference, Bob Timberlake Exhibit Announcement, North Carolina Museum of History, Raleigh

September 7, Fiftieth Anniversary of V-J Day, Fort Bragg

September 12, Governor's Awards for Excellence [state employees], Raleigh

September 13, Empire Industries, Glenoit Mills Expansion Announcement, Tarboro

September 13, Notes for Meeting with Tobacco Growers, [no location]*

September 14, Accepts Award for Economic Development Efforts, Raleigh Chamber of Commerce Luncheon, Raleigh

September 14, Press Briefing: Trade, Education, and Cultural Mission to Israel and Japan, Raleigh†

October 5, Colony Tire Plant Tour, Edenton

October 6, Veterans of Foreign Wars Reception, Raleigh*

October 6, Tyrrell County Visitor Center Dedication, Columbia

October 9, Billy Graham Carolinas Crusade Announcement, Charlotte†

October 9, North Carolina Extension Homemakers Association [notes], Charlotte

October 10, Governor's Awards for Outstanding Volunteer Service, Elon College [delivered October 11]

October 12, Installation of Michael Hooker as Chancellor [clear text], University of North Carolina at Chapel Hill

October 12, Installation of Michael Hooker as Chancellor [emended text], University of North Carolina at Chapel Hill

October 12, AmeriCorps Swearing-in, Raleigh

October 12, North Carolina League of Municipalities, Durham [delivered October 16]

October 13, North Carolina State Grange Convention, Raleigh

October 16, North Carolina State Museum of Natural Sciences, Raleigh

October 18, Health Corporation Announcement, Rocky Mount

October 18, Square D Recycling Center Dedication, Knightdale*

October 23, Reception for John Hope Franklin, Raleigh

October 25, North Carolina Association of Broadcasters, Greensboro*

October 26, Seniors' Town Meeting, Charlotte*

October 27, 1995 Entrepreneurial Schools Awards Ceremony, Raleigh

October 30, North Carolina Partnership for Accelerated Schools, Raleigh

October 31, Post-Campaign Rally, 1995 State Employees Combined Campaign, Raleigh†

November 1, ElectriCities Swearing-in Ceremony, Raleigh

November 1, Governor's Awards for Outstanding Volunteer Service, Washington

November 2, General Baptist State Convention, Greensboro

November 2, North Carolina Association of Colleges and Universities, Greensboro

November 3, Friends of Black Children [clear text], Research Triangle Park

November 3, Violence and Injury Prevention Roundtable, Raleigh

November 8, North Carolina Workforce Development Partnership Conference [clear text], Greensboro

November 13, Introduction of Vice-President Al Gore, Raleigh

November 13, 1995 North Carolina Awards Banquet [clear text], Raleigh

November 13, 1995 North Carolina Awards Banquet [emended text], Raleigh

November 16, Luncheon Honoring Jim Goodmon, Raleigh

November 17, Shaw University Founders' Day, Raleigh

November 17, Presentation, James B. Hunt Young Citizens Awards, Wake Forest University, Winston-Salem [not delivered]

November 18, Presentation, James B. Hunt Young Citizens Awards [emended text], Wake Forest University, Winston-Salem

November 18, North Carolina Jaycees Mid-Year Convention, Greensboro

November 21, Click It or Ticket News Conference [clear text], Raleigh

November 21, Click It or Ticket News Conference [emended text], Raleigh

November 21, Governor's Awards for Outstanding Volunteer Service, Fayetteville

November 27, Neuse River Council [clear text], New Bern

November 27, Neuse River Bridge Groundbreaking [U.S. 17], New Bern

November 27, New Bern Noon Rotary Club, New Bern*

November 28, State Employees Combined Campaign Awards Ceremony, Raleigh†

November 28, Opening Remarks, Governor's Summit on Agriculture, Raleigh*

November 29, Closing Remarks, Governor's Summit on Agriculture, Raleigh*

December 1, Richard Moore Swearing-in Ceremony [secretary, Dept. of Crime Control and Public Safety], Raleigh

December 1, Groundbreaking, Museum of Natural Sciences, Raleigh

December 4, ABB Power T&D Co., Inc., Dedication, Raleigh

December 4, Signing of Mutual Agreement with U.S. Department of Agriculture on Conservation of Natural Resources, Greensboro

December 5, Capitol Christmas Tree Lighting Ceremony, Raleigh

December 12, Statement on Rufus Edmisten, Raleigh

December 12, Global TransPark Authority Board of Directors, Raleigh

December 18, Hunters for the Hungry, Raleigh

December 20, Council of State: Railroad Lease Agreement Statement, Raleigh

1996

[First quarter], Safe School Efforts [notes; no location]

[First quarter], Senior Tar Heel Legislature [notes], Raleigh

January 2, Swearing-in of Colonel Everett Horton as Highway Patrol Commander, Raleigh

January 3, Governor's Crackdown for Children [clear text], Raleigh

January 9, I-73/74 Briefing, Winston-Salem Chamber of Commerce, Winston-Salem

January 9, Graham Street Extension Announcement, Charlotte

January 11, Community College Presidents' Luncheon, Raleigh
January 23, Leesville Road Middle School A and B Honor Roll, Raleigh [delivered January 24]
January 24, Wake County School Leader Appreciation Dinner, Raleigh
January 25, Council of State Meeting, Raleigh*
January 29, Elizabeth City Middle School, Elizabeth City
January 31, Receives Nationwide Insurance "On Your Side" Highway Safety Award for Booze It and Lose It Campaign, Raleigh†
January 31, Governor Morehead Proclamation Ceremony, Raleigh
February 1, Leadership for the Twenty-first Century, Raleigh
February 1, MATHCOUNTS Ceremony, Clyde Erwin Elementary School, Jacksonville
February 1, Richlands Area Chamber of Commerce, Richlands*
February 2, North Carolina Tobacco Growers Association, Raleigh
February 2, American Legion Reception, Research Triangle Park†
February 7, Leadership North Carolina Alumni Association, Raleigh [delivered February 9]
February 8, Children's Defense Fund, Charlotte*
February 9, Gaston Chamber of Commerce, Gastonia [delivered February 13]
February 14, Child Passenger Safety Awareness Week [Click It or Ticket], Raleigh*
February 19, NAACP [National Association for the Advancement of Colored People] Awards Banquet, Raleigh
February 19, State Employees Combined Campaign [notes], Raleigh
February 19, North Carolina JobReady Partnership Council, Raleigh
February 23, Leadership North Carolina, Raleigh [delivered February 9]
February 27, Roundtable on Alternative Schools, Cape Lookout High School, Carteret County
February 27, Habitat for Humanity Groundbreaking/JobReady, Carteret County
March 4, Global Forum Welcome, Raleigh
March 4, Governor's Global Forum [high technology], Raleigh
March 4, Governor's Global Forum [economic development], Raleigh
March 4, AdvantageWest Unveiling, Asheville
March 4, T. C. Roberson High School, Asheville
March 4, Asheville Chamber of Commerce, Asheville

March 6, West Charlotte High School Roundtable Discussion on School Violence, Charlotte

March 6, Reception, North Carolina Board of Transportation, Charlotte*

March 7, "Education—Everybody's Business" Coalition, Raleigh†

March 7, George Bason Swearing-in as ABC [Alcoholic Beverage Control] Commissioner, Raleigh

March 8, Indian Unity Conference, Raleigh†

March 12, Daniels Middle School Science Symposium/PTA Award, Raleigh

March 12, Press Release: Statement on Secretary Edmisten's Resignation, Raleigh

March 15, DODGE/Rockwell Automation Groundbreaking, Marion

March 15, McDowell County Rest Area and Visitor Center Dedication, Marion†

March 18, Continental General Tire Headquarters Dedication, Charlotte

March 19, Azalea Festival Kickoff, Raleigh†

March 19, Moore County Luncheon, Southern Pines*

March 19, Distinguished Women of North Carolina Awards, Raleigh

March 20, Hugh McColl Introduction, North Carolina Citizens for Business and Industry, Raleigh

March 20, Western Vance Secondary School Roundtable on Safe Schools, Henderson

March 21, Glen Raven Mills Expansion Celebration, Norlina*

March 22, North Carolina Entrepreneurial Development Board Meeting, Raleigh

March 23, Jefferson-Jackson Day Dinner, Raleigh

March 28, Key Risk Management Services Corporate Headquarters and Corporate Office Park Announcement, Greensboro

March 29, SAVE [Students Against Violence Everywhere] Summit, Raleigh

March 30, Swearing-in Ceremony, North Carolina Teen Democrats, Raleigh†

April 1, Eckerd Wilderness Camp Tour/Roundtable, Elizabethtown*

April 3, Chamber of Commerce-Rotary Luncheon, Lincolnton

April 3, Press Release: Reaction to Death of Ron Brown, Raleigh

April 11, Introduces Bill Gates, Small Business Expo, Raleigh

April 15, Orange County Smart Start Visit with Vice-President Al Gore, Chapel Hill

April 17, Swearing-in of Murial Offerman as Revenue Secretary, Raleigh

April 19, Statement on Smart Start Private Support, Raleigh
April 19, Symposium on Urban Livability, Chapel Hill†
April 22, Presentation, Phil Hughston Memorial Award, Charlotte
April 22, Wandel and Goltermann Plant Dedication, Research
    Triangle Park [delivered April 23]
April 25, Billy Graham Freeway Dedication [I-240], Asheville
April 25, Boys and Girls Club Dedication, Hendersonville
April 25, North Carolina/Eastern Band of Cherokee Indians
    Economic Development Task Force, Asheville
April 29, Recognition Banquet, North Carolina Department of
    Transportation Wins National Quality Initiative Award for I-440
    Beltline, Raleigh
May 1, Groundbreaking, Eisai Pharmatechnology, Inc., Research
    Triangle Park
May 1, Luncheon, Eisai Pharmatechnology, Inc., Research Triangle
    Park
May 1, Older Americans Month Reception, Raleigh
May 2, Paul Broyhill/Caldwell County Smart Start Donation, Lenoir
May 2, Coltec Industries, Inc., Announcement, Charlotte
May 3, Transportation 2001, Raleigh*
May 4, Commencement Address and Acceptance of Honorary
    Degree, East Carolina University, Greenville
May 6, Budget Statement, Raleigh
May 7, Assemblies of God, Winston-Salem*
May 7, Greensboro Citizens' Forum on Crime [clear text],
    Greensboro
May 9, Citizens' Forum on Education, Raleigh*
May 11, Commencement Address, Acceptance of Honorary Degree,
    Pembroke State University, Pembroke†
May 14, Accepts National "Outstanding Governor for 1995" Award
    from Biotechnology Industry Organization, Research Triangle
    Park
May 16, Project Induct Advisory Committee, Raleigh†
May 16, Education Reform, Raleigh
May 20, Presentation, Order of the Long Leaf Pine to Jeff Gordon,
    Raleigh
May 20, Presentation, Order of the Long Leaf Pine to Rick Hendrick,
    Raleigh
May 21, Environmental Lobby Day, Raleigh*
May 22, CitySearch Unveiling, Raleigh
May 23, Smart Start Celebration for Children, Raleigh
May 23, GTP/Foreign Trade Zone Press Conference, Raleigh

May 23, Animal Waste Talking Points, Raleigh

May 28, Greensboro Rotary Clubs, Greensboro

May 28, Greensboro Rotary Tree Planting, Schiffman Park, Greensboro

May 28, 1996 U.S. Women's Open Advisory Committee, Pinehurst [delivered May 29]

May 29, Jaycees Press Conference, Raleigh*

May 29, Exploris Children's Museum, Raleigh

May 29, Accepts Donation from Kuwaiti Ambassador for Persian Gulf War Memorial, Raleigh

May 30, Progress Board, Raleigh†

May 30, Leadership North Carolina, Raleigh†

June 4, Press Release: Text of Letter on Swine Industry to House Agriculture Committee, Raleigh*

June 4, Press Release: Reaction on Death of Frank Kenan, Raleigh

June 5, Animal Waste Press Conference, Raleigh

June 7, Teachers' Town Hall Meeting, Manteo

June 10, Tar Heel Boys State, Winston-Salem

June 12, North Carolina School Boards Association, Raleigh

June 12, Tar Heel Girls State, Greensboro [delivered June 10]

June 12, Roundtable with Business Leaders, Greensboro*

June 14, Older Workers Symposium, Raleigh*

June 14, American Legion Convention Talking Points [clear text], Greensboro

June 17, Ribbon-Cutting Ceremony, ASMO Plant Expansion, Greenville

June 17, Association of District Court Judges, Atlantic Beach*

June 18, State Employees Association of North Carolina Legislative Day Barbecue, Raleigh

June 18, North Carolina Association of Educators Summer Leadership Conference, Research Triangle Park

June 18, Press Release: Statement on House Proposal on Teacher Pay, Raleigh

June 19, White House Visit/Church Burnings, Washington, D.C.*

June 21, North Carolina Federation of Business and Professional Women's Clubs, Raleigh*

June 24, Teacher of the Year Reception, Raleigh

June 26, Bravery and Heroism Awards Presentation, Raleigh†

June 27, Press Release: Statement on Special Recall Session of General Assembly, Raleigh

June 28, Veterans of Foreign Wars Convention, Greensboro*

June 28, Year of the Mountains Luncheon and Meeting, Asheville

June 28, Ribbon-Cutting, Final Phase of U.S. 23/441, Asheville†
July 2, Talking Points for Citizens' Forum, Goldsboro
July 3, Talking Points for Citizens' Forum, Greensboro
July 3, Talking Points for Citizens' Forum, New Bern
July 8, NAACP [National Association for the Advancement of Colored People] National Convention, Charlotte*
July 9, Raleigh/Wake County Home Builders Association Scholarship Awards, Raleigh
July 10, Press Release: Statement on Low-Level Waste Management Authority, Raleigh
July 10, Press Release: Statement on Death of Bill Lee, Raleigh
July 12, Five-Year Anniversary Celebration, Matsushita Compressor Corporation of America, Mooresville
July 12, Work First Forum, Charlotte†
July 15, North Carolina Police Executives Association, Atlantic Beach*
July 17, North State Law Enforcement Officers Association Talking Points [clear text], Raleigh
July 17, North State Law Enforcement Officers Association Talking Points [emended text], Raleigh*
July 17, Work First Forum, Jamestown*
July 18, Testimony to U.S. Senate Subcommittee on Parks, Historic Preservation, and Recreation on S. 988: Oregon Inlet Protection Act [clear text], Washington, D.C.
July 19, School-to-Work Grant Announcement, Jacksonville
July 19, AT&T American Transtech Customer Care Center Announcement, Jacksonville
July 23, Work First Forum, Raleigh*
July 24, Prayer Service/Ministers Meeting on Church Burnings, Raleigh*
July 25, Border Belt Tobacco Market Opening, Fairmont
July 26, Statement on Legislature and State Budget, Raleigh
July 31, Burlington Police Department Junior Police Academy [notes], Burlington
August 1, Old Belt Tobacco Market Opening, [no location]*
August 14, I-26 Corridor Association, Mars Hill†
August 14, Economic Development Announcement, Mars Hill†
August 16, Buncombe County Partnership for Children Meeting, Asheville*
August 17, Babe Ruth Baseball World Series Talking Points, Manteo
August 21, Talking Points for Young Leaders Conference, American Council on Germany, Raleigh

August 21, Press Release: Statement on Food and Drug
Administration Position on Tobacco, Raleigh
August 26, Corning, Inc., Announcement, Concord
August 26, Polar Plastics Group, Inc., Announcement, Mooresville
August 26, Work First Roundtable, Monroe*
August 27, U.S. 220/I-73/I-74 Ribbon-Cutting Ceremony Talking
Points, Asheboro*
August 27, Economic Developers Meeting, Raleigh
August 28, Governor's Crackdown for Children, Greenville*
August 28, Governor's Awards for Outstanding Volunteer Service,
Greenville
September 3, State Emergency Response Team Recognition
Ceremony, Raleigh†
September 4, Work First Forum, Charlotte*
September 4, RF Micro Devices Expansion Announcement,
Greensboro
September 5, Baptist Children's Home Western Area Conference,
Clyde†
September 7, Governor's Youth Summit to Prevent Crime and
Violence, Raleigh†
September 11, Hurricane Fran: Debris Cleanup, Raleigh
September 14, Spencer Shops 100th Anniversary, Opening of North
Carolina Transportation Museum's Julian Roundhouse, Spencer†
September 16, Nypro Dedication, Arden
September 16, Governor's Awards for Outstanding Volunteer
Service, Asheville
September 19, Remington Arms Co., Inc., Worldwide Headquarters
Opening, Madison*
September 20, North Carolina Joining Tobacco Lawsuit, Wilson
September 26, Visit to S. Ray Lowder Elementary School, Lincoln
County
September 26, North Carolina Business Committee for Education,
Charlotte
September 26, Speaking Points, North Carolina Business Committee
For Education's Total Quality in Education Initiative, Charlotte
September 30, Drug Court, Charlotte
October 1, Press Conference, 1999 Special Olympics, Raleigh*
October 4, North Carolina Crime Prevention Awards Ceremony,
Raleigh
October 7, Goodwill Industries' Groundbreaking of the Goodwill
Employment Center, Greensboro*
October 7, Stanly County Smart Start Visit, Albemarle

October 8, Democratic Campaign Rally, Goldsboro†
October 9, Purolator Products/Work First Roundtable, Fayetteville
October 9, State Veterans Home Groundbreaking, Fayetteville*
October 9, Democratic Campaign Rally, Fayetteville†
October 10, Host Marriott/Work First, Charlotte*
October 10, Olympians' Reception, Raleigh
October 12, Economic Development Announcement, Asheville†
October 12, Vance-Aycock Dinner, Introduction of Gov. Gaston
 Caperton, Asheville†
October 14, North Carolina League of Municipalities, Winston-
 Salem†
October 14, Tri-County Campaign Rally, Halifax†
October 14, Nash County Campaign Rally, Rocky Mount††
October 15, Pitt County Campaign Rally, Rock Springs†
October 16, Davidson County Campaign Rally, Lexington†
October 17, Union County Campaign Rally, Monroe†
October 18, North Carolina Economic Developers Association,
 Charlotte†
October 18, Governor's Crackdown for Children, Charlotte*
October 18, Disabled Veterans of North Carolina, Charlotte†
October 18, Randolph County Campaign Rally, Asheboro†
October 23, Leadership Charlotte Awards Dinner, Introduction of Ed
 Shelton, Charlotte
October 29, Dedication of New Dormitory, Guilford Prison Farm,
 Gibsonville*
October 30, Leadership North Carolina, Raleigh
October 31, Police Corps Scholarship Ceremony, [no location]
October 31, SOS [Support Our Students] Expansion Announcement,
 Charlotte*
November 7, Fran-Tastic Tree Groundbreaking, Raleigh
November 8, Press Release: Statement by Governor Jim Hunt
 Regarding Erskine Bowles, Raleigh
November 12, Governor's Outstanding Volunteer Awards,
 Greensboro
November 14, Global TransPark Conference, Mount Olive
November 15, 1996 Entrepreneurial Schools Awards, Raleigh
November 15, Ketner Awards Ceremony, Raleigh
November 16, "Sepphoris in Galilee" Opening, Raleigh
November 16, James B. Hunt Young Citizen Awards, Winston-Salem
November 26, MADD [Mothers Against Drunk Driving] Press
 Conference, Raleigh*
December 9, Farm Bureau Conference, Winston-Salem

December 10, Governor's Christmas Tree Lighting Ceremony, Raleigh

December 16, Electoral College Talking Points, Raleigh

1997

January 6, Governor's Award for Excellence in Education, [notes], Charlotte

January 7, Soil and Water Conservation Hall of Fame Banquet, Charlotte†

January 8, Salute to Community Colleges, Durham

January 10, Young Citizens' Forum, Raleigh

January 10, Student Government Assembly Talking Points, Raleigh

January 10, College and University Student Body Presidents' Forum, Raleigh

January 10, Op-Ed Column, *Charlotte Observer*

EXECUTIVE ORDERS

[Governor Hunt issued 106 executive orders during his third term in office. Although space limitations prohibit the inclusion of these items in their entirety in this documentary, a listing of titles has been provided below. The complete texts of Hunt's executive orders, promulgated during the period from 1993 to 1997, are located as follows: numbers 1 through 20, *Session Laws of North Carolina, 1993*, 2:3166-3255; numbers 41 through 53, *Session Laws of North Carolina, 1993, Extra Session, 1994, Regular Session, 1994*, 3:1011-1057; numbers 54 through 82, *Session Laws of North Carolina, 1995*, 2:2072A-2160; numbers 83 through 106, *Session Laws of North Carolina, 1997*, 2:2507-2570. Numbers 21 through 40 were omitted from the Session Laws; full texts of those documents are available from the North Carolina State Archives, Raleigh.]

1993

Executive Order Number 1, established new North Carolina Board of Ethics, rescinded Executive Order Number 1 (Martin), January 9

Executive Order Number 2, established North Carolina Small Business Council, February 11

Executive Order Number 3, transferred Keep America Beautiful program from the Office of the Governor to the Department of Environment, Health, and Natural Resources, February 23

Executive Order Number 4, established the Commission on Workforce Preparedness and its Inter-Agency Coordinating Council, rescinded Executive Orders 143 and 159 (Martin), March 10

Executive Order Number 5, waived certain restrictions for motor vehicles aiding the winter storm disaster relief effort, March 18

Executive Order Number 6, established Entrepreneurial Development Board, April 12

Executive Order Number 7, abolished North Carolina Drug Cabinet, rescinded Executive Orders 108 and 117 (Martin), April 13

Executive Order Number 8, state government recycling, reduction of solid waste, and purchase of products with recycled content, April 22

Executive Order Number 9, established Commission for a Competitive North Carolina, May 5

Executive Order Number 10, established Quality Leadership Awards Council, rescinded Executive Orders 119 and 166 (Martin), May 5

Executive Order Number 11, established Governor's Council of Fiscal Advisors, rescinded Executive Order Number 122 (Martin), May 5

Executive Order Number 12, established Public School Administrator Task Force, May 7

Executive Order Number 13, amended Executive Order Number 10, Quality Leadership Awards Council, May 20

Executive Order Number 14, amended Executive Order Number 1, North Carolina Board of Ethics, May 20

Executive Order Number 15, established Coordinating Committee on the Americans with Disabilities Act, rescinded Executive Order Number 179 (Martin), May 20

Executive Order Number 16, reestablished Geographic Information Coordinating Council, rescinded Executive Order Number 147 (Martin), May 21

Executive Order Number 17, established North Carolina Emergency Response Commission, rescinded Executive Orders 43, 48, 50, and 165 (Martin), June 16

Executive Order Number 18, described Emergency Management Program, rescinded Executive Order Number 73 (Martin), June 16

Executive Order Number 19, established Center for the Prevention of School Violence, June 30

Executive Order Number 20, designated 1994 as Year of the Coast, created Coastal Futures Committee, July 15

Executive Order Number 21, established North Carolina Local Government Partnership Council, August 12

Executive Order Number 22, renewed equal employment opportunity policy for state employees, rescinded Executive Orders 18 and 76 (Martin), August 13

Executive Order Number 23, re-established Public School Administrator Task Force, rescinded Executive Order Number 12 (Hunt), August 26

Executive Order Number 24, emergency relief for damage caused by Hurricane Emily, September 7

Executive Order Number 25, rescinded Executive Orders 55, 101, and 161, establishing Martin Luther King, Jr., Holiday Commission (Martin), and Executive Orders 71, 94, and 125, establishing Governor's Task Force on Rail Passenger Service (Martin), September 7

Executive Order Number 26, established North Carolina Public Employee Deferred Compensation Plan Board of Trustees, rescinded Executive Orders 39 and 185 (Martin), September 7

Executive Order Number 27, established Governor's Commission for Recognition of State Employees, September 7

Executive Order Number 28, established Advisory Committee on Agriculture, Forestry, and the Seafood Industry, September 28

Executive Order Number 29, established Teacher Advisory
Committee, September 28
Executive Order Number 30, established Highway Beautification
Council, rescinded Executive Order Number 126 (Martin),
September 28
Executive Order Number 31, established State Commission on
National and Community Service, October 1
Executive Order Number 32, reestablished Governor's Advisory
Commission on Military Affairs, rescinded Executive Orders 151,
163, 170, and 185 (Martin), October 21
Executive Order Number 33, reestablished Persian Gulf War
Memorial Commission, rescinded Executive Orders 152, 160, and
167 (Martin), November 10
Executive Order Number 34, established Highway Safety
Commission, rescinded Executive Order Number 12 (Martin),
November 23
Executive Order Number 35, established Governor's State Employee
Action Commission, rescinded Executive Order Number 89
(Martin), November 29

1994

Executive Order Number 36, established Smoking Policy
Coordinating Committee, January 7
Executive Order Number 37, citizen access to public records
maintained by state government, January 28
Executive Order Number 38, established Council on Health Policy
Information, rescinded Executive Orders 162 and 174 (Martin),
February 4
Executive Order Number 39, amended Executive Order Number 23,
Public School Administrator Task Force, February 4
Executive Order Number 40, amended Executive Order Number 9,
Commission for a Competitive North Carolina, March 21
Executive Order Number 41, extended Executive Orders 99 and 185
(Martin), Governor's Commission on Reduction of Infant
Mortality, April 12
Executive Order Number 42, rescinded the following executive
orders enacted by Governor Martin: Number 78, Governor's Task
Force on Injury Prevention; Number 136, North Carolina
Advisory Council on Telecommunications in Education; Number
153, North Carolina 2000 Steering Committee; Number 110,
Advisory Council on International Trade; Number 36, Governor's

Commission for Recognition of State Employees; Number 28, Advisory Committee on Agriculture, Forestry, and the Seafood Industry; Number 29, Teacher Advisory Committee; Number 30, Highway Beautification Council; and Number 34, Highway Safety Commission. October 27

Executive Order Number 88, amended Statewide Flexible Benefits Program, October 27

Executive Order Number 89, directed state purchasing agents to meet with representatives of the blind and severely disabled, October 31

Executive Order Number 90, established workforce development boards, December 5

Executive Order Number 91, Persian Gulf War Memorial Commission, rescinded Executive Orders 33 and 82 (Hunt), December 13

Executive Order Number 92, established Council for Young Adult Drivers, December 13

Executive Order Number 93, established North Carolina/Eastern Band of Cherokee Indians Development Task Force, December 21

1996

Executive Order Number 94, established North Carolina Alliance for Competitive Technologies, rescinded Executive Orders 63 and 80 (Hunt), February 26

Executive Order Number 95, established Council on Health Policy Information, April 24

Executive Order Number 96, established Task Force on Racial or Religious Violence and Intimidation, June 14

Executive Order Number 97, emergency relief for damage caused by Hurricane Bertha, July 12

Executive Order Number 98, amended Executive Order Number 97, emergency relief for damage caused by Hurricane Bertha, August 9

Executive Order Number 99, emergency relief for damage caused by Hurricane Fran, September 5

Executive Order Number 100, established Government Information Locator Service Coordinating Committee, September 12

Executive Order Number 101, psychologists and social workers licensed or certified out of state permitted to provide crisis counseling for victims of Hurricane Fran, September 12

Executive Order Number 102, amended Executive Order Number 99, emergency relief for damage caused by Hurricane Fran, October 2

Executive Order Number 103, amended Executive Orders 99 and 102, emergency relief for damage caused by Hurricane Fran, October 10

Executive Order Number 104, established North Carolina Disaster Recovery Task Force, Center, and Action Team, October 10

Executive Order Number 105, amended Executive Orders 99, 102, and 103, emergency relief for damage caused by Hurricane Fran, December 2

Executive Order Number 106, Hurricane Fran disaster leave and compensation for state employees, December 11

NOTE ON APPOINTMENTS

During his third term in office, Governor Hunt named to state boards, commissions, and other bodies many individuals who served through or were reappointed during his fourth administration. To include an appointments section in the volume for each of those terms would entail repeating much information. Therefore, a list of the governor's designees to statutory entities, 1993-2001, will be published in the documentary chronicling his fourth administration.

INDEX